LC

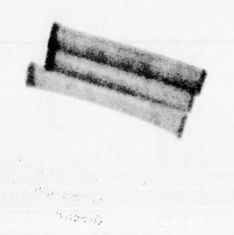

McGraw-Hill Series in Political Science

JOSEPH P. HARRIS, *Consulting Editor*

THE DYNAMICS OF DEMOCRATIC GOVERNMENT

McGraw-Hill Series in Political Science

JOSEPH P. HARRIS, *Consulting Editor*

THE DYNAMICS OF DEMOCRATIC GOVERNMENT

JOHN P. ROCHE

Haverford College

MURRAY S. STEDMAN, JR.

Swarthmore College

McGRAW-HILL BOOK COMPANY, INC.

NEW YORK   TORONTO   LONDON

1954

THE DYNAMICS OF DEMOCRATIC GOVERNMENT

To Constance and Susan
with love and gratitude

PREFACE

A STUDY OF the democratic political process which attempts to integrate contemporary developments with the traditions and precedents of the past courts the great risk of becoming dated almost by the date of publication. The "present" is elusive, becoming the "past" before we have even recognized it, and the status quo of today is the *ancien régime* of tomorrow. Yet, because we do not believe that the main body of our analysis will be seriously undermined by changing events, we have taken the risk and put ourselves at the mercy of time. Sir Winston Churchill may retire and Premier Malenkov may be unmasked as an American spy, but we feel that the principles underlying the democratic process will remain valid despite the dated nature of any of our specific statements.

We have attempted here to present the reader with what we believe to be significant generalizations about the nature of democratic government. In other words, this book presents a point of view, and we have tried to document our hypotheses with relevant and important facts drawn from the operation of democratic governments. While we have taken most of our data from the experience of the United States, Great Britain, and France, material on other democracies has been included at points where it is particularly significant. Furthermore, we must confess our bias: we are strong believers in democracy as a technique of government as well as a faith for living. Our religious and ethical assumptions are important in the formulation of our ideas, and we have made no attempt to hide them. At the same time, we suffer no illusions about our own infallibility and have made a great effort to avoid the arrogance of dogmatism. Our main goal is twofold: first, we want to present certain facts and ideas to the student; and, second, we want to supply the student with a framework for disagreement with us, if he is so inclined.

Obviously, many of the ideas set forth here are not original with us. We have tried to assign credit where credit is due, but we ask the indulgence of our friends if their cherished concepts turn up herein without a by-line. Many of the thoughts which we have expressed grew out of conversations with stimulating colleagues; others undoubtedly were absorbed, without benefit of identification, from our teachers.

Our greatest intellectual debts are unquestionably owed to our teachers at Cornell University and Columbia University, where we served our respective scholarly apprenticeships. To our colleagues in the Political Science Departments of Haverford and Swarthmore Colleges also go our thanks for their stimulating friendship and high intellectual standards. They have forced us to justify our hypotheses, and, indeed, to modify or abandon many of questionable validity. Our special thanks go to the following individuals who sacrificed their time and eyesight criticizing various portions of the manuscript: Professor Philip W. Bell, Department of Economics, Haverford College; Professor John D. Campbell, Department of Psychology, Haverford College; L. James Callaghan, M.P., London, England; Professor Mario Einaudi, Department of Government, Cornell University; Professor William A. Reitzel, Department of Political Science, Haverford College and The Brookings Institution; Professor Clinton L. Rossiter, Department of Government, Cornell University; and Dr. Jan Tinbergen, Director, Central Planning Office, Netherlands.

Finally, we must express our gratitude to our wives for their uncomplaining cooperation.

JOHN P. ROCHE
MURRAY S. STEDMAN, JR.

CONTENTS

PART I. THE BASIS OF DEMOCRATIC GOVERNMENT

Chapter 1

THE DEMOCRATIC POLITICAL PROCESS—
A THEORETICAL FRAMEWORK

"To HAVE doubted one's own first principles," observed Justice Oliver Wendell Holmes, "is the mark of a civilized man." He could have added with equal truth that such doubts are also the mark of the democrat. Democracy is a system of government based on the realization of man's fallibility, on the belief that no one person or small group of persons can possess Truth. Some democratic extremists would exclude from this company all those, notably Catholics, who believe that absolute truth exists, but this does not appear to be a legitimate criterion of exclusion. One may believe in the existence of natural law or absolute truth and still be a democrat providing that he is willing, like the great French philosopher Jacques Maritain, to concede man's inadequacy fully to apprehend this truth. Democracy thus rests squarely on the conception of shared truth. The democrat assumes that men in the aggregate pooling their resources—their shares of truth, so to speak—will in the long run do a better job of guiding their destiny than will any leader, no matter how able.

In this sense democracy is individualistic. It is based on an assumption, which cannot be verified empirically, that man has choice and that he has the power to choose between alternatives. To the democrat, life is no puppet show with various nonhuman forces directing the movements of men. On the contrary, although any sensible person recognizes that many of the things we do are an outgrowth of various conditioning factors, man stands at the center of the cosmos acting, believing, and struggling in the eternal search for the better life. Furthermore, democracy assumes that man is a responsible creature who must stand at the bar of history and be judged. In the democratic scheme of things, man cannot pass the blame for his errors to his libido, his childhood toilet habits, or the relationships of production of the society in which he lives.

The aim of institutions in a democratic state must therefore be to make this process of choice possible and, indeed, to maximize those factors which aid in making intelligent choice possible. To the democrat the life process and the political process are experimental. Institutions are tools which man has created to help him attain those objectives which he holds good, and man must be free to reject on the basis of experience those institutions which have not aided his forward movement. To put it another way, man must not become an automaton in the power of one of his own creations. Viewed in this perspective, the basic antidemocratic aspects of Nazi Germany, Fascist Italy, and Communist Russia become apparent. In each of these countries, institutions, *e.g.*, the Folk-state, the transcendent nation, and the Workers' State, which had been created in abortive attempts to liberate the people from some ostensible oppressor, ended up dominating the people who had created them or passively tolerated their creation. There was in Nazi Germany and Fascist Italy, and there is today in Soviet Russia, no possibility of rejecting these institutions and replacing them by others which might do a better job. Man in a totalitarian state loses his choice, loses his right to replace a bad tool with one better fitted for the project.

To this statement of the democratic premise the cynic may take exception. "This is all very well in theory," he will probably observe, "but how well does this system work?" Unfortunately, far too often the spokesmen for the democratic way of life have failed to enter the market place to refute this allegation of unworkability. Frequently antidemocratic causes have won the day almost by default. But far from being an unrealistic approach today to affairs, democracy is a demonstrably better system of government than any alternative so far presented. Judged by the wholly pragmatic standard of survival, for example, democratic societies have so far succeeded in maintaining their place in the world. Judged in terms of stability, another Hobbesian criterion, the democratic states have managed to withstand the tremendous impact of the industrial revolution and have, in fact, become more democratic and more stable. Historical graveyards are littered with the bones of absolutists.

The fact remains that democracy has been in practice the sole form of government that has institutionalized man's right to change tools. In the field of economics, for example, democratic societies have rejected laissez-faire capitalism, tried democratic socialism, experimented with limited capitalism, and even restored laissez-faire techniques without the slightest sign of violence. The objectives of the Democratic party are tried, found wanting, and replaced by the objectives of the Republican party. The latter is in turn found wanting and replaced by Democrats who have modified their former views, and the Republicans then begin a reconditioning aimed at improving their standing with the American people. The right to make demands and the right to vote for an alternative party with an alternative solution remain with the people. Similarly, the people of Britain experiment with various political instruments, retaining always the right to reject a tool that does not fulfill their expectations. Thus, in a democratic society, man has a fire escape. The defeat of democratic socialist governments in Australia, New Zealand, and Great Britain—in the first two nations, after long tenure—shows that this is far more than a hypothetical consideration.

To this the "practical man" may well say, "But look at the corruption and inefficiency that exist in democracies." In answering this objection two main contentions can be made. First, it appears that political life today in the democracies is far less corrupt and inefficient than it was half a century ago. It is indeed unfortunate that in the United States politics has become associated with smoke-filled hotel rooms, political bosses, and shady deals. This is not the place to engage in lengthy historical discussion, so it is suggested that the curious compare political life and the level of political morality that existed in the 1890's with those of today. Investigation will certainly support the contention that the standard of public morality in the United States has steadily improved.

Second, and more significantly, there appears to be no evidence to support the claim that dictatorships are more efficient and less corrupt than democracies. The extent of corruption, bribery, nepotism, and inefficiency in Nazi Germany and Fascist Italy is still insufficiently appreciated. Many German Jews and other anti-Nazis owe their lives to the fact that apparently no Nazi official was immune to bribery. With respect to the Jews, bribery was institutionalized, published price lists informing those interested what the cost of corruption would be. A considerable segment of the German General Staff was involved in plots of one sort or another, and the Chief of German Counter Intelligence, Admiral Canaris, used his office as a headquarters for anti-Nazi activities. The equivalent in the United States would be for the Chief of the Central Intelligence Agency to be a Soviet sympathizer! There is little need to discuss Fascist Italy, for it was a moral shambles in which, contrary to official claims, the trains did not run on time, and every public official of any standing inscribed on his banner *"enrichissez-moi."*

This myth of the efficiency of dictatorships is nourished by our ignorance of what actually takes place behind the barriers that totalitarian states invariably build between themselves and other lands. In the democracies the harsh klieg lights are thrown on official corruption and inefficiency, and the newspapers highlight instances of nepotism. In a dictatorship only an occasional public confession, denunciation, or purge, gives us any insight into actual conditions. Could one conceive, while Stalin ruled, of *Pravda* inquiring as to Vassily Stalin's qualifications for the post of Lieutenant General of Soviet Air Forces? One need only compare this example from the U.S.S.R. with the weekly forays that the anti-Roosevelt newspapers made during World War II against the appointment to high military positions of the President's sons Elliott and James to grasp the full force of this argument.

Recently the people of the United States have become worried about the Soviet dictatorship, and with considerable justification. To the average American the Soviet Union often appears as a monolithic, sinister state which seldom seems to make a mistake—a veritable Frankenstein's monster which moves without human weakness and proceeds mechanically toward its objectives. But when a future chronicler sits down to write the history of Stalin's dictatorship, we may well hear tales of governmental inefficiency and corruption that parallel the Nazi and Fascist experiences. The fact that Yagoda, Yezhov, and Beria, the last three chiefs of the secret police, were all, according to Soviet sources, imperialist spies indicates that some problems have troubled the regime. In the meanwhile the Soviet Union, protected by iron censorship, operates in a fog of mystery. We often confuse silent operation with efficient operation and, viewing events from our own frame of reference, assume that since the Soviet Union has had no Kefauver Committee it has no gambling or corruption.

Furthermore, the conditions of life in a dictatorship militate against efficiency. Efficiency is not merely a mechanical concept, for the most efficient worker is usually the one who uses his brains and devises short cuts, not the one who turns the largest number of nuts per hour. It is this type of creative efficiency, which has often in the industrial history of the United States cut minutes or even hours off the time needed to produce some article, that dictatorship stifles. When one's head is always in a noose, will he take a chance on some new idea or technique? As anyone who has ever served in any army can verify, the most efficient system of operation often involves flagrant disregard for official regulations, but if one's life is at stake, who will take the risk? Rather will the worker, soldier, farmer, scientist, or civil servant in the dictatorship adhere mechanically to prescribed rules. His slogan will be "Safety First."

The objections of the man from Marx remain to be considered. "Democracy," he will say, "is meaningless unless the people have full control over the instruments of production and distribution." He would further add that in the West we have "mere political democracy" which serves to camouflage economic inequality. This accusation has been a telling one in certain democratic countries, e.g., France, where economic inequality has been blatant and unameliorated. But the basic Marxist assumption does not hold up under close scrutiny. In all the democratic countries political democracy has been the lever that has been used to mitigate economic inequality. In Great Britain, for example, the Labor Government's policies won the support of the people at the polls and after taking office the Laborites proceeded substantially to alter the economic structure of the nation. In the United States the political victory of Roosevelt was the initial step in a significant reorganization of the American economy. At the other extreme, it also appears that Hitler used political power to subjugate the German economy, and in the Soviet Union itself, Lenin's seizure of political power in October, 1917, was the first step in the formation of the "Workers' State" and the economic transformation that accompanied it. Thus "mere political democracy," and indeed political power in general, assumes far more importance than the Marxist would admit. Man's actions as citizen seem to be more basic, except under certain limited circumstances, than his actions as an economic unit.

In summary, it is suggested that democracy is a form of government that stands the practical test of workability better than alternative methods of government, and in addition allows man to retain his essential individuality, his right to choose his tools. However, it should be noted that democracy is a difficult type of government which demands much of the citizen. The democrat must turn his back firmly on historical short cuts and "magic helpers." He is committed to the tedious, undramatic, and terribly exacting process of rational development. In the sections that follow an attempt will be made to discover what conditions, what institutional framework, seem to supply the best environment for the development of democratic government.

THE ROLE OF INSTITUTIONS

Before analyzing the institutions of democracy, a brief initial examination of the role of institutions may be in order. At one time democratic thinkers went a long way in the direction of assuming that institutions were autonomous forces. A thinker of the profundity of John Adams seemed to feel that all that was necessary for the creation of a republican form of government was a good constitution. Such an institution would proceed, apparently by its own force, to remold the lives and thoughts of members of a society into a democratic (Adams would have said "republican") pattern. This conviction appears to be part of a broader American tradition, that of faith in gadgets. In more recent years the Populists, whose naïve faith in political gadgets has not since been matched, put their main emphasis on demands for initiative, referendum, and recall of officials (including judges) and were thrown into consternation when these devices, on adoption in many states, did not automatically clean up politics. The traditional American fondness for laws as solutions to problems, a tradition which reached its zenith in the Eighteenth Amendment, is another aspect of this same belief in institutional autonomy.

But this flame no longer burns with its old brightness. Although American army officers are still prepared to translate the American Constitution into Japanese, German, or Swahili for the political guidance of the benighted natives, the latter no longer appear to consider the great American document as a magic formula. The nineteenth century saw too much of this. In nation after nation exuberant democrats in the first flush of power attempted to impose democratic constitutions on unprepared people and found to their dismay that a constitution of itself does little to change the way of life of a nation or existing patterns of power in a society. It seems conclusive that unless a constitution reflects the power relationships in a society, it will be ineffectual. Man will not be saved by institutions alone.

On the other hand, no democratic society can succeed in operating effectively unless it has adequate institutions. We might say that while institutions cannot save the day alone, they can play an important, if not vital, role in assisting a democratic society to survive. A good case can, for example, be made that the organization of executive power under the Weimar constitution played into the hands of Hitler. The German Republic had, in effect, a dual executive: the popularly elected President, and the Chancellor who was the leader of the government. This was an attempt to incorporate the supposedly better aspects of both the British and American executives, but like many attempts to get the best of both possible worlds, it succeeded only in intensifying difficulties. The President felt that, since he was the only public official elected by all the people, his authority was superior to that of the party leaders, and unfortunately, the constitution gave him the power to dismiss Chancellors. President Hindenburg's use of this power played a vital part in the rise of Hitler to power.

To turn the coin over, it seems demonstrable that the British system of election to Parliament has been a major contributing factor to Britain's strong, stable democratic system. If Frenchmen were forced at election time to choose between two alternative parties, which is what the single-member, plurality-election system requires of the voter, France might have a far stronger democratic government than it has today with the list system of proportional representation. Thus, given a certain minimum to work with, institutions can either make major positive contributions, or they can contribute to inadequacy and impotence.

THE PREREQUISITES OF DEMOCRACY

But what is this "certain minimum"? What factors must be present in society if institutions are to be of any significance? It has been suggested that if democratic institutions are to have any meaning they must reflect community sentiment. What is this sentiment? And how is it developed? These are the questions to which we must now turn our attention.

Sir Ernest Barker, the dean of British political scientists, has asserted that the two basic ingredients of a democratic community are national and social homogeneity. By national homogeneity Barker means that the people of a country must feel that it is their nation. National homogeneity does not depend on common descent from one ethnic source; it can be fed by a multitude of ethnic backgrounds. Among the democratic states France and Great Britain are prime instances of national homogeneity. Belgium and Canada, each with considerable internal friction between national groups, would fall at the other end of the scale. The United States would probably be somewhere in the middle, although as the years of large-scale immigration move farther and farther into the past and the number of foreign-born Americans decreases this country is rapidly becoming more homogeneous. By social homogeneity Barker implies the absence of class feeling, of economic cleavage, or of urban-rural hostility. Here France would be an outstanding example of a nation divided against itself. Not only are the rural French militantly opposed to the urban French, but the urban group is itself bitterly divided along class lines. The enormous Communist vote in France is less an indication of Soviet sympathy than it is an indication of the profound gap that separates the French worker from the other sectors of French society. The French worker recalls only too vividly the years of German occupation when the peasants were quite prepared to see him starve and the bosses were too often amenable to German direction. Great Britain and the Scandinavian democracies are the most unified. The importance of these two factors, national and social homogeneity, can be stated in a nutshell; if they are present, a society has community, a common frame of reference and common ideals.

To be more specific, let us analyze the United States for social homogeneity. In one sense, the United States is unique among the democracies. In no other has the working class so fully adapted itself to capitalism. In Australia, New Zealand, the Scandinavian countries, and in all the Western European democracies there is a special political party dedicated primarily to the interests of the worker. Even Canada has a vestigial party of this sort in the Cooperative Commonwealth Federation. But in the United States all attempts to organize a party around the interests of the worker have miscarried. Unquestionably there is a certain amount of economic cleavage in the United States, but it has not in recent years been sufficient to generate a labor or socialist party. The American worker apparently feels that his interests are adequately represented by the Democratic and Republican parties; in fact, it is dubious whether he even considers himself as a "worker."

While there appears to be very little of the "class struggle" in American life, there is a highly significant division between city and country. This nation was established by an overwhelmingly rural society, and this rural society left its imprint on American political life. The traditional virtues of the American— thrift, self-sufficiency, self-reliance—are the virtues of a rural society, and their governmental concomitant was the laissez-faire state, the "night-watchman state." However, as the United States became urbanized—and the process was accelerated tremendously after 1890—the realities of American life began radically to change. The city dweller does not have self-sufficiency and self-reliance inscribed on his banners. He is virtually helpless, for he must depend on others for the food that he eats, the water he drinks, the fuel to heat his home, and the very ground in which to bury him at the end of his days. The urban dweller cannot take the old folks into his three-room apartment when they get too old to work. Obviously this city man needs help and protection, and the logical organization to supply this help is the state. The farmer can cry "Down with the state!" and perhaps exist unassisted, although today this is becoming more and more difficult as farms become mechanized and electrified. The city dweller needs the state.

But the United States government and the governments of the states were all established to serve rural society, and the farmers have been reluctant to surrender their hold on political power. Not only are the rural areas vastly over-represented in the national legislature, but they still control such states as New York and Illinois where more than half the people live in great, and politically underrepresented, cities. Consequently, the demands of urban man that the state come to his aid have frequently been ignored by legislatures dominated by rural interest. This is not to suggest that the only cause of the recent demand for state intervention in economic life, the so-called demand for the "welfare state," is the growing urbanization of the United States, but rather to point out how urbanization can lead to the disruption of community. Viewed from this vantage point, the United States leaves something to be desired in terms of social homogeneity. It is probably significant that the democratic nation which seems to have the highest degree of social homogeneity, Great Britain, is also the most highly urbanized. A strong sense of community can probably exist at either the rural end of the scale, as in the United States of 1820, or at the urban end, as in Great Britain today, but at intermediate points the conflict between rural and urban interests can prove highly disruptive.

There is, however, a deeper community of values that is implicit in social and national homogeneity. A democracy is such not only because of the ideals that it espouses, but also, and more significantly, because of the methods it uses in achieving its ends. Presumably one could terminate the urban-rural split by forcibly destroying the power of the farmers. This, in essence, was the technique utilized in the Soviet Union. Obviously it is not a method to which democrats would lend their approval. Democracies, because they are based on the assumption of human fallibility, shy away from drastic solutions of an irrevocable nature. Although there may be acute conflicts between members and groups in a democratic society, these conflicts take place within an agreed frame of reference. A *modus vivendi,* or better, a *modus non vivendi,* has been achieved.

To put it another way, the democrat is willing to accede to a decision democratically arrived at even if it is against his interest, or what he believes to be his interest. He does this secure in the knowledge that he will not be destroyed, and that he will be allowed to continue to present his views to the public for possible later adoption. One basic factor which contributes to this willingness to accept a "wrong" decision is the knowledge that the democrat has, although he may never have consciously formulated it, of the diffusion of power in the democratic state. The democratic climate nourishes groups of all sorts, and the citizen working for a temporarily lost cause (no cause is ever, in the view of its supporters, permanently lost) may work through dozens of organizations to achieve his end. The McKinley Republican can retire to the Union League Club and find reassurance that the final triumph of real American principles is just around the corner. The defeated Socialist and his friends can always find a friendly cafeteria where they can reinvigorate themselves with coffee and the knowledge of their imminent victory. Man alone is man desperate, but man in a group is man secure.

True, there are always in any society a few extremists who will not accept the majority decision as binding, but the very nature of the political process tends to keep them disparate. In the first place, extremism is frequently a temperamental rather than an intellectual phenomenon. The extremist tends to be a prima donna who has difficulty getting along even with those who agree with him. The history of religious and political sectarianism bears testimony to this hypothesis. The man who has possession of the Truth is jealous of it, and tends to excommunicate those in Error rather than exchange views with them. Second, people are extremists about different things, which makes it additionally difficult to build a significant extremist organization. The absolute pacifist, the Communist, the Jehovah's Witness, the employer who will not tolerate a trade-union, and the businessman who will not pay his income tax have nothing in common except their rejection of society. Occasionally extremist organizations find conditions which nourish them, as in Czarist Russia or Weimar Germany, and infrequently they can find a working basis for unity, as the Nazis and Communists did for a time in Germany in 1932. But this would appear to be a symptom of the failure of the democratic community rather than a major cause of its collapse. Hitler wrote the obituary for a republic that had, in effect, been moribund for five years.

Thus the agreement to disagree is a vital part of national and social homogeneity, and in turn contributes to the strengthening of community. Once a society subdivides into autonomous microcosms, each with its own set of values and its own absolute truth, democracy withers. As in France today, where the spokesmen for the Communists and the extreme Gaullists no longer speak the same language as the center democrats, the absence of community tends to accelerate the process of disintegration. Democracy is indeed a delicate balance.

But to discuss the agreement to disagree in this fashion is to beg the even more basic question: How does this consensus develop? Obviously it does not materialize out of thin air. What then are the antecedents, the components, of consensus? Much thought has already been given to this problem by thinkers like Harold J. Laski, Ernest Barker, and Robert MacIver, and the following is essentially a synthesis of their views.

A homogeneous society is, almost by definition, a stable society. Thus stability appears to be a prime prerequisite for the development of democracy. The pattern of democratic development has generally proceeded in the following sequence: first, a stable authoritarian government; second, a stable semiauthoritarian constitutional government; and third, a democratic constitutional government. Although no attempt is made to posit this as a universal progression, it seems to portray accurately the course of events in Great

Britain, the United States, Sweden, and the nations of the British Commonwealth. Initially, in each of these countries, government was in the hands of an irresponsible elite. Gradually in the course of time, the elite was brought to heel, usually by the rising middle class, and irresponsible elitism was replaced by a system of partially responsible government. This partially responsible government was, in turn, enlarged through the progressive enfranchisement of the lower-class groups until universal suffrage resulted in fully responsible government. This process of enlargement appears to have taken place on an almost wholly pragmatic basis, with one faction of the dominant semiresponsible elite offering the vote to one lower-class section in hopes of achieving a permanent majority, and another faction making a counterbid to other unrepresented elements in the community. The British Reform Bill of 1867, which one authority feels was the most significant broadening of the British suffrage in the nineteenth century, was passed by Disraeli's Conservative Government in a frank effort to "dish the Whigs." The Prime Minister thought that the large group of lower-class voters enfranchised by the statute would remain permanently in the Conservative camp.

In the United States one can trace this same pragmatic process operating on many levels. The leaders of the so-called Jacksonian democracy were not idealists devoted to broadening the suffrage. On the contrary, they were largely aristocrats, judged by the criteria of that day, who based their political aspirations on the continued allegiance of those whom they had given the vote. But, as in Great Britain, the process of enfranchisement continued until no one, at least in theory, remained voteless, unless he were under age, incompetent mentally, or a convicted felon.

The facts seem to support the contention that in all the functioning democracies of the present day the institutions which play so important a role in these societies were originated by elite groups which were at best responsible to only a small fraction of the total members of their societies. This was certainly true of the United States Constitution and of the British North America Act which supplied the constitutional framework for the Dominion of Canada, and it can be seen in probably its most vivid terms in Great Britain, where the trappings of absolute monarchy still remain disguising one of the most advanced democracies in the world.

Obviously many other factors contribute to the development of consensus, but this slow movement of a nation toward democracy without encountering any tremendous or permanently disruptive experiences seems to be the most significant. It almost seems as though a democratic society must emerge in this fashion, for the attempts to establish democratic governments upon societies which had not gone through this process of evolution have invariably proved abortive. It may be said that to assert this is to justify authoritarian stewardship, is to approve of the domination of an emergent nation by a semiresponsible elite. In essence, this accusation is correct. The alternative to a period of domination by such an elite appears to be a period of domination by extremists speaking for the mob. It is folly to speak of turning authority over to an illiterate, backward people, for in reality they are unprepared and unable to exercise responsibility. What occurs in such instances is that an elite, whose sole claim to authority is that it has seduced the mob, takes over government and creates a shambles. Thus the alternatives are not government by a constitutional elite or government by the people, but government by a constitutional elite or government by an extremist elite, usually representatives of "one true faith" or "History." When such extremists seize power, the original enthusiasts, frequently idealistic, are soon replaced by bureaucrats of enthusiasm, *e.g.*, Stalin and Malenkov, who proceed to impose a totalitarian dictatorship and extirpate differing opinion. Furthermore, this differing opinion is not usually suppressed solely because it differs and therefore creates difficulties, but because it is heresy. In the course of history constitutional elites have imprisoned a good many dissenters, but not for heresy. The difference in attitude is immensely significant.

To take but one instance, let us look at the Russian revolutionaries of February, 1917. Essentially a middle-class group with a genuine belief in democratic ideals, the Kerensky provisional government was torn by schizophrenia. If they used the armed power of the state to suppress the Bolsheviks, they would be doing something undemocratic. Yet, the Bolsheviks represented a major threat, which was recognized by the government, to the development of democracy in Russia. Primarily because of timidity, the Bolsheviks were permitted by the government to achieve formidable organizational strength in the centers of population, and Lenin sneeringly referred to the Russia of that period as the "freest country in the world." If the Kerensky government had firmly smashed the Bolshevik organization, as it had easy opportunity to do, the subsequent history of Russia would be quite different, and there would be at least a good chance that Russia would have developed into a constitutional democracy. Would such action by the constitutional elite have been undemocratic?

On the other hand, the Indian Republic of today shows how effective a constitutional elite can be when it recognizes its responsibilities to the future. The Nehru Government is an elite composed of Indian democrats mostly trained in the British tradition. The government that has been formed in India is plagued by extremists on both wings: the Communists on one side, and the Hindu fanatics on the other. If the Communists were allowed freely to operate and utilize the techniques of agitation and mass communication, they could probably convince a considerable segment of India's illiterate peasantry that the government is not moving fast enough in the direction of land reform, and thus they could become leaders of a formidable mob. The real objective of such an organization, of course, would not be the achievement of land reform, but the seizure of power by the Communists. Nehru and his colleagues recognize this and have taken strong action to suppress communist organization. Indeed, India has internal-security regulations that exceed in severity those of most Western powers. In India, as in Pakistan, Indonesia, and the other nascent democracies of Asia, we are clearly faced with the alternatives of government by a democratic elite or government by a communist elite. Are the constitutional elitists wrong, and undemocratic, in their strong action against these other elites?

It is submitted that they are not. The objection may be raised that there is no difference between communist dictatorship and democratic dictatorship. After all, they are both dictatorships. But to object in this fashion is to take an essentially Manichaean view of life—to assume that in political affairs, as in western movies, we are faced with a choice between the "goods" and the "bads." But life is not patterned after western movies. We are faced with differences of degree, with choice between the half-truth and the eighth-truth. The recent course of Turkish history illustrates this very well. An elite group seized power in Turkey immediately following World War I with the objective of democratizing and westernizing Turkey. Politically the nation was run on an authoritarian pattern, with extremists of all varieties either silent, in exile, or in prison. However, generally speaking, Turkish social and economic life was revolutionized. In nonpolitical sectors, i.e., those areas of Turkish life which did not directly impinge on politics, a great deal of freedom existed. Illiteracy was largely eliminated. In short, while authoritarian, the Turkish government was *not* totalitarian. It did not seek to dominate every aspect of national life. Its checks were largely negative. When some aspect of life created political problems, the government would take action, and often strong action, but normally economic and social life were largely autonomous. After more than twenty-five years of such government, the constitutional elite decided that the time had come to liberate the political sector. The result was a free election in which the opposition succeeded in defeating the government. Today Turkey stands as a junior member of the democratic group of nations. If this experience is compared with that of the Soviet Union, the difference between domination by a constitutional elite and domination by believers in the "one true faith" becomes apparent.

THE PLACE OF POLITICAL PARTIES IN DEMOCRATIC SOCIETIES

There is one great difference that has yet to be considered between government by a constitutional elite and government by an extremist elite. This is the place and the role that political parties play in the two schemes of government. Here we find a tremendous and vital difference in attitude, which is the touchstone of antipodal viewpoints. To the constitutionalist, political parties are an accepted part of the mechanism of political life—so long, that is, as they remain political parties and not criminal conspiracies. On the other hand, the evangelist of the "one true faith" has no place in his scheme for parties. Usually he is vehement in his denunciation of the *party principle, e.g.,* Mussolini's statement, "We Fascists are not a party, but an anti-party." In practice, however, the extremists create a party based on the proposition that parties are bad.

Indeed, the clarion cry of the extremist has always been "Unity." He demands unity around the principles which he considers true and transcendent. Thinkers such as Machiavelli, Hobbes, and Rousseau set a precedent for this by holding that nothing was more disastrous to the state than factionalism, and political parties, of course, institutionalize factionalism. The modern totalitarian state has taken strong action against factions not only on the pragmatic ground that they create disturbances, but more significantly because to admit that parties have a role in the political universe is to concede that truth is not the private possession of the totalitarian elite. Political parties are the concrete realization on the level of practical politics of the basic democratic assumption of the shared truth.

To look at the leading example of our time, the Soviet Union is organized around the principle that the proletariat is the sole repository of political, social, and economic virtue. The supporters of the Soviet system maintain that this has been conclusively demonstrated by Marx, Engels, Lenin, and Stalin. Assuming, for the purpose of discussion, that this is the case, it follows that the proletarian party, the Communist party, has a corner on truth, and that all opponents of the proletarian party are not only mistaken but are *in Error, i.e.,* are heretics. Consequently, it is theoretically impossible to justify the existence of a party in opposition to the proletariat, for to do so would be tantamount to admitting that Truth and Error are equals. Truth in the Soviet Union is not something that is shared among the people; it is the private property of the Communist party elite.

Political parties are not alone interdicted by the totalitarians; the ban on parties logically applies to all groups which do not owe complete allegiance to the Truth as propounded by the elite. It is, for example, inconceivable that a totalitarian state should allow an independent trade-union movement to exist. The operation of such an organization is based upon the assumption that workers and industrialists have differing interests, and that the way to achieve a *modus vivendi* is for them to bargain with each other. But in the totalitarian state there can be no "class struggle," at least not in any legitimate form. The proper procedure is to extirpate those who are *wrong, i.e.,* those who claim individual or group interests to be essentially beyond the scope of state direction. Thus independent trade-unions and independent managerial associations cannot be tolerated, for their very existence controverts the totalitarian premise. In practice this has resulted in the Nazi Labor Front, fascist corporations, and the Soviet trade unions.

But the process of suppression does not stop even here. The modern totalitarian state demands not only outward conformity with official practice, but also conformity of thought. Even the remotest aspects of human knowledge must respect the Truth of the dominant elite. A Soviet biologist is not free to seek truth; he starts with Truth and must corroborate it. Individual expression is regulated not in terms of subjective intent, but of objective direction. As Arthur Koestler so brilliantly described in *Darkness at Noon,* a man is punished not necessarily for what he has done, but for what he should do if he believes as he does. By the application of an "escalator technique," the man who thinks Lysenko is wrong in his genetics has already taken the first step toward the overthrow of the regime and can therefore be punished for counter-revolutionary activity. Born and nourished in a conspiratorial atmosphere, the leaders of the totalitarian states view all others as potential, if not actual, conspirators and see to it that no ideas get abroad to serve as the rationale for future revolutions.

The democrat employs a radically different approach to the whole problem of organizations and individual activity. Groups are allowed tremendous autonomy, providing always that they do not engage in criminal conspiracies, and the history of democratic societies has been characterized by the enormous proliferation of groups, clubs, lodges, and like organizations which exist within society but owe only tenuous allegiance to the political objectives of the state. Even the relationship between members and organizations is largely, at least in the United States and Great Britain, unregulated by law. It is indicative of this high degree of organizational autonomy that only in the last generation have the United States courts, both state and Federal, come to grips with the problem of the authority of a trade-union over its members, of the power of local branches of the American Medical Association over physicians, of the right of a bar association to discipline a lawyer. Needless to add, religious organizations operate almost wholly unfettered by legislation.

There is, furthermore, method in this—as a totalitarian must think—madness. Democracy, although some of its apologizers and rationalizers have ascended into the philosophical stratosphere, is essentially a common-sense philosophy. Thus, although democrats may use the term the "will of the people," it has no transcendent overtones; it is not a moral will which adheres to society as a whole but not to its component members. Consequently, the discovery of the "will of the people" is a practical process, not a matter for philosophical divination, and there is no better way of finding out what the people want than by asking them. However, the developments of the nineteenth and twentieth centuries have made the simple "New England town meeting" procedure impossible except under very limited conditions. All men cannot be polled directly on important issues, and our system of geographical political representation has notable drawbacks. What better method, then, can be employed than finding out what the interested groups and organizations believe should be done?

Political parties are obviously the most significant organizations for this. But if these parties are to fulfill their function as creative forces in society, they must remain largely autonomous. The government is quite within its rights in requiring parties to operate honestly, but intervention to force or enforce doctrinal conceptions cannot be tolerated in a democracy. The parties should be allowed, and, indeed, encouraged, to bring their wares to the market place of ideas; the state should merely enforce the rules of the market.

Political parties in turn rely upon other organizations for their programs. Usually each party has a major constellation of interest groups which surround it and feed it. In the United States, for example, the Democratic party takes the views of the trade-unions very seriously, while the Republican party is traditionally receptive to the views of financial circles. In Great Britain a similar situation exists, with the trade-union movement in effect married to the Labor party and the Conservative party closely tied to the Federation of British Industries. At the same time, no party wants to become too closely identified with any one interest group or small group of organizations. The Republican party in the dry Western states lost votes in the 1948 presidential campaign through its identification in the public mind with the private power interests.

The degree to which small groups have succeeded in influencing the programs of the major American political parties can easily be ascertained by reading the speeches of the candidates for President. Seemingly each candidate has been given a long list of interest groups which he must seduce, ranging from the labor vote to those voters who enjoy fishing in stocked streams. The 1948 campaign was highlighted in New York State by a strenuous and disingenuous competition for the so-called "Jewish vote," with the candidates of the Democratic, Republican, and Progressive parties all promising aid, aid, and still more aid, to the nascent state of Israel. New York State apparently has no significant "Arab vote"!

Another interesting aspect of the American political scene which has been noted by many commentators is the fate of "reform movements." A small group of enthusiasts organize a movement to reform the currency. As long as they remain insignificant in numbers, neither major party pays much attention to their activities. But as soon as strength develops, the enthusiasts are likely to find that their issue has been stolen from them by one or both of the old parties. This is disheartening to the reformers, who usually retire to the wilderness muttering about the immorality of the old parties or the party system; yet it is plain evidence of the method by which the political parties renew themselves by periodic blood transfusions from other groups.

Democratic government is thus party government, and the parties themselves rely on other political, economic, and social groups for their inspiration. Robert MacIver has suggested that this is one of the great strengths of the democratic way of life—there are always alternative centers of power existing in society. A political party may decline, as the Liberal party has in Britain, but a new movement arises to replace it. Consequently there is little opportunity for a social vacuum to develop. Experience has shown that when a vacuum occurs in a society, when social needs are not filled by existing institutions, the ground is prepared for extremists. But in a democratic society there is always an organization waiting in the wings for some contingency to develop so that it can achieve star billing. This group stands prepared to solve the crisis, and usually its prescription is immediately stolen by a major party, which thus "muddles through." If neither party is prepared to accept the nostrum, the organization may go into politics for itself and achieve political power. This has been the case with the cooperators of Saskatchewan, the Canadian province, who were forced into political action by the indifference of the Conservatives and Liberals to the plight of the farmers and farm cooperatives. Their organization, the Cooperative Commonwealth Federation, has now dominated the province for more than a decade.

The group, the organization, the league, the party are thus the instruments which the individual uses to make his will known. Indeed, if individuals are to have any real say in government it must be through their groups. To demand of the individual, as the totalitarian does, that he abandon those groups which are not fully subservient to the state elite is equivalent to telling him to commit intellectual suicide. It is only through institutions that men can make their ideals meaningful, can implement their beliefs, and the competition of groups within a democratic society helps to ensure that the institutions of government do not break their moorings and instead of serving man, dominate him.

AUTHORITY IN THE DEMOCRATIC SOCIETY

Students of jurisprudence have long engaged in a pastime which may be described as ferreting out sovereignty. Following the British jurist, John Austin, many have felt that there is something which can be called integral sovereignty and which can in a quasi-mechanical fashion be located in a society. Thus Austin said that sovereignty in the United States resided in two-thirds of each house of Congress and in three-quarters of the state legislatures, since only with the cooperation of these two can the United States Constitution be amended.

Sovereignty—or, as we may better refer to it, final authority in society—is difficult to locate in a democratic nation. One can maintain with a fair degree of certainty that sovereignty in the Soviet Union is vested in the Presidium (formerly called the Politburo) of the Central Committee, but where is it in the United States? Examination shows that authority in the United States is tremendously diffused, with the President sovereign on certain matters, the Congress on others, the military having a final say in some decisions, the Farm Bureau Federation exercising final authority in others. The locus of final authority is elusive. Take the issue of recognition of the state of Israel, alluded to above. The decision to hold off recognizing Israel was apparently made by the State Department largely at the behest of the oil companies who wanted to avoid inflaming the Arab world. However, respect for the "Jewish vote" in the critical state of New York led in 1948 to a reversal of this decision. In short, authority on the Israel issue shifted from the oil companies to the New York Jewish community. Another example is the Yalta agreement which President Roosevelt accepted when informed by his military advisers that the entry of the U.S.S.R. into the Japanese war was essential for victory. The authority for this advice, considered disastrous by many, rested with the Joint Chiefs of Staff. However, in the dismissal of General MacArthur final decision-making power clearly rested with President Truman.

Under normal circumstances little attempt is made in the United States to discover who has the final say. In the event of conflict between the President and Congress, each side makes all possible effort to avoid reaching a decision. To put it bluntly, each side is afraid that it will lose, and only in the event that compromises fail will any serious effort be made to see who is boss. A knock-down, drag-out fight usually helps nobody in the long run. President Truman's efforts to achieve cooperation with General MacArthur, including even a presidential flight to Wake Island, are an instance of the lengths to which the constitutional commander in chief will go in order to avoid a final assertion of his legitimate power.

Another instance of this caution is the reluctance of the government, whether it be a Democratic national administration or a Republican state administration, to utilize the injunctive process against strikes. Not only are these officials wary of alienating the "labor vote," but they are also frightened that the unions may successfully defy the injunctions. Suppose an injunction is defied—what do you do next? Send in the National Guard? It is better not to come to bridges you do not want to cross.

To a lesser extent this same process operates in more highly centralized Britain. The election of the Churchill Government in 1951 immediately created a problem for the trade-unions and, needless to say, for the Conservatives. In a straight fight, could the Government down the Trades Union Congress? This question will probably never be answered, for with the election of Churchill a conspiracy was initiated to avoid finding out. The unions have tacitly agreed not to engage in frontal assaults on the Government, and the Government will certainly not undertake any Taft-Hartley Act.

It can even be suggested that a good indication of the degree of stability that exists within a society is the extent to which issues are taken to a final conclusion. In an unstable society such as that of France or Italy hardly a week passes without the government's being forced to break a strike, or exercise its sovereignty in some other aspect of national life. In the United States great potential conflicts are oftener than not settled well below the level of governmental action. Both the automobile manufacturers and the automobile workers, for example, may be completely convinced that justice is on their side, but each is afraid that the government, if invoked in a dispute, may hold for the other. Consequently, each is prepared to bargain and compromise to avoid a possible final loss, a decision which might be irrevocable.

This same process of avoiding final decisions on divisive issues takes place within private organizations. For many years, for example, the Democratic party sedulously refused to reach a final decision on the question of civil rights. The party platform contained a studiedly ambiguous affirmation of the principle of civil rights which the Southern Democrats ignored and the Northern Democrats played up. However, in 1948 a liberal Democratic caucus at the party convention forced the civil-rights issue in specific terms and, after several attempts to sidetrack the matter failed, won the day. The result was a split in the Democratic party which, although not too important in 1948, probably contributed to Stevenson's defeat in the election of 1952. It is interesting that President Truman, according to the memoirs of Secretary of Defense James Forrestal, regretted that the issue had been brought to the fore and even added that he sympathized with the Southern delegates. Thus final assertions and demonstrations of authority offend dissidents and frequently lead them to extreme action. Southerners who were prepared to accept a new compromise on civil rights, conceding some of the issues, refused to accept the final decision. In the former instance, they knew that they could come back to fight again another day; in the latter, they felt that their position within the Democratic party was untenable. At the time, a cynic was heard to observe, "If we clarify about three more planks in the platform, there will be nobody left to stand on it!"

BASES OF PARTY ORGANIZATION

This diffusion of authority, of sovereignty, as it exists in the vast, sprawling United States, and to a lesser degree in the other democracies, has had profound implications on the organization of political parties. In addition, the unique constitutional framework of the United States has added some special factors in this country. Let us examine first the generic issue of the effect of diffusion on democratic parties, and second the special conditions that exist in the United States.

Since in a democracy the political parties are not the sole instruments of popular will but must operate side by side with functional pressure groups, the parties must attempt to channel the political activities of these groups. Otherwise, as has been pointed out, the groups are likely themselves to become political parties. As a consequence, the parties must possess a high degree of flexibility, must be prepared to reconsider their premises the minute that a substantial portion of their followers begin to look elsewhere for political leadership. This makes it very difficult for an ideological party, a party built around a rigid doctrinal approach, to succeed.

At first glance, the party systems of many foreign democratic nations seem to refute this generalization. Britain, the British Commonwealth nations, the Scandinavian countries, and France all seem to have large, successful ideological parties. It is submitted, however, that this is not the case. While many of the labor and socialist parties of today originated as ideological parties, the closer they approached power the less ideological they became. The British Labor Party, for instance, achieved power in 1945 because of the adherence to its objectives of a substantial segment of the British middle class. In 1950, at the celebration of the Labor party's fiftieth anniversary, the leaders explicitly rejected the class-war doctrines of the early leader James Keir Hardie and asserted that the party now represented the aspirations not alone of the British workers, but also of the British middle class.

Another British example comes to mind. When the Labor party's program for the election of February, 1950, was first enunciated, it contained a plank calling for the nationalization of insurance. Immediately the cooperative movement, which has tremendous insurance assets, announced its opposition to this move. Faced with this opposition from a group which has traditionally given the Labor party firm support, the party strategists changed the campaign demand to "mutualization" of insurance, or ownership by the insured. This, of course, satisfied the cooperators, since their insurance firms are owned by the insured!

Likewise, the British Conservative party is far from ideological. It is estimated by Labor party experts that one British worker in four votes Conservative, and the Conservative party will certainly take no action to alienate this support. To move to the Continent, it certainly appears that French political parties have a far larger dose of doctrine in their make-up than the British, but again the extent of this ideological base has been exaggerated. It should be noted, first, that the Communist parties of France and Italy, although there can be no doubt of their ideological affiliation to Moscow, are not acting in public like ideological parties. Recently the communist leadership in both France and Italy offered the right hand of fellowship to anybody, regardless of class origins or position, who would oppose the North Atlantic Treaty and support "Peace." The French Socialist party, like the German Social Democratic party, is almost totally unable to achieve agreement among its members as to what the party does stand for, and consequently it makes frequently contradictory appeals to various sectors of the community. It is likewise with the Christian Democrats of Italy, who are internally divided among left-, center-, and right-wing factions and, as a result, unite only on the lowest common denominator of anticommunism. This analysis could be continued from country to country, but would fail to show any major party outside the Communists—and the Communists are insignificant in all the stable democracies—which fits the definition of ideological. True, some are more ideological than others, but it is difficult to locate any that have not, when faced with the possible antipathy of a large section of the electorate if a certain course were continued, risen above their principles.

Interestingly enough, there appears to be a similar tendency away from doctrine in the trade-union movements of Britain and Western Europe—although this is far less marked than in the political sphere. One example of this was a report on public ownership presented by the executive to the 1950 meeting of the British Trades Union Congress. This report, while endorsing the measures of nationalization undertaken by the Labor Government, suggested that before any further action along this line was initiated a thorough study be made of the effectiveness of public ownership and of possible alternative techniques of public control. This "go slow" policy was reasserted at the Congress's 1953 meeting. The *Force Ouvrière*, anticommunist trade-union center organized in France in 1948, although closely aligned to the Socialist party, maintains a technically nonpolitical position, and there are some influential leaders of the organization who urge that it break loose from the remaining ties with the Socialists. The free German trade-unionists, traditionally split into socialist and nonsocialist centers, have in the period since World War II unified into one large organization which, while friendly to the Social Democratic party, is officially nonpartisan and has not hesitated to oppose the SDP on certain issues. It should be added that the Adenauer Government felt that this neutrality was compromised in the 1953 German election, and demanded that more Christian Democrats be put on the board of directors of the confederation as a guarantee of future nonpartisanship.

To summarize, it seems that the nature of democratic society militates against ideological parties and, indeed, against any large functional group with an ideological foundation. The reason for this may be that any group which organizes rigidly around the "one true faith" finds itself unable to deal effectively with the other groups in society. If such a group had its way, it would "unify" society around itself, but being unable to employ force, it must either learn to compromise or relegate itself to political limbo. Furthermore, if a position on any issue is rigidly maintained, those holding it lose their bargaining power. No Republican in 1860 bothered to consult the abolitionists about the party's presidential nominee; the abolitionists had nowhere else to go! To take another instance, a trade-union organized on a purely ideological basis cannot afford to be beaten. If its ideological enemies take power, its bargaining power is zero and opponents can maintain that they have a mandate to break the organization. Many American trade-unionists secretly rue the day that they became closely affiliated with the left wing of the New Deal, for they feel that this made a Taft-Hartley Act inevitable with the resurgence of the Republican party. This is only a minor instance, for American unionism is primarily anti-ideological, but it brings out the force of the argument.

In addition, the democratic climate of opinion works against ideological organization. Democracy is essentially a rational system, and the democrat is traditionally suspicious of the ideologue with his claim to infallibility. Notoriously easygoing, the democrat can tolerate many rational vices in his leaders, but he reacts unfavorably to the "man sent from God." General MacArthur appealed tremendously to many Americans as a great military leader and as a focus, as well, for anti-Truman sentiment, but the General's almost fanatical approach to world problems seems to have alienated most of his original constituency. While many Americans contribute to religious missionary activity of some sort, it should be noted carefully that the missionary is a comic figure in American folklore. In fact, democrats seem to avoid choosing leaders with outstanding ability, much less with a sense of mission. Fear of the unpredictable Winston Churchill appears to have led many Britons to vote for the unassuming Attlee. As a partial consequence of this, aspiring leaders in a democracy usually hide their lights under bushels of seeming mediocrity.

As a consequence of these factors, and others, which will be treated in detail in later chapters, political parties in the various democratic nations resemble each other far more than any one of them resembles a totalitarian party. Generally they are based on a more or less stable constellation of pressure groups, although seldom is an interest group irrevocably committed to a party. They tend to proceed pragmatically from issue to issue, testing in each case the reaction of the public to their points of view. They eschew controversial doctrine to the greatest possible extent, and excommunicate only as a last resort. Opposing parties tend to resemble each other; indeed, in Great Britain the Laborites and Conservatives today resemble each other far more than either resembles its ancestors! In short, accepting the democratic political process and the diffusion of power which is its concomitant, each party attempts to gain the allegiance of as many loci of power as it can. There are few democratic parties that explicitly exclude anyone. The French Christian Democrats, although ostensibly a Catholic party, welcome Protestant members, as does the German Christian Democratic Union. Regional parties exist in a few countries, Canada, for example, but they are not regional by choice or in program. Agrarian parties, where they operate, as in Sweden, are constantly seeking urban allies. Although it may be rash to generalize on this theme, it almost appears that any party which is consciously and explicitly exclusionary is verging on extremism and departing from the democratic stream.

As mentioned before, there are in the United States additional forces at work which act as an almost complete barrier to ideological party organization. The outstanding institutional factor is the absolute majority needed in the electoral college to elect a President. A noted pundit once observed that in American politics there are not two sides to every question, but only two sides to the White House—inside and outside. To get its man inside the White House is the major objective of an American party, and there is no second prize. Achieving this end in a nation the size of the United States with regional differences, urban-rural conflict, and other problems too numerous to note, is exceptionally difficult on any basis but a pragmatic one. Traditionally this problem has been handled through the federal organization of the parties, with a coalition being formed every four years to run a candidate for the Presidency. Each party has within it almost every point of view in abundance, and no common view has been required—only a common candidate. The New York State Democrat is far closer to the New York State Republican than he is to the Texas or Iowa Democrat. The California Democrat, conversely, is in far more agreement with the New York Democrat than he is with the California Republican. Thus each party runs its affairs state by state and then, when the time comes to nominate a President, tries to find someone who offends no significant constituency.

This extraordinary looseness and diverseness of party has, as will be discussed in detail in a later chapter, been a major contributing factor to the development of pressure groups as active political forces in the United States. The lowest common denominator in the United States is so low that interest groups feel that they must individually implement their claims. The British do not have this problem, largely because the common denominator there is sufficiently high that interests can with some safety leave their aspirations in the hands of the politicians. But even in Britain, lobbies are not unknown and are not without effectiveness. The pacifist group in the Labor party created tremendous problems for the Labor Government, and the Federation of British Industries is constantly exerting pressure on the Conservatives.

CONCLUSION

The purpose of this introductory chapter is to present the democratic political process in its broadest terms. In the chapters that follow, various generalizations contained here are examined in detail, and the experience of various democratic nations is integrated on the functional level. Using the United States as a point of reference, the institutions of other democracies are analyzed as they are found relevant to the subject under discussion. The integration operates at each level, e.g., when the electoral process is discussed, the experience of other democracies is brought in for purpose of comparison with that of the United States. Although the main comparisons will be with British and French experiences, developments in other democracies will be examined whenever they are relevant to the discussion. Some countries lend themselves better to the analysis of certain problems than others, and when this is true, they are used and the other democracies largely passed over. But fundamentally the discussion is not of countries, but of issues and problems of the democratic way of life. The analysis has been centered around the United States because those who use this book will mostly be Americans, concerned first and foremost with the operation and perhaps improvement of the American democratic process.

PART II. THE SOURCES OF PUBLIC POLICY:
POLITICAL PARTIES AND PUBLIC OPINION

Chapter 2

POLITICAL PARTIES—FUNCTIONS
AND ORGANIZATION

IN ABSTRACT theory, democracy rests upon the belief that, through the pooling of the views of individuals, society can develop, widen its vistas, and find the better life. But this abstraction must find institutional meaning. Some supposed democrats, like Jean Jacques Rousseau or the leaders of the French Revolution, eloquently advanced an abstract democratic theory but, when the time came to talk of the practical, forbade "faction" in their societies. The basis for this interdiction of association was the belief that groups tend to pervert the individual, to lead him off down the primrose path of personal interest. Presumably, the more associations an individual belonged to, the less concern he would have for the public interest. In short, this view is posited on the assumption that there is a conflict between public and private interest. The result of such a scheme is that the individual *as individual* may possibly believe as he chooses, but he is powerless to implement his views except through the state. It is conceivable that a political system based on this direct approach could work in a very small state, but it is inconceivable that it would operate in a large, complex, industrial society. Some cynical observers have even questioned the *bona fides* of the New England town meeting, feeling that, while free discussion is always present at these gatherings, few real decisions are made without prior caucus agreement.

Thus the right to organize interest groups becomes the heart of the democratic political process. Operating on the assumption that private and public interests interlock rather than conflict, democrats rush to form organizations which will advance their views. The impersonalization of industrial societies has probably, as Erich Fromm suggests in his brilliant analysis *Escape from Freedom*, contributed tremendously to the growth of organizations. The individual in our society feels a psychological need for associates and associations because he no longer thinks that society, government, business, or labor will respond to individual pressure as they once did. In a period when huge unions negotiate with giant industries, the individual, be he worker or businessman, cannot successfully go it alone except under extraordinary circumstances.

The result has, of course, been the enormous development of associations or

27

interest groups in democratic societies. Those concerned with governmental and political matters may be classified either as political parties or as pressure or interest groups. The main distinction between parties and pressure groups is that parties run candidates for office while pressure groups do not—or, at least, not openly. In addition, parties try to mobilize, hence convince, majorities, while interest groups work on legislators and administrators already in office. Some interests may engage in both types of activity: the prohibitionists, for example, have pressure organizations such as the Anti-Saloon League as well as a Prohibition party which runs presidential candidates every four years. But normally a political party, if it is seriously engaged in the quest for power, must be far broader than any one interest group. The remainder of this chapter will be concerned with the parties, while a discussion of pressure groups will be found in a subsequent chapter.

The role that political parties play in democratic political theory should be clear, but an important and complex question remains to be discussed: What are the appropriate concrete functions that parties fulfill in a democratic society? A discussion of the organization of the parties can be valuable only if it is conducted in terms of certain standards, so before undertaking an analysis of actual party operations in the major democracies, criteria for evaluation should be established. It is, therefore, to the question of proper party functions, and their implications, that we must next turn our attention.

The governmental process can, for convenience, be subdivided into two broad components: the formulation of policy and the implementation of policy. It should be emphasized that this is a convenient subdivision, for there obviously is no watertight compartment between the two categories. They act and interact continuously. But the broad distinction is valid in the same sense that there is a recognizable difference between hot and cold, although one may not be able to state accurately where hot ends and cold begins. Politically speaking, there are groups at work in society concerned primarily with the formulation of new governmental policies and, in the case of political parties, with presenting potential leaders who will, it is asserted, implement the proposed policy innovations. These new programs are presented to the electorate on formal political occasions, e.g., elections or referendums, and are constantly being urged upon the public through the less formal mechanism of the propaganda campaign.

The major value of the policy-formulation function of political parties lies not so much in promises to undertake actions X, Y, or Z as in the establishment of a frame of reference, a climate of opinion, which will condition the actions of policy implementors. It is obviously impossible for the party to commit itself to the electorate on the hundreds of thousands of specific decisions that its administrators will make. All it can do is announce its general approaches to certain major issues and encourage the electorate to extrapolate from these its probable views on the minutiae of administration. A citizen who casts his ballot for a low-tariff candidate for President, or an organization which supports a candidate because of his position on lowering tariff barriers, does not ask the candidate to promise that he will appoint low-tariff spokesmen to the Tariff Commission. Conversely, a President elected on a conservative position would not be asked whether he would appoint socialists to the various government regulatory bodies. In both cases, the electorate would assume, perhaps with too much faith, that the specific actions of administration would flow logically from the general climate of opinion represented by the candidate.

On the other hand, the implementation of policy takes place on a somewhat different level. Here the actual task of execution is usually turned over to experts who are given general instructions on what is to be accomplished and are left to choose, within the bounds of reason and political expediency, what techniques they will utilize. Particularly in the highly industrialized state, the service of experts is vital to the success of proposed measures of public policy. A government decision to regulate coal-mine safety, for example, is almost wholly dependent for implementation upon the employment of highly trained inspectors. In recent years, the trend has been for national legislation merely to establish a framework within which administrative experts will operate, rather than to attempt an exact delineation of how the job shall be done. Again it should be reiterated that policy execution cannot be completely divorced from policy formulation, for frequently the method of implementation can frustrate the original purpose of a statute. But because in a democracy the executives operate under the watchful eyes of all interested groups, this does not often happen. When experts do tend to become semiautonomous, it is usually because they have no eagle-eyed constituency overseeing their activities. The Visa Division of the State Department, whose constituents are voteless foreigners, has far more autonomy than the Office of Education, which operates under the surveillance of the National Education Association, the American Council on Education, and various teachers' organizations. It is important to note, furthermore, that an interest group which had sufficient influence to get its views incorporated in legislation usually has sufficient power to ensure that the execution of the adopted policy proceeds without sabotage.

Assuming this division between the formulation and the implementation of public policy, the query may be raised: To what extent are these functions within the proper jurisdiction of political parties? Should the parties formulate *and* implement public policy? Or should they establish the framework of policy, supply political leadership, but leave the implementation of policy to others? To put the question another way, we may ask: To what extent should the actions of government be subject to the control of nongovernmental party officials and party decisions? Further, and of great significance in this era of *expertise*, should party service rather than technical proficiency serve as the basis for appointment to administrative positions?

For many years, Americans seemed to feel that parties properly should exercise both policy-formulation and policy-implementation functions. Beginning in the Jacksonian period, the tradition developed that election to office constituted qualification for office. This was carried to great extremes in the states, with the election of judges without any required legal qualifications, of coroners who might be totally lacking in medical knowledge, and of auditors who might be incapable of solving simple problems in mathematics. Furthermore, with respect to appointed offices of the Federal government, the Jacksonian attitude was—as expressed by Secretary of State Marcy—"to the victors belong the spoils." The unfortunate American attitude toward government officials may in large part spring from the fact that for many years appointment to office was based on party service rather than on qualifications for the position. The Foreign Service was, with few exceptions, staffed by party hacks, with wealthy party contributors occupying the embassies, and the President's Cabinet was a top political pie. Although conscientious Presidents undertook to put able men in key Cabinet posts, they often found that pre-convention promises gave them very little leeway. President Lincoln's famous comment about the Secretary of War whom his managers foisted upon him, that Cameron "wouldn't steal a red-hot stove," comes to mind at this point. While one may enjoy the President's witticism, it should be remembered that the Union was then on the edge of disunity and civil war, and the character of the Secretary of War should have been a matter of some concern to the nation.

The Pendleton Act of 1883, which established the Civil Service Commission and initiated the merit system on a small scale, was the first major step on the road back to President Washington's conception of "fitness for office" as a prime requisite for appointment. However, the passage of this measure was motivated more by sheer disgust with the political practices of the day than by any thought-out philosophy of clean government. It is also possible that, as American history texts uniformly point out, the shooting of President Garfield by a "disappointed office seeker" was instrumental in the passage of the act, although it is not clear how the Pendleton Act would remedy such disappointment. In fact, if the philosophy latent in the Pendleton Act had ever taken hold in the Washington of 1883, it would appear that disappointment and presumably assassination would have increased.

The principle that merit should be the main criterion for appointment to a government post was gradually expanded over the intervening years until today well over 90 per cent of the employees of the national government are under civil service. One of the last remaining strongholds of patronage, the Collectors of Internal Revenue, fell before the onslaughts of reform in 1952 following a wave of scandals. It should be noted that the "fall of the mink dynasty," as gleeful Republicans called it, and its replacement by the merit system was based less on an a priori concept of good government than on a deep conviction among Democrats that unless they undertook some conspicuous political penance, the Republicans would have a choice election issue. Indeed, Republican success in the 1952 presidential election may have been partly due to the strong public reaction against venality in the tax offices.

But, however achieved, the principle of merit is of vital significance to the functioning of a democratic society in the atomic age. American society in the 1840's, or even in the 1920's, could blunder along with incompetents in high places and eventually a vital democracy would see to it that the worst blunderers were fired and the ship of state returned to course. But today, when prompt decisions on matters of world-shaking importance are required, democracies must have the services of their best-qualified citizens. The American Ambassador to the Soviet Union, for example, should not be a wealthy party contributor with a taste for caviar; he should be a man who appreciates both the realities of international politics and the niceties of communist dogma. This need for people with expert knowledge is everywhere apparent, and it must be met if the United States is not to blunder once too often.

Consequently, it is suggested that the proper function of political parties is to formulate public policies, supply governmental majorities, and fill high political offices, but not to attempt the implementation of policy. This is not for a moment to suggest that parties have no governmental function, but rather to propose that this function is somewhat different from what is usually supposed. It is the party's job to propose a policy, or more usually a body of policies, to the public, to supply leaders—a political class—who will incorporate these views into public policy, and, very significantly, to punish leaders for policy deviations. In short, the party supplies what might be described as the climate of government and the instruments of government—a majority and a political class—but it does not govern. Government is the task of the political class which, while owing its leadership to party auspices and operating within the climate of government created by the party, has far broader responsibilities than have party leaders who are in opposition or are not members of the government. Few would contend, for example, that President Dwight Eisenhower or Sir Winston Churchill should solely concern themselves with the welfare of American Republicans or British Consevatives. Parties are by definition only parts, while the political class is responsible to the totality; President Eisenhower is responsible to the 27 million Americans who voted for Governor Stevenson as well as to his own 35 million.

To some critics this distinction between party and governmental functions may smack of mysticism. "After all," the criticism may run, "when party leaders become government leaders, they do not undergo a transformation—they are the same men with different titles." There is, of course, some truth in this observation, but in a deeper sense the success of the democratic way of life is posited on its fundamental falsity. Democracy is not simply majority rule; as Sir Ernest Barker has suggested, democracy is rule by the majority for the whole. Rule by a majority simply for its own benefit is political and social brigandage and is one of the characteristics of societies in disintegration, *e.g.,* France, Weimar Germany. Although the party function is a necessary prerequisite to the governmental function, the two are not identical. The governmental function is more inclusive, and because this is the case the political class, supplied by the party, becomes responsible to the wider constituency. Thus the distinction between party and governmental functions and the concomitant assumption that party leaders do undergo a transformation on assuming office might be considered one of the vital political myths of democratic government, and fortunately empirical examination of the actions of American Presidents and British Prime Ministers indicates that such a transformation, a widening of vistas, does in fact occur. President Eisenhower's bitter struggle with members of his own party to extend the excess-profit tax might be cited in evidence here.

If this distinction is accepted, then certain functions are associated with the party, and another set of functions are within the jurisdiction of the government. In the same sense that it is not a proper function of government to regulate the opinion-forming activities, or to dominate the internal structure, of political parties, it is not the function of the party to supply directives to the government or to fill technical state positions with party hacks. Except among barbarians, governing is more than simply distributing loot to one's followers. Once the party has supplied the political class and the climate of government within which the political class will operate, the job of implementing policy should be placed in the hands of those best qualified to do the job. The experts must, of course, work under the supervision of the political class— which retains the prerogative of replacing experts who reject the climate of government—and the political leaders must accept responsibility before the party and the electorate for the techniques of administration. Such a system would allow for both flexibility and responsibility: flexibility, in that highly skilled administrators can adapt the agreed-upon policies to rapidly changing national and international conditions; responsibility, in that the electorate retains the final right to reject the policies and the political class responsible for them.

This still leaves the parties with vital functions to perform. Although not governing, the party—as was suggested above—lays the foundations of government, creates the atmosphere within which the officials operate, mobilizes majorities for policies, provides the political class, and last, but not least, acts as an effective link between the people and the state. Each of these functions is significant for the smooth operation of democratic government, for, as will be demonstrated below, parties that supply leaders but not policy create great difficulties, and a party system that contributes policies but no effective political class leaves much to be desired.

With this discussion in mind, let us now begin our examination of the political party systems that exist in the major democratic states and see to what degree the actual parties fulfill the ideal requirements stated above.

THE UNITED STATES

It is generally said that the United States has a two-party system, but this is a deceptive generalization. Actually what one should say is that in any specific election district at election time there are seldom more than two significant contenders for office. Indeed, in about half the election districts in the United States there is only one significant contender, for in these areas the minority party is too weak to offer an effective challenge to the party in power. Furthermore, the two parties running candidates in one state may have little resemblance to the two parties in another state, although they wear the same Republican and Democratic labels. For example, the New York State Republicans are unquestionably more liberal than the Iowa Democrats. As E. E. Schattschneider demonstrated in his incisive study *Party Government,* national parties are in the United States a myth: the Democratic and Republican parties are essentially loose confederations of state and local parties that close ranks every four years to contest the Presidency of the United States.

Thus it is an office that supplies the common denominator for the American parties. The constitutional requirement that a President must receive a majority of the electoral votes forces the formation of two major blocs every four years. The alternative form of election if no presidential candidate receives a majority of the electoral votes, *i.e.,* election by the House of Representatives, is apparently too horrible to contemplate! A possible reason for this dread of seeing the election go into the House, aside from the historical fact that both times it has been tried trouble developed, may be that the urban sections of both the Democratic and Republican parties fear action by the rurally weighted House of Representatives.

One of the most fascinating aspects of American political life is the virtually private nature of the selection of presidential candidates. The national conventions that nominate presidential candidates are regulated by no law; they are, in effect, glorified club meetings where delegates come as private citizens to choose a potential occupant of the most powerful office in the nation. Delegates may come committed to some candidate, but there is no way that such a promise may be enforced in law. The presidential primaries that are held in some states are actually only state-subsidized public-opinion polls from which powerful contenders for presidential office frequently abstain. These polls may have some psychological influence on the choice of candidates, as was the case in the 1948 Oregon struggle between Thomas E. Dewey and Harold Stassen, but in legal terms they decide nothing. A delegate who refuses to abide by the presidential-primary result in his state may be guilty of a political double cross, but by the time anything can be done about it, the party will have nominated its candidate. Once the ball is over the goal line, there is no penalty, even for the dirtiest of dirty playing, that will bring it back fifteen yards and cancel the touchdown.

These nominating conventions are in a sense small editions of the national legislature, for contained within them are all sorts and types. The liberal who must appeal to the labor vote is present, demanding a progressive plank on labor legislation. The conservative who wants an end to the welfare state except for business, the farmer in search of price protection, the public-power advocates—all are there with their demands. Some time is spent on drafting a platform, but this is usually turned over to sonorous rhetoricians with a gift for studied ambiguity. The main job is the selection of someone to win the top post. And here, too, local concerns are forcefully interjected. The chosen candidate for President must be a man who can help the party back home. What shall it avail a local party if its candidate gains the Presidency but loses its own district? The New York State Republicans were throughout 1952 going in deadly fright that Senator Taft would be the Republican candidate for President. This was not because they were certain Taft would lose, but because they were virtually certain Taft would lose New York. A Republican national victory which left them out in the cold did not have much appeal.

Consequently, the major prerequisite for a presidential nominee must be that he can appeal to the marginal voter and at the same time not be offensive to any significant group in the party. We can with some justice call American national politics the search for the common denominator, or, to be specific, the search for a man who appears forward-looking enough to satisfy the more liberal urban elements of the party and does not unsettle the conservative rural segment.

Many who have observed this process at work have reached the conclusion that there is no place for issues or principles in American politics. But this is not a fair generalization, for issues play a very vital role in American political life on the local level, particularly in urban areas. In many cities pressure groups have developed with the major purpose of forcing the parties to pay more attention to issues, and in at least one instance, Philadelphia, the pressure group concerned, municipal reformers working through Americans for Democratic Action, itself took over the Democratic party and won power in 1950 on issues. But because the American party system is so decentralized, and because the Philadelphia liberal Democrats need the support of the Alabama conservative Democrats to maintain a Democrat of any sort as President, few issues float up to the stratospheric level of national politics within the parties. When they do get injected into national politics they can cause great difficulties, as evidenced by what the civil-rights issue did to the Democrats in 1948.

Another inadequate generalization about American politics is that patronage holds the parties together—that the reason the Southern Democrats supported Truman, to the extent that they did, was their fear that the President would withdraw patronage from them. There is, of course, some validity in this contention, but it fails to take into consideration the fact that where the local politicians depend least on national patronage is precisely in these safe areas of the party's strength. The Democrats have complete control of the local and state governmental apparatus, and while a few added Federal plums would be nice, they are not essential to hold the machine together. Actually there is another consideration that plays a far more important role in holding the allegiance of the Southern Democrats to a liberal Democratic President, and that is congressional status. The Southerners know that if a Democrat is going to carry New York, California, Illinois, and the other vital urban states, he must be fairly liberal and advance views that are anathema to the South. But if these Southern Congressmen are to remain in their vastly powerful committee posts—and a very large percentage of the Democratic committee chairmen come from the South—the Democrats must carry the urban areas. If the Republicans carry the urban sector, there will be unfortunate episodes like the Eightieth Congress (1946 to 1948) and the Eighty-third Congress (1952 to 1954) in which the ancient masters of power, the Democratic committee chairmen, have had to move away from the head of the table. Therefore the conservatives need a liberal President and are prepared to put up with a lot of campaign nonsense, secure in the knowledge that when the matters so loosely and liberally discussed before Northern liberal audiences come before Congress in the form of legislation, they will be sitting in the real seats of power. The President can propose, the committee chairmen dispose.

It has often been suggested that the American political scene would be much improved if the national parties formulated some ideological basis for membership, with all the conservatives in one bag and all the liberals in another. This might make politics somewhat simpler to understand, but it would also result, at least under present circumstances, in the type of bitter quarrels that characterize present-day French democracy. The United States is not a homogeneous nation, and it is highly questionable whether, if divisions were made ideologically, only two parties would result. More probably there would be three or four. The Republicans and the Southern Democrats may work well together in frustrating liberal proposals, but it is doubtful how much agreement there would be between them on positive measures. Moreover, as Thomas E. Dewey has suggested, the conservatives would always lose to the liberals, if two parties of principle developed. Under present conditions each party tries to get as many of the different interests into its camp as it can, and the result is that many of the more bitter political problems are compromised to some degree on the party level. There is, in addition, a good deal of feeling that the party should tiptoe around sleeping dogmas rather than fight out divisive solutions. In a society like that of the United States, with tremendous latent economic and regional antagonisms, any additional level of compromise may be to the good. The American political process, engaged in the pragmatic quest for compromise, has so far succeeded in blunting the razor's edge of divisive interest, and it is doubtful whether a neat ideological division in party alignment would contribute significantly to American political life except in the negative sense.

On the basis of this discussion, it can be seen that the American political party system, to the extent that it operates nationally, specializes in supplying leadership, or, to be more precise, in supplying a President. After the election, the national parties disappear for a four-year hibernation broken only by a few committee meetings. This leaves a President in office, but what else? To take the specific case of President Truman's victory in 1948, did the people give the President a mandate? If so, what was it? Some claimed that Truman was clearly given the green light for his liberal program, but the facts of the election seem to belie this assertion. Unquestionably, many in the North voted for the President because they supported his civil-rights and pro-labor views. But the farmers of Iowa, who voted for Truman, also voted for Gillette for the Senate, a conservative Democrat. They supported Truman for his agricultural policy—not for his liberalism. Similarly, Truman carried most of the South despite the strong opposition to his civil-rights program. The Far Westerners seemed to support the President's views on public power and irrigation. The farmers backed his views on farm supports which serve to keep the prices of some commodities quite high to consumers, while many city consumers voted for Truman as the man who might bring solace from high food prices. Thus one can take the so-called Truman "mandate" and break it down into about five or six mandates, several of them contradictory.

The conclusion is obvious: the man who is elected to the highest office in the United States seldom enters the Presidency with a body of clear-cut policy. In all probability if he had one, he would not have been elected. Even President Franklin D. Roosevelt, considered by some to be a doctrinaire, seldom got specific in his campaign speeches and went to great pains to avoid antagonizing the Southern Democrats. Admirers and detractors of Roosevelt can, with retrospective omniscience, turn the New Deal into a consistent body of dogma, but if one analyzes Roosevelt's legislative program dispassionately, it appears as a succession of frequently ill-related measures, with not a little internal inconsistency, designed to appease the various segments of the "New Deal mandate." One of the reasons Roosevelt was such a superb politician was that he was so little of an ideologue. If his picture hung in many a Harlem tenement, it also was displayed in the Georgia "cracker's" shanty.

This is not to maintain that it makes no difference which party controls the Presidency and Congress. Not only the direction of the President, but also the dominant beliefs of the majority party in Congress are important in determining the color of legislation. There is a big difference between a Republican Congress of the twenties, which attempted no great regulatory measures, and the New Deal Congresses of the thirties, which passed such significant statutes as the Social Security and Wagner Acts. It is true that rural-urban, or agrarian-industrial, or conservative-liberal divisions occur more frequently in Congress than party divisions. Yet, the effect of this should not be exaggerated. In the United States, majority rule is achieved by legislative, not party, majorities; while in Britain, majority rule is attained by majority-party domination. But no one has ever definitely demonstrated that laws passed by a majority of a British majority party are necessarily more reflective of public opinion generally than laws passed by an American Congress on a nonparty basis. To make matters even more complex, it should be noted that neither the Labor party in 1945 nor the Conservative party in 1951 obtained a majority of the electorate, but each won a legislative majority. In Britain, decision on issues is sought at the polls; in the United States, it is obtained in the legislature after the election.

Leadership, then, and not policy, is the matrix of American national politics. Naturally enough, different leadership implies certain policy differences, for Senator Russell would obviously take a different view of civil rights from Senator Lehman. But the central point remains valid; it is the man who is elected, not the policy. Consequently the national party "organizations," such as they are, cannot supply the policies for the American government, and the President, if he chooses to try to formulate policy in a vigorous manner, cannot rely on any national party machine to help him implement his views. It is to the Congress that he must go, and because of the decentralization of the parties, the party whip rests lightly on most members of Congress. Discussion of the legislative process is reserved for treatment in a later chapter, so little more will be said at this point. However, it might be worthwhile to add one important observation which may help to explain the constant warfare between President and Congress. A large proportion of the votes which elect any President comes from urban areas. But in the Congress, because of maldistribution of seats by rurally dominated state legislatures, these urban areas are uniformly underrepresented, thus putting any President who tries to stand in well with his urban supporters in a jam. If a President advocates programs favored by city voters, he must frequently do it at the cost of impotence with Congress, and if he works closely with Congress, he may well suffer for it in the urban election districts. Another problem reserved for later discussion, that of the role of lobbies, should also be alluded to here, for it is the weakness of the American political party system that helps to give the pressure groups such an important place in American government.

In addition to the decentralization of American political parties and their emphasis on supplying national leadership rather than national policy, there is another unique characteristic that deserves mentioning. In the other democracies, one usually finds the outstanding leaders of all parties occupying niches in the formal governmental, or, in the case of opposition parties, in the parliamentary structure. In the United States, party leaders are frequently members of an informal power structure that has no institutional foundation. Indeed, the system of presidential election in the United States automatically relegates the defeated candidate to relative obscurity. Thus the formal leadership of the minority party, to the extent that it exists, rests with a state governor like Dewey, a private citizen like Stevenson or Willkie, or an ex-President like Truman or Hoover—none of whom can command a national rostrum ex officio. There is no official leader of the opposition. In passing, it might be noted that American parties are usually financially bankrupt at the national level.

This informal power structure is not only characteristic of the minority party on the national level; it exists in both parties at all levels. The "boss" who holds no official job is a recurrent figure in American political mythology, going back at least to Alexander Hamilton, who attempted to run the Adams administration from his home in New York. The term "kitchen cabinet," referring to these informal advisers, was coined during the administration of President Jackson. Space does not permit an examination of this phenomenon on the state and local level, but certain hypotheses can be advanced for its prevalence at the national. In the case of the majority party which has succeeded in electing the President, we generally find that the chief executive's formal advisory structure—the Cabinet—is of little value to him in determining over-all policy. Cabinet appointments are not usually allocated solely on merit, but as political plums designed to assuage the various sections of the victorious party. Consequently, the typical Cabinet contains men who are identified with various pressure interests in the nation and who tend to fight the President in behalf of these interests rather than fighting the interests in behalf of presidential policy.

Since his official family is riddled with special pleaders, the President must seek his advisers elsewhere. As a consequence of this and other related factors, the United States has had a series of "Gray Eminences" like Harry Hopkins, Colonel House, and Bernard Baruch, who have scuttled freely up and down the back stairs of the White House. Needless to add, what is true of the Cabinet is doubly true of the Vice-Presidency, which is generally given as a consolation prize to a leader of the opposite wing of the party from the President. Institutionally speaking, the President has no friends.

As far as the minority party is concerned, there are several major reasons for the development of an informal power structure. The lack of an institutional niche for the defeated presidential candidate, such as that occupied in Great Britain by the leader of the Opposition, is one. Between presidential elections, the only real bond that unites the members of the majority party, to the extent that it works, is the fact that they have elected their President and he speaks as their national leader. But this glue, thin and watery as it is, is not available to the minority which returns to its tents, not its tent, to prepare for a new assault four years thence. The first effect of the defeat is to bring bitter recrimination upon the standard-bearer, and yet there is seldom agreement upon the reasons for defeat. One wing of the party denounces "me-tooism" and demands an independent position, while the other claims that the cause of defeat was insufficient "me-tooism." Take the defeat of Governor Dewey in

1948, for example. Many Republicans felt that Dewey's loss was due to his refusal to take an independent, Republican stand on the issues of the day. Yet others, particularly in the agricultural states of the Middle West, felt that it was Dewey's qualified opposition to farm subsidies, his apparent devotion to free, unsubsidized enterprise, that led to his loss of these critical states. In any case, what national leadership there may be in the minority party is informal when it is not invisible.

It would seem as though this situation could be remedied by agreeing upon some leading minority member of the House or Senate as party spokesman, and indeed from 1948 to 1952 the influence of Senator Robert A. Taft was working in this direction. But the fact is that members of Congress are very seldom in positions of real party power. It should be recalled that the basic level of party organization is the state and that a Congressman, who must spend much of his time in Washington, is not in any position to manage the day-to-day operation of a political machine. A simple comparison of the number of state governors who have been Presidents or candidates for the Presidency with the number of candidates drawn from Congress should suffice to make this point. Since the Civil War the steppingstone to the presidential nomination has usually been the governorship of a large two-party state such as New York or Ohio. For the governor of such a state to take a seat in the Senate is, in effect, a waiver of his chances for the Presidency. Furthermore, there is little correlation between power in Congress and power in the party. The most powerful members of Congress, those who occupy the seats of power on the crucial committees, are there because they come from one-party states; *i.e.*, they have seniority based on perpetual reelection. A Senator from a two-party state, New York, for example, is lucky if he can be reelected twice, while a Senator from South Carolina will generally hold his seat until he dies or tires of the job. But it is precisely these marginal, two-party, highly industrialized and urbanized states that must be carried by any party that wants to elect a President, although in Congress the representatives from such states may have little power and less seniority.

This brings up another reason for the growth of informal party leadership; the underrepresentation of urban areas. The United States has a formal legislative structure designed for a rural society, and the urban regions have far less say in policy determination than they are entitled to on the basis of population. But, as has been noted before, the President must carry the urban districts to win, or, at least, a large percentage of them. Thus a President is forced to find informal advisers from the cities, although formally speaking the city party organizations may have little say in the decisions of the party's members of Congress. The only time the city vote is really crucial on a national scale is in the election of a President. The minority party is in the same dilemma.

Once we have brushed aside the myth of the American national party, we find two broad congeries of warring factions whose operations are almost wholly directed and financed from the state level. Effective party organizations are almost totally absent from the national picture, where the elected President sits as the leader of his party but without any institution upon which he can rely to reward his fellow Democrats or Republicans for accepting his leadership or to punish them for opposing his position. The minority party does not even have this much cohesion. In this day of radio and television, the opposition frequently finds itself in great difficulty because there is no one who can automatically shoulder the task of replying to the President in the battle for public opinion. In Britain, the Prime Minister and the leader of the Loyal Opposition will always get facilities for public argument, but when the President of the United States makes a partisan address, he may be answered by the president of a university, a Senator, or a governor—or by all three—and none of them can speak authoritatively for the opposition. Needless to say, this makes it very difficult for the electorate to exercise its judgment on the issues involved, and it may be one of the reasons for the high percentage of nonvoters in the United States. It should be added that this process is frequently complicated further by the fact that there may be several majority spokesmen in addition to the President, who repudiate or seriously modify his views. Thus the act of decision by the electorate, the casting of the ballot, frequently bears more resemblance to a bingo game than to an intelligent choice between alternatives.

One final aspect of American party life deserves discussion: the consistent rewarding of infidelity. Or, to put the question in a more specific context, why are not Democratic Presidents chosen from the faithful, solid South? Here again the constitutional framework, which requires a majority of the electoral college to elect a President, has to be taken into consideration. Each party has certain states in its bag: the Democrats usually have the South, and the Republicans can count on Maine and Vermont, Kansas, Nebraska, and the Dakotas virtually through thick and thin. Consequently, when the party conventions are held to choose presidential candidates, the major question before both parties is victory in New York, Pennsylvania, Illinois, California, and similar states. Each party then tries to find a candidate, preferably a governor from one of these states, whom it believes to have urban appeal. Some states are eliminated from the picture immediately; for example, the constitution of the Commonwealth of Pennsylvania prohibits a governor from holding two successive terms, thus making it unlikely that a strong governor will emerge. But the main result is clear: the nomination will generally go to a strong candidate from a big two-party state. Thus the marginal large states, the ones which could fall into the hands of either party, are the ones that win the Presidency. This seems to be one reason why in these big states neither party wants to change the arrangement whereby all the state's electoral votes go to the candidate with a plurality. A state law would suffice to change this—al-

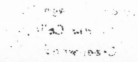

though a constitutional amendment has been urged—but both the Democratic and Republican delegates like to go to conventions representing the New York State organization with the heady offer of forty-five electoral votes if their man is nominated. The minute a state becomes "sure," it loses its bargaining power.

To summarize, it seems apparent that the main function of American political parties, in so far as they operate on the national level, is to supply Presidents. The parties, reflecting as they do the heterogeneity of American society, are highly decentralized organizations that find their real achievement on the state and local level. It might be added that in some states too the parties are largely fictional bodies, less significant in the determining of state policy than some pressure groups, while in others, as V. O. Key has pointed out in his monumental *Southern Politics,* the parties are merely loose associations of "friends and neighbors." The strength of party organization appears to vary directly with the degree of urbanization. But whatever the situation may be in the states, the point remains that nationally speaking the political parties do not supply policy or political responsibility. Consequently, since policy and responsibility must exist in American national politics, other institutions must fill this vacuum. These institutions, however, are the subjects of later chapters.

THE ELECTION OF 1952—A CASE STUDY IN AMERICAN POLITICAL DYNAMICS

All American presidential elections are exciting and important, but certain ones, such as those of 1896, 1912, 1932, and 1952, stand out. Not only were the campaigns of these years striking, but their outcomes represented significant watersheds in American political history. To be precise, in each of these elections the electorate's final decision symbolized a basic policy reorientation as well as a realignment of fundamental political interests. The 1952 campaign offers these in abundance, for not only did General Eisenhower's victory return the Republicans to executive power after twenty lean years, but it was accompanied by such breaks with tradition as the capture of the votes of the Southern urban middle class for the GOP and the pathetic collapse of the Democratic big-city machines.

In retrospect, it is clear that the most significant battle of the entire campaign was not the one on November 4 when the ballots were cast, but rather the internal struggle in the Republican party which erupted like a volcano at the nominating convention in July, 1952. The issue in the Republican party was clearly between Senator Robert A. Taft of Ohio and General of the Army Dwight D. Eisenhower, and the contest was a savage one with no holds barred.

Behind each candidate for the nomination there lined up various clusters of personal and economic interests. Senator Taft—"Mr. Republican" to millions of Americans—enjoyed the support of the party professionals. He had complete control of the Republican National Committee, and his followers

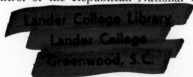

dominated the convention committees which made the preliminary arrangements on speakers, rules, and credentials. Generally speaking, outside the South, Taft's followers came from safe Republican areas, and in addition, the Senator's men dominated the moribund Republican apparatus in the Southern states. Taft entered the convention with a formidable head start over General Eisenhower; indeed if his followers held the line, he appeared certain to win the nomination.

General Eisenhower made life very difficult for his supporters in the months before the convention. Obviously reluctant to enter politics, Eisenhower had refused in 1948 to be considered for the Presidency, explaining that, in his view, a man with a civilian background would be better qualified for the job. However, during the last months of 1951 and the early months of 1952, a constant stream of visitors went to the headquarters of the North Atlantic Treaty Organization in Paris to urge him to reconsider his previous decision. Clarifying previous rumors, General Eisenhower suddenly announced in midspring that, although he would not campaign for the nomination, if it were awarded to him he would run. With the delicacy and respect that had always characterized his relationships with the civil authorities, Eisenhower did not feel that he could make any explicit policy commitments until he doffed his uniform—he merely made it clear that he was a Republican.

But this highly laudable circumspection put his supporters in a quandary, for nominations, like elections, are won as much by promises as by personality. When the early backers of the General, such as Paul Hoffman, approached leaders of various Republican organizations, they were often accused of having a phantom candidate. Nevertheless, Eisenhower strength began to grow, nourished by two main sources: amateurs with unbounded enthusiasm for the General and his talents, and anti-Taft professionals of the international wing of the GOP. While the former made the most noise, it was the latter group, brilliantly marshaled by Governor Thomas E. Dewey of New York and his grand vizier Herbert Brownell, which eventually won the day. In terms of economic interests, Eisenhower had the strong backing of New York financial circles, of the exporting corporations, including such a significant industrial complex as the automobile industry, and of the new urban middle class in the South, particularly in such states as Texas and Florida. But the Eisenhower strategists realized that unless they could somehow crack the Taft organization, their chances of carrying the convention would not be very good. Their answer to Taft's domination of the party apparatus was a tremendous public-opinion campaign aimed at convincing the American people that "Taft could not win," hoping by this to intimidate the Taft rank and file to such an extent that they would not dare to employ their vaunted steam roller.

On the other hand, the Democratic picture going into the convention was thoroughly confused. The leading public contender was undoubtedly Senator Estes Kefauver of Tennessee, who had won an impressive series of presidential

primaries—even decisively defeating President Truman in New Hampshire. But the Tennessean, who had built a formidable reputation for himself as chairman of the Senate Crime Investigation Committee, was anathema to the party professionals, who considered him a "Boy Scout." In particular, Kefauver's willingness to indict Democratic big-city machines in his investigation seemed to the pros to be an unforgivable display of nonpartisanship. Thus the Tennessee Senator was in the unfortunate position of having nobody behind him but the rank and file, and the ranks and files do not win presidential nominations.

In addition to Kefauver, Senator Richard Russell of Georgia and W. Averell Harriman of New York were presidential hopefuls. Both were sectional candidates, representing opposed viewpoints within the loosely knit Democratic party. Behind Harriman stood organized labor and Americans for Democratic Action, sometimes described as the "New Deal government in exile." Harriman stood firmly for strong civil-rights legislation, repeal of the Taft-Hartley Act, and an extension of the social gains of the New Deal. Russell, on the other hand, was the candidate of the Southern Democrats, opposing virtually everything Harriman stood for. In a sense, Russell was not a serious candidate any more than Harriman was; rather, each was engaging in political blackmail, hoping by marshaling his strength to force the nomination of a candidate who was agreeable to him. Governor Adlai Stevenson of Illinois was widely supported, in spite of his protestations that he was not a candidate, for it was felt that he would be a compromise candidate around whom all the factions in the party might rally.

Public-opinion surveys showed that Eisenhower was head and shoulders above Taft for the GOP nomination, and although the preferences on the Democratic side were less marked, Senator Kefauver led the pack. An interesting indication about Eisenhower's potential support was that many Democrats seemed prepared to cross party lines and vote for him—a fact which the Dewey forces used to great advantage in their campaign to immobilize Taft.

Meeting shortly before the Democrats, the Republicans assembled in convention proceeded to engage in a savage internecine battle, to the great delight of millions of television viewers. The crucial question was: Could the Eisenhower forces build up a force sufficiently powerful to neutralize the initial Taft control over the convention? The issue came to a head early in the convention over the question of seating Southern delegates, and the Taft forces, bombarded by a tremendous wave of letters, telegrams, and newspaper editorials, cracked. In one of the most brilliant political maneuvers of the century, the Dewey strategists assaulted Taft, supposedly a paragon of Republican virtue, on the moral issue of "fair play," claiming that the Taft delegations from Texas, Louisiana, and Georgia were unrepresentative and had obtained their credentials fraudulently. Under the strain, and in the full view of millions of television screens, the Taft leadership lost its nerve, misplayed its parliamentary cards, and allowed the Eisenhower forces to go to the floor of the convention on high moral grounds—although in fact the Eisenhower delegations from the Southern states were anything but immaculate. The outcome was the crushing of the Taft forces, and the nomination of General Eisenhower was assured. To broaden the ticket ideologically and geographically, Senator Richard Nixon of California, a right-winger in the state GOP, was named vice-presidential candidate. Nixon possessed the additional virtues of being a veteran and only thirty-nine years old. A further highlight of the convention was the final interment of the political aspirations of General Douglas MacArthur, whose highly touted keynote speech, designed rhetorically to exorcise Eisenhower, faded away into boredom and scattered, absent-minded applause.

By contrast, the Democratic convention was dull. Its tenor was revealed on the first day, when Adlai Stevenson, appearing in his role as Illinois host, received a tremendous ovation from the delegates. Initially managed by a group of enthusiastic amateurs, the Stevenson candidacy was soon taken over by professionals such as former Senator Francis E. Meyers of Pennsylvania and Jack Arvey, boss of the Cook County Democratic machine. Although the governor was a very reluctant bridegroom, and insisted in the strongest possible language that he was neither interested in nor qualified for the Presidency, the other candidates soon realized that he was the major contender. Because of the conservative character of Stevenson's organizational support, the liberal Democrats attempted to coalesce against him, but this effort foundered on the inability of Kefauver and Harriman to agree on who should head the ticket. Kefauver supporters frankly admitted that if their candidate did not receive a majority on the first ballot, his chances of winning would be very slight—a prediction which proved to be correct. After two indecisive ballots, Harriman threw his support to the Illinois governor and the battle was over. In an attempt to assuage the South, Senator John Sparkman of Alabama, an economic liberal with a poor record on civil rights, was nominated for the Vice-Presidency. Generally speaking, the worst consequence of the convention was the residue of bitterness it left among the Kefauver supporters, who felt—with considerable justice—that the "people's choice" had been frustrated by the professional politicians. However, there was some feeling among political realists that, as one of them put it, "the Boy Scout should be thrown to the wolves in '52, so we can save Adlai for '56." This sentiment was held mostly by those who thought Eisenhower was unbeatable, and there is some evidence to suggest that perhaps it was a view shared by Governor Stevenson in the preconvention period.

In terms of power and control, what occurred at the Republican convention was a factional struggle between the dominant elements of the party organization, largely rurally based, and an opposition group of an essentially urban character. This "Dewey" group, urban-based, justified its claim to predominance by the fact that the votes it claimed for its candidate were not "sure"

Republican votes, but were, on the other hand, the votes of the marginal, independent voters needed to carry an election. Conversely, the Democratic nomination illustrated the more familiar device of political accommodation, *i.e.,* Stevenson was a common denominator who was least unacceptable to all wings of the party.

The Eisenhower campaign differed tremendously from that of Stevenson. While the Republican candidate called for a "Crusade" and tended to express himself in broad ambiguous terms, the governor spoke specifically, giving the public a detailed account of his views on various important matters. The two men approached the public in different fashions: Eisenhower was friendly, "folksy," and, with few exceptions, largely negative—his campaign slogan "Time for a Change" was essentially a variation on the old negative theme beloved by oppositions, "Turn the rascals out"—while Stevenson was intellectual, somewhat distant, and, as befitted a defender of the "ins," positive in urging the people not to "let them take it away." Toward the end of the campaign Eisenhower promised, if elected, to go to Korea and personally investigate the situation there—a political coup which the Democrats were unable adequately to counter. In addition, while the Republican campaign was run with clockwork efficiency, the Democratic was badly mismanaged—it was largely and conspicuously run by amateurs in the attempt to counteract the charge that Stevenson was the "machine candidate." A good practical example of the managerial inefficiency of the Democrats was the abuse of precious television time; frequently the viewers had to listen to ten minutes of introduction by local Democratic leaders before Stevenson came to the screen, and the governor was frequently cut off before he finished his speeches. The Republican managers did not subject their viewing public to any such agonies; Eisenhower went on the screens, delivered his speeches, and went off with military precision. It was probably true that the Democrats had nothing like the financial resources available to their opponents, but they hardly utilized what they had effectively.

Television, indeed, came of age in the 1952 campaign. Both parties made extensive use of it, although the Democrats emphasized this medium more heavily in the attempt to counteract their opponents' dominance of the press. The effects on the voter have been, and will be, analyzed and discussed by political scientists and social psychologists at great length, but whatever conclusions are finally reached, one fact emerges beyond dispute: the new medium is frightfully expensive. Another technological development of the campaign was the tremendous use of air transportation. To the newspaper reader, radio listener, or television viewer, the impression was often given that both candidates were in several places at once. Alistair Cooke, the American correspondent of the *Manchester Guardian,* humorously complained that he preferred the old whistle-stop type of campaign because it simplified political geography for his British readers.

In order to counteract the tremendous appeal of Eisenhower's vertical issues—*i.e.*, those like Korea, communism, and corruption which appealed to
all elements of the community regardless of economic, geographic, or ethnic
affiliation—the Democrats stressed class or horizontal issues. Telling the lower-
income groups that they "never had it so good," the Democrats made an effective, if ungrammatical, appeal to self-interest, and promised to continue the
social gains of the New and Fair Deals into the indefinite future. They further
insinuated that Herbert Hoover, or even William McKinley, was the real
Republican nominee, and that a GOP victory would immediately result in all
clocks being turned back twenty, thirty, or fifty years.

An unusual campaign occurrence was the so-called "Nixon affair." In the
midst of the campaign it was suddenly revealed that Senator Richard Nixon,
the GOP nominee for the Vice-Presidency, had received special financial assistance from a secret fund established when he went to the Senate by some
California supporters. For a while it appeared as though Nixon might resign
his candidacy as a consequence of this revelation; indeed, such a distinguished
Republican journal as the *New York Herald-Tribune* immediately demanded
that he step down. But in a sensational national television address, the Senator
discussed his fund, stressed his honesty in financial matters, and implied that
his critics were misinformed radicals. Although the Democrats immediately
labeled Nixon's address a soap opera, "Dick's Other Fund," he remained on
the ticket with public support, and the Democrats were almost simultaneously
put on the defensive by the disclosure that Governor Stevenson, too, had a
secret fund, used in his case not to finance his own activities but to give bonuses
to low-paid key officials in the Illinois state government. Stevenson and his
running mate Sparkman immediately riposted by making public their income-
tax returns for the preceding decade and inviting their opponents to do likewise. Although General Eisenhower did make his returns public, Senator Nixon
refused, but the Democrats found that by this time the public was bored with
bookkeeping and made little capital out of the refusal.

The campaign was further complicated by the presence of two ringers, one
on each side. Indeed, at one point in October a foreign observer noted that it
was difficult to tell whether Eisenhower was running against Stevenson, or
Senator Joseph McCarthy against President Truman. The Wisconsin Senator
made two nationwide television appearances, privately financed, in the effort
to identify the Democrats with communism. His logic may be exemplified by
one excerpt: Stevenson, he submitted, was demonstrably the communist candidate since the *Daily Worker* had not denounced him as strongly as it did Eisenhower. However, the Senator's charges, which were later dissected and refuted
in brilliant fashion by the editor of the Jesuit weekly *America,* seemed to have
little influence on the outcome of the election. In any event, in the November
election McCarthy ran 200,000 votes behind Eisenhower in the Wisconsin
voting, winning his seat in the Senate by only 100,000 votes.

President Truman took as his personal mission the arousing of the labor and minority vote. Whether in the over-all picture he helped or hindered Stevenson will be long debated, but there can be no doubt that, by some of his intemperate remarks, he gave the GOP useful campaign ammunition. In particular, a Truman statement to the effect that Eisenhower was allied with Nazi-type elements was employed effectively by the Republicans to show the depths to which the Democrats could sink in their desperate quest for office. In doing this, they misquoted the President, but the latter should have been experienced enough in politics to anticipate this move and forestall it. On the other hand, the President's whistle-stop tour did galvanize the loyal party workers into action. As often as not, Stevenson had been too busy writing his superb speeches to shake the right hands, and the President attempted to compensate for this unpardonable political sin. Stevenson's distaste for ghost writers, although largely overcome by the end of the campaign, diverted a great deal of his time from political leg work which plays an important part in winning campaigns. In any case, with Truman in the North, Eisenhower in the Northwest, Nixon in the Middle West, McCarthy in Chicago, Sparkman in the South, and Stevenson in California—all simultaneously—the 1952 campaign certainly broke all records for hyperthyroid political activity.

There is one further note on the Truman safari that seems worth recording. In a sense, Stevenson and Truman worked at cross-purposes, for the upper-middle-class groups to whom Stevenson's moderation, his freedom from association with corruption, and his intellectual integrity had a strong appeal tended to be antagonized by Truman's unrestrained denunciation of everything Republican, by his administration's record of corruption, and by his frank class appeal. However, the President did arouse the minority vote and the labor vote—to the extent that either of these exists—which had been somewhat alienated by Stevenson's rather professorial lectures and his conservative backing at the convention. But the President's presence on the field made it extremely difficult for Governor Stevenson to disassociate himself from some of the more unsavory aspects of the Truman administration, a situation which the Republicans capitalized on by referring to the governor as a "captive candidate."

But Stevenson was not the only purported "captive candidate," for the Democrats attempted to convince the American people that Eisenhower had betrayed his original internationalist supporters and become a "Taft stooge." The basis for this charge was the famous conference on Morningside Heights, referred to as "Munich at Morningside" by the Democrats, at which Taft and Eisenhower reached agreement on their aims, and the Ohio Senator swung his full support behind the General. In retrospect, it seems undeniable that the GOP candidate took a temporary tack to the political right, but in the light of later events such as Cabinet appointments, this could hardly be classed as a sellout. In fact, both candidates, troubled by wide schisms in their parties,

had to make tactical shifts. Governor Stevenson, for example, originally opposed compulsory FEPC legislation and repeal of the Taft-Hartley Act, but
later—as Eisenhower was moving to the right to consolidate Taft positions—
shifted to the left to hold the Northern urban vote.

The outcome of the election can be described fairly as an Eisenhower, as
distinguished from a Republican, victory. The total of some 62 million votes
in itself broke all previous records for voter participation, with 63 per cent
of the potential voters, that is, adult citizens, casting their ballots. To illustrate
the size of the vote, one need only recall that the next highest figure was attained in 1940, when 50 million votes were cast in the Roosevelt-Willkie contest. The election was unique in one major respect, for in almost all the states
in the Union the presidential and congressional elections were treated by the
voters as separate processes. Although Eisenhower received over 55 per cent
of the total vote, the Republicans took control of the Senate with a majority
of 1 and the House with a majority of 10. This may be compared with the results in 1948, when President Truman won by far less than a landslide, but
obtained a majority of 12 in the Senate and 92 in the House! It would appear
that Eisenhower received a tremendous personal vote of confidence, but that
the voters were somewhat less enthusiastic about the Republican party's congressional record. Furthermore, the right wing of the Republican party in the
Senate had quite a rough time of it; Senators Kem, Ecton, and Cain were
defeated in states that went for Eisenhower, and Senators McCarthy, Jenner,
and Martin ran well behind General Eisenhower in their states. Conversely,
Governor Stevenson led the Democratic slate in votes in only nine states, although he polled the highest popular vote ever given a loser—some 27 million
votes.

In the electoral college, the Eisenhower victory was even more pronounced.
There the General received 442 votes to Stevenson's 89. Ironically, the Democratic candidate who had concentrated his fire power in the urban, industrial
states, failed to carry a single one; all his electoral votes were from the Deep
South or border states.

Once again, as in 1948, the public-opinion polls proved unsatisfactory as
predictive devices. Crossley, Gallup, and Roper all indicated that the election
was a tossup which could easily go either way. What they all missed was the
enormous personal popularity of General Eisenhower. In several pivotal states
which the pollsters considered to be "close," the General's margin turned out
to be very substantial, e.g., in New York, rated a 50-50 split by Gallup, Eisenhower outdistanced Stevenson by 850,000 votes!

As a result of the 1952 election, some traditional dogmas of American politics required substantial revision. The myth that the bigger the vote, the more
Democratic it would be was shown to be just that. The belief that the voters
would put party preference ahead of presidential preference was also disproved.
In this election, a substantial margin of the electorate told public-opinion

pollsters that the Democratic party was more nearly identified with their own personal interests than the Republican, but, at the polls, millions of persons historically identified with the Democratic party, notably in the South, voted for the GOP presidential candidate.

It was also shown, on the basis of election returns from counties adjacent to Washington, D.C., which are heavily populated by commuting Federal employees, that such government personnel and their families do not blindly vote for the party in power. On the contrary, these counties went for the GOP candidate by large margins. Another effect of the election was to discount the role played by minority and labor groups in winning elections. Although Negroes were fairly solidly for Stevenson, this fact did not affect the outcome, and except for the city of Philadelphia, Michigan, West Virginia, and possibly a few other areas, labor solidarity was less in evidence than in 1948. Indeed, many union political workers complained that while the men were almost solidly for Stevenson, their wives were voting for Eisenhower. Farmers quite clearly returned to the Republican ranks. All in all, Eisenhower's personal popularity, plus the vertical impact on all classes and regions of the issues of corruption, Korea, and communism, were the significant factors in the Republican presidential triumph. These issues seem to have worked with particular force on women and on persons voting for the first time.

On the morrow of the election, many exuberant analysts claimed that the days of the one-party South were over, that the Eisenhower victory in Florida, Louisiana, Texas, Virginia, and several border states marked the beginning of a two-party era in that region. These conclusions did not follow from the election results and have been substantially disproved by subsequent developments. What 1952 actually saw was a two-candidate South rather than a two-party South, for grass-roots Republican organizations did not carry the day for the General. Where he won, he won because substantial elements of the Democratic organization, reflecting widespread Southern discontent with the policies of the Truman administration, came to his support. Thus in Virginia, Senator Harry Byrd and his machine lent implicit aid and comfort to the General; in Texas, Governor Shivers and his supporters openly backed Eisenhower. But this aid was to Eisenhower alone; no nonsense, such as support for Republican congressional candidates, was tolerated. Indeed, the Texas Republicans, in order to advance Eisenhower's cause, endorsed every Democratic candidate below the top lines! Moreover, in a state such as Georgia, where the party apparatus went solidly to bat for Stevenson and no defections were winked at, the Democrats won a thumping victory. In short, Eisenhower carried these Southern states because the Democratic professionals, or at least a substantial body of them, lined up behind him. The Republican party in the South is as wraithlike as ever, and in a sense is worse off than before because Eisenhower's debt, in patronage terms, is not to them but to elements of the Democratic party.

Thus, in summary, it might be said that the 1952 presidential election was a Democratic defeat, but not a Republican victory. The candidate Eisenhower seemed, in the minds of millions of Americans, to transcend party lines and slogans. Thus the people of the state of Washington voted for Eisenhower, but sent a militant New Dealer, Henry Jackson, to the Senate. Massachusetts went for Eisenhower, yet rejected the General's convention stalwart, Henry Cabot Lodge, Jr., as Senator in favor of a liberal Democrat, John Kennedy. In other states, Eisenhower was paired with conservative Republicans (Ohio, Pennsylvania, Wisconsin), liberal Republicans (New York, Kentucky), conservative Democrats (Missouri, New Mexico), and, of course, Southern Democrats (Texas, Florida). Obviously, there is no ideological common denominator here; the one thing that binds all these areas together is the unique personal standing of General Eisenhower. Consequently, the 1952 presidential election is a remarkable case study of the impact of a personality on the American political process, and of the degree to which party lines are flexible or nonexistent when the Presidency is at stake. American politics is still sufficiently fluid that personality can be considered more significant than ideology.

BRITISH POLITICAL PARTIES

Many American political commentators have, in their despair over the lack of party organization and responsibility in the United States, looked across the Atlantic to Great Britain for their model of what a democratic political party should be and should do. This may be an enjoyable pastime, but it is hardly a fruitful one, for British political parties are an outgrowth of British conditions, which are significantly different from those existing in the United States. It is indeed the case that British parties fulfill to a large degree those functions that, it has been suggested, a democratic party should fulfill, and we can certainly learn valuable lessons from the British experience. But the proposals that the United States should adopt a cabinet form of government on the British model are hardly worth consideration.

If it is the task of the political party to formulate public policy and supply a majority for this policy, but not itself to implement the policy, the British system is obviously the most advanced in the democratic world. However, before we investigate the British party system, it might be well to look at the conditions that have led to this development.

Great Britain is geographically a small nation—smaller, in fact, than the state of Oregon, not to mention Texas, Montana, or California. In addition Britain has a highly homogeneous population with few ethnic minorities, and this population is highly concentrated in urban areas. Thus most Englishmen share roughly the same environment and national background, and tend to look upon national problems from similar viewpoints. The large and powerful agricultural sector of the United States has no counterpart in Britain, and while the United States still espouses many of the values of an agrarian society, most Englishmen have been living in an urban context long enough to know that "self-reliance" is illusory. Moreover, there have been historical reasons why most Britons accept the state and its works without strenuous objections. Consequently there is a basic unity to British politics that is largely lacking in the United States. Both the Labor party and the Conservative party speak for urban constituencies and—while there may be real differences of opinion between them—they are both prepared to use the state for large-scale intervention in economic life. A laissez-faire movement did flourish in Britain throughout the nineteenth century, but the decline and collapse of the Liberal party seems to mark the end of this tradition.

Furthermore, Britain is a highly centralized country with a unitary system of government. There are no states or provinces such as we find in a country organized on federal principles that can hinder the activities of the central government, and the powers exercised by British local governments are wholly derived from Parliament. All these factors contribute to the centralization of British political parties, and their concentration at the national level. It is the national Parliament that has final authority on all matters, and thus the major task of the party is to obtain a majority in the House of Commons.

Strong national party organization is a relatively new phenonmenon in Britain. Prior to the rise of the Labor party, the Conservatives and Liberals were organized in a fairly loose manner around local chieftains such as the Chamberlains in Birmingham. When the Labor party came on the scene, the beginnings of national parties were visible in the National Liberal Federation and the Conservative National Union, but the Laborites—who immediately set to work to build a strong centralized party—acted as the catalyst. Nevertheless, it was not until 1950 that the Conservatives, under the organizational genius of Lord Woolton, succeeded in matching Labor in this field. In a homogeneous nation like Britain, where it is virtually impossible to build up a regional or functional political stronghold such as we have with the Democratic South or the "farm bloc" in the United States, a political party's survival may well depend upon the efficiency with which it organizes nationally. The downfall of the once mighty British Liberal party may be attributed partly to its reluctance to build a centralized party machine.

Two strong parties thus vie with each other for the 625 seats in the House of Commons, with the party obtaining a majority supplying the executive. There is no separation of powers between the executive and the legislature, and consequently pressure groups cannot play the one off against the other as they can in the United States. This means that the interest groups must attempt to gain their influence on the party level rather than on the governmental level, and each party gathers around itself a constellation of interests. For example, the cooperative movement, the Trades Union Congress, and the anti-imperialist organizations support the Labor Party, while the National Union of Farmers and the Federation of British Industries work with the Conservatives. By the time a party's program has been hammered out, it usually has real significance because it represents the views of those sectors of the community that support the party. If a pressure group does not act on the party level, it forefeits most of its influence. As a discussion of pressure groups will follow in a later chapter, suffice it to say that a political platform in Britain has real institutional meaning, for—unlike the United States—there is no higher court of appeal for the interest which is unrepresented at the party level.

British political parties therefore supply both leadership and policy, and British political institutions tend to force the electorate to make a clear choice between the two alternative programs. Any group suggesting a third alternative must begin its campaign for power by cutting into the votes of the party with which it is most in agreement. For example, if a new group to the right of the Conservatives enters the electoral lists, its candidates will draw votes from the Conservatives, not the Laborites. In a system of election like Britain's, with single-member constituencies and election going to the candidate with the most votes, few politicians are prepared to cut the throats of their nearest allies as a first step in defeating their bitterest enemies. True, the Labor party succeeded in doing this at the expense of the Liberals, but it should be recalled that parties were not then organized in so centralized or national a fashion as is now the case. It is highly doubtful if this could happen in contemporary Britain.

The functions of supplying leadership and policy and of organizing the electorate are carried out by the British parties, but to what extent do they go on from there and attempt to implement policy? To put the question another way: Is the basic responsibility of the Churchill Government to the people of Great Britain or to the Conservative party members? Here the answer seems clear: the parties have refrained from direct intervention in the process of government and have been contented with the negative control that they have over the future careers of Members of Parliament and Ministers. When the Labor party first took office in 1945 and formed its first majority Government, it was feared in some circles that Attlee and his colleagues would be creatures of the Trades Union Congress, which supplies the bulk of the Labor party's funds and votes. However, the Labor Government soon made it clear that it was "His Majesty's Government," not the Trades Union Congress's Government, and the TUC never attempted to meddle directly in the implementation of public policy. In 1952, when certain irresponsible elements in the unions threatened to call a political strike against the Churchill Government, Herbert Morrison, former Labor Foreign Secretary, declared flatly that "efforts at industrial coercion against an elected Parliament . . . would be wrong in principle." Similarly, when the Labor Government established public corporations to administer the nationalized industries, it did appoint prominent trade-unionists to some positions, but it declared that they must resign their union positions and act as representatives of the national interest rather than as delegates from their unions. That this policy was quite successful can be ascertained by the fact that the Conservative Government did not feel called upon to dismiss board members appointed by the Laborites upon Churchill's 1951 accession to power. Furthermore, both the Conservative body of M.P.'s and the Parliamentary Labor party, composed of Labor Members, are self-governing entities that establish their own rules of procedure and are in no immediate sense responsible to the party executives.

It is quite difficult to find a prominent British politician who does not occupy some position in the Parliamentary or governmental structure, so that the formal party apparatus generally is identical with the real allocation of party power and influence. Because Parliament does adequately reflect the British community, there is no need such as exists in the United States to go outside the formal institutions in search of advisers. In addition, the British Cabinet—although it may often contain dissident factions—is a collective unit representing the majority in Commons, and the Prime Minister must rely upon his Ministers for advice and assistance. Since the function of the Cabinet is to govern, there can be no place in it for one who refuses to accept the policy determinations that are made. A Minister who disagrees with his colleagues is faced with either of two alternative courses of action: he can swallow his objections and continue in the Government, or he can state his objections in public and resign from the Cabinet. It was the latter course of procedure that Aneurin Bevan took when he disagreed with the Labor Government's decision to charge a fee for spectacles and dentures under the National Health Service. Thus the Cabinet always presents a united front to Parliament and the public, and Parliament and the public are in the fortunate position, often denied to the American Congress and people, of knowing who is responsible for any policy that is formulated. The central pillar of cabinet government is unified responsibility. In the United States, the President is frequently blamed for anything that happens during his administration regardless of his actual responsibility, and despite the fact that he often has insufficient power to deal with a crisis. In Britain, the Government is held responsible for crises, but is simultaneously given adequate power to cope with difficulties. The search for responsibility in American institutions can be compared to a shell game where one is never sure which shell the pea is under, and occasionally there may be no pea at all under any of the shells. In the British system of government, the pea is always under the Government shell. This sometimes results in an unfair assessment of blame when a Government is handed problems which are not of its making and with which no one nation can adequately cope, *e.g.*, the dollar shortage, but it does make it possible for the British electorate to exercise a definite decision on the basis of clearly drawn lines of responsibility. No Prime Minister can ever blame Parliament for his difficulties.

Nor can a Prime Minister blame the Opposition. Except in extraordinary situations, there is little chance of the Opposition undermining Government policy. Indeed, the role of the Opposition in the British Parliament is not to obstruct, but rather to use the debate over policy as a technique for influencing the electorate. In order to achieve this, the Government party whips and the Opposition whips, who usually arrange these matters, decide before an important debate just what sections of a bill will be discussed at length, which briefly, and which ignored. In the debate itself, the Government attempts to make the strongest possible case for the measure, and the Opposition sends in its top authorities on the subject to try to convince the people that the Government is misguided. Most Parliamentary debate is aimed not at the Members, but at the external audience—the electorate.

True, the Opposition can engage in irresponsible tactics, but it dare not go too far in these matters. The Prime Minister can at any time dissolve Commons and "go to the country," *i.e.*, hold a general election. Consequently, the Opposition is constantly aware that if it acts in too rash a fashion, it may have to face the public on the matter. A United States Senator knows that nothing can terminate his six years in office except death or the grossest of misconduct, and can cheerfully lambaste the President or the opposition Senators without having any fear that he may be called to immediate account for his irresponsibility. The fact that some desultory political maneuver can land one face to face with the electorate is a notable muffler on irresponsibility. Can one conceive of the House of Representatives voting, as it did at one point in 1948, to deprive Britain of Marshall Plan assistance until she consented to a unified Ireland, if the Congressmen had faced the possiblity of justifying their actions to their constituents in an immediate election? It is probable that Congressmen would celebrate St. Patrick's Day in a less legislative fashion.

One of the unique consequences of British political-party organization is the permanence in the House of Commons of top party leadership. Each party sees to it that its ablest spokesmen remain and survive even disastrous elections. The method used by both parties takes full advantage of certain electoral realities. Each party has a certain number of "safe constituencies" in which no opposition candidate has a remote chance of election. These seats are reserved by the party leadership for its top echelon. It should be recalled that there is no requirement in Britain that a Member of Parliament live in the district he represents, and a Member can run in one constituency one year and in another five years later. As a Member ascends the party ladder and demonstrates his ability, he usually moves from a marginal district to a safe one. Thus a typical career of a young British aspirant for Parliament might begin with his running in a hopeless district where his party has no chance of victory. If he puts up a good fight and impresses the party leadership, he may be given a somewhat better opportunity at the next election. Eventually, after he has been elected and has shown the party that he is a valuable Parliamentary asset, he may receive a safe seat. Occasionally, a party leader gets defeated. The case of Sir Frank Soskice, Solicitor-General of the Labor Government, who was defeated for reelection in 1950 is a good example. Shortly after Parliament convened, a Labor Member from a safe district "resigned." (The term is put in quotation marks because in theory it is impossible to resign from Parliament. An elaborate technique is employed whereby the Member desiring to resign from Parliament is appointed Steward of the Chiltern Hundreds. Since no back-bench Member of Parliament can hold office under the Crown, the Member thus succeeds in his purpose.) Sir Frank Soskice won the seat in a by-election and took his place in the Government.

As may be surmised from this discussion, there is a high degree of centralized control in the party organizations. In theory, each constituency has a Conservative and a Labor Association which nominate the candidates for Commons. But the party central office must be consulted and its approval secured, and of course upon such approval is contingent financial and organizational support. A local Labor Constituency Association can, for example, run someone who opposes the national party program, but in all probability their candidate will not receive the approval and support of Transport House, Labor party headquarters, and must therefore run as an independent. The pressure upon the constituencies to follow the lead of the central party leadership is consequently tremendous and usually successful. It should be added that this conformity is not wholly due to financial pressure; it is also an outgrowth of experience in running independent candidates. For example, the Labor party expelled five Members of Parliament from the party in 1950 for procommunist activities. All of them were widely known and had previously received large majorities in their constituencies, but when they ran as Independents in the 1950 general election against virtually unknown Labor opponents, they were beaten by enormous majorities. Apparently the British voter votes for the party and not for the man.

Thus British democracy is served by two large centralized parties which share a broad area of agreement and which have similar foundations in the needs of urban constituents. A highly homogeneous society has produced a highly homogeneous party system in which the main distinction between the Laborite and the Tory seems to be based on a psychological factor: the Tories move backward into the future, looking to the traditions of a glorious past and attempting to mitigate the speed of change, while the Laborites move ahead confidently with a sanguine confidence in the power of man to hoist himself up by his own bootstraps.

Furthermore, centuries of political practice have led to the delineation of the proper sphere of the political party. It is the task of the party to promulgate new policies for the consideration of the electorate, to select Members of Parliament who will implement these policies, to organize the electorate behind these Members and policies. But it is not the task of the party to impinge directly on the functions of government: here the parties pass the torch on to a new runner, the Government, which is charged with the implementation of party policy, but—and the distinction is important—not as *party* policy. What the Government proceeds to carry out is national policy directed toward the well-being of all Her Majesty's loyal subjects, and because of its wider responsibilities, the Government has tremendous discretion as to the method and pace of policy implementation.

FRENCH POLITICAL PARTIES

In the course of the recent struggle of the Tunisians for full independence from France, a Tunisian politician raised the question, "Is France qualified for self-government?" This is a query which many Americans have echoed over the years in one formulation or another. Perhaps too few American political scientists have appreciated what a lesson French political life can offer to the United States, for there is good reason to believe that if the United States did not have the Presidency to serve as a unifying force in American political life, American parties would respond to the same centrifugal force as have the French.

French society resembles American far more than it does British. Like the United States, France is a nation with a profound urban-rural schism and with strong regional loyalties. True, there are Scots and Welsh in Great Britain, but there is no uniform voting pattern for these groups: Labor and Conservative affiliations divide both. However, in both the United States and France there are strong regional political strongholds. The "Solid South" is comparable to the Catholic bastions of Brittany and Alsace. In addition, France has what the United States does not have—a deep division along class lines between the workers and the employers. France, in short, does not have a united community, but rather three or even four separate communities sharing one national bed.

It is against this background of heterogeneity that one must discuss the French political-party system. The central drawback of French political life is that there is no unifying institution such as the American Presidency which forces the warring factions to come to terms at least once every four years. On the contrary, French political institutions aggravate the centrifugal tendencies of French society. The use of proportional representation, which will be discussed in detail in another chapter, encourages the political party to "go it alone" and rewards intransigence. There is no bonus for compromise except a rather involved procedure incorporated in the 1951 electoral law which awards all the seats in a district to any alliance of parties which obtains 51 per cent of the vote. But this is only temporary, for once the electoral triumph is under their belt, these victorious allies divide up the spoils proportionately and go on their different ways.

French parties certainly fulfill the function of formulating policies. In fact, they overdo it considerably. When a voter is called upon to exercise his choice, he is not presented with two broad alternative programs as is the British voter, but is handed a political spectrum from which he can choose any hue he likes. If he wants socialism and God, he can vote MRP; if he wants socialism without God, he can vote SFIO. Various shadings of free enterprise are also possible, as well as communism with or without Malenkov. The French voter is not called upon to exercise responsibility; he is encouraged to vent his prejudices. It would be gross oversimplification to attribute this political fragmentation solely to proportional representation, for it existed under the single-member constituency system in use, with but slight modifications, throughout the Third Republic. But the system of proportional representation is certainly the worst possible under the circumstances, assuming that stable government is the end to be desired and the one toward which political institutions should be directed.

It is apparent that French parties do formulate policy, but they do little to organize the electorate behind a practical policy. A French election can with justice be described as an institutionalized campaign to disorganize the electorate. Similarly, the election results supply leadership for five or six different policy complexes, to mention only the leading parties, and consequently the problem of organizing a government is one almost entirely separated from the electoral process. Traditionally the French people have voted "left" only to have French governments march steadily to the "right" from virtually the day after the election. As can be imagined, this has led to a certain cynicism about the democratic process and has accelerated the developments of extremist groups on both the "right" and the "left."

Because of the complex nature of French party politics, it might be well to analyze in some detail the various groups that compete for the favor of the electorate. Moving from "left" to "right," using these terms only in their symbolic sense as they represent the seating arrangements in the National Assembly, there is first the PCF (*Parti Communiste Français*) or French Communist party. The Communists are the best-organized party in France and have succeeded in developing considerable mass appeal since the Liberation and the reconstitution of the French Republic. Although the French Communist party has clearly stated its loyalty to the Soviet Union and is no more than the French section of the international communist movement, it has managed to gain great support from discontented elements in the French community—notably the working class. Most French workers are not Communists, but they feel that the Communist party is the only political movement that advances their cause and register what are essentially protest votes in the communist column. There is a dynamism and life to the Communist party which is notably lacking in the other groups, and the existence of this *élan* has brought into the communist ranks many who share the anticapitalistic nostalgia so common in Europe today and are searching for an alternative to "bourgeois degeneracy." The Communists have been noticeably successful in their agitation among young people, who often feel that the other parties are dominated by old men who think only of preserving what they have. As Domenach has pointed out, the

Communists have built in France a new society in embryo existing within the greater French society, but denying its jurisdiction and offering instead a whole new set of values and loyalties. To become a Communist is not just to join a party, but to reject one way of life in favor of another, to be converted to a new faith. Consequently, the French Communist party is brimming with enthusiasm, with converts eager to win their spurs, with crusaders who fulfill their orders with a religious zeal. Those militants act as yeast in the dough of discontent and turn every failing of the democrats, of which there are unfortunately many, to their own advantage. The party, like a parasite, fattens on the weakness of French democracy.

Next to the Communists in the National Assembly sit the dwindling band of Socialists known collectively as the SFIO (*Section Française de l'Internationale Ouvrière*). But to refer to the Socialists collectively would be to give an erroneous impression at the start, for there are almost as many socialist viewpoints as there are Socialists. Initially, at the beginning of this century, a militant party supported by the French workers, the Socialists have been flanked on the left by the Communists and have lost almost all their working-class strength. The tragedy of French socialism is, in a sense, the tragedy of French democracy, for the factor which played an outstanding role in the decline of the SFIO was its willingness to act as a responsible party and not an aggregation of phrenetic sectarians. However, the minute the Socialists began to rise above party considerations and their great leader Léon Blum induced them to look to the national interest, they began to decline in strength. The workers, disgusted at the socialist unwillingness to accept union demands unconditionally, switched to the Communists, who would always demand 150 per cent more than responsible Socialists were willing to concede. Sectarian enthusiasts, who were prepared to do socialist leg work and ring doorbells seven days a week for the "cause," lost interest in a party which was prepared to undertake the prosaic labors of responsibility. The result was that by 1954 the SFIO was largely composed of civil servants and school teachers and, fearing further depletion, moved erratically from responsible to irresponsible political activity with unnerving suddenness. Today the SFIO is essentially a middle-class democratic party trapped between its radical past and its bourgeois composition. It is incapable of radicalism, but unwilling to concede to bourgeois realities, and as a consequence suffers from acute political schizophrenia.

The Popular Republicans, or MRP (*Mouvement Républicain Populaire*), are a postwar phenomenon, having grown from virtually nothing to tremendous proportions in a brief span. But this growth was in large part illusory, for most of the MRP's surprising strength in 1945 to 1946 came from right-wing voters who sought temporary shelter under a "safe" umbrella until the obloquy of collaboration with the Nazis wore off. The parties of the "right" were thoroughly discredited in 1945, and to many a rightist the Catholic basis of the MRP guaranteed that nothing too radical would come of supporting it. The larger the MRP representation was in the National and Constituent Assemblies, the better chance there would be of frustrating the frankly collectivist intentions of the Communist and Socialist parties, then engaged in common activity. The resurgence of the "right" in recent French elections has been accompanied by an increasing deflation of MRP strength. The program of the MRP is both Catholic and socialist. It is attached to the Christian Democratic movement, but on economic matters it is far to the left of the other Christian Democratic parties in Western Europe. Its leaders gained great prestige during the war when they took a leading part in the National Council of the Resistance, but few of them—with the exception of Robert Schuman—maintained their reputation into the postwar period. Today the MRP is, like the Socialists, torn by internal dissent as some members move toward the right and power, while others stand by the leftist principles of the party.

Between the MRP and the Gaullists can be found a galaxy of rightist parties with little in common except their distrust of collectivism and their reluctance to yield to De Gaulle. But beyond this negative common denominator, the rightists have little in common. Some, like the Radical Socialists (*Parti Radical et Radical Socialiste*), are anticlerical, while others give their full support to state subsidization of parochial schools. There are also differences of opinion on the proper method of alleviating the economic crisis. This sector of the political spectrum is the breeding ground par excellence of the "independent" deputy who resists "regimentation" or organization with an almost religious fervor and who looks upon the fall of a government with the aesthetic pleasure that an artist gets from a beautiful sunset. To the "independent," the state is the enemy of freedom, and he consequently feels little responsibility for maintaining a stable government. In short, irresponsibility is rationalized into doctrine. This is not to suggest that the French "independent" is not a believer in democracy; he is, and frequently with a passionate fervor. But democracy to him is synonymous with *laissez faire*, with the "night-watchman state," and he sees governmental instability as one technique of frustrating the march toward collectivist serfdom. Obviously a government that cannot even collect taxes is no threat to the liberties of people, and perhaps the best way to protect the rights of man is to keep the government too weak to collect taxes! The nonauthoritarian right then resembles a conference of Indian tribes: chiefs and their personal followings united only in the physical sense that they are in one tent.

The Rally of the French People, or RPF (*Rassemblement du Peuple Français*), is not a political party. At least, this is what we are told by its guiding genius, General Charles de Gaulle. The RPF is on the contrary a movement dedicated to lifting Frenchmen "above party." One is suddenly reminded of Benito Mussolini's claim that the Fascists were not a party but "an antiparty." Like the Communists the RPF has capitalized on the weakness of the center, the so-called "Third Force" often referred to by punning Frenchmen as

"Troisième Faiblesse" or third weakness. De Gaulle stands for "unity," for "French sovereignty," and presumably for God and motherhood, but beyond this he has hardly tipped his hand. On the practical level De Gaulle has advocated changes in the French constitutional structure which would supply a strong executive on the American model, a fact which has tended to confuse the picture because many non-Gaullists agree with him on this, but feel that to advocate these changes would strengthen the General's hand. De Gaulle's views on economics seem to stem from the old right-wing Catholic doctrine of "associationism," the view that employers and employees in an industry should form economic associations to manage their affairs, and this to many French Catholics as well as non-Catholics smacks of the "corporate state" and fascism. The General's following is a heterogeneous lot, composed of some democrats like René Capitant who support De Gaulle's constitutional views and feel that he could be controlled in power, and a large body of the old anti-democratic Pétainist right who feel that the General is the only alternative to the "stinking, godless, Masonic Republic." It is questionable whether this odd congregation can long hold together, for the De Gaulle policy of voting with the Communists against the center, based on the premise that when catastrophe strikes De Gaulle's hour will come, is repugnant to many of his followers, particularly the moderates. In 1952 the first rebellion occurred when some twenty Gaullist deputies insisted on supporting the rightist government of Premier Pinay, and this revolt was only the harbinger of more to come. In 1953, after the RPF had been decisively defeated in municipal elections, De Gaulle formally withdrew his faithful remnant from the political arena, although a quasi-Gaullist bloc still remains in the National Assembly. This history of decline of the once powerful RPF points up the difficulty faced by a political party which lacks totalitarian control over its members when it attempts to follow a policy aimed at catalyzing catastrophe.

It has been necessary to describe French political parties in somewhat more detail than American and British because without some understanding of the five main parliamentary groups it is impossible to understand the difficulties that the French party system places in the way of stable government. Furthermore, the French party system has a distinct generic relationship to the systems in Belgium, Holland, Western Germany, and even Denmark. It will probably be true of Italy also, for the amorphous Christian Democratic party which obtained a majority in the election of 1948 is on the verge of fragmentation, having lost its majority in the election of 1953.

Let us examine in detail the difficulties faced by a French statesman who wishes to form a government. He begins with the opposition of the Communists and the Gaullists and thus must seek his support from the Socialists, the MRP, and the right. The Socialists and the MRP demand a fairly radical economic policy, but this is anathema to the right. The MRP and some of the rightists insist on state support for Catholic schools, but this is rejected by the Socialists and some anticlerical rightists. Forming a government consequently becomes a political game of ticktacktoe, with an infinite number of possible frustrations.

But the difficulties do not cease with the formation of a government. Assuming that a Premier does succeed in getting the support of the SFIO, the MRP, and the right, and forms a government with the important Cabinet positions doled out to the various groups, he still has no collectively responsible ministry. The Cabinet Ministers look upon themselves as ambassadors from their respective parties, responsible not to the French people, the Premier, or even to the National Assembly, but to their parties and the programs the latter have endorsed. Collective responsibility under these conditions becomes a farce. The Socialist Premier Ramadier attempted in 1947 to set a precedent along British lines when he refused to abide by a decision of the National Executive Committee of his party and declared his responsibility to the whole French nation, but a precedent to be a precedent must be followed, and this one died a-borning.

In summary, French parties intrude far too much on the process of government. Unwilling merely to formulate policy and pass it on to the formal structure of government, they dominate, or attempt to dominate, the whole political process. However, the result of this is paradoxical, for France must be governed by someone, and since the parties so signally fail, others must do the job. The day-to-day business of government falls into the hands of the bureaucracy who, because of the lack of ministerial stability, proceed with virtual autonomy to run France. Since administration is the proper subject of another chapter, suffice it to say here that French parties try too much to dominate the government directly and, in large part as a consequence of their overambition, succeed only in buttressing the power of an irresponsible bureaucracy.

There is little point in examining other democratic party systems, for they largely fall into two classifications: one set such as Australia, New Zealand, Canada, and Sweden similar to the British model; and the other, which is notable in most Western European democracies, resembling the French. The party system of the United States of America is *sui generis:* no other nation which can be included among the major democracies has a system remotely resembling the American.

In conclusion, it might be worthwhile to compare the three systems at several levels and see if any significant generalizations can be formulated. First, we might examine the degree of responsibility of government to people that exists under each. Here it would seem that the United States is the most directly responsive, if not overresponsive. The weakness of the party system is a direct causal factor in this sensitivity. In Britain and France the political parties stand as buffers between popular sentiment and governmental action, while in the United States politicians tend to ride the crest of sentiment with unbridled pleasure. Part of the great popularity of public-opinion polls in the United States, to be discussed later in this book, can probably be attributed to this desire of American politicians to know which way the crowd is going so they can be its leaders. Because American political parties have so little ideological ballast, they tend to look for their ideas in "public opinion" and they hesitate to stand up against a wave of public sentiment. A British or French party leader, with well-formulated ideas of his own, is often ready to resist momentary enthusiasms with some firmness. Of course, if some public concern assumes major proportions, the British or French parties will trim their sails to the wind, but there tends to be some delay in the process. Incidentally, it is probably because American politicians respond so readily to public enthusiasm, not to say hysteria, that the system of checks and balances has gained its unique status in government. Since the American party system does not provide a "cooling-off period," and apparently the American people want protection against their momentary effusions, a braking system has been installed in the formal structure of government to guarantee some delay, some time for second thoughts.

Second, it might again be noted that democratic political parties seem to operate most effectively in a homogeneous society. This may sound like a commonplace statement, but it helps to explain the disorganization of French politics and the loose nature of American political parties. When the electorate tends to be quite uniform as in Great Britain, the parties share many more characteristics than they do in nations like France or the United States where there are not one but several electorates. The real significance of this point, if it is valid, lies in the future, for as the United States and France become more urbanized and homogeneous, their party systems may gain in stability and common values.

Third, the role that institutions play should be noted. It has been suggested earlier that the central unifying factor in American politics is the Presidency, and that if the United States had a cabinet form of government, it might be on the French model rather than the British. While this is all on a hypothetical level, it seems completely improbable that the United States would have only two parties; three or four would be more likely. On the other hand, French institutions seem to accelerate the process of disorganization. The system of proportional representation, for example, encourages people who in the United States or Great Britain would rely on pressure tactics or lobbying for their influence to go into politics for themselves. Similarly, the absence of a strong executive with the power, as it exists in Britain, to dissolve the legislature and force the deputies to justify their actions to the voters in effect guarantees the French legislators a five-year open season in which they can shoot down governments as often as they choose. If the French had to elect a strong President patterned after the American model, it might well alter considerably their present political landscape.

Last, the question of the responsibility of the administrator to the politically elected leaders, although it is properly the subject matter of another chapter, must be briefly alluded to. Modern democracies need experts, but these experts must be kept "on tap, but not on top." How then do these three political systems keep the bureaucrats responsible? The answer in two cases is obvious: the French do not keep their administrators responsible, and the British have their experts well leashed to politically responsible Ministers. A British Minister can speak with authority and the civil servants under him know that he is backed up by his party majority in Commons. The French administrator on the other hand lives in the serene knowledge that the Minister who is here today will, in all probability, be gone tomorrow, or next week, or next month, and that the Minister's authority is at best tenuous. The American technique of maintaining responsibility is unique, for it does not depend on the formal political structure so much as it does on the informal authority of the pressure groups and the power that these interests have with congressional committees and with individual Congressmen. Administrators tend to be responsible to a pressure group–congressional committee coalition rather than to executive officials with a party background. The parties, as such, play a very small role in holding the experts in line.

Chapter 3

INTEREST GROUPS IN MODERN SOCIETY

MODERN DEMOCRATIC society is everywhere characterized by the existence of numerous groups and associations which are free from governmental control, or at least from direct governmental control. We tend to take the existence of these groups so for granted that it is easy to forget that such more or less autonomous subsocieties have not always existed. True, groups have always existed, but historically they have been carefully controlled by various social forces and institutions such as churches, aristocracies, and governments. Although the Middle Ages, as Gierke has pointed out, were the golden age of associations, the *right* of free association was virtually nonexistent. Individuals were assigned to groups by a more or less arbitrary fate, and strenuous attempts were made to see to it that they did not escape from their assigned compartments. With the rise of the national states based on a monolithic concept of the state-society or the society-state, groups came under strict government control.

In the sixteenth century, the wars of religion resulted in the precarious establishment in some countries of one kind of freedom of association—the right to associate for religious worship with members of one's own faith. Thus the precedent was established, although frequently not adhered to, that the existence of different religious groups inside one nation-state does not necessarily threaten that state's governmental stability. In fact, there is some evidence that the supporters of religious toleration such as John Locke and Jean Bodin felt that stability could develop within a state only by removing the area of religion from the political sector—taking religion "out of politics," so to speak —and making religious affiliation a matter of private conscience.

The sector of freedom of association was at first limited to the sphere of religion, but when the Industrial Revolution began, the prototype was there waiting to be followed. The example of the peaceful coexistence of various religious faiths laid the groundwork for the virtually full freedom of association that characterizes the modern democratic state. The Industrial Revolution, and the social forces that came in its wake, shattered the old sense of unity which had been largely based on the homogeneity of an agrarian society. The division and specialization of labor which plays the part of Lucifer in Marx's

Paradise Lost shattered agricultural homogeneity and helped develop a society increasingly interdependent, specialized, and mobile. In the field of political theory, the old concept of monolithic unity was replaced by a new idea of many unities existing side by side within the geographical borders of one state.

The increasing interdependence of human beings made associations and organizations of various types mandatory. National markets were created for the first time. In addition, the growing degree of industrial and even agricultural specialization led men of like interests to unite in trade and business organizations for their own protection and to further their common interests. Simultaneously, the ancient barriers of caste and class began to wither in the face of increasing mobility of population and the establishment of a new touchstone of virtue—capital.

What was true in the world of commerce and trade was also true in other areas. State control over art and literature became abhorrent to the intelligentsia and—perhaps even more important—became more and more difficult to enforce. The British Crown could forbid the publication of seditious pamphlets, but there were always printers in Amsterdam open for seditious business. New cultural movements were fostered by this increasing freedom and soon achieved the virtual autonomy in matters nonpornographic that they have today. Labor organizations fought their way toward legality, and in many countries formed the basis for political movements. In short, from whatever angle one views the situation, it is clear that in the course of three centuries the right of free association became generally accepted in the nations which are today the Western democracies.

Technological advance also resulted in the proliferation of groups and associations in countries which were by no means evolving into the typical patterns of democracy. But this proliferation proceeded under the watchful eye of the state, and was channeled into harmless or progovernment directions. Authoritarian states have always assumed some form of over-all control of private groups which might possibly form the nucleuses of opposition movements. But it remained for the modern totalitarian countries to take over nearly all hitherto private groups and make them into virtual agencies of the state.

The effort in modern dictatorships is to create at all costs a sense of organic unity. To do this, all phases of life must be "coordinated," or, in other words, politicized. Thus, in the name of unity, German art under the Nazis had to display "Aryan" characteristics. In the Soviet Union, which has gone much further in this direction, such diverse fields as genetics, architecture, literature, and music are forced to advertise the virtues of class struggle and the unique invincibility of the Soviet Union. Señora Peron, in the guise of a humanitarian, took over the once free Argentine labor movement and harnessed it to the purposes of the present dictatorship. Examples could be multiplied endlessly. The principal point is that the totalitarian regimes do not dare permit freedom of association in any form familiar to the Western world. Whether this suppression is based on devotion to an ideology of the "organic state" or on a sheerly pragmatic fear of freedom is immaterial. The end result is the same; many groups are created or taken over, but these organizations are intended merely to serve the ends of the ruling class or clique of the totalitarian state. Modern dictators are much wiser than their predecessors. Rather than try to eliminate groups from society, they accept groups on the condition that the latter contribute to the purpose of the state.

BASES FOR GROUP ORGANIZATION

Not all groups are political in nature. Indeed, most organizations have no stated political objectives. The vast majority are concerned with cultural, professional, economic, or merely recreational ends. Among the groups listed in the *World Almanac,* for example, the following point up this diversity: Abraham Lincoln Association, National Academy of Sciences, Air Force Association, Alcoholics Anonymous, Anti-profanity League, Automobile Old Timers, Society for the Preservation and Encouragement of Barber Shop Quartet Singing in America, Society of Biblical Literature and Exegesis, Blizzard Men of 1888, Bill of Rights Commemorative Society, National Button Society of America, League for Industrial Democracy, Child Conservation League of America, Society for the Preservation of Circus Street Parades, Daughters of the British Empire in the U.S.A., Daughters of Ohio in New York, Duodecimal Society of America, First Avenue Boys, Society of the Friends of De Grasse, American Historical Association, Izaak Walton League of America, Loyal Knights of the Round Table, Military Order of the Carabao, Guild of Former Pipe Organ Pumpers, Workers Defense League, American Polar Society, Women Descendants of the Ancient and Honorable Artillery Company, World Calendar Association, Save the Redwoods League, American Society of Zoologists.

This listing, which is a typical cross section, illustrates the observation that most groups and associations have few, if any, political objectives. Yet most of them are potential political forces under special circumstances. The number of such organizations is staggering. A recent student of the subject, Dayton McKean, estimates that there are in the neighborhood of 100,000 different associations in the United States! The same proliferation of associations is seen in Great Britain. *Whitakers Almanac* lists approximately 1,500 societies and organizations. These range from the Fabian Society and the Royal Society to the National Council for the Unmarried Mother and Her Child, Inc.; the Royal National Mission to Deep Sea Fishermen; the Cremation Society; and the Empire Day Movement.

In political analysis it is customary to limit attention to those groups which systematically attempt to influence either legislation or administration. These are generally called "interest" or "pressure" groups. Thus the great groups of concern to students of politics are those representing labor, business, agriculture, commerce, the professions, religion, and veterans. Any association which is effective in determining the course of the political process, at any point in the continuum, is worthy of examination, although the amount of examination is, of course, determined by the efficacy of the group in influencing public policy. While it is not always the case, it is usually true that the great private organizations representing the basic divisions in modern society are vitally concerned with the economic functions of government. Veterans' organizations want bonus bills; farm organizations want price supports; industry groups push protective tariffs; labor groups demand regularized collective-bargaining procedure. However, it is not accurate to say that all groups are concerned with economic power or that they reflect a fixed economic bias. Even the industrial community, for example, is split on the question of the protective tariff, and there are many groups which lack any apparent interest, unless viewed through magic Marxist glasses, in the economic processes. All the major groups are obviously concerned with the locus and direction of economic power, but this is simply a recognition of the fact that economic motivation is very great in political affairs.

It is possible to distinguish between pressure and interest groups, but the semantic game is hardly worth the candle. The term "pressure group" is often considered one of reproach, while "interest group" has the advantage of being emotionally neutral. A recent writer, David Truman, defines an interest group as "a shared-attitude group that makes certain claims upon other groups in the society. If and when it makes its claims through or upon any of the institutions of government, it becomes a political interest group." A somewhat more restrictive definition is given by V. O. Key, who refers to pressure groups as "private associations formed to influence public policy." In any event, it is the element of influence on public policy that is important. Any group may function as a pressure group, but only the most influential are of concern here.

Interest groups can be classified according to subject matter or clientele. An example of the first is the Save the Redwoods League; an example of the second is the American Legion. It is not always possible to determine from the title of an organization what its political interests are. In some cases the titles are quite ambiguous. It is difficult, for example, to determine from their titles the objectives of such politically oriented groups as the Committee for Constitutional Government, National Council for American Education, Southern Conference for Human Welfare, or the Wheel of Progress.

The great pressure organizations in the United States are those which deal with labor, business, agriculture, veterans and patriotic affairs, the professions, and religion. It should be understood that no organization ever speaks for 100 per cent of its members, yet the principal organizations are important precisely because they have convinced the legislators or administrators that they can, on occasion, deliver the votes of their members.

The following survey describes only the most important American organizations.

FARM ORGANIZATIONS

The most significant farm groups are the National Grange, the American Farm Bureau Federation, the National Farmers' Educational and Cooperative Union of America (Farmers' Union), and the National Council of Farm Cooperatives. In accordance with Jefferson's dictum that "those who labor in the earth are the chosen people of God," the farm organizations have long been in politics to ensure that the "chosen people" receive their just deserts.

In the period immediately after the Civil War, there was a rash of farmers' political parties, but these organizations did not succeed in winning political power and in 1896 the last significant one amalgamated with the Democrats. This decline in farmers' parties is significant, for it appears that the farmers early learned that more could be gained by pressure tactics than by frontal assault on governmental offices. The politics of farming in recent years has thus been pressure rather than party politics.

The leader among early farm groups was the Grange, formed by Oliver H. Kelley and his associates in 1867. Patterned on the Masonic order, the Grange at first grew slowly. Today it has about 800,000 members. The Grange quickly entered politics, the designation "Granger laws" attesting to its influence in forcing through state regulatory legislation, aimed primarily at the railroads, in the 1870's. In recent years, it has become politically rather conservative, opposing reciprocal trade legislation and the Brannan Plan, but continuing its interest in educational matters.

In terms of seniority, the Farmers' Union comes next. Established in 1902 to encourage the spread of cooperatives, it spread from Texas up the Mississippi Valley. In strength it has fallen far below its peak 1928 membership of more than 900,000 to a present membership of about 125,000 families. Although habitually accused of "radicalism," the Farmers' Union today is really nothing more than pro–New Deal. It favors social security, the Brannan Plan, and reciprocal trade legislation. Its ideal is the perpetuation of the family-sized farm. The Union has recently won libel suits against persons terming it "communist."

By all odds the most powerful of the farm organizations is the American Farm Bureau Federation. In some respects it is a governmental agency, acting both for the states and for the Agriculture Department in Washington. The Farm Bureau developed from the legislation which established the famous county-agent system. Local bureaus were established to support the agent, and in time the local bureaus federated into state organizations and thence, in 1920, to the level of a national federation. The Farm Bureau now claims more than a million and a quarter members, principally in the corn belt.

The Farm Bureau stands solidly for free, government-subsidized enterprise.

It claims credit, perhaps somewhat exaggeratedly, for nearly every major piece of farm legislation passed in Washington since 1920. The farm bloc in Congress was organized in the Bureau's Washington office, and the actual drafting of the first Agricultural Administration Act (AAA) was also undertaken in its national headquarters. Generally the Bureau opposes specific pro-labor proposals and reciprocal trade, and it has fought bitterly against the Brannan Plan. Its main constituency appears to be high-income farmers.

The last major farm grouping is the National Council of Farmer Cooperatives. This organization cuts across the membership of the previously mentioned groups, and only a small indication of its importance can be given here. A recent writer estimates that marketing and purchasing cooperatives together have more than 3 million members and do more than 2 billion dollars worth of business annually. In some respects the two types of cooperatives are rivals. The National Council speaks for about half the 10,000 producer's co-ops in the country. The California Fruit Growers' Exchange (Sunkist brand) is an example of such a cooperative.

In buying and selling, cooperatives are often alleged to possess preferential tax exemptions. These come under constant criticism in both Congress and the state legislatures. The cooperatives tend to view organized labor with suspicion. In California and Texas some producers' cooperatives are accustomed to using cheap Mexican labor during harvesting seasons, and it has been suggested that they have been parties to illegal or "wetback" immigration. This has resulted in head-on collision with both organized labor and the Farmers' Union.

LABOR ORGANIZATIONS

In the United States there are at present over 60 million in the labor force. About 20 million are women. Only about one-third of them are organized into unions, although the figure is far higher among men than among women. Of the latter it is reliably estimated that less than 20 per cent are organized. The potential political strength of organized labor is therefore only in small part realized. In addition, the two leading labor organizations—the American Federation of Labor and the Congress of Industrial Organizations—are frequently at cross-purposes on political issues.

Although labor organization has a long history in the United States, the rise of the modern labor movement can be dated by the formation of the American Federation of Labor in 1886. Representing primarily craft unions—although in recent years, with the growth of the International Ladies' Garment Workers' Union and the International Association of Machinists on an industrial basis, this emphasis has tended to decrease—the AFL has generally followed a politically nonpartisan line. Its great leader, Samuel Gompers, president from 1886 until 1924 except for one year, advocated a policy of "rewarding one's friends and punishing one's enemies." Thus, candidates were endorsed by local affiliates on the basis of their labor record in Congress, state legislatures, or city councils. This has led to such an anomaly as the local AFL in New Jersey supporting in 1940 the candidacy for Congress of Fred Hartley, later to be a sponsor of the Taft-Hartley Act! At the same time, the Federation, with the exception of endorsing La Follette in 1924, and Stevenson in 1952, has been careful to follow a generally nonpartisan policy. Despite much agitation within its ranks by socialists of various sectarian affiliations, the AFL has steadfastly refused to support the formation of an independent labor party in the United States.

In recent years the AFL has tended to become more politically unified. Prior to the 1948 presidential election it formed an organization known as Labor's League for Political Education. The League attempted to defeat those Senators and Congressmen who had voted for the Taft-Hartley Act. However, at the same time certain union leaders, notably Hutcheson of the Carpenters, were active in the Republican party which had sponsored the labor legislation under attack. In 1949 the League announced that it would operate on a permanent basis, and that it would subsidize labor members of state legislatures in those states where salaries were very low. This is a practice which has been followed by the British Labor party for many years.

More spectacular in the political arena has been the Congress of Industrial Organizations. Originating within the AFL as a committee for the organization of semiskilled and unskilled industrial workers, the CIO seceded from the parent organization in 1936. John L. Lewis of the Mine Workers, who instigated the organization and the breakoff from the AFL, subsequently returned to the AFL, only to disaffiliate once more. The United Mine Workers are today living in a state of melodramatic independence. Somehow both the AFL and the CIO have survived Lewis's exoduses, but they remain as far apart as ever. At present there appears to be little prospect that the two giant labor organizations will combine.

In 1943 the CIO established a Political Action Committee to support President Roosevelt's campaign and aid Roosevelt supporters. The CIO, pleased with the election results of 1944, decided to continue the PAC and spent a prodigious amount of time and energy in the 1946 congressional campaign. The results were extremely discouraging. The *CIO News* referred to the election as "Black Tuesday," as only 73 of the 318 congressional and 5 of the 21 senatorial candidates endorsed by the CIO were elected. Indeed, in some political circles not unfriendly to labor, CIO endorsement was referred to as the "kiss of death." Leaders of the United Automobile Workers union began to resuscitate plans for an independent labor party, but nothing developed from these rumblings. The CIO, like the AFL, was apparently firmly committed to working within the existing political framework.

The new Congress, controlled by the Republicans, did not allow the unions to make the retreat from politics that many proposed as the proper policy. The proposed Taft-Hartley Act, enacted into law as the Labor-Management Relations Act of 1947, brought interfederation labor unity to a new high. Stung by what they designated, with unnecessary exaggeration, as the "Taft-Hartley slave-labor act," the CIO, AFL, and Railway Brotherhoods engaged in unprecedented grass-roots cooperation. State-wide joint labor organizations were established, and funds were pooled. Although in 1948 President Truman was reelected and the Democrats took command of both houses of Congress, the ensuing legislation was not appreciably pro-labor. Once again in 1950 labor went into the campaign, but as in the off-year election of 1946, the labor-endorsed candidates took a fearful drubbing. This was particularly true in Ohio where, after a tremendous labor campaign against him, Senator Robert A. Taft was reelected by an unprecedented majority.

The Korean crisis and the beginnings of national mobilization saw the formation by the AFL, the CIO, the Railway Brotherhoods, and the then independent Machinists (who later returned to the AFL) of the United Labor Policy Committee. The aim of the committee was to ensure that organized labor's views received adequate attention at the top level of government, principally through labor participation in the making of key decisions. After some nine months of cooperative effort, the unity thus achieved was broken when the AFL left the committee in August, 1951. William Green, president of the AFL, declared that the ULPC had been intended to be merely temporary, that its purposes had been accomplished, and that further cooperation could be best achieved through "organic unity" of the two great labor organizations. Neutral observers felt that the AFL was piqued by what it considered administration favoritism toward the CIO. In the early days of the Eisenhower administration, the shoe was on the other foot: the CIO contended that the administration, with AFL leader Martin Durkin as Secretary of Labor, favored its opponents. However, when Secretary Durkin, in October, 1953, resigned as a protest against the administration's refusal to accept his views on Taft-Hartley revision, his action was acclaimed by AFL and CIO alike. A new surge of rumor had it that Walter Reuther and George Meany, the new presidents of the CIO and AFL, were engaged in serious unity negotiations, and Durkin's resignation was, at least in part, a gesture by the AFL designed to assure the CIO that the older federation would not succumb to Republican blandishments.

Future agreement is by no means assured, for each of the giant federations and the large independent unions has vested interests to defend. The CIO speaks largely for the mass-production industries, while the AFL looks after the more highly skilled craftsmen. The interests of these two groups are not necessarily, particularly in the short run, identical. Take, for example, the future of prefabricated housing. If there is a boom in prefabricated housing, a new mass-production industry will be created and the price of homes will be brought within reach of many industrial workers who cannot afford one. On the other hand, prefabricated housing has been fought bitterly by the AFL building-trades unions, who are here engaging in what has been termed by their enemies "security-minded sabotage." Thus labor, like industry and farming, can present a united front on very few issues.

BUSINESS GROUPS

Like trade-unionists and farmers, businessmen come in different-sized packages with different labels. It is misleading to speak of "business" as if it were a homogeneous, monolithic organization—an error into which many European intellectuals fall. In the first place, there is competition not only between individual firms, but also between types of business. Railroads and steel companies, both giants, are in complete disagreement over the proposed conveyor-belt system to unite the ports on Lake Erie with the inland steel cities. A similar clash of interests exists with respect to the proposed St. Lawrence seaway, with the railroads united with New York City shipping interests in opposition.

In the second place, the conflict between retailer and wholesaler, between manufacturer and distributor, can be very real. During the summer of 1951, the price war between Macy's, Gimbel's, and other leading New York department stores illustrated the reality of the conflict between retailers and manufacturers of so-called "fair-priced" items. Not only did some manufacturers, like Squibb, take injunctive action against the department stores, but some smaller stores attempted legal action against the larger ones. The selling price of certain popular novels and certain drugs was reported as being far less than the wholesale price.

Another consideration is the competition between the same industries in different sections. The classic example is the textile industry, where New England has for years faced growing Southern competition. In the garment trades one often finds unionized manufacturers cooperating with the unions in an attempt to block the establishment of nonunion "runaway shops," which can take advantage of wage differentials to undercut the unionized manufacturers. Recently textile plants have been set up in Puerto Rico in an attempt to take advantage of nonunion wage scales and tax preferences not available on the mainland. Some unionized textile manufacturers have gone to the Textile Workers Union of America and, in effect, suggested an organization campaign on that island. These examples will give some inkling of the complexity of the industrial picture.

Granted that there exists continual warfare among many types of businesses and between individual companies, it is still true that some business associations are much more powerful politically than others. Incidentally, the term "businessman" requires some refinement. If one includes under this heading all proprietors and managers, exclusive of foremen, professionals, and farm owners, the total comes to something like $3\frac{3}{4}$ million persons. If foremen and others who fulfill managerial functions are included, the total approaches 5 million.

Acting as general spokesman for a large segment of the business community is the Chamber of Commerce of the United States. With several thousand chapters, the Chamber seeks to integrate local and state opinion on the national level. However, the Chamber has often encountered opposition on specific issues from other business groups. For example, its position on price controls in 1946 was at variance with that of both the National Association of Manufacturers and the Committee for Economic Development. The individual chapters are particularly effective at the local government level. Frequently they engage in much work of a nonpolitical type such as educational and charitable activities. However, the general tenor of the national organization may be ascertained from its slogan: "What is good for business is good for the country."

The National Association of Manufacturers was founded in 1895, some fifteen years before the Chamber of Commerce. It is set up as a nonprofit organization comprised of about 16,500 corporations, and admits neither individuals nor associations to membership. The determination of NAM policy apparently rests with the professional secretariat in Washington; the membership is not polled on issues.

Associated with the NAM are state organizations usually designated "manufacturers' associations" or "associated industries." These state federations are extremely powerful in industrial states, maintaining both a central headquarters and legislative agents ("lobbyists"). Although the NAM professes to believe in collective bargaining and the right to organize, it has opposed nearly everything that organized labor has favored. Much more than the United States Chamber of Commerce, the NAM concentrates on labor questions. Furthermore, the NAM opposed virtually every significant law passed by the national government from the early 1930's well into the war years. The NAM has been positive in support of legislation only when some form of assistance to business was a stake.

The organization carries on a tremendous "educational" campaign, spending between 3 and 4 million dollars a year. Most of this money goes into advertising, while the remainder is apportioned to public meetings and the distribution of numerous pamphlets and leaflets. All in all, the NAM conducts one of the most effective and shrewdly conceived publicity campaigns in the country.

Although the Chamber and the NAM are the outstanding business organizations, there are thousands of other smaller groups. According to the Department of Commerce there are about 8,000 such organizations with a membership totaling approximately 600,000. Some of the activities of such trade associations have no immediate relationship to government, but the great majority probably exist mostly for the purpose of influencing the national and state governments. In addition to claims for special preference, the general demands for efficiency in government, lower taxes, and hostility to government support of nonbusiness activities, known as "socialism," are everywhere made.

PROFESSIONAL ORGANIZATIONS

In the United States, members of professional groups have been quite wary of joining any organization which might be called a union. Whether motivated by the conviction that professionals are above unionism, or by a simple belief that unions have no economic function for those whose rewards are proportional to their ability, professionals have generally eschewed strong organizations. However, physicians, lawyers, and musicians are exceptions to this rule.

The largest single category of professional persons consists of school teachers. Over a million strong, they have traditionally been hostile to joining organizations. Only about a third of them even belong to the National Education Association, an organization which has been noted for timidity and nonpartisanship. Most unionized teachers, a small number indeed, are members of the American Federation of Teachers, AFL; a very few belong to the left-wing Teachers Union. Despite relatively low pay, nonprofessional social status, and the compulsion of special loyalty oaths for teachers, the profession has generally been most conservative in politics.

College professors are almost totally unorganized except along functional lines. For example, members of the American Historical Association meet annually to exchange footnotes and jobs, but play no collective role in politics. However, the recent imposition of "loyalty oaths" by several state legislatures, notably California, has resulted in some political activity by various functional groups, particularly the psychologists.

Best-organized among professional groups are the doctors, lawyers, and musicians. The American Federation of Musicians is admittedly a union which has achieved monopoly status in the industry and succeeded temporarily in staving off unemployment and hunger among musicians. The doctors and lawyers do not class their "associations" among unions, although they serve much the same functions. The American Medical Association, founded in 1847, is far more significant than the American Bar Association, and discussion here will be confined to it.

The American Medical Association, with its affiliated county and state medical associations, has for many years devoted itself to keeping "politics out of medicine." Its method of proceeding has been to take medicine into politics with a vengeance. An instance of this pressure was the AMA's campaign against President Truman's health-insurance proposals in 1949–1950. In the course of this struggle, the association assessed each of its 140,000 members $25 to implement its nonpolitical stand. A high-powered advertising firm was employed to flood the country with denunciations of President Truman, Federal Security Administrator Oscar Ewing, the British Labor Government, and "socialized medicine." The administration's proposal never got far in Congress, but the struggle appears to be only beginning. The medical politicos of the AMA are girding themselves for a long battle with the "political medicine" favored by labor, the liberal Democrats, and a few dissident doctors.

VETERANS' ORGANIZATIONS

So long as there are wars, there will be veterans' organizations. The American Legion, the British Legion, the Canadian Legion, the Steel Front of Weimar Germany are notable examples. In the United States the veterans' organizations have always professed outstanding and disinterested patriotism. At the same time, they have with considerable success pushed through their own legislative programs.

While veterans' organizations were established after the Revolutionary War, it remained for the Grand Army of the Republic to set the pattern for future veteran groups. Founded in 1866, the GAR immediately allied itself with the Republican party, and was particularly successful in securing the passage of pension legislation by Congress. The Veterans of Foreign Wars grew out of the Spanish-American War; the American Legion, out of World War I.

Undoubtedly the outstanding veterans' organization in terms of influence and membership is the American Legion. With more than 3 million members, its size alone makes it a political force of the first magnitude. When the aura of patriotism is added, the Legion becomes—at least in the minds of legislators—well-nigh irresistible. The Legion is based on local posts which exist in nearly every sizable community in the country. Particularly in rural areas, the Legion hall is often a center of community activities with a bar as an added attraction. National conventions are lively affairs on the social side, although most decisions taken at the meeting itself follow exhortation rather than debate and are usually "unanimous."

In fact, the average member of the American Legion has very little to say about Legion policy. The latter is determined by a small group of self-perpetuating officials who co-opt new "kingmakers" into their exclusive club; they draft most resolutions, dominate the national conventions, and are believed to control the elections. This has led to strange ambivalences. An estimated 500,000 members of the Legion, for example, are trade-unionists, but the Legion has invariably taken an attitude hostile to labor. President Roosevelt vetoed the Bonus Act in 1935 and the Legion immediately promised to end his political career, but 1936 saw no swing of the "veteran vote" to the Republican column.

However, most politicians are unwilling to test empirically the strength of the veterans' organizations, and the American Legion, closely allied with the VFW, has moved from legislative triumph to legislative triumph. Veterans' bonus bills have been put through many state legislatures; civil-service preference for veterans is universal, although the form differs from state to state. The veterans' organizations, with the exception of the small American Veterans' Committee founded after World War II, show a boisterous degree of patriotism and tend to be highly suspicious of foreigners.

The great drawing card of the veterans' organizations, in addition to excellently appointed clubhouses, is their stranglehold on the United States Veterans Administration. Any effort to streamline that organization, or to amalgamate some of its functions, *e.g.,* medical, within other government agencies, is steadfastly opposed. The ironic aspect of this is that the conservative veterans' groups have often, in practice, been the foremost supporters of "socialized medicine" for the millions of Americans who have served in the armed forces. This has not escaped the vigilant eye of the American Medical Association, which has often taken up the cudgels against the expansion of Veterans Administration medical facilities. A conflict of this sort between two powerful pressure groups may place a Congressman or state legislator in a genuine predicament.

RELIGIOUS ORGANIZATIONS

Religious organizations have always been active in American politics. Yet, with the exception of the pre–Civil War "Know-Nothings," a party of bigoted Protestants, the United States has never known what the Europeans call a "confessional party." Organized religions have preferred pressure tactics to party tactics, and have followed the usual custom of rewarding their friends and punishing their enemies. The reason is not to be found in any philosophical allegiance to the separation of church and state, although that certainly plays a part in the reasoning of some of the more intellectual religious groups. In large measure it has been the very diversity of religious groups, particularly of Protestant sects, and the fact that no group has any substantial geographical dominance, that have tended to prevent the formation of religious political parties.

As a whole, the country is overwhelmingly Protestant, either by direct membership or by association. In 1950 total Protestant membership was set at about 49 million, but this figure was deceptively small and did not include large numbers of children enrolled in Sunday schools. Total Roman Catholic membership was about 28 million, while Jewish congregations counted some 5 million adherents. Even accepting the above figures as roughly accurate, some 70 million Americans appeared not to be formally affiliated with any church. But it should be kept in mind that the great bulk of the unaffiliated probably consider themselves, however remotely, to be Protestants. In World War II the Army often formalized this by stamping the dogtag of any soldier who admitted to no denomination "P" for Protestant.

The diversity of Protestant sects accounts for the lack of unity on political matters, and even within one denomination a wide range of theological views running from fundamentalism at one extreme to modernism at the other can be found. A Northern Presbyterian, for example, has more in common by and large with a Northern Baptist than either has in common with his Southern coreligionist. As denominational difference makes a united Protestant party an impossibility, so the concentration of Roman Catholics in urban centers makes the formation of a national Catholic or Christian Democratic party impossible. Massachusetts and Rhode Island are the only states in the union with an absolute majority of Catholic citizens. Thus a party founded solely on Catholicism would receive very few votes indeed—even assuming the improbable event that every Catholic voted for the Catholic party—in a presidential election.

However, it should not be inferred from the above statements that religious interests are not active in the political process. In large cities with mixed religious populations every school-board election tends to be a struggle for power among competing sects. In some cities the appointment of public-school teachers is based on an understood quota system, a kind of proportional representation of leading religious elements. Where, as in New Jersey, the question of legalizing such a form of gambling as bingo is a perennial issue, the conflict between the Methodist Board of Prohibition, Temperance and Public Morals, and the Knights of Columbus is real and open. In Connecticut and Massachusetts, the last states with anti–birth-control legislation, the Catholic Church has led the opposition to repeal, to date successfully. In numerous states the extent of state aid to Catholic parochial schools is a lively issue. Nor is amusement exempted from clerical pressure. Most of the so-called Sunday blue laws, *e.g.*, the amusement curfew in Pennsylvania, date from early Protestant efforts to regulate morals by legislation. Another type of problem was illustrated in New York City when the Catholic Church demanded that the Italian film *The Miracle* be banned as blasphemous and temporarily succeeded in invoking state authority for this purpose.

The most spectacular demonstrations of religious power over national legislation in this century have been national prohibition and Federal aid to education. In the first case, militant—even fanatic—Protestantism was successful in forcing adoption of the Eighteenth Amendment, prohibiting the manufacture and consumption of intoxicating beverages. The Anti-Saloon League, which spearheaded the drive, received the bulk of its support from the Methodist, Baptist, and Presbyterian churches, abetted by fundamentalist sects. This is the only instance in American history of a religious bloc amending the Constitution, although the power exists potentially to repeat the performance.

Catholic pressure on Congress was revealed in the debates of the Eighty-first Congress over the Barden bill. This proposal, which would have given funds to state educational systems, barred the use of such monies to support private and parochial schools. A combination of Republicans and Northern Democrats (from urban centers) succeeded in defeating the bill. The implication was that there could be no Federal aid to education unless parochial schools were included with public schools among the beneficiaries.

The battles relating to separation of church and state, state aid to confessional schools, marriage and divorce legislation, gambling, and child labor will continue. In addition, disputes break out regularly in the realm of foreign policy. The questions of aiding Israel and the desirability of having a diplomatic representative at the Holy See are recurrent examples.

INTERNAL ORGANIZATION OF INTEREST GROUPS

It has been traditional and probably natural for interest groups in the United States to employ a federal form of organization. Labor organizations are a case in point. Both the AFL and the CIO have local unions. These in turn are federated into a city council with mainly coordinative powers, and into state federations. The final step in the hierarchy is the national convention attended by representatives of all constituent unions. As in the political parties, the real power in the trade-unions is usually not at the top but at the bottom. In most unions the locals have a high degree of autonomy. Less complex but similar in general pattern is the structure of the American Farm Bureau Federation. The United States Chamber of Commerce is also, in essence, a federal organization.

An example of a unitary structure is that of the National Association of Manufacturers. The National Catholic Welfare Conference, which coordinates Catholic activities, may be regarded as a highly integrated organization. A few trade-unions such as the United Mine Workers also fall into this category.

In between the extremes of unitary and federal organization there are many variations. There appears to be little correlation between the structure of an organization and the methods it employs or the ends it advocates. It is not possible to predict political or other action by American interest groups on the basis of their constitutional structures. Leadership, control techniques, devotion of the led to the leaders, and other intangible factors are often far more important than formal devices. A democratic union constitution, for example, is no proof of democratic objectives—the United Electrical Workers, a Communist-dominated union, is an example for consideration here. Only close examination of past practices can be helpful in predicting the stand or tactics any given organization is likely to employ.

THE ENLARGEMENT OF THE POLITICAL SECTOR

One of the outstanding developments in modern industrial society has been the enlargement of the political sector. A hundred years ago political activity was confined to a fairly limited sphere, while the economy proceeded on rules of its own making and many groups, *e.g.*, doctors and lawyers, lived in a guild world of autoregulation. However, the last century has seen the increased politicization of life; the government has moved into one sphere of life after another to regulate in the public interest. The laissez-faire economy has been replaced by a mixed economy in which the government plays an increasingly important role. This has been true not only of the United States but also of the other leading industrial states.

The world-wide trend toward government intervention in economic life was undoubtably accelerated by World War II, but it was in evidence decades before 1939. In the United States it was the Great Depression which marked the end of an old era and the beginning of a new. The New Deal administration initiated Federal relief, enlarged the Reconstruction Finance Corporation to aid business, established the Tennessee Valley Authority, sponsored social security on a national basis, and regularized collective-bargaining procedure. During World War II the Federal government assumed virtually complete control over American manufacturing, distribution, and consumption. Indirect controls over the labor supply were established; price control and rent control became part of the national pattern. With the Korean crisis, new controls over production were initiated, and selective service began once more to assume wartime proportions. The result, for better or for worse, has been the direct intervention of the national government into economic life and into personal life. There are few autonomous spheres.

These developments have had a profound effect on interest groups. Organizations which historically tended to avoid the most obvious forms of pressure politics found it expedient or even necessary for self-defense to enter the arena of political combat. When government action can mean the life or death of an industry, e.g., the whisky manufacturers and brewers under the Eighteenth Amendment, pressure action is inevitable. As mentioned before, the doctors—traditionally apolitical—have not retained their disinterest in the face of government action in the field of health insurance. It is difficult to think of any economic or professional group which does not today keep its finger on the pulse of political activity.

THE VULNERABILITY OF AMERICAN GOVERNMENT TO PRESSURE

In the United States the proliferation of interest groups has been most marked. This is not only due to the politicization of group interests. Numerous foreign observers from Alexis De Tocqueville and Lord Bryce to Harold Laski have noted that Americans are "joiners." Whatever the cultural reasons for this may be, there are strong political factors which work in the same direction.

Federalism, bicameralism, and the system of checks and balances make national party government in the British sense unattainable in the United States. Under the American presidential system of government an interest group may conceivably apply influence at innumerable pressure points. Not only is the President himself an object of solicitation, but also every responsible administrative officer and the 531 members of Congress. In addition, recourse may be had to the courts to defeat the combined will of the President and Congress.

This latter procedure has been developed to a new high by the Communist party, which floods judges in communist cases with telegrams and petitions and even pickets courthouses.

Further pressure points are obvious. Interest groups may seek either to influence the decisions of administrators or to affect their enforcement of policies already agreed upon. Since this entire process may be duplicated, in miniature, another forty-eight times in the separate states, it is not surprising that the United States is a happy hunting ground for pressure groups. The most complicated governmental structure the world has seen since the Venetian Republic protects itself against pressure groups with papier-mâché armor. It follows logically that frequently the private, relatively uncontrolled interest groups are more important in the American political process than are the weak but highly advertised political parties. Some governmental agencies have gone to the point of organizing their own interest groups to see that they are not neglected by Congress and the President. It is generally believed, for example, that the Departments of Agriculture, Commerce, and Labor are more responsible to the Farm Bureau, the NAM and the United States Chamber of Commerce, and the AFL and CIO, respectively, than to any concept of the general interest. It is further interesting to note that no matter which political party is in office, the Department of State is constantly under attack from many sources, while other departments seem relatively immune. The answer seems to be that the Department of State is the one major administrative division that has no constituency, no constellation of interest groups which look after its interests in the way the Farm Bureau protects the Department of Agriculture. When an agricultural appropriation is cut by Congress, the protests pour in from indignant farmers, but the State Department has no farmers.

In the one-third of the forty-eight individual states where the two-party system is really operative, party discipline tends to be stronger than at the national level. But the same phenomenon of proliferation of interest groups is observable. Studies of pressure politics in New Jersey, New York, Rhode Island, and other states show that a great deal of legislation as well as administrative action, or inaction, is the result of pressure, not party politics.

THE IMPERFECT MOBILIZATION OF INTERESTS

In all democratic societies the same persons are likely to be members of different organizations which are in conflict on specific issues. In such circumstances the individual has the option of subordinating one interest to another, or of doing nothing. (In a totalitarian state where the government coordinates all major, and even minor, group activities, these embarrassments presumably do not arise.) The social psychologist would refer to such a person as a victim of "cross-pressures."

A few examples will show the complexity of the pressures. Suppose a mother is both a member of a parent-teacher association, committed among other things to Federal aid to education, and a Catholic. A conflict obviously exists. Assume that a man is both a member of a junior chamber of commerce, interested in getting the Hoover Commission report enacted into law, and an American Legionnaire. If he sides with the chamber, he comes into conflict with the Legion which, among other things, strongly disapproved of the Hoover Commission's recommendation that control over veterans' hospitals be taken from the Veterans Administration.

In a democratic society all of us are frequently in similar situations. There is a political corollary to this which is of great importance. Professor E. E. Schattschneider has termed it "the law of the imperfect mobilization of political interests." This means that in a free society no economic or political interest can ever be mobilized 100 per cent. Thus, *all* labor will not oppose the Taft-Hartley Act, *all* Protestants will not be opposed to state aid to parochial schools, and *all* businessmen are not in sympathy with the NAM.

It might be possible with scientific polling techniques to find out exactly how many workers favor Taft-Hartley, or how many businessmen oppose the NAM, but this is seldom undertaken. The reason is simple: each side is afraid it will lose the poll! Their whole organizational appeal is built on the assumption of homogeneity, and they cannot risk a finding of dissidence. From a propagandistic point of view, it is more convenient for a leader to speak, or claim to speak, for 90 per cent of the industry or 90 per cent of the workers. "Ninety percent" is a round figure that seems to engender considerable respect from legislators and administrators alike. A scientific poll might have the same effect as a cold shower.

INTEREST GROUPS AS SUPPLEMENTAL FORMS OF REPRESENTATION

With but few exceptions, modern democracy operates through the device of representation. In the ancient Greek city-states, where all citizens participated directly in the quite simple governmental process, no problem of adequate representation existed. But as the size of governmental units increased, direct democracy proved less and less feasible and was replaced by various systems of representation. Of course, this problem existed only in areas where democracy of some sort survived the competition of tyrants or triumvirates.

The history of the development of representation is obscured by the fog that covers so much of the period between the fall of Rome and the twelfth century. The councils called by the Church were probably one major source; the meetings of the Germanic tribes which early led to the creation of embryonic parliaments in Iceland, Denmark, and other areas were probably another. An important stride toward modernity was made in 1265 when Simon de Montfort called representatives from the British shires and boroughs to

Westminster. From this date on, the development of democratic institutions was closely associated with the rise of the British Parliament.

It should be noted that although election is the modern basis for determining representation, this has not always been the case and is not necessarily the case today. Historically representation was frequently based on a system of "estates." In some countries there were three estates—nobility, clergy, and merchant elements from the cities (burgesses)—while in others there might be four, as in Sweden until 1866, or two, as in Britain. England narrowly escaped a tripartite parliament, but the division of the clergy into lords and commons resulted in bicameralism. A peculiar form of the "estate" system survives today in areas like the Union of South Africa, where the Negro community is allotted a certain number of seats in the parliament; in Pakistan, where minority religious communities are allocated a fixed number of seats in the legislature; and in the Gold Coast, where a certain percentage of seats in the legislature are reserved for the Ashanti tribes.

Up until about the beginning of the nineteenth century, the British shires tended to be bona fide communities. Populated by inhabitants who shared common interests, the shires served as an adequate basis for political representation. With the extension of the suffrage and the growth of communications, and the urbanization that accompanied the Industrial Revolution, the shires gradually disintegrated as communities. City dwellers in one shire had far more in common with city dwellers in the next shire than they had with the countryfolk in their own. In short, the unity of the shires became merely geographical rather than economic or cultural.

A similar process took place in other countries where the Industrial Revolution likewise emasculated geographical subdivisions of any functional meaning they previously possessed. This led to a demand for supplementing the existing system of political representation, which was formulated in terms of these archaic geographical units, with some techniques that would more adequately reflect real community sentiment. As pointed out above, "industrial man," as Peter Drucker has labeled the inhabitant of modern industrial society, is typically a member of one or more significant economic interest groups, and, logically enough, attempts were made to base this supplemental representation on an economic foundation. Incidentally, precedent existed for this combination in the British House of Commons where the "City" or financial section of London possessed separate representation in the chamber. Several attempts at combining economic and political representation deserve investigation.

Functional representation; *i.e.*, representation based on occupation or economic activity rather than on geographical location, was incorporated in the 1919 constitution of the German Republic. Subsequently, the Economic Chamber or *Reichswirtschaftsrat* was established to advise the *Reichstag* on "sociopolitical measures of fundamental importance." The Economic Chamber had 326 members drawn from ten groups including agriculture; forestry; horticulture; fisheries; industry, banking, and commerce; insurance; consumers; professions; transportation; etc. Although formally appointed to membership in the Chamber by the Minister for Economic Affairs, the members were actually designated by the great interest groups in the several areas. In each of the producing groups, as distinct from the technicians, employers and employees were given equal representation. It was hoped that the members of these groups would look upon economic problems from a broad perspective rather than from the point of view of the trade-unions or employer associations which had designated them to membership in the council. While it is unnecessary here to investigate in detail the *Reichwirtschaftsrat*'s gloomy history of importune impotence, it is pertinent to note some of the difficulties that were encountered in its operation. First and foremost, the leaders of the political parties were very suspicious of the functional chamber and its activities. They felt that it was designed to supersede, or at least encroach upon, the work of the political chamber, and set out to make it impossible for the economic council to accomplish anything of significance. This was done by refusing to refer important measures to the new chamber, by treating its opinions with indifference if not contempt, and even by petty niggling at the transportation subsidy accorded by the state to the members of the *Reichwirtschaftsrat*. The only recourse at the disposal of the members of the economic body was to write letters to the newspapers.

Second, and in some respects equally significant, there was not unity within the economic council. The employers banded together irrespective of field of activity and the workers did likewise, so that instead of having a body above class politics which could serenely analyze the national interest, there developed a microcosm of society at large with the acute split between workers and management that characterized the politics of the Weimar Republic. In short, agricultural workers considered themselves workers rather than agrarian experts, and the employers of agricultural workers thought of themselves as employers rather than as dispassionate seekers for a "true" agrarian policy.

The dream of taking economics out of politics did not, however, die with the debacle of the *Reichswirtschaftsrat*. In Britain, the Guild Socialists, bellwethered by the Webbs and G. D. H. Cole, long urged the creation of a "third house of Parliament" to deal with economic affairs; in France a National Economic Council was set up in 1925 to advise the Chamber of Deputies on economic matters, with no visible consequences; and in the early pseudo-idealistic phase of Italian Fascism a Council of Corporations was established to transcend petty selfishness and economic shortsightedness by determining the national interest. One has a distinct suspicion that the British Socialist advocacy of an economic chamber was in part a perhaps unconscious political maneuver designed to establish at least one house where the workers would determine policy. In any case, once the Labor party appeared to be on the road to power in the House of Commons, little more was heard of the proposal. Above and beyond this unsubstantiatable accusation, the Guild Socialists themselves divided bitterly on the functions and basis of representation of the chamber.

The French NEC operated in an inconspicuously innocuous fashion and was replaced in the Constitution of the Fourth Republic by a similar body. It would perhaps be well here to detail the composition of this contemporary council, for it is a choice example of French devotion to detail: 45 persons are designated by the most representative organizations of the workers, salaried employees, civil servants, technicians, engineers and supervisory personnel; 40 representatives are selected from industrial enterprises (including 10 representatives of the artisans); 35 delegates are named for agriculture; 9 representatives from the cooperatives (both producers' and consumers'); 15 are named from the overseas territories; 10 qualified representatives of French thought are included, presumably to lend dignity to the proceedings; 8 persons represent family associations; and finally 2 delegates represent war victims' associations. This formidable gathering, once the fairly complex matter of selection has been solved, must be consulted by the Government on all economic proposals except the budget—which is the most significant economic enactment and the one which is basic to all others! This would appear to be a triumph of wasted effort.

The Fascist and Soviet addiction to economic bodies is in a somewhat different category from that in democratic societies. In France and Britain, there has always appeared to be an expedient motive at work in the demands for such bodies. To be more precise, the demand for another house of Parliament or a strong economic council has been heard most loudly from those underrepresented or in a minority in the political chambers, i.e., the workers. However, in totalitarian societies where individual interest is theoretically subordinated to the "general will" as determined by its self-appointed prophets, Councils of Corporations, Labor Fronts, and similar bodies are a practical way of enforcing the demands of the dictators. Dictatorships cannot tolerate the give-and-take of individual or group interests and replace it as rapidly as possible by enforced conformity with the views of party experts. In effect, a totalitarian state is government by irresponsible experts who maintain that they have possession of the national interest. Economic councils thus serve as echo boards for the decisions of the party technicians whose rationale for their actions is that they speak for the "long-run public good," and who can denounce anyone who disagrees with their decisions as selfishly devoted to his own "petty" interest. One of the first portents of totalitarian regimes is the demand that the individual subordinate his interests to the national will. In Argentina, Spain, or the Soviet Union interest groups are not supplemental instruments of representation, but rather are transmission belts carrying instructions from the elite at the top to the individual at the bottom.

Few Americans have ever urged the creation of an economic house of Congress. Even fewer have suggested the abolition of the present representative bodies and their replacement by a "social parliament." To the average American such proposals would sound quixotic if not un-American. On the other hand, a very broad type of functional representation is in fact achieved in the United States by less spectacular methods. The most effective of these is control over legislators and administrators exercised by pressure or interest groups.

Attention has already been called to the extreme proliferation and diversity of interest groups in the United States. A few words of analysis are in order to account for the obvious success of these groups. It will be recalled that in a previous chapter the American party system was said to be characterized by extreme decentralization, that is, by localization of political power.

This can be noted particularly in the national Congress where voting on important issues usually runs across and not along party lines. A classic example was the Senate's refusal to sustain President Truman's veto of the Taft-Hartley Act: the Democrats split about evenly on the question, and the veto was overridden. This example is particularly significant since Mr. Truman banked heavily on repeal of Taft-Hartley as a campaign issue in 1948, and since his party became the majority party in both houses of Congress as an outcome of the election. Without burdening the reader with too many illustrations of a fairly obvious point, attention may also be called to the 1948 platforms of the Democratic and Republican parties. Both espoused, with slight verbal differences, the creation of a permanent Fair Employment Practices Commission. Yet no national FEPC has been established by Congress!

In short, the President cannot control his own party in Congress, and consequently the only national party figure is in a position where he is unable to redeem his campaign pledges or implement the party platform. The Congressmen and the President are responsible to different constituencies, one of which dominates the election of legislators and the other the selection of the Chief Executive. Once again it is valuable to note that urban voters have a far more decisive role in the election of the President than they do in the selection of Congressmen, and as a result of this, party platforms, in a presidential election year, tend to pay lip-service to the demands of urban voters. The promise of FEPC was obviously aimed at securing the electoral support of the Negroes, who play an important role in presidential elections in the Northern industrial states, but who are in a position to elect relatively few Congressmen. Thus it was quite predictable that no FEPC legislation would pass the rurally dominated Congress.

It is easy to get wrought up about situations of this sort, but it is also important to realize that knavery and chicanery play a relatively small part in this swindling of the urban voter. Although the refusal of the states to give adequate congressional representation to the city areas does play a significant role in this process, the basic cause is the loose organization of the party system which makes party government impossible. If a President is to furnish concrete redemptions for his urban supporters, he must first sell at least part of his soul to one of the rural blocs. Thus President Franklin D. Roosevelt effected a workable coalition for a time between the Southern Congressmen and the representatives of the urban North, but the price demanded by the Southerners was a stiff one, being in effect a full subsidization of Southern agriculture plus a "hands-off" policy on civil rights. Under these conditions government can operate, but it must proceed on the basis of continual compromise and political expediency, not of principle, promise, and delivery.

As Professor E. E. Schattschneider, a leading American apostle of party government, has observed, there is a "vacuum in the power to govern." The President can rarely impose his will on Congress, while simultaneously Congress itself cannot organize to govern along precommitted, that is, party, lines. The situation is ready-made for pressure groups to step in to fill this vacuum, and this they do with conspicuous alacrity. What the parties are unwilling or unable to tackle, the interest groups are ready and willing to handle.

Why can they do this? Fundamentally because a powerful pressure group with nationwide interests can mobilize tremendous force. This force is brought to bear where it is most effective, in the Congressman's own constituency. It is true that pressure groups distort and exaggerate their own effectiveness, but the American Legion, the Farm Bureau, and other potent groups can unseat recalcitrant legislators. Conversely, such groups may aid legislators who demonstrate their willingness to follow the "public interest" as defined by the groups themselves. Inside Congress functional groupings are commonplace; e.g., the farm bloc, the silver bloc, the labor bloc. James Burns in his study *Congress on Trial* has pointed out that in reality a multiparty system exists in the national legislature. These blocs are much more real and effective than the two parties, which lose their minimum cohesion once the Speaker of the House, majority and minority leaders, and committee members have been selected. Some Senators have made no bones about their functional allegiances; "Cotton Ed" Smith, for example, was proud to be known by that title. Burns calls such men "pressure politicians."

Not only do pressure groups supplement, and sometimes virtually take over, the legislative process, but they can also effectively influence the decisions of government administrators. Evidence of pressure-group activities in this sphere is less well documented than with legislatures, but it is nonetheless convincing. Here again the perniciousness of the lobbyists has been greatly exaggerated. Administrators, operating in a universe which unlike Britain has no clear lines of responsibility, must have ways of predicting the effects of possible administrative action. When a high executive official cannot count on the support of his party in the legislature, he must find his support among those people most likely to be affected by his activities, and frequently he must modify his decisions in terms of their wishes. They have Congressmen and he does not. To put it another way, when an administrator is not supplied with any criteria of consensus by the political parties, he must supply his own antennas for ascertaining what the people want. This necessarily puts him in close touch with the interest groups which speak for the segment of national life with which he is dealing. As noted elsewhere, most agencies now have "advisory committees" populated by the leading pressure groups in their areas whose specific job it is to keep the administrators in touch with "public opinion." In this fashion, the functions of administrative pressure groups have been institutionalized and given recognition.

There are other governmental agencies which are in effect colonial dependencies of large pressure groups or complexes. The Veterans Administration is a good example of this category, for such large veterans' organizations as the American Legion and the Veterans of Foreign Wars have far more control over the policies and procedures of the VA than does the President or Congress. Here there exists a virtually autonomous agency which finds that it runs very smoothly so long as it follows the advice of its pressure mentors, and which knows that its pressure constituents will supply it with defense in depth against possible congressional or presidential inroads into its functions.

Other ways of making group interest felt in the administration include the policy, used extensively during World War II, of bringing industrial leaders into government agencies charged with handling the sectors of the economy with which they were associated. Prominent examples of this included the War Production Board, the Office of Defense Transportation, and the Petroleum Administration. The theory behind this was that the petroleum industry, for example, would accept government regulation much more readily if the regulators were former leaders of the industry. A recent prominent example of this was former President Truman's appointment of Charles Wilson of the General Electric Company as Defense Mobilizer. However, this procedure raised some rather acute problems of divided loyalty, and the conscientious businessman-administrator was frequently assailed by his former colleagues as a "deserter" if he took action contrary to their wishes, while he was almost automatically attacked by labor circles as a "stooge" of business.

Another technique, frequently employed in the selection of judges, is for the appointing authority to ask the professional organization to supply a slate of worthy candidates. The bar associations, in such cases, propose certain men and the executive chooses his man from among them. While this is not often employed on the national level, in 1951, when President Truman nominated candidates for Illinois Federal judgeships other than those proposed by Senator Paul Douglas of Illinois, the Senator polled the Chicago Bar Association. The poll showed that Douglas's candidates were preferred to Truman's, so the Senator invoked "senatorial courtesy" to block confirmation of the President's nominees.

From these illustrations it is apparent that interest groups—particularly in the United States—supplement the traditional geographic basis of representation. The power of interest groups is greatest where the political-party system lacks cohesion, while in nations like Britain with strong party government, pressure must be brought on the political parties rather than on the legislature and the interest groups tend to become directly associated with one party or the other. In nations like France where government is invariably based on coalition, interest groups tend to become political parties. The system of proportional representation, which contributes to this fragmentation, rewards intransigence. However, this subject has already been discussed in another context and will be passed over here.

Many Americans feel that too much power has been transferred to interest groups at the expense of a responsible political system, but it must be noted that the present situation will not easily be altered. At the same time, most Americans view with considerable suspicion the formal transfer of political power to private groups. Not only ethical, but also constitutional, issues arise from such a transfer. Occasionally such an attempt is rebuffed by the courts, as occurred recently in New York where it was judicially determined that the legislature had improperly delegated the power to control horse racing to the Jockey Club. However, the practice of establishing advisory boards to represent specific interest groups in administrative agencies continues to grow. In a sense, this is administrative pluralism and attests to the flexibility of the administrative process. The effect that it has had upon the traditional American doctrine of the separation of powers has never been adequately investigated, but it would seem that the creation of independent feudal baronies in the executive branch does great violence to that concept.

RELATIONSHIPS BETWEEN PARTIES AND PRESSURE GROUPS

It becomes important at this time to examine briefly the relationships that exist in the democratic nations between parties and pressure groups, although this has already been discussed to some extent in the chapter on political parties.

Several conclusions about this relationship are apparent. First, in nations like Great Britain with a parliamentary form of democracy and strong party systems, pressure groups tend to be identified with the major parties and to work for their goals through the parties. Thus in Sweden the labor movement works through the Social Democratic party—which is, however, far broader in membership than merely trade-unionist. Similarly, in Britain the National Farmers' Union is closely affiliated with the Conservative party. In countries of this sort, the pressure process operates, but not upon the legislature—at least not to any extent. Rather the lobbyists concentrate their efforts on the internal decisions of the parties, knowing that attempts to influence the decisions of the legislature will be frustrated by party discipline. To put it another way, pressure groups adjust their activities to efficient operation in these nations, and since the level of decision making is not the legislature but the party, they do not waste time on unrewarding legislative pressure.

Second, in weak-party parliamentary systems like that in France, the pressure process takes another form. Such nations are usually characterized by community fragmentation which, operating through the mirrorlike electoral mechanism of proportional representation, is reflected in a fragmented legislature governed by precarious coalitions. There is little consensus, and each major interest in the nation, far from trusting its future to any other group, intervenes directly into the political process. In short, pressure groups become political parties, and the legislature, instead of being the forum for government by discussion between parties based on compromised interests, is the battlefield on which the fragments of the community fight for survival. The coalition governments that are formed have no collective personality as does the British Government; they are composed of ambassadors from the pressure parties who are there more to defend their own castles than to seek broad perspective on national issues. Indeed, as the recent history of the French Socialist party shows, the attempt to achieve broad national and social perspective can be suicidal. Attempting, under the leadership of Léon Blum and Paul Ramadier, to compromise their views on wages with those of the other center parties, the Socialists found that their efforts to achieve a long-run solution to the problem of inflation were condemned as treason by many workers, interested only in raising their pitifully low pay. The outcome of this effort at compromise was that the Communist party, always ready to raise extreme demands, stole most of the Socialist party's working-class support. The moral of the story as far as the Socialists were concerned was that irresponsible intransigence pays political dividends, and—with Blum dead—they soon returned to their old ways. In the land of the blind, as H. G. Wells once pointed out, the one-eyed man is not necessarily king. Thus in democracies on the French pattern there is a blurred line between parties and pressure groups. True, there are groups such as the French Stamp Collectors Association that are not in politics, but all the major national interests—workers, farmers, businessmen, Catholics—have one or more parties dedicated primarily to pursuing their pressure goals.

Third, in the United States we find a ninety-six–party system operating along geographical lines and supplying the members of the national legislature. Because the parties are federally organized, with the real power at the bottom, it is fruitless to expect them to supply cohesive policies on a national scale. Should one, for example, expect the Texas Democrats who supported General Eisenhower in the 1952 election—but who remained Democrats nonetheless— to have any real policy ties with the urban Northern Democrats? Consequently, to reiterate Burns's point, we have in effect a multiparty national legislature. If our executive were chosen as is the French, we might well have impotent coalitions, shifting from day to day or from issue to issue. However, the independently elected President supplies continuity to the executive, and our legislature is faced only with the problem of forging legislative policy. Since the Congress is the level at which decisions on policy are made, it is understandable that the pressure groups do not waste much time with the parties as parties, but pack their bags and come to Washington. And, inasmuch as the parties cannot supply legislative policies, the pressure groups leap in to fill the void. The key to the strength of lobbies in the United States, it cannot be emphasized too often, is not the innate corruptibility of *Homo americanus* but the policy vacuum created by the lack of strong national parties. Legislators are elected to serve the best interests of *their districts,* and who is in a better position to tell them how to implement this ambition than the groups that represent the functional interests of their constituents?

Those who bewail this lack of political authority and bow three times daily toward Westminster, "the seat of responsible government," should take solace from two factors that are not often considered adequately. First, they can imagine how much worse off the United States would be without an independent President who need not seek votes of confidence in Congress. Second, they should note that gradually the major pressure groups in the United States are becoming more closely identified with one party label or the other. If one compares the present explicit support, as in the 1952 presidential election, which the major union confederations give to the Democratic party with the earlier activities of the powerful Anti-Saloon League, which supported any "dry" irrespective of his party affiliation, he can get some insight into this significant development. As these modern industrial pressure groups broaden their base, the politicians they influence will tend to unite irrespective of geographical lines. An urban, labor-supported Democrat from San Francisco, for example, will vote with urban, labor-supported Democrats from New York, Chicago, or Detroit. An analysis of the vote in Congress on any crucial issue will show how far this process has already gone. This development, if continued for another generation, could lead to the domination of Congress by two major parties, one urban-centered and the other rural-centered, each supported by a complexus of interest groups. Under these circumstances, the activities of pressure groups would probably shift, as they have in Britain, from the task of influencing the legislature to the job of bringing pressure on the parties.

REGULATION OF INTEREST GROUPS

Since pressure groups are outstandingly an American phenomenon, most attempts at regulating their activities have occurred in the United States. True, a few years ago the British, stirred by all the furor about lobbying across the Atlantic, decided to investigate the extent to which it was taking place in Britain. A dignified search revealed that a few government employees were accepting cigarettes and an occasional lunch from lobbyists, and after a few sonorous moral blasts had been emitted by the Opposition, the matter was dropped. But as we have seen, this investigation, considered as a quest for lobbying in the American sense and not as a hunt for corruption in government, was misconceived; there is virtually no occasion for American-style lobbying in Britain. We are dealing with an American problem.

To understand the efforts that have been made on the national level—there has also been action in the states—it is necessary first to analyze the techniques of the lobbyist. In Congress, as in the states, the control over legislation generally resides in the standing committees. Usually the legislature will follow the advice of its committees. This greatly facilitates the task of interest groups, since it is easier to convince a small committee than an entire Congress. Furthermore, committee activities are seldom well publicized, so that representatives of special interests can often operate in relative secrecy and can express their views with little opposition.

How do these groups operate? Once the interest has achieved some measure of organization, a national headquarters staff with full-time employees is established. Frequently the executive secretary who manages this office is the real policymaker in the organization. Attached to the legislative staff there may be one or more legislative agents. It is the agent's business to present the organization's viewpoint before individual legislators, congressional committees, or government administrators. He may cajole, persuade, or threaten, but he may not—under penalty of imprisonment—offer any bribes. Legislative agents—as lobbyists prefer to call themselves—must be personable, must know their way through the mazes of legislative and administrative procedures, and must peddle their programs with constant zeal. It is apparent that ex-Congressmen fulfill these conditions fairly well, and it is not uncommon to find them joining the Washington staffs of national interest groups after a defeat at the polls. Less obvious is the fact that many former administrative employees find private employment by pressure groups interesting and profitable. Often such former office holders are members of the Washington offices of corporations which find it wise to keep a trained eye on administrative developments of interest to their business.

From the national headquarters of the pressure group comes a steady stream of propaganda. The objective of this is more often to influence opinion makers in key positions—newspaper editors, ministers, educators—than to affect directly the mass public. But in addition, genuine mass organizations can, at the appropriate signal, mobilize local chapters and flood Congressmen with letters, petitions, and telegrams. The greater the geographic spread of the membership, the more effective such pressure campaigns are likely to be.

Probably more important is the function of bill drafting, which is carried on by the national headquarters of virtually all groups. Bills are prepared forwarding the objectives of the group, and it is seldom difficult to find a legislator willing to introduce a bill given to him by the legal counsel of an important lobby. In some cases the legislator may note on the bill that he is introducing it "By Request," which tips off his colleagues to the fact that he has no great and abiding interest in the subject matter, but a strikingly high proportion of acts of Congress originate in the office of an interest group. If one considers the administration an interest group, which is virtually its status on Capitol Hill, the proportion goes even higher.

Once the bill is introduced, the legislative agents nurse it through the various preliminary stages. This involves testifying before the congressional committee charged with handling the proposal, talking privately to members of this committee, and sometimes taking wider action in Congress to force the committee to give adequate consideration to the measure. If hearings are held by the committee, the legislative agents marshal experts to support their views. In order to get a major enactment through Congress, it is usually necessary to build an *ad hoc* alliance with other interest groups on the basis of "You scratch my back, and I'll scratch yours." Thus the farm-bloc lobbyists may agree with the labor lobbyists to support low-income housing if the latter will line up for agricultural subsidies. Sometimes, as in the struggle for the passage of the Fair Labor Standards Act of 1938, a major pressure group will change its line two or three times, making life extremely difficult for the Congressmen who look to it for policy advice.

Sometimes a pressure group will be more successful in one house of Congress than in the other, in which event it becomes vitally important to influence the actions of the conference committee which is appointed from both houses to reconcile differences. Although the main job here is to get the "right" men appointed to the conference committee, it is also important to have access to the members after they go into executive, *i.e.*, secret, session. The importance of having ex-Congressmen as lobbyists is at this time most apparent. It should be added that conference committees have tremendous powers and can, in effect, rewrite a bill in a manner significantly different from either of the two versions before it. Furthermore, the recommendations of such committees are usually immune to amendment on the floor; they must be accepted or rejected *in toto*. Since there are few important bills which do not end up in conference, pressure at this level is in real terms most rewarding.

So far in this analysis there is nothing necessarily dishonest or unethical about the procedures of the pressure groups. It appears to be merely an elaboration of the freedom of petition guaranteed by the First Amendment of the Constitution. Granted that the system is open to abuse by dishonest lobbyists, there are few persons who would urge the elimination of the principle of petition. Why, then, is there so much furor about the practice of lobbying?

The principal criticism stems from the fact that all interests are not organized in accordance with their potential strength. For example, consumers as a group have little voice in policy determination. But beyond this, it is not even the case that all economic interests are represented. In the hearings which preceded action on the Smoot-Hawley tariff bill of 1930, for example, the importing interests of New York City were virtually unrepresented, while manufacturers and farm organizations were present in abundance. At the same hearings few persons presumed to speak for the consumers. Even when groups do try to present the consumers' viewpoint to Congress, their case is weakened by the fact that the Congressmen know that the consumers are disorganized and that the groups which speak for them are self-appointed.

Even in those few situations where representation before committees may be said to reflect a genuine cross section of American society, the competing organizations are never equal in terms of economic strength or prestige. The ideal situation, in which the varying interest groups would simply cancel each other out, never exists. In this respect Madison's famous analysis of "factions," contained in issue No. 10 of *The Federalist,* proved to be an incorrect prediction. Ideally, the answer to this criticism would be for each interest to achieve maximum organization, but while this might alleviate the imbalance in the long run, it is no solution to the immediate problem.

There is likewise continual doubt whether a given representative of an organization does in reality speak for the interest of its membership. The phenomenon of cross pressures, highlighted by the fact that many an American belongs to several interest groups with potentially conflicting interests, makes it unlikely that the lobbyist's perpetual claim to represent "90 per cent" of his functional constituency can be taken seriously. There are, implicit in this discussion, two problems which continually plague the analyst: first, what interest is really represented by the interest group? and second, what percentage of the group's membership really shares the expressed views? Basically the dilemma is how to permit group representation while at the same time protecting the general welfare from highly specialized raids.

In an effort to solve these problems, Congress and about three-quarters of the state legislatures have passed legislation dealing with lobbying. It cannot be said that the legislation has been very effective, but on the other hand, it has served to focus continual public attention upon the activity of lobbyists.

Although there were Federal laws regulating specific forms of lobbying long before 1946, the La Follette–Monroney Act of that year was the first general attempt to deal with the problem. Title III of this enactment, known as the Regulation of Lobbying Act, provides that anyone, or any corporation, who is paid to influence directly or indirectly the passage or defeat of Congressional legislation must register and file a quarterly financial statement with the Clerk of the House or the Secretary of the Senate. The information collected in this manner is published quarterly in the *Congressional Record.* Criminal prosecution is provided for violation of this statute. Certain persons are exempted from these provisions, including anyone who merely appears before a committee to express his views on a proposal but receives no pay for so doing, an employee of a newspaper acting in the regular course of business, and any public official acting in his governmental capacity.

This law has resulted in a monumental accumulation of data on lobbyists. By the end of 1949 a total of 2,878 persons and groups had registered and informed the record that they had collected more than 55 million dollars and spent some 27 million dollars. But, in spite of the value of this publicity, there has been general dissatisfaction with the operation of the statute. Its wording is ambiguous; it is not adequately enforced; it has numerous loopholes and exemptions which make the collection of comprehensive data virtually impossible. Nonetheless the "Lobby Index," published by the House of Representatives, provides fascinating materials for students of the political process. It was particularly interesting to note that, by the end of 1947 alone, some thirty former Senators and Representatives were registered as lobbyists.

What more should be done? The customary American approach to the problem of sin is either to enjoy it or pass a law against it, or do both. Thus it was with prohibition, and thus it is now with "excessive spending" in political campaigns. In the case of lobbying, the regulation has not been very effective for reasons listed above, but there is a significant problem of democratic principle implicit in the question of how much further such regulation should go. A drastic approach such as has been urged in some quarters would include the regulation of the internal affairs of the pressure groups in the effort to protect the representative character of the group and to eliminate certain undesirable practices.

While the undemocratic organization of many pressure groups is to be deplored, it may be seriously questioned whether government regulation of the internal activities might not be far more dangerous to the democratic tradition. Such regulations as aim at curbing the dishonest actions of pressure groups—for example, forcing them to disclose the sources of their funds and the explicit use to which they are put—are one thing, and a great deal may be said for them. But to invade the sphere of free association, except when —as in the instance of monopolistic activities—the groups directly violate the laws, is something quite different. As has been suggested before, these groups are the dynamic of the democratic process, supplying new ideas and leadership, and for the government to invade this area—even on an idealistic pretext— could tend to enforce conformity and cut off this energizing flow of new insights. In addition to this philosophical objection, it is also possible that such internal regulation might be held invalid as a violation of the First Amendment. Certainly the free speech and petition provisions of this amendment stand as a bulwark against Federal regulation of the internal conduct of pressure groups. One of the significant characteristics of totalitarian regimes is the effort to "coordinate" the groups that exist in society and lead them to "true" ways of thinking and behaving. Democracies must be wary of taking a step so fraught with danger to the democratic political process.

Chapter 4

PUBLIC OPINION

DEMOCRACY, AS has already been suggested in earlier chapters, is firmly postulated upon the rule of the majority, or—to put it in a slightly different fashion —upon rule with the consent of the majority. This proposition may seem to be so self-evident as to be beyond dispute, but it is often quite difficult to reconcile the functions of political parties with the doctrine of majority rule. It is obvious, in the first place, that one does not include in the "majority" criminals, the mentally disordered, or minors. But the narrowing of the "majority" does not stop here: in the presidential election of 1948 only about half the potential electorate of 100 million cast their votes. The "majority" thus becomes half plus 1 of those exercising their franchise or, to return to the 1948 election, about one-sixth of the national population.

Second, even if a majority of all duly qualified citizens participated in an election, it would still be difficult to assess the result in terms of a specific issue. True, the election will decide who is to be President, governor, or mayor, but beyond this expression of personal confidence or popularity, what is indicated? In 1932, for example, the Democrats promised to cut the Federal budget 25 per cent if Roosevelt were elected. This was not done. To what extent were the supporters of the Democratic presidential and congressional candidates misled? Was the election of Roosevelt a mandate for Federal miserliness?

Questions of this sort are virtually unanswerable. All that can be said with certainty is that elections decide who will hold office. They do not supply mandates on specific issues. Furthermore the political parties which dominate the American scene are not parties of principle and tend to equivocate on issues. This results in the exclusion of the determination of public opinion on issues from the formal electoral process on the national level.

It is clear then that democracy is, in fact, much more than mere majority rule, and, similarly, public opinion is somewhat different from the opinion of the majority. At one time it was the fashion to conceive of public opinion as a mystical, unified whole, roughly comparable to Rousseau's "general will." Such a doctrine, while mystically attractive, is of little value in determining legislative and administrative policy. More specific guides to action must be discovered.

Today, it is universally conceded that there are many publics and many opinions. With the exception of extremely simple questions, it is highly doubtful if a majority opinion exists in most areas. Yet, it remains necessary, by whatever mathematical means, to create at least the fiction of agreement, even if at a relatively low level. It is this function of creating the fiction of consensus that is fulfilled, to a greater or lesser degree, by democratic political parties and party systems. But if we identify the parties as the principal transmission belts of public opinion, it is clear that many questions of great public concern are of little political significance. Most persons, for example, hold strong views on such questions as sex, diet, family structure, and religion, but on the whole these subjects lie outside the area of political action and therefore have little direct impact on the formation of public policy.

If we view democracy largely as a process, underpinned by a belief in the rationality of man and the dignity of the individual, and not as a set of static values or goals, the role of public opinion is sharply illuminated. In contrast to other forms of government, democracy not only tolerates the free organization of opinion but draws strength from it. Freedom of expression, of political agitation, form the very lifeblood of the democratic process. For democracy, based on the general consent of the governed, must respond to popular pressures and shifts of opinion; the alternative is oligarchy, rule by an irresponsible minority. Only in a democracy is the government committed to altering its policies in response to changes in opinion. Obviously, the most effective technique for determining opinion shifts is the electoral process, but since elections cannot be held daily, it is imperative that alternate methods of discovering significant variations in public thinking be utilized. The following sections contain an evaluation of ideas about public opinion, the formation and measurement of public opinion, and in conclusion some observations are offered on the sensitivity of different types of democratic government to changes in public opinion.

THE NATURE OF PUBLIC OPINION

On most issues, public opinion is in reality a minority opinion which is accepted by the majority. Such an operational definition does not harm our definition of democracy, for it is assumed that a majority could, if it chose, override this opinion and substitute another in its place. The important point about public opinion in a democracy is not that a mathematical majority must accept an idea before it is considered valid. It is virtually impossible to compute opinion holdings with exactitude. The key factor for a democracy is the existence of a peaceful and effective technique of substituting one view for another.

A major criticism of public opinion—one that is concerned not with quantitative but with qualitative evaluation—must be examined at this point: the allegation that all human behavior is irrational. From this premise certain observers have gone on to doubt whether the public can ever be sufficiently rational to manage its own affairs, and consequently to these critics democracy becomes a wholly illusory utopia.

It is neither necessary nor desirable to review the entire debate on this issue; several examples will suffice. Gustave LeBon, the famous French sociologist, asserted his emphatic conviction that peoples and nations do not act in accordance with their real best interest. Furthermore, LeBon maintained, the world was entering the "era of crowds" in which individualism would be engulfed by the mass mind, and the mass mind was essentially irrationally motivated. Obviously democracy could not operate in such an environment, for opinion could neither be formulated rationally nor implemented logically. This concept of the mass mind appeared also in the thought of the Englishman Graham Wallas and the Spaniard Ortega y Gassett.

A generation later the noted columnist and student of public affairs Walter Lippmann advanced the idea in his *Public Opinion* (1922) that most persons think in terms of stereotypes. By this he meant that ideas on subjects such as the attributes of an Italian or an American are determined long before one makes any contact with an Italian or an American. In other words, people do not proceed empirically to make judgments, but cling to irrational stereotypes despite evidence to the contrary. It follows, then, that public opinion is largely based on myths, which may be true or false, but which are considered to be immune to empirical refutation.

Both LeBon and Lippmann agree, however, that not all persons and actions are irrational—they would certainly insist that LeBon and Lippmann and their respective analyses were superbly rational. What little optimism one can gain from this qualification tends rapidly to disappear when he examines the psychoanalytical writings of the last half century. Starting with the works of the master, Sigmund Freud, and continuing to the present, the Freudians have called our attention to the irrational, "the unconscious," in man's behavior. While some recent psychoanalysts such as Fromm and Horney have quarreled with parts of the original Freudian thesis, there is still general agreement on the point that a great deal of human activity is irrationally motivated. The recognition of the role of irrationality is, of course, a rational act, and the power gained from this recognition can be applied to many ends. It was used by Dr. Goebbels to glorify the Nazi ideology; it can be used by democrats to further democratic statesmanship. Massive studies such as Adorno's *The Authoritarian Personality* are attempts to apply this knowledge to the concrete problem of what leads people to abandon democracy in favor of authoritarian creeds. Other, less quantitative, attempts in the same direction have been undertaken by Erich Fromm in his *Escape from Freedom* and by Eric Hoffer in *The True Believer*.

As if these two assaults on public rationality were not enough, a third has recently come into the foreground; the accusation from cultural anthropologists that opinion is culture-linked. George Bernard Shaw long ago suggested in his *Caesar and Cleopatra* that when Britannus, the comic Briton, used the term "natural law," he confused it with primitive tribal customs. It remained for the anthropologists to document this germinal insight. Ruth Benedict in her analysis *Patterns of Culture* (1934) brought it dramatically to the attention of the American people, and as a result of this and other work in the field by Margaret Mead, Alexander Leighton, Clyde Kluckhohn—to mention only a few—many of our earlier ideas on human conduct have been drastically modified.

It was traditionally believed that human nature was a constant; that people react similarly to similar stimuli whether they live in Cairo, Illinois, or Cairo, Egypt. We now know that, far from this being the case, each culture supplies its own behavior patterns, its central values around which the society is integrated. Some anthropologists have pushed this generalization too far, asserting dogmatically that each culture is and should be the final judge of its own standards and that it is wrong to interfere, say, with the head-hunting proclivities of the Igorots because our intervention is based only on our cultural judgment that head-hunting is wrong, while to the Igorots it is quite normal and ethical. But there are very few ideas that, if pushed to their logical extremes, do not lead to absurdity. The intelligent approach is to avoid logical extremes—which do not occur except in logic textbooks—and attempt to apply insights to the immediate practical problems of life. On this level, there is much to be learned from the cultural anthropologist. He has made us aware of the tentative nature of our mores and of the degree that American social, economic, and political conditions have conditioned American opinion. He should also make us somewhat suspicious of the exportability of various American institutions which may not have universal application. And for the student of the political process, the entire series of anthropological investigations serves as a warning not to read into the cultures of other peoples concepts and ideas which are peculiarly American, or Western, or Christian.

Individual psychologists, social psychologists, sociologists, or cultural anthropologists may or may not be democratically inclined. But to the student of the democratic process it is the research, not the individual's bias, that is important. By calling attention to the irrational, the group, and the cultural factors which influence men's conduct and thought, these social scientists have performed an outstanding service that may be utilized by those interested in perpetuating democracy. In large part their contributions have been rationally presented and formulated, which in itself is a deep bow to the rationality of the potential reader. Freud's unconscious certainly influenced him in a profoundly rational—not to say ponderous—fashion, and apparently no culture is so completely unique as to defy understanding and analysis by some eager American anthropologist!

Thus rational discussion, even of the irrational, becomes the objective to be desired, and it is consequently of crucial importance to democratic societies that the basic organs of public-opinion formulation—the press and radio—be free, uncoerced, and dedicated to the rational analysis of public issues.

THE FORMULATION OF PUBLIC OPINION

In the preceding paragraphs it has been implied that public opinion is not the same thing as deeply ingrained cultural behavior patterns. The distinction is an important one. Cultural behavior patterns may be likened to a great stream, with eddies, channels, and pools. In the deepest channels may be found the principal buttresses of a society—the myths and institutions that are basic to that particular society. Ideas about religion, about happiness, about sex, about warfare are formed in this lower, more substantial, slower-moving part of the stream. Institutions such as churches, schools, armies, bureaucracies find their support at this level.

On and near the surface of the stream, the patterns are different. Gusts of wind may turn a smooth surface into a cauldron; crosscurrents may blind one to the deep, undisturbed current beneath. It is at this top level that changing ideas characterized as public opinion are most likely to be noticed. In addition to dress, sports, and entertainment fads, one finds in democratic nations electoral demonstrations, campaign trends, and current political issues at this level.

Public-opinion polls may measure candidate preference, the comparative status of political parties, or the type of automobile most in demand by the consuming public. Polls of this sort serve a useful and practical purpose. In stable democracies, shifts in opinion in peripheral areas may be absorbed, adjustments made, new courses of action followed. This is the situation in the United States and Great Britain. In less stable countries, where there is a greater absence of fundamental consensus, such polling is of little value. It is not difficult to recognize the symptoms of a diseased community, but the cure is at best uncertain, at worst nonexistent, because of the difficulty of deliberately reshaping through the democratic process the basic myths and institutions of a society.

Consider, for instance, the influence of attitudes toward the family on attitudes toward government. It has been suggested quite plausibly that the German pattern of patriarchical authoritarianism made the acceptance of democracy more difficult than would have been the case if the American attitude toward fathers had been the accepted standard. As another example, compare the attitude toward government engendered by the congregational form of church organization in eighteenth-century New England with the situation a century earlier. Puritan Presbyterianism did not encourage democratic attitudes toward government; Congregationalism tended to spread responsibility in church organization and government and thus laid a groundwork for similar changes in the political area.

These basic institutions—the church, the family, the educational system

—evolve much more slowly than political systems and frequently fall behind the needs of the day. This is what the socoiologists call an "institutional lag." If this lag is too great, if the basic institutions get too far removed from reality, peaceful change is often foreclosed and violent revolution occurs. All great class revolutions bear witness to this truth. The problem for democratic statesmanship is to keep the basic myths and institutions in line with reality.

It is through the political process that this must be done, for only in this fashion can the necessary changes be made in an orderly, gradual manner. The great merit of democracy is that it provides a technique by which change can be made according to recognized rules of the game and in response to genuine popular pressures. Democracy is always in a state of delicate equilibrium, an equilibrium which can be destroyed only too easily under certain circumstances. The problem, in positive terms, is how to transmit popular pressures and change direction, while at the same time maintaining a fundamental balance.

In democracies with strong party systems, this all-important function is largely entrusted to the parties. In all democratic nations pressure groups operate to a greater or lesser degree in their role of supplementing the parties. The question is, how can a democratic government, in the absence of a clear party decision and with no unanimity among the interest groups, determine public opinion? It seems hardly necessary to add that this is the usual situation in the United States!

There are numerous techniques for ascertaining public opinion. One is to analyze the direction of newspaper editorials and magazine commentaries. Another is to determine the prevailing opinion among radio commentators, public speakers, clergymen, etc. A last method is to go directly to the public with a public-opinion poll. But whatever technique is utilized, the final result will be determined by two forces: the institutions which mold behavior patterns, the family, churches, schools; and the instruments which form public opinion, the press, radio, television, the movies, and various minor media. The institutional influences are so long-range as to be outside the discussion of the formation of public opinion in any immediate sense; it is a task for the historian to assess the relative weight to be given to each basic institution and their interplay. However, the organs of immediate public opinion fall properly within the scope of this analysis. It is to these media that we turn for the facts and hypotheses that we base our judgments on; these are the organs that can force a legislature or an executive to act in some given way. If the total picture given by these media is distorted, or false, or misleading, the effect is likely to be felt at once. On the other hand, it is doubtful whether newspaper ideas on the nature of God would evoke any quick change in people's attitudes on God. Let us now turn our attention to the most significant media of mass communication and evaluate the role that they play in the formulation of public opinion.

THE PRESS AND PUBLIC OPINION

The common-sense judgment that in literate nations the press is the out-standing medium for the communication of views on public policy has, in addition, been confirmed by scientific public-opinion polls. There are numerous reasons for this predominant position, among them the relative cheapness of printed material, the ease of distribution, almost universal literacy, and the conviction that the written word carries more authority than the spoken. Great victories in the realm of freeing ideas from state control and censorship have centered around freedom of the press, and in our own time attempts to censor textbooks, to ban books or magazines from sale, or to destroy material objectionable to the regime (as in Nazi Germany and Soviet Russia) evoke more heated opposition than do attempts to censor motion pictures, radio, or drama. Without a free press, the free formulation of ideas becomes terribly difficult, if not impossible.

While all democracies are in theory agreed upon this proposition, in practice the methods for implementing this principle vary considerably. It is generally believed in the United States that the best guarantee of a free press is the absence of government ownership or control. Government is considered the natural enemy of civil liberty, and the constitutional framework of the United States, as well as those of many of the separate states, incorporates this antistate sentiment. The First Amendment to the Constitution, for example, provides that "Congress shall make no law . . . abridging the freedom of speech or of the press . . . ," and the constitution of the state of Rhode Island and Providence Plantations put it even more strongly: "The liberty of the press being essential to the security of freedom in a state, any person may publish his sentiments on any subject, being responsible for the abuse of that liberty. . . ."

This principle of noninterference in the operations of the press necessarily assumes private ownership. With the exception of the Fourth French Republic, where almost all newspaper plants are owned by the state, and of occasional hidden subsidies to "inspired" journals such as have occurred in the United States, particularly during the early days of the republic, and in other nations, private ownership has been the general rule. Of course, this does not mean that the government does not issue bulletins, pamphlets, journals, and magazines —most modern governments do—but rather that the principal newspapers and magazines are privately directed.

However, in recent times a new problem has developed. Consonant with the general tendency toward business concentration, the press in the United States and Great Britain has become in the past fifty years more and more concentrated in fewer and fewer hands. This has created an issue quite distinct from that of government censorship: that of private censorship. Put another way, the question is, has ownership of the press become so concentrated that a free press, in the sense of a competitive press presenting different viewpoints on public issues, has become an anachronism?

Consider, for example, some recent figures that seem to give substance to this contention. Since 1909, the total number of daily newspapers in the United States has been decreasing. It has been estimated that fewer than 200 American cities have any newspaper competition, and in many of these instances the competition is more theoretical than actual. Some ten states have no daily newspapers in competition at all. Powell, a recent writer on the subject, states: "In 91.6% of the cities in which dailies are published, publication conditions are non-competitive." Newspaper chains are sometimes considered more of a threat to the free press than the factor of noncompetition. This alleged menace comes not from circulation—according to Irion, another student of the problem, the sixty-three chains control only 37 per cent of total United States daily circulation—but from the concentration of ownership. Irion declares that "less than 100 individuals control more than 50% of the total circulation" of newspapers in the United States.

It is also pointed out that newspapers own a considerable number of American radio stations. Thus, it is possible for one owner or group to control all sources of information that originate in a city. Lazarsfeld, a sociological analyst of public opinion, has asserted that about 25 per cent of all commercial stations are owned outright by newspapers, while the figure is much higher if partial ownership is taken into consideration. Newspaper ownership of FM stations is substantially larger, and the newspapers also have a large stake in television.

Another assault on the American and British press came, particularly in the 1930's, from those who claimed that the newspapers were subservient to their advertisers. This was buttressed by the fact that newspaper income today, as contrasted with a century ago, comes primarily from advertising, not circulation. But the allegation that advertisers consequently controlled editorial policy has not been substantiated. In one-newspaper cities, the advertiser has nowhere else to go and is hardly in a position to dictate to the editors. Even in competitive areas, the papers are generally stronger than any individual advertiser. It is, for example, preposterous to imagine that the *New York Times* or *Washington Post* would censor a news story at the demand of an advertiser.

A more serious charge against the press, and one rooted in a real philosophical problem, has been that, since the newspapers are big business and the newspaper owners are big businessmen, the newspapers reflect the economic and social prejudices of business. It is not that newspaper executives are individually dishonest, but that they cannot escape from the "class" attitudes of upper-income businessmen. This view, strongly maintained by Marxists as well as by such ideological mavericks as Harold Laski and Max Lerner, contributed to attempts both in the United States and Britain to analyze the health of the press. To this end, the British Royal Commission on the Press and the privately supported American Commission on Freedom of the Press investigated the situation in their respective countries. The Royal Commission, while finding a very large degree of ownership concentration—about 76 per cent of the daily circulation in 1948 was controlled by five great chains—came to the conclusion that this fact in itself was no great menace to the traditional British desire for competition in ideas. The American Commission, although it recommended extreme vigilance and deplored sensationalism, felt that the situation in general was less black than many had feared. The most radical suggestion that this body had to offer was that it might be desirable for the government to guarantee competition under certain circumstances.

On a different level, both British and American newspapers—to say nothing of French—have been accused of sensationalism and bad taste. In the United States it is undeniably true that the newspapers with the largest circulations are the most sensational. But this quantitative fact should not be considered adequate evidence that these sensational papers are the most influential. Exhaustive studies of reader interest have been made in this country, and the results seem to indicate that this assumption cannot be made. Pictures and cartoons, followed by general news, are the best-read sections of the paper. The sports section rates highly with men, while women consider the advertisements and obituaries about as impelling as front-page lead stories. Relatively few persons of either sex read editorials.

But this still does not give us any insight into newspaper influence. While the *New York Daily News,* with the largest circulation in the city, has apparently exercised little editorial influence over its readers, can one assume that the less-circulated *New York Times* exercises significant influence? There is no adequate evidence on this subject, but a generalization seems apparent. The commanding attention given to the editorial views of the London *Times,* the *Manchester Guardian,* the *New York Times,* the *New York Herald-Tribune,* and the *Washington Post,* to cite a few outstanding papers, would seem to indicate that these journals should be given a weight of influence out of proportion to their circulation. In a sense, papers of this type are read by public-opinion "makers"—the governors as distinguished from the governed—and hence deserve more serious consideration. The *Chicago Tribune,* for example, is expertly edited and has an enormous circulation, but—if elections are any indication—its antedeluvian political views have been by-passed by the reader on his hurried way to the brilliant sports section. On the other hand, the *Washington Post*'s editorial views have frequently ruined breakfast for both Congressmen and Federal administrators—although one should not deny the drawing power of the *Post*'s tremendous assortment of comic strips.

The problem narrows down to how much the editorial views of the newspaper influence its reporting of news. As long as editorializing stays securely on the editorial page, the reader can pass it by, but when it turns up in the "straight" news story, the reader begins to drink from a poisoned well. Probably editorial views have more influence on the selection and spacing of news, and particularly on the wording of headlines, than most American editors would admit—though few papers approach the *Chicago Tribune* in these respects. Furthermore, this distinction between editorializing and news writing can be overemphasized; undoubtedly an editor's view of good journalism will influence his employment policy, and it is natural for people to want associates who share their general frame of reference. But the point remains that when one reads the news stories in the average British or American paper, he emerges with a sufficiently undistorted factual presentation to allow him to reach an independent judgment on the matter.

On the basis of this discussion, the question may well be asked: How much influence does the press have on public opinion? The answer that comes to mind is that, at least in the United States and Great Britain, the press creates public opinion but does not direct it. To put it another way, public interest in contemporary issues grows largely from the information on these matters that is put out through the newspapers, but the view that the public takes of the matters does not seem to be press-controlled. To use only the most startling examples, one can examine press opinion on British and American elections. According to Dayton McKean, Roosevelt's press support was highest in 1932, when newspapers controlling about 40 per cent of the national circulation were behind him. By 1944, when F.D.R. was elected to his fourth term as President, his press support had fallen to 17 per cent. In Britain, the Labor party has always been tremendously outgunned in the newspaper arena. Unquestionably, both the British and American newspapers contributed tremendously to public interest in the elections and public knowledge of the issues involved, but they can hardly be accused of exercising a decisive influence on the outcome. If one piece of evidence is any indication—and it is admittedly an extreme case—the American people seem to be profoundly suspicious of the political activities of their newspapers: a National Opinion Research Poll taken in 1946 revealed that 81 per cent of those polled thought the radio stations "were fair," while only 39 per cent would say this of the newspapers.

One important difference between the press in the United States and that of most other democracies is the almost total absence of a party-owned press. While most American newspapers have nominal political allegiance to either the Democratic or Republican party, neither of these parties has an official organ. True, the American Communists have the *Daily Worker,* but this is hardly a newspaper in the accepted sense of the term, being more like a daily catechism of the faithful. However, in Britain the Labor party has its own press establishment and publishes, under trade-union auspices, the *Daily Herald,* and in France and the other Western European democracies most of the newspapers are under party direction. It should be said, by way of qualification, that the journals published in the United States by interest groups often serve a similar function. The *CIO News* and other union publications tend to speak for the urban wing of the Democratic party, while various business journals support the Republicans. But the structure and nature of American parties, the necessity to compromise on most important issues because of sectional and functional differences, makes direct party ownership of papers too risky to contemplate.

Those who feel that the American and British newspapers distort the news should spend some time in France, Italy, or Western Germany. In these nations, most newspapers are run and subsidized by the various political parties, and one frequently gets the impression that objectivity has long since gone the way of the gold standard. In the whole of France there is but one journal, *Le Monde*, which presents its readers with unadorned facts, and it is easily the dullest paper in France. The Socialists, the Christian Democrats, the Communists, and the various parties of the center and right carry on constant journalistic warfare, and the purpose of party journalism is to convince the convinced. One American government emissary who was invited to breakfast by a French Premier was amazed to note that the latter was reading the European edition of the *New York Herald-Tribune*. He expressed his surprise at this, and was told by the French statesman, "For twenty-five years I read my party paper and was daily whipped up to a frenzy. But now I have a weak heart, I am one of the chiefs of the party, and I need information!"

Generally the more ideological the politics of a country, the more partisan-slanted and party-financed the press will be. Anyone who wishes to conduct an interesting case study into the nature of truth should collect all the French newspapers for one week, preferably an election week, and see what similarities they bear to each other and to the same news as reported in, say, the *Christian Science Monitor*—an American journal with outstanding foreign coverage—or the *Times* of London.

The situation in Switzerland and Scandinavia more nearly approximates the British scene. Both areas have great, commercially supported newspapers, dedicated to high standards of journalism, while, at the same time, there are a considerable number of party-supported papers.

In summary, the press of the United States and Britain, while containing a lunatic fringe, ranks with any in the world in terms of fairness and objectivity. At the same time, this press is predominantly conservative in editorial bias. In these papers, it should be noted, great emphasis is placed on nonpolitical matters. In both countries, the norm is private ownership supported by advertising revenues. The press, in short, is big business and shares business ideals. It is interesting to note in passing that even in Britain, where there is a strong Labor party with the allegiance of half the electorate, the Labor *Daily Herald* has tough sledding. It has recently been tremendously outdistanced in circulation by a new pro-Labor commercial daily, the *Daily Mirror*, which does not find a Labor sermon in every world event, domestic situation, or in the falling of a sparrow, as the *Herald* tends to do. The *Herald* grew up at a time when British politics were far more ideological than they are today, and as British politics have grown in homogeneity, the paper has lost much of its constituency.

The situation is about the same throughout the English-speaking areas of the Commonwealth. On the Continent, various Scandinavian and Swiss papers approximate, if not equal, the British and American ideal, but in France, Italy, and Western Germany, ideological tensions plus economic considerations that largely eliminate the possibility of a commercially supported press result in a partisan and, for the most part, party-supported press with wholly utilitarian objectives. The moral is not that a free-enterprise economy results in a free press, but that a politically stable society is more apt to support a nonbiased press than is a society rent by basic ideological fissures. Applying this hypothesis to India or Pakistan, one would not expect to see the emergence of a free press in the American sense for some decades, and until this stability develops, there will probably be pretty rigorous governmental restrictions aimed at preventing journals from poisoning the wells of public opinion.

RADIO, TELEVISION, AND PUBLIC OPINION

Less important than the press as sources of information for the higher socio-economic groups, but more relied on by other groups, are radio and television. Both are relatively new industries, and only radio has been extensively studied by social scientists in terms of its influence on the public.

In all totalitarian countries, radio and television are rigidly controlled by the state. In democratic nations, while the form of ownership varies widely, the principle that a considerable amount of competition in ideas is valuable is maintained. At one end of the ownership scale is the United States, which allows private broadcasting within a loose framework of government regulation, and at the other end are Great Britain, France, and Italy, where radio and television are owned and operated by the government. A middle position is found in Canada, Australia, and New Zealand, with both public corporations and private broadcasting stations operating side by side.

For all practical purposes, each of these systems permits about the same amount of freedom in the expression of political views. Each system has its vigorous adherents, who believe that their system is the best in the world; while perhaps less vociferous in expressing their views than American radio and TV executives, the managers of foreign broadcasting systems are equally convinced of the superiority of their own approach.

Outside the United States, it is uncommon to hear paeans of praise sung for the American system of broadcasting. If imitation is the greatest flattery, commercially supported privately operated broadcasting on the American model has received little homage. With few exceptions, this technique has been accepted only in countries close to American influence, such as Mexico. In Britain and France, although radio is a state monopoly, the government does not concern itself with day-to-day programing. Denmark follows this pattern. In Sweden, however, the industry is operated by a private public-service corporation in which the press, radio, and government cooperate. Italian radio is operated by a public corporation with some government control over content.

In the United States, and in those Latin-American nations permitting private commercial broadcasting, the costs of radio are borne in the first instance by advertisers. This method of sustenance gives the impression to the casual listener that the radio programs are as free to him as the air he breathes. Of course, this is only illusory, since the costs of advertising are passed on to the consuming public. Since the consuming public and the radio public are, at least in the United States where there are many more radios than families, about the same, the general public is in fact paying for its radio fare through a system of private taxation.

At the other end of the scale are those nations which operate radio and television as state monopolies. In Britain financing is generally obtained by an annual tax on all receiving sets—£1, or $2.80, or £2 for those with television sets. As about 90 per cent of all families own radio sets, it is clear that the public in general is footing the bill. In some other countries, like France, where ownership of sets is less widespread, the radio-listening families may be only half the total number of families, and here it is much more the radio listener who pays the costs of broadcasting. A relatively large group which neither owns radios nor listens regularly to radio broadcasting escapes entirely from paying.

In Britain and Canada, as in the United States, radio broadcasting began as a commercial venture, but today in both these nations other techniques are applied. Canadian radio is only partly commercial in character. In 1929, the Aird Commission recommended that radio be made a state monopoly, and, although this was never put into practice, a public corporation, the Canadian Broadcasting Corporation, was established in 1936. The CBC immediately began to construct stations in the principal cities and planned to absorb existing private facilities, but for financial reasons this has never occurred. The license fee of $2.50 per annum raises only about 5 million dollars, which is a small sum indeed when compared with the 400 or more million dollars raised by advertising in the United States. Because of its impecuniousness, the CBC made arrangements for network services with various private stations which, now, collectively, have almost twice the annual income of the CBC. The corporation proper owns and operates less than twenty stations, about half of which are high-powered. With affiliated private stations, mostly in the thickly settled areas, these government transmitters constitute the network which covers all Canada. When not transmitting network programs, the affiliated stations are free to resume local broadcasting.

The most famous and thoroughly studied government radio monopoly in the world is the British Broadcasting Corporation. Formed in 1927, when the British state took over the privately run British Broadcasting Company, the

BBC was, among other things, a striking example of public ownership motivated by antisocialist conceptions. The major reason for the nationalization of
British radio was that the Conservative Government had found radio to be a
highly valuable way of getting directions to the country during the general
strike of 1926 when many of the newspaper unions were refusing to work. It
was felt that so powerful a medium of mass communication should not be left
in private hands, where it could be paralyzed by strike action in the event of
an industrial crisis. In structure, the BBC is similar to other public corporations. The Board of Governors, appointed by the Prime Minister not on a
political basis but on the characteristic British ground of fitness for public
service, operate through the Director General and his staff, who are employed
at the discretion of the Governors. In both practice and intent, the BBC is
absolutely divorced from governmental control of its day-to-day operations;
indeed, the Governors of the BBC are as independent of government dictation
as any American private broadcaster. The corporation is not entirely financed
from license fees; a considerable amount of additional revenue is raised by sale
of the *Radio Times* and the *Listener,* the former having in 1948 a circulation
of more than 7 million copies.

Broadcasting in the United States is too familiar to warrant a detailed examination of its history. At first, broadcasting was under the control of radio-set
manufacturers who wanted to increase sales. When Pittsburgh's station KDKA
broadcast the election returns in 1920, public interest in radio soared. At that
time, few persons thought of radio as a money-making proposition. General
Electric and Westinghouse and their sales company, Radio Corporation of
America, viewed broadcasting primarily as a means of selling their equipment.
Advertising on the radio was rare and apologetic. The development of new stations, grabbing any handy frequency, resulted in public and industry demands
for governmental regulation. Finally, Congress passed the Radio Act of 1927,
creating the Federal Radio Commission.

The permanent structure of American radio was established under the Communications Act of 1934 which created the Federal Communications Commission as an over-all regulatory agency. The basic intention of the act was
to safeguard the public interest through general regulation, but, at the same
time, Congress made it clear that the FCC was not to exercise any substantive
control over the content of radio programs. It was to insist on the observation of certain ground rules—notably, the utilization of frequencies and the
power of stations—but to have no censorial powers.

Since 1934 there have been two major developments in American radio: first,
radio advertising and broadcasting have become big business; and, second,
control of radio programing has become highly centralized in four great networks. Let us examine these points and their implications. Advertising, at first
shunned, is today widely hailed as the savior of radio. A large proportion of

the advertising return that radio stations receive is from certain major accounts: soap manufacturers, cigarette concerns, automobiles, etc. These accounts are handled by a few large advertising agencies which, in practice, control most of the paid network broadcasting time. In other words, advertisers and sponsors dominate American radio. The local station proprietor has virtually nothing to say about the programs that his station will put on at the better listening hours; this is handled by the networks. The networks do a very efficient job, and in most cases the caliber of the programs on the local station would be lower if the proprietor were left to his own devices. But the fact remains that American radio has become a highly centralized affair with the program content at thousands of local stations dominated by four major program centers. Even when it comes to producing sustaining programs, those without sponsorship, the networks are able, because of their superior resources, to do better shows than the local station, which traditionally relied on hillbilly bands and piano nocturnes.

Upon examination, then, it is clear that American broadcasting, despite the large number of stations and genuine competition among the networks, is not likely to supply much new merchandise to the market place of ideas. A newspaper is able to adjust itself to a locality and can swing its ax with abandon, never worrying about what people a thousand miles away will think of its views. However, a local radio station is dependent upon its network advertisers, and by the time the network shows are over, there is little time left for originality except the hours from midnight to seven in the morning. Furthermore, an advertising agency out working for a big client wants a program that will appeal to all parts of the country and offend none, and by the time national programs have been watered down to the lowest common denominator of the mass radio market it is safe to say that little in the way of injecting new ideas into the public consciousness takes place. The networks will not even tolerate an announcer with a Southern accent, much less someone with an idea that might offend.

All public-opinion polls taken on the question show that Americans believe radio to be much fairer in reporting news than is the press. This is, of course, the opposite side of the coin described in the paragraph above. Radio is conspicuously neutral—a fact that has assets as well as liabilities. But in any case, the educational power of radio is potentially enormous in the United States, for Americans in the aggregate spend much more time listening to the radio than they do reading newspapers and magazines. This is particularly true among the lower socio-economic levels. This power has to date been used in the main to sell products on the national market. It is, of course, true that all networks and many independent stations produce excellent music, dramatic and documentary programs, but yet the fact remains that the main dedication of radio is to exploiting the mass market via mass advertisement. Obviously such procedure may adversely affect cultural standards in the long run, since the appeal must be to the lowest common denominator. In actual fact, the American press is far more diversified than is radio.

It is at this point that American radio stands out so conspicuously from foreign radio. The BBC, for example, seems to feel that one of its major functions is to raise the cultural standards of its listeners. The BBC does entertain, it does offer a variety of programs at the same hour, it makes an effort to appeal to different tastes in the population. But at the same time, the conscious effort to raise public standards is always apparent, and sometimes a bit tedious. The government corporations in the Commonwealth nations share this dedication, even if they are less zealous in applying it. When this approach is suggested to American radio executives, they usually reply defensively that they are running an entertainment industry, not a school, and that the American public gets what it wants. This may be true, since there is no accurate way of finding out except by asking the public whether it likes what it gets, and when this has been done the result, in both the United States and Britain, has been public satisfaction. Unquestionably, there is some dissatisfaction in Britain with the programming of the BBC, but a sizable proportion of Americans also consistently state in their responses to polls that they would like less or no advertising on American radio.

Even if it were conceded that the principal purpose of American radio is to make money, and the principal purpose of British radio is to raise standards, it might still be contended that such observations are largely irrelevant. What difference does it make how an industry is owned or operated, providing that it contributes to freedom of information? Or, to put it another way, does one system make a more positive contribution to the free formation of public opinion than the other? To answer this question, two further queries must be disposed of: First, is censorship exercised over political statements? Second, do the contending parties or groups receive equal facilities for the presentation of their views?

The first query can be disposed of simply. Within the framework of the laws of libel, broadcasting systems in all democratic countries permit political speakers to fire whatever shot they may have in their arsenals. The content of political speeches is not at the mercy of the broadcasters. However, the answer to the second query cannot be made in so peremptory a fashion. Equal facilities can be defined in different ways. For example, in Britain, during campaigns, the BBC allots time for five election broadcasts to each major party, with a lesser number to any minor party. For this there is no charge. *Radiodiffusion Française* operates on the same principle, the amount of time allocated being determined by the strength of the respective parties in the last election. In America, the Communications Act of 1934 provided that if a station permits a candidate to use its facilities, it must afford "equal opportunities" to other candidates. If the time was given free as a public service, the others must receive free time, but if the candidate paid for it, the others can be charged equivalently. In many situations, then, this means that all candidates must have equal access to radio time, although many of them may not be able to afford to take advantage of the opportunity. But "equality" is the ideal: rich candidates and poor candidates must be given an equal chance to buy radio time.

Whether opposing opinions, as distinct from opposing candidates, receive the same consideration is an entirely different matter. The BBC has tried to solve this problem by avoiding controversial matters as much as possible; *i.e.,* by sticking to "straight news" and ignoring interpretation. Even if this solution were possible in the United States, it might not be desirable. The position of the FCC is that a reasonable balance of opinion should be presented on the air. Thus, it is customary to allot time on Sundays to all major religious groups, not merely to one. The FCC may also insist in specific instances that both sides of controversial issues be presented to the public, and in the event that a radio station flatly refuses to present a balanced picture, the Commission may refuse to renew the station license when it runs out. However, such drastic action as this—or even the threat of drastic action—is seldom necessary.

What does complicate the situation is not the planned presentation of different points of view, or the sale of time on an equal basis to candidates for office, but the commercial sponsorship of certain opinion broadcasts. News broadcasts sponsored by networks or stations generally have a high degree of objectivity. At the same time, networks and stations sell time to commentators who do not speak for radio interests, but for a private sponsor. It is at this point that a large degree of opinion imbalance results.

The total time on the air of commentators John W. Vandercook, Fulton Lewis, Jr., Henry Taylor, or George Edwards may not be large. Yet, these and other commentators command large audiences at favorable program times. They are not merely entertaining; they are actually "reporting" and "interpreting" data that for the listener may form the basis for future attitudes and opinions. Now any "interpreter" starts with various biases, prejudices, or "slants," and thus you may find two commentators coming to opposite conclusions on the significance of the same event. Presumably, Vandercook and Lewis are honest men, but they come to antithetical conclusions calling the shots as they see them. Yet, if a significant sector of the listening public regularly follows one or more commentators of the same "pitch," they are not getting the whole story, but only selected parts of it. The way out of this dilemma might lie along either of two lines. First, if opposing views were presented in about equal proportion, few persons would object. In this case, those who were convinced by the Lewises could listen only to the Lewises, and those in the Vandercook camp only to the Vandercooks, but both would be available. However, since the war, sponsored news analyses have tended to become more and more conservative, and the net effect is that in certain areas it is impossible to find a "liberal" commentator on the local stations. No one is going to suggest that sponsors must support commentators because they are liberal, but the problem of distorted analyses must be met in some fashion, particularly when one set of "impartial analysts" have the stage virtually to themselves. One solution is for those organizations that support liberal views to sponsor liberal commentators, and this has been done to some extent. The American Federation of Labor, for instance, supports a daily fifteen-minute program. But by and large, liberal organizations do not have the funds to pay for such radio time, particularly when it is at a choice listening hour such as seven-thirty in the evening.

Assuming that it will be impossible to obtain an equitable distribution of time between different viewpoints because one will ordinarily hold an economic advantage over the other, the next best thing would be to discover and publicize the degree to which bias exists. This was suggested by the American privately sponsored Commission on the Freedom of the Press, which urged the creation of an auditing bureau for both press and radio that would do detailed content analyses and appraise for the benefit of the public the objectivity of both media. This suggestion, mild though it was, met with immediate rejection by both press and radio interests. However, there is no inherent reason why it could not be carried out with relative ease if the necessary funds could be obtained. Strangely enough, some people feel that there is no reason why so-called "liberals" should be heard on the air, and they maintain that any attempt to get a hearing for "liberal" ideas is merely special pleading. These people apparently do not understand that freedom of information involves publicity both for one's own views and for the "wrong" views of his opponent. If the day ever comes when the shoes are reversed, many of the people who are now struggling to get a hearing for "liberalism" would be equally concerned that "conservatism" get fair play. The major point is that all significant viewpoints in the American community should be able to get a fair hearing over the air waves.

The problems inherent in commercially sponsored broadcasting are likewise present in television. As a result of the development of television by already existing radio networks, the same group of advertisers and advertising agencies that now control the programing of American radio also have at their disposal the new, unique, and revolutionary medium. Like radio, television has experimented with voluntary standards designed to protect the public interest and ward off government censorship. Up to the present, at least, attempts at preperformance censorship by local governments have been repelled, although it is perhaps only a question of time until some form of censorship will be established either by the FCC or by an unofficial body such as serves the movie industry. Public taste will permit the "TV neckline" to go only so far.

At first, radio feared that its new competitor would drive broadcasting out of business. It is now apparent that such fears were exaggerated, although in half a dozen metropolitan areas the TV audience already outnumbers the radio listeners. Beyond question, with the completion of new TV stations and relay points, the television audience will increase spectacularly. Already radio advertising rates have fallen sharply. Despite the high costs of operation, TV has in some places proved profitable and may be expected with larger audiences to become more so.

While the development of television has led to a veritable sociological field day, with pollers asking questions and counting the unmistakable aerials, most of the analysis to date deals with viewing habits and little with the intensity and influence of TV on the viewer. While television is extremely popular with children and only barely less so with adults, its influence on opinion formation and behavior remains to be studied. That the medium can be used to good political advantage is undisputed. Thomas E. Dewey, Rudolph Halley, and Senator Estes Kefauver have all used it to good advantage. Although it is not known for certain how much TV campaigning has to do with winning votes, there is no doubt that telecasts under the right circumstances may win initial popularity. This was dramatically illustrated in 1951 by the activities of the Senate Crime Investigating Committee under the chairmanship of Senator Kefauver with Halley as Chief Counsel. Since the proceedings were televised and featured some of America's most notorious racketeers, the viewing audience even at midday ran into the millions. It was a grand show, and Halley's role may have played a large part in his later victory in the race for President of the New York City Council on a minor-party ticket.

Another illustration of the power of TV occurred in 1952 when Senator Kefauver announced that he would seek the Democratic nomination for the Presidency and had tremendous success in the preferential primaries. Perhaps to discourage such future candidacies, Speaker Sam Rayburn of the House of Representatives ruled in February, 1952, that in the future no telecasts of House committee activities would be permitted. In spite of Republican protests, Rayburn's ruling was sustained by the House. However, when the Republicans took control of Congress in 1953, the decision as to whether or not to permit televised hearings was left in the hands of the individual committees.

The televising of congressional investigations has created some new problems in the field of civil rights which have yet to be dealt with in a comprehensive manner by the courts—the difficulty, for example, of obtaining an unbiased jury in the case of a man who has refused to testify before such a committee. Refusal to testify is no admission of guilt—at least, not in law. But in the minds of the viewers, the impression of guilt would be virtually ineradicable.

What TV does is to highlight personality. Its impact is much sharper than either a week-old newsreel or a radio broadcast. Scientific studies now under way on the 1952 presidential campaign may be expected to throw more light on the actual influence of television on the voter's decision and decision-making process. Suffice it to say that both parties felt that TV could not be overlooked as a vital medium for influencing public opinion in the campaign, and this resulted, among other things, in a considerable change in the strategy and atmosphere of the two nominating conventions.

MOTION PICTURES AND PUBLIC OPINION

According to the psychologists, one of the major problems that any society faces is that of reconciling the real world with the one desired. To a large extent the motion picture industry exists to bridge this gap, if only for a two- or three-hour interlude. The films permit the member of the audience to transport himself to a make-believe world, far removed from the prosaic day-to-day existence he knows in the world without. Psychologically, the process is a complicated one. A motion picture fan may identify himself with both the actors and the situations. This, in itself, is no different from reactions to other forms of drama. But the unique contribution of the cinema is to present large doses of human behavior of a type that is frequently neither socially nor religiously desirable, always climaxed by the triumph of virtue. Thus, while the heroine may have been somewhat wild in her courting days, upon marriage to the hero she settles down to an ideal existence in a white cottage and never lets her eyes linger on another man. From the point of view of an adolescent, the moral would seem to be that you can sow wild oats before marriage, but that somehow matrimony will result in a new-found stability and virtue. This is a comforting, if somewhat unrealistic, message.

The American motion picture industry specializes in the forbidden: illegal sexual relationships, acts of violence and crime, glorification of types of people who would hardly be welcome in actual society; e.g., the hard-boiled "private eye" à la Raymond Chandler. The one thing that puts Hollywood into nervous palpitation is the fear that a film will be too "highbrow"; i.e., that it will be aimed at a level over the heads of the audience. This level has generally been calculated as being in the middle or late teens, and it is this group that forms the bulk of American motion picture audiences. In addition, 30 to 40 per cent of the industry's profits come from foreign sales, and foreign audiences often react, understandably, in a negative fashion when confronted with epics designed to titillate American teen-agers. Not that the European or British film industry is any better: those who exclaim at the humor of *Tight Little Island* or the restrained brutality and tragedy of *The Bicycle Thief* should remember, before they begin to demolish Hollywood for its lack of perception, that as a rule only the best foreign films are imported to the United States. On the other hand, highly developed American sales techniques have led to the exploitation of both good and bad American pictures in Europe. There are American films that match almost anything produced in Europe or Britain in both humor and tragedy, but unfortunately they are not the only ones that make the transatlantic crossing. If they were, Europeans generally might have a higher view of American culture.

Pictorial representation through the cinema is widely believed to have great influence on the audience. Since, in the United States, the weekly number of motion picture patrons is numerically equal to about half the total population of the nation, serious attempts have been made to study the degree to which films influence American behavior. The most famous investigation was that conducted under the auspices of the Payne Fund nearly a generation ago. From this, the only point of unchallenged accuracy that emerged was that motion pictures have an effect on the emotional behavior of children. Later specialized studies dealing with adult reactions have thrown little light on the problem. In several experiments using control groups, some measurements have been attempted but the results are far from conclusive. Many sociologists, anthropologists, and psychologists have come up with devastating criticism of the motion picture industry, but, boiled down, their observations amount to little more than an attack on American cultural patterns and behavior. In short, while many indictments have been drawn up, the truth of the matter is that no one knows whether, in the long run, American behavior is much affected by the motion pictures, always excepting highly emotional persons or those of a tender age. Some pressure groups seem to feel that specific films have harmed them; e.g., when Clark Gable appeared in *It Happened One Night* without an undershirt, the underwear manufacturers objected strenuously, and the cigar manufacturers have for years been urging that Hollywood have some heroes smoke cigars instead of leaving that excellent tobacco product as the symbol of the racketeer. The Hatters Union has also urged that all the men in films laid in present-day America wear hats! Hollywood has tried to comply with these various requests, but the industrial results are unknown.

That motion pictures can be used to put over a "message," educational or otherwise, has long been recognized. Both governments and educators have employed the cinema to put over certain points of view or to illustrate vividly certain techniques. Because of the high cost of production, motion pictures have not been as widely used for educational aids as many educators think would be desirable. However, current criticisms of the motion pictures are not primarily aimed at educational films, but rather at the commercial Hollywood product. The criticism is mostly on the ground of taste, the alleged lowering of cultural standards, and the deception of youth. As instruments of direct education or propaganda, such as an Army film on sex hygiene or a government film on soil conservation, motion pictures are highly effective. But the number of people who attend all such educational films is minute compared with the enormous body of Americans who go for sheer entertainment. A further distinction between these film types should be noted. The person who attends an educational picture usually goes with a purpose, and if the film is a good one, it may influence him profoundly. However, the normal movie-goer is not seeking education. His set is entirely in the direction of entertainment, and it is doubtful how much influence a film could have upon him when his basic design is to escape from reality to a completely artificial world which he does not associate with his normal environment.

Both the American and foreign film industries have had difficulty in getting governments to treat them as adults. For many years, the United States Supreme Court refused to treat the motion picture as a medium of information, but rather held that its primary function was entertainment. The consequence of this was that films did not fall within the categories of mass media that were protected from arbitrary censorship by the First and Fourteenth Amendments. The position of the cinema, legally speaking, was thus roughly equivalent to that of a burlesque show: anything believed offensive to public morals could be censored in advance of showing by public authorities, and almost any grounds for objection would suffice to ban a film.

However, in 1952 the Supreme Court radically revised its approach to the motion picture. The immediate cause of this major shift was the banning by New York State authorities of the Italian film *The Miracle*. This film, which had been shown in Italy and Eire with little clerical opposition, was denounced by Cardinal Spellman as "sacrilegious" and Catholic pickets were soon marching back and forth in front of the theater which was showing the offensive picture. This, however, succeeded only in improving the theater's business, and legal steps were taken to ban *The Miracle*. After some rather complex legal maneuvers, the New York State Board of Regents banned the film from New York State on the ground that it was "sacrilegious." When the case reached the Supreme Court, the justices unanimously reversed the New York decisions and incorporated motion pictures into the media of mass communication which are protected from arbitrary state action by the due-process clause of the Fourteenth Amendment. However, the Court pointed out that there are special problems connected with motion pictures that may justify their being treated in a somewhat different fashion from the press or the soap-box orator. What forms of motion picture censorship; *i.e.*, what techniques of public regulation, the Court will permit remains to be discovered from future litigation—of which there will undoubtedly be plenty. The unofficial types of coercion, moreover, are very difficult to deal with legally. For example, in the instance of *The Miracle,* the New York Fire Department suddenly began to take an active interest in the theater showing the picture! If a theater is closed for violations of the fire regulations, who could maintain that the owner was being denied any constitutional rights? The picket line is another form of coercion which is quite legitimate, but its effectiveness is quite limited. Indeed, the free publicity resulting from picketing is such that some theater owners are rumored to have hired pickets themselves to picket their shows.

Actually, film censorship in America is vastly complex. The industry itself, through the Production Code Administration, attempts to enforce certain standards upon its members. The code, drafted principally by the Jesuit priest Father Daniel Lord, is administered by the Production Code Administration under the present direction of Joseph I. Breen. In addition to previous censorship exercised by the industry, other forms of private censorship exist. The Legion of Decency, a Catholic organization, brings pressure on the industry not to film certain scenes and stories and also to eliminate certain passages from finished pictures. Literally scores of other groups, both religious and secular, also attempt to influence the content of films.

Even if a picture has been approved by the Breen office and has survived the unofficial scrutiny of other organizations, it must still run the gauntlet of government censorship in nine states and about fifty cities. Various minority groups again bring pressure, this time on the state or city officials, to eliminate pictures that misrepresent, distort, or inflame. Thus, in addition to the case of *The Miracle* mentioned above, Jewish groups have demanded that *Oliver Twist*, a British film, be banned as engendering anti-Semitism, and some Protestants succeeded, on a city basis, in prohibiting Ingrid Bergman's vehicle *Stromboli* on the interesting basis that Miss Bergman's marital arrangements were somewhat extraordinary. Veterans' organizations also keep a close watch on motion pictures to prevent any unpatriotic pictures from reaching the screen, and the American Legion recently objected to Charles Chaplin's film *Limelight* on the ground that the actor is a "subversive."

The relative timidity of the film industry is thus quite understandable. Everyone must be pleased; no one can be offended. This is a difficult feat to perform. One might have supposed that the industry, under these pressures, was sufficiently pure from an ideological standpoint, but this has apparently not been established to the satisfaction of the House Committee on Un-American Activities. The committee periodically investigates Hollywood in search of "reds" and has succeeded in turning up a sufficient number to justify its activities to some newspapers. However, in the broad picture, it does not appear on the record that the Communists ever succeeded in getting a significant toe hold in the industry, much less in getting films produced that echoed the party line. At a time when conservative Americans were supporting Russia's fight against Germany, Hollywood picked up the beat and made a few pro-Russian films. But this only proves how closely the industry watches the pulse of American society; not that it was un-American. Going a step further than the committee, Senator Edwin Johnson of Colorado sponsored a bill in 1950 that would have licensed all performers. This measure died in the Senate, but the possibility always remains that the Federal government may some day find itself in the business of regulating the motion picture industry. However, since the Supreme Court has now ruled that films lie within the protection of the First Amendment, it hardly seems possible for the national government to embark upon a course which amounts to censorship of them.

In other democratic countries, censorship enjoys less of a vogue than in the United States. Usually, as in Denmark, there is a state board for this purpose. In Great Britain censorship is exercised by a voluntary body set up by the industry: the British Board of Film Censors. Local governments generally enforce the decision of this Board on theater owners, although the London County Council has been known to authorize showings of films interdicted by the censors. British censorship centers more on standards of taste than on political orthodoxy; *e.g.*, it is not uncommon for American films portraying bobbysoxers to be banned on the ground that such adolescent activity is in bad taste and should not spread to young British ladies. In Latin-American nations, Hollywood's favorite clutching kisses are regularly eliminated from films, although there is seldom any ban on nudity. In short, given all the hurdles that a motion picture must leap if it is to be a financial success, it is surprising that so many pictures considered "good" or "excellent" by "highbrow" audiences are in fact produced. There is also the consoling thought that motion picture attendance is a voluntary activity and can, if one desires, be omitted.

THE IMPACT OF OTHER MEDIA OF COMMUNICATIONS

The press, the radio, the cinema, and now television are the great mass media. From them is obtained most of the information upon which people base their conscious decisions. Other media exist in abundance, but their influence is secondary. While various types of advertising, cartoons, public addresses, books, and magazines also furnish information on which action may be based, the cumulative effect of these media is slight when compared to the great mass opinion industries. However, this analysis would not be complete without taking these minor media into consideration.

The most conspicuous American popular magazine is the *Reader's Digest*. With a monthly circulation of more than 15 million copies, it clearly reaches a large part of the American as well as a considerable foreign public. Yet, at the very most, not more than one literate American in three reads it regularly. In fact, surveys have shown that, comic books aside, only one literate American in three reads any magazine. Purportedly "high-brow" magazines such as *The Atlantic* and *Harper's* have monthly distributions of less than 160,000 copies.

Although the *Reader's Digest* does perform various adult-education services, its primary purpose, like that of various less-circulated magazines, is to show a profit from publishing, not to disturb the public unnecessarily. In addition to great mass-distribution magazines, there are, of course, in all democratic countries, various journals of opinion. The more opinionated of these, which specialize in exhorting their faithful constituents to greater faith, make little contribution to the formation of public opinion. But other news magazines and journals of opinion, with a less introverted approach, may have considerable indirect influence. To the extent that such magazines influence the thinking of "opinion leaders"—clergymen, business executives, editors, teachers, politicians—they are probably much more important than circulation figures would imply. Unfortunately, little research has been undertaken into this potentially fruitful area of the role of "opinion leaders" and the sources of their information. There are, in addition, professional journals such as the *American Political Science Review* or the *American Sociological Review* in which professors and other specialists exchange information, but these are in fact subsidized by scholarly associations and make no dent in the opinion market.

In summary it would seem that public opinion has deep roots in the soil of a society and in the institutions like the family, the churches, the schools, and the political forms which that soil has nourished. The media of communications which have been examined may alter the surface manifestations of this basic social "set," but it is questionable whether they can alone radically alter the "inarticulate major premises" of a society. To be frank, the process of basic change is still, in spite of much illuminating sociological and anthropological research, largely shrouded in mystery. We know that societies do change, and change radically, and we know that certain factors contribute to this transformation, but the formula of change and the role that mass media or propaganda play in it remains undetermined. This much we do know: in totalitarian states public opinion is considered to be a vital weapon in the defense of the dictatorship, and great emphasis is placed on manipulation and organized opinion formation. In a democracy, on the other hand, while opinion manipulation is not unknown, the opinions of the people, or public opinion collectively, plays a significant part in the formation of public policy. It is trite but accurate to observe that only a public which is informed can serve as a reliable basis for democratic government. As President Washington observed: "In proportion as the structure of government gives force to public opinion, it is essential that public opinion shall be enlightened." An obvious prerequisite of public enlightenment is that no one point of view shall gain a monopoly of the media of mass communications.

THE MEASUREMENT OF PUBLIC OPINION

Assuming that public opinion should play a determining role in the formulation of democratic public policy, the next problem which arises is how public opinion can be ascertained. Scientific methods for the determination of public opinion are of fairly recent origin. Early in this century it was fashionable to observe, with Lord Bryce, that democracy should be based on public opinion, but that unfortunately public opinion was essentially unmeasurable. The entire science of public-opinion analysis became possible only with the development of adequate statistical theory. In order to understand the implications of public-opinion research on public policy, it is necessary to examine in some detail the most common measurement technique: polling. Happily, we can sidestep the statistical theory which supports this device; suffice it to note that further advances in the application of polling techniques depend on the adequacy of mathematical and psychological theories, and that polling does not operate automatically in a social vacuum.

The basic assumption underlying polling is that it is unnecessary, in order to test opinion on a question, to query every member of the public. A representative sample should give about the same results, and much more quickly and cheaply. Therefore polling is, in principle, an extension of an older method of obtaining information—the social survey. As developed in Great Britain more than a century ago, and later in the United States, social surveys were principally concerned with social and economic conditions in particular cities or communities. Recent examples of this technique may be found in the Lynds' *Middletown* and the subsequent *Middletown in Transition*. More familiar examples are probably the United States government surveys, of which the decennial census is the most obvious. From a scientific point of view, the work of the Bureau of Agricultural Economics has been outstanding. This Bureau has made unique and vital contributions to the development of sampling techniques, and its statistics, derived from questioning a small proportion of the population, are considered by some scholars to be more reliable than those obtained by universal questioning in the census! This is not mere scholarly bias, for the census, conducted as it is by amateurs, tends to be quite inaccurate at some points.

Other common methods of determining opinion fall under the heading of market surveys, used to determine the marketability of various commercial products, and of radio audience research, used to determine listener preference. However, students of government are primarily interested in public-opinion polls and closely related devices.

The genealogy of these polls is of interest. As early as 1824, straw votes were taken by at least two newspapers in an effort to predict the outcome of the presidential election. These straw or trial polls were in no sense scientific, but were intended mainly to stir up reader interest as well as to gauge political opinion. In our own time, newspaper polls have broadened out into wider areas, but these polls are all regional in character.

Magazines also entered the picture, when, as early as 1912, the *Farm Journal* polled its readers on the forthcoming presidential race. The famous, but ill-fated, *Literary Digest* poll began in 1916 and terminated abruptly in 1936 after predicting that Landon would trounce Roosevelt. The *Digest*'s technique was simple, although the operation itself was enormous: to millions of telephone subscribers and car owners, ballots were mailed. About a quarter of those queried responded. Until 1936, the *Digest* poll was quite accurate; in 1932, for example, it predicted the vote of the top presidential candidates within 1.4 per cent. However, in 1936, when the poll not only failed to predict the winner but was also 20 per cent off in its estimate of the popular vote distribution, the magazine and poll collapsed in joint ignominy. It should be noted that the *Digest* poll, as well as others patterned on it, did not confine its polling proclivities only to elections, but also sought out opinion on issues such as prohibition and tax plans.

The demise of the *Digest* focused attention on rival polls which had been much more successful in forecasting the 1936 results. Among these polls were the Fortune Survey, conducted for *Fortune* magazine by Paul T. Cherington and Elmo B. Roper; the Crossley poll, under the direction of Archibald M. Crossley; and the Gallup poll, organized by George Gallup in 1935 under the title of the American Institute of Public Opinion. All these organizations forecast with remarkable accuracy the outcome of the 1940 and 1944 presidential elections, but for various reasons they all miscalled the 1948 election. The main reason for the 1948 fiasco appears to have been overconfidence: Governor Dewey apparently had complete faith in the polls, and the pollsters seem to have had full confidence in Governor Dewey. As a consequence, the Fortune Survey discontinued polling, which is a very expensive proposition, in September, 1948, and Gallup ceased sampling two weeks before election day. Subsequent studies have shown that during this backstretch period the greatest shift of voters from Dewey to Truman occurred, but the transfer was completely missed by the pollsters. In 1952, imbued with hypercaution, the pollsters completely missed the Eisenhower landslide.

Elections give glamour to public-opinion polling, but it should be emphasized that most sampling is more concerned with obtaining public views on issues than with election forecasting. Organizations such as the National Opinion Research Center in Chicago, the Princeton Office of Public Opinion Research, and the Survey Research Center at the University of Michigan conduct a great many confidential surveys for government agencies while eschewing the limelight and danger of election prediction, while the periodical Gallup and Roper analyses of public opinion on various significant issues of the day appear in many newspapers and periodicals.

Despite the fiasco which overcame the professional forecasters in 1948, polling is here to stay. Its uses are obvious and valuable. A few words on polling methods are therefore in order. According to Irion, there are some eight stages in a polling operation: selection of the topic, selection of the "universe" or whole to be examined, determining the sample, preparing questions, pretesting the questions, interviewing, preparing results, presenting the results. All these stages present problems, but the most difficult area is the determination of the sample.

Upon reflection, it will be conceded that men's objective activities, as distinguished perhaps from their subjective motives, can be measured. In this men are less different from other parts of the universe than is sometimes imagined. For example, to test the presence of typhoid germs in water, it is not necessary to test all the water in the lake, but merely to test a sample of it. Again, to test the presence of sugar in the human blood stream, a doctor does not drain out all the patient's blood, but only takes a drop or so. The presence of fixed characteristics, whether in wheat, blood, water, or human beings, lies at the basis of all sampling procedures.

There are four general methods of sampling. The first, random sampling, operates on the assumption that every person stands an equal chance of being examined. The sample is chosen at random by taking every fifth name in the tax rolls or in the telephone book, or such similar devices as were employed by the *Literary Digest* in its presidential polls. The second, stratified sampling, is much more complex for here quota controls are established on the basis of known facts about the "universe" under examination. For example, if 50 per cent of the people in the community under examination are known to be Unitarians, 50 per cent of those questioned should be members of this religious body, and so on with other characteristics such as sex, income, age, or marital status. This is the method used most by commercial pollsters. The third, purposive sampling, deliberately confines questioning to some specific group or element in the community, as when college professors of political science are asked whom they support for President, or "men of distinction" are queried on their brand of whisky. The fourth, a variation of the second and third, attempts to combine both stratified and purpose sampling. It should be noted that all these methods of sampling are based on the assumption that basic data on the population must be available and accurate. Since even the United States census contains inaccuracies, and Americans tend to move around rather freely, these basic statistics are sometimes distorted. Statistical methods can give valid results only if the raw material employed is itself accurate.

Keeping this information in mind, it might be well to examine the so-called "1948 debacle." It should be emphasized again that, while predicting presidential races is the most advertised form of polling, it is not the most important or valuable use to which polls are put. In a presidential year, the pollsters are asked just one question: Who will win? If they deliver the correct reply, few will bother to analyze the methods employed to reach it; most will acclaim the poll as prescient. Thus in November, 1948, a Los Angeles swami had a brief moment of glory when it turned out that his prediction of a Truman victory, based on a close analysis of the relative position of Jupiter and Mars, was correct. Although this method has little to recommend it, the swami received the accolade of the newspapers for coming through with the right answer.

In 1936, for example, the pollsters, Roper excepted, were far less accurate in their election predictions as far as comparative votes were concerned than they were in 1948. But they picked Roosevelt and the crowd cheered. The best year prior to 1948 was 1944, when no poll was far from the actual Democratic percentage of the two-party vote, and Roper was only two-tenths of a percentage point off the actual vote. This feat led the public to believe that polling had indeed reached the point of scientific accuracy and was infallible.

The 1948 election returns were eye-opening. While Crossley, Gallup, and

Roper had given Governor Dewey respectively 49.9 per cent, 49.5 per cent, and 52.2 per cent, the Republican candidate in fact received only 45.1 per cent of the total vote. These were errors of the first magnitude, for, to take the case of Roper, a miscalculation of 7.1 per cent in the popular vote led to an overprediction of 16 per cent in Dewey's favor. However, the statistical distortion can lead to unfair exaggeration of the degree of error. Crossley, for instance, was nine-tenths of a percentage point off in his estimate of Wallace's vote, but in terms of the Wallace percentage of the total vote he was 37.5 per cent too high!

After the 1948 election results were known, the pollsters publicly ate crow—to the great delight of those who believe firmly in the unpredictability of human behavior. The Social Science Research Council, however, immediately spearheaded efforts to determine the basic causes of failure. In its report, the Council's committee called attention to two principal sources of error: one in quota sampling and interviewing, and the other in the allocation of undecided voters. The percentage of undecided voters was in fact very high—about 15 per cent. When the pollsters decided to cease their sampling operations—which was well before election day—these voters were distributed to the two parties in the same proportion as those who had made up their mind; i.e., if the ratio of Republicans to Democrats among those voters who had made up their minds was 3 to 2, the undecided voters were distributed on the same basis. Prior to 1948, this technique had worked with seeming satisfaction and accuracy. Immediately after the election both Gallup and Roper took polls to ask respondents whether they had voted, for whom, and when they had made up their minds. The Social Science Research Council Committee, commenting on the information gathered from this poll, remarked, "In other words, if we were to take these data at face value, we would say that about one voter in seven made up his mind within the last two weeks and three fourths of them voted for Truman." Data from other sources tended to reinforce this hypothesis.

In the future, it appears that polls will be taken right up to the date of the election, and special attention will be given to trends and shifts. For prestige purposes, more expensive techniques, ignored by the commercial pollsters before 1948, will also undoubtedly be employed. In 1950 Gallup claimed remarkable accuracy in forecasting the election results. During the same year, the British Institute of Public Opinion predicted British election results to within 1.3 percentage points for Labor and five-thousands of a percentage point for the Conservatives!

It has been suggested that, while predicting presidential winners is great—and hazardous—sport, it is in reality a minor utilization of measurement techniques. What, then, has been learned from public-opinion measurement? The reader need only turn to a current issue of the *Public Opinion Quarterly* to see in summary form the questions and answers given to scores of separate polls.

The variety of questions is bewildering, and some seem trivial. Yet, it is only through such polls over a period of time that it is possible to trace the strength of sentiments of first-rate political importance. For example, public attitudes toward the regulation of railroads or government ownership of certain industries have merely been estimated in the past. The change, or lack of change, in views on these and other similar subjects can now be studied in some detail over a stretch of years. In 1951, the Princeton University Press published a monumental volume entitled *Public Opinion 1935–1946*. Prepared under the editorial direction of Hadley Cantril of the Office of Public Opinion Research, this work contains summaries of surveys conducted by twenty-three organizations in sixteen countries for the twelve-year period. Poll results are presented chronologically by subject matter. For attitude research, whether on "immortality" or on "political parties," the Princeton compilation is indispensable.

A great deal of what is known about voting behavior has come from public-opinion polls. For example, it is now established that poorer groups tend to vote less than wealthier groups, and that college graduates are much more likely to vote than non-college graduates. It has also been shown that college graduates are more likely to be "independent voters" than are other groups in the population. Additional techniques for measuring attitudes and behavior have also been developed. Various attitude scales may be employed to gauge opinion; for example, the Thurstone and Likert scales. Depth interviews, which attempt to measure the intensity of opinion, may be utilized to answer the charge that public-opinion polls gather only superficial data. The Kinsey reports on the sexual behavior of the human male and female used this technique. The panel, or repeated interview method, was employed by Lazarsfeld and his associates in their study of how voters in Erie County, Ohio, made up their minds in the 1940 presidential campaign. *The People's Choice* and various follow-up studies have shown that voters, in the mass, express themselves politically in about the same way as the groups to which they belong. Socio-economic status (SES), *i.e.*, social and economic position in the community, is directly related to party affiliation, but no less important is religious affiliation. At the same time, the higher the SES rating, the greater is the participation in elections. The Lazarsfeld and other related studies indicate that, given sufficient knowledge of an area, its history, its inhabitants, fairly accurate predictions about political behavior can be made.

Another technique of opinion forecasting has been developed by Louis Bean, formerly of the U.S. Department of Agriculture. In *How to Predict Elections* (1948), Bean explained his system of prognostication, which has proved remarkably accurate. Using a historical-statistical method, Bean continues past trends into the future, making allowances for change as measured by recent elections, referendums, or public-opinion polls. Although his critics maintain that his method smacks of witchcraft, Bean's success in predicting election results has been amazing.

POLLS AND REPRESENTATIVE GOVERNMENT

Do techniques which measure public opinion and attempt to predict future public attitudes constitute a threat to democratic government? Social scientists often find themselves, somewhat unwillingly, in a position similar to that of the atomic physicists who have seen their discoveries employed primarily for destructive purposes. The discoveries of social scientists—polls, interviews, mass observation, and all the rest—are in themselves politically neutral. However, they can be employed in ways which, in the opinion of individual social scientists, may be either socially constructive or socially destructive. Neither the physicist nor the social scientist should be blamed merely because his techniques are applied to attain bad ends.

In practice, the measurement of public opinion has proved a blessing to American administrators—practically every major department of the United States government attempts by varying means to judge probable reactions to proposed plans. If indications are that the proposals will receive hostile receptions, changes may be made to assuage the potential critics. The Treasury's bond drives, the conservation programs of the Department of Agriculture, and the work of many other agencies have leaned heavily upon accurate polling methods.

In a more narrowly political sense, extensive use is continually made of the newer techniques for measuring opinion. Legislators can, for example, determine whether a noisy pressure group in fact speaks for as many people as it claims. It has become apparent, to cite just one instance, that labor leaders exaggerated the degree to which union members disliked the Taft-Hartley "slave labor" act. This act, which did by its complexity serve as a lawyer's full-employment measure, was patently not a slave-labor act, and the workers refused to support this extreme claim. It is probable that a realization of this weak support was one factor which restrained Congress from repealing the act as the President had demanded. Other illustrations can be drawn from campaign politics where it is common to find candidates measuring opinion through polls before they take a final plunge of commitment on some issue.

A frequent criticism of polling, heard less frequently since 1948, is that the polls create a "band-wagon" effect. The argument is that people want to be on the winning side and use the polls to pick the winner. However, numerous studies have revealed that there is little relationship between a candidate's standing in the preelection polls and an increase, or decrease, in the final election tallies. Reliance on polls has notably decreased since the 1948 shambles, and the 1952 presidential campaign saw a bitter struggle right down to Election Day, with no reliance on a purported "band-wagon" psychology.

A further criticism, advanced more often in Great Britain than in the United States, is that excessive reliance on public-opinion polls may undermine the integrity of the legislature. This argument assumes that the legislator will become merely a rubber stamp, following public opinion and never daring to stand up for his own views. There is little empirical evidence to support this criticism, and a good case may be developed in refutation of it. Issues are rarely presented in a yes-or-no fashion either to the legislator or to the public in opinion polls. Furthermore, it seems doubtful that present mass testing devices offer a very accurate gauge of the intensity of opinion, which is perhaps more important to a representative than a mere arithmetic plurality of opinion. There is also evidence to suggest that after an action is taken, it may become popular; for example, polls taken in the United States in 1940 and 1941 at first revealed majority opposition to lend-lease aid for those nations fighting Germany, but after the legislation was passed public opinion shifted to support it.

To the degree that a government operates apart from direct party pressures, the need for other devices than mere legislative divisions to measure opinion bcomes proportionally more important. In the American form of government, with its tradition of independent executives, longer terms for Senators than for Representatives, and staggered elections, voting divisions in the legislature as well as elections themselves offer only very rough indices of opinion. Therefore it is not surprising that American governmental agencies, as well as legislators and chief executives, make far more extensive use of polling information than is common elsewhere.

The British Government, which cannot in practice be overthrown in the House of Commons, is in a very different position. It must assume responsibility for its actions to the electorate at large; support in the House may generally be taken for granted. There opinion changes may be gauged in a variety of ways; for example, in the periodic conferences between backbenchers and Ministers, or by the results of by-elections which occur upon the death of Members. If sufficient grass-roots opposition to its actions seems to be developing, the Government may alter its policies. At the same time, the British Government does in fact maintain a unit charged with measuring opinion and opinion changes, and so do the major party organizations. There are also private polling organizations that operate along similar lines to those in the United States.

Under a hair-trigger system of parliamentary government such as exists in France, parliamentary debates and elections register public opinion far more accurately than they do in the United States or in Britain. The many parties which submit finely shaded programs to the electorate convert elections into public-opinion polls where the voter may register his views at any point along the scale. This does not occur in Britain or the United States where the voter is given, in effect, a yes-or-no choice between two major parties—with both of which he may be in substantial disagreement. To take but one instance, the American isolationist has not been able to vote his convictions in a presidential campaign for at least twenty years, while his French counterpart can always find a political home. As a result, although various polling organizations exist in France, the impact of their findings is of little political significance. Changes in opinion are quickly, even violently, recorded in the National Assembly. It would seem superfluous in a multiparty nation employing proportional representation to depend upon polls, content analyses, or other methods of measuring public opinion. Thus the charge, considered above, that public-opinion polls may undermine faith in representative government is purely relative to the government under consideration. Even those most strongly opposed to polling would scarcely contend that polls constitute a menace to the stability of the French government!

PUBLIC OPINION AND CHANGES IN GOVERNMENTAL POLICY

To what extent should governmental policy reflect changes in public opinion? In answering this question, two separate but related points must be considered. First, there is the problem of nonparticipation and its implications; second, the adequacy of the mechanisms for the transmission of opinion changes must be examined. To put it another way, we must first discuss the criteria for discovering whether the people are *really* demanding change, and then evaluate the techniques that exist for implementing this desire.

Under the first heading, let us look at the United States. In the total population there is probably a segment of about 20 per cent which is militantly in favor of change, and another 20 per cent strongly in favor of maintaining the *status quo*. In between these two poles lies the great bulk of the population, which can take change or leave it alone depending upon the circumstances. When a national election takes place, the two extreme segments march to the polls en masse and cast their ballots, but a good proportion of the in-betweens do not even take the trouble to vote. Can any inference be drawn from their inaction?

Educators, civic-minded reformers, and some politicians profess to find great danger in such displays of apathy. The voting percentage in the United States, where from 50 to 60 per cent of those of voting age participate in presidential elections, is unfavorably compared with that of Britain, France, Italy, Germany and other democratic nations, where huge electoral turnouts are the rule. However, the fears of the civic-minded are somewhat exaggerated. In nations where everybody is excited about politics, most people vote, and the fact that people stay home from the polls in the United States may be considered an indication of confidence in the basic governmental process; *i.e.*, that either way the election goes things will work out all right. In addition, it should be noted that elaborate residence requirements disfranchise many highly mobile Americans, and that deliberate chicanery has been employed to keep Negroes from exercising their proper place in the electorate.

Aside from such shameful attempts to thwart the democratic process for the benefit of specific racial or economic groups, nonparticipation may in fact indicate a high degree of satisfaction with government. To revert to previous terminology, voluntary abstinence from voting may indicate a high degree of consensus in a democratic society. On the other hand, tremendous electoral participation, coupled with frantic party activity, political strikes, and riots may indicate a high degree of citizen participation but a low degree of consensus. Thus in a society with a relatively low degree of political participation, it might be suggested that the nonvoter votes against change by simply staying home. This is not intended as a cynical commentary, for there clearly are many benefits to be gained from increased participation in government. However, in the objective situation it is difficult to build a case for basic change when a third or more of the voting population refuse to get excited enough to vote.

It could be suggested that the reason so many stay home is that neither party offers any real change, and so the voter, disgusted, refuses to choose between a Republican and a Democrat who may hold very similar views. This paralysis of perfectionism may affect some voters—unquestionably some militant Taft supporters refused to vote for the "internationalist" Eisenhower in 1952. But this argument fails to take into consideration the function of the American political party which will shift its direction at a moment's notice to capture a sizable segment of the electorate. The reason Eisenhower was nominated over Taft was precisely that the Republicans assembled in convention felt that the changes purportedly advocated by Taft would not be acceptable to the American people. Similarly, if the voters are really disgusted with the two old parties, one would expect a large increase in the vote of minor parties advocating extensive change, an increase which has not materialized. It would seem that few American nonvoters are ideologically motivated.

As was suggested in the last section, it is the high degree of political nonparticipation in the United States which helps to give the technique of opinion polling its unique American significance. In other nations—where often, as in Belgium and Italy, voting is compulsory—nonparticipation does not present the problems it does in the United States, and demands for change are directly tabulated on the electoral register.

A second major consideration deals with the adequacy of the mechanisms for the transmission and implementation of opinion at the governmental level. This is the heart of the democratic political process, and, in one way or another, this volume is concerned with aspects of that central and crucial problem. It may be reiterated at this point that some mechanisms are more adequate than others to accomplish these ends. The type of party system and the type of parliamentary system are factors to be considered here. The American type of presidential system is notoriously unresponsive to opinion shifts as measured by elections. Other means of measurement, such as opinion polls and the pressure process, tend to compensate for this deficiency. Under parliamentary systems, the principal distinction is between the British and the French types. The British party system admirably transmits general opinion from the electorate to the government, although here it should be noted that vested party interests, such as the trade-union movement in the Labor party, act as a strong deterrent to sudden change. On specific issues, some pressure-group activity exists in Britain, but—as has already been indicated—these lobbies act primarily within the parties rather than directly on the legislative process. In the French parliamentary system, where the parties are often pressure groups in political guise, the transmission of opinion is highly efficient, but the means for implementing this opinion and translating it into concrete policies are virtually nonexistent.

In summary, both the intensity of public opinion and the mechanisms for its transmission condition the sensitivity of government to opinion shifts. Once more it is necessary to return to the fundamental concept of consensus, and to observe that if a high degree of basic community agreement exists, mechanisms are likely to offer few difficulties. On the other hand, if little fundamental consensus exists on the utility and value of democratic procedures, mechanical changes alone will not remedy the difficulties. The basic problem is whether release and response mechanisms can change on an evolutionary basis to correspond with shifts in public opinion. If the shifts are sudden, or if the mechanisms are unresponsive, a revolutionary situation is likely to be present. Public opinion, today often deified, can be no better or no worse than the community which it reflects. There are no magic formulas, including the proposals that political participation be made compulsory by fining nonvoters, which can guarantee sudden self-improvement.

Chapter 5

ELECTORAL SYSTEMS

THE DEMOCRATIC "class struggle" takes place in polling booths rather than in the streets. Yet the very real conflicts that exist—of party versus party, of interest against interest, of section versus section—would not be kept within manageable limits were it not for explicit, understood rules of procedure, usually embedded in law as well as in custom.

Depending upon the country under analysis, its laws and its traditions, there is widespread divergence in the techniques whereby ballots are substituted for bullets as the basis for decision making. In the following pages, an effort is made to analyze some of the significant similarities and dissimilarities in the electoral systems of various leading democratic nations. In a previous chapter, attention was focused upon the implications of party organization. Here the concern is with the rules under which the game is played. What are the principal means by which nominations are made, ballots counted, campaigns and voting regulated? Under any system there are certain ground rules which define the conditions of contest, and the professionals in politics are as much bound to observe them as are their counterparts on the baseball diamond or the football gridiron. The reader should be forewarned that we are not merely interested in description or in historical analysis. Even more, we are concerned with the power struggle that is the essence of politics. At the same time, it should be remembered that laws, including those governing electoral activity, are made by men who are partisans, and that laws so passed inevitably reflect past tensions and decisions. It would be improbable, therefore, that electoral laws in general would stand a disinterested, idealized test of utopian fairness. But this is simply to call attention once more to the imperfection of human beings, including those residing in the great democracies.

NOMINATIONS

To begin, let us raise the question as to why the nominating process is important. It is important because, in the real sense, the nominating level is the decisive level of party decision making. A party makes its bid for power with its nominees, and the quality of the nominees is a direct outgrowth of the functioning of the nomination system. Thus, at this level, are fought the bitterest internecine battles of American politics; here the various elements in the party

—conservative, liberal, urban, agrarian—show their hands in the effort to win the party label for their man.

It is also important to remember that in about half the nation's election districts the two-party system does not exist except in embryonic form, for the minority party is too weak seriously to contest the general election. Consequently, in these areas, the nominating battle within the dominant party is in effect the conclusive conflict. If, for example, one holds a conservative point of view that in California would lead him to enroll in the Republican party, but lives in Georgia, he seldom wastes his time in the GOP. Rather than refighting the Civil War each November, which is what running as a Republican in Georgia entails, the practical American generally devotes his efforts to capturing the Democratic party for his viewpoint and the candidate that represents it. To do this, the nomination must be captured, and the wide diversity of viewpoint that characterizes both Democrats and Republicans in Congress is a vivid testimony to the widespread success of this process of boring from within. It is unfortunate that the nominating process has generally been neglected by students of American government, for in all areas of the nation it is a decisive phase of politics and in many sections it is conclusive. Generally speaking, the nominating function is much more significant than the electing function.

As has been noted earlier, the American national parties are prize examples of political decentralization. That is to say, the power to make nominations to Federal offices is diffused among national conventions, state conventions, and state-wide primaries. In another context, this results in voting divisions in Congress, and in many state legislatures, customarily following regional, economic, or functional lines, depriving the party designations of most of their significance. Some might object to attributing the decentralization of political parties to the diffusion of the nominating power, and indeed this is by no means the whole story, but the usual allocation of blame for weak parties which places the onus on federalism is more inadequate. Both Canada and Australia have governments organized on the federal principle, but possess quite strong centralized party systems. Thus federalism does not automatically result in party decentralization, and the characteristics of the American party systems appear to be a logical outgrowth of the tremendously diffused, decentralized nominating system.

Nomination to office in the Federalist era of American history was a fairly simple affair. Those who were rich, well-born, and civic-minded merely nominated themselves! Of course, some organization was necessary, and by the end of the eighteenth century the legislative caucus—which got its name from a famous colonial patriotic club, the North End Caucus of Boston—had become the standard nominating instrument. Such a caucus, consisting of party members in Congress, was responsible for naming both presidential candidates in 1800.

The legislative caucus was quick, inexpensive, and decisive. As practiced by the Republicans until Jackson overthrew "King Caucus," the party legislators simply gathered and nominated party leaders for the Presidency and Vice-Presidency. Thus for almost a quarter of a century a relatively centralized nominating system, with strong overtones of legislative supremacy, was employed in choosing chief executives. A President thus chosen had points of close resemblance to the Prime Minister of a parliamentary government, for he owed his status to his prestige in Congress and his renomination would obviously depend upon maintaining cordial relations with the legislators.

Jackson and his followers, strongly opposing a system which they considered oligarchic, preferred the convention to the caucus as a nominating device. This was part of the general trend of Jacksonian democracy which worked to broaden the base of the republic by getting greater public participation in the political process. As early as 1804 a state convention was held in New Jersey, and this seemed to be an ideal way to get popular control of nominations. On its surface, the convention system appeared to be remarkably democratic. At the base of the party pyramid in the states, the voters chose the delegates to state conventions, which in turn chose representatives to national party conventions. These latter bodies, fully representative of the wills of the various internal party segments, would then pick a national candidate. Between conventions, party committees functioned as the agents of the supreme body, the convention. In 1828, the various parties employed different nominating techniques and only the Anti-Masonic relied on a convention. But by 1832 the convention system began to assert its supremacy. Accompanying the acceptance of the convention system was a tremendous diffusion of party power. The President no longer was the choice of a legislative clique which could hand the job out to men of its choice; he rather became an official with an autonomous constituency. In a real sense, the separation between President and Congress dates from this time.

Except on the national level, the convention system in time became discredited and was replaced by new devices for choosing nominees on the state level. For this there were several reasons. In the first place, the Jacksonian Democrats apparently assumed that the citizen had boundless time and energy to devote to politics. This proved not to be the case, as the great bulk of the citizenry was quite apathetic. In the second place, as an outgrowth of this indifference, the professionals took over the conventions. In many areas the primary, either oral or written, conducted by the parties to select the convention delegates was corrupt. Tammany Hall primaries in the days of Boss Tweed come to mind as illustrations of this point.

Reformers counterattacked with two types of proposals, one category aimed at cutting down the number of elective positions, and the other designed to fortify the election machinery itself against manipulation. The major proposal of the first type was the establishment of the merit system of civil service which was calculated to remove many government jobs from politics. In the latter category was the agitation for the Australian ballot, printed by the state and filled out by the voter under more or less secret conditions. Prior to this time—and it should be noted that the Australian ballot penetrated South Carolina only very recently—each party printed its own distinctive ballot, and anyone who wanted to vote for its candidates would pick one up at the poll. Obviously this established ideal conditions for keeping the voters in line. It would, for example, have taken a brave man, if not one with a martyr complex, to request a Republican ballot at a Southern poll in the election of 1880!

Although the introduction of the Australian ballot did clean politics up somewhat—machine politicians began to complain, for instance, that they could no longer be sure that bought votes stayed bought—it did not purify the conventions. The reformers, always ready with new gadgets, soon came forward with a device that challenged the representative principle itself—the direct primary. The theory behind the direct primary was that instead of choosing potentially corruptible delegates to decidedly corruptible conventions, the party voters could choose their nominees directly. We can, from our position of eminence, look back with some cynicism on the sublime faith of the reformers, their conviction that the people (Good) would reform politics if only the politicians (Bad) could be excluded from the political process. However, they went to work with a vengeance on behalf of their new panacea and by 1910 the direct primary was in almost universal operation. Today, only Connecticut has not adopted it.

There are in the United States two principal types of primary. Under the "closed" system, only enrolled party voters are permitted to vote in the party primary. The purpose of this is to prevent raiding by the other side. On the other hand, in those states which have "open" primaries, there is no test of party affiliation, so that any qualified voter may choose whichever party ballot he prefers. The "open" primary is, of course, ideal for raiding purposes—all the Democrats may decide to vote in the Republican primary in order to defeat a strong potential Republican nominee—and it leads to fantastic maneuvering. The best technique so far devised to keep the raiders home is for each party to see to it that the other one has a contest in its primary, for if, say, the Democrats have a primary fight, they will be too busy fighting each other to raid the Republicans! An interesting variety of the "open" primary exists in the state of Washington, known as the "blanket" primary. Under this system, the voter is given one ballot which contains the nominations of all parties, and is free to help nominate a Republican for governor, a Democrat for lieutenant governor, and so on. Although this system may seem to be the epitome of party irresponsibility, it does provide the voter with an opportunity to penalize a political party for poor nominations, and it does, ironically enough, help sustain the two-party system by giving the minority party an opportunity to capitalize on failures of the majority party.

To be more precise, if the Democrats are the dominant party in an area, the tendency will be for voters to register Democratic not only because they believe it is the effective technique for getting their views heard, but also because registered Republicans may find themselves discriminated against by local government authorities, e.g., the assessments on Republican property may be uniformly higher than on apparently equivalent Democratic property. In the usual primary election, the voter must name his party, or be a registered member of it, to obtain a ballot, so that if all the nominees are unacceptable to him, he is left with no way of registering his disgust except voting for the opposition later at the general election, an alternative frequently unacceptable to him. However, under the Washington system, the voter is given a consolidated ballot with all parties on it, and if a Democrat wants to reject his party's nominees, he can do so by voting in the Republican primary, either for some offices or for all of them. Recent studies have, however, shown that the average Washington voter sticks to one party rather than roaming around at will.

Ordinarily, it is quite simple for a person to get his name on a primary ballot. All that is required is membership in the party and a sufficient number of signatures, as provided by state law, on a nominating petition. Some states, following the example of Colorado, have attempted to combine the convention and the primary systems, providing for a preprimary party conference which can name an official slate of nominees to run in the primary. This is an attempt to retain the party responsibility inherent in the convention system while eliminating the corruption which generally accompanied that system. The party decision is given a prominent part in nomination, but the people retain, through the primary election, the power to repudiate an unacceptable decision.

In some states, the candidates may seek nomination from more than one party. Called "double" or "cross" filing, this practice is most common in California. In the 1952 senatorial election in California, for example, William Knowland ran on both the Republican and Democratic tickets, having won both primaries. Once nominated by both major parties, a candidate is virtually assured of election, for his only opposition is that of minor party or independent candidates. An additional variation is found in those areas of the country where some officials are elected on a nonpartisan basis. The outstanding example of this is in Nebraska, where all the members of the state legislature are chosen in this fashion. To be nominated on a nonpartisan ballot requires either a petition or a nonpartisan primary. If a primary is used, the usual practice is to have the top two candidates compete with each other at the general election. In practice, it is doubtful whether nonpartisan primaries and elections are always as free from party control as the term would imply. For example, elections to the Chicago city council follow the nonpartisan format, but despite the absence of party designations on the ballot, there is seldom any doubt as to the candidates' political affiliations. The parties, of course, are free to put up "nonpartisan" candidates, and sometimes the election is between nonpartisan Democrats and nonpartisan Republicans. However, what nonpartisan techniques have succeeded in doing in many areas is to produce a new type of political framework in which party labels lose their significance. In the great majority of local elections conducted on a nonpartisan basis the voters neither know nor care what the party affiliation of candidates is. This makes it possible to fight local elections on local issues rather than having them an adjunct of national politics.

The result of a century and a half of development of American nominating procedure is that the caucus and convention have largely given way before the direct primary. The convention has survived nationally for the nomination of Presidents and Vice-Presidents, and is still employed in a few states, largely by Republicans in the South, as a device for nominating state officials. In some states its use is optional. In the remaining states, the direct primary supplies nominees, although it should be noted in passing that it is possible, though often extremely difficult, to nominate candidates by state-wide petition. The petition method is generally employed by minor parties to get on the ballot, and in the effort to cut down flanking attacks by such sects, the major parties have—particularly in the large industrial states—set tremendous petition requirements. This has played a significant part in the decline of minor parties, since any group with a political panacea—unless it has totally lost touch with political reality—attempts to operate at the primary level within the two major parties, rather than as a minor party in the general election.

In contrast with the situation twenty-five years ago, few Americans today would wax lyrical in describing the virtues of the direct primary. Indeed, many would concur in the judgment of Professor Joseph P. Harris that "the most essential function of the party—that of bidding for power by offering a slate of candidates—is virtually outlawed by the direct primary." Like most political nostrums for which great things have been prophesied, the primary has not resulted in any noticeable purification of American politics. It would appear that the many substantial advances that have been made, especially since 1945, should be attributed to increased civic consciousness and related factors. If an electorate once becomes really aroused about, say, corruption in government, almost any conceivable election system will prove responsive. In a sense, the old faith in political gadgets was an outgrowth of political laziness: the citizen was to be "saved," with no effort upon his part, by the autonomous action of some electoral or governmental mechanism.

Viewed from the vantage point of power politics, the direct primary system has been vigorously attacked on the ground that it tends to destroy party responsibility and unity. For example, a party's nominees for governor, lieutenant governor, attorney general, and other officials may be in complete disagreement on fundamental issues—all they have in common is victory in the party primary. This situation recurs constantly, and in order to eliminate this disunity at the state-wide level New York State repealed in 1921 the provision of its primary law relating to nominees for state-wide offices and returned to the convention system. The theory of this was that whichever group controlled the state party apparatus would nominate a ticket composed of men in basic agreement on political issues, thus eliminating the type of situation in which a governor from the liberal wing of the party would be surrounded on the ticket by nominees from the right flank with whom he would be at hopeless odds in a governing situation. Both in terms of the caliber of candidates nominated and of policy agreement among the nominees, the New York plan has generally yielded excellent results. This is not to say that an occasional convention does not slip up—the Democratic nomination of John Cashmore to oppose Irving Ives for the United States Senate in 1952 was an obvious blunder—but to suggest that a ticket so selected is demonstrably better in terms of party responsibility and usually equal to if not better than those chosen by primaries in terms of ability. The New York solution does supply party unity and responsibility, while at the same time retaining the right of the rank-and-file citizens to utilize the primaries at the local levels of state government.

Before analyzing that most unique American political institution, the national nominating convention, it may be well at this point to make a few comparisons with the systems employed in other democratic nations. No other country has such a complicated system of nomination as the United States. Not only is the nominating process simpler elsewhere, it is usually under less governmental control. Although local party organizations in Western Europe, for example, are not precisely closed corporations, they do not witness the free-for-all nominating battles that often occur in the United States. The reason is simple: the nominating there is done by what Americans would call a "machine"; i.e., a meeting of party officialdom. Power to nominate is thus centralized in the party central committee, and even if party pressure can force these "apparatus men" to include some maverick on the party ballot, they can see to it that his name is put far enough down to ensure his defeat. To understand this, one must recall that under the system of proportional representation used in France, Italy, Germany, and other Western European nations, a district may be assigned, say, five seats in the legislature with the occupants distributed among the parties in terms of their percentage of the vote. Thus if two-fifths of the voters of this district are Socialist, two Socialists will be elected, and—with certain possible exceptions as in Italy—the top two men on the ticket will get the jobs. Consequently, if the party central committee wants to keep some "wild man" out of the legislature, but does not dare to refuse to run him, it can simply put him fifth on the list in a district where only the two top candidates can possibly be elected. The primary originated in the United States and has remained an almost exclusively American institution. On the other hand, party conventions are widely used for nomination purposes throughout the democratic world; for example, in Norway and in Canada.

The ease of the nominating process in Britain is likely to startle Americans.

Since a British parliamentary election campaign takes only about three weeks from start to finish, little time can be lost in getting nominees in the field. Nominations are made eight days after the dissolution of Parliament or after the expiration of the five-year term of office. Nominations are filed on what is known as "Election Day," and ballots are cast on "Polling Day." So far as the legal provisions governing candidacy are concerned, simplicity is the rule. A candidate turns into the returning office a petition containing ten signatures, including a proposer and a seconder. With this petition he makes a deposit of £150 ($420), to be returned if he receives one-eighth of the constituency vote. Actually, there is a great deal more to securing a nomination than merely meeting the minimum legal requirements. A candidate not backed by one of the two great parties has little chance of visiting Parliament except as a tourist, and crackpot candidacies are discouraged by the deposit.

It is customary for the local party organization to name a nominating committee, which examines the field and invites a likely person to stand for office. The local committee may ask the party central office for advice or, conversely, the central office may recommend a candidate to the constituency organization. In passing, it should be noted that the candidates need not be local talent, but can come from any part of the realm. According to its rules, the Labor party central office must give its approval before a candidate may run under the party label; in practice, the Conservative party also exercises considerable authority over nominations. The refusal of the Labor central office to approve a candidate does not mean that the latter cannot run; it merely means that if he does run, he does it as an independent. As a result, the Labor party in particular, and the Conservatives to a lesser extent, have a strong mechanism for dealing with rebels, for without the moral and financial support of the central office, a candidate has little chance of victory. The degree to which this is effective can be illustrated by the 1950 election in the Gravesend constituency in which the Labor party refused to endorse the candidacy of Konni Zilliacus, a long-time maverick, and ran a candidate against him. Although Zilliacus had represented the district for many years and his opponent was relatively unknown, the nominee with the party label won easily. For British local elections the same procedure is utilized except that no deposit is required.

While in Great Britain the victory of one party over the other automatically supplies the nation with a chief executive, in the United States an elaborate process is required to select the nominees of the Democratic and Republican parties for the independently elected executive. The strange thing about this process of selection is that it is almost entirely unregulated by law. The selection of a presidential candidate by a party is legally in the same category as the choosing of a Chief Eagle by the benevolent order of Eagles! The technique of selecting presidential candidates by national nominating conventions originated in the Jacksonian period, and remained unchallenged for almost a century. Then the tide turned and it appeared, especially after 1912, that the political gadgeteers of the progressive movement would substitute some form of nationwide primary as a nominating device.

In 1912, the presidential preference primaries and the election results both demonstrated that the rank-and-file Republicans preferred Theodore Roosevelt to William Howard Taft, who was selected by the Republican convention. In 1913, President Wilson called upon Congress to provide for presidential preference primaries without "the intervention of nominating conventions." In this, Wilson the political scientist obviously dominated Wilson the politician, for without the split in the Republican ranks, Wilson would have been an unemployed college president! In addition, he proposed the establishment of a party council, with the responsibility for drafting the party platform.

While a Democratic Congress, composed of politicians rather than moralists, failed to act on Wilson's recommendations, the states continued to pass presidential primary laws of varying types. By 1916 half the states had such legislation; today the number has dropped somewhat to about a third. The essence of these laws is to ask the party voters to select convention delegates who are pledged to specified presidential candidates, although some of them are informative only.

In practice, the presidential primary system is quite unsatisfactory. Great difficulties arise from the fact that different states hold them at different times, some candidates may withdraw after receiving endorsement, and strong candidates may refuse to run in states where they know they will do badly. In addition, the pledged delegates are under no legal sanction at the convention; if they violate their trust, punitive action may be taken upon their return home, but by then the damage is done. For example, at the 1952 Democratic convention, one of the delegates from the state of Washington, pledged to Kefauver after the latter swept the state's presidential primary, shifted to Stevenson before Kefauver released his delegates. The chairman of the Washington delegation insisted on a public poll of the delegation to reveal the name of the deserter, but the fact that the latter joined the winning team made further reprisals somewhat difficult. Perhaps if he had switched to Russell, the Democrats back home could have made him regret it. Incidentally, the desire to expose deserters is behind many of the endless delegation polls which take up so much of the convention time, although on other occasions this technique is used to stall for time while maneuvers are in process. Another weakness of the presidential primary is that often a state's delegation will be pledged to a "native son"; that is, a person who will drop out on an early ballot after negotiating with his state's strength for a maximum political reward. As a consequence, the presidential primaries are far less valuable than public-opinion polls in predicting the outcome of conventions.

As a solution to these problems, it has been urged many times since Wilson first brought the matter up for general discussion in 1913 that Congress establish a nationwide presidential primary election, financed by the Federal government but using state electoral machinery. Generally it is proposed that such a primary be suggestive or even morally binding, but of no legal force. In some ways proposals of this character are appealing as an affirmation of belief in direct democracy. But the other side of the coin must also be taken into consideration; the voters might nominate a ticket that would be almost sure to lose because of failure to balance the slate. To be specific, consider the Democratic situation in the summer of 1952. Senator Kefauver was unquestionably the leading choice of rank-and-file Democrats, as was demonstrated by both presidential primaries and public-opinion polls. Yet the convention nominated Governor Adlai Stevenson of Illinois. Why? The choice of Stevenson was prompted by the fact that he was the best candidate from the point of view of all sections of the party. The urban East preferred Harriman, a militant Fair Dealer; the South wanted Russell, an able, nondemagogic conservative; the border states and the West stood for Kefauver, the slayer of corrupt dragons; but the convention took its stand on Stevenson, a liberal-conservative, an opponent of corruption, a magnificent speaker, and the successful governor of a state with a large block of electoral votes. Could considerations of this sort, essential to party success, be handled through national primaries?

The national nominating conventions are, of course, open to criticism on many counts. To a certain extent they are not representative; at the conventions as in Congress, the strength of the rural areas is exaggerated. Thus, in Republican conventions, the key to nomination may be control over delegations from states which rarely, if ever, wind up in the Republican column on Election Day. Senator Taft almost won the Republican nomination in 1952 through his control of the Southern delegations; the loss of Texas, Mississippi, and Louisiana cost him his margin of victory. Until the two-thirds rule was abolished by the Democrats in 1936, the South had an absolute veto over presidential candidacies, since no one could get two-thirds of the votes without Southern support.

It is also charged that the conventions are dominated by a relatively small group of men, mostly state and local leaders, who make all the significant decisions in "smoke-filled back rooms." Thus it was authoritatively stated by various pundits that the Democratic convention of 1952 was run by the big city bosses, the labor bosses, Americans for Democratic Action, and President Truman. Democratic observers, on the other hand, were not slow to spot the invisible hand guiding the Republican convention, and variously identified it as belonging to General Motors, General MacArthur, and Governor Dewey.

To a certain extent all these analyses are true, since each important segment in the party plays an important role in the decision making, and each one has its leaders. But what it boils down to in the end is a truism that any group, if it is going to be successful in obtaining its objectives, has organization and leadership. The similar charge that conventions are too unwieldy to make policy decisions is also exaggerated, for no large body ever really makes policy decisions. Policy decisions must, by their very nature, be made by small groups, and so long as the leaders who make these decisions represent their constituents' interests adequately, there is little cause for complaint. For example, Senator Sparkman met with the leaders of the Northern Democrats in Chicago and agreed to a fairly strong civil-rights plank for the Democratic platform, but there is little evidence to suggest that he was not speaking on behalf of the great bulk of Southern Democrats, who had little interest in losing an election.

Some observers, following Woodrow Wilson, have pleaded for an approximation of the British system in which the leadership of the party would be centralized and constant. A forceful case was made for this viewpoint by the Committee on Political Parties of the American Political Science Association. However, the program committees of both 1952 major party conventions rejected the suggestions as theoretical and impractical. The party committees were not altogether mistaken, for there were two fundamental weaknesses in the recommendations of the political scientists. First, their proposals amounted to an effort to change the locus of power within the parties by legerdemain. However, the location and impact of power cannot be dealt with purely by verbal formulas or magic incantations. Second, the 1952 conventions nominated candidates who were universally acclaimed as being first-rate presidential timber—Governor Stevenson and General Eisenhower, thus dampening the powder of the critics. From the long-range point of view, changes in the location of power in the major parties seem likely to result from the operation of two forces: urbanization and the growing primacy of foreign-policy issues. Should this happen, issues would be debated on other than sectional grounds, but in the meantime, the presidential nominating conventions, and the tremendous decentralization of party power that they symbolize, appear to be here to stay. Although, to paraphrase Bagehot, success in a crap game is no logical argument for crap games, in the mind of the average American it would appear to be a fairly strong practical motive to go on with the game.

ELECTION DISTRICTS

While the key to the internal distribution of party power is to be found in the nominating process, the basic contributing factor in the existence of a two-party as opposed to a multiparty system is the type of election district. The single-member district system, widely used throughout the English-speaking world, strongly contributes toward the maintenance of a two-party system. A multimember district usually results in the converse. This is not to suggest for a moment that any electoral mechanism is responsible for the form of a party system—the French have not developed a two-party system under any variation—but rather to point out the role that institutions can play if basic consensus exists in a society. In the pages that follow an attempt will be made to evaluate the different types of districting, while proportional representation, because of its intrinsic interest, will be treated as a special case in a subsequent section. The discussion will be largely confined to the systems that exist in the United States, Great Britain, and France.

Like United States Congressmen, Members of the British House of Commons are elected from single-member constituencies which follow geographic lines. While, with some exceptions, this practice has normally been followed in the United States, the last remnants of functional representation were not swept from the House of Commons until 1948, when the twelve "university seats" were abolished. In addition, although an 1885 statute definitely committed Britain to the single-member district plan, a few multimember districts remained until 1948. Today the single-member district is typical in the United States, Britain, and the Commonwealth.

Normally, under the single-member district plan, a plurality is sufficient for election; i.e., the top man wins no matter what percentage of the vote he receives. An exception occurs in election to the lower house of the Australian parliament, where a system of preferential voting has been in effect since the end of World War I. This does not appear to have weakened the tradition of two-party rule, for—despite appearances—the real division is between pro- and anti-labor coalitions. Although the history of South Africa and of France under the Third Republic point in the other direction, the experience of America, Britain, Canada, New Zealand, and Australia strongly suggests that single-member election districts tend toward the creation of a two-party system.

If this assertion were grounded in history alone, it still might be misleading as regards the future, but there is a certain logic in the proposition that can easily be expounded and perceived. When single-member districts are coupled with plurality election, the formation of a third party weakens those closest to the new party in viewpoint, and strengthens the party farthest away. For example, if Colonel McCormick had succeeded in getting his American party into the American presidential election of 1952, the new party's candidate would not have cut into the voting strength of Governor Stevenson, but into that of General Eisenhower. The presence of the American party might, in effect, have guaranteed the victory of the Democrats, whom Colonel McCormick certainly considers more "un-American" than the Republicans.

Consequently there is a very understandable and practical tendency for the opposition to group around one party, or—to put it another way—the second major party accumulates a monopoly of the opposition, eliminating third, fourth, and other minor parties in the real struggle for power. This in itself only helps the formation of a two-party system in each individual district; it is conceivable, for example, that in one district the Democrats would be the major party and the Republicans the minor party while in the next district the Republicans would be on top with the Socialists holding a monopoly of opposition. However, the increasing centralization of parties on a state-by-state basis, joined with the fact that the big parties tend to have financial resources unavailable to the small ones, has made it increasingly difficult for small parties to hold on to isolated baronies. A good example of this was the defeat of Vito Marcantonio in the New York Seventeenth Congressional District, long the bailiwick of the American Labor party. First, the Democrats and Republicans, by state law, made it impossible for Marcantonio to run on two tickets—he had previously managed to capture both the ALP and the Republican nominations—and then they united against him. He was defeated in 1950, and his ALP successor Vito Macri was similarly beaten by a coalition candidate in 1952.

An excellent example of this same process at work in Britain is the decline and fall of the once powerful Liberal party. Beginning with the election of January, 1910, the Liberal delegation in Commons had steadily diminished until after the election of October, 1951, it amounted to only six Members. The reason for this is not hard to find: the rise of the highly centralized Labor party which early in the century captured most of the urban strength of the Liberals. The Laborites initially made few inroads into Conservative strength, which was strongly centered in rural areas, so that the Conservative and Labor parties soon stood as the two great contenders for political power. This put the Liberal voters, who were mostly anti-Labor, in an acute dilemma, for if they voted for Liberal candidates, they were splitting the anti-socialist vote and aiding the Labor party. Eventually, in 1951, the Liberal party, in effect, gave up the ghost and the bulk of its remaining voters went Conservative, playing a decisive role in defeating Labor in many marginal districts.

But while the single-member district may make a major contribution to governmental stability by making it difficult for many parties to arise, it should be emphasized again that this is predicated upon the existence of a considerable degree of consensus and homogeneity in a society. For example, if there is strong sectional feeling in an area, sectional candidates will be elected in the constituencies, and will go to the national legislature as a third-party bloc. The remaining Liberal strength in Britain is centered in Celtic districts, largely in Wales, and apparently nothing will dissuade the voters of these districts from sending Liberal Members to Westminster. A similar situation existed in the United States during the 1880's and 1890's, when Populist and Greenback congressmen were sent to Washington by rural districts. However, once a nation has become politically standardized—as is the case in Britain—or, as in the United States, standardization has taken place on a state basis, the electoral system tends to squeeze out minor-party candidates.

It should also be kept in mind that, although stability is a great virtue, it is often achieved by gross distortion of the popular vote in the single-member system. Three examples taken from the United States and one from Britain should serve to illustrate this point. In the New York City aldermanic election of Nov. 7, 1933, the Democrats and their allies won 52.2 per cent of the popular vote, but received 75.4 per cent of the offices. In the 1935 election for the same body, the Democrats polled 66.4 per cent of the votes, and received 95.4 per cent of the seats! In the city of Philadelphia, to take another illustration, no Democrat was elected to the city council at regular council elections from 1919 until 1939!

In Britain, the Liberal party again supplies a good instance of distortion, operating there on the national level. In 1945, it took about 200,000 Liberal votes to secure one Liberal seat in Commons, and in 1950, this figure rose to about 280,000. In the latter year, the Labor party held one seat for each 42,000 votes cast for its candidates. One can understand why the Liberal voter deserted; the wonder is that so many stayed so long.

In addition to mathematical distortions of this type, other difficulties often arise with the single-member district system. In particular, every time shifts in populations require redistricting, the problem arises as to where the new boundaries shall run. This history of this thorny problem, which has vexed American politics for a century and a half, will not be elaborated here. Suffice it to say that the Constitution requires redistricting after each decennial census, but this redrawing of congressional districts must be performed by the states themselves. If a state refuses to act, as Illinois has refused since 1910, or if it acts in such a way as to defeat the purposes of equitable representation, as is the case in almost every state in the Union, there is no possible recourse to the Federal courts for corrective action. Instead, the only appeal possible is to the legislature which created the injustice or failed to eradicate the injustice. Needless to add, it has almost become part of the American political tradition for rurally dominated state legislatures to divide up the states in such a way that urban areas are underrepresented in Congress and, of course, in the state legislatures.

Gerrymandering—drawing district lines in such a way as to exaggerate the strength of one party and diminish that of the other—is not limited to the United States. Americans, used to having election districts resembling dumbbells, snakes, or umbrellas, would have recognized familiar characteristics in electoral maps of the Third French Republic. In the English-speaking world, the most notorious system of gerrymandering now existent is that in Northern Ireland, where the Protestant majority has vigorously utilized geographical manipulation to keep the Catholic minority underrepresented at the Belfast parliament.

The House of Commons itself, after three hundred years of loose practices in the matter, finally incorporated a nearly automatic technique of redistricting in the Redistribution of Seats Act of 1944. As the law now stands, four "boundary commissions," composed of civil servants, are empowered to draw district lines, and it is anticipated that future recommendations of these bodies will be put into effect administratively; i.e., by Orders in Council. Thus, Parliament will not again be faced with the problem of redistricting, unless it wishes to do so.

As an alternative to the single-member district system, it is possible to set up a plan under which everyone runs from one very large district. When city councilmen are elected at large, this is the technique employed. On reflection, it seems clear that when applied to an extremely large area, a state, for instance, it is unwise and unfair to elect all legislators at large. Such a practice would not only offend local sensibilities, it would also result in grossly distorted distribution of legislative seats. An additional argument of great practical force which has probably worked to keep enthusiasm for state-wide elections at large at a minimum is that if this system were utilized, the city vote in many states would be sufficient to defeat the "up-staters" and elect a whole slate of legislators. Elections to national legislatures are, therefore, based on single-member districts, or on many multimember districts. On the Continent the general practice is to elect from numerous multimember districts, employing, however, party lists and proportional representation. Thus, the minority, or minorities, are always assured of some representation. A brief survey of French experience with electoral systems may throw some light on the type of problem involved.

By decree of Mar. 5, 1848, France established a system known as *scrutin de liste*, or general-ticket system, with the departments serving as electoral districts. Each voter was permitted to select as many candidates as there were seats to be filled. The Second Empire replaced this system with the *scrutin uninominal*, or single-member district, by the decree of Feb. 2, 1852. To be elected, a candidate had to receive an absolute majority. Failing this, a second election was held in which a plurality sufficed to elect.

For nearly forty years, the French alternated between variations of these two systems. Finally, by the law of Feb. 13, 1889, the *scrutin uninominal à deux tours* was reestablished, with one deputy to be chosen from each *arrondissement*. If no one received a majority in the first ballot, a runoff election was held a week later and the high man emerged as victor.

Dissatisfaction with this technique resulted in the establishment in 1919 of a highly complex general-ticket system which confused everybody and satisfied even fewer than had the earlier method. On July 12, 1927, with a distinctly audible sigh of relief, the French returned to the "classic" system— majority election from a district, with a runoff, if necessary, won by the candidate with a plurality. This, as might have been predicted, did not end the dissatisfaction, which was particularly strong on the political "left." The distribution of seats in the Chamber of Deputies did not necessarily reflect accurately the popular vote, and, in addition, gerrymandering was all too frequent.

After World War II, France established a system of proportional representation—long the dream of the "left"—using the departments as electoral districts with certain exceptions in heavily populated areas. Straight party voting was required; it was impossible to split a ticket. The purpose of the law was admittedly to strengthen the larger parties, but the development of the "Cold War" and the rise of Gaullism on the "right" presented the center parties—the Third Force—with the problem of cutting down the legislative power of the Communists and the Gaullists—both large parties. In short, the electoral system had to be modified in such a fashion as to aid the center and militate against the two extremes.

An ingenious law was soon on the books to serve this function. The act of May 7, 1951, provided for election of deputies by proportional representation except that if a single party or a coalition received a majority of the votes in any district, it would receive all the seats to be allocated. But a neat wrinkle was inserted by permitting only national parties, defined as those parties which were nominating candidates in at least thirty districts, to form coalitions! Once a coalition received a majority in a district, thus winning all the seats, it was to divide the winnings among its members in terms of their relative contribution to victory. For example, if the Socialists and the Christian Democrats (MRP) formed a coalition in a district with six representatives and received a majority of the votes—with the Socialists supplying 50 per cent of the total and the MRP 50 per cent—the Socialists would receive three seats and the MRP three. This would be true even if their combined vote at the election was 51 per cent of the total. The law did not, however, stop there. It specifically excluded two Paris districts from its scope, since it was felt that the Gaullists might conceivably receive a majority there! So straight proportional representation operated in Paris.

The general expectation was, of course, that the Gaullists and the Communists, having no friends, would be unable to form coalitions, and the Third Force would therefore triumph. In actual fact, while the law did cut down communist representation considerably, it did not fulfill its positive purpose. In the election of June 17, 1951, the Third Force obtained only 289 seats of a total of 627, far short of the anticipated majority. The reason for this was the intervention of new groups in the election which won many seats to the right of the Third Force, although not connected with the Gaullists.

French experience has been surveyed at some length to demonstrate that the type of electoral system is not decisive in shaping the party system. France has had a multiparty system regardless of whether the single-member, general-ticket, or proportional-representation technique was employed at elections. Even if one discounts the parties as such, and considers only the parliamentary alliances, *groupes,* it is evident that the agreement on fundamental principles that characterizes the House of Commons and the United States Congress is conspicuous by its absence. Apparently the causes of the multiple-party system in France are so deeply rooted in French history and tradition as to be beyond remedial treatment by changes in the electoral mechanism. In addition, it is doubtful whether the French consider a two-party system to be a necessary symbol of political wisdom. An advocate of the two-party system there might well be a candidate for extended interrogation by a Committee on un-French Activities.

PROPORTIONAL REPRESENTATION

So many nations are today employing one variety or another of proportional representation that it would be valuable to examine this electoral technique at some length. The purpose of PR, as it will henceforth be abbreviated, is to secure in the legislature an accurate reflection of popular sentiment. In other words, if four parties contest an election and receive respectively 40 per cent, 30 per cent, 20 per cent, and 10 per cent of the vote, they should receive respectively 40 per cent, 30 per cent, 20 per cent, and 10 per cent of the seats in the legislature. In order to avoid unnecessary complications, attention will be confined here to the two principal forms of PR—the Hare system and the list system. Various forms of preferential and limited balloting, while intended to secure minority representation, are in reality quite different from PR. At the same time, the analysis of PR will be limited to fundamental principles, since the mechanical techniques employed vary widely from place to place and are of little fundamental significance.

In English-speaking nations, the type of PR most widely employed is the Hare system, named after the English barrister Thomas Hare, who was one of its originators. In 1859, Hare published a book on the subject, and his views had the distinction of winning the endorsement of John Stuart Mill, the great political philosopher of that day. The purpose of this system is to avoid the landslide effects possible under the general-ticket technique as well as the distortions which are likely with the single-member district. The essence of the Hare system is the single transferrable vote, which ensures that ballots which are surplus can be transferred to other candidates, thus wasting few votes and assuring minorities of proper representation.

As a case in point, suppose that a city council of five aldermen is to be chosen. If they are all elected at large, whichever slate is highest will normally get all five seats, even if it receives less than a majority of the total vote. On the other hand, if they are chosen from five different wards, the distribution of the votes of the losers can be such that all five seats are won by a party with only a slight majority or even with a plurality. Under the Hare system of PR, the election might work out as in the following illustration.

The city as a whole forms one election district and anyone can vote for as many candidates as there are listed on the ballot. He votes for them in terms of his preference, putting a number "1," "2," "3," etc., before the names. Suppose that in the election 120,000 valid ballots are cast in this manner. Now, the first step is to determine a "quota," *i.e.*, the number of votes needed to elect a candidate. In our example, this is found by dividing the number of seats plus 1 (six) into the total number of ballots (120,000). The result is 20,000, and to it we add 1, making the quota 20,001.

The ballots are then counted. Any candidate who receives 20,001 first-choice designations, or more, is declared elected. It is at this point that the transferrable-vote feature comes into action. Normally, a candidate who receives 25,000 first-choice ballots would have 4,999 surplus, or wasted, ballots. But not under the Hare system. Suppose Candidate A in this aldermanic election receives 25,000 first choices, thus having a bonus of 4,999 extra votes. His ballots are then reexamined and the second-choice designations of 4,999 of them are transferred to the appropriate other candidates. It makes practically no mathematical difference whether any 4,999 ballots are taken at random from his pile, or only the last 4,999. These second choices are then added to the totals of candidates who have not yet attained the 20,001 quota.

With the distribution of Candidate A's surplus ballots, some other candidate may now have attained the quota of 20,001 votes. If so, he too is declared elected. If not, the candidate with the smallest number of first-choice votes is declared eliminated and his second-choice votes are assigned to the other candidates. This process of eliminating the bottom man continues until five candidates have passed the quota, and the membership in the city council is determined. If the city as a whole is about 60 per cent Republican and 40 per cent Democratic, the council will reflect this division by having three Republican members and two Democrats. Thus, a sizable minority receives representation which it might not obtain under any other system.

Several features of the Hare system merit attention. Since nomination is usually by petition, no primaries are necessary. One election will suffice, for PR itself serves the function of sorting out the strong and the weak candidates, normally the job of the primary. Usually some technique is used to keep out frivolous candidates. For example, during the period that New York City employed this election method, 2,000 signatures were needed on a nominating petition. Fewer signatures are required in Canadian and Irish elections, but a deposit is made by the candidates, returnable only if a certain minimum percentage of votes is obtained.

In many American cities PR has been associated with nonpartisan elections. There is, however, no essential relationship between the two, and in New York City party designations appeared on the ballot, with the county committees of the respective parties determining who could be so designated. PR elections cannot ordinarily be handled by election machines, so paper ballots are used. Undoubtedly voting machines could be devised for this type of election, and at one point in the history of PR in New York City a machine was reportedly prepared to fill this need. Rumor has it that the old party leaders, who were strongly opposed to PR and finally succeeded in eliminating it, promised to run enormous lists of candidates which no machine could handle, and thus kept the new voting machine out of action. If it had been possible to use voting machines, one of the major arguments against PR, its complexity to the average voter, would have been eliminated.

The Hare system is widely used in Commonwealth countries for the election of city governments, and is employed on a nationwide basis in Eire. In 1920, the British Parliament provided for PR elections for all Ireland, and the system was retained by the Irish Free State after it achieved its independence in 1922. In Ulster, where the dominant party saw no virtue in ensuring representation to the Catholic minority, the system was abolished. However, PR has been used by the Irish Republic continuously since 1922. In Britain, the Liberal party, for reasons which should be obvious in view of the discussion earlier, has long agitated for PR, but to no avail. South Africa employs PR for indirect election to its upper house, and the Australian Senate is also chosen by this method. The most significant experience has been in Ireland, where normally PR has resulted in a single party receiving a majority of the seats in the legislature. The election of May 30, 1951, was an exception to this rule, and we have yet to discover whether a new trend will develop in the other direction.

Advocates of the Hare system maintain that it is indeed the answer to democracy's prayers. For example, George Hallet, in his book *Proportional Representation*, alleges that PR ensures minority representation, guarantees no wasted votes, supplies adequate majority representation, provides freedom for the voter, checks the dominance of political machines, eliminates the gerrymander, develops leadership, reduces fraud, raises voter interest, and furnishes increased cooperation and good feeling.

On the other hand, critics of the Hare system, who feel that Mr. Hallett is more the amorous swain than the objective analyst, claim that it has two crucial weaknesses. First, they allege that it creates splinter parties; and, second, they maintain that it encourages bloc voting and extremism. Unfortunately, few detailed studies of the validity of these charges are available. However, one excellent study of the operation of the New York City system was prepared by two distinguished political scientists, Belle Zeller and Hugh A. Bone, which analyzes the principal charges made against PR in that city.

It was found that, in contrast with the assertions of critics, PR never resulted in coalition government in New York City. Throughout the ten-year period from 1937 to 1947 in which the system was employed, the Democrats had a majority on the City Council. It was also reported by Zeller and Bone that PR did not appear to exaggerate racial and religious voting. It had been asserted by critics that a Jewish voter would favor Jewish candidates irrespective of party, an Irish voter, Irish candidates, and Italian voter, Italian candidates, etc., but an examination of the transfer of votes made by the political scientists seemed to indicate that party regularity was stronger than any purported racial or religious bond. In other words, a Jewish Democrat would vote for Democrats irrespective of national origins, while a Catholic Republican would give his support to Republican candidates irrespective of religious affiliation. Thus the New York City experience, while not supporting Mr.

Hallett's extreme statement of the virtues of PR, lends no support to the critics who have denounced the system so vigorously.

On the European continent the prevalent form of PR is the list system. Under both the Hare and the list systems, the election district is plural; *i.e.*, there must be more than one person elected to represent it. But here the similarity with the Hare system ends, for while Hare emphasizes the individuality of the candidate and allows the electorate to select candidates in terms of individual choice, the list system binds the voter to a party. The voter must choose between the lists of various parties, and once he has chosen, he cannot, with few exceptions as in Italy, alter the order of the candidates on the ballot. It was pointed out earlier in this chapter how this practice leaves the nominating power in the hands of party professionals and hands the voter a pig in a poke.

There is in practice a great deal of diversity in the actual operation of the list system in various nations. Without analyzing the intricacies of the various national plans, a few observations of a general nature may be in order. The prototypical list system was that devised for the Weimar Republic, which was in turn based on the experience of the German state of Baden. As applied to the nation at large, the plan had these characteristics: Germany was divided into thirty-five electoral districts, within each district a bloc of 60,000 votes entitled a party to one seat in the *Reichstag,* and the useless votes of the parties were pooled in either of two fashions to ensure a minimum of vote wastage. Supposing, for example, that the Socialist party ended up in one district with 119,000 votes. It would receive one seat, and have 59,000 votes extra. The party leaders could then pool this surplus with its surpluses in one or two other districts and receive one seat for each 60,000, or transfer its district surplus to a national pool where seats were allocated on the same principle. It should be noted that the size of the *Reichstag* was not fixed, but varied according to the number of votes cast in the country. This Weimar system might be described as a mathematician's dream, for it turned the *Reichstag* into an almost exact mirror of national sentiment.

But mathematics is not based on compromise—no mathematician ever compromised with a student who maintained that 2 and 2 is 5—and politics is. Thus while the Weimar method impressed some political scientists who felt that precision is a virtue in human affairs, it was strongly criticized by others less influenced by the mystical quality of numerical exactitude. The major charge was that the plan eliminated compromise from the electoral process and fostered the formation and continuation of extremist splinter parties. The job of a democratic legislature, it was suggested, was both to discuss and to decide, and this electoral technique, by making coalition government the norm rather than the exception, turned the *Reichstag* into a debating club with little decision-making function. Some critics also objected to the high degree of control placed in the hands of party leaders, who actually nominated the candidates on the ballot. Indeed, so strongly was party emphasized above personality that the ballots did not even carry the full list of party candidates, but only the names of the first four! However, once again we must be cautious in suggesting that the downfall of the Weimar Republic was caused by PR. Undoubtedly PR played a part in the complexus of causality—if the *Reichstag* had not reflected so brilliantly the fragmented German community, the crises of the twenties might have been surmounted—but as has been emphasized before, the "gadget theory of history," like the "devil theory of history," is in the last analysis a vast oversimplification of a highly complex historical problem. No institution can supply consensus to a bitterly divided society, and, conversely, no institution can single-handed destroy a viable community.

Since the French system has already been discussed in some detail, we shall pass on to an examination of the contemporary Italian variety of PR. The law of 1946 provided for large districts, but, in contrast to most other European nations, full preferential voting is permitted; *i.e.*, the electorate, not the party, determines which individual candidates shall hold office. In a sense, this is a combination of the list and Hare systems, for once the number of seats allocated to a party is known, the individual ballots are examined to discover to which of the candidates the voters have given first preference, and elimination proceeds until the requisite seats have been filled. Pooling of unused votes is permitted, but with a provision that only a party having at least one candidate elected may pool its votes. The effect of this in the election of 1948 was that while all the minor parties garnered 15 per cent of the votes cast, they received only 10 per cent of the seats in the Chamber of Deputies. In the same election, the Communists—who had succeeded in getting the Nenni faction of the Socialist party to form a common electoral front with them—used the preferential system to striking advantage. Their disciplined voters, accepting the popular-front list, proceeded to give highly systematic preference to the Communists within it, and the result was that although the Socialists contributed 40 per cent of the voters for the combined list, they received only 20 per cent of the popular-front deputies! This created considerable discontent in the ranks of the Nenni Socialists, who were not averse to selling out socialism, but did feel that they were entitled to a *bona fide* pay-off. The Communists retorted, more in sorrow than in anger, that it was sheer coincidence. In an attempt to cut down the size of the Communist contingent in the Chamber of Deputies, the Italians devised for the 1953 election an election law which, drawing from French experience, attempted to encourage compromise around the center coalition. This bill provided that if a coalition received an absolute majority of the popular votes, it would receive 65 per cent of the seats in the Chamber. There was vigorous objection to "Scelba's Steal" (Scelba was Minister of the Interior in the Government and introduced the measure), particularly from the Communists, and when the votes were counted, it was reported that the governing coalition had failed by a tiny margin to gain the required majority.

However, it has since become apparent that the De Gasperi coalition was counted out of its victory: many votes were ruled out as invalid when initially counted, but were subsequently validated. By the time this information became common knowledge, Italy was in the clutches of impotent cabinets lacking stable parliamentary majorities, and no one was in a position where he could declare—and enforce—a reallocation of seats in the Chamber based on the actual election results!

The new German Federal Republic has adopted a complicated electoral form which includes both PR and the use of single-member districts. According to the law of May 10, 1949, election to the lower federal chamber, the *Bundestag*, is handled as follows: First, an over-all total of 400 seats was established, and this in turn was subdivided among the *Länder*, or states, in terms of population. Second, each *Land* divides its allotment so that 60 per cent of its delegation to the *Bundestag* is elected from single-member districts under the plurality system (as in Britain or the United States), while the remaining 40 per cent are chosen by PR. Consequently, each German voter has, in effect, two votes; one for a specific candidate in his election district, the other for a PR party slate. Although he votes only once, his vote is given two functions. The technique by which the allocation of seats under PR is worked out is highly complex, and will be passed over here. One wrinkle in the law does, however, deserve mention—that providing that no party receiving less than 5 per cent of the vote in a *Land* can get any seats from PR unless it has succeeded in electing at least one member for a geographical district. This cut down the representation of the Communist party, and minor regional parties, considerably, for while the Communists received over-all 5.7 per cent of the votes cast in the election of Aug. 14, 1949, they elected no member from a geographical district and in many *Länder* received less than 5 per cent of the votes. As it worked out, the KPD required about 90,000 votes to elect one deputy to the *Bundestag*, while 55,000 sufficed for the major parties. In the 1953 election, the Communists failed to get a single seat. It is still much too early to pass judgment on this peculiar amalgam of the single-member and PR systems, but if the election of 1949 is any criterion, it is doubtful whether the introduction of the single-member district will break the strangle hold of the parties on the electoral process, the "tyranny of party," which led to its introduction.

There are other variations of PR, but they are all basically similar. Some, such as are employed in Scandinavia, emphasize voter preference within the party list; others, such as that used in Switzerland, operate only in areas where a substantial number of representatives are to be chosen. The only European state that has abandoned PR in recent years is Greece, and there the fact that PR is "un-American" seemed to be the decisive factor.

It is difficult to assess the faults and virtues of the list system of PR because of the absence of generally accepted criteria of judgment. It is certainly an electoral system which militates against stability of government, but some nations may put a higher premium on accurate representation of public views than on attaining stability at the expense of diversity. And even if one grants the accusation that PR has in France and Germany contributed to the weakness of the government, there is always the Scandinavian experience on the other side of the ledger to demonstrate that PR can be coupled with stability. Returning to the theme emphasized throughout this book, it appears that electoral devices, while frequently significant, are less vital contributors to stability than is ideological agreement on the ground rules of democratic government. Where there is democratic consensus, almost any electoral system can be made to yield stable government, and the fact that this stability may be achieved either through the domination of one party or of a coalition, as has been true in Sweden for years, indicates that coalition government is not automatically weak government. Weak government springs from far more basic sources.

CAMPAIGN PRACTICES AND REGULATIONS

A conspicuous contrast between the United States and other modern democracies lies in the frequency of American elections. In a normal twelve-year period, the average Democrat or Republican will be asked to vote in thirty-six elections; his British counterpart will vote in only six! Not only do Americans suffer from acute "electionitis," but they are also constantly exposed to a virulent virus which we shall call "campaignosis." One cannot be precise about this, but it appears that the average American presidential campaign, beginning with preconvention maneuvers and running through Election Day, must last about fourteen months. Certainly the Eisenhower build-up, undertaken by the liberal wing of the Republican party to counteract Taft's impressive control of the Republican National Committee, began in 1951, if not earlier, and developed strength for more than a year before the victory of November, 1952. During the same period Harold Stassen toured the world to broaden his understanding of world problems—an understanding hardly essential to the proper fulfillment of his task as president of the University of Pennsylvania. Others were busily engaged in building up General MacArthur for the American shogunate, although—in fairness to MacArthur—it should be pointed out that he was not responsible for his supporters, some of whom were, like Gerald L. K. Smith, highly disreputable, and that he did nothing to encourage them. Where his name appeared on the presidential ballot in 1952 on a "Christian Nationalist" line, as it did in California, it was without MacArthur's permission and over his protest.

It is highly questionable whether the average American is as interested in lengthy campaigns as these phrenetic activities would imply, and an interesting contrast is offered by the British campaign system. Following either the dissolution or the expiration of Parliament, British law permits three weeks for nominating, campaigning, and electing! As in the United States, pollsters nose about, candidates tour their constituencies, and national figures talk over the facilities of the BBC. But the whole procedure is over in a very short time, and the new government is instantly formed.

In France, and generally on the Continent, campaigning is held to a minimum. Third Republic practice was for the Minister of the Interior to issue a decree calling for an election only twenty days before the actual election. Immediately each party center issued a sonorous manifesto, stating its principles and promises, and the usual campaign practices came into operation. An American would note one major difference from practice in the United States— the elaborate and extensive use of billboards and placards. At election time the French tend to desert their national sport, soccer, in favor of another and hardly less rough form of recreation known as billboard warfare. The object is to paste the propaganda of one's own party over that of opposition parties on the billboards, and each party has offensive as well as defensive teams in the field.

Regulation of campaigns is more detailed in the United States than in most other countries, principally because each of the forty-eight states has legislation outlawing various practices. Certain acts of Congress are also aimed at the elimination of "corrupt practices" from Federal elections. Some of these laws place limitations on the amounts of money that can be raised, while others attempt to prohibit contributions from certain sources. For example, a national statute of 1907 forbids any national bank or corporation from making contributions, and in 1943 this was extended to include trade-unions. In 1947, the Taft-Hartley Act extended previous prohibitions on union expenditures to include primaries and conventions as well as the Federal elections themselves. Finally, the Hatch Act of 1940 limited the contribution of any individual, committee, or association to the cause of any candidate to $5,000, and simultaneously provided that no political committee operating in three or more states may spend more than 3 million dollars in any one calendar year. This last provision was an enlargement of the Federal Corrupt Practices Act of 1925, which placed limits on the amounts that might be spent by candidates for Federal office.

In practice, congressional legislation has proved inadequate, and it is difficult to know what can be done to make it stronger and more effective. For example, the Hatch Act set the maximum outlay of a national party committee in a presidential election at 3 million dollars, but the unofficial estimates of the cost of the two presidential campaigns in 1952 hover around 85 million dollars. How can this discrepancy be explained?

The fact of the matter is that the Hatch Act does not limit campaign expenditures at all. In the 1940 campaign, the Associated Willkie Clubs maintained that each separate club could spend up to the 3-million-dollar limit, and this viewpoint has been accepted ever since. In a sense, the Hatch Act contributed to the decentralization of political parties by establishing such a limit, for the other groups which grow up to aid the election of a candidate raise and spend their own money and are thus well out from under the control of the campaign headquarters. The same thing is true with respect to local party authorities. It might be noted here that this may, at least in part, have motivated the framers of the Hatch Act who often seemed more concerned with the threat of a national party machine growing up than with corruption in campaigns. The Hatch Act's restrictions on the political activity of Federal officeholders, who might have served as local agents of the national party leader, the President, should also be viewed in this light.

In truth, the American people do not seem to be greatly concerned with the problem of money in elections, and the Congress seems to reflect this disinterest. The main problem does not seem to be one of honesty, but rather one of fairness. Few people would be willing to see elections consistently won by the party with the fattest pocketbook, but there is no indication that this has actually occurred in recent presidential elections. The superior financial resources of the Republicans aided them to victory in 1952, but not in the previous five contests. There are, it is true, new difficulties growing out of the high cost of television—in 1952, the cost to the parties was $30,000 to $60,000 per half hour—but it is yet to be demonstrated that television can win or lose an election any more than the newspapers have been able to do so in the past. In fact, if one party so dominated television that the other had little opportunity to present its case, it is quite possible that this superior spending power would backfire in its face. In the past, the fact that an overwhelming proportion of the newspapers supported the Republican candidates seemed to create in the public mind a feeling that a moneyed conspiracy was out to get the Democrats, and may have led to support for the Democrats as the underdog.

However, it would be unwise to underestimate the problem of financing elections and its implications. Candidates who must conduct million-dollar campaigns, as is the case in most state-wide struggles in large states such as California, New York, or Illinois, cannot be elected without being under heavy obligation to business, labor, or the other interests that underwrote the expense of the battle. Although the cost of campaigning for the House of Representatives is considerably less, a candidate without large independent resources must similarly seek substantial subsidization from interest groups. Obviously, the groups which will put up large sums of money to aid a candidate are not merely engaging in philanthropic activity; on the contrary, they are willing to sign the check because they anticipate a concrete return on their investment. This financial tie between elected officials and interest groups helps to explain the general subordination of party loyalty to pressure-group loyalty in Congress. While it would be an oversimplification to say that elections can be bought, it is clear that a candidate without financial resources starts out with two strikes against him irrespective of his character or the issues he presents.

To a lesser extent, various other nations have also tackled the general problem of the relationship between money and free elections. British law imposes rigid limits on what a candidate for Parliament may spend. These limits are set at fivepence per elector in a borough and sixpence per elector in a county district. Thus in a borough of 50,000 qualified voters the top expenditure would be a little over $4,000 per candidate. While this figure is not large by American standards, its presence does tend to diminish the financial advantage enjoyed by wealthy candidates.

In Britain, from the moment a candidate has been adopted by a party, he and his agent are alone responsible for observing the law. The party association which is backing him is both dissolved and absolved. The campaign agent, a functionary unknown in the United States, is the key figure in British pre-electoral activity. He opens an account at the local bank, pays into it whatever sums the candidate may receive, makes payments out of this fund, and at the end of the campaign presents a financial statement to the returning officer. In due time this statement is published in the local press, and the opposition gets a good chance to investigate it item by item for discrepancies. To get around the possibility that someone may spend money on a candidate's behalf without the latter's knowledge, a 1918 statute specifically prohibits unauthorized expenditures.

Since the agent is such a key figure in the campaign, his talents are carefully cultivated. Both major parties run schools to train agents, and publish books outlining their principal duties. The agent must know something of finance and accounting and a great deal about public relations; he must be both civil and energetic at the same time. If the local party association is prosperous, the agent may hold a permanent, full-time job, while in less advantageous constituencies, he may come in only at election time. Even an independent candidate is required to have an agent.

French elections are also expensive, but there is little legal regulation of campaign expenditures. The larger parties of the left have traditionally given substantial assistance to their local candidates, while the generally decentralized parties of the right have relied on local resources to a greater extent. However, despite the relative shortage of laws governing expenditures, there has been little electoral corruption in France in recent years.

Another aspect of election regulation is concerned with the identity of the voters. Nowadays in the United States it is necessary to register with governmental officials in order to vote in primaries and at general elections. When the United States was predominantly rural, less formal methods of identification were employed. Early in the nineteenth century, Massachusetts, and other New England states passed registration laws to cut down fraudulent voting, and other states soon followed suit. Today only Texas and Arkansas are without such provisions, and in these states the presentation of a poll-tax receipt accomplishes the purpose.

Where the voter must himself assume the responsibility of registering, the system most commonly used in the United States, the term "personal registration" is employed. Where the government assumes this responsibility, as is the case in most European countries, the term "nonpersonal registration" is used. For many years, expert opinion in the United States has favored the adoption of a system of personal registration on a permanent basis. Once registered, a voter need not reregister unless he moves to a new address or, by failing to vote in a certain number of successive elections, is dropped from the roll. Most of the heavily populated sections of the United States now use this system, the most notable exception being New York State where there is permanent personal registration only in the rural areas. In the cities of that state it is necessary to go through the time-consuming process of reregistering before each election. The reason for this discrimination appears to be that the rurally dominated legislature feels that in this manner it can cut down the proportion of the state's vote cast by the urban, and strongly Democratic, areas.

In Britain, the preparation of the register is the job of the local registration officer. If the unit of local government coincides with the Parliamentary constituency, one officer suffices to keep both rolls. If the areas are not coterminal, there is a registration officer for each. No registration effort by the voter is necessary, for it is the duty of these officials to keep their lists up to date by inquiry and canvass.

The French system is equally simple. A permanent electoral list is maintained at the town hall of each commune and is revised annually by a committee of local officials. The type of plan used in Britain and France is generally employed throughout Europe, and it should be noted that the proportion of persons of voting age who actually vote is uniformly higher than in the United States. There is nothing intrinsically complicated about devising a fair and efficient registration system, and there are several techniques of almost equal feasibility. If the American states were to adopt the European plan it is possible, but by no means certain, that a higher proportion of the potential electorate would actually go to the polls.

Just as government has regularized registration procedures, it has also taken over the administrative machinery of elections. The voter is identified by government—not necessarily national government—officials, the polling booths are under the control of election officers, and the counting of the ballots is performed by agents of the government. In the United States, the usual regulatory device is a bipartisan precinct election board whose members are generally appointed on the advice of party managers; *i.e.*, on the basis of patronage.

The board usually opens the polls at 8 A.M., although the hour varies somewhat from state to state, and keeps them open for ten or twelve hours. When the polls close, the board and the clerks, in the presence of party "watchers," count the ballots and record the totals on tally sheets. These sheets are then forwarded to the central election authority, which adds, or "canvasses," the totals and announces results. Official results, as distinguished from unofficial preliminary announcements, are not known until the appropriate officials have certified the winners, although this is usually a *pro forma* action since the preliminary results are seldom significantly altered. In contested cases, the courts or central election boards determine the winners, except that legislative bodies act as their own judges in contested elections.

The procedure is similar elsewhere. In Britain, for instance, when the polls are closed, the ballot boxes are taken under police protection to a central counting place. The returning officer opens the boxes in the presence of the candidates and their counting agents and, when the count is completed, announces the results. In the event of a tie in a local election, the returning officer may cast the deciding vote, except that in London this must be done by lot. The statute of 1948 provided that when a tie occurs in a Parliamentary contest, it is decided by lot. When corruption is charged, the whole matter is turned over to the courts.

In all democratic countries, voting is now by secret ballot, except perhaps in some minor local elections. The form of ballot used in the United States is called the Australian ballot, first introduced in Massachusetts and Kentucky in 1888 and now employed throughout the country. The essence of the Australian ballot is that the government prints and distributes the ballots, and they are marked in privacy. There are two main types used in the United States: the Massachusetts office-block type and the Indiana party-column type. The office-block ballot forces the voter to discriminate in his voting, while the party-column ballot facilitates straight party voting. Under the latter plan, the candidates of each party are listed in a single column and the voter may, by placing one mark at the top, vote for the entire ticket. It is obvious why the politicians have generally tended to favor the Indiana rather than the Massachusetts variety! Yet, sometimes, expediency dictates a change in the other direction, as when, in 1950, Ohio adopted the office-block ballot in a move calculated to increase Senator Taft's vote by about 100,000. It was feared that the exceptional popularity of the Democratic candidate for governor, Frank Lausche, might lead many to vote the straight Democratic ticket, so ticket-splitting was encouraged by installing the office-block ballot. It was thus ensured that "Jumping Joe" Ferguson, Taft's opponent, would not ride into the Senate on Lausche's coattails.

Although some unknown Russian may have invented the voting machine in the fourteenth century, about the time other Russians were devising baseball, to date the credit for this achievement has rested with the Americans. It was a most useful creation, for Americans have been addicted to the long ballot, and the machine automatically counts the votes which, if done manually, usually takes many hours. In nations where few officials are elected, paper ballots ordinarily suffice. Indeed in a British Parliamentary election, the ballot is no larger than a postal card, and merely lists the names of the candidates, their addresses, and their occupations. A ballot several feet long remains a strictly American phenomenon and reflects, of course, the dispersion of political authority onto national, state, and local levels.

UNITED STATES PRESIDENTIAL ELECTIONS

Elsewhere in this book reference is made to the electoral college and its influence on American politics, so that no effort will be made here to reiterate the points discussed there. The purpose here is to call attention to some of the basic elements of the system in an effort to underscore the contrast with other democracies.

As we know, the Founding Fathers envisaged the electoral college as a sifting device, designed to remove the selection of the President from popular control—from domination by the "mobility," as one of them put it—and to raise it above mass passions. Each state was accorded one electoral vote for each Senator and Representative, with the manner of selection left entirely in the hands of the several states. At first, the electors in most states were chosen by the state legislatures, but by 1832, only South Carolina refused to choose presidential electors by popular vote. In effect, the electoral college became a recording device.

Any independence which the electors might still have possessed was further sacrificed when the district system of election was cast aside for the general-ticket plan. Under the district system, the electoral votes of a state were divided among the parties in terms of which districts of the state were carried by the respective party candidates, and thus the vote of a state might be fairly evenly divided. But the general-ticket system, under which the high slate on a state-wide basis captured the whole electoral vote, gave certain advantages to state politicians, particularly if the state was one with a large number of electoral votes. New York, for example, would not have the power it does at both Democratic and Republican nominating conventions if the state's electoral votes were divided on Election Day proportionally between the parties. It is the prospect of forty-five solid votes that leads the party schemers to pay great heed when New York speaks. Except for a temporary aberration in Michigan in 1891, this has long been universal practice.

The result is that today the American voter casts his ballot directly for presidential candidates, for although the electoral college remains, its members are pledged by the party. Legally speaking they are still free agents, as was demonstrated in 1948 when one of Tennessee's electors voted for Thurmond although Truman carried that state, but morally they are bound. However, this is not the principal problem involved in the continuance of the electoral college. The primary difficulty is that the distribution of electoral votes may not correspond to the distribution of popular votes throughout the nation. Thus, it is possible to elect men to the Presidency who have received less than a majority of the popular vote. In fact, this has happened ten times, the most recent example being the election of President Truman in 1948. But along with Lincoln in 1860 and Wilson in 1912, Truman did receive a plurality of the national vote. What is more difficult to explain is the victory of Hayes over Tilden in 1876, a classic case of electoral larceny, when Tilden had a 200,000-vote margin over his opponent. Again, in 1888, the man who received the most popular votes failed to garner a majority of the electoral votes. This situation arises because it is possible to carry several large states with large blocks of electoral votes by slender majorities, while losing a good many other states by lop-sided margins.

In 1948, the presidential election narrowly missed decision by the House of Representatives. Truman received 24,100,000 popular and 303 electoral votes, while Dewey obtained 21,900,000 popular and 189 electoral votes. Yet, a shift of 3,554 votes in Ohio and of 8,933 in California would have relegated the election to the House, since no candidate would have received the required majority, or 266 of the 531 electoral votes. Had the House undertaken the job of electing the President, Dewey would probably have become President, since each state delegation casts only one vote, and the number of Republican plus States'-Rights delegations exceeded the number of pro-Truman Democratic delegations. In 1952, although Eisenhower obtained 55 per cent of the popular vote, the electoral college exaggerated his victory by awarding him 442 electoral votes or 82.6 per cent of the total. In short, the electoral college does not adequately reflect the breakdown of national sentiment in terms of popular vote.

The danger latent in the type of situation which occurred in 1948 has not gone unnoticed. Shortly after the election, Senator Lodge of Massachusetts and Representative Gossett of Texas introduced a proposed constitutional amendment aimed at radically altering the electoral machinery. This proposal passed the Senate in 1950, but failed to receive the necessary two-thirds vote in the House. In its final form, this proposal undertook to introduce three major changes in electoral procedure. First, it would have abolished presidential electors, although retaining state electoral votes as at present. The objective of this was to prevent electors from acting on their own judgment as the one Tennessee elector did in 1948. Second, instead of a majority of the electoral vote being required for election, a plurality would suffice, provided that the high candidate received at least 40 per cent of the national total. If he did not, the two highest candidates would compete in Congress which, in joint session and by constitutional majority, would select the President. Third, the general-ticket system would be abolished and in its place the electoral vote of each state would be divided among the candidates proportionately to their popular vote. This last was the most basic provision of the suggested amendment, and its effect would be profound.

With no particular premium placed on the electoral vote of any one state, the "pivotal" states, *i.e.*, those with doubtful allegiance and large electoral votes, would cease to be pivotal. For example, in the 1952 presidential election, General Eisenhower would, if this system had been in operation, have received only 25 of New York's 45 electoral votes, while Governor Stevenson would have obtained the other 20. Similarly, Eisenhower would have gathered in only 18 of California's 32, with Stevenson receiving the other 14. Consequently, this amendment would make really nationwide campaigning profitable and would make it possible for a Democratic candidate to be nominated from Texas, or a Republican candidate to be named from a normally Democratic stronghold such as Massachusetts. However, it would do nothing to remedy the state-to-state disparity between popular and electoral votes; for example, in 1952, each electoral vote in Georgia represented 42,419 votes, in Kentucky, 87,784, and in New York 154,993. There is no electoral bonus for a high turnout.

It seems doubtful whether this amendment, at least in its present form, will ever be approved by the House of Representatives, which cherishes its rusty prerogative to choose the President if no candidate gets a majority in the electoral college. However, there are other alternatives. One possibility would be to provide for the direct popular election of the President, but this proposal would immediately alienate the rural Representatives and Senators and would have no chance of acceptance. An alternative plan, requiring no tinkering with the Constitution, would be to return to the former district system, but this conception would meet with opposition from the larger states which now, in effect, control the nominating process because their massed electoral votes are so vital to election. A last suggestion would be to tie in congressional and presidential elections by permitting the representatives of the party which won the presidential-year election to the House to act as presidential electors. On the basis of recent history, this would work against the Republicans, who, in spite of Eisenhower's landslide in 1952, obtained only a bare majority in the House. More importantly, it would probably revolutionize American politics by centralizing the parties, so that the time is certainly not ripe for such a development. If the parties became centralized, such a technique might meet with favor, but until then such devices must remain in limbo.

THE IMPORTANCE OF ELECTORAL SYSTEMS

Basic to the study of politics is the belief that men may learn from experience. If this is not the case, political scientists and all other varieties of educators are merely playing games. But as a practical matter, statesmen, legislators, politicians do seem to learn from the experience of others—not much, perhaps, but something. Thus, when after World War II it became necessary for half a dozen nations to reestablish governments, constitutional architects began by not only surveying their own experience but also examining those systems in operation elsewhere.

One of the fundamental problems faced by these constitution makers and lawmakers was the nature of the electoral system to be instituted. As has been suggested above, this is not merely a matter of copying electoral blueprints on one hand, or of slavish addiction to historical precedent on the other. It is fundamentally a question of attempting to achieve certain objectives, and achieve them within the constitutional and customary pattern of the particular nation concerned. Once made, such decisions are likely to have long-lasting effects, and the electoral and party systems become forces working for, or, on the other hand, enervating, the fiber of the nation.

As in the past, Americans and Britons will doubtless continue in the future to feel a moral superiority to Europeans and their multiparty systems, while Europeans will exhibit moral disdain at the thought of the "unprincipled" two-party systems in the United States and Britain. But although one may conclude, with traditional Anglo-Saxon bias, that an electoral-political system which contributes to majority government is superior to one that fails to do so, this is not the primary consideration. The basic issue is whether the system, whatever it may be, works sufficiently well to receive the confidence of the electorate. To conclude on a philosophical note, it might be observed that any electoral system which the people feel answers the needs of their society is probably the right one for them. While we may feel that such a system is unworkable, we must also recall that democratic government is not an outgrowth of gadgetary innovation, but rather of basic social agreement—and basic social agreement can operate through any one of a number of electoral instruments.

PART III. THE IMPLEMENTATION OF PUBLIC POLICY

Chapter 6

LEGISLATIVE STRUCTURE AND ORGANIZATION

HISTORICALLY, BOTH the doctrine of constitutionalism and the rise of representative legislatures are integrally associated with the development of democratic government. Modern democracy is possible only through the functioning of freely operating political parties, and, in this sense, democracy as a form of government is not much more than a hundred years old. But the parties must perform their policy-making functions somewhere, and the place for this in democratic states is preeminently the legislature. In this and the following chapter we shall analyze some of the more important structural, organizational, and functional aspects of modern legislatures. Primarily, our interest is in the dynamics of the legislative process. However, some historic material is necessary for a clear understanding of this process as between democratic countries. For illustrative purposes, attention is focused primarily on the great modern democracies of the United States, Great Britain, and France.

RISE OF LEGISLATURES

No one can say for certain exactly when or where the idea of representative assemblies, as contrasted with direct democratic procedures, specifically originated. There is no question that such assemblies existed from time to time in the ancient world. It is also possible that the impetus to establish representative assemblies came not from the example of England alone but also from medieval Spain. Be that as it may, the rise of the English Parliament beyond any doubt furnished the most important model for legislative development in other nations. In the case of the United States and the Commonwealth countries, this connection is obvious. The expression applied to the assembly at Westminster —"the Mother of Parliaments"—is not simply a figure of speech.

The history of Parliament, in any detail, would require several volumes, and these alone would be insufficient to capture the spirit of constitutional developments. Our concern here is more limited, and attention will be directed to a few outstanding features. Magna Carta, the Great Charter of June 15, 1215, had little to do with democratic government. Its importance lay rather in a feudally imposed restriction upon unlimited royal power. Even before that,

King John, in 1213, had summoned four knights from each county to meet with his Great Council. Gradually, because of the need for more funds, the representation was broadened. The so-called "model Parliament" met at the command of Edward I in 1295, and thereafter Parliament began to be part of the political order.

Within a hundred years of the model Parliament, tricameralism gave way to the bicameral order familiar ever since to the English-speaking world when the British clergy, instead of forming a separate estate, were divided between Lords, *i.e.*, Bishops, and Commons. In 1407, King Henry IV was forced to pledge that money grants would be considered in the first instance by the House of Commons. This set the precedent that money matters should primarily be the concern of the more popular house of a bicameral legislature, a precedent which eventually became a principle. The idea that Parliament could make law also developed slowly. Originally, the Parliament simply assented to royal decrees. From the custom of presenting individual petitions to the Crown there grew the idea of collective petitions by the Commons as a body. Eventually, the principle was established that lawmaking as well as taxation should be in the hands of Parliament.

It should be understood that these ideas did not gain immediate acceptance, nor was their importance particularly appreciated at the time. During the sixteenth century, Tudor ideas of absolutism seemed to give the country only an unhappy choice of strong monarchs or feudal anarchy. With considerably less tact, the Stuarts attempted during the seventeenth century to implement absolutism, with the result that, after half a century of conflict, royal supremacy was definitely overthrown by the bloodless revolution of 1688.

It is difficult to exaggerate the importance of the "Glorious Revolution" of 1688 and of the Bill of Rights adopted by Parliament during the next year. Rule by divine right was buried as a doctrine unacceptable to Englishmen. Henceforth, supremacy rested in Parliament; the succession to the throne itself became a matter, in a crisis, for Parliamentary determination. That sovereignty was exercised through Parliament was never again seriously contested. The philosophical basis for these developments was promulgated, after the fact, by John Locke, who in his famous *Two Treatises of Government*, published in 1690, read the funeral service for royal absolutism.

English constitutional development did not stop at this point. In the last two and one-half centuries significant changes have occurred, including the lessening of royal power and limitation of it to purely ceremonial functions, the rise of the cabinet system, the decline in the power of the House of Lords, the increase in power of Commons and its democratization, and the side-by-side growth of the cabinet and party system. Simultaneously the models for development in other countries tended to come from Britain. For example, the American Declaration of Independence comes straight from the Bill of Rights of 1689 and from John Locke. At a later date, the model for constitutional monarchies came from Britain as well. It is impossible to comprehend modern government without some familiarity with British constitutional history. From the point of view of the present discussion, the factor warranting emphasis is that it was in England that the principle was first developed that the legislature could make—as against announce or interpret—law. Except for dictatorships, it is now universally accepted that the source of law is the people, acting through elected legislatures. Even in dictatorships, rubber-stamp agencies, such as the Supreme Soviet or the Nazi *Reichstag,* go through the formalities of expressing the popular will. In actual practice, of course, the source of law in monolithic one-party dictatorships is the elite in control of the party.

THE PLACE OF THE LEGISLATURE IN DEMOCRATIC THEORY

The place assigned to the legislatures in democratic theory varies with both the time and the country. While the Parliament in Great Britain is legally supreme, control over the Parliament rests, as we have seen, in the Cabinet. Far from being simply an executive committee of the Parliament, the Cabinet, operating through party control, is in practice the chief lawmaker of Britain. The distribution of power, however, does not alter the legal status of the legislature, which might, if it chose, overthrow the Cabinet.

Assessment of the role of legislatures has undergone considerable change in the United States. During and immediately after the Revolution, practically all governmental power was entrusted to the state legislatures. Abuse of this power led to popular demand that the legislatures be restricted by constitutional devices, and that the power of the executive be correspondingly increased. Given the American disposition both for limited government and for the checks-and-balances principle, these developments are completely understandable.

The Federal Constitution itself reflects this. The first article deals with the structure and powers of Congress, thus recognizing the key importance of the legislature. On the other hand, the powers of the Congress were limited in various ways. According to the basic premise of federalism, in certain areas the national government was to have no lawmaking power. According to the checks-and-balances principle, the executive and the judiciary were to serve as checks upon the power of the lawmakers. To complicate matters further, certain executive powers were given to the Senate, while the power to veto— a legislative power—was given to the President.

Under the American system, the executive—president, governor, or mayor— possesses some powers quite independently of the legislature. It is not therefore accurate to refer to Congress alone as the instrumentality of the popular will, for the executive also is chosen by and is responsible to a plurality or majority of popular will as expressed through elections. Indeed, the distrust of legislatures and the consequent tendency to enhance executive power seems to have been an active force in American politics from the very beginning. It is not surprising that, although American legislatures act as freer agents than the British Parliament, they command less respect. This feeling has been accompanied by an increased interest in representative aspects of the executive, and, in particular, by mounting demands that executive and administrative agencies be in some sense representative.

While the British recognize parliamentary supremacy, and the Americans do not, French views must be described in plural terms. Authoritarian French politicians and political philosophers, going back to the days before the French Revolution, have always been impressed with the desirability of independent executive power. Sometimes these advocates have taken a position approximating Louis XIV–style absolutism; at other times, they have come close to the American view. The most noted contemporary exponent of the view that French executive power should be independent of the National Assembly is General Charles de Gaulle. The other French extreme is illustrated by the position of the Communists during the debates of the Constituent Assembly in 1946. The proposed constitution, which followed the views of the Communists in this respect, would have given the principal lawmaking and policy-determination powers to a unicameral assembly. As the result of a referendum of May 5, 1946, this so-called Cot constitution was rejected by the French people.

The Communist and Socialist argument in favor of a unicameral legislature with concentrated powers was based theoretically on the contention that the legislature, as the organ of popular will, should be supreme. Superficially, this may seem to coincide with the current British viewpoint, but actually, theory had little to do with the Communist position, which was rather based on the possibility that a Communist and Socialist majority could proceed quickly with basic "readjustments" in the French economic and social order. Subsequently, it became apparent that the Communist view was unacceptable to the great mass of the French people as well as to the other political parties who realized, particularly after the Czechoslovak coup, the full implication of Communist "democracy." On the other hand, despite repeated cabinet crises which make that country appear at times ridiculous before world opinion, France has no intention of creating the American type of independent executive authority. The distrust of centralized political power, as against centralized administration, goes back to the French Revolution. The end result is that the French parliament—with its two houses, the National Assembly and the Council of the Republic—is simultaneously unable itself to govern and yet strong enough to prevent the executive from taking power. As has been pointed out earlier, it is this stalemate which gives the French bureaucracy its tremendous authority.

This type of analysis could be continued with other modern democracies. It is important to note, however, that only in Britain is the doctrine of complete parliamentary sovereignty accepted. Every other major country in the world has a written constitution of one form or another. For all practical purposes, only in Britain does the legislature act as a standing constitutional convention. Yet, in actual fact, the British Parliament is not unlimited in what it may do. Limitations of custom, of tradition, of public opinion exceed and transcend the freedom theoretically given the Parliament to act. The chief limiting device is public opinion, as exercised and transmitted by the party system. In both the United States and France other devices exist for the limiting of legislative power.

THE LEGISLATIVE FUNCTIONS

Representation may most profitably be discussed in connection with electoral systems, and this has already been done in Chapter 5. However, at the risk of repetition, it is appropriate to call attention once more to the representative function of legislatures. Legislatures do much more than make laws. Increasingly, laws are in fact made by agencies other than legislatures. Legislators are considered representatives and as such are responsible to the represented, *i.e.*, the electorate. The very act of electing representatives to a legislature is an act of political integration. Representation is a very real and fundamental form of integration, for in the process of selecting a legislature a series of separate and opposed views are integrated into some form of national unity. Even if the legislature is disposed to act in an irrational manner, it nonetheless represents an effort to arrive at a democratic consensus. From this it follows to some extent even in the United States, that the primary general function of a legislature is no longer to legislate but to act as a forum of public opinion for the purpose of settling conflicting viewpoints. In short, legislatures have become more important as educational sounding boards than as lawmaking organizations, though the techniques vary greatly under different democratic systems. Under modern dictatorships the reverse is true. Legislatures such as the Supreme Soviet exist, but their function is to act as a transmission belt from the party above to the citizenry below. In other words, they are conceived as of convenient instruments by which the governors are aided in governing. Integration is achieved outside the legislature and is in fact enforced by the total weight of state power. Such integration is the opposite of the democratic method. It is, in reality, an attempt to create an artificial sense of unity or conformity by liquidating the diversity of opinion and of group organization associated with modern democracy. It requires no elaboration to point out that this kind of unity can be maintained only through totalitarian police methods.

How effectively any given legislature functions is determined not only by considerations of social homogeneity and consensus within a particular country but also by the institutions of government. Rarely do theories of government completely account for institutions; usually, the institutions grow and the theories follow. The exact features of any legislative system are determined by a multiplicity of factors, including custom, constitutional structure, and the party system. Once it was decided, for example, that the United States should have federalism and checks and balances, a strong impetus was given to establishing certain governmental practices. The function of legislatures, either state or national, are certain to be different from what they would be under a unitary system without checks and balances. Similar observations may be made about party systems. A two-party system, as noted earlier, does tend to produce a stability not always associated with a multiparty system. This stability, or lack of it, is particularly noticeable in parliamentary governments, where the cabinet is dependent upon legislative support. Or, again, whether the power of dissolution exists may be a question of considerable importance. If the Third Republic had permitted the President to exercise his theoretical right to dissolve a recalcitrant Chamber of Deputies, thus forcing new elections, the history of France might have been different. British governmental stability may be attributed as much to the power of dissolution as to a two-party system. These factors have been mentioned, not in order to weight them in any mathematical sense, but merely to call attention to the diversity in legislative structure, organization, and functioning. Proceeding from general to specific considerations, let us now examine in some detail the legislative structures of the major modern democracies.

UNICAMERAL AND BICAMERAL LEGISLATURES

Practically everywhere federalism and bicameralism have gone hand and glove. At the Philadelphia convention in 1787, one of the earliest questions considered was whether to establish a unicameral or a bicameral national legislature. The Congress at that time consisted of one chamber only, and New Jersey proposed that unicameralism be adopted by the convention. On the other hand, the British model, state experience, and the desire to balance off economic and sectional groups, worked toward the adoption of a two-chamber system. The plan proposed by Virginia, although it favored the larger states, urged bicameralism. The convention during its first week accepted the principle of a two-chamber legislature. Subsequently the Connecticut Compromise worked out the details, the convention agreeing that the Senate should represent the states and the House the popular electorate from uniformly sized districts. The Philadelphia decision was in no sense unique. Other countries emerging from colonialism and faced with the problem of large areas and sparse populations also adopted federalism, and with it, bicameralism. The examples of Canada, Australia, and most of the Latin-American states come readily to mind. Although some of these factors were of course not present in Western Germany, Pakistan, and India, it is significant that in these countries federalism was associated with representation of the states or provinces in the upper chamber.

At the heart of the problem of how many chambers a legislature should have is the question of representation. The American Founding Fathers clearly and explicitly felt that the Senate would and should represent different interests than the House of Representatives, and implemented this belief by providing for indirect election of Senators. The rationale for this approach vanished with the passage of the Seventeenth Amendment, providing for the direct election of Senators. However, upper chambers in the United States, through deliberate or accidental underrepresentation of urban areas, have tended for many years to be weighted in favor of economic, regional, or ethnic minorities. It is difficult if not impossible under universal suffrage to justify such a situation. Yet, except for the state of Nebraska, which in 1937 established a one-chamber legislature, no state has accepted the unicameral principle. The implicit reason, rarely stated baldly, is simply fear of urban majorities.

Representation is also the crucial matter when one considers the British House of Lords. For centuries the House of Lords occupied an important and exalted position in British government. Indeed, until the middle of the nineteenth century it was more important than its counterpart. The decline of the Lords dates from the gradual extension of the suffrage and, hence, the rise of nationwide British political parties. In a period when, for all practical purposes, both Lords and Commoners represented special class interests—the established church, the army, the landed gentry—there could be little serious conflict between the two chambers. But once the great national parties, based on universal suffrage, were in existence, the inevitable clash occurred. It became necessary for the parties, in order to win elections, to attack special privileged groups and interests. The process of decline in the prestige of the Lords was greatly accelerated by the crises within the Liberal party over the Irish question which resulted in a large number of Liberals, including lords, permanently deserting the Liberal party for the Conservatives.

The rise of the Labor party during the present century has aggravated the situation further, for Labor was doomed to be a perpetual minority in the upper house. The chief complaint of Labor has been the failure of the Lords to represent the working and artisan classes of Britain. When one considers the membership of the Lords, this complaint seems well founded. Although socialist lords are not today unknown, they are made and not born! In August, 1949, the membership of the House was 860; a figure which included 3 royal peers, 2 archbishops, 21 dukes, 27 marquesses, 133 earls, 92 viscounts, 24 bishops, 523 barons, 12 life peers, 16 representative peers from Scotland, and 7 Irish representative peers. In Britain there are more women than men, but since no woman may sit in the House of Lords, more than half the electorate is unrepresented in that chamber. It is not surprising that the general view is that the Lords represent only themselves, and do not do too good a job of that. There are seldom more than fifty members of the chamber present at a sitting, and a quorum for business is only three! One can frequently find more peers at a fox hunt than there are attending sessions of the House of Lords.

Until 1911, the Lords possessed full power to reject bills passed by Commons. However, in that year, after a bitter battle and two elections, the Lords yielded and agreed to a substantial modification of their powers. This was only done after the Liberal Government had threatened to have enough new peers created of its persuasion to obtain a majority in the Lords, and the upper house chose a limitation of its prerogatives as the alternative to a horrendous act of aristocratic inflation. By the terms of the Parliament Act of 1911, the Lords lost all power to veto financial measures and could only delay the passage of other types of legislation for two years. The Parliament Act of 1949 further depreciated the power of the Lords by reducing the period of delay to one year.

What functions, then, are served by having a House of Lords at all? It was to this question that the Marquis of Salisbury addressed himself during a debate on proposed reform of the Lords in 1947. He listed three main functions which, in his view, were performed by the Lords: first, the bringing to bear of expert opinion on the questions of the day; second, the amending or improving of bills sent over from Commons; third, the delaying of action on bills where there had been no mandate from the people in order to permit opinion in the country to crystallize. The Labor Government was not sufficiently convinced by these arguments to modify its bill, and the Parliament Act of 1949 went through, as scheduled, over the opposition of the Lords. However, Labor spokesmen did agree that the Lords had proved quite useful in discovering and amending weak provisions in measures passed necessarily in great haste, by Commons. In fact, most amendments of this sort suggested by the House of Lords have been accepted without argument or debate by Commons.

This parliamentary debate illustrates, however, an argument frequently advanced for bicameralism: that a second chamber acts as a check on the first. At the Philadelphia convention of 1787 the American Founding Fathers accepted this argument as well as that dealing with indirect election of Senators. Essentially an argument for limited government, this conception is based on the theory that legislators may be hasty and volatile and may at times be restrained from folly by delay. From another point of view, it is a sheer distrust of majorities, and it was from this elitist eminence that James Madison defended an indirectly elected Senate. In contemporary America, with universal suffrage and practically universal literacy, the Madisonian arguments would not be made publicly. Indeed, much of the force of the argument is lost if the same persons vote for members of both lower and upper houses. The chief remaining argument for bicameralism, then, is that it delays hasty legislation. Given the weak organization of American political parties and the tendency of American legislatures to pass ill-considered legislation, there is some merit in this position. On the other hand, where either party discipline or unicameralism, as in Nebraska, forces serious consideration of bills from the start, the contention loses practically all its force.

Outside the United States there is, even in nations with federal systems, a tendency for upper chambers to lose their former importance. The Senate of Canada, for example, is commonly thought of as a place where aged or no longer important party politicians may be given a place of prestige and respectability. It is of no significance either in legislation or in party control. Since Canadian Senators are not elected but are appointed for life by the Government, it is inconceivable that they should be given any real power. On the other hand, where members of the upper chamber are elected, but simply from larger districts than members of the lower house, they may possess important if not always coordinate powers of legislation, as is the case, for example, in Australia.

A good example of the loss of faith in second chambers comes from France. At the time of the constitutional laws of 1875, republicans in general favored a unicameral assembly, while various shades of rightists preferred two chambers. The conservative viewpoint prevailed, with the result that the French parliament consisted of a Senate and a Chamber of Deputies. From a constitutional point of view, the chambers had equal power, except that money bills had to originate with the lower house. On the whole, the standing of the Senate was remarkably high.

Originally composed of both life members and indirectly elected members, the Senate after 1918 consisted entirely of Senators chosen by an electoral college within each department. The electoral colleges of each department consisted of representatives from the Chamber of Deputies, members of the elective general council, members of *arrondissement* councils, and delegates from each communal council in the department. One-third of Senate seats fell vacant every three years, and each Senator served for nine years.

Normally, the Senate gave way before prolonged pressure from the Deputies. Yet, it was generally conceded that the Senate under the Third Republic was one of the most effective and most able legislative chambers in the world. As has been noted, the first French postwar constitutions, drafted in 1946 but rejected by the voters, provided for a unicameral legislature. The second constitution provided for a second chamber called the Council of the Republic, and named the lower chamber the National Assembly. In appearance, France has retained bicameralism, but in actuality the Council has little power and is only a shadow of the former Senate. The Council may delay bills for two months but cannot defeat them. Even in the election of the President, the Council plays a minor role. For such electoral purposes both chambers sit together, with the result that the National Assembly has about twice the voting power of the Council.

In Germany the decline in influence of the upper chamber has also been felt.

Under the Empire, the *Bundesrat* was extremely powerful. Structurally, the *Reichsrat* of the Weimar Republic was quite similar to the old *Bundesrat*, but both in constitution amending and in legislation it possessed merely a suspensive veto. The most successful phase of the *Reichsrat's* work related to its position in *Reich-Länder* affairs. By custom and usage, the upper house —which was eventually a council of states—gained considerable influence in executive and administrative affairs relating to the states. The constitution of the Bonn Republic continues the principle that an upper house should represent the states. Although not elected but appointed by the state governments, the *Bundesrat* possesses considerable powers in various areas, notably in amending the constitution, in taxation, and in the issuance of administrative orders. The *Bundestag*, or lower house, popularly elected, is far more powerful, for the Chancellor and his government are responsible to it. The uniqueness of the present arrangement lies, however, not in any drastic departures from past legislative organization, but rather in the powerful position occupied by the Chancellor and his cabinet.

In summary, it is fair to say that the decline in the prestige of upper chambers has been world-wide. The most notable exception is the Senate of the United States. That this exception is due to other factors than federalism becomes clear from the preceding analysis, since in various other federal countries upper chambers have not been exempt from the nearly universal tendency described, and in the United States itself federalism has since the Civil War been increasingly moribund.

THE COMPOSITION OF THE LEGISLATURE

Just as a basic premise of democracy is the free organization of opinion, a basic premise of democratic legislatures is freedom of discussion. This proposition, which today seems almost self-evident, was arrived at only after long and bitter fights between the English monarch and the English Parliament. Without freedom in matters of attendance, speaking, and voting, a legislature can hardly be expected to perform the duties expected of it in a democratic society.

The Bill of Rights of 1689 included in its enumeration of principles the following: "That the freedom of speech and debates or proceedings in parliament ought not to be impeached or questioned in any court or place out of parliament." The Constitution of the United States contains a similar guarantee in Section VI, paragraph 1, of Article I: "The Senators and Representatives . . . shall, in all cases except treason, felony, and breach of the peace, be privileged from arrest, during their attendance at the session of their respective houses, and in going to and returning from the same; and for any speech or debate in either house they shall not be questioned in any other place."

The immunity from arrest is not of practical importance, since the phrase as construed in the United States does not exempt a Senator or Representative from ordinary processes of criminal law. On the other hand, the provision relating to speech or debate is of critical importance and has been broadly construed. In practice, Congressmen may not be sued for anything said before either house or before a committee of either house—a protection which also extends to written reports. The immunity from the laws of libel and slander may, of course, be abused. A notable series of examples were the attacks of Senator Joseph McCarthy of Wisconsin on various employees, or one-time employees, of the Department of State. However, the only corrective action which can legally be taken in such circumstances is by the legislative branch itself. Charging that Senator McCarthy had abused his privileges, Senator William Benton of Connecticut was able in 1951–1952 to present to the Senate a motion that Senator McCarthy be expelled for violation of Senate rules. The matter was referred to a Senate subcommittee which did not, however, recommend expulsion. Yet the very fact that a committee of the Senate even considered the motion may serve as a reminder to other legislators that flagrant abuse of privileges involves the possibility of reprimand or even of expulsion.

The idea that speeches made in the course of legislative sessions should be privileged has long been accepted in the democratic world. On the other hand, this right is not absolute, and may be curtailed by action of a legislative assembly, by action of its officials, or even by hostile public opinion. The immunity granted is legal only; political vengeance is not interdicted by it.

Another constitutional right given American Senators and Representatives is to determine their own salaries by law. Since 1855, Congressmen have received annual salaries which today, under the La Follette–Monroney reorganization act of 1946, are set at $12,500 per year. Although this sum makes American national legislators now the highest paid in the world, in view of the enormous expenses of campaigning (particularly for House members, who must campaign every two years), this figure is probably not high enough. Stronger national parties with centralized fiscal resources might be able partially to defray campaign expenses for Congressmen, thus weakening their ties with the interests that now aid them, but such parties do not appear to be in sight. Another alternative, often advanced, is that campaign expenses be paid for by general grants from the Treasury. The reasoning behind this proposal is that wealthier individuals, and their backers, may obtain an undue financial advantage in elections. As we have seen, Congress has attempted to limit the amounts of money which may be spent in electioneering, but the present legislation contains so many loopholes that enforcement is next to impossible. However, until either stronger parties with great financial resources are established in the United States, or the Treasury is authorized to give grants to all candidates for Federal office, membership in Congress will continue to be an expensive proposition. A survey conducted by the *New York Times* in 1952 indicated that on the average a Congressman must earn, through speeches or writing, about $3,000 a year beyond his salary to make ends meet.

What the American Congress, and lesser American legislatures, have been facing is essentially a manifestation of a deeper problem, which arose in Britain about a century ago. In simplest form, the question was whether government service as a legislator was the duty of a privileged and monied group, or whether salaries should be paid to legislators so that all classes could afford to run for office. So long as Britain was governed by landed gentry ,no salaries were necessary. But as the class basis of British politics changed, demands were increasingly heard that Members of the House of Commons be paid. Finally, in 1911, a regular salary of £400 was voted for members not already on the government payroll, a figure which was in 1946 increased to £1,000. Members of the House of Lords receive no salaries for their services, unless they are government officials. The present salary is, of course, not sufficient to support an M.P., so that most members must continue as best they can with their regular occupations or professions. This is one reason why Commons do not meet in the morning. Since, financially, being an M.P. is not a self-sustaining occupation, the practice of paying low annual salaries in effect penalizes members of the Labor party. Recognizing this to be the case, that party has for some years subsidized those of its Members in Commons who require additional income in order to serve.

The question as to whether to pay legislators and, if so, how much, is closely related to the class status of the lawmakers. Thus, in Britain, the Conservative party, most of whose members have nongovernmental sources of income, still adheres to the ideal of service with no pay. In a brilliant political maneuver, Winston Churchill shortly after assuming the office of Prime Minister in 1951, dramatically lowered the salaries paid to himself and his principal assistants in the Cabinet. Although this step saved little money, it attracted, as intended, widespread publicity.

Studies of various sessions of Congress have thrown some light on the class and occupational backgrounds of the members. One fact stands out above all others: the middle-class nature of Congress. In terms of occupation about 60 per cent of Congressmen are lawyers. Religiously, they divide in about the same proportions as the entire country. A very high percentage have held public office previous to their election to Congress. In contrast to the British Parliament, manual labor is virtually unrepresented, although some Congressmen may at one time or another have been so engaged. Another interesting fact is that, despite the enthusiasm of Senators and Representatives from agricultural areas for the welfare of the farmers, few *bona fide* farmers are members of Congress.

Mr. J. F. S. Ross, in his work *Parliamentary Representation*, analyzed intensively the personnel of the House of Commons from 1918 to 1935. According to Ross, there were, in the average prewar House, some 56 members not gainfully employed (nearly all of whom were Conservatives), 200 professional men, 139 company directors; 69 men in finance or commerce; and 76 in the public service. At the other end of the social-economic ladder there were 125 workers and 79 union officials.

Another distinguished British observer, Mr. L. S. Amery, in *Thoughts on the Constitution,* noted that in 1947 professional men numbered about 250, while some 170 manual workers or former manual workers constituted the second largest group. The balance of the House, primarily Conservatives, were divided between businessmen and the old landowning and service class. Even in the Labor party a disproportionate number of M.P.'s had received expensive private and university educations. Labor usually had a higher proportion of women Members of Parliament; for example, in the 1951 election, eleven women were elected by the Laborites, while only six sit for Conservative constituencies.

Under the Third French Republic the most interesting characteristic of parliamentary personnel lay in the difference in background between Senators and Deputies. Lawyers formed the largest single group in the Chamber, more than one-third of the total membership of 615. After the lawyers came farmers, manufacturers, teachers, and members of other professional and business groups. On the other hand, the Senate tended to have a much more aristocratic background, both in terms of wealth and in terms of national distinction in the fields of science and letters.

LEGISLATIVE ORGANIZATION

From the point of view of setting and pageantry, the most colorful legislative assembly in the world is the British Parliament. The daily routine in Commons calls for the Speaker to enter, in wig and gown, to the shout of "Hats off, Strangers!" The robed chaplain and the sergeant-at-arms (carrying a mace) add to the occasion. If a new session of Parliament is to begin, the ceremonies assume formidable proportions. The Commons go to the chamber of the House of Lords, where the monarch or an assistant reads the Speech from the Throne. The Commons then return to their own chamber and give "humble thanks" to the monarch for his or her "glorious speech." In debates in Commons extreme courtesy is usually the rule, although on occasion the debates have the lack of decorum associated with lower houses of American state assemblies. A Member wishing to make a point of order must be covered, so that, in order to obtain the floor, it is sometimes necessary for hats to be thrown around from one Member to another.

A feature of the House of Commons which distinguishes it from the typical Continental chamber is its rectangular shape. The British have great respect for this characteristic. After the House was destroyed by fire as a result of a German air raid on the night of May 10, 1941, a few foolhardy souls suggested that the building be substantially altered in rebuilding. Churchill would have none of this, emphasizing that a chamber too small to seat all its members had the advantage of simultaneously creating both a sense of urgency and one of intimacy. He stressed the "depressing atmosphere" of a large house that might be half empty. He also called attention to the fact that the British party system was "much favored by an oblong form of chamber," his point being that the semicircular type of Continental chamber encouraged a multi-party system with numerous party gradations.

Under normal circumstances Parliament is in session from the end of January to about July or August, and from the beginning of September until Christmas. The life of a Parliament, under the Parliament Act of 1911, is set at a maximum of five years. Dissolution, controlled by the Cabinet, almost always happens before the expiration of a five-year period. Parliament may extend its own life, as was done during both World Wars, when the five-year limitation was overruled by a vote of that body.

Both the structure and the spirit of the French National Assembly are in great contrast to the House of Commons. The hall in the Palais Bourbon used by the National Assembly is a semicircular auditorium, with curved benches rising in tiers from the central rostrum occupied by the President of the Assembly. To the left, facing the auditorium, are the Communists; at the far right sits the Gaullist remnant. Left of center are the Socialists, while the Popular Republicans are shaded into the right. The symbolic function of these seating arrangements can perhaps be better appreciated if it is realized that one of the bitterest interparty squabbles of the immediate postwar period was between the Christian Democrats (MRP) and the Radical Socialists, each of which demanded that its members be seated to the left of the other.

The merit of the British seating plan is that one is either with or against the Government physically, if not spiritually. Under the French plan the many differences in party affiliation are reflected in the seating arrangement. In addition, to make an address, a French deputy must march to the front and mount the pulpitlike tribune. Once there, he sees around him a captive audience of no mean proportions, and tends to readjust his remarks to fit the formal atmosphere and the combination of physical circumstances that has made him the inevitable center of attention. In the House of Commons, on the other hand, members merely rise in their places and state their views in conversational fashion. The use of elaborate notes is frowned upon, and one certain way of emptying the House is to read a prepared speech. The rapier-like wit of expert hecklers also tends to discourage pomposity and tendentiousness.

The seating plan in the United States Senate is to place all Republicans on one side of the aisle, if possible, and all Democrats on the other. The chamber is built like an amphitheater. From the position of the Vice-President, the Republicans are on the left side and the Democrats on the right, an arrangement with no apparent symbolic overtones. Seats are assigned on either side of the aisle in terms of seniority. Since the seats are arranged in a semicircle, the net pictorial effect is not unlike that of the National Assembly. In the House the problem is more complicated because of the larger number of members. Eight groups of seats are arranged in a large semicircle, in front of which is the Speaker's desk and the reporters' table. Seating is in terms of the large center aisle, which bisects the semicircle, and of seniority.

Members of the National Assembly are chosen for a period of five years. This term can theoretically be shortened if the ministry dissolves the Assembly. However, this can be done only under conditions which are not likely to exist. Under no circumstances can an Assembly be dissolved in the first eighteen months of its session. After that period has expired, if two ministerial crises— and a ministerial crisis is narrowly defined as a failure to gain a formal vote of confidence, with a twenty-four-hour cooling-off period required between the time the vote is asked for and the time it is taken—occur within eighteen months, the Premier may dissolve the Assembly, simultaneously resigning his office. Critics seem to agree that in fact the power of dissolution is as non-existent in the Fourth Republic as it was in the Third, and some French leaders, notably Paul Reynaud and Pierre Mendès-France, have urged the amendment of the constitution to make the power of dissolution meaningful.

An American legislator, once in office, may feel certain that he will, health permitting, serve out his full term. It is provided in the Constitution that Representatives be elected every two years, while one-third of the Senate is chosen every two years. The Senate is thus a continuous body, while the House must reorganize at the beginning of each biennial period. Technically, each two-year period is called a "Congress," and sessions are identified as the first, second, third (as the case may be) of each Congress. Each house may be called into special session by the President; in such a situation, it has full constitutional powers and is not limited, as is the case in most states, to matters proposed by the executive. Prior to the passage of the Twentieth Amendment in 1933, a new Congress which had been elected in November did not meet until some thirteen months had passed, unless called sooner in special session. Meanwhile, the old or repudiated Congress met from December until March 4. The Amendment changed this by moving the inaugural date of a President back to January 20 and by requiring the new Congress to meet on January 3.

The principle of a fixed term of office is accepted in all American legislatures; given a separation of executive and legislative functions, this is obviously necessary. Under parliamentary government, where the basic principle is fusion of executive and legislative powers, the ideal is to set a maximum term for legislators subject to possible dissolution by the cabinet. In actual practice the legislators, except most notably in Great Britain, usually serve out their full terms. This is because the power of dissolution, though theoretically in existence in France, Western Germany, and the Scandinavian countries, is rarely exercised. The practice of dissolution is normally associated with Britain and Commonwealth countries only.

THE PRESIDING OFFICER

One of the most interesting contrasts between British and American governments lies in the relative position of the Speaker of the House of Commons and the Speaker of the House of Representatives. While the latter position was derived from the former, the comparison at present is more semantic than actual. A spokesman existed for the House of Commons from very early times, but it was in the "Good Parliament" of 1376 that Sir Peter de la Mare emerged as the prototype of the modern Speaker. He was not called by that title, which began with his successor, Thomas de Hungerford, in the Parliament of 1377. Thenceforth for several centuries, while the position of the Speaker was established, his accountability was not. Like the dean of the faculty at an American university, who is usually either denounced by the faculty as a Judas or by the administration as a Tom Paine, the Speaker of the House of Commons had the difficult, if not impossible, task of trying to please two masters. In the contest over the attempt by Commons to elect Sir Edmund Seymour as Speaker, Charles II rejected the choice of Commons, but that body stoutly maintained that the selection lay within its province. As late as the time of George III royal influence was felt in the choosing of the Speaker; on the other hand, after 1694 royal influence was exercised by indirect, not by overt, means.

The elimination of royal influence marked the first state in the development of the position of Speaker to its present eminence. A second phase related to the surrender of party connections by the Speaker. The requirement that the chair be impartial gradually resulted in the separation of the office from active politics. When Arthur Onslow resigned his treasurership in the Navy upon becoming Speaker in 1727, a significant step was made. The House was aware of Onslow's efforts to achieve independence and impartiality and showed this by voting him a pension upon his retirement from office in 1761.

Fiscal independence from royal authority was pinned down in 1790, when a fixed sum was set for the Speaker's annual salary. At the same time, he was forbidden to hold any place for profit under the Crown. The last great phase in the development of the Speaker's position was establishment during the term of Shaw-Lefevre (1839–1857). Previously, although the Speaker had been impartial when in the chair, he had felt free to become involved in partisan affairs out of the chair. Shaw-Lefevre completed the last phase of the development when he set the precedent that the Speaker should have no connnection with party in or out of the chair. For many years thereafter the tradition existed that a Speaker should be returned to the House with no contest. In recent years, however, in order to maintain its constituency organization in the Speaker's home district, the Labor party has contested the parliamentary seat. Customarily, even so, Labor supported any Conservative Speaker seeking reelection by the House if he had won at the polling booths. Lately, even this tradition has been shattered, as Labor in Commons has refused to give the customary unanimous vote to the Conservative candidate for Speaker. However, once the Speaker had been so elected Labor joined with the Conservatives in eulogizing the virtues of the new "Mr. Speaker."

The Speaker in the American House of Representatives is above all a party leader. At the same time he is, of course, an official of the House, as provided for briefly in the Constitution. Originally, the Speaker was simply the presiding officer, carrying out what were thought of as routine duties. Under the regime of Henry Clay (three times Speaker between 1811 and 1825), the potentialities of the office for party leadership were in part realized. These potentialities were further developed under Thomas B. Reed (Speaker, except for four years, from 1889 to 1899), who earned the title "Czar Reed" by his strong tactics. In particular, his refusal to recognize dilatory motions and his counting of members present to constitute a quorum, contributed to his fame. The power of the Speaker reached its fullest height under Joseph G. Cannon in the period from 1903 to 1910.

At this time the authority of the Speaker was indeed awesome. He selected the members of all committees of the House, including the Rules Committee, of which he was chairman. It was impossible to pass legislation without the agreement of the Speaker, who had become, after the President, the second most powerful figure in American government. From the point of view of strong party government, the power of the Speaker was to be welcomed. Never have the relationships between Congress and the President been on so sound a basis as they were when Cannon was Speaker and Theodore Roosevelt President, for Cannon could deliver and could therefore bargain realistically with the Chief Executive. Similarly, the President did not have to scurry around interviewing Congressmen to find out where Congress stood on some proposal; the Speaker served as a central channel for the transmission of congressional views. But in the eyes of the Democratic minority and Republican insurgents, the Speaker's powers constituted dictatorship. Long-standing dissatisfaction finally came to the top in 1910, when the Speaker was removed from the Rules Committee; one year later, he was stripped of his power to name members of standing committees.

From the "revolution" of 1910–1911 the speakership has never fully recovered, but it still holds tremendous powers, *e.g.*, recognition on the floor, interpretation of rules, the steering of bills to standing committees. In addition, the Speaker, if of the President's party, constitutes, along with the president of the Senate and the majority floor leaders of both houses, a part of the Big Four of the President's strategy staff. Under the Presidential Succession Act of 1947, if the President dies, and there is no Vice-President, the order of presidential succession puts the Speaker first in line, then the president *pro tempore* of the Senate, then (as under earlier laws), the heads of departments beginning with the Secretary of State.

Throughout the Commonwealth, the position of the Speaker in lower houses has followed the British, not the American, tradition. In the French Third Republic the presidents of each chamber were elected by the members thereof. The elections took place at the beginning of each session. In terms of prestige, the president of the Senate ranked after the President of the Republic, but while the presiding officer of the Senate often had little to do, his counterpart in the Chamber of Deputies often found his position irksome and trying. In cases of extreme disorder, he might use the *droit de chapeau,* that is, put on his hat, thus signifying that he might suspend the sitting and go home unless the disorder subsided. Before the war it was customary for the president of the Chamber to act impartially in matters of recognition and to refrain from both debating and voting. The situation is roughly similar with the office of the president of the National Assembly under the Fourth Republic. Chosen by majority vote—if necessary, by a plurality if two votes fail to produce a majority—the president has powers comparable to those of his predecessor. However, he retains his party position and is neutral only in the narrowest sense of the word. Thus Edouard Herriot, President of the National Assembly and venerable leader of the Radical Socialists, did not hesitate in 1952 to state his strong negative views on the proposal for a European army, and his successor in 1954, the Socialist André Le Troquer, is similarly outspoken. Furthermore, the job of presiding over the tumultuous National Assembly is not always easy, particularly since the Communist deputies and the extremists of the right have taken to inkwell throwing and desk-top slamming as techniques of legislative procedure.

COMMITTEE STRUCTURE

An outstanding characteristic of modern legislatures is that most of the law-making activity is carried on by legislative committees. Although the emphasis varies under different systems, it remains true, whether the committee is a committee of the whole or a standing or *ad hoc* body, that the bulk of the real work is done here. There is nothing particularly novel in the use of committees, for in reality this is simply the application of the age-old principle of the division of labor. The result of utilizing this principle may be twofold; on the one hand, the business of the legislature can be expedited; on the other, the committees, under some systems, may develop a high degree of specialization. An offshoot of this specialization, as illustrated in both the United States and France, is that the legislature as a whole is usually loath to overrule the recommendations of one of its committees.

The committee principle goes far back in English history—almost, in fact, to the beginnings of Parliament. On a continuous basis, however, the use of committees in Parliament began about the middle of the sixteenth century. By the time of Elizabeth, it had become the practice to commit public bills to committees. However, both then and now, committees of Parliament have played a distinctly subsidiary role in the legislative process, for they have been kept subservient to the entire legislature. The records show that the technique of committal to committees began with single bills, but that, at least as early as 1571, the practice had been inaugurated of using committees for areas of subject matter, *e.g.*, for "Matters of Religion." The next step was to appoint standing committees, empowered to deal with identical subject matter throughout an entire session, and by the middle of the seventeenth century there were five committees which were regularly appointed.

Objections arose at about the same time to the use of select committees. In the first place, royal influence was apparent in the selection and use of such committees. Therefore, in 1621, the House ordered that all committee meetings be open to all House members, whether members of the committees or not. Another factor in the abandonment of select committees was the general feeling that all House members should participate in important decisions, for example, those dealing with money matters. A third factor was the reluctance to see debates presided over by the Speaker, who at this time was a royal servant. There arose, as a result of these influences, a preference for the use of committees of the whole House.

The procedure which was established in dealing with money bills has retained its form since the seventeenth century. In 1668 the House resolved that bills relating to money should be referred to a committee of the whole House for action. The practice actually precedes this time, for the Committee of Supply was set up in 1620 and the Committee of Ways and Means in 1641. Both are committees of the whole House. The Committee of Supply votes expenditures for the fiscal year, while the Ways and Means Committee authorizes taxation.

This brief historical review is intended to underline the fact that the use of committees is not of recent origin. At the same time, it should be borne in mind that both the structure of government and the party system affect the use and the vitality of committees. There is thus a wide variety in committee practices in the leading democratic countries. The rise of the cabinet and party systems in eighteenth-century Britain inevitably tended to play down the lawmaking role of Parliament. As we know, this has resulted in the fact that public laws in Britain are today under the control of the Cabinet. Consequently, the most important function of Parliament is no longer lawmaking per se; this function has been imperceptibly shifted from the legislature to the Cabinet. The role of committees in Parliament has likewise been altered to fit this new reality. The present structure of the committee system in Commons will be discussed at a later point; what is being emphasized here is that committees no longer play a decision-making role in Parliament.

In contrast, the committees in both the United States Congress and the French parliament are of great importance. Again, both the structure of government and the party system must be viewed as affecting the role of committees. With a weak national party system, the Congress has developed in the direction of committee domination of the legislative process rather than party domination of committees. As a result, committee decisions are much more important than party views in the American national legislature, even though committees are chosen with regard to party considerations, among others. A more extreme example of committee autonomy comes from France, where the executive has even less authority vis-à-vis the National Assembly than is the case in the House of Representatives. This committee authority is based on multiparty support and draws its legal power from the National Assembly. With a necessarily pusillanimous Cabinet and a highly divided Assembly, only the committees are left as possible instruments for the exercise of legislative power. Under the American system, the President can, if he will, appeal over the heads of Congress and its committees to the people. Under the French system, it is not in practice possible for the Premier to do this, since this would be an open invitation to the Assembly to overthrow the government. In order to bring out the differences in committee systems most sharply, the following analysis will deal with the United States, Britain, and France in that order.

The initial efforts of the House of Representatives in trying to deal with nearly all matters in committee of the whole ended, as readers of these pages might have anticipated, in failure. Within a generation after the First Congress there were about a dozen standing committees to which bills dealing with a particular subject matter were referred for action, and this has remained the pattern ever since. For many years the relatively small size of the House and the small number of committees presented no insurmountable problems of committee membership. But, as memberships in the House grew, and more standing committees were established to deal with new matters of legislative concern, members became overburdened with committee assignments. By 1927, there were 61 standing committees. Although this number was later reduced, at the time of the La Follette–Monroney Act of 1946 some 48 committees still remained. This act, aimed at streamlining congressional procedure, reduced drastically the number of standing committees, so that at present there are 19. Under the former system, most Representatives served on at least four or five committees; under the reorganized system, members generally serve on only one committee. The Senate, of course, also makes use of committees. The reorganization act of 1946 reduced the number of standing committees in the Senate from 33 to 15, with the result that Senators usually serve on only two committees.

In addition to standing committees, both houses of the Congress make use of special committees and of joint committees. A special committee is usually organized to deal with a specific problem, e.g., an investigation, and dies after having performed its function. A joint committee consists of members from both houses. Such a committee may be merely a housekeeping device, as is the committee on the Library of Congress, or it may be concerned with substantive matters, as are the joint committees dealing with atomic energy, labor-management relations, and the President's economic report. In both houses there is a rules committee, which, starting out as a special committee, became a standing committee dealing with procedure. Without this committee's consent it is virtually impossible, in the crowded sessions characteristic of the postwar era, to bring a bill up for the consideration of the House. In the Senate the Committee on Rules and Administration has never enjoyed the authority and prestige of its counterpart in the House. Mention should also be made of the very significant conference committees which are established on an *ad hoc* basis when it becomes necessary to iron out differences between Senate and House versions of a bill dealing with the same subject matter. Because such differences arise on virtually all important pieces of legislation, and because the conference committees have great discretion in working out the final form of the statute, these committees often play a key role in the legislative processs.

In both houses, the assignment of members to committees is the task of party selection committees, or "committees on committees," chosen by party caucus. Generally, these committees have little discretion as far as membership on key committees is concerned, for senior party members may usually write their own committee ticket. In 1953, however, the Democrats in the Senate deviated from usual practice by assigning Stuart Symington of Missouri, a freshman Senator who previously served as Secretary of the Air Force, to the Senate Armed Services Committee—a powerful committee usually reserved for senior Democrats and Republicans. The committee assignments of both parties are then ratified by the whole Senate or House with practically no discussion.

Each committee chairman is usually a member of the majority party, which also supplies a majority of the members on the committee. Until 1953, it would have been true to say that the committee chairman was invariably a member of the majority party, but in that year, the Republicans continued Senator Harry Byrd of Virginia, a Democrat, as chairman of the Joint Committee on Reduction of Nonessential Federal Expenditures—a major break with tradition, although the committee is one with minor functions. The position of the committee chairman is one of great importance. In practice, he can often determine, unilaterally, the fate of pending legislation by refusing to call his committee together to consider a bill, by creating procedural difficulties for the committee through his control of staff research, or by devious parliamentary maneuvers. Rarely does a committee revolt against the actions of a chairman, although in 1953, one full-scale and one partial insurrection did take place. In the former instance, Republican and Democratic members of the House Government Operations Committee acted in virtual unanimity to clip the wings of Chairman Clare E. Hoffman; in the latter case, the Democratic members of an investigatory subcommittee of the Senate Committee on

Government Operations withdrew in protest against Chairman McCarthy's claim that he had sole authority over staff appointments and stayed away until a compromise was reached on the matter in January, 1954.

In the event that a committee refuses to take action on a proposed statute, or is unable to do so because of sabotage by its chairman, it is possible through involved procedures to extract the bill from committee for debate on the floor of the legislature. One technique that can be thus employed is a petition signed by half the membership of the House, but in 1953, in the course of the struggle to get action by the Ways and Means Committee on a bill extending the excess-profits tax for six months, the Republican leadership in the House of Representatives utilized the Rules Committee for this purpose. After a special rule had been prepared which circumvented the committee, and aroused tremendous argument on both sides of the House, members of the Ways and Means Committee averted the drastic action, and precedent, by agreeing to take cognizance of the tax bill.

At first glance, it might seem strange that a committee chairman should often be in a position to defy both his own party and a majority of the house. The explanation for this phenomenon lies in two considerations: first, the manner of selection of chairmen; and second, the composition of the committees. Chairmen under the American system are chosen on the basis of seniority, that is, on the basis of longest continuous service on the committee as a member of the majority party. What this means is that committee chairmen tend to come from safe constituencies, from areas which are normally one-party districts or states and hence far removed from national "tides" as evinced in presidential elections.

In years when the Congress is controlled by the Democrats, therefore, an undue proportion of committee chairmen come from Southern states. Yet, these are the areas which tend most strongly to oppose Democratic Presidents on certain issues, notably civil rights. The same situation occurs when the Republicans control either house; chairmen tend always to come from areas least removed from the great opinion tides manifested in the general election. The chairmen represent safe, unchanging one-party areas, while the successful presidential candidate represents the entire country.

Furthermore, the committee system is unrepresentative in another respect. Senate and House members are desirous of being assigned to committees which deal with subject matter dear to the hearts of their constituents. This is understandable, and the selection committees usually cooperate in the fulfillment of this desire. Thus, a committee on agriculture normally has few representatives of urban areas; a committee on merchant marine and fisheries does not adequately represent the inland sections of the country. Yet, city dwellers eat corn and people in the midlands eat fish. Since neither house will normally overrule one of its own committees, the unrepresentative character of both chairmen and committee members frequently results in the frustration of legislative majority rule, to say nothing of frustration of national party claims as made in presidential campaigns. An example of this, happily now merely history, was the series of attempts to repeal the discriminatory tax on oleomargarine. The agricultural committees, reflecting the preferences of dairy farmers to the almost complete neglect of urban consumers, succeeded in preventing repeal of the tax for half a century. When in the Senate, the repeal bill was finally referred to the Finance Committee, an urban majority was eventually able to have its way. The triumph of the urban majority was not, however, altogether a matter of principle. In the final showdown, Southern Senators lined up with Senators from industrial states to gain victory. The Southern preference for untaxed margarine was attributed to the fact that, increasingly, oleomargarine is today being made from cottonseed oil instead of from meat fats!

In various states the same battle has been fought in miniature over the issue of whether oleomargarine colored yellow could be sold to housewives. Since urban underrepresentation is also characteristic of the states, these battles were frequently bitter and savage, even in industrial states like Pennsylvania and New York. In New York State the problem was complicated by virtue of the fact that the Republican legislative majority relied heavily upon rural constituents for its voting strength. In addition, it should be observed that cotton is not among the staples produced in either the Empire or Keystone states.

If we may summarize the consequences of the present committee system in Congress, we are led to agree with Professor Schattschneider that the decisive role in legislative decision making is in the hands of the least representative bodies. In effect, Congress does not operate as a whole in any real sense, but rather it creates a fiction of general action by ratifying the decision of its necessarily parochial committees. The impact of this abnegation of over-all responsibility upon the operation of representative government in the United States cannot be underestimated. The theory of democratic legislation is that through the process of discussion consensus will be attained, and consequently the end result of legislative action will be a measure in the general interest. However, the Congress makes no serious effort at general consideration of policy; it simply accepts the frequently contradictory recommendations of its committees. In short, the particular has swallowed up the general. It is this congressional particularism that has led to much conflict between the legislature and the President, for the latter is forced by his position to take a general view of public policy.

A further objection to the present arrangement whereby standing committees exist on the same subject matter in each house is that the practice entails considerable duplication of effort. Not only do the committees often cover the same ground, but interested witnesses must appear, often at considerable inconvenience, before different committees to give the same testimony. While a professional lobbyist is not likely to be annoyed by this drain on his time —he is paid for his activity—the average interested citizen may find committee appearances burdensome. Of course, the lobbyist and the interested citizen are not the only ones whose time is thus consumed. Spokesmen from the great governmental agencies are continually called up to testify. In testifying on behalf of a foreign policy, for example, the Secretary of State may have to go over the same field four times—in the Senate Foreign Relations and Appropriations Committees, and in the House Foreign Affairs and Appropriations Committees. Indeed, a standard complaint of high-ranking officials is that an inordinate amount of their time is given to committee appearances, thus detracting from their principal administrative tasks. Presumably, congressional committees could get all their information from inferior agency officials—indeed, these are the men who usually brief their chiefs on the material to be covered in the hearing—but Congress feels that it has the right to hear the top man, not some "office boy." One of the reasons the Pentagon is so top-heavy with general officers is that congressional committees get a grieved look if anyone with less than two stars on his shoulders comes in to represent the military establishment.

One partial solution would be to make wider use of joint committees, as is now done in the field of atomic energy. At least thirteen states use joint committees; yet in only three New England states—Connecticut, Maine, and Massachusetts—do the committees perform most of the work on the important subjects. Of more interest to students of comparative government may be the example of Sweden. There are nine joint standing committees of the Riksdag, through which most of the bills pass. Given wide powers, these committees are research agencies of major importance. In addition, in the event of disputes between the two chambers of the parliament, the committees act as mediators. Finally, these Swedish committees may act as quasi-governmental bodies during periods of minority government. The last point is summarized by Neil Elder in these words: "In sum, during periods of minority government the committees undertake to formulate the broad lines of policy, often compelling acceptance by the government. If we may judge by experience in the 1920's, such committee activity at least ensures that some legislation is forthcoming in periods of party chaos."

In contrast to American and Swedish committees, the committees of the House of Commons are no longer of great substantive importance. Under British usage, when a bill has passed its second reading it is ordered either to a committee of the whole House or to one of the six standing committees. The committee of the whole House is used for money and tax bills. It is also used to confirm provisional orders and to handle legislation of great constitutional importance. Otherwise, after the second reading, a bill is committed to a standing committee. These are known as Committees A, B, C, D, and E, and the Scottish Grand Committee, composed of all Scottish members in the House, which deals with internal legislation for Scotland.

Members of standing committees are chosen in proportion to the party strength in the House, and normally number about sixty. These committees are, in effect, small replicas of the entire body which are employed to save time. They do not acquire power and autonomy like their American counterparts. In addition, specialists may be assigned to a committee when a particular bill seems to warrant extra attention. Assignment to committee (except for Scottish bills) is by simple rotation, and once the committee has finished with a specific bill, it dissolves. The presiding officer of a committee is a member of the Speaker's panel of chairmen. While the House of Lords makes no general use of standing committees, the Lords, like the Commons, often appoint select committees.

The purpose of select committees is to investigate or study a given subject and report to the House. Formerly select committees exercised functions of information gathering which are now performed largely by royal commissions and by departmental and interdepartmental committees. Recent examples of select committees include the Select Committee on National Expenditure, the Select Committee on Procedure, and the Select Committee on Members' Expenses. Select committees of the House of Commons are given power to send for persons and documents. Witnesses must answer questions, but the House protects such witnesses from subsequent prosecution in the courts for what has been said before the committee.

Superficially, at least, the committee system under the Third French Republic closely resembled the American system. In both cases the standing committees were concerned with a particular subject matter, and the list of committees closely approximated the titles of the principal government agencies themselves. Early in the Third Republic the ministries realized that subject-matter standing committees would become enemies and competitors of the Cabinet, and so it eventually turned out. In 1882 the Chamber finally established standing committees, to be followed by the Senate in 1921. Each year, the Bureau, or Secretariat, of the Chamber assigned committee quotas to the parliamentary groups, each group being rewarded in proportion to the size of its membership. Each group caucused and made its nominations, which were then printed in the Official Journal and stood unless fifty deputies challenged any list. In that event, the Chamber voted on committee membership. The procedure was similar in the Senate. Committee chairmen were elected by their respective committees, not chosen by the American principle of seniority.

All bills, whether supported by the ministry or merely by a private member, were referred to the appropriate committee. The committees took their work seriously, often to the embarrassment of the ministry. Under the Third Republic the committees voted secretly, and public hearings were not held, in contrast with usual practice in the United States. The Fourth Republic, in order to meet the secrecy charge, permits any bill to be brought forth to a public vote upon demand of three committee members.

Under both Third and Fourth Republics an outstanding feature of the French committee system is the institution of the *rapporteur,* or reporter. A committee instructs one of its number to study a bill and make a report on its merits. True, the committee may amend or modify the effort of its *rapporteur,* but this is less likely than that the *rapporteur* will alter the ministry's proposals. Contrary to the American custom, where normally the committee chairman defends and explains a bill on the floor, this function in France is performed by the *rapporteur.* On occasion the temptation was and is too much, for great emphasis is placed on making most of the opportunity to dazzle the government and the Assembly with wit and rhetoric. In power terms, what this means is that an ordinary member may be in command of the situation, taking precedence both over a minister and over his own committee chairman. This is, of course, even more splinterizing than the American example, for even the most cantankerous member of Congress feels the responsibility of a committee chairmanship and usually tries to work with the administration, if it is of his party, and with the party leaders. An American chairman is unlikely to waste his time on a bill of little importance, since he has more than one bill to worry about; but a *rapporteur,* with no other major legislative care in the world, may make a mountain out of a molehill. The power of the committees, along with the weak party structure, seriously weakened the Third Republic, and there is every indication that this identical process is taking place under the Fourth Republic. The Finance Committee of the National Assembly already has the scalps of at least three Premiers of postwar governments hanging from its wigwam.

PARTY ORGANIZATION WITHIN LEGISLATURES

Any discussion of the democratic political process necessarily involves the subject of political parties at many points. Previously, the implications of party organization have been pursued at some length. The present analysis is limited to considering the party structures inside the legislative assemblies of the principal democracies. In so doing, the distinction between formal and informal structures of party power should be kept in mind.

The parliamentary party group in Great Britain consists of three elements: the members of the party in the House of Commons, commonly referred to as the Parliamentary party; the leaders of the party; and the whips. Since the Conservatives and Liberals operate in roughly the same manner, they will be treated together. On the other hand, certain peculiarities of Labor organization deserve separate attention.

In theory, members of the Conservative (or Liberal) party get together from time to time to determine both their leaders and their policies. On the basis of frequent party conferences of the Parliamentary party it is possible for the leaders to test back-bench opinion and, if necessary, to alter their programs in the face of intraparty opposition. In practice, the Conservative party leadership is practically self-perpetuating. If the party is in power, the Cabinet, and especially the Prime Minister, can count on nearly complete support from party members in the House. It is the party leadership, not any conference or congress, which in reality makes the key legislative decisions.

With Labor the situation is somewhat different. Of the three principal British parties, only Labor has a formal written constitution. Supreme authority, including the authority to amend the constitution, is vested in an annual conference. Each year the conference elects a national executive committee, which, though completely subordinate to the conference, carries on the detailed work between conferences. The executive committee also supervises the work of the party headquarters, or central office, at London. Any Labor aspirant to Parliament must agree, in advance, to act in accordance with the party constitution and its standing orders.

When Labor is in the Opposition, the national executive committee has more authority over the activities of the Labor M.P.'s than is the case when Labor is the government, and the Parliamentary Labor party insists on a high degree of autonomy. While bound as to general principles, it is the Parliamentary party which chooses its party leader and his deputy, appoints the whips, and decides on tactics. For example, in 1952 Herbert Morrison was defeated in his attempt to gain reelection to the national executive committee, but was shortly thereafter retained as deputy chairman of the Parliamentary Labor party. A Labor Prime Minister is in no real sense subject to the orders of the national executive. Indeed, Prime Minister Attlee, in 1945, made it perfectly clear that he was the King's first Minister, not a marionette who would respond to strings pulled by the national executive committee of the Labor party or the Trades Union Congress. In America there was considerable misunderstanding on this point at the time of the Labor victory in 1945. The chairmanship of the national executive, which rotates yearly and is purely honorific, was at that time held by Professor Harold J. Laski. With a monumental lack of tact, Laski proceeded to hold press conferences, at which he indicated what course the new Prime Minister, Clement Attlee, might be expected to follow vis-à-vis the Russians. Laski's statements were taken as Labor gospel in America; in Britain they were largely dismissed as merely the individual opinions of one man. Needless to add, the British evaluation was the correct one.

The leaders of each Parliamentary party choose whips, whose main functions are to keep the party members in line, to make sure members turn out to vote at the proper time, and to act as intermediaries between the leadership and the party. Since party discipline is all-important under the British type of parliamentary government, these men hold posts of considerable significance.

There are usually four Government whips—a chief whip and three assistants. In the first case, the title is Parliamentary Secretary to the Treasury; in the others, Junior Lords of the Treasury. As ministers, the whips are of course paid from public funds. Opposition whips usually number three for each party and are unsalaried. In the House of Lords each party has two whips.

The term "whip" is also used to denote a weekly circular detailing forthcoming parliamentary business. The amount of underlining (one, two, or three lines) indicates the importance of the bill or discussion to be undertaken at a specific time. If the statement "Your attendance is requested" is underlined once, the discussion may be dismissed; if it is underlined twice, attendance is expected; if this expression is underlined three times, failure to attend without excellent reason may result in expulsion from the party. In the last few years it is said that four- and five-line whips have been employed. The record of six set in the seventeenth century is believed not to have been surpassed by either the Attlee or Churchill Goverments.

Party organization in the House of Representatives is at the same time more formidable and less effective than in Commons. The Speaker, the chairmen, the committees are all agencies of the House. Partly paralleling this official organization is a network of party agencies, including the majority and minority parties, the caucuses of each party, steering committees, floor leaders, whips, and assistants. Unfortunately, the term caucus has fallen on evil days, so that both parties tend to steer clear of it as much as possible. From this it does not follow, however, that caucuses are never held. The majority-party caucus is much in evidence when a new House is being organized. It selects officers, including the Speaker, and through its committee on committees it indirectly, subject to formal and usually automatic House approval, selects the majority members of the standing committees. Similar functions are performed by the caucus of the minority party. Neither the Democrats nor the Republicans have succeeded in using the caucus as an instrument of party discipline, or even shown much interest in doing so, although the Republicans have employed it frequently for discussion purposes. There has been some talk of this, but given the present system of congressional election, such proposals constitute little more than waving an empty gun.

Returning to the question of party control, it must also be noted that the majority party caucus chooses a majority steering committee and a majority floor leader. The steering committee performs the job of selecting the bills which the party managers wish considered on the floor and of making sure that such consideration is in fact given. The majority floor leader, who is chairman of the steering committee, has very real control over the course of debates as well as the selection of bills. In reality, after the Speaker, he is usually the most powerful person in the House, and he works hand in glove with his committee chairmen.

The majority and minority whips may appoint any number of assistants.

Their formal functions are similar to those ascribed to their British counterparts, although in terms of authority the situation compares unfavorably with that in Commons. The reason for this is that, lacking any power of expulsion or discipline, the caucuses have little control over their members. Official, as well as party, organization is less pronounced in the Senate. There is more emphasis placed upon individuality in the smaller legislative body. Like the House, the Senate has majority and minority leaders, whips, and assistants. In addition, there are also majority and minority "policy committees" in the Senate. A provision for such committees in both houses had been inserted into the draft of the Senate version of the 1946 legislative organization act. This provision did not survive the House, but the Senate put into an appropriation bill authority for the Senate alone to set up such committees.

Based on a series of proposals made by Robert Heller in January, 1945, and supported by various influential Congressmen, the majority policy committees were to gather together party leaders and committee chairmen with the intention of constructiong long-range legislative programs compatible with the national interest. This proposal failed in the House primarily because it seemed to challenge the existing authority of the Speaker, by making him a member of a seven-man majority policy committee. It was the Republicans, in the Senate, who first established such a committee, following their victory in the 1946 elections. Senator Robert A. Taft was chosen by the Republican conference to be chairman of the policy committee and under his leadership the body was employed extensively and effectively. However, when the Republicans lost control of the Senate after the 1948 election, the Democrats made little use of their own policy committee, preferring presidential leadership and guidance. For the Democrats the policy committee was merely an organization performing traffic control functions. Thus, the potentialities of policy committees have not thus far been realized. This is another way of saying that no effective means of party control have yet been discovered, whether for the majority or minority party.

The organization of French parties in the National Assembly is so complicated by individual variations that only a few brief generalizations may be hazarded. The situation at present is not unlike that which obtained in the Chamber of Deputies under the Third Republic. Following the elections, individual deputies arrived in Paris for the organization of the Chamber. At that point, party names could mean much or little, depending on the deputy. In any event, individual deputies formed parliamentary groups—in essence, parliamentary parties. The standing committees were made up of men from these groups.

In order to govern, arrangements had to be made among groups, that is, blocs had to be organized consisting of several groups. The bartering was thereupon done between blocs. Not only did the blocs have no authority over their component groups, but the groups had no control over their individual members. With individuals constantly changing groups, both the groups and the blocs showed remarkable instability.

As has been previously noted, there is evidence that some parties in a more accurate meaning of the term are presently developing in France. These include the Popular Republican Movement, the Socialists, and the Communists. These parties, notably the Communists, exercise considerably more control over their parliamentary members than was customary under the Third Republic. Still, party organization is extremely weak in the present National Assembly, as the continued instability of ministries attests. Without attempting to be cynical, it might be observed that the rewards for party loyalty are so slight in France that there is no overwhelming motivation for individual members of the Assembly to feel bound to either electoral or parliamentary alliances. On the other hand, if only in terms of prestige, the rewards in Britain and even in the United States may be high.

STRUCTURAL TENDENCIES

One of the most interesting phenomena that the student becomes aware of as he examines the comparative virtues and vices of democratic legislative forms is the persistence of certain institutional characteristics. Each of the major democracies, it would appear, has a certain basic set, a basic institutional bias, which seems to mold the legislative institutions.

The central American constitutional principle, for example, is the tripartite division of the institutions of national government, often miscalled the separation of powers. As has been noted above, the Constitution makes no clear division of powers between the three branches of government, but rather contented itself with simply establishing the three functional divisions of executive, legislature, and judiciary, then turning them loose to fight with each other for their proper prerogatives. Indeed, it is the absence of any real separation of powers that has generated the continuing conflict between the legislature and the executive, for, like chess players, each new Congress and new President set out to enlarge their holdings, to seize new positions of strength, and to hold positions already taken. Although there was no compulsion on the individual states to follow this pattern, they have, without exception, provided for the tripartite system of organization. Like Pythagoras, Americans seem to have a mystical faith in the potency of the number three.

The same characteristic of structural permanence may be observed in British government. There the essential principle is the fusion of executive and legislative functions. It is, of course, true that this fusion has not always existed in its present form, and that it is a consequence of the party-cabinet system rather than of philosophical theorizing. Nevertheless, the practice of having a collegial, cabinet-type executive has permeated all levels of British government from the national government down through the city, county, and borough councils. The commission exercising legislative, executive, and even some judicial functions is as typical an institution of British governance as the three-headed structure is of American.

Similarly, the French experience seems to demonstrate the permanence of a certain institutional set—in this case, one which is composed of centralized administration and decentralized political authority. All recent attempts to decentralize the administration or to institute strong political control of the administrative elite have, as David Thomson has shown in his brilliant *Democracy in France*, come to nought. If one looks at the span of years since 1875, it appears that certain basic French prejudices, *e.g.*, fear of a strong executive, distrust of strong parties, have conquered the reformers who have attempted, largely by tinkering with the legislative structure, to reform the patent weaknesses of French politics.

Thus it would be superfluous to indicate at any further length the truism that basic societal prejudices, or sets, will find their way to operate through the institutions of government, and will, if necessary, mold the institutions to their basic purpose. Consequently, while the forms and structures of legislatures are of importance to the student of politics, more important is the interaction between legislative organization, legislative process, and party process. Underneath legislative forms lie political processes, and underneath political processes lie the group interactions which form the core of modern society; beneath the groups lie the fundamental societal patterns and sets which control to a large degree the direction and content of our culture. The political process is thus far wider and deeper than the term "politics" customarily implies. In the next chapter, we shall develop this analysis further by inquiring into the dynamics of the legislative process—one of the focal points of the whole political universe.

Chapter 7

LEGISLATIVE OPERATION

THE PRIMARY function of legislative bodies has always been to declare law, to make law, or to act as a forum in which the merits of particular laws can be discussed. Nevertheless, all legislative bodies in democratic countries have additional functions to perform. Some of these duties arise sporadically, others are performed with considerable regularity.

Where there is a written constitution, the legislature normally participates in the process of constitution amending. Under the American system, proposed constitutional amendments usually originate with the legislature and are then submitted to a wider electorate for final approval. Thus, the national Constitution may be amended after a two-thirds vote has been accorded a proposed amendment in each house of Congress, followed by approval of three-quarters of the states. The approval of the states may be by majority vote in the state legislatures, or by approval given by a special convention called for ratification purposes. In all cases but the repeal of the Eighteenth Amendment (prohibition) by the Twenty-first Amendment, Congress has directed that the ratification or rejection be undertaken by state legislatures. On the issue of prohibition tempers ran so hot that Congress wisely decreed the calling of special conventions in the states. This technique achieved the desired effect of taking the state legislators off an uncomfortably warm seat by permitting the "drys" to place the onus for repeal upon amateurs elected for one purpose only.

The alternative method of originating a constitutional amendment, initiation by two-thirds of the states followed by the calling of a national convention by Congress, has never been used. Failure to use this method has not been for lack of effort. Currently a proposed amendment, which would limit national taxation to 25 per cent of personal and corporate income, has been passed by the legislatures of about twenty-eight states. The chances are, however, that before calling a constitutional convention, Congress would itself pass any proposed amendment which seemed to have any possibility of final acceptance. The reason for this is that Congress might be unwilling to face the possibility that a constitutional convention could rewrite the entire Constitution. In any event, even if two-thirds of the states did ask for a constitutional convention, there is no way to force Congress to call one. There is no legal way to force a legislature to live up to such a constitutional provision. The people, can, of course, have their vengeance—if they choose—by defeating recalcitrant Congressmen at the polls.

Under the parliamentary form of government the national assemblies also participate, but much more directly, in constitution amending. In the French Third Republic the only distinction between ordinary law and constitutional amendment lay in the size of the parliamentary majority. Meeting jointly as the National Assembly, the senators and deputies had to approve a proposed amendment or revision by an absolute majority of their total membership. At the present time, under the Fourth Republic, the procedure is somewhat different. The new element which has been introduced is the possibility of holding a popular referendum to approve of an amendment. The role of the Council of the Republic is not important, since amendments must originate in the lower house, the National Assembly. If the National Assembly can pass the amendment by a two-thirds vote, it becomes effective. Failing to obtain this majority on the second reading in the Assembly, or to obtain a three-fifths majority in both houses on final passage, the amendment is then sent to the public for acceptance or rejection. In all likelihood, the procedure under the constitution of the Fourth Republic is, despite appearances of complexity, actually simpler than that prevailing under the Third Republic.

Italy has adopted a procedure similar to that of France. Under the provisions of Article 138 of the present constitution, constitutional laws must be passed by each chamber in two successive deliberations at an interval of not less than three months. On the second voting they must be approved by an absolute majority in each chamber. The laws must be submitted to popular referendum on demand of one-fifth of the members of either chamber, or by 500,000 electors, or by five regional councils. In the referendum a majority of valid ballots in favor of the proposal is required before the law is promulgated. On the other hand, a referendum is not held if a proposed constitutional law has been approved in its second voting by a two-thirds majority of the members of each chamber.

Constitutional amendments in Italy and France do not ordinarily provoke feelings so bitter that the stability of the country is at stake. In the United States, although such questions as the passage and later repeal of prohibition arouse heated controversy, the difficulty of constitutional amendment usually guarantees that a sizable majority of the population, widely spread geographically, approves of the amendment. The Eighteenth and Twenty-first Amendments, initiating and ending prohibition, may, in this light, be viewed as representing a basic shift of majority opinion over a period of time, although H. L. Mencken's observation that many Americans will vote for prohibition as long as they can stagger to the polls should also be kept in mind here. A somewhat similar safeguard is provided in both France and Italy. In South Africa the process is quite different. The very ease with which the South African basic law may be amended (except in two particulars) almost guarantees continuous tension. Unlike Britain, where the basic law may also be changed by ordinary legislation, South Africa is definitely not an example of a country enjoying a large measure of national and social homogeneity. Indeed, quite the reverse is true.

The South African constitution may be amended by majority vote in both houses of the legislature, except that to alter the right of certain "colored" (*i.e.*, half-caste) elements to be represented by white representatives or to abolish the legal equality of the English language with Afrikaans requires a two-thirds vote in each chamber. Early in 1952 the Supreme Court of South Africa voided a bill passed by the Malan Government which would have deprived "colored" elements of their historic representation in Parliament. The Court did this on the ground that under the British statute which set up the Union of South Africa such deprivation could be accomplished only after a two-thirds majority had been obtained in the legislature. Responding to the challenge, the National- ists demanded "constitutional reform" so that the two-thirds requirement could be ignored, even if the Supreme Court were made directly subservient to a simple legislative majority in the process. With what must have struck many observers as delightful irony, the Nationalists pointed to the example of Great Britain, where, of course, the courts have no right to hold an act of Parliament invalid, while the United party, which stood to lose several seats in the legisla- ture if the Malan Government succeeded in its efforts, pointed lovingly to the United States and the American practice of judicial review and declared the latter worthy of emulation. The irony of this becomes clear when one realizes that the Malan or Nationalist party is bitterly anti-British, while the United party has always prided itself on its loyalty to British traditions!

The struggle between the Supreme Court and the Malan Government entered another phase when the South African Parliament proceeded to make itself the High Court of the Union and in this capacity overruled the Supreme Court. However, the courageous judges refused to be taken in by this semantic ma- neuver and promptly declared the act of the High Court unconstitutional. At this point the Government backed down, for the time being. The reason for this retreat appeared to be political rather than moral. The Nationalist party was not so much inhibited by respect for the judiciary as it was by the fact that its opponent, the United party, was suddenly given a commanding moral height from which to fight. The United party has never been particularly con- cerned with the unfortunate "colored" people or the Bantu and had been in the difficult position of defending the Negroes in spite of itself. But the Supreme Court's decision turned the tables and made the United party the defenders of "law and order" and of the Constitution instead of "Bantu lovers." At the time of its retreat, however, the Government threatened to take the issue to the voters, as it did successfully in April, 1953. After his electoral success, Malan, however, appeared to abandon the frontal assault on the courts in favor of a court-packing technique which would accomplish the same end with less publicity.

In addition to constitution amending, legislatures frequently act as electoral bodies. The American Constitution provides that the House of Representatives shall choose the President if no candidate for President received a majority of the electoral votes. In this contingency, the House chooses from among the three candidates with the highest electoral votes, with each state delegation having one vote and a majority needed to elect. If no candidate for Vice-President receives a majority of the electoral vote, the names of the two highest candidates are sent to the Senate. There, each member has one vote, and a majority is required to elect. The selection of the President has been thrown to the House of Representatives on only two occasions—in 1800 and again in 1824.

In both France and Italy the President is chosen by the legislature. The Constitution of the Fourth Republic provides that both houses shall sit together to select a President. While the constitution is silent on the type of ballot and also on the size of the majority needed, Vincent Auriol was chosen President in 1947 by a secret ballot and by a simple majority of the votes cast. The same requirement was used in 1954, when it took thirteen ballots to elect President Coty, thus indicating that a "simple majority" is not necessarily simple to obtain.

The Constitution of Italy contains provisions similar to those in effect in France. Election of the President is by parliament meeting in joint session, with a two-thirds majority required until the fourth ballot. If such a majority cannot be obtained after the third ballot, an absolute majority suffices. In establishing the basic law of the Bonn Republic, the German founding fathers determined to avoid the risk, which occurred under the Weimar Republic, that a popularly elected President might compete for power with a *Reichstag*-chosen Chancellor. As a result of a decision to follow French practice, the federal President is chosen by a special convention, composed of all members of the *Bundestag* (lower house), and an equal number of representatives chosen by the popular branches of the state legislatures. Consequently it is reasonably certain that the President will not be a competitor of the Chancellor. When the first President, Theodor Heuss, attempted to force cabinet appointments on the first Chancellor, Konrad Adenauer, the latter held his ground, with the result that the position of Chancellor may in the future be exempt from direct presidential pressure. If so, the course of action planned by the Bonn constitution writers will have been justified in practice.

Some national legislatures are entrusted with judicial functions. In the Congress this is limited to impeachment proceedings. The House of Representatives acts as a grand jury, in effect returning an indictment. The Senate acts as a trial jury, with a two-thirds vote necessary to convict. In all, the Senate has sat as a court of impeachment on only 12 occasions. Of these the most notable was the trial of President Andrew Johnson in 1868. In perspective, the attempt to remove Johnson from office represented the high-water mark in a series of attempts by Radical Republicans to substitute congressional for presidential government. Johnson escaped conviction by a single vote. The only penalty on conviction is dismissal from office, and impeachment proceedings can be brought only against the President, Vice-President, Federal judges, and civil (not military) officers of the United States.

In Britain, the House of Lords has traditionally been the highest court of civil appeals, but because of the legal ignorance of most of their Lordships this function gradually fell upon those peers with legal qualifications. In 1876, to assure the presence of expert jurists, the Lords of Appeal were introduced into the House. Nine distinguished jurists are given life peerages and, with the Lord Chancellor—the top government law officer—they handle all judicial business. In addition, for centuries, a peer had the right to be tried by the House for a criminal offense, but this, perhaps because the behavior of peers has improved somewhat in recent decades, gradually became obsolete and was abolished in 1948.

With the writing of their postwar constitutions, both the French and Italian constituent assemblies were faced with the question of whether to provide for some measure of judicial review. The French set up a Constitutional Committee to determine questions of constitutionality. This committee is composed of the presidents of both chambers, eleven persons chosen by the parliament from outside its own membership, and the President of the Republic as chairman. The Italian constitution provides for a Constitutional Court, composed of fifteen judges. One-third of the judges are named by the President of the Republic, one-third by parliament in joint session, and one-third by the supreme judicial bodies. Such a court was in any case made necessary by the establishment of regions, with separate powers, under the new constitution. In addition, the court has jurisdiction over laws passed by the national parliament itself. That this innovation was not greeted enthusiastically by Italian politicians may be deduced from the fact that the statute actually establishing the Court did not pass parliament until March of 1953, and a year later the Court still remained unorganized. One bone of contention seemed to be the right of the President of the Republic to make his own appointments. Apparently Premier De Gasperi felt that the judges should be named in fact by the Government, while President Einaudi believed that the constitution gave him free choice. Several German states, Korea, Venezuela, and Japan have also in their new constitutions adopted the American principle of judicial review. The Bonn constitution establishes a Federal Constitutional Court, which may judge the constitutionality of both federal and state law. In choosing the members of this court the legislature is all-important, since half the members are chosen by each house.

Besides performing constituent, electoral, and judicial functions, many legislatures have additional duties than lawmaking to perform. The United States Senate, for example, acts as an executive council when approving, or disapproving, of nominations and treaties submitted for consideration by the President. Furthermore, Congress is, in effect, a bicameral city council for the District of Columbia. The role that legislatures play, usually on an informal or indirect basis, in directing administrative establishments is reserved for treatment in another chapter.

LAWMAKING: RULES

The rules or regulations in effect in the British House of Commons came into being in a manner reminiscent of the growth of English common law. Based on custom and precedent, unwritten parliamentary rules were adequate for the leisurely debate characteristic of the predemocratic era. After the great Reform Acts of the nineteenth century revolutionized the character of British politics, it was necessary to refine the procedural rules in order to expedite legislation. At the present time, therefore, most of the rules remain in effect after adoption as "standing orders." In addition, there are also "sessional orders" which remain valid for one session only. The rules may be amended, repealed, or revised by simple majority vote. Yet it should be observed that customs and precedents continue to play a very large role in House of Commons procedure.

As in many other areas of the legislative process, English experience has also served as the basis for parliamentary procedure for other countries. In the case of the United States the lineage is obvious. Congress adopted in large measure the rules under which the Confederation Congress operated; these in turn were derived from the practices of the colonial legislatures; and these, finally, were based upon English practice in the seventeenth and eighteenth centuries. The Constitution lays down a few requirements governing legislative procedure. More important is the *Manual of Parliamentary Practice,* prepared for the Senate by Thomas Jefferson, as a partial defense against the boredom of the Vice-Presidency. In 1937 the House of Representatives adopted the same manual. In addition, each house has standing rules and orders, as well as a long series of precedents and decisions of Speakers which govern proceedings.

It is no longer possible to master American parliamentary rules easily. In fact, few members of either house ever achieve more than partial understanding of the remarkably complex rules of procedure. This observation holds particularly true for the House, whose rules may be scanned by the reader by examining a volume (always kept up to date) entitled *Constitution, Jefferson's Manual, and Rules of the House of Representatives of the United States.* The Senate's rules are printed in a volume entitled *Senate Manual, Containing the Standing Rules, Orders, Laws, and Resolutions Affecting the Business of the United States Senate.*

Pierre Dumont's treatise, based on British practice, was important as a basis for parliamentary procedure in European parliaments established during the earlier half of the nineteenth century. Throughout the Commonwealth, the procedure of Westminster is followed unless a legislature rules to the contrary on any given point.

LAWMAKING: STAGES OF BILLS

The most important single fact about the British legislative process is Cabinet control over the passage of bills. Still, in order to throw some light on the procedures in other countries, it seems advisable to describe in some detail the stages through which bills pass Parliament. This discussion should be read with the point noted that it is the Cabinet, through party control, which determines both the substance and the timing of all important legislation.

Unlike the practice in America, there are never competing bills on the same subject before Parliament. In both houses the same bill is considered. The Government's legislative program is announced at the opening of each session of Parliament by the Queen's speech. The pragmatic utility of the Crown is beautifully exemplified by this speech, for in 1945 it featured a socialist monarch expounding the ideals of the Fabians, while in 1953, a Conservative Queen delivered Churchillian sentiments to the lawmakers. If the Labor party should win the next election, the Queen will simultaneously alter her official sentiments, for the speech is always prepared by the Government in office and comprises a general statement of governmental policy. The day-to-day order is determined each Thursday when, in response to a question from the leader of the Opposition, the leader of the House details the weekly program.

There are two types of bills: public and private. Public bills deal with national policy and are invariably introduced by members of the Government. In the event that a private member introduces a bill relating to questions of national policy, the bill is known as a private member's bill. Private bills deal with a locality or an enterprise, e.g., a township or a water board.

If the Government is about to introduce an important measure, it is customary to give public notice of such an intention. The purpose of such notice is to alert interested groups and to obtain their recommendations before actually drafting the proposal. These recommendations may be obtained, as noted before, by the use of royal commissions, or of select committees, or of departmental and interdepartmental committees. It is not possible for a government department to introduce a bill on its own initiative. On the contrary, the department must obtain Cabinet approval in principle before any action is undertaken. Having obtained approval, the department then consults organized groups to obtain their views as to details. The department then draws up the lines on which the bill is to be drafted, and the proposal is then sent to the Treasury, where the Parliamentary Counsel (established in 1869) proceeds to the technical business of drafting. In so doing, the Counsel must determine which previous laws must be amended or repealed. This completed, the bill is ready for presentation to Parliament, which almost always means the House of Commons.

In case of a private member's bill, the member must arrange for his own drafting, although after the second reading the Government may offer help. The Government offers no help in the drafting of private bills. Once any bill has been drafted, it is ready for presentation to the House under long-established procedures. The first reading is a formality. Having given its permission to present the bill, the House merely requires that a copy of the bill be given to the Clerk. Without going into the complexities of the matter, it should be noted that great hurdles have to be passed before a private member may introduce a bill. There is seldom room in the tight parliamentary schedule for them, so the number that can be introduced may be severely limited—or even completely blocked by the Government.

The first opportunity for debate on a public bill occurs on the second reading. After the bill has been introduced by the appropriate minister, debate is held on the principles of the proposal. Detailed discussion is reserved for a further stage. If the Opposition objects to the bill on principle, it is theoretically possible to defeat it at the second reading. This would involve, of course, the overthrow of the Government, provided that the bill were an important one. On occasion, the Opposition may be strong enough to force postponement of consideration of a bill, which in a busy Parliament could mean rejection.

Following the second reading, the bill is ordered committed either to a committee of the whole house or to one of the standing committees. Under either form of committee, a member may speak more than once in the same debate (which he may not do on other occasions). At the committee stage the objective is the detailed analysis and possible amendment of the bill. Hence the bill is voted on clause by clause. Two stages remain. In the first of these, the report stage, the committee passes on to the whole House its recommendations. The House may recommit the bill in whole or in part to a committee. If it does not, the bill is ready for the last stage, the third reading.

Here, the debate concerns only general principles. Only oral amendments are permitted. When passed by the House, the bill is sent to the Lords, with the request that they concur in the draft. The identical procedure described in the House occurs in the House of Lords. If the bill is amended by the Lords, it is returned to Commons for consideration of amendments. On each of these amendments a vote must be taken. In the event of prolonged disagreement, the Commons merely apply the provisions of the Parliament Act of 1949; in effect, they ignore the Lords' amendments or objections. If there is no disagreement, or if the disagreement has been ironed out, the bill is ready for the Royal Assent. This is given in the House of Lords, almost always by a Royal Commission under the Great Seal. This bill is then an Act of Parliament.

The procedure in the United States House of Representatives is similar at nearly every point to that in the House of Commons. Similarity in procedure and in terminology, however, should not leave the impression that the total process in power terms is identical. In the following discussion, those differences which are most significant are pointed out. Once again, the reader is cautioned that the distinctiveness of the British system lies in the fusion of executive and legislature, specifically, in Cabinet control over the Parliament. With these words of warning, an analysis of procedure in the House of Representatives is in order.

Each bill must be introduced by a member of the legislature. If a bill concerns some matter of general application, it is called a "public" bill; if it deals with a particular person or place, it is known as a "private" or "special" bill. The bill may appear in either house, except that under the Constitution revenue bills must originate in the House. In practice, this restriction is of little importance, since the Senate may amend a bill in such a manner as virtually to draft a new one.

To a large extent, the bills which are introduced are not actually originated by members of Congress, although Lawrence H. Chamberlain found that a somewhat larger number of bills owe their start to congressional initiative than is often supposed. Be that as it may, about half of all major public bills come from the executive branch of the government. They must be introduced by members of Congress, but the drafts themselves are often worked out in detail by some executive agency. Numerous bills originate outside the government entirely, from private interests, individuals, associations, and so on. Frequently a member of Congress may satisfy a constituent by introducing a bill into the legislative hopper, but adding "By Request" at the top of the draft followed by the legislator's initials. What this means is that the bill will almost always be automatically killed in committee, while, at the same time, the Representative or Senator is in a position to assure his constituent that the bill has been forwarded to a committee for appropriate action.

Once introduced, the bill is assigned in the name of the Speaker to an appropriate subject-matter committee. Usually, the assignment is automatic, and is actually done by the Clerk. On occasion, however, reference to an unfavorable committee can ensure defeat of the bill. To overrule the Speaker's decision a majority vote is required, so that, in actual fact, he is seldom overruled on the committee assignment of a bill.

The great bulk of the 10,000 to 12,000 bills introduced during each session have little or no merit, and quite properly die in committee after cursory examination. If the committee decides that the bill warrants attention, the next step is to acquire information upon which to proceed intelligently. Especially in the Senate, though often in the House, senior members of the committee may be experts on the subject under discussion and may therefore offer expert opinion. Even so, additional information is normally required. This may be obtained in a variety of ways, including the committee's own professional staff, government officials, and lobbyists. It is also rather common to obtain information from basic inquiries or investigations, especially when the subject is of first-rate importance, and to place that information at the disposal of the committee.

An example of this type of approach is afforded by the reports of the Hoover Commission in 1949, which served as the basis both for reorganization proposals submitted by the President and for legislative enactments. In addition, the typically American device of holding public hearings will almost always be employed if the subject of the bill is of great importance. At such hearings anyone affected by proposed legislation will normally be permitted to comment on the bill. In contrast, appearances before investigating committees are usually at the invitation of the committee, sometimes enforced on unwilling witnesses through the power of subpoena. The interested reader will find that the easiest way to find out which organizations appeared for and against a given bill is to examine the *Congressional Quarterly,* a private publication originally intended for newspaper editors but now in most public and college libraries. This remarkable publication, which has weekly summaries of congressional action both on the floor and in committee, as well as an annual summary, is invaluable for all serious students of Congress.

The final decisions of a committee are reached in executive, *i.e.,* private sessions. This practice has been defended on the ground that it permits deliberation outside the scope of public attention and pressure. It is not always possible, however, to maintain a high degree of secrecy, since there are many sources of leaks to interested newsmen and radio commentators. Barring objections by the Speaker or by the Rules Committee, a committee report in favor of a measure is likely to be accepted by the whole House. It is possible for a committee to make an adverse report, but this is rarely done. Most bills which are unacceptable are simply pigeonholed by the committee.

From the foregoing discussion, it will be apparent that it is the committees of Congress which constitute, in Woodrow Wilson's phrase, "Congress at work." Viewed from the position of a casual visitor in the House or Senate gallery, Congress may appear indeed to be a desultory organization. Yet, when it is recalled that most of the real work is done in committee, an entirely different impression may emerge. Formerly, a committee chairman sometimes killed a bill, despite favorable committee action, by failing to report it. This practice has been curtailed, if not eliminated, by a provision of the Legislative Reorganization Act of 1946 which requires prompt reporting of approved bills by all chairmen.

The power of a committee to kill a bill, however, raises a serious problem when it is recalled that congressional committees are not in reality representative of their entire bodies. In fact, as was pointed out in the previous chapter, they are the least representative bodies in the government. If a house wishes to overrule one of its committees, it can legally do so. Under House Rule XXVII, a majority of the House can force a committee to report, that is, to give over custody of the bill to the entire House. In practice, this is difficult to obtain. During the twenty-four-year period from 1924 to 1948, only seventeen bills were thus discharged from committees. The reason for this reluctance seems to be a fear that if the whole House overruled one committee, it could overrule others—a custom which might make it virtually impossible to accomplish anything in Congress except reciprocal decision upsetting. Thus the basic rule has become "You go along with our committee, and we'll go along with yours." Congress as a whole is obviously incapable of detailed action, so it has to depend upon its component committees for this. The alternative, lacking strong party controls, would be legislative anarchy.

The handling of bills after the committee stage is complicated by the presence of numerous calendars which may serve as guides to the order of precedence. No useful purpose is served by an overly detailed discussion at this point; the reader is referred to Floyd M. Riddick's authoritative *The United States Congress; Organization and Procedure* for details. Here we shall confine the discussion to broad outlines. When a bill is returned from committee, it is placed on a list known as a "calendar." A bill dealing with money goes on the Calendar of the Whole House on the State of the Union (Union Calendar); a public bill not relating to money goes on the House Calendar; a private bill goes on the Calendar of the Committee of the Whole House (Private Calendar). In addition, there is a Consent Calendar, consisting of unopposed bills which can be disposed of by unanimous consent, and a Discharge Calendar, relating to motions to discharge bills from committee.

The fact that there exists a House rule providing that bills shall be called up in their calendar order is not of great practical importance. The Rules Committee, in effect, determines priorities by bringing in special rules or orders making specified bills the regular business of the House. One result of this is that hundreds of bills on calendars are never called up for consideration and permanently disappear at the end of the session.

The device most commonly employed by the House for consideration of a bill, after the committee stage, is the committee of the whole. The advantage of the committee of the whole is that a quorum consists of only 100 members, the chair is occupied by a special chairman designated by the Speaker, debate is informal with each speaker allowed only five minutes (except by unanimous consent), divisions are taken by voice vote or rising vote or tellers instead of resorting to endless roll calls. When the House has finished playing out its disguise, the chairman reports the committee's action to the Speaker, who in turn asks the formal House whether it approves the decision of the committee of the whole. Needless to say, it usually does! Perhaps 90 to 95 per cent of the House's business is transacted in committee of the whole; all finance and most other important bills are handled in this manner.

Also derived directly from British procedure is the device of three readings for all bills (except those disposed of by unanimous consent). Going back to the days when the average Member of Parliament could not read, the custom of three readings no longer serves any great purpose in an age of nearly universal literacy. The first reading in Congress now consists of merely printing the title of a bill. After the committee stage, the second reading takes place. This is an actual reading of the proposal, section by section, either in committee of the whole or before the entire House. Debate occurs and amendments may be offered at this point. Finally, the bill as amended is put to vote—"Shall the bill be engrossed?" If the answer is favorable, the third reading takes place (normally by title of the bill only) and the House is ready to vote on final passage.

Procedure in the United States Senate is similar to that in the House. The most important differences are three: (1) the Senate no longer uses the committee of the whole except for the consideration of treaties; (2) there is little privileged business before the Senate, except for important appropriation bills; (3) the Senate usually does not attempt to limit debate by its individual members. To this last point we shall return later. First, a few observations on the comparable legislative procedure under the Fourth Republic will be offered.

Both the Third and Fourth Republics have utilized a distinction between Cabinet bills and private members' bills. Cabinet bills are called *projets de loi,* while private members' bills are known as *propositions de loi.* In actual fact, the distinction is rather meaningless, since both Government and members' bills must take their chances before the Assembly. Nothing like the British system of giving priority to Government bills has ever existed. Once prepared in writing, the bills are assigned in the name of the President of the Assembly to the appropriate committees. The role of the committee, and especially of its reporter, has already been noted.

When ready for presentation, the bill is given to the President, who along with other officials of the Assembly determines when it shall fit in with the "order of the day." Thenceforth, the procedure, in outline, is as follows: There is general discussion, a vote is taken to authorize proceeding to read the articles of the bill, the articles are debated in detail and voted upon, a vote is then taken on the measure as a whole. Upon passage, the measure is sent to the Council of the Republic. In the event of any prolonged conflict, the Assembly may make its will felt over the relatively weak Council.

LAWMAKING: THE EFFECTUATION OF MAJORITY RULE

From the foregoing discussion it might be assumed, unfairly, that democratic legislative bodies are so tightly bound to their own rules of procedure that the views of the majority may easily be obstructed by a garrulous minority. The necessity to protect the majority from an obstreperous minority has long been recognized. Indeed, the device of "calling the previous question," *i.e.,* demanding a vote at once on a bill, was adopted by the House of Commons in 1604. Although useful both in Commons and in the United States House of Representatives, this method is not sufficient in the face of a determined and organized minority, *e.g.,* Irish Nationalists in nineteenth-century Britain. As a result, both houses have adopted further means of curtailing debate, which come under the general term of closure.

There are three principal devices in use in the House of Commons. The first of these is a simple majority vote ("simple closure") which has the effect of stopping debate and precipitating a vote. Satisfactory for uncomplicated measures, this device failed to solve the problem of shortening debate on involved, multifaceted proposals. A new method grew up in the late nineteenth century, known as "the guillotine," or closure by compartments of a bill. The House agrees in advance as to the time to be allowed to each part of the bill. When the allotted time has terminated, a vote is taken on that particular section. The third and most recent closure method is known as "kangaroo" closure. Under this procedure, the Speaker is authorized to pick out amendments to a motion which he deems worthy of debate, a job which he does with the advice of the leaders of both parties. These and only these amendments are then debated and voted upon, but it should be emphasized that there are generally only a few key provisions in a proposed enactment, and these the Opposition has its opportunity to amend.

In Britain the decision to invoke closure is made, in effect, by the Cabinet. In the National Assembly it is the deputies themselves who decide to terminate discussion. *Clôture* can be obtained by a simple majority vote. Under another device, however, it is possible to provide for immediate consideration of a measure by using a procedure known as Urgent Discussion. Widely used in the earlier days of the Fourth Republic, this method soon became normal, while the ordinary procedure ceased to be employed. On demand of the ministry, a general committee, or even the proposer of a private member's bill, Urgent Discussion results in immediate consideration of a bill which continues until a decision is reached. Under the new procedural rules adopted in 1950, Urgent Discussion has been used less frequently than in the period from 1947 to 1950. The new rules strengthen the position of the ministry in forcing early consideration of one of its own bills.

Closure is not a serious problem in the House of Representatives. By voting to consider "the previous question," the House may bring debate to a halt and force a vote on the measure. In addition, each member is limited to a speech of not more than one hour under a rule adopted in 1841. More important, however, is the custom of obtaining from opposing party leaders advance agreements to limit debate, and then if necessary writing this agreement into a special order made by the Rules Committee. The story in the Senate is quite different. Obstruction in that body through filibustering is a perennial issue.

If the Senators wish to do so, they can dispose of business very promptly. Thanks to the device of unanimous consent, the Senate in the last few sessions has actually passed more legislative measures than the House, and the great bulk of its business, quantitatively speaking, is disposed of in this manner. On the other hand, when a hotly contested issue is before the upper chamber, it is not uncommon for Senators who oppose a given measure to talk it to death. Against this practice the majority of the Senators have little defense, for the "previous question" device has not been employed since 1806. Senators may, and customarily do, agree in advance to vote on pending measures and amendments at a specified time. But this must get unanimous agreement, so it is hardly a form of closure.

A crisis of the first magnitude arose in 1917 after a tiny group of Senators blocked, by filibuster, voting on a bill, supported by President Wilson and passed by the House, which called for the arming of American merchant shipping. Public opinion heavily backed the President, and, more important, most Senators were enraged. As a result, the Senate for the first time adopted a procedure which could limit debate. Under the provisions of Rule XXII, one-sixth of the Senators must sign a petition to close debate. Two days later the roll had to be called on the question of stopping debate. If two-thirds of the Senators present voted in favor of the question, the measure had to be entertained until disposed of. No Senator was allowed to speak more than an hour on the bill, amendments were permissible only with unanimous consent, and dilatory motions were outlawed.

Compared to the procedure in other legislative bodies, Rule XXII was not a severe form of closure, but it was nevertheless difficult to put it into effect. Closure was invoked only four times up to 1949. In recent years considerable opposition to killing measures by filibuster has developed, particularly over the issue of civil rights.

In his State of the Union address of January of 1949, President Truman called on Congress to pass several measures relating to civil rights endorsed in the Democratic party platform for 1948. Southern opposition was instantaneous. When the principal measures—fair-employment-practices legislation, outlawing of poll taxes in Federal elections, making lynching a Federal crime —finally were reported from committee, a filibuster by Southern Senators prevented Senate consideration of the proposals. The filibuster was thus employed not only to prevent action on the bills, but also to prevent their formal consideration! Not content with getting the withdrawal of the civil-rights proposals, the Southern bloc proceeded to work for the amendment of the closure rule itself.

In 1948, the President *pro tempore*, Senator Vandenberg of Michigan, had ruled that closure could be invoked only to close debate on a bill, not to close debate on a procedural motion to bring a bill up for consideration and action. A year later Vice-President Barkley reversed Senator Vandenberg's ruling, by including both the motion to consider a bill as well as the debate on a bill's substance subject to action under Rule XXII, but his ruling was reversed by the Senate. The Senate finally amended Rule XXII in such a way as to make closure more difficult than ever. First, the two-thirds vote necessary to obtain closure was changed from two-thirds of a Senate quorum, a quorum being forty-nine Senators, to two-thirds of the total membership of the Senate. In the past closure could be ordered by a minimum of thirty-three Senators; as amended in 1949, the procedure now requires a minimum of sixty-four. Secondly, the rule was amended to provide that no motion to change the Senate's rules was subject to closure. The immediate effect was to make impossible the passage of various civil-rights measures; the long-range effect is to give control of the Senate to any determined minority which can muster a total of at least thirty-three Senators. Another effect was to delay indefinitely the admission into the Union of Hawaii and Alaska as states. While it was anticipated that Hawaii's Senators would be Republican and Alaska's would be Democratic, the potential party line-up had nothing to do with the admission question. At stake, as Southern Senators saw it, was the admission of four new Senators who would probably support civil-rights legislation. In order to maintain an advantage of only one vote against the invoking of Rule XXII, Southern Senators were prepared to keep the territories out of the Union!

It should not be thought that filibusters occur only over civil-rights legislation, or that they are practiced only by Southern Democrats. In the debate over the question of overriding President Truman's veto of the Taft-Hartley Act, Senator Wayne Morse of Oregon (then a Republican) staged with Senator Glen Taylor of Idaho (then a Democrat) a marathon filibuster calculated to delay Senate consideration of the proposal. In defense of his action, Senator Morse distinguished between "good" and "bad" filibusters. A good filibuster is intended, he said, merely to delay action until the country may be heard from; a bad filibuster, according to the Senator, is one which seeks to kill the legislation outright. Though Senator Morse did not invent this distinction, there is something to be said for a temporary delaying action intended to give public opinion a chance to express itself. In 1953, the Senate opponents of the measure ceding title to offshore oil resources to the states employed a similar delaying tactic, though without success.

On the other hand, a bloc filibuster which has as its purpose the prevention of voting on the merits of a bill is difficult to defend on rational grounds. The most interesting defense of unlimited Senate debate was made a quarter of a century ago by Professor Lindsay Rogers in *The American Senate*. In the contest between the President and the Congress, Mr. Rogers said, the advantage is altogether with the President. The House in particular finds itself overshadowed by the Chief Executive. Only in the Senate, Mr. Rogers asserted, does the legislative branch have a chance to compete with the executive on even terms, and in the Senate only because of the freedom of debate. A Senate critic of the administration cannot be silenced and can often force investigatory action. While freedom of debate may be abused, as in a filibuster, in Rogers's view it was eminently worth preserving as the only way in which to preserve the independence of the Senate. Mr. Rogers also pointed out that very few bills, once defeated by filibuster, were ever again raised as serious issues before the Senate, indicating, he believed, an absence of popular support. In general, Mr. Rogers's observations on this last point were correct, but he assumed that because the items filibustered were not again brought before the Senate, they were of little substantive significance. On the other hand, it could be argued that the reason these measures did not return was the knowledge on the part of the committee chairmen and members that they would be talked to death if sent out. Rogers's argument has lost whatever force it may have had when it comes to the issue of civil-rights legislation, where the majority of the country (as shown by public-opinion surveys) as well as the majority of the Congress find their will thwarted by a minority of Senators.

LAWMAKING: LEADERSHIP OUTSIDE THE LEGISLATURE

If the Government has a substantial legislative majority, parliamentary leadership presents no problems of mechanics, at least not in Great Britain. The only problems are likely to be those of policy. If, on the other hand, the Cabinet should be a coalition of several parties, as in France, the techniques of parliamentary leadership as well as the policies to be pursued become formidable problems. At Westminster leadership is supplied readily and willingly by the majority party through the Cabinet.

Despite the 1950 changes in rules (as noted above), the French National Assembly is itself a law-originating body, not merely a ratifying agency for ministerial proposals. As a result, leadership is divided among several groups —the coalition cabinet, the parliamentary committees, the parliamentary *groupes* and parties. Leadership from outside the legislature makes itself felt primarily because of the necessity for the committees to receive information from the government departments. Because of the rapid turnover in ministries, real executive leadership tends to reside not in the amateur Ministers but in the permanent heads of departments. The degree of liaison between department heads and strategically placed committee chairmen is often more significant than the liaison between the Ministers and the committees. By a process approaching default, leadership—especially during periods of prolonged ministerial crises—reverts to the professional civil servants.

In addition, the monolithic or potentially disciplined political parties such as the Communists, Socialists, Gaullists, or MRP have a split leadership, *i.e.*, there is a party executive or central committee which has certain supposed— or, in the case of the Communists, real—authority over the decisions of the deputies, and the parliamentary leaders of these parties. This problem has, in particular, plagued the Socialists and Christian Democrats, for in both the SFIO and the MRP there is a constant conflict raging between the "rank and file," *i.e.*, those leaders of the party not in office and their friends, and the parliamentary leadership. In general, these parliamentary leaders manage to escape dictation, but it is done at the cost of either clear-cut policy enunciation or "grass-roots" support. Again, the consequence is to leave real decision-making power in the hands of the one institutional group that knows what it is doing —the administrative class.

Before the passage of the Twentieth Amendment, a somewhat similar situation could arise in the United States in the closing session of Congress following a President's defeat for reelection, *e.g.*, the last few months of President Hoover's term of office. One should not overdo the comparison, because deadlock and strife between executive and legislative branches were deliberately institutionalized in the Constitution. Yet it may be observed that whatever leadership the President may give to the legislative process does in fact tend to evaporate once it is known that he will not seek reelection. The Twenty-second Amendment, which limits the President's term in office to two terms, makes it virtually certain that the Chief Executive will have little control over Congress during the latter part of a second term. Likewise, a decision not to run again for office weakens the President's authority over Congress, as President Truman discovered in 1952.

Despite these reservations, the President may exert a considerable, even at times a dominant, influence over legislation. He may do this through messages to Congress, through party control, and by mobilizing public opinion behind his own legislative program. The President is required by Article II of the Constitution "to give to the Congress information of the state of the Union" and to "recommend to their consideration such measures as he shall judge necessary and expedient." As a consequence, it has become customary for the President to deliver such an address at the start of each regular session of Congress. In his address, the President discusses public affairs and recommends the passage of appropriate legislation. With millions of persons watching the event on their television screens and millions more listening over radios, the occasion is a momentous one.

In addition, under the Employment Act of 1946, the President is required to forward to Congress an economic report. Although the objective of the report is to recommend policies necessary to maintain high employment, President Truman used the economic report to cover a wide area of economic policy. A third message, also transmitted early in January, is the budget message. The proposed budget itself is a weighty and detailed document, but in his message of transmittal, the President has again the opportunity to discuss his legislative proposals, this time as related to dollars and cents.

The President has not always been a prime initiator of legislation. At first, acting for George Washington, Secretary of the Treasury Alexander Hamilton tended to view his own position as comparable to that of the British Prime Minister. This attitude produced the inevitable reaction from Congress and was not repeated by the Jeffersonians. Except for a few Presidents, such as Jackson, Lincoln, and Cleveland, executive initiative in legislative matters was only sporadic or nonexistent until the accession to the White House of

Theodore Roosevelt. The tradition established by Roosevelt was followed and strengthened by Woodrow Wilson, Franklin Roosevelt, and Harry Truman.

In a parliamentary system of government, executive leadership comes not from exhortatory messages but from party control. The general inability of the President to control members of his own party in Congress has previously been analyzed, but it should be noted that, on occasion, a President such as Jefferson or Franklin Roosevelt, by his personal distinction or through threats to withhold patronage or by a combination of both, may be the active leader of the congressional wing of his own party and force through some of his legislative program. Because of the committee system, and especially because of the seniority method of selecting committee chairmen, the more normal situation is that the President may be opposed by powerful congressional leaders of his own party on the very issues for which he was presumably elected by the public. Although some Presidents, notably Wilson and Franklin Roosevelt, have succeeded, at least for a time, in making party lines hold around their legislative programs, this sort of leadership is exceptional.

By themselves, the constitutional devices of a State of the Union message and of presidential veto would not earn for the President the title of "chief legislator." As was hinted at above, the secret weapon of the President lies in his potential ability to mobilize public opinion behind him. A striking illustration of this occurred in the 1948 presidential campaign, when President Truman campaigned effectively against what he termed "the do-nothing Eightieth Congress." Yet the Democratic Congress which convened in January of 1949 proved to be equally unsusceptible to the blandishments of the President, and did even less than the Eightieth!

Both Theodore Roosevelt and Wilson sent special messages to Congress with the twofold aim of stimulating public discussion and of requesting congressional action along recommended lines. In his noted "fireside chats," delivered over a nationwide radio hookup, President Franklin Roosevelt repeatedly sought both to inform the country and to arouse public opinion in favor of particular legislative measures. At one point, these "chats" were so effective that all Roosevelt had to do to bring an important Southern Democratic Senator into line was caress a microphone as they discussed their differences! On occasion, a President reports by radio on the nature of some impending crisis. For example, President Truman in 1946 spoke before a joint session of the Congress on the crisis caused by railroad strikes, and urged immediate enactment of legislation to draft the strikers. He followed a variation of the same technique in 1952 when, in view of a threatening steel strike, he broadcast to the country the essence of his Executive order seizing the industry and putting it under government operation. There is nothing mysterious about the increased control exercised by the President over legislation, emergency or otherwise, during the present century. The public, particularly in the area of foreign affairs, expects the President to supply initiative and leadership. In the event of what seems to him unreasonable obstruction in Congress, the President can and does appeal directly to the country. The rationale for this situation is that the public believes that the President must represent the national interest, while there is often considerable doubt as to whether Congress does.

Besides direct intervention by the President, the executive branch generally initiates a considerable amount of the legislation passed by Congress. Much of this is noncontroversial, but frequently ideas of major importance originate with the departments and bureaus. In addition, some legislation springs directly from the fertile minds of representatives of various interest groups. Access to the legislative process is widely shared under the American system of divided authority. In this respect, the comparison with the British Parliament is striking indeed.

LEGISLATIVE CONTROL OVER ADMINISTRATION

In democratic states it is assumed that administrators may be held accountable to the public through their representatives in the legislature. The American President has, of course, considerable powers which do not grow directly from congressional action, but, at the same time, any effective exercise of presidential power must be buttressed by congressional support.

The first way in which a legislature may control the administration is by passing the statutes which create administrative agencies and which define the duties of these agencies. In addition to the statutes which create agencies and thus define general policies, annual appropriations also afford a substantial legislative weapon for the control of administration. In all democratic countries authorizations to spend money must come from the legislature. In Britain, where the Cabinet—operating, of course, subject to ultimate parliamentary checks—controls the fiscal process, there is no possibility of a deadlock between executive and legislature on this issue. But in the United States Congress the degree of control exercised over appropriations is an effective means of asserting congressional authority over administrative agencies.

Some examples may help to make this clear. In 1946, one of the problems facing Congress and the country was whether to extend price-control legislation. This legislation, favored by the President, was in time extended, but some months later the congressional appropriations committees appropriated insufficient funds for the administrative agency—the Office of Price Administration—to function effectively. This action effectively emasculated the price-control program which Congress had earlier voted to continue. Under American procedure a substantive (subject-matter) committee acts on bills involving programs, but this is only the first step. Once authorized, most programs would die unless funds were appropriated to put them into effect. At this point, an entirely different committee steps into the picture to appropriate the money. The distinction between an authorization and an appropriation in American legislatures is basic. As President Franklin Roosevelt once observed, "An authorization is like a New Year's resolution," *i.e.*, it may or may not be actually followed up.

It is thus commonly necessary for administrative officials to appear before two sets of committees in each house of Congress, one to authorize a program, the other to appropriate funds. At the hearings of the appropriation committees (and subcommittees) officials must appear to defend their estimates of proposed expenditures. While these hearings may be perfunctory, they often are searching in their scope.

Some officials, indeed, are usually able to get more funds than the President and the Bureau of the Budget originally recommended in the proposed budget. For instance, the Director of the Federal Bureau of Investigation usually has no trouble in getting at least the minimum amount of monies requested, and the Department of Agriculture was granted, in 1953, 14 million dollars more than had been requested in the budget. Other officials fare less well, especially if they are from agencies without a voting clientele, such as the Department of State. A perennial whipping boy is the Voice of America program. It is not unusual for Congress to criticize the administration on the ground that its propaganda directed against the Soviets is weak, then to authorize an expansion of the program, then to make expansion impossible by refusing to vote the funds. Regardless of the merits of this procedure, it may be observed that appropriations are a tremendous weapon for the assertion of congressional control over administrative policy. Naturally, this may be carried too far, as when a legislative body itemizes the details of expenditures in such a fashion as to destroy administrative discretion entirely. On the other hand, the annual necessity for justifying expenditures before appropriations committees results frequently in constructive suggestions and policies.

Another method of legislative control, at least potentially, is through the audit. The objective is to discover whether the funds actually appropriated by the legislature have been legally and honestly spent by public officials. In Britain, this function is entrusted to the Comptroller and Auditor-General who is, for all practical purposes, an agent of Parliament. He makes his reports to the Committee on Public Accounts, headed by a chairman from the Opposition. This committee, abjuring sensationalistic publicity, then engages in a thorough, dispassionate appraisal of seeming illegalities and reports to Parliament. A somewhat analogous American institution is the General Accounting Office, headed by the Comptroller General, which is responsible to Congress. However, the Comptroller General is not in the position to conduct a real postaudit or to criticize government expenditures, since his prior approval is required before actual departmental expenditures can be disbursed from the Treasury. Once he has held that an expenditure is valid, it is doubtful whether he would engage in criticism of his own decision. Furthermore, congressional action following up the work of the GAO has been difficult because of the tardiness of that body in reporting. The Government Operations Committees of the House and Senate, established by the Legislative Reorganization Act of 1946, were given the power to examine the reports of the GAO, but their activities have been directed more toward political goals than toward the careful financial scrutiny of government activities that characterizes the work of the British Committee on Public Accounts.

In the amount of control exercised over the administration through appropriations, the extreme situations are represented by Britain and France. As we have seen, Parliament has in fact surrendered its power over taxation and appropriation measures to the Cabinet, keeping only the power of auditing. In France, control over executive policy through appropriations is not merely a theoretical possibility; it is a nightmarish reality. The budget is introduced in the same manner as any other government measure. If a budget has not actually been drawn up before the beginning of the summer recess, the Finance Committee sweats away the summer working on the budget, while other deputies are comfortably vacationing.

Primarily the Finance Committee is concerned with the annual budgets. In fact, however, the committee examines practically all bills which have any relationship to public finance. Since such examination involves a large number of bills, the committee really consists of a group of reporters. The committee holds hearings featuring numerous appearances by members of the executive. When the committee makes its reports, the proposals originally submitted by the ministry are found to have undergone great changes. In practice French budgets come from two sources, the ministry and the committee. General reports made by the committee freely discuss foreign affairs, the armed forces, and other matters of high policy. Discussion is thus by no means limited to purely financial questions. As might be anticipated, one result of such a procedure is to weaken seriously executive leadership and governmental stability. In the financial debate on the committee reports, there is a tendency for the general reporter of the committee to view the Minister of Finance as an unworthy adversary, a feeling which is also shared by the special reporters. As a result, voting on financial measures may give a good indication as to whether a particular ministry will last or is on its way out. American and British observers for the most part condemn the French appropriation procedure on the ground that no legislative committee can exercise intelligently the kind of power given the Finance Committee. The proper function of a legislature, they would agree, is not to encroach on the legitimate sphere of the executive but rather to confine its attention to broad issues. Wearisome as the American congressional procedure may seem at times, it is infinitely less dangerous to the stability of the republic than that followed in the Third and Fourth Republics.

Furthermore, there is a real element of irony in the role of the Finance Committee. The committee's very success in checking or destroying the policies of the "political class," *i.e.,* the Premier and his Cabinet, helps to guarantee the autonomy of the "administrative class," *i.e.,* the *fonctionnaires.* The excessive degree of responsibility of the Cabinet deprives it of the authority necessary to keep the bureaucracy in hand. Although little research has been done in this area, some evidence would suggest that the administrative class works hand in glove with the Finance Committee to forestall strong executive authority. Generally the administrators and a majority of the Finance Committee have a common goal—they are both against change. David Thomson has suggested that no significant alteration in French policy can be effected unless it has the support of the administrative class.

INVESTIGATING COMMITTEES

Since the Glorious Revolution of 1688, the fount of governing power in English-speaking countries has been the legislature. In the preceding chapter, we have noted the varying offshoots from the model of the English Parliament. It has also been emphasized that in Britain the theory of legislative supremacy has been replaced by the fact of Cabinet dominance. Nonetheless, in all democratic countries, there exist ways and means whereby the legislature may exercise a considerable degree of control over administrators.

One such means is through the use of investigating committees, *i.e.,* legislative committees which are given by a Parliament or Congress extraordinary authority to inquire into the operations of government. In the classic home of parliamentary democracy—Great Britain—the use of investigating committees has become less important as the Cabinet has assumed *de facto* authority over Parliament. At the same time, the Parliament continues to make some use of "select committees," for the purpose of studying a given subject on which legislation may be proposed. To a very large extent, however, Parliament nowadays prefers to gather information by using royal commissions or by employing departmental committees.

The French equivalent of the parliamentary investigating committee is the *"enquête,"* which means an investigation undertaken by either a general committee or a special committee. By authority of the house the committee may be given power to compel testimony from witnesses under oath. The findings of committees of investigation are not usually of much importance; frequently the hearings merely provide a setting for partisan fireworks.

It is in the United States Congress, largely as a result of the lack of executive-legislative integration, that investigating committees have reached their greatest development. There is nothing new about congressional investigations. The first use of this device occurred in 1792, when the House sought to inquire into the causes of the St. Clair disaster in the Indian war. Leading students of Congress generally cite three legitimate reasons for the holding of congressional investigations. First, there is the need for Congress to obtain adequate information upon which to base legislation. For example, the Pecora investigation of

1933 led to the establishment of the Securities and Exchange Commission. Second, there is the use of committees to supervise or check the work of administrative agencies. Examples would include the joint House-Senate probe of the TVA in 1938 and the investigations into the RFC conducted in 1951–1952. Third, there is the use of committees to influence public opinion by giving circulation to certain facts or ideas. It is at this point that tempers frequently wax hot. The treatment of representatives of industry by the La Follette Civil Liberties Committee during the 1930's was anything but tender; and the House Committee on Un-American Activities has been notoriously rough on those suspected of, or accused of, communist affiliations.

Four general types of criticisms have from time to time been directed against congressional investigating committees. The oldest, used by Senator Sumner in 1860, is that the committees pry into the private lives of citizens. It is not possible to take this criticism seriously. Another equally frivolous criticism is that the committees take time and cost money. This may be true, but to argue that committees should be abolished as an economy measure is tantamount to cutting off one's nose to spite his face; to legislate intelligently, Congress must have sources of information other than those made available by the administration, in the same way that it must be able to pry into the private lives of government officials in search of malversation and peculation—which may be rife. It is also alleged that on occasion the committees are motivated by partisan considerations, e.g., the Tydings subcommittee was split almost exactly along party lines in its report to the Senate on the validity of Senator McCarthy's charges of alleged communist influences in the State Department. Yet, those who would take partisanship from Congress may be accused in turn of aspiring to either a Platonic ideal of government, a Hitleresque type of nonpartisanship, or a Milquetoastian utopianism.

The most valid of current criticisms of the committees is that they frequently use unfair methods. Specifically, witnesses are often browbeaten, sometimes they do not have a chance to present their side of the controversy, often publicity "leaks" damage irreparably the reputations of wholly innocent individuals. For this there is only only one answer: Congress itself must establish a procedure to be followed by its committees which meets the elemental requirements of due process. To require that the committees behave like courts would be to eliminate much of the usefulness of those committees. What is needed is some measure of congressional restraint in the interests of fair play. In addition, a good deal of the information now obtained by committees could be better obtained from other sources, for example, from presidential commissions on the order of the justly famed Hoover Commission. Too many congressional investigations in progress at one time tend not only to deter Congress from the consideration of more important business but also to confuse and bewilder the public. The all-time record, set in the second session of the

Eighty-second Congress prior to the 1952 presidential election, resulted in numerous charges and countercharges but in little public law.

QUESTIONS AND INTERPELLATIONS

Except for its limited use in Wisconsin since 1915, the device known to the British as the question period has not been employed by major units of American government. Frequently, it is true, one hears of proposals that Cabinet members be permitted to speak and to be questioned on the floor of Congress. In practice, it is doubtful that such a move would do anything other than create a maximum of ill will. In any event, in committee hearings, Congressmen may question top-level administrative officials as much as they wish. Secretary of State Dean Acheson once tried the experiment of addressing as many members of Congress as cared to hear him report on the world situation. The meeting, although not held on Capitol Hill, was well attended. After the Secretary's speech was finished, he entertained questions from the floor, but the procedure proved definitely unsatisfactory. Some Congressmen felt that they had been caught in a classroom with a professor setting rhetorical traps for them to fall into, and openly promised to work the Secretary of State over the next time he came before their committees when they would have the rhetorical advantage. It is doubtful whether this experiment will ever be repeated.

Although the American system of separation of functions is not conducive to question-and-answer sessions between legislators and administrators, at least on the floors of legislatures, the British have employed such a device since at least 1721. At the present time the number of questions presented daily is around 130. A fairly elaborate code of what may or may not be asked has been developed. For example, the following types of questions are not permitted: those which are in effect a short speech, questions seeking an expression of opinion, questions introducing the name of or containing reflections on the sovereign or royal family. Every member of the House of Commons may raise questions, provided they are addressed in writing to an appropriate Minister, that they conform to the general rules, and that notice is given at least two days in advance. There is no requirement, other than the requirements of common sense and political *savoir-faire*, that a Minister answer a question directed to him.

While the questioning of Ministers is one of the principal devices by which Members of the House of Commons may hold the government accountable, the questions are rarely followed by a debate or by a vote. A vote of censure, in the form of a motion to decrease his salary, may be directed against an individual Cabinet member, and it is possible, though improbable, that the Cabinet will drop him. The majority party will mobilize its forces to prevent such a vote from being held or, if held, from passing. Of course, if a Minister has become a political liability, he will be dropped, but not by direction of the Opposition. Usually in such a case, *e.g.,* Minister of Fuel and Power Shinwell in the 1945 Labor Government, the Government first defeats the Opposition's motion of censure and then, after a decent interval, shifts the man in question to a less significant post. A final method of enforcing accountability—and the extreme one—is for the leader of the Opposition to offer a motion of no confidence in the government. This is not directed against a specific Minister, as in a vote of censure, but against the entire Cabinet. Should the vote be carried, the Cabinet will resign or will call for a general election. Today the Cabinet is never defeated on a motion of no confidence, thanks to the party discipline be-hind the Government.

Thus, in effect, the question period is much more important than the vote of censure or the vote of no confidence at Westminster. In France, the situation is almost the reverse. Theoretically the Fourth Republic's Assembly permits "oral questions," in which the questioner reads his question, the appropriate Minister answers, and the questioner is entitled to five minutes' reply. Actually, the monthly sitting devoted to oral questions is not held. Much more satisfactory is the system whereby members may submit written questions, to which they receive written answers.

A more effective method of French parliamentary control is the interpellation, by which a member asks a Minister or the Premier to explain a policy of the Government. Requests are forwarded to the Conference of Presidents, which determines which requests shall be submitted for answering. The Minister has the option of agreeing to full debate or to refusing debate. If the latter, a short debate will actually take place on the refusal to allow a full debate. If a full-fledged debate is permitted, the discussion is naturally much longer and more carefully developed. Since the Cabinet exercises control over which requests shall be debated, it is not likely that the government will be overturned as the result of interpellation. However, on losing a formal vote of censure or a formal vote of no confidence, the Ministers are required to resign collectively. In contrast to British practice, votes of no confidence, followed by the resignation of the ministry, are as common in the Fourth Republic as they were under the Third Republic.

SPECIAL CHARACTERISTICS OF LEGISLATIVE CONTROL

Despite the different means by which legislatures may hold administrators responsible for their actions, the degree of accountability which may be achieved varies not only from system to system but also from time to time under the same system. Generalization is thus difficult. Nevertheless, a statement of some of the problems raised under the American, British, and French forms of legislative organization may be helpful.

The very nature of the congressional system of committees tends to fragmentize American administration. Since the committee system to some extent parallels the administrative structure, the tendency for administrators to deal directly with their congressional counterparts is marked. This administrative-legislative nexus is discussed elsewhere at some length; suffice it here to note that in the course of obtaining adequate funds, it is often more important for an administrator to please an appropriations subcommittee than to convince either the President or the Bureau of the Budget. Under such circumstances, over-all fiscal (and personnel) planning becomes difficult. Frequently Congress goes too far in laying down, largely through the framework of annual appropriations, the details of operation which properly belong in the administrative province.

In addition, the executive-legislative separation seems at times to encourage in Congress a boyish sense of irresponsibility. An example of this is the perennial attempt in the House to deny funds to the British unless the latter agree to put Northern Ireland under the jurisdiction of the Dublin government. Such an effort may be pleasing to some of the Rhode Island constituents of Representative John E. Fogarty, but this is hardly statesmanship. Over a period of years the House was in the habit of passing fustian resolutions demanding that the British leave Palestine or India, in effect, usurping the job of conscience-keeper for the British Empire. Needless to say, the British took a dim view of these moral-uplift homilies.

If the question is merely an expression of opinion, intended for the consumption of constituents, such a didactic resolution may do no lasting harm. Where funds committed to the furtherance of American foreign policy are at stake, the results may be anything but amusing. Fortunately, the House usually recovers from its moral fervor the next day and reverses itself, as it did with Congressman Fogarty's initially accepted amendment denying European Co-operation Administration funds to Britain so long as Ireland remains divided.

At the same time, it is not difficult to understand the frustration of the average Congressman. Confronted on all sides with demands for economy, with demands for closer surveillance of administrative activities, his two chief weapons remain the control over appropriations and the use of investigating committees. Particularly where government corporations such as the TVA are involved, it is extremely difficult for Congress to obtain the information upon which to base intelligent judgment.

In the House of Commons a somewhat similar problem arises. If the government refuses to answer questions put to it, or gives evasive answers, there is little that the average Member of Parliament can do. Particularly in an age of large-scale government ownership through public corporations, a Member of the House of Commons is likely to feel that his questions receive inadequate answers. For example, one Member stated recently that while he could complain with some measure of success about the lateness of trains when they were under private ownership, he is now told by the Minister of Transport to read the government corporations' annual reports! In addition, in an era of economic specialization, it is difficult even to ask intelligent questions.

The French problem is entirely different. Boiled down to its simplest dimensions, it is: Who controls whom? As we have seen, methods exist by which the Assembly may control the ministry. Yet no practical method exists by which the ministry may be assured of control over the Assembly. The situation is one-sided, with power being centered in the legislature. Under these circumstances, power gravitates toward the all-powerful committees. If the committees are unable to act, by default governing power is left to the *fonctionnaires* in the administrative departments of the government. Previously, it has been noted that this impotence is closely related to the multiparty system and to the lack of the power of dissolution. In an even more basic sense, this situation may be attributed to the fundamental lack of agreement in French society. Nonetheless, the problems which are presented to Frenchmen desirous of preserving democratic methods are enormous. These problems are aggravated by the power relationship existing among the ministry, the Assembly, and the bureaucracy.

LEGISLATURES AS FORUMS OF PUBLIC OPINION

Compared to parliamentary legislatures, the American Congress remains a relatively strong law-originating body. Yet the principal characteristic of the Congress is that divisions on important questions occur on nearly every possible basis other than party. The regionalism, even parochialism, of American national politics is nowhere better illustrated than in the national legislature. In other words, the ties between a Congressman and his constituents are far stronger than the ties between the Congressman and his national party. As a result, there is in reality a multiparty system in Congress, a system which is not stable but which fluctuates with the ebb and flow of issues.

There is no use in pretending that the American people do not approve of the current arrangements. Even when critical of Congress as an institution, the majority of persons interviewed on the question of party realignment consistently prefer to retain the present system. The rationale for this lies in the belief that consensus should be established at the legislative level, not at the election level preceding congressional sessions. Given the size and diversity of the country, this belief is defensible. One result, however, is to place a premium on individualism in the legislative halls, and another is to make it possible for all shades of opinion (except the extreme left) to be expressed in Congress. Of course, Congress in a mathematical sense is rarely expressive of public opinion on any given issue. At the same time, even though oratory may swing but few votes, Congress does act as an extremely effective forum for the expression of varying facets of public opinion. The point to emphasize is that this expression of opinion is not normally an expression of party opinion. It is here that the difference between Congress and the House of Commons is so marked.

Even so, it would serve no useful purpose to overlook the fact that party, in

Congress, is a factor of importance in legislative divisions. The importance depends on the issue. For example, when the question is one of patronage, the Congressmen split along party lines. A more significant illustration is the Democratic preference for low tariffs as opposed to the Republican leaning toward high tariffs. This difference has also been present in voting on reciprocal trade legislation. On the questions of government action, social and labor problems, and farm support a recent writer, Julius Turner, has also found party differences to be relatively sharp. Turner has also pointed out that party cohesion, as measured by roll-call votes in various important bills, has been steadily falling since the time of McKinley in 1900. Up till the present, in any event, the lowest point ever reached in party unity was the period following the coming of the New Deal.

In contrast, the primary function of the House of Commons is no longer to initiate legislation or even to oversee public administration. Rather it is to act as a forum for the expression of public opinion. In performing this function, both the Government and the Opposition are in effect addressing their words to the country at large. Since an election may be called at any time without much prior notice, both major parties must of necessity attempt to give the impression of a constructive position on important issues. There is, of course, no fixed term of immunity from elections such as is so characteristic of the American system. A favorable public opinion must be cultivated now, not two or six years from now; furthermore, the opinion to be cultivated is a national one, not merely that of a single constituency.

If these observations are accurate, one would anticipate a high degree of internal party cohesion in the House of Commons. Upon investigation, this surmise turns out to be true. During the 1920's the percentage of party votes in Commons averaged 94.9 per cent. A party vote is defined by Turner as a roll call on which 90 per cent of one party votes "yea" and 90 per cent of the other party votes "nay."

Thus proceedings in the House of Commons take on the appearance of a marionette show, with the party leaders manipulating the strings. This explains, at least in large part, why the rigorous closure provisions do not create more discontent: the Opposition is not trying to defeat the measure under discussion; it is trying to influence the country against the party in power. Consequently, the Opposition can pick the salient and most vulnerable aspects of a proposal, send its best men into battle against them, and allow most of the bill to pass without debate.

Similarly, criticisms of administrative decisions are not aimed at defeating the Government *in* the House of Commons. They are, rather, designed to convince the people of Britain that the Government is arbitrary, bureaucratic, and fundamentally unfit to rule. The consequences of these attacks are seen at the polls, not in the division lobbies at Westminster. While figures have not been compiled for more recent years, there is every reason to suspect that party solidarity has increased. In the American House of Representatives the low point during the 1920's occurred in 1928, when only 7.1 per cent of the votes were party votes!

In analyzing the French legislature, still another set of characteristics become apparent. The National Assembly is a forum of public opinion par excellence, but as has been noted previously, the Assembly is so representative of shifts in public opinion that it is not able either to govern or to furnish the necessary majorities for ministerial leadership. To compare British or American with French parties on the basis of a party vote is impossible, since such a technique of analysis depends on the existence of only two parties. However, by employing methods developed by Stuart Rice, it has been possible to develop "an index of cohesion." On this basis, perfect cohesion is 100, while the lowest possible cohesion is 0.

A study of the French Chamber of Deputies in 1930, undertaken by Ralph Burton, showed that the large class parties had a very high degree of cohesion. For example, the Communists rated 100 and the Socialists 98. On the other hand, the smallest *groupes* had a very low degree of cohesion. Today, the two extremes, the Communists and the remaining Gaullists, have a great deal of cohesion, but the groups between are much less integrated. If one excludes the two extremes, the degree of cohesion seems to be a direct correlate of position on the left-right continuum, with the parties to the left (SFIO, MRP) more cohesive, and the parties to the right (Radical Socialists, peasant groups) most undisciplined.

IMPROVEMENT OF LEGISLATURES: THE AMERICAN APPROACH

The most significant attempt in many years to improve the internal structure and operations of Congress was the Legislative Reorganization Act of 1946. At various points in the preceding analysis the leading provisions of this legislation have been mentioned. It is unnecessary here to analyze the law in detail. On the other hand, it is pertinent to inquire into the performance of Congress since the La Follette–Monroney proposal became public law. Fortunately, George B. Galloway, of the staff of the Library of Congress, has made an intensive examination of the operations of the law in terms of its objectives. The following is a summary of Mr. Galloway's conclusions.

In general, he finds, the act has worked out very well. Gains have been achieved in lessening the numbers of committees, in improving committee procedure, and in the staffing of the committees with professional experts. However, only in the Senate have party policy committees functioned. Nor has the work load of Congress been lightened under the act. Many private bills should be handled by some other agency than Congress. The fiscal provisions of the act either have been ignored or have not in practice proved workable. Although some additional information has been obtained under the lobby registration provisions of the act, clarification is needed. Congressional salaries were raised and a substantial majority of Congressmen are participating in the Federal retirement plan.

While he does not commit himself specifically, Mr. Galloway leaves the clear impression that much remains to be done. Along with others, he asserts, "Congress is the central citadel of American democracy and our chief defense against dictatorship." Hence, further improvement is of first-rate importance. It is a matter of considerable debate, however, whether mere internal improvement of Congress gets close to the heart of reform. The record of Congress itself has been far from encouraging, notwithstanding the 1946 effort.

At one extreme in the general debate stand those who contend that internal reform of Congress can come about only after a general reform of the national party structure. Given cohesive national parties, this school argues, Congress could reform its procedure and organization in short order. Representative of this approach are Elmer E. Schattschneider and James M. Burns, two recognized authorities on American national politics. At the other extreme stands Ernest S. Griffith, the distinguished Director of the Legislative Reference Service of the Library of Congress. Mr. Griffith believes that Congress is doing a good job as it is, although he sees room for improvements in such areas as organization and staffing. In particular, Mr. Griffith pays tribute to the sense of responsibility of the American Congress and is critical of scholars who advocate more disciplined national parties.

The truth probably lies, as it usually does, somewhere between these extremes. Even Mr. Griffith sees room for congressional improvement, although, in his view, this improvement is an internal affair. Professors Schattschneider and Burns tend to view congressional improvement as an external affair, something which would inevitably follow upon a reorganization of the existing national parties. Whatever the abstract merits of congressional reform via party reorganization may be, the plain fact of the matter is that the American people at the present time are not prepared to pay the price which party reorganization along the lines advocated by Professor Schattschneider would entail. The best that can be hoped for is that Congress, encouraged by the results of the 1946 legislation, will continue with the job of internal improvement.

THE BRITISH APPROACH

Despite the fact that it is considered by many non-Britons, as well as Britons, to be an irreproachable model, the British Parliament is frequently criticized by the British themselves on various grounds. Except for a few Liberals and others associated with minor parties, this criticism has little to do with party structure. True, there exist internal difficulties inside each Parliamentary party, and it is not always easy to reconcile differences. At the same time, cabinet government is so accepted by the British that it would be unthinkable to tinker with its basic mechanism.

The criticism most commonly heard is that Parliament has lost control of the fiscal process. In particular it is claimed that the Parliament does not have at its disposal an adequate amount of time to consider budgetary matters. Whether steps in the direction of greater parliamentary control would represent progress is doubtful. The party in power would be unlikely to agree to any such "reforms," and the party out of power would be unlikely to continue such "reforms" once it had achieved cabinet control. If it is agreed that the essence of British democracy lies in the choice at general elections between parties, it is difficult to take seriously charges of "cabinet dictatorship" and the like. So long as the electorate retains final authority to replace the "ins" with the "outs," there can be no substantial basis to the charge. It is noteworthy that no Briton of any standing whatever has ever advocated either the adoption of the presidential form of government on the American model or that of the parliamentary form on the French model.

PROBLEMS OF THE NATIONAL ASSEMBLY

Nearly all authorities on French government are agreed that the basic difficulties in France cannot be attributed merely to the National Assembly. Improvements could certainly be made by the Assembly itself, *e.g.*, by limiting the powers of the Finance Committee. Yet these reforms would be relatively trivial compared to the basic questions of dissolution, the electoral system, the multiparty system. Recognition of this has resulted in the creation of a prolific literature on the desirability of general reorganization of French government. On the other hand, relatively little attention has been given by French writers to the question of internal reform of the National Assembly. As we have noted, the situation in America is (except for a few academic authorities) almost completely the reverse.

THE GENERAL TREND TOWARD ENHANCEMENT
OF EXECUTIVE AUTHORITY

Except in France, the universal trend during the twentieth century has been to enhance the prestige and authority of the executive. There has been a corresponding decline in the position of democratic legislatures. Particularly since the Reorganization Act of 1939, the President of the United States has in fact become "chief administrator." His position as "chief legislator" has also been strengthened, particularly in times of sudden emergencies, such as the Korean War or strikes in crucial industries. At these junctures the public looks to the President, not to Congress, for leadership, and is inclined to be extremely critical of the President when leadership is not supplied.

During the last 100 years a similar evolution has taken place in Great Britain, as increased party discipline in Commons, changed social conditions, and military emergencies have joined to increase the prestige of the collegial executive or cabinet. The German executive under the Bonn Republic has registered spectacular gains over the relatively weak executive under the Weimar Republic.

These developments, and similar ones in other democratic countries, do not signify, as is often charged, the imminent demise of democratic government. What they point to is the increased necessity for executive leadership in an age of economic specialization and military emergency. One result is the lessened importance of legislatures as law-initiating bodies. At the same time, greater emphasis is placed upon legislative oversight of administrative agencies as well as upon legislatures as forums for the expression of public opinion. These are important functions, not to be dismissed lightly.

In succeeding chapters, the political process will for convenience be examined in terms of administrative, judicial, and executive functions. At nearly every point, however, it will be necessary to call attention to the key role of legislatures in democratic societies.

Chapter 8

THE ADMINISTRATIVE PROCESS

JUDGED IN eighteenth- or nineteenth-century terms, the modern democratic state is decidedly hyperthyroid. Everywhere that one turns, he finds state activity, and most of this activity is included under the term public administration. Since most of the work of the state is performed by agents of the executive branch of the government, it is with the organization and structure of this division that we are here concerned. The adjective "public" before the word "administration" is intended to underline the fact that the problems of administration are not limited to governmental organizations. Indeed, much of the most significant research on problems of organization and administration has come from nongovernmental bodies; for example, industrial corporations and churches. The relationship between governmental administration and administration in other areas is further revealed by the current jargon of public administration. As cases in point, the expression "chain of command" and the word "hierarchy," frequently employed in the writings of experts in this field, come directly from military and church usage.

Public administration is concerned, in the phrase of Marshall Dimock, with the "what" and the "how" of government. The "what" is subject matter— public health, reforestation, and the hundreds of other activities of government —while the "how" is management techniques. Viewed in this light, public administration includes not only the highly specialized activities and functions so characteristic of modern government, but also such over-all problems as personnel management, fiscal management, and methods of planning and leadership. In both the area of subject matter and that of technique it is clear that public administration in any given country reflects the cumulative skills and talents available in society. For example, a highly industrialized nation has no difficulty in securing the services of specialists in finance, in management, and in operating techniques. At the other extreme, the government of Iran, left to its own resources, has had great difficulty in conducting petroleum operations since the expulsion of the Anglo-Iranian Oil Company. At the time of expropriation, the Iranian government did not have at its disposal citizens who were specialists and top-level managers. Training an administrative and managerial elite is a difficult and arduous process for a nonindustrialized country. In contrast, the United States, during a military or other emergency such as the present "Cold War," can and does tap the civilian supply of specialists and managers, many of whom leave their businesses for temporary administrative posts with the United States.

In the traditional view, public administration is mainly concerned with getting things done. In recent years this view has been questioned by some who would say that the essence of administration is policy. The disagreement is more a matter of philosophical orientation than a sharp difference in interpreting observed facts. For example, traditionally, democratic theorists have insisted that the legislature must be considered the fount of policy formulation. Yet, it is apparent in all modern governments that, more and more, actual policy formulation is being undertaken by top-level administrators, with at times only a cursory inspection from the legislative solons. The distinction between politics (policy) and administration (getting things done) has, in short, become unrealistic. In actual fact, the best type of public administrator today is concerned primarily with policies, programs, and objectives, not with routine operations.

In this and in the succeeding chapter, we shall touch only incidentally upon the formulation of public policy, for the entire book, essentially, deals with this broad question, and with the related question of political responsibility. The relationship between policy formulation and policy execution is reciprocal, but for analytical purposes, much is to be gained by treating administration as though it were a separate province of government. A word of caution is, however, in order. The reader should bear in mind that administration deals with human units, with human beings, that the forms and techniques of public administration are used to affect human activities, and that the same group processes, noted in earlier chapters, are also operative in bureaucracies, departments, and agencies. With this in mind, we can proceed to a more detailed examination of the place and role of public administration in modern democracies.

Public administration is a subdivision of political science. However, it has specific elements which distinguish it from the larger area. Charles Beard listed the elements of public administration as organization, finance, accounting and recording, personnel administration, purchasing of materials, and technical methods. Under the last heading, Beard included such things as the technology of public hygiene and water-supply engineering.

From this list it would seem that public administration differs from traditional political science in being nonnormative, that is, ethically neutral. In addition, many of the elements of public administration are scientific in nature. Nevertheless, it is generally agreed that administration is more an art than a science, although Professor Beard once remarked, dissenting at least in part from this, that public administration is "as much of a general science as economics or psychology or biology, more of a science than history or politics."

As further advances in technology are inevitably forthcoming, some aspects of administration will probably become ever more technological and scientific in character. The preparation of a budget, for example, obviously requires considerable statistical skill.

Beside the debate over whether public administration is an art or a science, a great deal of paper and ink has been wasted trying to distinguish politics from administration. This dichotomy, suggested in 1900 by Frank J. Goodnow, was intended by Goodnow to emphasize the two primary functions of the state —to declare the will of the public and to execute that will. While still suggestive, this distinction has been found less valid by subsequent scholars. As more and more concrete studies of policy formulation have been made, it has become increasingly clear that administrators frequently originate policy, or at least have a decisive role in the actual impact of generalized policy statements. At the same time, it is often painfully apparent that legislatures frequently exceed the boundaries of policy formulation by passing special acts which are really administrative ordinances.

Further difficulties in the study of public administration are suggested by the frequent use of derogatory expressions such as "bureaucracy" or "red tape" as applied to governmental activities. The impression meant to be conveyed is that somehow government administrators are different, emotionally and intellectually, from business, or trade-union, or university administrators. For example, in 1932, former Solicitor General James M. Beck published a work entitled *Our Wonderland of Bureaucracy*. Among the many unusual comments in this book is the statement that "the constantly growing strength of bureaucracy, the demands of groups of legislation and large appropriations, and the impotence of Congress to maintain its power are leading the American Government toward an absolutism worthy of Moscow, but unworthy of Philadelphia, where the Constitution was framed." Another variation on the same theme is Laurence Sullivan's *The Dead Hand of Bureaucracy,* which informs us that "bureaucracy is representative government suffering a nervous breakdown." While no doubt amusing, texts of this sort are not in reality attacks upon public administration, but are essentially criticisms of the twentieth century.

Pleasant though it might be, we cannot in actuality return to any supposed "golden age." Such critics of bureaucracy could as well devote their time and energy to the activities of the Society for Preserving the Horse and Buggy. Intemperate criticisms of governmental operation should be counterbalanced by reading such a book as Paul Appleby's *Big Democracy*. A top civil servant for many years, now with the Maxwell School at Syracuse University, Dr. Appleby clears up many popular misconceptions of American government. He points out, for example, that even red tape, properly understood as regularized procedure, is a valuable safeguard against capricious, irresponsible action. It is, after all, a fundamental disregard for red tape, otherwise known as procedural safeguards, that characterizes Soviet totalitarianism. Appleby also suggests that any large organization, business, ecclesiastical, or governmental, runs into difficult problems purely because of bigness.

The fact of the matter is that administration, both as subject matter and as technique, is a fundamental part of modern complex industrial society. Though it may be used for bad ends, it is also apparent that it may be used to promote human welfare and happiness. At least, in the great democracies, this is the objective.

EXPANSION OF GOVERNMENTAL ACTIVITIES

At one time the functions of the state were simple. They consisted of tax collection, maintenance of internal order, and military defense. On the other hand, today nearly everywhere we have the service state, which in the advanced democracies is in the process of becoming a mutual-assurance state. The days of "anarchy plus a constable" are gone. Britain has gone further in the direction of taking the risk out of life than the other democracies, yet, in the United States, one need only consider such developments as social-security legislation, minimum-wage laws, agricultural price supports, subsidies for aviation and shipping firms, to realize that this country, too, is continually tending toward a "pool the risk" society.

It may be wondered why this is so. Although there is no simple answer, it is fairly apparent that the rise in governmental functions in the last seventy-five years has to a very great extent paralleled the rise of modern technology. Technological advance generally implies industrialization on a large scale, and, with it, urbanization. In the process, the self-reliant rural man gave way before the dependent urban man. Relying on others for goods and services, the city dweller was placed at the mercy of forces beyond his control. When such forces became antisocial or reactionary, the tendency was for the urbanites to band together to force government into positive remedial action. The same phenomenon was evident with farmers. At one time agrarians were largely self-sufficient, existing, in a sense, outside the market place. But today, farming has become more a business than a way of life. Agricultural specialization, whether in America, Canada, or Australia, has placed large-scale farmers in a situation comparable to that of city dwellers. No individual farmer, for example, can control the price of wheat or wool. If the free-market price falls below a level at which the farmer can support himself and his family, he bands together with his friends and neighbors to force government intervention on his behalf.

It is in these terms that the Interstate Commerce Act of 1887 and the Sherman Antitrust Act of 1890 are to be explained. Moreover, at the same time that powerful elements of the public were demanding regulation of railroads and trusts, these and other elements were also demanding more in the way of positive services. An early example is furnished by the rise in the United States, and later in Britain, of free public education. Later extension of this principle include public parks, public housing, greatly expanded medical facilities, and the like.

Coming somewhat later chronologically than the demands for regulation or services were outright subsidies to support certain fields of endeavor. In the United States tariff subsidies began with the initial meeting of Congress in 1790, but except for state gifts to railroad and canal companies, it was not until the present century that the principle of government subsidies was nearly universally adopted. At the present time, Federal subsidies in one form or another are given to extensive sectors of the economy and to various segments of the populace. Included in the former group are such industries as aviation, shipping, housing, agriculture; included in the latter are most large-scale farmers, veterans, government contractors, dependent women and children, and the blind.

The most extreme extension of the principle of government intervention is outright government ownership of industries and plants. Of all the great democracies, Britain has carried this to the furthest extent. Yet, in the United States, Scandinavia, and other countries not enamored of nationalization, municipal and local government ownership and operation of transportation services and public utilities have been common for several generations. Many conservative communities in the United States would be startled to discover that, in the opinion of some, their ownership of their water-supply systems indicates a local triumph of socialism.

Whether nationalization on the British model, regulation on the American, or cooperativism on the Scandinavian is the best of all courses to follow is beyond our consideration at this point. But all will agree that it is possible to meet the demands of the public for regulation, subsidies, services, and perhaps ownership, only with a vastly expanded governmental apparatus. The 1950 census listed 5.5 million persons as civilian government workers in the United States, of whom slightly fewer than 2 million were employed by the national government.

Mobilizations and wars always increase the duties and functions of government. Since the start of the present "Cold War," civil employment by the Federal government has steadily risen until it is now close to the World War II peak. At the present time, more than half the Federal civil servants are employed by the defense and mobilization establishments.

THE TRAINING OF ADMINISTRATORS

For many years American colleges have given courses in American government and administration, and most colleges now give courses in administration as such. The procedure is to treat administration as a part of the larger totality of the political process. Since few undergraduates are, therefore, in a position to "major" in public administration, it is difficult to assess the validity of that part of the political science curriculum by itself. Nonetheless, there is today abundant opportunity for the college graduate to enter the service as an administrator. Leaving aside the many positions filled by technicians, *e.g.*, engineers, biologists, or soil conservationists, it remains the case that many thousands of college graduates are recruited annually to posts such as junior management assistant, analyst, and intern. In most cases, majors in any of the social sciences, but especially in political science and in economics, may with aptitude qualify for such beginning administrative positions.

At the graduate-school level the emphasis is, of course, somewhat different. In the first place, the training is more intensive, and, as a consequence, graduates of public-administration schools are generally able to command more lucrative beginning positions. In the second place, there has been a distinct trend toward autonomy on the part of these graduate schools. That is, there has been a steady increase in the number of such institutions devoted almost exclusively to the study of public administration. Provided that the undergraduate training was sufficiently broad, this is not, of course, an indictment, but it does represent a possible difficulty.

Some persons who judge mainly by British standards are apt to be disappointed at the relative failure to develop a bona fide career service in the United States. But the emphasis should be placed on the term "relative," for the truth of the matter is that the expansion of the career service in the national government, and in many of the states, since 1920 has been phenomenal. On the other hand, before handing the Americans too many plaudits, note should be taken of two problems, both currently debated among public-administration educators, which have not yet been satisfactorily resolved.

Not only have politicians and university boards of trustees taken a mixed view toward training for public service; educators themselves have been in serious disagreement. At the heart of the problem is the question as to whether it is possible to train a person to be an administrator, in the abstract, or whether he should be trained to administer *something*. For example, should an administrator first become a specialist in agriculture, or public health, or engineering, and then rise up the escalator of power; or should he simply be college-trained without any functional specialty? Assuming that a liberal-arts education is a good background for a potential administrator, should such an education be followed by graduate instruction or should the college graduate learn while on the job?

A related problem plaguing the graduate schools of administration is the type of curriculum to follow. In general, the emphasis has been placed upon training for staff functions, *e.g.*, personnel and fiscal work. However, the crying need is for capable persons to take charge of actual operations—to be "generalists," not "specialists"—and this, of course, in turn requires previous experience. A vicious circle is thus created. It should be pointed out, however, that graduate schools that prepare candidates for specific posts have been relatively successful in placing their graduates. In such a situation the premium is placed upon personal contact among the students, the professors, and the hiring agencies. The Institute of Public Administration at the University of Michigan and the Maxwell School of Citizenship at Syracuse University have been outstanding in this regard.

In Britain, the teaching of public administration has never been a problem, for the simple reason that it is rarely taught at all. British recruitment has followed the recommendation of the Northcote-Trevelyan and Macaulay reports of 1853–1854 to the effect that the highest-ranking university graduate should be hired regardless of specialization. These "generalists" are then trained in many specific administrative functions and become the administrative elite which gives great administrative stability to British government. On the Continent, since the war's end, there has been a resurgence of the belief that public administration constitutes a serious academic discipline, a "science." For example, France in 1945 established a National School of Administration to train top-flight civil servants.

GENERAL RULES OF ADMINISTRATION

Organization occurs everywhere, in both the physical and human worlds. Since organization is a universal phenomenon, many observers have been led to seek the basic principles of organization as revealed in all forms of human group activity. As related to public administration, the objective has been to find such principles and then to apply them to existing administrative structures.

In his *Principles of Public Administration,* published in 1927, W. F. Willoughby attempted an analysis of American national government in these deductive terms. An elaborate application of alleged principles of organization was presented in 1931 by James B. Mooney and Allen C. Reiley in *Onward Industry!* Despite these and similar expositions, the term "principle" as applied to administration has tended to lose popularity with later writers—perhaps because each writer tended to come up with his own set of universally valid "principles." The search for generally valid propositions continues, but such propositions are no longer commonly spoken of in terms of eternal principles. Modern students of government have tended here, as in related areas, to shy away from the natural-law universe assumed by their scholarly ancestors.

Nonetheless, there is widespread agreement that certain generalizations are usually valid and ought to be observed in any administrative structure. First, organization should be hierarchical in nature in order that control over a large enterprise may be exercised from a central point. That is, lines of authority should run upward and downward, with a single head at the top of the pyramid of power. This phenomenon is sometimes referred to, in the language of public administrators, as the scalar process.

Associated with the scalar process is unity of command. By this is meant the allocation of responsibility and authority throughout the hierarchy, with the person at the top ultimately responsible for the entire unit. The term "chain of command," as used by the military or by government administrators, refers to the channels through which directing and coordinating powers are exercised. Another military usage which is also employed in this connection by public administrators is the distinction between "command" and "technical" channels. This distinction may be illustrated by a simple example. In a military post, the commanding general is responsible for all activities under his command. Orders from the general are passed down to various subordinate echelons through command channels, that is, in each echelon the commanding officer is responsible for the execution of orders in his own jurisdiction. However, at each large military post there are numerous technical services, *e.g.*, Ordnance, Signal Corps, and Medical Corps. For purposes of general direction, these smaller groups are, of course, under the command of the general. At the same time, these specialized groups receive instructions regarding methods, care of equipment, and techniques through what are called "technical channels." For example, directives from the Chief of Chaplains in Washington go directly to the post's chaplain, not through the commanding officer of the post. The larger any organization becomes, the more likely it is to be forced to distinguish between command and technical channels.

As Arthur Macmahon and John Millet have pointed out, on occasion a conflict may come between line officers operating in the chain of command and staff or advisory specialists operating partly through technical channels. This conflict was termed by Macmahon as "the rival claims of hierarchy and specialty." As a case in point, assume that a technical adviser to the State Department is ordered to formulate a policy which he, as a specialist, believes to be unsound. At this point, it is clear that an acute conflict between hierarchy and specialty would occur.

Another generalization with seeming validity is that subdivisions immediately under the chief of an organization should be grouped in terms of functions or of general purposes. In the American national government, the departments are arranged in this fashion, as the names Department of Agriculture, Department of Commerce, illustrate. Within major organizational units, subdivisions are generally on process lines, *e.g.*, a medical or legal subdivision.

The number of departments reporting to a chief should ideally be small enough to enable him to exercise a "span of control." This technical term is based on the psychological fact that no person is able to master more than a relatively small number of continuing relationships. According to the French management specialist, V. A. Graicunas, six persons reporting continually to one superior is about the maximum. Beyond that number, he declares, the relationships become hazy and blurred. One need not quibble about the number six; the point is that any executive who has any more than six persons reporting to him regularly or consulting with him is unlikely to be doing the most effective job. The validity of this observation has been assumed by most large

American corporations who limit the executive span of control to about six subordinates. But, even if the span of control be enlarged to ten persons, it is clear that most American government executives do not possess effective control over their principal subordinates. In this country the Hoover Commission experts and others have long argued that it is impossible for the President to execute his many responsibilities adequately, since too many heads of departments and agencies—no less than sixty-five—have direct access to him. To get around this difficulty, Presidents tend to establish "kitchen cabinets," or small groups of intimate advisers, thus by-passing the established channel. This may entail serious administrative consequences, with the alternative being to allow unsupervised officials a dangerous degree of autonomy. During World War II, the British, with their usual practicality, institutionalized a "kitchen cabinet" when Churchill established a small "war cabinet" of a few key individuals, most of whom were very close personal friends of the Prime Minister.

The military and industry have pioneered in reducing the number of subordinates who report directly to a chief, maintaining that operating efficiency is thus increased. Government has been much more reluctant to adopt this procedure, which has been a major contributing factor to the lack of administrative responsibility which characterizes so much American governmental administration. Obviously, unless a superior is in a position to maintain effective control over his inferiors, the latter will tend to become independent of him. The counterpart to span of control is, of course, the delegation of authority to subordinates. There is little point to having effective span of control, numerically, if the superior insists upon doing over all the work of his subordinates.

It is generally agreed that legislative bodies should not specify the details of organizational structure. In American city and state governments this remains the exception rather than the rule. Congress likewise is often guilty of exceeding the proper limits of legislative wisdom by drafting overly confining and restricting laws which cramp administrative flexibility. For example, in 1951 the national legislature provided that a Director for Mutual Security should be appointed in the Executive Office of the President, and that the same man who was appointed to this task should also administer the huge operating agency, the Mutual Security Agency. The Executive Office of the President was designed as a staff body to give the President technical advice; yet, Congress in this statute imposed line functions upon a staff officer. In a nation with a cabinet system of government such as Great Britain this situation need not arise.

It might be well at this point to further clarify several terms which have been used and will be employed again. Reference has already been made to the distinction between "line" and "staff" functions. The line, or line officers, are those in the direct line of command. In issuing orders and supervising their subordinates, these officers are directly involved in achieving the functional objective of the organization. The staff, or staff officers, perform work which is largely advisory or consultative in nature. It is their job to give technical advice to line officers.

A good deal of mystery sometimes needlessly surrounds the concept of staff. To some extent, this mystery has been created by academicians who, perhaps because of their own bias, overemphasize the importance of staff to the exclusion of line functions. Returning to our previous military example, the officers and men at the general headquarters of a military post who perform duties relating to personnel, intelligence, supplies, finances, transportation, and training, are all performing staff functions. These staff personnel are not permitted to issue orders which go down the chain of command. Instead, recommendations are made, when necessary, to the general, who will himself see to it that the recommendations are transmitted as orders through the chain of command. Needless to say, staff officers often have a decisive role in determining what policy ought to be followed, but they have no authority to issue direct commands.

The expression "general staff" refers to top-level groups of advisers whose main function is to filter information so that the executive may be as free as possible for the handling of important decisions. As might be anticipated, the best examples come from the general staffs of armed forces, but there are also numerous civilian illustrations. The Executive Office of the President, but not the Cabinet, performs general staff functions for the Chief Executive, and a similar staff may be found assisting the Secretary of Agriculture.

An auxiliary staff is one which performs duties of a "housekeeping" nature, that is, jobs which are done in every department of the government regardless of the special purpose of that department. At every level of organization, for example, people must be paid and personnel procedures must be regularized, and consequently personnel and finance fall under the heading of auxiliary staff activities.

However, one must be careful in employing such terms as line and staff. In a small organization, e.g., an infantry platoon, no distinction is necessary. But as one proceeds from smaller to larger organizations, it becomes more and more imperative to distinguish line from staff functions. Fundamentally, the purpose of this distinction is to enable the line officers more adequately to fulfill their primary mission: command. But if line officers are to do their jobs properly, they must have good advice and sound planning at their disposal, so that, as John Millet and Herman Somers have clearly demonstrated, planning is an administrative responsibility that line officers can only ignore at their peril. Many Republicans who felt that the Eisenhower victory in 1952 would put an end to the activities of the "long-hairs" or "egg-heads" in Washington have been startled to discover that the professors and other technical specialists, whether long-haired or egg-headed, are still giving advice. But these hopes were obviously utopian, for President Eisenhower did not rise to a position of military eminence by disdaining staff assistance. Indeed, on the contrary, much of his genius in the field consisted of a fine ability to utilize his technical advisers to the maximum. Many a government line officer has been sonorously anti-intellectual—until he was faced with his first complex decision.

It is important to discuss the general rules of public administration as they have been formulated by various analysts, but the student should not be misled by this into believing that public administration is an applied science. It is not. Indeed, some organizations violate every rule in the administrator's handbook, and yet operate successfully because of superior personnel or a fine *esprit de corps*. For example, consider British municipal government. British boroughs are run by elected councils, and most of the administrative work of the boroughs is supervised by various council committees. At one swoop, a host of general rules is violated. The patent effectiveness of British local government must be explained in terms of traditions of public service rather than by criteria of sound administrative organization. Or, to take an even more horrible breach of the general rules, consider the Swiss plural federal executive which actually manages Swiss affairs rather efficiently.

In part as an outgrowth of this persistent refusal of facts to conform to theories, a substantial amount of attention has been given in recent years to the psychology and sociology of organizations. Some army units are much better than others with similar tables of organization; some administrative departments perform their duties far more competently than others with similar internal structure. Why? There have been numerous attempts to answer this question. During World War II, the United States Army subsidized a tremendous psychological and sociological analysis of the problems of military organization, the results of which were published in three volumes as *The American Soldier*. The best analysis of this sort to date in the area of government administration is *Public Administration* by Herbert Simon, Donald W. Smithburg, and Victor A. Thompson, in which theory and description are combined in the effort to uncover and analyze the underlying issues of administration.

SOME ORGANIZATIONAL PROBLEMS IN AMERICAN GOVERNMENT

Just as custom and tradition are important factors in legislative procedure, so also are they significant forces in the shaping of an administrative tradition. Ever since the Revolution, France has maintained a strongly centralized administrative system. Despite occasional dreams of devolution or regionalism, it is unlikely that French administration will undergo any major shift from past practice. Nor is it easy for outsiders to impose on a conquered country a new system of administration. Although the Americans decentralized Japanese government during the occupation period, it remains to be seen how long the Japanese, now independent once more, will forego the obvious advantages which centralization brings to a small area.

American administration is likewise firmly rooted in the soil of the past. Indeed, as Leonard White has demonstrated in his remarkable study *The Federalists,* the fundamental pattern of national administration was evolved and established prior to Jefferson's victory in 1800. The work of the Federalists, much of which can be attributed to the genius of Alexander Hamilton, has demonstrated remarkable durability, even withstanding at most key points the onslaught of egalitarian and semianarchistic Jacksonian democracy. Current proposals to strengthen the executive department of the government are essentially Hamiltonian in nature.

Federalism and the conception of checks and balances, often miscalled the "separation of powers," were unquestionably the most significant factors in the shaping of the American administrative tradition. The decision that the nation should be organized on a federal, rather than on a confederal or on a unitary, basis meant an inevitable duplication and overlapping of the functions of the states and the national government. At the same time, the checks-and-balances doctrine implied that executive control over administration would be tempered by a jealous legislature and brought under ceaseless judicial scrutiny. This fact in itself demonstrates the inaccuracy of the traditional term "separation of powers," which has misled many a student into believing that the American national government is divided into three watertight compartments. The President, for example, exercises executive functions, but has no clearly defined body of executive power. He must wage relentless war with Congress to gain new authority and to hold on to earlier conquests, and a seeming victory may, as in the steel-seizure case of 1952, be snatched from his grasp by the Supreme Court.

Because the boundaries between presidential and congressional bailiwicks are so indistinct and are subject to such incessant redelineation, the sort of administrative responsibility that is characteristic of Great Britain is very difficult to obtain. For whom does a Federal administrator work? Is the President the man whose orders he should obey? Or, does his department lie within the colonial empire of some powerful congressional committee? Take, for example, the Passport Division of the Department of State, which for many years was, in effect, a protectorate of Chairman Pat McCarran of the Senate Judiciary Committee. A Secretary of State could attempt to enforce his views of passport policy on this department, but he did so at his peril. The Senate Judiciary Committee in a showdown had all the aces, for it could cripple the administration by refusing necessary approval to vital legislation, and could, indirectly, wield great power over the Department of State's appropriations. If the Chairman of the Judiciary Committee suggested to his colleague the Chairman of the Appropriations Committee that the State Department had requested far more money than it needed, his views received very serious consideration. In fact, they were given such serious consideration that sensible Secretaries of State avoided argument and conceded defeat. This is only one example, and there are hundreds more. The consequence is that American national adminis-tration is a modern form of feudalism in which the President has the titular authority of a feudal king, but real authority often resides in independent baronies jointly run by congressional committees and cooperating administra-tors. The classic statement of this is the United States Army Engineers' un-official description of their function as "the engineer consultants to, and con-tractors for, the Congress of the United States."

In short, the framers of the Constitution guaranteed perpetual civil war within the national government not by precisely dividing and separating pow-ers, but by interweaving, through checks and balances, legislative, executive, and judicial power, and giving each branch of government a chance and an invitation to enlarge its functions. No doubt the decisions made in 1787 were politically and logically justified at the time they were made, but a consider-able price has been paid for them by succeeding generations. As one of the con-sequences, at least in part, of federalism, for instance, we have in the United States an incredible number of governmental units—no less than 119,465 in 1951, and this represented a considerable decrease over the total of previous years!

Compared with a unitary country such as Britain, governmental power in the United States is remarkably diffused. In fact, no other nation in the world offers its citizens so many points of access to decision makers. Thus coordina-tion, the primary problem of organization, is exceptionally difficult to achieve, not only within the Federal level of government, but also between Federal, state, and local levels. As was suggested above, it is sometimes a fairly difficult job to discover who really makes administrative decisions in the national gov-ernment, and it is even more difficult to obtain coordination. One can, for ex-ample, put the Secretary of State and the Secretary of Defense on a coordinat-ing committee, but their attempts to work together on policy may not be binding on the Passport Division of State or the Army Corps of Engineers, who look to congressional committees for direction.

The classic battle for coordination was fought over the issue of unification of the armed services in 1947 to 1949. A Secretary of Defense was established to integrate the Army, Navy, and Air Force into a unified command, and the three services began fighting a bitter delaying action. Those interested in the bloody details of the struggle should turn to the *Forrestal Diaries,* where the first Secretary of Defense kept a day-to-day account of the maneuvering. Suf-fice it to say that each service rushed to its congressional friends, congressional committees began investigations, admirals denounced generals, the Air Force claimed it could sink any Navy ship, and the Navy replied that it could bring down any Air Force plane, and the Marine Corps offered to take on the other three services combined. Finally, unification of sorts was achieved, mainly through the iron will and bitter determination of Forrestal. But to this battle can be attributed, at least in large part, the later derangement and suicide of the extremely able Secretary. In clandestine fashion the struggle still goes on, largely over what would be called in trade-union circles jurisdictional issues. Should the Marines have their own air arm, or should they depend on the Air Force? What is the strategic role of carrier planes? In obtaining solutions to these, and similar problems, the individual services still invoke the aid of their friends in Congress—although much less flagrantly than before.

Related to the problem of coordination is the question of how much centralization should exist within an agency. Whenever authority is delegated, as it must be in any large-scale administrative operation, that authority is to some extent decentralized. The most obvious type of decentralization is by a geographical distribution of functions; for instance, in tax collecting or in delivering the mail. The Bureau of Internal Revenue of necessity has field or regional offices where a tremendous amount of its work is done. However, when this is done, the problem of maintaining standard procedures while still allowing the regional chiefs to exercise some discretion immediately arises. The most notable example of an agency which has consciously attempted to push its administration down to the "grass roots" is the Tennessee Valley Authority. But no one pattern has universal validity. To decentralize the Department of State by scattering its bureaus throughout the nation might seriously weaken its effectiveness. On the other hand, to conduct all the work of the National Labor Relations Board in Washington would be to invite trouble in the field of labor relations.

Another type of decentralization is that set up along functional lines. Here, the problem is related to departmentalization generally. For example, should each agency executive have his own car and driver, or should there be a central motor pool for the agency or a group of agencies? Should supplies be purchased by a central unit, or should each division do its own buying? Again, there are no certain answers; the solution must be worked out in the light of available facts.

A constant conflict occurs in all large organizations between the two principles of organization by area and organization by function. It will be agreed that in any city there should be only one police force, and the city should be subdivided into police precincts on a geographical basis. But assume that a riot breaks out in one precinct. Should that precinct have its own riot squad, or should the riot squad be assigned to central police headquarters and sent to emergencies? If a murder is committed in this precinct, should it be handled by detectives from that area, or should specialists from headquarters be detailed to solve the case?

At more complicated levels of government, the conflict between areal and functional organization becomes much more involved. For example, should there be a separate Petroleum Division of the Department of State, or should each geographical bureau have its own petroleum experts? What about research and intelligence specialists? In this sort of situation a decision, often an unpleasant one, has to be made, and there is no magic formula to help the Secretary of State make up his mind. Experience and investigation seem to be the only guides to making decisions such as this.

In short, centralization versus decentralization, areal versus functional organization, administrative control versus administrative discretion, all pose weighty and difficult questions for administrators. And, furthermore, in the United States, decisions of this sort are made even more complicated by the fact that top-level government administrators have to adjust their decision making to congressional realities, as well as the imperatives of the federal system.

THE ORGANIZATION OF AMERICAN ADMINISTRATION

A bird's-eye view of American national government would reveal a bewildering variety of shapes, forms, and nomenclatures. Only an exceptionally ill-informed person, or one hypnotized by a chart of Federal organization, could believe that one man, the President, can personally supervise the thousands of activities of nearly two thousand major units of government. This myth of responsibility does, however, play an important part in American politics. The President is always—in the public mind, at least—held responsible for administrative fumbling, although frequently he has very little effective control over the activities of the department in question. This is, of course, particularly true when the department held up to public blame is a crown colony of some important congressional committee, or the protectorate of an important pressure group as is the Veterans Administration.

But, while the student should keep the realities of American administration in mind throughout, our concern here is with the technical aspects of governmental organization. There are five major types of organization in the executive branch of the government. First, there is the President's immediate staff centered in the Executive Office of the President and containing, among other units, the Bureau of the Budget, and the Council of Economic Advisers. Second, there are the ten great line departments: State, Defense, Treasury, Labor, Justice, Commerce, Agriculture, Interior, Post Office, and Health. Third, there are two units which are departments in all but name: the General Services Administration and the Housing and Home Finance Agency. Fourth, there are about fifty government corporations. Fifth, there are several dozen boards, commissions, and "independent agencies" which defy inclusion in any of the above categories.

A century ago the picture was by no means so complex, as most government activities were carried on within the framework of great executive departments directly under the President. For a variety of reasons, not the least of which is distrust of growing presidential power, Congress in the interim has established a large number of agencies either only remotely under the President's authority, or beyond his jurisdiction altogether. As a result, it is not possible to draw neat, symmetrical charts which depict in any realistic fashion the flow of authority and responsibility in the government as a whole.

Needless to say, this has made the President's administrative task a most difficult one. It seems possible to assert that a President's qualitative control over the bureaucracy is far less today than it was in the days of Washington and Adams. Or, to put it another way, the United States, instead of marching steadily toward bureaucratic collectivism under the aegis of an increasingly powerful Chief Executive, has in reality moved in the direction of bureaucratic pluralism, in which the President has had a perpetually decreasing role in actual administrative decision making. Absolutely, the President's power today is greater than it has ever been, but relatively, he appears to have less power than ever before. That the Congress considers this to be an eminently desirable situation can be deduced from the strenuous congressional objections to measures designed to make the Presidency more efficient. There is an old observation in army circles that the more complex the organization, the more power at the bottom. Thus, while Congress cannot limit the theoretical scope of executive authority, it can throttle the Presidency by insisting on highly complex executive organization.

Furthermore, the President does not start with very clear powers. The framers of the Constitution—who, it should be noted, looked upon constant civil war between the President and Congress as one of the buttresses of freedom—did not define the President's administrative duties in any precise fashion. He is to see to it that "the laws are faithfully executed," but this provision, interpreted narrowly, would make the President little more than an arm of Congress. In fact, it would seem as though the Founding Fathers considered "executive power" to be more military and political than administrative. But in this area, as elsewhere, the Constitution has grown by a slow process of accretion. Under the Federalists, the Presidents took their administrative duties seriously. After Jackson, the prestige of the office dropped, reaching an all-time low in the administration of Andrew Johnson. Even Lincoln, while a great President in most respects, was a poor administrator—perhaps because he had so much else on his mind. In this century, both Roosevelts and Wilson have reestablished the prestige and status of the office. These three Presidents, while continuing to exercise all the traditional prerogatives of the Chief Executive, built the Presidency into an institution for popular leadership and to a lesser extent developed the concept that the President is and ought to be "Chief Administrator." It is with this last aspect that we are here concerned.

For those who like business comparisons, the President may be considered the general manager of the United States government. What are the major administrative duties of the Chief Executive? Following Leonard D. White, a leading authority on this subject, we can note six distinguishable functions. First, the President must determine the main lines of administrative policy. A major instrument of this policy coordination is the Bureau of the Budget, which acts for the President in approving or rejecting all proposals for legislation initiated by the various departments. Second, the President must issue the necessary orders, directions, and commands to his subordinates. While many orders may be given orally and informally, on most important matters the President issues Executive orders or Proclamations which are collected and published in the *Federal Register*. Third, the Chief Executive must coordinate the activities of the organization, which is, as we have seen, the primary problem of public administration. If coordination cannot be achieved at lower levels, then the President himself must act as the final court of appeal. Under Franklin D. Roosevelt, who seldom trusted a subordinate with real power, this latter was quite common; under Harry Truman and particularly under Dwight D. Eisenhower, authority has been delegated much more broadly, perhaps at the sacrifice of control. Fourth, the President should control the structure of organization. Congress has seldom given the President much leeway here, but the Reorganization Acts of 1939, 1945, 1949, and 1953 have supplied the Chief Executive with some needed authority in this area. Fifth, the President should control the management of finances. Since 1921, the preparation of the budget has been an executive function, and, once completed, the budget is submitted to Congress. However, the President has little control over congressional reaction to his budget, and frequently when money is appropriated it is turned over to the President with elaborate provisions for spending which give little flexibility to the executive.

Finally, and deserving somewhat more extended treatment, the President must have the power to appoint and remove personnel. At the lower and middle levels of Federal employment, the President generally has little voice in hiring and firing. These matters are handled under the direction of the Civil Service Commission by rather elaborate rules and regulations. According to the terms of the Constitution, the President must submit to the Senate for approval his nominees for ambassadors, consuls, and Justices of the Supreme Court. Congress may enlarge this list, and has done so at various times, generally as a thinly disguised technique of expanding patronage. At the present time, exclusive of military and naval officers whose approval is usually automatic, and some 21,000 postmasters, the President and Senate together appoint only a few thousand of the more than 2 million persons in Federal civilian employment. Although postmasters of the first three classes must obtain favorable Senate action, they have been under classified civil service since 1938. In June, 1952, the Senate rejected three reorganization proposals submitted by President Truman with the endorsement of the Hoover Commission which would have placed all postmasters, all United States marshals, and all customs collectors under competitive civil service. As a consequence of this, marshals and customs collectors remain entirely without the merit system, while postmasters retain their highly ambiguous status. In effect, postmasterships continue to be disposed of according to the spoils system, with a veneer of the merit system applied later. The technique is this: most postmasters are chosen by members of the House of Representatives belonging to the party in power (majority Senators may choose the postmasters for their home towns!) and receive Senate confirmation. Once appointed to office on a "temporary" basis, these appointees subsequently take what is in theory a "competitive" examination and come under the protection of the civil service system. Actually, the competitive element in the examination is nonexistent.

President Truman was successful earlier in 1952 in bringing collectors of internal revenue fully under the merit system. He lost on postmasters, marshals, and customs collectors for two main reasons: first, considerable Republican opposition developed against the idea that Democratic appointees should be frozen in office; and, second, the old-line Democratic committee chairmen in the Senate realized that their power would be reduced by these measures and joined the opposition. The success of Truman's proposal on revenue collectors may in large part be attributed to the fact that it came shortly after several scandals involving these officials, and few Senators were willing to risk possible identification with "corruption" by voting against the measure.

There is no uniform rule governing the extent of the requirement of senatorial approval. In the Department of State, for example, bureau chiefs are career officials who need not pass senatorial scrutiny, while in other departments inferior officers—postmasters, for instance—must be given a clean bill of health by the upper house. As a matter of courtesy, Cabinet nominees are usually given automatic approval, although recent years have seen several bitter attacks on proposed Secretaries. However, such attacks were more a utilization of a good forum to attack administration policies than denunciations of the individuals concerned.

Impressive though the President's power of appointment is, there are restrictions which limit his authority. Reference has already been made to "senatorial courtesy," that is, the requirement that the President, if he is to get Senate approval for certain appointments, clear them with the senior Senator of his party from the state in which the job exists. On this matter, the Senators band together like fraternity brothers, and if the President disregards the wishes of one of his Senators, he will have little chance of getting the appointment approved. The old rule of "you scratch my back, and I'll scratch yours" operates most effectively among the members of what has been described as Washington's top club.

While the above description of senatorial courtesy is somewhat frivolous, there is a somber element to the picture. One clear result of senatorial courtesy is to retain patronage appointment for many routine positions which ought to be part of the career service. In addition, some positions which are far from routine, e.g., Federal judgeships, have been kept in patronage politics because of the necessity of senatorial confirmation. It is to be doubted whether the requirement of Senate approval has elevated the standards of appointments to any class of positions. True, it has led to vigorous battles on the Senate floor and in the press, but these struggles have been motivated in general by a desire to embarrass the administration. Rarely have they been joined over the technical qualifications of the nominee. So far as parties are concerned, senatorial courtesy weakens the presidential or national organization by building up parochial loyalties to individual Senators.

Implicit in the business of joint presidential-senatorial approval of certain officers is the question of who has the right to fire them. Can the President do it of his own volition? Or must he get senatorial approval? Although discussed in the first years of American government, this problem was side-stepped for three-quarters of a century. It was tacitly accepted that the President could dismiss such appointees without consulting the Senate. However, in 1867, Congress reopened the controversy by passing the Tenure of Office Act which forbade the President to remove any joint appointees without the permission of the Senate. This restriction even applied to members of the President's Cabinet, and was, indeed, in part designed to stop President Johnson from firing Secretary of War Stanton, a pet of the radical Congress. Although the original Tenure of Office Act was repealed in 1887, an act of 1876 retained the principle and applied it to most classes of postmasters.

In 1926, in the famous case of *Myers v. United States*, the Supreme Court took a long overdue look at the act of 1876 and declared it to have been thoroughly unconstitutional. The Court declared that the President had the right to discharge without the concurrence of the Senate any executive officer, in this instance a first-class postmaster. However, in 1935, the Court revised its views somewhat by redefining "executive officer." The case grew out of President Roosevelt's dismissal of Federal Trade Commissioner William E. Humphrey on what were unquestionably political grounds. Roosevelt took strong exception to Humphrey's stated view that the FTC should wither away at the earliest possible moment, and decided to replace the stalwart Republican with someone more in line with administration policy. This was done, but Humphrey contested the dismissal on the ground that the President could fire Federal Trade Commissioners only on the bases provided by Congress, "inefficiency, neglect of duty, or malfeasance in office," and not on mere political grounds. In *Rathbun v. United States* the Supreme Court agreed with Humphrey—or rather with his executor, since Humphrey had since died—and pointed out that while the President had complete authority over executive officers, Humphrey was not an executive officer, but rather a quasi-legislative or quasi-judicial official. In instances of the latter sort, the President can dismiss only on the grounds stipulated by Congress. However, the Court did not take the time to define a quasi-legislative, quasi-judicial function, or to delineate the boundary between such offices and those of an executive nature. This mystical border has not since been marked out, so that today the student who wishes to find out which agencies are quasi-legislative, quasi-judicial in essence must look to the provisions in the act setting up the body to see if the President's removal power is limited! Those which have limited removal power are "quasis," while those which do not are executive; and, conversely, those which are "quasis" have limited removal power. This is reminiscent of the early dictionary which defined a violin as a small cello, and a cello as a large violin.

Although Congress may abolish an agency altogether, it may not force, at least in theory, the removal of individuals from executive offices. Several years ago Congress provided that no money from an appropriations bill should go to pay the salaries of three named Federal officers, but the Supreme Court declared that this was an unconstitutional bill of attainder. However, Congress, not to be put off by any judicial niceties, soon devised a foolproof technique of attaining the same objective. Desiring to eliminate a certain bureau chief from the Bureau of Reclamation, the legislators merely provided, in voting an appropriation to pay the salary of this official, that he must be a graduate engineer—which the individual in question was not! Obviously this was not a bill of attainder; it was simply Congress establishing adequate qualifications for an executive office. Congress has provided that it alone may remove the Comptroller General of the United States, and also that it has the power to discharge Directors of the Tennessee Valley Authority, but the constitutionality of these provisions remains questionable.

The President's powers of appointment and removal have been given extended treatment both because they are vital to the operation of the administrative machine and because there remains such a significant area of fog in such a key function. While the President's power to dismiss in ninety-nine cases out of a hundred is open and shut, the hundredth official is often very significant. The quasi-legislative bodies with respect to whose members the President must proceed with great circumspection play a very important part in American government. They are known as the independent regulatory commissions, and will be discussed in some detail later in this chapter. Suffice it here to note that when the Treasury announces one policy and the Federal Reserve Board simultaneously proposes one diametrically opposed, as occurred under the Truman administration with some regularity, the cause of this hodgepodge is not far to seek: the Secretary of the Treasury works for the President, while the members of the FRB are "quasis," virtually beyond the reach of presidential authority and discipline. The issue is not whether the FRB or the Treasury is correct in its views; the basic problem goes far deeper and touches the very heart of democratic government. It is this: How can democratic government function adequately when an elected Chief Executive is not given the power to promulgate and implement policies throughout the administration?

Although the preceding analysis discusses or mentions most of the administrative duties of the President, it might be well to add three more: to supervise and control administrative operations, to investigate, and to conduct public relations. From this imposing roster of duties and functions the conclusion inescapably emerges that the President cannot adequately perform his administrative duties without a sizable and properly trained staff of assistants. Even with them, the job of Chief Administrator remains a killing one, but the adequacy of the presidential staff remains to be discussed before such an evaluation can be undertaken.

Only by institutionalizing the Presidency—dividing it up into several units, each assigned to be part President—is it possible for the Chief Executive to do his job. At first glance, there might seem to be no particular problem involved in this. Why could the Cabinet not perform this function? Why could the Vice-President not be given the job of administrative general manager? In considering these questions, it is well to keep in mind the type of duty which the President, as general manager, is called upon to perform.

Initially, it is evident that the Cabinet is not, and cannot be made into, a general staff. Department heads are generally selected on the basis of various party, geographical, religious, and ethnic considerations, not for their technical ability in the fields assigned them. What they have in common is political *expertise*, and quite frequently several members of the Cabinet have the presidential bug buzzing among their ambitions. Indeed, a wise President may take his party rivals into the Cabinet to neutralize them, as it were, by enmeshing them in his policies. Lincoln did this, having no less than three would-be Presidents in his Cabinet at one time—Chase, Seward, and Stanton—and outmaneuvering them all the way. Wilson likewise "hung the albatross of Bryan around his neck," as one contemporary put it, by taking one of his rivals for the Democratic nomination in 1912 into the Cabinet as Secretary of State. Politicians seem to have become wiser since then, as evidenced by Senator Taft's obvious unwillingness in 1953 to have anything to do with a Cabinet post. This system of appointment has decided assets, among them that it keeps technicians from making policies according to their somewhat rigid versions of "Truth," but the price which must be paid for it is the surrender of the possibility that the Cabinet can give the President any detailed technical advice. The Cabinet is a political body whose principal task today is reconciling the demands of pressure groups with the imperatives of public policy. A good example of what can happen when a technician gets a Cabinet post occurred during the Truman administration when the President appointed a career post-office official, Jesse M. Donaldson, to be Postmaster General. So long as this post was occupied by top Democratic party officials and was, in effect, the clearinghouse for patronage, Congress kept its hands off the Post Office, but as soon as Donaldson took over the job, the department's appropriation was cut. President Eisenhower's appointment of Arthur Summerfield to this position may return the department to its previous immunity, enjoyed for so long under James A. Farley, Robert E. Hannegan, and others who knew very little about the mails but a great deal about jobs.

Furthermore, the Cabinet is entirely the President's creation, to be consulted, enlivened, or ignored as the latter sees fit. It may be merely a showcase to keep some leading party functionaries out in the open, while the President seeks his advice from others with no place on the organizational charts. Sometimes a Cabinet may be forced upon a President as the price of victory in the election, which immediately leads to the formation of a "kitchen cabinet" of advisers whom the President can trust. In addition, vast areas of government policy are not under the jurisdiction of the ten department heads, but are the bailiwicks of other officials. For example, the Defense Mobilizer and the Director of the Foreign Operations Administration report directly to the President, although neither is in the Cabinet.

From time to time it has been proposed that the Vice-President be put to work. As Clinton Rossiter has shown, there have been repeated proposals to this end since 1787. Beyond presiding over the Senate, the Vice-President has only a handful of duties to perform, and these are mostly inconsequential. Senator Monroney of Oklahoma once proposed that there be two Vice-Presidents, one to preside over the Senate and succeed, if necessary, to the Presidency; the other to act as executive manager. To achieve this goal, the Constitution would have to be amended.

However, as Rossiter points out, much could be achieved without an amendment provided that a President really tried to utilize the skills of a Vice-President. In the 1948 Presidential campaign, Governor Dewey declared that if he won, he would make extensive use of the abilities of his Vice-President, Governor Earl Warren of California. Vice-President Alben W. Barkley did perform valuable services to President Truman both as a peacemaker within the Democratic party and as a campaign orator, but he showed no interest in the problems of administration. However, it should once again be emphasized that the main problem here, as with the Cabinet, is a political one. Since vice-presidential nominees are generally chosen to balance the ticket, it seems unlikely that most Presidents would be likely to entrust much responsibility to a man who represents a different segment of the party. Both Governor Dewey and Governor Warren were, it should be noted, from the liberal wing of the Republican party, which may account for Dewey's purported willingness to give Warren substantial authority. The present instance is more typical, for President Eisenhower was the choice of the liberal wing of the GOP while Senator (now Vice-President) Nixon came from the anti-Warren right wing of the California Republicans. Even so, it appears that Nixon has undertaken the task of legislative trouble shooter for the President.

While it is possible that reform of the Cabinet and of the Vice-Presidency could strengthen the Presidency, immediate assistance has come from another quarter. Under the terms of the Reorganization Act of 1939, an Executive Office of the President was created into which were shifted various managerial agencies responsible to the President. Thus, for the first time, the central administrative position of the President was recognized.

The components of the Executive Office of the President change from time to time, but its principal current units are the Bureau of the Budget, the White House Office, the Council of Economic Advisers, the National Security Council, and the Office of Defense Mobilization. The work of the Bureau of the Budget is discussed later in this chapter; suffice it here to note that the Bureau, established in the Treasury in 1921, but shifted to the Executive Office in 1939, handles budgeting and the clearance of legislation for the President. The White House Office, established in 1939, includes presidential secretaries and administrative assistants assigned to help the President perform routine duties. On occasion, however, these duties may be much more than routine, *e.g.*, John Steelman, one of Truman's administrative assistants, was also one of the President's top labor trouble shooters.

Established in 1946, the Council of Economic Advisers reports to the President on the state of the economy, while the National Security Council, established with its twin the National Security Resources Board in 1947, handles matters affecting foreign policy and mobilization for war. The Central Intelligence Agency is subordinate to the National Security Council. The Office of Defense Mobilization was established in 1950 to coordinate defense efforts growing out of the "Cold War." For all practical purposes, its first Director, Charles Wilson, was general manager of the American economy.

It is now possible to set up a balance sheet on which the powers of the executive in the abstract may be contrasted with the actual managerial powers of the President. Ideally, an executive would have administrative, fiscal, and personnel control over his organization. However, Americans must take for granted the fact that no President, no matter how overwhelmingly elected or how friendly to Congressmen, will ever be trusted by Congress. We have, built into our Constitution and traditions, institutional animosity between these two great branches of government which is reflected by constant congressional attempts to limit the authority of the executive and, conversely, by persistent presidential action to enlarge executive jurisdiction. Given this incessant guerrilla warfare, we can never expect the President to attain the ideal level of administrative control. However, the Presidency has in recent years steadily increased in administrative effectiveness. Indeed, the progress since 1939 in the direction of strengthening the managerial functions of the executive has surpassed the dreams of even the rosiest reformers of the 1930's. Still, even within the framework of executive-legislative conflict, there is much more that can be done.

PARLIAMENTARY ADMINISTRATIVE ORGANIZATION

Given favorable operating conditions, there is no question but that a cabinet form of government meets the ideal criteria of sound administration better than its counterpart, the presidential system. As we have seen, the essence of sound administration is coordination, and a cabinet in a parliamentary form of democracy represents coordination at the highest level. On the other hand, since human beings rarely, if ever, achieve perfection, actual cabinet performance sometimes falls far short of ideal goals. Since policy formulation under the British and French types of cabinet government is considered elsewhere, our concern here will be centered upon cabinets as administrative devices.

The key agency of British government is the Cabinet, and almost all British administrative units are directly responsible to it. A few semi-independent boards and public corporations—of which the British Broadcasting Corporation is the best example—operate outside of the control of the Cabinet, but their number has decreased in recent years. In the early years of the development of the public corporation, the tendency was to give these organizations large autonomous jurisdictions, but when the Labor Government nationalized substantial segments of the economy in the period from 1945 to 1950, the public corporations established to manage the public enterprises, e.g., the National Coal Board, were made responsible to a member of the Cabinet who has to approve all long-range policy determinations. Thus, the government is responsible for what these agencies do, and if the corporations fail to fulfill their tasks, the people can with justice blame the failure on the government in power. The decrease in the autonomy of these organizations has resulted in an increase in responsibility, for under the old system, when things went wrong, the government could disclaim responsibility and the people had no way of taking action against the corporations themselves. Interestingly enough, there has been far less of this economic feudalism, of this turning large segments of the economy over to irresponsible, autonomous experts, in Britain than in the United States. The British apparently do not share the American dream— or nightmare, as it has turned out—of "taking economics out of politics."

Although in recent years there have been sixty or more Ministers in the British Government, only about a third of them are actually members of the Cabinet. The Ministry is thus far larger than the Cabinet. The posts which carry with them Cabinet status also shift from government to government, and, as any realistic analyst would expect, not all Cabinet members are actually of equal power. Under any government, for example, the Chancellor of the Exchequer is far more powerful than most of his colleagues. Since 1916, when Prime Minister Lloyd George established a war Cabinet composed of only five members, four of whom did not head departments, the tendency has been for power to be exercised by an inner group of the Cabinet. During World War II, Winston Churchill established a war Cabinet on the Lloyd George model, and after his return to office in 1951, he again created several "super-Ministers" whose main function was to coordinate functional areas of British life. These "overlords," as they were called colloquially, were chosen from the House of Lords so that they would not be burdened with the pressure of work in Commons, and were given no direct administrative duties in the effort to free their time for the job of policy coordination. There were objections to the fact that these officials were beyond reach of inquiry in Commons, and some felt that they confused the lines of responsibility. In any case, in late 1953, the experiment was abandoned and the "overlordships" abolished. The Labor Government also had an inner Cabinet throughout its years in power, the main members of which were Prime Minister Attlee, Chancellor of the Exchequer Cripps, Foreign Secretary Bevin, and Lord President Morrison.

However, no handful of men, no matter how able, could cope with all the administrative duties of the British Cabinet. Consequently a Cabinet Office and a Secretariat are attached to the Cabinet to collect information of various types needed by the executive or by cabinet committees. In addition, the Cabinet itself is subdivided into various functional committees, and, although the names of these subcommittees are never made public, it is clear that they deal with important economic, planning, defense, and other similar high-level problems.

Since it must be consulted by all ministries on any policy having financial implications, the Treasury is the leading agency for administrative coordination at ministerial and lower levels of British government. Through its control over estimates, it performs a role somewhat analogous to that of the Bureau of the Budget in the United States. As Hiram Stout has pointed out in a recent book, it is indicative of the increasing importance of the Treasury that its staff grew from only 140 persons prior to World War I to more than 1,500 in 1953. The fact that the Prime Minister is nominal head (First Lord) of the Treasury underlines the importance of this organization.

As an administrative device, the French Cabinet suffers by comparison with the British. In the first place, the average life of a Cabinet is about seven months, hardly enough time for the ministers to become even remotely acquainted with the work of their departments. In the second place, there is no French counterpart of the British Treasury, and the Finance Committee of the National Assembly is able to operate in such a fashion as to limit the Cabinet's authority in fiscal matters. In the third place, the necessity of forming coalition Cabinets has meant that coordination inside the Cabinet is difficult to obtain. Ministers are more ambassadors from their own political parties than they are members of a collectivity, the Cabinet. For all these reasons, a French Cabinet resembles a holding company far more than a high command, and the actual direction of administration consequently falls into the hands of the professional civil servants.

The implications of this last point are profound. Many observers have noted that no matter what is happening on the Cabinet level, French government goes on, but they have seldom realized the full meaning of this seeming stability. In effect, with certain rare exceptions, France is governed by an administrative elite which is irresponsible, autonomous, and self-perpetuating. An old Swabian saying asserts that "when the masters divide, the servants rule," and this is an accurate characterization of modern France. But what this means in practice is that much of French administration has been "taken out of politics" in the sense that the administrators are not responsive to the political process or in any real way to the will of the electorate. For example, when Marshal Pétain established his quasi-fascist French government at Vichy in 1941, almost all the top civil servants joined him. Indeed, almost the only top-level civil servant of the Third Republic who refused allegiance to Pétain and fled abroad was Alexis Léger, former Secretary-General of the Ministry of Foreign Affairs. This was a most effective commentary on the degree to which the political ideals of French society had permeated into the bureaucracy.

Another point which should be brought up here is the close resemblance between the French and American systems of administration in the degree to which the legislature could intervene directly in the administrative process. As in the United States, the functional committees of the French legislature formed close ententes with segments of the bureaucracy, but in France the centralizing force of the American Presidency has been totally absent. This paragraph has been put in the past tense because as yet there are no studies which relate whether this is as true under the Fourth Republic as it was under the Third, but what evidence there is would tend to indicate that it is still true. Certainly the conditions which gave rise to this situation have not been modified since the war. Unfortunately, few French political scientists concern themselves with problems of this sort, rather preferring to bask in the sunny fields of political philosophy.

DEPARTMENTAL ORGANIZATION

Having examined the top-level administrative organization in both the presidential and cabinet systems of government, it might now be advisable to look briefly at the organizational forms which operate on lower levels. The first category is the executive department which exists in different forms in all major democracies.

The ten great executive departments of American national government are organized along traditional, hierarchical lines. Justice excepted, the top official is known as the secretary, and in all but two departments, an undersecretary acts as the alter ego of the secretary. The State Department has two undersecretaries, one of whom deals with substantive policy questions while the other acts as the departmental business manager. Each department has one or more assistant secretaries—State has had as many as eight—who are responsible for major areas of the department's work. Close to the top level are grouped various important operating agencies, known as bureaus, offices, services, etc., usually headed by a single officer termed head, chief, or director. For example, in the Department of State may be found the Visa Division, the Passport Division, etc., each headed by a chief. Further down the hierarchical ladder, the subdivisions become increasingly smaller in size. There is little standardization in terminology.

While on paper the basic pattern is similar throughout the ten great departments, there are in fact great dissimilarities. For example, the Department of State is far more integrated in structure and operation than the Department of Agriculture, which is actually a holding company for scores of virtually autonomous operating agencies. The Department of State makes a noble effort at policy coordination which is, with the exception of one or two quasi-autonomous baronies such as the Passport and Visa Divisions, quite successful. On the other hand, there is little top-level coordination in Agriculture, which bears a certain resemblance to the late Holy Roman Empire both in the multitude of independent feudal states within it, and with respect to the Secretary's actual power over his purported vassals.

To an outsider, British departmental organization presents far less symmetry than American. One reason for this is the fact that the departments have varying legal and institutional origins. The Treasury and the Admiralty, for instance, are survivals of ancient times; the Foreign Office traces its beginnings to the King's private secretary; the Board of Trade began as a committee of the Privy Council; and the Ministry of Defense was created by an act of Parliament. In addition, the shape of British administration is constantly changing under the impact of changes in public policy, e.g., the Labor Government's nationalization of the steel industry replaced the regulatory Iron and Steel Board by a public corporation. Nor is the pattern of administration identical in all parts of Britain; Scottish administration in such fields as health and education varies considerably from that in England, and Northern Ireland has achieved a large degree of autonomy in those areas which would in the United States be left to state jurisdiction.

Some British departments are headed by a Minister, but in other cases, authority resides in a board. In the latter event, one member of the board is usually designated president or chairman, and is in practice comparable to a Minister, e.g., the President of the Board of Trade. As is the case in the United States, the department heads are amateurs in most fields except politics, where their competence may be taken for granted. Under the Minister is a Parliamentary secretary, a post which is used to give able young Members of Parliament of the ruling party the opportunity to demonstrate their talents. Thereafter, each department has one or more permanent undersecretaries who are career civil-service officials. From this point on down through the organization, the bureaucratic structure is similar to that in the United States.

The most striking difference between the American and the British departments is not structural; it is the difference in the echelon to which career officials may aspire. In the United States, all secretaries, undersecretaries, and assistant secretaries and many bureau chiefs are appointed by the President with the consent of the Senate. If an administration changes, these men lose their jobs and are replaced by members of the winning party. A professional civil servant cannot hope to be permanently appointed to any job above that of bureau chief, and in many cases even this is beyond his reach. In short, professionalization stops relatively far down the hierarchical ladder, while amateurism extends quite a distance down from the top. By contrast, a British permanent undersecretary is the No. 2 man in his department, *i.e.*, he is just below the Minister. Consequently, in the event of a turnover in British Government, the administration is relatively unaffected and is assured of a large measure of operating continuity. This is not to suggest that British civil servants run the administration in terms of their own views on policy. Although some critics have suggested that the permanent undersecretaries have sabotaged policy changes, there is no evidence to support this claim. On the contrary, the political stability of British Governments gives the Ministers plenty of time to learn their jobs, and the permanent civil servants, whether through dedication or realism, adjust themselves to new situations and policies with remarkable ease.

Under both the Third and Fourth French Republics, the administrative structure has remained highly uniform. Each department is headed by a Minister, who in several of the more important agencies is assisted by an undersecretary. As is the case in Britain, the Minister must be prepared to defend his actions on the floor of the legislature. The departments are subdivided into various bureaus, headed by permanent civil servants. A curious feature of French administration, which has no parallel in Britain or in the United States, is the cabinet of the Minister. Based on the theory that a Minister coming into office will be surrounded by hostile bureaucrats, the Minister's cabinet is composed of intimates and cronies of his own choice. Although they receive no official salaries, these quasi officials often exercise considerable authority and were sometimes in the past rewarded by being slipped into high-salaried civil-service posts—a fact which of course tended to weaken their subsequent loyalty to their supposed chiefs and led them to act as agents within the state for their patrons. To the career civil servants, the Minister's cabinet represents a menace and a species of constant espionage. Although there seems to be little justification for this unique institution, tradition apparently forced the Fourth Republic to continue it.

French administration generally is highly centralized, as it has been with but slight intervals since the French Revolution. When the postwar reorganization was initiated, the Christian Democratic Party (MRP) attempted to insert some decentralizing provisions in the new constitution. Its efforts were almost entirely in vain, and where it did gain a measure of success—as, for instance, in attempting to give local authorities some power over the naming of the prefect, the tremendously powerful local agent of the national government—little seems to have come of the changes. However, centralization is not synonymous with efficiency or with integration, and it would appear that much of the activity undertaken by the central government, *e.g.*, education, could better be left to the local authorities. While British local governmental authorities like the French are in theory completely at the mercy of the central government, the British have wisely devolved large administrative areas to local government, with the House of Commons and the Cabinet merely exercising negative restrictions and setting minimum standards of performance. This the French, imbued with the tradition of centralization as the counterforce to reactionary antirepublican regionalism, have refused to do. In addition, the tradition of bureaucratic autonomy in French government makes real integration at the departmental level difficult to achieve. As has been noted, coordination at the Cabinet level is likewise hard to attain.

NONDEPARTMENTAL ADMINISTRATIVE ORGANIZATIONS

In addition to those functions which are administered by regular departments, the United States, France, and to a lesser degree Britain, all have organizations of an administrative nature outside the regular executive agencies. Indeed, about half of all the agencies in the United States government above the "division" level are located outside the ten regular departments. Some, like the General Services Administration, are patterned after departments, and the change in status of the Federal Security Agency from agency to department in 1953 presented no great administrative problem. There is also a plethora of boards, commissions, and corporations. The most unique bodies are certainly the so-called independent regulatory commissions—the Interstate Commerce Commission, the Federal Trade Commission, the Federal Reserve Board, and six more—which exercise legislative and judicial power, often softened by a "quasi," in addition to executive power and whose members cannot be removed by the President throughout their fairly long stipulated terms of office except on specified grounds.

These commissions, which are often referred to by Congressmen as agents of Congress rather than as parts of the executive branch, and have been accorded a status of this kind by the courts, have created considerable confusion among analysts of American government. Some have suggested that they operate in a distinguishably different fashion from executive agencies. Unfortunately, no such distinction will hold up, for many executive agencies also exercise legislative and judicial authority. The Secretary of Agriculture, for example, exercises functions with respect to crop regulation which are completely analogous to those of an independent regulatory commission. As was suggested earlier, the only sure clue to the existence of an independent regulatory commission, a member of the so-called "headless fourth branch of government," is that the members are appointed for long terms with restrictions on the President's removal power. These organizations cannot be given a niche in the rational administrative universe no matter how much intellectual effort is put into the job; they remain administrative freaks.

In addition to agencies, administrations, commissions, and boards, the Federal government has made extensive use of the corporate device. Once again, there is no uniform pattern of organization. Among the almost eighty government corporations there are some, like the Tennessee Valley Authority, which operate almost wholly independently of the President in their day-to-day operations, while others, like the Commodity Credit Corporation, are located within the jurisdiction of a line department—in the case of the CCC, within that of the Department of Agriculture.

A formidable series of arguments can be mustered on behalf of the government corporation as an administrative device. In essence, as the President's Committee on Administrative Management stated the case, "its peculiar value lies in freedom of operation, flexibility, business efficiency, and opportunity for experimentation." Viewed in perspective, government corporations in the period prior to 1935 possessed a considerable amount of financial autonomy. In general, they were not required to submit annual budgets, were allowed to use their own earnings instead of turning them over to the Treasury, and were not subject to the auditing power of the Comptroller General. In addition, corporations were exempted from civil-service procedures and could purchase and contract without observing the customary government rules.

Since 1935, the freedom of corporations in all these areas has been curtailed. Corporate autonomy outside the regular line departments ran counter both to congressional demands for constant scrutiny of corporate activities and to the increasing interests and effort to concentrate executive responsibility. As a result of plans submitted by the President and approved by Congress under the Reorganization Act of 1939, all corporations then existing except the Tennessee Valley Authority and the Federal Deposit Insurance Corporation were put into line departments or into over-all "agencies." In 1945, Congress again limited the fiscal autonomy of corporations by passing the Government Corporation Control Act.

The government corporation has a long history in Britain, but it was not until after World War II that corporations were given substantial roles to play in the national economy. As in the United States, early British corporations had considerable autonomy, but this tradition has been changed substantially in recent developments. An old-style corporation, for example, the British Broadcasting Corporation, was—and still is—in no real sense responsible to the government of the day. Its directors are appointed for long terms with secure tenure, resembling, in this respect, members of American independent regulatory commissions. However, when the Labor Government beginning in 1945 undertook to nationalize substantial segments of the economy, the corporations that were set up to operate these nationalized industries were given decidedly limited prerogatives. For example, the Gas Act of 1948, which nationalized the production and distribution of gas, provided for the establishment of a government corporation, the Gas Council, and subsidiary Area Gas Boards, the members of which were to hold their positions at the discretion of the Minister of Fuel and Power. Furthermore, the act clearly stated that the

Minister could give these bodies "such directions of a general character as to the exercise and performance . . . of their functions as appear to the Minister to be requisite in the national interest." In short, the powers of these new corporations, while extensive so far as day-to-day operations are concerned, are curbed in the interest of executive responsibility. The feeling among the Laborites seemed to be that national planning was incompatible with the existence of powerful, autonomous corporations. Obviously, the government could not plan coal production in any sensible fashion unless it had the power to enforce its decisions on the National Coal Board, the public corporation which runs the coal industry. However, although the Labor Government took steps to control the policies of the corporations, it did not require them to operate under the rules and fiscal controls of the ordinary government departments. As a result, employees of the corporations remain outside the regular civil service.

The French too have employed public, or mixed public and private, corporations for some time. Indeed, the tradition of state enterprise in France can be traced back to Colbert, the brilliant finance minister to King Louis XIV. The mixed corporation is a phenomenon quite common in Europe, but almost totally nonexistent in Britain, where the Manchester Ship Canal is almost the only example. It consists of a corporation which is owned partly by the state and partly by private individuals. Generally, the state holds a majority interest, as is the case in the *Société Nationale des Chemins de Fer Français*, established in 1937 to run the French railroads, and as is true of the more significant French mixed corporations. Occasionally the state owns a minority interest in an organization, for example, less than 3 per cent of the stock of the *Société Française des Nouvelles-Hébrides* is held by the government.

However, after World War II, the French nationalized a fairly extensive sector of their economy and established straight public corporations to do the job. The main industries taken over by the state were coal, gas and electricity, banking, civil aviation, and the bulk of the insurance business. In addition, some individual factories whose owners had cooperated with the German invader were expropriated as punishment for collaboration. When it came to organizing the governing boards of the corporations, the French introduced a new wrinkle: interest representation. For example, the *Charbonnages de France*, the French equivalent of the British National Coal Board, is composed of eighteen members, six representing the state, six the workers, and six the consumers of coal. There are detailed instructions on how these members are to be chosen, one example of which should suffice us here. The six government representatives are to be selected in the following manner: two by the Minister of Mines, one by the Minister of National Economy, one by the Minister of Finance, one by the Minister of Labor, and one by the Minister of Transport.

Thus the principle of interest representation, which the British sternly rejected, turns the governing boards of nationalized corporations into small replicas of the national legislature, with all manner of viewpoints represented. This may be an excellent formula for a debating society, but it is hardly a realistic fashion of running a coal industry. But there is more to it than that, for, with the exception of the chairman of the board, no member receives any pay for his services, and the director-general, the man who actually directs the day-to-day operation of the industry, is appointed by the state! Any acute and realistic student of public administration could predict the outcome: the board may propose, may denounce, may implore, but the director-general runs the industry, subject only to what ministerial control may exist. The director-general may get memoranda from the board, but he gets his pay from the central government.

Basically, interest representation on these boards is a form of institutionalized irresponsibility, representing a complete rejection, in theory, by the French of the principle of executive control. However, once again, the basic direction of French political institutions, bureaucratized centralism, has proved stronger than the hopes of the reformers. The result is that control over French nationalized industries appears to lie in the hands of the *"fonctionnaires,"* the bureaucrats, rather than with the Cabinet or with the tripartite boards.

CONCLUSIONS

The basic problem of public administration in a democracy is that of responsibility. Obviously, the people cannot themselves elect administrators to fill the many technical jobs that modern government has created, but they have every right to demand that these bureaucrats—and it should be emphasized that this term is not employed as profanity—do the jobs the people want done and do them in the way the people believe appropriate. Aristotle observed that the guest is a better judge of the meal than the cook, and what democrats are trying to devise is a method whereby the guest can implement his views and, if necessary, fire the cook.

The best technique so far devised to achieve this end is executive responsibility. The people choose an executive, either a President in the United States, or, indirectly, a Prime Minister in Britain and France, and hold the executive responsible for what the administration does. Thus, if an administrative policy becomes unbearable, the people can vote in the opposition; while the knowledge that this is possible tends to keep the executive on its toes so far as keeping the administration in line. A good instance of this process at work was the American presidential election of 1952. There had been some conspicuous corruption in the Truman administration which the Republicans capitalized upon in the campaign. In spite of the fact that few people believed that Governor Stevenson would not take strong action against dishonesty in government, the people voted Eisenhower in by a huge majority. This was, at least in part, a punishment meted out to the Democrats for their laxness, and the Republicans were faced with the prospect of devoting themselves to keeping their record clean.

But if this process is going to be effective, the executive must have control over his administration. Let us look at a hypothetical example. Suppose that the Secretary of the United States Treasury announces that unless stringent controls are put upon installment buying, the nation's economy may take a terrible inflationary leap. Two days later, the Chairman of the Federal Reserve Board declares that unless controls are taken from installment buying, a depression will result. To the man on the street, both these pronouncements come from the "government." But only one of them represents executive policy. The voter is patently put in a very confusing position, for inevitably the party in power will quote whichever agency turned out to be right as an indication of its foresightedness! If the people are to judge—and this is the basic premise of democratic government—they must have the evidence before them in a clear fashion. Thus clean, clear lines of administrative responsibility are the basic prerequisite for regulating the regulators.

Chapter 9

TECHNIQUES OF ADMINISTRATIVE MANAGEMENT

In the previous chapter, we attempted an exploration of the dynamics of the administrative process—attempted, as it were, an operational analysis. In this chapter, however, our attention will shift to the perhaps less interesting, but nevertheless, vitally important subject of administrative methods as they exist in the major democracies. This calls for an examination of personnel management, fiscal management, techniques of policy formulation and revision, and the methods of implementing administrative decisions.

PERSONNEL MANAGEMENT

It was once observed that "the men of Massachusetts could make any constitution work," and although we may not share our ancestors' optimism, it remains true that no administrative system can be better than the people who operate it. Thus it becomes vital to the success of administration that competent people be obtained to fill government jobs. The United States government got off to a good start when President Washington made his appointments to office on a nonpartisan merit basis, but the Jeffersonians watered this system down considerably by keeping most earlier appointees in office but allocating new jobs to their political supporters. During the period from 1816 to 1828, the so-called "Era of Good Feelings," when the nation had for all intents and purposes a one-party system, considerable administrative stability developed and patronage presented few problems. However, in the states, particularly the Northern states, the slogan "To the victor belong the spoils" was gaining strong support, with the result that there developed a close relationship between party and bureaucracy.

With the accession to power of President Jackson in 1829, the national scene quickly changed. Believing in rotation of office as a matter of democratic principle, Jackson soon put his beliefs into practice. In a message to Congress in December, 1829, the President declared: "The duties of all public officers are, or at least admit of being made, so plain and simple that men of intelligence may readily qualify themselves for their performance; and I can not but believe that more is lost by the long continuance of men in office than is generally

261

to be gained by their experience." The President therefore requested Congress legally to limit tenure in Federal office to four years.

That Jackson's philosophy—a clear repudiation of the earlier tradition that there was a need for continuance in office of trained, experienced government employees—was widely approved throughout the nation seems beyond question, but the results were serious and of long duration. Obviously under conditions of this sort, administrative stability becomes a will-o'-the-wisp. The consequences were soon appreciated by Secretaries of State, Secretaries of War, and other administrators charged with obtaining efficient government, but despite repeated pious pledges of reform in the platforms of the major parties, it was not until 1883 that Congress took remedial action. Although the Pendleton Act of 1883 applied to only a few thousand positions in Federal service, it supplied the foundation for the present merit system which, since the Ramspeck Act of 1940, regulates the employment of virtually all Federal employees. The merit system does not, and should not, protect the top, so-called "policy-making," administrators such as the secretaries and undersecretaries, but there is some difference of opinion as to which positions are in fact policy-making. The Eisenhower administration, maintaining that the Democrats had brought many policy-making jobs under civil-service protection in order to keep their men in office in the event of a change in administration, took action in 1953 to strip several thousand high civil servants of their jobs. This action was bitterly condemned by the Democrats, who claimed it was a first step toward a return to the spoils system, while Republicans generally maintained that administration control over these positions was essential to obtain responsibility in the bureaucracy. There is some justice in both claims, for the principle of merit appointment with tenure tends to conflict at many points with the principle of administrative responsibility, and one's decision between the two is likely to be colored by whether it is his party which is taking action to ensure administrative responsibility to the American people or the opposition party which is undermining good government. The only Federal agency which is wholly exempt from the provisions of the Ramspeck Act is the Tennessee Valley Authority, which has a personnel system of its own.

In the states, the situation is much less satisfactory, nor can it be said that more than a few cities have really adopted a merit system of appointment. However, the worst area from the personnel point of view is archaic American county government, where the traditional spoils system remains nearly unscathed by the reform movements of the last seventy-five years.

Neither Britain nor France has ever had anything on a national scale approaching the Jacksonian spoils system. During the eighteenth and first half of the nineteenth centuries, the British civil service was looked upon largely as the private preserve of the aristocracy. In a sense, it was a form of institutionalized unemployment characterized by a good deal of incompetence, but not on a party basis. In 1855, a Civil Service Commission was created, but it was not until after 1870 that appointment based on competitive examination became the rule.

French development took a different form. In the early days of the Third Republic, office was frequently given to friends and neighbors of leading politicians. However, this was not done on any large-scale party basis for the excellent reason that no one party was ever in a position to dominate the scene. Nor was there any extensive application of the doctrine "Sweep the rascals out," since in a multiparty system it was difficult to agree on the identity of the rascals. In contrast to Britain and the United States, France did not centralize its personnel system under a civil-service commission. Gradually nearly all departments have been brought under various plans of competitive recruitment. A general law of Oct. 19, 1946, established the recent framework within which the departments operate in selection, but there is still a wide diversity of technique throughout the administration.

Only in the United States, of all the great democracies, is it still seriously maintained that political party workers should be repaid for their services from the public treasury. Why is this the case? One explanation is financial in nature; the American election system is staggeringly expensive. Although contributions can usually be obtained in presidential elections, relatively few persons contribute money for local party work. Yet the funds must come from somewhere, and one good source is to put party workers on the government payroll —and it should be emphasized here that this is largely on the state and local level. After the Democrats took control of the Philadelphia city government in 1950, they discovered numerous sewer inspectors, inspectors of weights and measures, and other employees who had not even put in an appearance at their jobs for years. Some were found to be holding jobs in private employment at the same time they were carried on the city payroll, the implication being that their remuneration from the city went directly into the party treasury.

It is often argued, with much justice, that while civic-minded citizens will contribute money and energy to dramatic and high-level political contests, they tend to stay home when the issues seem dull and drab, as is the case in most local elections. But someone must ring doorbells, engage in canvassing, organize the electorate, and it often turns out that only persons holding sinecures can take the time for these vital but boring political chores. A final explanation is that American politics tends to be singularly devoid of ideological considerations—much more so, in fact, at the state and local level than at the presidential. When an issue can be posed in ideological terms, there is usually little difficulty in rallying supporters who will devote a tremendous amount of time and energy to "the Cause." This is certainly the case in France and Italy, and is true to a lesser extent in Britain. In the United States, people of principle all too often devote their talents to nonpartisan political groups such as the

League of Women Voters, to the exclusion of party work. Thus while the relationship between party and bureaucracy presents problems everywhere, these problems are most sharply etched in the United States.

From this discussion it is apparent that a spoils system is thoroughly incompatible with scientific personnel management. Gradually, even at state and local levels of government in the United States, the personnel-management school is gaining ground, and in the long run—although it may be a very long run—will probably win the day from the spoilsmen.

THE DEVELOPMENT OF PERSONNEL MANAGEMENT

One of the basic elements of personnel management is the presence of a central personnel agency. Prior to 1883, each department in the United States government handled its own personnel problems, subject only to a few general statutes. With the passage of the Pendleton Act, the Civil Service Commission was created, and with it came the concept that appointments to office should be based on competitive examination for all but the top-level government employees. Today this three-member bipartisan Commission has far more extensive responsibilities than was originally the case. In addition to giving examinations and preparing lists of persons eligible for appointment, the Commission also classifies positions in terms of the degree of skill required to perform them, establishes procedures governing dismissal from service, and keeps an elaborate record system up to date. With several thousand persons in its employ, the Commission has fourteen regional offices and numerous branch offices throughout the country.

By the terms of an Executive order of 1938, each department and major independent establishment was required to set up a personnel office of its own, and to coordinate the work of the Commission, the department personnel officers, and the Bureau of the Budget, a Federal Personnel Council was established, which is now attached to the Commission. But elaborate though the Federal personnel management system has become, it has still failed to satisfy its numerous critics. Both the President's Committee on Administrative Management and the Hoover Commission recommended changes.

In 1937, the President's Committee suggested that the Civil Service Commission be replaced by a single administrator responsible to the President. Thus, along with the Bureau of the Budget and the National Resources Planning Board, the national personnel organization would have constituted one of the three administrative aids to the President. The committee also recommended the creation of a personnel board, with advisory powers only, to serve as the "watchdog" of the merit system. Commissions and boards, the committee said, were unsuitable for administrative work; rather they should be employed only for advisory, quasi-legislative, or quasi-judicial functions.

Congress, traditionally hostile to measures giving the President increased control over the bureaucracy, rejected this proposal. Nor did the Hoover Commission revive the idea of a single administrator, although it did recommend a number of changes in personnel management, notably the concentration of the Commission's administrative power in the hands of a chairman and the decentralization of recruiting. While rejecting some of these suggestions, Congress did agree to the creation of the post of chairman with full administrative powers. In the meantime, the recruitment of employees has more and more been entrusted to the departments and agencies themselves.

During World War II, formal procedures were waived because of the desperate need to recruit Federal employees in a hurry, but the merit system was not abandoned. Those recruited in this expeditious fashion were accorded only temporary status for the duration of the emergency. Following the termination of the conflict, President Truman ordered the reinstitution of normal standards. Thus today, with the exception of officials appointed by the President with the consent of the Senate, the merit system includes virtually all Federal civil servants. Viewed in the perspective of seventy-five years, this represents a remarkable achievement.

When compared to the United States, Britain has had, since 1870, fewer spectacular battles in building up a central personnel agency. At the same time, the steps in the British progression have been fairly analogous with those in the United States. Today, the chief difference lies in the great strength of the Treasury as a fiscal and personnel control agency when contrasted with the American establishment.

Like the United States, Britain has a Civil Service Commission. The three commissioners are appointed by the Crown after consultation with the Treasury and hold office indefinitely—which, in practice, means until eligible for retirement. Since the commissioners are almost always drawn from the permanent civil service and have had no political experience, they are not required to represent different political parties. The principal business of the Commission is examination and certification, for actual appointments are made by the operating departments, subject to Treasury approval. Classification, salary, in fact everything but discipline, comes under Treasury control. The Permanent Secretary of the Treasury is the highest paid individual in the British civil service and bears the title "Head of the Civil Service." The Treasury has no control over local government service. Moreover, it has no control over employees of public corporations, since they do not technically fall into the category of civil servants. Such employees are recruited directly by the corporations which, subject to over-all governmental controls, also handle such matters as wages, hours, and size of establishment. The Tennessee Valley Authority in the United States operates in closely analogous fashion. Each ministry has its own personnel office, so that the central and departmental personnel agencies are roughly similar to those in the United States.

In France the tradition has been for each department to establish its own criteria for appointment and administer an appropriate examination to competitors for office. At the top level, these examinations were exceptionally difficult and drew strong competition, particularly from graduates of the law schools. Since graduates of these same schools, risen to high posts in the administration, were generally responsible for making up and administering the examinations, it was often charged that the examinations tended to favor candidates with similar backgrounds. Thus graduates of the *École Polytechnique* tended to dominate technical positions and to load the competitive examinations for such jobs in such a fashion that more graduates of the school joined them in office. But this is more evidence of egotism than it is of corruption, and there appears to be little political patronage in the French civil service today. Since the war, the French have innovated top-level recruitment by establishing a National School of Administration which combines academic training with on-the-job experience over a three-year period. Admission is on a severely competitive basis. This school may serve to centralize recruitment for top jobs, but all other positions are still filled on a decentralized basis.

RECRUITMENT AND CAREER SERVICE

Despite the structural similarities between the American and other personnel organizations, vast differences occur in the areas of recruitment and career services. At base, these differences reflect opposed philosophies which, in turn, reflect differing national traditions. Both in Britain and on the Continent, special privileges surround, to use Leonard White's phrase, "career groups in general administration." A brief contrast of American with British experience will be helpful in illustrating this wide philosophical divergence.

In Britain, as in the European democracies, a career in general administration embodies several principles, including a university background in law, literature, the humanities, or philosophy; direct recruitment to the top level and assignment to responsible duties at an early stage in one's career; and promotion on merit, possibly to a position of permanent secretary. To illustrate this process in specific terms, let us examine the British "administrative class." If he is between twenty-one and twenty-four years of age and has received a university degree, a candidate is eligible to take the examinations given by the Civil Service Commission. Little or no specialization is required on the examinations, since the objective is to recruit "generalists" who are capable of further development. The examinations for February, 1949, for instance, allowed two hours for an essay on any one of such questions as: "War is an extension of politics. Discuss"; "Consider the view that the artist, no less than the scientist, deserves well of the State"; and "Is it true that goodness consists simply in concern for human welfare?" Other parts of the same examination required a condensation of a 1,200-word excerpt from John Stuart Mill, the writing of a rebuttal to a printed speech, or a treatment of the similarities and differences in two poems.

The situation in Britain is similar to that in France in at least this respect:

the examiners themselves are members of the university faculties which furnish the candidates. Thus this process of recruitment has tended to take on some of the characteristics of a closed corporation. Partly because of complaints on this score, but to a larger extent because of the tremendously expanded requirements for "generalists" immediately after World War II, an alternative method of recruitment was devised known as "Method II" to distinguish it from "Method I" above. Under this new plan, anyone with a first- or second-class honors degree from a university may take a qualifying examination. If successful, the candidate is then given an intensive battery of tests, many of the problem-solving type, at a country manor during an extended week end. Method II, originally devised during the war to choose military officer candidates, has proved sufficiently successful to be retained as a permanent technique. At one time it was virtually impossible for anyone to enter the administrative class from a lower level of the civil service, but the Labor Government recently instituted some reforms in this area. However, such movement up the ladder is still highly uncommon.

Although membership in the administrative class carries with it assignment to responsible positions, promotion within the class tends to be quite slow for the average member. While exceptionally brilliant men have moved up rapidly, a 1938 analysis showed that the average assistant secretary, the median grade two above the bottom and two below the top, had been in service over twenty-three years. With the great expansion since the war, this time in grade may have been cut down somewhat. Promotion to the top ranks of permanent secretary and deputy secretary is based on ability, but this ability is judged largely by the so-called "undersecretaries' ring," the informal group of top civil servants who advise the Head of the Civil Service. Consequently, while there is little question but that the men promoted to top positions are able, they tend to be very much of a pattern. No imaginative genius could hope to slip through this screening process built around the principle of conformity.

Beneath the administrative class, and separated from it by a virtually watertight bulkhead, is the executive class. This group is recruited at the age level of eighteen to nineteen from persons with a secondary-school education. Next comes the clerical class, and at the bottom is the clerical-assistant class. In addition, there is a professional, technical, and scientific class, recruited on the basis of much more specific examinations following technical training.

In contrast, nearly all the 1,700 or more examinations administered by the United States Civil Service Commission are technical in nature, are aimed at specific positions, and are intended to measure qualifications for immediate assignment rather than capacity. Under such circumstances, it is difficult to build up career services, although such do exist in such technical areas as the Forest Service and the Public Health Service. The only notable career group recruited on anything like the British basis is the Foreign Service of the Department of State. Since the Rogers Act of 1924, examinations for the Foreign

Service stress general background and potential ability rather than concrete mastery of details. Furthermore, since 1934, the Civil Service Commission has established a few registers intended to recruit persons of general ability and college education, for example, those for Junior Professional Assistant and Junior Management Assistant, and a substantial number of recruits has been obtained in this fashion with excellent results.

There is one notable aspect of the American civil service which deserves mention here: its fluidity. As Herman Somers has pointed out in a significant analysis, there is a high degree of interchange between government and private employment, and the United States frequently "borrows" businessmen, tradeunionists, or scholars for temporary positions in government. Somers makes note of the fact that there are far fewer career Foreign Service officers representing the United States abroad than there are citizens from various walks of life who have been given special, generally temporary, assignments, and he suggests that the significance of this fluidity is far-reaching. In effect, it brings the public and the bureaucracy into far closer contact than is the case in Britain or France, gives a great many influential businessmen and others experience in and an understanding of administration, and suppresses the development of a professional class of civil servants set apart from the public.

Beyond doubt, the United States will not, and probably should not, imitate the British system of recruitment, at least not without substantial modifications. At the same time, some reforms of the present system of recruitment seem in order. For example, if examinations were more closely geared to school and college curriculums, instead of the present emphasis on technical knowledge and experience, better results might be expected. The question of veterans' preference, first introduced after the Civil War, also deserves reconsideration. Under a 1944 statute, honorably discharged service personnel with service-connected disabilities receive a 10-point bonus on examinations, in certain lower-paid positions all such veterans who get at least 70 on the examination go to the head of the registers, and all honorably discharged veterans with no disabilities get a 5-point bonus and precedence over nonveterans with equal ratings. Thus a disabled veteran who receives 82 on his examination takes appointment preference over any nonveteran who received less than 93, and it may be questioned whether the best interests of the government are served by this policy.

But it should not be assumed that all Britons are ecstatic about their civil service. On the contrary, the British system has come in for some searching criticism. At one time, the charge was repeatedly made—particularly by the Laborites—that the administrative class, composed as it was primarily of Oxford and Cambridge graduates, rested on family and money. There is less substance to this charge today, since most university students in Britain are now given substantial assistance through government grants and scholarships. But perplexing new problems have arisen. At the upper echelons of government, clashes between members of the administrative class and members of the professional, technical, and scientific class are becoming more common. On occasion, the government unquestionably needs a good economist on top in preference to a man who forty years ago took first-degree honors in Greek at Oxford. As administrative work becomes ever more specialized and technical in nature, there appear to be limits to what untrained generalists can accomplish. While the British have developed a genuine career service which attracts able recruits, they have not solved the conflict between "hierarchy" and "specialty," alluded to in the previous chapter. The root of the matter is a basic change in the nature of governmental activities. A century ago, the duties of government were comparable to those of a referee, but at present the British government must act not only as referee but also as coach, trainer, and manager. It is likely that the ideal temperament and training of a referee is quite different from that of a coach or manager. At least, the problem centers around the reconciliation of these two roles.

UNIONS IN PUBLIC SERVICE

Sterling Spero pointed out in 1948 that one out of every ten workers in the United States is employed in the public service, and that more than 1 million civil servants belong to some sort of employee organization. This listing does, of course, include all levels of American government, but the total remains impressive.

Generally governments in their capacities as employers have forbidden the strike as an instrument of employee bargaining. On the other hand, the right of employees to organize into protective associations is generally conceded. In 1902, President Theodore Roosevelt forbade by Executive order Federal employees to attempt to influence Congress except through hierarchical channels, but in 1912, the Lloyd–La Follette Act removed this restriction and not only recognized the right of association, but also permitted Federal employees to affiliate with outside labor organizations.

Although the courts have long held it illegal to strike against the sovereign, the Taft-Hartley Act of 1947 contained a provision reinforcing this common-law rule, and provided further that any government employee participating in a strike loses his job and cannot be reemployed by the government for three years. However, aside from seized industries, notably coal, the Federal government has never been plagued with strikes, either of economic or political origin, such as have occurred continually in France and Italy. Outside the industrial and postal services, employee organization in the national government is weak. Printers, plumbers, and other skilled workers employed by the government have belonged to the American Federation of Labor for generations.

The potential conflict between the competing claims of loyalty to the sovereign state and labor solidarity, although illustrated by the Boston police strike of 1919, has rarely burst into reality in this country. In contrast, the

British general strike of 1926 squarely posed this problem for thousands of unionized British civil servants. Although government employees did not participate in this strike in any numbers, they made their sympathies with the strikers perfectly clear. As a result, Parliament passed a law in 1927 which prohibited government workers from belonging to outside unions. In 1946, partly to fulfill its campaign promise, and partly to ensure trade-union support for future nationalization of industry, the Labor Government repealed this statute. In the 1951 election campaign the Conservatives went on record to the effect that, if successful, they would not reinstitute the 1927 measure.

Legislation of the type of the Trade Disputes Act of 1927 is negative in nature. A much more constructive approach to the problems raised by the government as employer is embodied in the work of the Whitley Councils. Since 1919, the British have employed these councils to foster collective bargaining between high-ranking government officials and the rank and file or "staff." At the top, there is a National Whitley Council which concerns itself almost entirely with general problems. About seventy departments have departmental councils, and since it is at this level that most of the actual bargaining is performed, these councils do most of the actual work. In the event that there is a disagreement over wages, that is, if staff and the Treasury cannot agree, there is recourse to arbitration. For nonindustrial personnel, wage disagreements are submitted to the Civil Service Arbitration Tribunal; for industrial personnel, to the Industrial Court. Decisions of these labor courts are binding unless overruled by Parliament.

In nationalized industries entirely different problems arise. Although workers have continued to remain in the same unions and are not civil servants in the technical sense, they find that the government is in a much stronger bargaining position than any former individual employer enjoyed. Also, the interests of the union and the government may differ as, for example, in 1952 when Italian coal miners had to be sent back home when British miners refused to work alongside them. While the British miners wanted to keep coal mining as a preserve for British labor, the Government, as owner of the mines and with the general welfare in mind, strove to produce more coal.

While the policy of some British unions in nationalized industries has on occasion posed problems affecting British economic stability, the same unions offer no political threat to the government. In France the picture is much more complex. As in other Western European democracies, the current struggle among Catholics, Socialists, and Communists for control over labor organizations is by no means confined to nationalized industries, but the postwar French nationalization and the communist domination of the leading trade-union federations have created broad new problems, both of economics and of ideology. At the same time, the French inheritance of union militancy has always, even in more traditional areas, proved of constant embarrassment to the government. Beginning in 1894, French law permitted state railway employees to organize. However, the right to organize was not construed as the right to employ the strike weapon, as was illustrated when a nationwide strike on the railroads in 1909 resulted in Premier Briand's calling the strikers into uniform, thus breaking the strike. Government functionaries worked for over half a century to gain full recognition for their unions, but this was not granted until October, 1946. The main problem plaguing the contemporary French labor scene is the political strike, usually of communist inspiration. Fortunately, most French trade-unionists have little enthusiasm for the political strike, so that even workers affiliated with communist-dominated trade-unions tend to be reluctant when it comes to leaving their jobs to protest a North Atlantic Treaty, or whatever the current bête noire of the party leadership may be. The last successful, or at least widespread, *political* strikes in France occurred in March of 1948 and led the government to pass a law forbidding the use of the strike weapon for political purposes. Recently a large percentage of the French public, including trade-unionists, appeared to have supported the successful efforts of the Pinay Government to smash a communist-inspired general strike which was called following the arrest of Jacques Duclos in 1952 on the charge of endangering the security of the state. The 1953 strike wave, while it had definite political overtones, was essentially founded on economic grievances.

LOYALTY

There are three principal approaches to the problem of disloyalty in government service. First, a government may sit idly by and do nothing. This was essentially the course followed by the Third Republic in the period before World War II. German penetration into high places went unchecked, a fact which undoubtedly contributed to the success of the Nazi attack on France in 1940. Second, a government may proceed with discretion to discharge or to transfer from sensitive agencies persons whose disloyalty has been proved. Since 1948, Britain has empowered Ministers to transfer or to suspend Communists, but only after a secret hearing. No publicity is given to the Minister's actions. Third, an over-all approach may be employed, in which all civil servants are presumed to be capable of guilt until proved innocent. It is this approach which has been used in the United States.

Among the influences shaping the Federal government's program, the most important is the work of the House Committee on Un-American Activities. Beginning in 1938, this committee gradually convinced the House, and, eventually, large segments of the public, that the government had been infiltrated by subversive employees. Congress specified in the Hatch Act of 1939 that no funds should be paid to any employee who was a member of any organization advocating the violent overthrow of the American government, and the Civil Service Commission incorporated this rule into its administrative regulations. Finally, on the recommendations of President Truman's Temporary Commission on Employee Loyalty, various criteria were established for determining loyalty. These criteria were incorporated in Executive Order 9835 of Mar. 22, 1947.

Under the terms of this order, the Attorney General was required to list all subversive organizations, membership in any one of which was to be considered prima facie evidence of disloyalty. In addition, the Federal Bureau of Investigation, which had earlier completed a check on all government employees, was ordered to check upon the loyalty of all new appointees. A person found by his department to be a poor loyalty or security risk—the latter category including employees who, while not held disloyal, were believed because of drunkenness or other personal failings to be potential disclosers of secrets—could appeal this decision to a departmental appeal board, and a Loyalty Review Board was set up by the Civil Service Commission to act as the court of last resort. A final administrative determination of disloyalty could, of course, be appealed to the judiciary, but the Federal courts, following the lead of the Supreme Court, have shown little willingness to interfere with the techniques of administrative screening. However, this system of appeals was not applicable to the so-called "sensitive agencies"—State Department, Atomic Energy Commission, and Department of Defense—which could discharge a person as a poor risk without a hearing or any right of appeal. The Eisenhower administration modified this system somewhat by abolishing the Loyalty Review Board, increasing the authority of agency heads in matters of personnel security, and eliminating the distinction between loyalty and security risks.

Although only a handful of persons were actually dismissed under the loyalty program from 1947 to 1953, with a larger group resigning while under investigation, the broad impact of the program on the Federal service was unquestionably bad. While few would question the right of the government to demand loyalty from its employees, the basic problem is the proper definition of loyalty and disloyalty, and the establishment of procedures to be used in making decisions in individual cases. For example, persons accused of disloyalty are not necessarily presented with the evidence that had been used to prepare the accusation. The purpose of this is to protect FBI informants from exposure, a justification not in itself without merit, but one which nonetheless runs contrary to the basic principle of Anglo-American justice that the accused has the right to full examination of the evidence against him. Actions of individual departments, many of them reversed on appeal by loyalty review boards, have frequently seemed to be based on an identification of loyalty and conformity, and, however unjustifiably, the word has gotten around among the civil servants that ideas are dangerous. Thus, although the actual firings have been few, the psychological impact of the loyalty program on the Federal bureaucracy has been profound and deleterious. Even if one has a perfectly clear conscience, a rare phenomenon anywhere, it is difficult to engage in constructive work in an atmosphere of espionage and suspicion.

In addition, the Federal loyalty program established a precedent which was soon followed by many states and cities, which tended to build their loyalty programs upon foundations even less secure. Not to be outdone in vigilance, various private industries, *e.g.*, radio, motion pictures, and television, in effect instituted their own private programs directed toward weeding out subversives. The basic problem here as in government was how to define and identify a "subversive." In actual fact, some persons whose only sin was nonconformity were relieved of their employment in private industry. Amateur Communist hunters who could not distinguish a Communist from a unicorn tended to run roughshod over individuals accused of communist sympathies.

While the threat of communist infiltration, particularly in sensitive government agencies and in industries engaged in secret defense work, is a real one, the job of spotting communist agents is not one for amateurs. While it is often said that amateurs, in the sense we are using the word here, brought Alger Hiss to justice, it must be remembered that Whittaker Chambers gave evidence to the amateurs which he had previously withheld from the professionals. If Chambers had turned over the "pumpkin papers" to the FBI, the same end could have been attained with much less furor. Furthermore, it may be suggested that those who hurl loose charges of communist affiliation may, by creating an atmosphere of suspicion and confusion, be aiding the Communists more than they hinder them.

FISCAL MANAGEMENT

Administration and finance are so integrally interwoven that it is not possible to separate them. The association is as close as that between administration and legislation. Since all administration requires funds, and since most laws require funds for execution and enforcement, finances play a key role in the governmental process. Since most of the field of public finance lies beyond the scope of this book, the following paragraphs are limited to the organization of fiscal management. More specifically, our interest lies in the organization of the executive in this area.

As was pointed out in the preceding chapter, fiscal control is a vital executive function. In line with the world-wide trend toward the enhancement of executive authority, it is not strange to find that in all democratic governments the powers of executives over the fiscal process have been steadily increased. The development has not, however, been uniform, but has varied with each country, its needs and its conditions.

As an inheritance from British tradition at the time of the American Revolution, it was quite predictable that the American Congress would exercise most of the powers in the fiscal area. Indeed, in creating the Treasury Department, Congress recognized a peculiar relationship between that agency and itself. The first Secretary of the Treasury, Alexander Hamilton, looked upon his job as approximating that of the British Prime Minister, and planned to report in person to Congress on his activities. Congress, however, already jealous of its prerogatives, refused the Secretary the right to appear in person, and Hamilton's hopes were among the first sacrificed on the altar of executive-legislative rivalry. At the same time, in states and cities, as well as the Federal government, the executive possessed little fiscal authority. Legislative bodies granted money directly to the spending agencies without executive intervention. Especially in the states it was common to create tax commissions and debt commissions which were in no sense coordinated with each other or with the already established financial agencies. In this respect the record of the Federal government has been generally superior to that of the American states and cities, although both the depression and post–World War II inflation caused the latter to renew their efforts to centralize fiscal administration.

Before 1921, and the passage of the Budget and Accounting Act, Federal finances were handled in a haphazard manner. As many as nine committees in the House and fifteen in the Senate had authority to draft appropriation bills. With no coordination, bills originating in the executive branch were collected and turned over to Congress. The congressional committees paid little or no attention to over-all spending ceilings, and cared little for the state of the Treasury. By the Budget and Accounting Act the United States became the last great democracy to establish an executive budgetary system. It was able to postpone the obvious for so long only because it was the richest of the democracies, but the expenses of World War I forced the adoption of a more methodical approach.

As was noted earlier, this act established the Bureau of the Budget, with authority not only to prepare an executive budget, but also to control departmental expenditures after Congress had voted appropriations. While the mechanics of the process are too technical to be gone into in detail, the following steps illustrate in outline form what is done: By September 15 of every year, each agency under the executive branch must submit a proposed estimate of expenses for the next fiscal year to the Bureau. The fiscal officers of the agencies are then required, in periodic conferences, to justify their estimates to the Bureau. While the Director of the Bureau is given considerable discretion by the President, he must, of course, confer with his chief on the most substantial questions. The Secretary of the Treasury collects data on expected revenues and makes any recommendations on changes in the tax laws. When all the information has been secured, about the first of December, the officials of the Bureau prepare a budget of perhaps 1,500 pages. After this bulky document has received the approval of the President, it is ready for him to transmit to Congress during the first week of January. The point to this procedure is that the President's recommendations are all-inclusive, covering expenditures, revenues, and proposals for new revenue measures.

In order to adapt its procedure to the new budgeting method, Congress in 1920 reorganized the committee structure for handling appropriations. From that time on, only one appropriations committee in each house received appropriation bills, while revenue measures were channeled to another single committee in each chamber. Although this procedure represented some improvement over previous practice, the appropriations committees soon divided into numerous subcommittees so that Congress was still not provided with a review of the whole budget at one time or the opportunity to weigh the needs of one program against the needs of another. In the hope of improving this procedure further, the La Follette–Monroney Act of 1946 provided for a huge joint committee consisting of both appropriations and both revenue committees, charged with the preparation of a legislative budget setting a ceiling on expenditures. This legislative budget was to be prepared by February 15 of each year, but in practice, Congress has not yet achieved this objective.

While the budgetary system has proved its worth, there is still room for improvement. Under prodding by the Hoover Commission, the Congress and the President established a "performance budget." As embodied in the budget presented for the first time in 1950 in January, this document separated ordinary from capital expenditures and also listed expenditures by functions instead of by departments. Under such a performance budget, it is possible to discover exactly how much money is being appropriated for each function of government, while under the old system some money for a department might have been included in many varying sections. To take the Hoover Commission's example, it was formerly next to impossible to determine the requested expenditures for the Bethesda Naval Hospital, while today this information can be gained in a moment. More helpful in the long run would be the adoption by Congress of the principle—employed in Britain—that it would not appropriate money except on request by the executive. By constitutional amendment, the President could also be given the power to veto specific items of appropriation bills, a reform which, if the experience of most of the states where governors have this power is any indication, would undoubtedly save millions of dollars by preventing needless expenditures.

While generally in accord with the budgetary system set up by the 1921 legislation, the President's Committee on Administrative Management recommended in 1937 that the Bureau of the Budget give more attention to supervising departmental spending. This suggestion has to a large extent been adopted. At the present time, there remain only two major weak links in the fiscal process. The first of these is the failure of Congress to coordinate expenditures with revenues, as it agreed to do in 1946; the second is the somewhat ambiguous position of the General Accounting Office.

An agency of Congress, the General Accounting Office, incurred the wrath of the New Deal when its director, the Comptroller General, disallowed various expenditures made by the New Deal agencies. The ground for disallowal was that Congress had not appropriated funds for the specific purposes for which money had been spent. In particular, the battle between the General Accounting Office and the Tennessee Valley Authority was far-ranging and notably bitter. The main difficulty arose from the fact that in making his decisions the Comptroller General refused to accept the decisions of Federal courts or of the Attorney General as precedents for his own holdings. The President's Committee recommended abolition of the General Accounting Office, the transfer of the preauditing functions to the Treasury, and the creation of a new agency for postauditing. Nothing came of these proposals, but they were repeated before the Hoover Commission a decade later. That commission urged retention of the General Accounting Office but favored increasing the executive authority in the area of preauditing and in the prescribing of accounting forms. These latter functions were to be performed in the Treasury Department. Some, but not all, of the Hoover Commission's specific recommendations for change were adopted.

At the heart of the controversy is the question as to the appropriate functions of an auditor. In commercial usage, auditing is done by outside experts who check the corporation's books and report to the board of directors. In a very real way, this constitutes a check on the financial integrity of the corporation's officers. It is generally agreed that the General Accounting Office should perform this function and should report to its principal—Congress—any discrepancies. At the same time, to pursue the commercial analogy, the actual financial controlling of a corporation's affairs is an executive function. The comptroller is responsible, along with the president and other officers, to the board of directors. What he does is make sure the funds are being spent in accordance with over-all instructions, and that the operating departments are being held strictly to their allotments. The difficulty with the General Accounting Office is that, in spite of recent reforms, it violates this principle by not only checking up on how executive agencies spend their funds, but also prescribing in detail the accounting forms and techniques to be employed by these agencies. The General Accounting Office also has the essentially judicial function of determining whether proposed expenditures fall within the allowed jurisdiction of the agency, but has never, in exercising this function, utilized judicial procedures or even applied the rule of *stare decisis* with respect to its own decisions. Thus every questioned action of an administrative agency has been decided upon its individual merits by the Comptroller General, and the agencies are never sure in advance what line of reasoning this officer will follow. Therefore the Comptroller General and the General Accounting Office reach into the heart of the administrative process and challenge administrators for control over their departments. The Comptroller General is considered by many experts on American politics as the second most powerful individual in the government—exceeded in power only by the President.

In its actual operations, the General Accounting Office has been more of an accounting than an auditing agency, despite the declared intention of Congress in 1921. By concentrating more on legality than auditing, it has tended to hamper administration. In the long run, the blame for the General Accounting Office's unsatisfactory performance rests largely on Congress itself. This is because the Comptroller General has been assigned two incompatible functions—auditing and accounting—and also because Congress has created no agency within itself to which the General Accounting Office can report. As a result of the Hoover Commission's recommendations, two minor improvements were noted: the departments were given more extensive accounting functions, subject to supervision from the General Accounting Office; and auditing was thereafter to be performed in the field where the records and vouchers had accumulated rather than in the central office of the General Accounting Office.

It is in the area of fiscal management that the American system of built-in legislative-executive hostility is seen to its worst advantage. As has been noted before, in Britain the budget is prepared by the Treasury and is accepted by the House of Commons as a matter of confidence in the Government. In preparing the annual budget, the Treasury operates in about the same manner as the Bureau of the Budget in the United States. In the United States, a member of Congress may force the executive department to justify its proposed expenditures and may, with the aid of like-minded friends, disrupt budgetary proceedings to an almost unbelievable extent. The major objection to the British system of financial legislation is that the ordinary member of Parliament cannot be well informed on what is going on. While a British budget, or "Supply Bill," as it is called, will contain enormous and far-reaching policy decisions, it will be put through the House of Commons by a well-oiled Government majority in twenty days. Once funds have been appropriated, the Treasury supervises expenditures. Finally, the Comptroller and Auditor General, enjoying virtually the independence of a judge, reports irregularities to the Treasury and, in an annual report, to the Committee on Public Accounts of the House of Commons. Chaired by a leader of the Opposition, this committee normally performs its duties with commendable fairness. Throughout the British Commonwealth, the organization for fiscal management is based on British precedent. The chief exception lies in the relative weakness of ministers of finance when contrasted with the British Treasury.

As might be expected, French fiscal management is less effectively organized than British. Although the Ministry of Finance is comparatively strong, it lacks the power of the British Treasury or of the American Bureau of the Budget to curtail expenditures. Legislative interference with the budget, as presented, occurs frequently. The Finance Committee of the National Assembly exercises powers over executive recommendations that resemble the procedure in the American Congress. In addition, the Minister himself does not have powers comparable to those of the Chancellor of the Exchequer or to the director of the American Bureau of the Budget in terms of his influence over administrative officials. Once appropriations have been made, the ministry possesses but little supervisory authority, and there is no effective system of preauditing or of controlling. A Court of Accounts performs general auditing duties and has the power to report to the National Assembly. In retrospect, it seems generally agreed that the Court is more effective today than it was under the Third Republic.

INTERNAL MANAGEMENT

Fiscal and personnel management are not objectives in themselves; they are tools for the accomplishment of purposes defined by statute or by Executive order. What is to be accomplished by an administrative agency, and how it is to be accomplished, become the concerns of internal management. W. Brooke Graves has identified the various components of internal management control as planning, organizational production, supervision, and leadership in administration.

The technique of administration—deciding what is to be done—and of management—deciding how it is to be done—exceed the scope of this work. What will be done here is to call attention to various types of problems and situations which arise in the area of internal management. First, of course, is the law or order which establishes an agency. The amount of administrative discretion permitted the agency will ordinarily be defined by statute. Thus, a framework is established within which management must operate.

To get the agency established and its program under way is a problem. An agency may have been granted wide jurisdiction by Congress in the statute which created it, but obviously unless it is organized in such a fashion as to implement in practice this grant of power, it may not be able to accomplish its objectives. However, it is ordinarily possible to obtain plenty of expert assistance. Specialists in the British Treasury, or from the Bureau of the Budget, for example, who are skilled in the procedures of internal management may be loaned to the agency during its initial period. If the agency is to be part of an existing department, management planning officials of that department will play an active role at the time of inception. In some cases, nongovernmental consultants may be called upon to work out control or related procedures. The tools of internal management available to these experts include such procedures as organization analysis, work-load analysis, channels of command, and standards of performance.

The mental climate surrounding any agency—especially a new agency—is of great importance. If it is believed that the organization is only a temporary one, the morale of the employees will ordinarily be low. On the other hand, a new agency created to administer a new program usually has little difficulty in finding able personnel. There is generally a great deal of interest in a new program, and potential employees hope to get in on the ground floor of a dynamic organization. Similarly, well-established agencies have little difficulty recruiting, *e.g.*, the prestige of the Treasury Department is sufficiently great so that recruitment in most of its agencies offers few problems. An agency under constant attack from the legislature may find the recruiting of first-rate managers more difficult than an agency which enjoys relative immunity from legislative criticism.

Top-level administrators rarely enjoy the peace and quiet implied by the phrase "span of control." In practice, a top-level administrator is forced to give a considerable portion of this time to such problems as public relations, appeasement of various interest groups, and his agency's relationship with key legislators. Despite a flood of material on the administrative process, both in the United States and in Britain, little is actually known about decision-making per se. The most ambitious attempt to explore this area has been undertaken by the Inter-university Case Program, a private organization with headquarters at Swarthmore College. The Program has so far published more than thirty case studies of administrative decision making, with the primary aim of making the material available as teaching aids in public-administration courses. From the cases so far collected, two general conclusions appear to emerge: first, in making an actual decision, the administrator usually has at his command only a small fraction of the key facts and figures; second, decisions are made under such tremendous pressures and tensions that, in retrospect, a great many mistakes are made in judgment.

Nor is enough known about successful administrators so that it is possible to isolate administrative traits as such and make use of this knowledge in training and recruiting administrators. There appears to be no uniform set of administrative virtues, or, on the other hand, of vices. Some able administrators are dictatorial, others are democratic; some are conscientious, others appear to be lazy. The long-range objective of scientific studies in the field of public administration is, of course, to develop the techniques of management to such an extent that few mistakes will be made in operation. This goal, which may be utopian, would have, if achieved, the necessary consequence of severely limiting administrative discretion.

A key task of internal management is planning, which is another way of looking at policy formulation. It may be doubted whether it is possible to escape planning in this sense, for it is clearly a function of administrative leadership to attempt to foresee future problems and come up with possible solutions before the problems become serious. "Planning," of course, is a word with many meanings, but as used here it refers to surveying the program, anticipating future needs and policies, and preparing the necessary administrative organization. The emergence throughout American government of internal planning units—often called "control units" or "plans and training sections" —illustrates the increased attention given this variety of planning.

Another function of internal management is the training of personnel. In the American government, this is best exemplified by the Graduate School of the Department of Agriculture, which is virtually a full-scale university for in-service training. Another example is the Foreign Service Institute of the Department of State. At the Institute persons who pass the necessary foreign-service examinations are given intensive language and area studies before being sent abroad on specific assignments.

In recent years, a good deal of attention has been given by sociologists, social anthropologists, and psychologists to such problems in internal management as the conditions of maximum worker morale, the effectiveness of rank-and-file participation in managerial decisions, and the type of leadership which obtains the best results from the group. In Britain, the Whitley Councils represent a group approach to problems of wages and hours, and, in this country, the Tennessee Valley Authority has approximated the same procedure. In addition, such investigators as Elton Mayo, Kurt Lewin, and Rensis Likert have undertaken controlled experiments in various aspects of these problems. A whole literature has developed from Mayo's experiments in the conditions of maximum worker productivity at the Western Electric plant in Hawthorne, Illinois, and a new field of research known as "human relations in industry" has developed largely as a consequence of Mayo's pioneering. Lewin's concern was not with specific industrial problems, but rather with theoretical considerations of group dynamics. However, his suggestive experiments, designed to test whether democratic leadership, authoritarian leadership, or laissez-faire leadership obtained the most effective group work, undertaken initially at Iowa State College, have stimulated research into techniques of industrial and governmental leadership. Likert and his associates at the University of Michigan's Institute for Social Research have engaged in some very interesting experiments with industrial groups such as railroad section gangs in the effort to isolate and analyze the psychological components of effective organization and worker morale.

While these social scientists would be the last to claim that their research into problems of internal management has supplied a blueprint for government or industrial organizations to follow, some of the implications of their studies are clearly relevant to the problem of achieving and maintaining an effective bureaucracy. During World War II, drawing upon techniques developed earlier in Britain and Germany, the Office of Strategic Services instituted a testing program for potential "cloak and dagger" men designed to assess personality and group interaction. The recruits were assembled and given jobs that were to be handled in group fashion, while a number of "ringers" supplied by the OSS attempted to frustrate group action in one way or another. Careful note was made of the way various members of the training section responded to challenge and frustration, and those who lost their tempers or were incapable of effective group work were weeded out. While the American government has made little subsequent use of this screening technique, the British Civil Service Selection Board has instituted a week-end testing period along similar lines conducted initially at a country estate, Stoke-d'Abernon, and more recently at a house in London. Certain applicants for positions in the administrative class spend the week end together engaging in various group activities while their actions are evaluated by a panel of experts. The British feel that this testing device has been quite useful in eliminating potential misfits from the service.

ADMINISTRATIVE POWERS

How do administrators secure compliance with their suggestions, threats, commands, and orders? In face-to-face contacts with citizens, what forms of action are available for administrators? These questions, involving the wide range of administrative powers from noncoercive persuasion to coercive threats, form the subject of the following paragraphs. It should be noted that this is not a mere catalogue of government activities—such as flood control or public-health services or maintenance of air-force bases—but rather a consideration of the techniques of external administrative control.

At the start, it must be emphasized that many forms of administrative action are noncoercive in nature. A declaration of government policy is usually only suggestive; at the same time, it may be widely accepted. For example, following intervention of the Chinese Communists in the Korean War, the Department of State asked American shippers not to trade with Red China. With every legal right to do so, some shippers ignored the declared American policy. A possible consequence of this independence could have been a reluctance on the part of the American government to assist the shipping concern if one of its ships got into trouble with the Chinese Nationalists on Formosa. Similarly, it is customary to take the advice of the Department of State on the question of making foreign loans. During World War II, the United States government employed "indirect sanctions" in many areas; for example, the race tracks were, in effect, closed by a press release and the "dim-out" was imposed by the same technique.

When the government establishes commercial standards, as it has with cotton and grains, commercial traders are not obliged to observe such standards. Yet, in practice, these standards tend to become accepted. Related to this is the custom of having the government act as a model employer, as exemplified by the leadership of the Federal authorities in adopting the eight-hour working day. A more recent illustration arose in 1936 with the Walsh-Healey Act, in which Congress imposed standards of wages and hours on contractors supplying materials over a given value to the United States government, and it was hoped that these standards would serve as a model for private employers beyond the purview of the act.

Through educational campaigns and demonstrations, government is able to sell many programs to the public. The sale of defense bonds in all democracies rests largely upon patriotism. Conservation demonstrations by agricultural agencies are designed to teach farmers superior planting methods. In both cases, the forms of action are noncoercive. Often a favorable response can be obtained through conferences between government officials and contending forces in society, especially in the field of labor relations. The Federal Mediation and Conciliation Service is devoted to this sort of noncoercive coercion.

Going further in the direction of compulsory measure, governments often buy consent, directly or indirectly. For example, the U.S. Department of Agriculture pays farmers for not growing certain soil-depleting crops. The French government attempts to encourage a higher birth rate by exempting fathers of large families from military service. Often United States government agencies, such as the Federal Housing Administration, will subsidize activities only if they are to be established or run in conformance with certain minimum standards. Related, but still different, is the use of a government establishment as a yardstick device. When the Tennessee Valley Authority was first established, much was made of the argument that TVA's power costs and rates would furnish a guide, a "yardstick," to determine what constituted just charges on the part of the privately owned utility corporations. Countless additional illustrations of suggestive, educational, promotional, and piloting devices could be given, but the actual categories are of no particular significance. What is important is the realization that much compliance with government policy may easily be secured without recourse to threats of prison sentences. Indeed, a government which finds itself in a position where it can enforce its rules and regulations only by direct threats has obviously lost much of its democratic character, for law enforcement, like democracy itself, is an outgrowth of consensus.

INSPECTION AND LICENSING

Inspection in one form or another is probably as old as government itself. It was widely used by public authorities in medieval towns, as well as in colonial America. In its more modern application, inspection consists of examining a situation to make sure that it comes up to the minimum standards established by the public policy. All governments use inspection for health work and for the maintenance of adequate standards in factories. In the United States the Federal government inspects a wide variety of articles in interstate commerce, including locomotives, airplanes, meats, and drugs. While coercion is often used if a situation does not improve following inspection and criticism, this device is more an educational than a coercive one.

In contrast, licensing involves the use of power, either by denying a license or by revoking it. As Ernst Freund has pointed out, licensing is the lifting of a legislative prohibition. In general, something may not be done; then a license is granted, which permits an exemption from the general ban. Whenever a government requires registration, it is illustrating this point. For example, firms and persons engaged in the munitions trade are required by law to register with the Department of State. There is no general grant of permission to buy or sell armaments; for the public welfare, controls must be exercised. Again, the Civil Aeronautics Administration may issue and revoke certificates to pilots.

No one knows exactly when and where the process of licensing began, but its origins go far back in British common law. Before 1900, Federal licenses in the United States were rare, but at the present time, among other activities, the Federal authorities issue licenses to warehouse operators, owners of stockyards, grain-exchange operators, radio and television broadcasters, armament manufacturers, and manufacturers of fissionable materials.

Even more extensive use is made of the licensing power by the American states, which commonly regulate through this device matters such as the professions, health and safety, and various business enterprises. Automobile drivers' licenses, liquor licenses, firearms permits, and barbers' licenses are common examples of this power in practice.

ADMINISTRATIVE LEGISLATION

While inspecting and licensing have long histories, administrative legislation is a development of more recent vintage. Administrative legislation is the issuing of orders applying to an individual or of rules and regulations of general application by an administrative authority. This authority may be an individual, a board, or a commission. Both the individual orders and the general rules may have the force of law. Executive orders and proclamations issued by the American President and published in the *Federal Register* have been previously analyzed as illustrations of the President's directory and supervisory powers. For purposes of the present analysis, Executive orders and proclamations are excluded from the discussion of administrative legislation.

The use of, and need for, administrative orders arise when a legislative body, unwilling to write a highly detailed statute to govern all foreseeable contingencies—and, indeed, incapable of so doing—authorizes an administrator to promulgate the specific applications of a general policy. Such delegation does not arise from legislative laziness, but from the fact that the subjects governed by legislation have become in recent decades so technical in nature that the legislature must of necessity delegate to expert administrators the function of filling in the details of a broadly defined legislative policy. In the early days of the republic this technique was seldom employed. Beginning with the Interstate Commerce Act of 1887, however, the technique of issuing "cease and desist" orders began to be more widely employed. If a railroad violated a law, or a regulation passed by the commission, the commissioners not only notified the carrier but also ordered the violation to be stopped. This type of directing power has become basic for government regulation of American business, for example, by the Federal Trade Commission, the Federal Communications Commission, the Secretary of Agriculture as administrator of the Packers' Act, or the National Labor Relations Board. It is also possible, of course, for an administrative agency to be authorized by law to grant orders of exemption, as occurs when a city zoning board grants an exemption to existing zoning regulations.

In contrast to orders of individual application, there exist rules of general application with the effect of law. The use of this technique goes back to the earliest days of the country. However, it has been since 1890, under the impact of urbanization and industrialization, that the practice of issuing rules of this sort has flourished. Excluding the code authorities under the National Recovery Administration declared invalid by the Supreme Court in 1935, Professor Leonard White tells us that rule-making power in 1936 "was vested in 115 Federal agencies, on the basis of 964 statutory provisions and 71 executive orders or proclamations." No one knows exactly the volume of sublegislation which comes from these authorizations to issue rules, but it has been estimated that the published rules exceed in numbers of pages the Acts of Congress by eight or ten to one. Government by rule is today the customary method of procedure.

The delegation of rule-making power by the legislature to the executive is carried even further in Great Britain and France. Under the Stuart kings, the issuance of "prerogative orders," that is, orders based not on law but on supposed inherent royal authority, was one of the bones of contention between the monarch and Parliament. However, after 1689, Parliament from time to time conferred authority upon the government to issue "statutory orders." It was not until late in the nineteenth century that the practice of administrative legislation on a fairly extensive basis was accepted as normal. The present century has witnessed tremendous extension of this practice. Now the great bulk of regulation in such fields as agriculture, industry, health and education is by administrative legislation, not by act of Parliament. In all countries the basic reason for the growth of administrative rule making was the increased inability of the legislature to pass on highly complex technical questions. Of necessity, the flesh and blood of statutes had to be supplied by the executive— the institution which was confronted with the day-to-day job of adjusting general policy considerations to specific situations. In addition, under the sheer pressure of time, legislatures were forced to write general laws. Under British practice, "statutory instruments," that is, administrative regulations, must lie before the House of Commons for forty days before becoming effective. A select committee of the House is charged with the task of examining the regulations, not in the attempt to evaluate their wisdom, but solely to see that they are justified under the statutes. Furthermore, any regulations issued as "provisional orders" must pass both houses before becoming valid. While these checks are more cursory than might be imagined, the fact remains that Parliament does, if only in theory, continue to hold the reins. It is also significant that orders and rules normally possess no immunity from judicial review, as do acts of Parliament. A court may hold an order *ultra vires* if it is not based on adequate legal authority.

In both Britain and the United States the growth of delegated legislation has been viewed with horror by many persons. In particular, jurists versed in the common law have tended to regard administrative legislation as representing a surrender of legislative functions to the executive. An outstanding explosion occurred with the publication in 1929 of a work entitled *The New Despotism*, written by Lord Hewart of Bury, the Lord Chief Justice of Britain. His Lordship savagely criticized Parliament for giving rule-making powers to administrative authorities, maintaining that this procedure was eroding away British liberty. The Government set up a committee to explore these charges, and subsequently, in 1932, that body produced a document known as *The Report of the Committee on Ministers' Powers*. The commissioners exonerated the British administrative system from Lord Hewart's charges, but, at the same time, suggested certain possible improvements, most of which were later adopted. A minority of the commissioners favored the creation of an administrative court system, as in France. The majority rejected this proposal on the ground that such a system would be incompatible with the sovereignty of Parliament and the supremacy of the law. It might be noted here that the problem of delegated legislation, which has aroused much controversy in Britain and the United States, has hardly troubled the French because of their elaborate system of administrative law, and administrative courts charged with implementing it. Since French administrative law is discussed elsewhere in this book, it will be passed over here.

A similar suggestion was made by the Committee on Administrative Law of the American Bar Association in the early 1930's, but the Association refused to endorse the proposal. The President's Committee on Administrative Management in 1937 recommended the separation of judicial from all other functions in the independent regulatory commissions. The Walter-Logan bill, representing an attempt to force administrative agencies into a judicial mold, passed Congress, but was vetoed by President Roosevelt. Subsequently, taking up a suggestion of Attorney General Frank Murphy, the President authorized the Attorney General to appoint a committee to explore the entire problem. The report of the Attorney General's Committee on Administrative Procedures was a balanced approach to the question and served as the basis for the Administrative Procedure Act of 1946. By the terms of this act, Congress required announcement in the *Federal Register* of intent to propose an administrative rule, and permitted interested parties to give their views before such a rule was adopted. Excluded from the provisions of the act were matters relating to the military, foreign affairs, and government loan contracts.

ADMINISTRATIVE ADJUDICATION

The final category of forms of administrative action is adjudication, which is the most formal type of coercive administrative action. Concerned with property and personal rights, administrative tribunals command great respect by virtue of the importance of the questions with which they deal. The problems presented by judicial review of administrative action, as well as the desirability of an administrative court system, are discussed in the next chapter and may be passed over at this point. Here, we are concerned with adjudication by administrative officials or tribunals as a means of law enforcement.

The same general influences which forced legislatures to delegate rule-making authority to administrators also forced the delegation of adjudicative authority. Administrative adjudication, in the words of Professor White, "means the investigation and settling of a dispute involving a private party on the basis of law and fact by an administrative agency." In the United States as in Britain, though not on the Continent, there is a wide diversity of administrative authorities authorized to adjudicate disputes involving private parties. Some, like the United States Customs Court, are independent administrative courts, while others, like the Board of Veterans' Appeals in the Veterans Administration, are administrative tribunals established inside a larger agency. Numerically small but of great importance are the regulatory establishments, such as the Interstate Commerce Commission, which exercise quasi-judicial as well as administrative and rule-making powers. In addition, there are various licensing authorities, such as the Civil Aeronautics Administration, which perform a semijudicial function in licensing pilots and aircraft. And last but not least, certain administrative officers, such as the Secretary of State, the Attorney General, or the Secretary of Agriculture are endowed with certain judicial functions. The Attorney General, for instance, has the power to overrule the Board of Immigration Appeals on matters of deportation or exclusion from the United States.

While British government is less diffused than that in the United States, a detailed examination of British administration would show that there, too, the power of administrative bodies to perform functions of adjudication is widely scattered throughout government agencies. In administering the housing acts, for example, the Ministry of Health acts as an appeals court; so does the Home Office when it decides questions involving British citizenship. Town and country planning laws and nationalized health legislation resulted in enlarging considerably the area of administrative adjudication.

While Lord Hewart attacked administrative legislation in his *The New Despotism,* he reserved his most biting criticism for the field of administrative adjudication. The Ministers' committee here, too, rejected most of the Chief Justice's charges but made various recommendations for improvement. In the United States, although the states for many years have been using commissions to decide workmen's compensation cases and the Interstate Commerce Commission has now been handling reparations cases for half a century, criticism of administrative adjudication did not boil over until the late 1930's. In particular, it was often alleged that the National Labor Relations Board's hearing examiners were biased, and that, as in the case of the Federal Trade Commission, the commission acted simultaneously as prosecutor, judge, and jury.

Congress, in passing the Federal Administrative Procedure Act of 1946, attempted to meet complaints of this type by laying down new procedures to be met by administrative authorities when acting in adjudicative capacities. Many of the provisions of this act were designed to guarantee a fair hearing, with the result that much customary judicial procedure was adopted. At the same time, hearing examiners were placed rather directly under the Civil Service Commission, and were rotated in their assignments. Finally, the grounds for appealing from an administrative tribunal to the regular courts were substantially broadened. Whether these moves are likely unduly to hamper the freedom and effectiveness of administrative agencies remains uncertain. However, they do represent a real attempt to fit the emerging techniques of administrative adjudication into the American constitutional firmament.

Chapter 10

THE FUNCTIONS OF THE JUDICIARY

To MOST Europeans, the American emphasis on the role of the judiciary in government seems quite puzzling. This is understandable, for outside the United States there is no democracy in which the judges have so decisive a say in the determination of public policy. While it would be overstating the case to say that nowhere else do the judges have a political role—the current battle in the Union of South Africa between the Supreme Court and the Parliament shows the inadequacy of this generalization—it does seem fair to say that in most democracies the judiciary is much more insulated from the political process than is the case in the United States. Judges in the United States suffer from institutional schizophrenia, that is, they are actually called upon to fulfill both political and legal functions. Elsewhere, their work is largely confined to fairly narrow legal confines, delineated by a Parliament that has the last word.

The distinction between legal and political functions requires some elaboration and justification. As is usually the case with such distinctions, the line of demarcation cannot be drawn between the two categories with absolute precision. However, if we define the legal activities of a court as those in which it operates within a framework of law established by the legislature, we can then define the political functions as those in which the judges act upon the framework of law and, in effect, play a part in the lawmaking process itself. In the first instance, the judges are merely technicians highly trained and skilled, whose task it is to apply the decisions made by the Queen in Parliament, or by the National Assembly, to the problem situations that develop in the implementation of the law. Indeed, the decisions of the judiciary may water down the meaning of a law, but the lawmaking authority can always return to the lists and restate its views in unambiguous terms incapable of being watered down. In short, the judges are stuck with the laws, whether they like them or not, and judges, realizing this, seldom attempt to frustrate the wishes of the legislature.

In the second instance, where the courts have a hand in the lawmaking process, we find a different set of rules operating. Here the judges are not alone concerned with the application of the law, but are also, to an extent that varies with circumstances, prepared to evaluate the wisdom of the lawmakers in terms of their own particular criteria of justice or "constitutionality." For the judges to undertake this political role, something more is required: a written constitution which supplies certain tests, necessarily of a highly general nature if they are to be effective over any length of time, which can be applied to the work of the legislature. To put it another way, if judicial review of the validity of legislation is to be effective, the judges must have an external yardstick against which they can measure any statute. The best example of this sort of system in operation is the American judicial process, to which we now turn our attention.

THE AMERICAN JUDICIAL PROCESS

The United States presents the unusual spectacle of a nation in which any court of competent jurisdiction, state or Federal, may declare an act of Congress to be unconstitutional. Although the United States Supreme Court has the last say in such matters, and few cases originate outside the Federal court system, it is conceivable that a country justice of the peace could hold a national statute invalid. Needless to add, the state courts have the same power with respect to state legislation.

The reason for this is that the Constitution explicitly established a national government of limited powers, *i.e.*, Congress was only to exercise jurisdiction over the areas listed in Article I of the Constitution, with the remaining authority reserved to the states and to the people. Furthermore, certain restrictions on the way Congress exercised its power were incorporated in the document, for example, bills of attainder and ex post facto laws were interdicted by Article I, and the Bill of Rights added in 1791 forbade, among other things, the limitation of freedom of speech, press, assembly, or religion and the deprivation of individual life, liberty, or property without "due process of law." In sum, the founders of the new nation were highly distrustful of government in general, and while they desired the national government to have sufficient power to create a workable federation, they wanted to keep this new creation on a fairly tight leash.

But governments, as the French experience demonstrates, are not limited by pious phraseology, and limitations are meaningless unless they are institutionalized. Consequently, the question arises: If Congress passed an ex post facto law, perhaps over a presidential veto, who would do anything about it? It is at this point that one appreciates the function of the judiciary, and it would seem—although the issue is still controversial among scholars—that the framers intended that the Federal courts should have the power to declare such laws invalid. Hamilton asserted in *Federalist* No. 78 that this was a proper, indeed an indispensable, judicial prerogative, and Jefferson, later to become the archenemy of judicial review, in a letter to Madison, criticized the proposed Constitution because it did not explicitly endow the Federal courts with this power. The cry "It's unconstitutional!" and the accompanying demand for judicial action dates back to the earliest days of the republic. In fact, the Jeffersonians tried hard but vainly to get the Federal courts to declare the Sedition Act of 1798 unconstitutional.

However, this is of antiquarian interest, for in 1803 the Supreme Court ruled that it did have the power to invalidate acts of Congress, and although the Court did not again disallow a statute until 1857, the precedent established by John Marshall in *Marbury v. Madison* has not since been seriously contested. While Marshall engaged in some dubious legerdemain in his opinion in the Marbury case, the central proposition was sound. In effect, Marshall asserted, there is no point in having a written constitution if its terms are meaningless and subject to perpetual alteration at the whim of the legislature. Judicial review was thus enshrined as a central institution of American government.

There are two aspects of judicial review as it operates in the United States. The first, described above, occurs when the Federal courts evaluate and perhaps void an act of the national legislature. The second, which Justice Holmes believed to be far more important to the American frame of government than the first, takes place when the Supreme Court strikes down an enactment of a state legislature on the grounds that it conflicts with the Constitution or some Federal law or is an intrusion into an area where the states are without jurisdiction. The Supreme Court's power in this area is a natural concomitant of the supremacy clause of the Constitution which provided that the Constitution and laws enacted under it were to be the "supreme law of the land." Armed with these two varieties of judicial review, the Court was to be the umpire of the Federal system, seeing to it that the national government remained within its allocated area of jurisdiction, while simultaneously checking usurpations of power by the states.

Similarly, the actions of the President are subject to judicial scrutiny and may be declared unconstitutional, or, more frequently, *ultra vires* a congressional delegation of authority. This latter situation develops when the President, or one of his administrative officials, claims some authority under a law, but a court holds that the law does not in fact authorize the executive's claim. Sometimes a court will simultaneously void both an executive action and the law upon which it is based—as occurred several times in the period between 1933 and 1937.

AMERICAN JUDICIAL STRUCTURE

There are in the United States forty-nine different judicial systems, but for our purposes here the state systems may be largely ignored. The Federal court system is arranged in three tiers: at the bottom, the district courts, next, the courts of appeal, and, atop the pyramid, the United States Supreme Court. The district courts are the courts of original jurisdiction, that is, they are the courts in which litigation commences. From the district courts, as well as from certain regulatory agencies such as the National Labor Relations Board, appeals may be taken to the courts of appeal, which are the last stop for most contests. Finally, and usually at the discretion of the Court itself, appeals may be taken to the Supreme Court for final settlement. There are a few ways of short-circuiting this arrangement, but they need not concern us here. Also it should be mentioned that in rare cases, specified in Article III of the Constitution, cases may be initially tried in the Supreme Court.

In its capacity as regulator of the Federal system, the Supreme Court also has jurisdiction, initially granted by the Judiciary Act of 1789, over the decisions of state courts of final jurisdiction. In the event that it can be demonstrated that the decision of a state court runs counter to the Constitution or to congressional enactment, the Supreme Court may overrule it. This occurs fairly frequently, although not as frequently as one might imagine would be necessary to keep forty-eight state judiciaries out of the Federal pasture.

The jurisdiction of the Federal courts is based on a twofold grant of authority in Article III of the Constitution. They may hear cases growing out of Federal laws or administrative actions (which are known as Federal questions), and they have jurisdiction over cases between citizens of different states (which is referred to as diversity of citizenship). In the former instance, they simply interpret the Federal statutes or ordinances, while in the latter, their job is far more complex since they have to apply state law. For example, if a citizen of New York State sues a citizen of Kansas for trespass in the United States District Court for the Southern District of New York, the district judge must apply the New York State law of trespass.

THE WORK OF THE COURTS

Following the distinction established above between political and legal functions, a study of the work of the Federal courts reveals that the vast bulk of their time is spent on litigation in the legal category. Most cases have no direct political implications; in only a few do the courts exercise their prerogative of judicial review. Indeed, most judges scrupulously avoid intervening in the political sphere if they can possibly do so. The Supreme Court makes it a rule never to discuss the constitutionality of a statute if the matter at issue in a case can be settled without reference to the Constitution. If it is possible to interpret a statute in such a fashion as to circumvent the issue of constitutionality, the high Court will so interpret it.

Substantively speaking, the job of the Federal judiciary is to supply the specific sanctions that bind the individual to the community. Congress of necessity writes laws in large type; the courts must supply the small type, the specific meaning of a law in a specific situation. In a massively complex society such as that of the United States, each important law results in hundreds of anomalies, that is, of situations to which the law does not seem to fit. Many of these are today remedied by administrative agencies which, acting under authority vested in them by law, make special rules for the special cases. But still a considerable number end up in court, for the decisions of administrative agencies may be reviewed by the judiciary.

Similarly, the courts are responsible for the trial of those who violate the United States Criminal Code. It is not true to say that in a democracy the courts or the police enforce the laws—they do not, and this is one of the distinctions between democracies and totalitarian states. In democracies, the community enforces the laws, and the Federal courts are the forums in which the decisions are made, by juries, as to which laws it wants maintained and which it wants undermined. The judge is the umpire who sees to it that certain ground rules, designed to ensure fair play, are maintained, and who is charged with the task of making clear to the jury exactly what the issues are. In the event that the community, speaking through the jury, feels that the existing law is wrong, even when a person on trial has clearly violated it, the judge and the police are powerless, and the accused goes free. This occurred regularly during prohibition to the point where the government virtually ceased prosecutions under the law.

LAW AND COMMUNITY SENTIMENT

Indeed, legally speaking, the United States is highly collectivistic. American law, built around the jury system, is community-centered law. For better or for worse, the jury reflects community sentiment. California gold-field justice, developed around the assumption "Give a man a fair trial and hang him," was a vivid example of this proposition in action. Similarly, if the community sympathizes with a mercy killer—as it often seems to do—the individual who has committed "murder" walks from the courtroom scot free. If the community shares white-supremacy convictions, it will hardly deal harshly with lynchers who have "put an uppity Negro in his place." In short, the judicial process, rather than being a pillar of individualism, is more often an instrument of conformity, enforcing the views of the collectivist-minded community upon the eccentric, the deviant, the subversive. Of course, this coin has another side. The jury may also stand with the man unjustly persecuted by a spiteful authority, with the newspaper editor accused of libel by the crooked politician. To put it another way, the norms of behavior accepted by the community, whether they be good, bad, or indifferent in terms of varying ethical standards, are those which the juries apply in their work.

But is community sentiment necessarily "right"? This is another form of the question, "What is justice?" with which Socrates plagued the Athenians, and it is a question which has haunted thinking men ever since. Some thinkers, accepting a natural-law framework, have maintained that the actions of the community are just only if they conform to certain transcendent criteria of right and wrong. They assert that right is not right one day and then, because of an adverse nose count, wrong the next. One does not obtain justice or determine the nature of good and evil by counting noses. Others have asserted just as strongly the supremacy of nose-counting, that right is what people say is right. This, they claim, is democracy, and they point out that the natural-law thinkers always seem to identify natural law with their own peculiar prejudices. They point with glee to the classic statement of the Milford, Connecticut, town meeting, which in 1640 stated its territorial claims in the following resolution: "Voted, that the earth is the Lord's and the fulness thereof; voted, that the earth is given to the Saints; voted, that we are the Saints."

Obviously, this dilemma is incapable of solution here. We can recognize the fact that communities have made mistakes, and it does not seem sensible to say that an anti-Negro decision of an anti-Negro community, such as those which occasionally occur when lynchers are turned free by juries, is "right." Yet, those who denounce the advocates of natural law also have a measure of justice on their side, particularly when one notes that no two major natural-law thinkers have been in agreement on exactly what comprises natural law. In a sense, democracies try to operate between these two extremes by establishing what might be called operational absolutes. These operational absolutes are built around the proposition of human fallibility and the substance of the democratic ethic, the ideal of free development in a free society. Thus when a jury acquits a lyncher, the democrat can assert that this is wrong because it is a fundamental violation of the democratic ethic, of the very precepts on which the society is based. He will admit that the democratic ethic is not necessarily true for all times and places, and that his belief must be subject to constant reexamination, but that on the basis of the evidence he feels that lynching violates the ground rules of democratic government and is thus wrong in terms of the ethical imperatives which are an integral part of the democratic faith.

THE POLITICAL ROLE OF THE JUDICIARY

Although most of the work of the Federal courts is of a legal character, as we have employed the term legal here, the most important function from the point of view of the student of American government is that which sees the courts directly intervening in the political process. Again it should be noted that while state courts exercise parallel functions with respect to state constitutions, our concern here is specifically with the activities of the Federal courts.

To understand the full implications of the political role of the United States courts, it is important to examine briefly the Constitution of the United States which serves as the point of reference for declarations of unconstitutionality. The first significant point of interest is the broadness of the documents—its provisions regulate an immense area of governmental activity. Second, it is refreshingly brief, particularly when compared with the constitutions of many American states or of other democratic nations. The new Indian constitution of 1949, for example, fills a book of 254 pages, and is far closer to a statutory code than it is to a constitution. It is difficult to think of any aspect of Indian life that is not discussed in the Constitution; Article 340 (I), for instance, authorizes the President to appoint a commission to investigate the conditions of the socially and educationally backward classes. This sort of encyclopedic constitution has been favored by many of the American states.

But the Constitution of the United States is both brief and general. The framers of the Constitution did not attempt to usurp the prerogatives of the future Congress and President, and consequently contented themselves with establishing the major outlines of the new government, leaving specific decisions on public policies to later authorities. Furthermore, when the framers got into an argument over some point, they were quite capable of inserting an enigmatic phrase into the document—a technique which often solved the immediate problem but left the divination of intent to future generations. There were, for instance, two schools of thought on the basis for citizenship in the new nation: one group, led by Hamilton, asserted that national citizenship should take precedence over state citizenship; while the other, with states'-rights orientation, maintained that the states were the basic units of citizenship, and that national citizenship should be derived from citizenship in a state. After several severe arguments on the subject, the framers solved the problem by simply using the term "citizen of the United States" but never defining it! In actual fact, citizenship was not clearly defined until after the Civil War, when the Fourteenth Amendment explicitly stated that state citizenship was subordinate to national citizenship.

Thus the Constitution is a Pandora's box of ambiguities. It used such phrases as "interstate commerce," "uniformity" with respect to excise taxation and naturalization, and "due process of law," but did not define what they meant. Problems such as these have supplied constitutional lawyers with headaches— and fees—almost since the beginning of the republic, and many a judge has wished that the framers might have taken the trouble to be more explicit. However, it may be suggested that this very lack of conciseness has supplied the American Constitution with a dynamic that the encyclopedic constitutions lack. Each generation can supply new meanings to the old phrases—pour new wine in old bottles, so to speak—and thus adapt the Constitution to changing social conditions. This has been the process of American constitutional development, and the courts, notably the Supreme Court, have served as a continuing constitutional convention, bringing the document up to date. It is this possibility of development which accounts for the fact that the Constitution has moved from a simple agrarian era to an age of industrial complexity with virtually no significant formal amendments. The most significant constitutional amendment from this point of view is the Sixteenth, authorizing the income tax, and it should be noted that the passage of this amendment was forced by the refusal of the Supreme Court to permit an income tax. Usually the Court does not put the people to this trouble.

It would be a mistake to think that the job of constitutional revision lies wholly with the courts; on the contrary, much innovation comes from the legislature and from the executive. But the courts, and particularly the Supreme Court, serve as the filterers of change. The legislature and the executive may alter the pattern of government, but the courts have the final say on the validity of these changes.

LIMITATIONS ON THE EXERCISE OF JUDICIAL REVIEW

To have a power is one thing; to maintain it is another. As will be discussed shortly, there is a large area of potential conflict between the courts, which tend to be dominated by old men set in old ways, and the legislative and executive branches of the government, which are more sensitive to new requirements and new public demands. Indeed, this smoldering conflict has broken into open flame at several points in American history, most recently during the years 1933 to 1937 when the Supreme Court declared half a dozen significant New Deal innovations unconstitutional. However, it is surprising that this open conflict had not occurred more frequently. The main reason that it has not taken place more often must be sought in the nature and composition of the United States Supreme Court.

Clemenceau once observed that war was too important a business to be left to the generals, and we might paraphrase this for our purposes here to the statement that interpreting the Constitution is far too significant to be left in the hands of legal technicians. The legal profession has often complained about the character of Supreme Court Justices, maintaining in essence that they are "political lawyers," but it might be suggested that it is precisely this fact that has given the Court its great power. Indeed, the first great "political lawyer" was Chief Justice John Marshall, and today the high tribunal is occupied by two ex-Attorneys General, three ex-Senators, a former Solicitor General, a former Chairman of the Securities and Exchange Commission, a former state governor, and only one justice of a predominantly "legal" background— an ex-professor of law. Obviously the road to the Supreme Court is paved with politics, not law!

Thus while the legal training of the Justices may not be of the best, most of them are acutely aware of the political realities that exist at any given time. They are also aware of the weakness of the Supreme Court which, in the words of John Marshall, has neither the purse nor the sword, and are seldom willing to engage in quixotic ventures. To put it another way, the Court is generally far too wise to attempt to resist a strong majority; its power of rejection is really effective only when the majority is fragmented. Obviously, assessing the internal cohesion of majorities is no job for technicians; such a task calls for men with extensive experience in politics.

This is not to suggest that the Court consciously weighs the state of the majority before undertaking an important political decision. (Again it should be noted that "political" decisions make up a small proportion of the Court's work, although it is, from our point of view, the most significant proportion.) Rather, it is to offer the hypothesis that public opinion rather than the wording of the Constitution is often the decisive factor—and appropriately so—in such decisions. Let us briefly examine recent American constitutional history for evidence to support this hypothesis.

First, it is significant to note that very rarely does a cohesive majority exist in the United States. Normally, as was suggested earlier in this book, political power in the United States is diffused widely among political parties, pressure groups, and the Presidency. Wartimes tend to create monolithic majorities, particularly on issues related to adequate defense, and it is during wartime that the Supreme Court tends to go into constitutional hibernation. For instance, during both World War I and, to a lesser extent, World War II, there were extensive violations of civil rights in the interests of "winning the war." By peacetime standards, most of these—such as the incarceration of 70,000 American citizens of Japanese ancestry in relocation centers in 1942—were clearly unconstitutional. But when the Japanese-Americans tried to get the Supreme Court to declare the imprisonment, based on the possession of enemy ancestors, unconstitutional, all the Court would observe was that war was hard on everybody. Congress and the President had been in full agreement in 1942 that protective custody was the solution to the presumed threat to the Pacific Coast area offered by the Japanese and Japanese-Americans, and in 1944, the Supreme Court would not substitute its wisdom for that of the other branches of government combined.

In other words, when the President and Congress are moving arm in arm, the Court tends to be most cautious in intervening. The actions of the anti-Roosevelt Court in the years of 1933 to 1937 would seem to contradict this assertion, but a special set of circumstances appear to have been operating at that time. There is every reason to believe that the conservative Justices felt that they, and not Roosevelt and Congress, were sustained by real political power. This illusion was buttressed by the press, which hailed each declaration of unconstitutionality as a victory in the war to restore a government of laws and not of men. In effect, perhaps because of their advanced age, the Justices did not have their fingers on the pulse of public sentiment, but felt that the New Deal was a momentary aberration which would receive frenzied attention for a brief period of time, and then be consigned to the political curiosity shelf along with the Populists, the Greenbackers, the Anti-Masons and the Know-Nothings. Roosevelt's resounding victory in the 1936 election ended this mirage. Precisely because it was insufficiently political-minded, the 1933-to-1937 Court was facing open defeat and curtailment of its powers when in 1937 President Roosevelt presented his famous "court-packing" proposal to Congress. However, Congress, the press, and the people bristled at this attack on a treasured American ideal, judicial supremacy, and the reorganization failed. Although the President lost this battle, he won the war. Subsequent Court decisions upheld New Deal legislation, and several of the oldest and most conservative Justices soon retired, to be replaced by Roosevelt appointees.

But normally in the United States, for reasons that have already been discussed in earlier chapters, the majority is fragmented and political power is diffused among congressional committees, executive bureaus, the President, pressure groups, and state governments. Usually civil wars are raging within both parties, and simultaneously Congress and the President are locked in ceaseless conflict. Configurations of pressure groups form, ally themselves with administrative agencies, utilize friendly congressional committees, and then, having achieved their objective, break up, only to re-form, in different patterns, on the next significant issue. This fragmentation of the majority gives the Supreme Court great freedom of movement, for when the balance of forces is delicate, its power, thrown on one side or the other, can be decisive.

Thus, it seems clear that *in an emergency* the President has the power to seize an industry. However, in 1952, the Supreme Court held that President Truman's seizure of the steel industry was an unconstitutional exercise of executive power. True, the President had no statutory warrant for seizing the steel works, but other presidents had taken over industries without congressional authority, and the Court had failed to intervene. But in the other instances, full-scale wars were in progress, Congress was quiescent, and the public seemed to approve the executive's actions as forwarding the winning of the war. In short, emergencies existed. On the other hand, Congress was notably opposed to Truman's seizure, the press was outraged, and the public seemed to feel that the President had gone too far. To put it another way, there certainly was no monolithic majority in favor of seizure, and the Court struck down the President's order. In effect, the Court, appreciating the fact that the American people and the Congress did not consider the Korean War and the Cold War to be full-scale crises, rhetorically exorcised the emergency and insisted on the limitations of the peacetime Constitution. The lesson would seem to be that when there is an *emergency,* the President has unusual powers, but that the presence or absence of an emergency is determined by the Court in terms of whether or not a coherent majority exists on the issue, and more specifically by whether Congress supports or opposes the action.

Consequently, and paradoxically, the key to judicial power in the United States is judicial self-restraint. No powerful, cohesive majority can permit a judicial body to frustrate its response to the demands of the electorate—at least not for any length of time. Conversely, when the majority is tentative and fragmented, the influence of the judiciary can be profound. The skeptic may question this, pointing to the few instances in which the Supreme Court has declared either acts of Congress unconstitutional, or the President out of bounds. But to examine this situation quantitatively is to miss the basic level of judicial influence—the formative levels of public policy. The fear of judicial interdiction has prevented many an executive action, and similarly when Congress prepares a law the possible views of the Supreme Court are taken into serious consideration. A disciplined majority would be prepared to pass a law that violated existing canons of constitutionality and confront the Court with it; a fragmented majority is seldom willing to do this.

THE RATIONALE OF JUDICIAL LEGISLATION

It is clear that the American Federal judiciary does in effect exercise political decision-making power, does act as a sort of superlegislature. True, its actions are based on a written Constitution, but the Constitution is so written that virtually any criteria of legality can be based on it. Consequently, whether they admit it or not, judges are called upon to evaluate the wisdom of government action, rather than its mechanical conformance to the Constitution. For example, the club of "due process of law" which the courts can employ to belabor the state and Federal governments is not solid and objective like the policeman's nightstick. On the contrary, the meaning of "due process of law" has changed several times in the history of the Republic and may change again. What one judge considers to be due process may be unconstitutional tyranny to another occupant of the bench.

But in the United States the courts, armed with these subjective criteria of constitutionality, may reinterpret and strike down the actions of the executive and the legislature, substituting their conceptions of public policy and of common good for those of the popularly elected government functionaries. The question immediately arises: Why do the people tolerate this interference with majority rule? Why does a democratic nation permit nine politically irresponsible Supreme Court Justices, who may have been appointed to the bench a generation earlier, to intervene decisively in the decision-making process?

Whole books have been written on this subject. Radicals have raved and ranted, radical political movements such as the Populists and the Progressives of 1924 have demanded an end to this situation, Marxists have cynically noted the coincidence between the views of liberty held by the Court and those held by "Wall Street." But the fact remains that the American people have never gotten particularly unsettled about the role of the Supreme Court, and have even—if Roosevelt's experience in trying to tamper with the Court is any indication—cherished the concept of judicial supremacy. In the light of the controversy that exists on the subject, and the absence of evidence which might point conclusively one way or the other, one must skirt this subject with some circumspection. But some tentative conclusions may be suggested.

First, it would appear that the Court has a certain symbolic function in American political psychology. Like the British Crown, it is permanent. Presidents and Congresses come and go at regular intervals, but the Supreme Court changes only slowly and virtually unnoticeably. There is very little permanence in American politics—even the American flag is changed every time a new state enters the Union—and it may be suggested that the Court, as the living personification of the Constitution, serves as a symbol of state stability in the midst of governmental flux. Obviously there is an irrational bond between the American people and the Court, for only in irrational terms can one explain the impassioned and fervent manner in which Americans who loved Roosevelt and supported his policies leaped to the defense of the "nine old men" who had stood in the way of the New Deal. Democracies in action tend to resemble adding machines which mechanically compute majorities, register the winners of elections, and proceed to the solution of public problems in a quantitative fashion. While we cannot deprecate this procedure, we must realize that it is frequently a cold and impersonal one, highly rational in essence. Yet recent studies in social psychology have clearly revealed that men do not act wholly on a rational basis, and much of the appeal of the Nazi dictatorship was that it offered warmth and symbols to a nation in which democracy had been notably uninspired and desiccated, impersonal and mechanical.

If we view the Constitution as the central symbol of American political life, the mystical functions of the Supreme Court become apparent. The Justices may be likened to the keepers of the sacred flame, the permanent guardians of the principles of the republic in an atmosphere characterized by rapid change and social instability. Cynics may scoff at this, and political scientists may analyze statistically the nine sets of prejudices of the nine Justices, but the value of such a symbol of permanence in a dynamic and in many ways rootless society should not be underestimated.

Second, and on a highly utilitarian level, it may be suggested that the American people accept the political role of the Supreme Court because they believe that it is a good idea to "sleep on" important decisions. As was noted earlier, the American Congress and the President are highly responsive to public sentiment, and it is possible for important pieces of public policy to be enacted on the crest of a wave of passion. In Britain, the tightly organized political parties serve as a buffer between public enthusiasm and public policy, so that before the public mood can be reflected in legislation or administrative action, a considerable process of discussion, both within Parliament and without, must take place. However, American political parties offer no such temporizing effect, so that the check on hasty and impassioned majority action has been incorporated in the institutions of government. The Supreme Court is the final forum of delay with respect both to state and to Federal actions. The Court supplies an institutional opportunity for revised judgment.

Viewed from this standpoint, the job of the Court is not so much the imposition of certain substantive policy views as it is the enforcement of the rules of the democratic game. If one interprets the decision in the steel-seizure case in this light, he might say that what the Court actually did was tell the President that by acting without a majority he was breaking the ground rules of government by discussion. It was not the seizure that was wrong, but the method employed by the executive. Similarly, when the Court reverses a conviction in a state court on the ground that a confession was tortured from the accused, it is not asserting that the man is innocent; it is rather insisting that he be tried in conformity with the broad principles of democratic justice.

Another practical factor that should be taken into consideration here is the effect of delay itself on public judgment. An old Croatian proverb has it that delay is the handmaiden of justice, and many an accused criminal owes his life to the fact that the protracted judicial process supplied time for public sentiment against him to wane. Certainly by the time a case has wended its leisurely way to the Supreme Court, one is in a better position to exercise balanced judgment and perspective. In short, it is suggested that the American people, perhaps subconsciously, believe there should be a "cooling-off period," and the Supreme Court, utilizing the technique of judicial review, implements this slowdown.

But, as the instance of the Court versus the New Deal illustrates, the justices have to be well attuned to public sentiment. They should inhibit passion, but not restrain marriage. Thus when a majority, after discussion, seems set upon certain policy formulations, the Court, in the interests of its own prestige, must perform the marriage ceremony between the Constitution and the policy innovations. Perhaps the majority is still "wrong" by the criteria held by the Justices, but that is another question. The "vital myth" that the President and Congress are subject to the decisions of the Supreme Court depends for its survival upon a wise Court which will refuse to engage in combat with a cohesive majority or attempt to solve problems that are not judicially solvable. The Dred Scott case stands as a monument to judicial egotism; the attempt by Chief Justice Taney in this instance to solve once and for all the slavery problem nearly resulted in the destruction of the concept of judicial supremacy. Ironically, the power of the Court depends in large part upon its unwillingness to be drawn into unequal combat.

But when all this has been said, it is important to conclude by emphasizing that judicial review is not a trick played by the judges on the people. One of the basic themes of American political theory has traditionally been the limitation of government power, and judicial review has been one of the principal weapons employed, particularly in the states, to subordinate lawmakers and administrators to general constitutional principles. To say that judges are human and that they accumulate their opinions as to what is right and wrong as do other human beings is not to be cynical. Indeed, what is striking throughout most of American history is the degree to which strong-minded judges, and particularly Supreme Court Justices, have shown reluctance in substituting their judgment for that of the elected organs of the government. One can scoff at this self-restraint on the ground that it was political realism, but it is probably closer to the truth to believe that this reluctance was largely motivated by a deep sense of responsibility. Furthermore, when one reads the recent decisions of the Supreme Court of the Union of South Africa, confronted as it is by a legislature dedicated to racist fanaticism, he can gain a new appreciation of the positive values of judicial review. From the point of view of political realism, the South African judges are committing suicide, but they have nonetheless struck a noble blow for freedom and justice.

THE BRITISH JUDICIARY

Although at one time in the late sixteenth century it appeared that judicial review of Parliamentary enactments might become a part of the British system of government, the tradition died in the cradle. Certainly since 1689, and the accession of William and Mary by Act of Parliament, there has been no advocacy of judicial supremacy worth mentioning. The job of the British courts has been the application of Parliamentary enactments to specific instances, not the evaluation of the wisdom of the legislature. Again it should be noted that occasionally a court can by the process of interpretation modify an act of Parliament, thus momentarily substituting its views on public policy for those of the legislators, but Parliament has the last word and can pass a declaratory act, binding on the courts, stating exactly what it did mean and what it wants enforced. Against this the courts have no recourse, and realizing that Parliament has the whip hand, few judges will even attempt the fruitless task of sabotage by interpretation. In short, the British courts do not have the power to hold an act of Parliament "unconstitutional."

But this is not to suggest for a moment that the British judiciary does not have an important limiting function. While the courts do not have a hand in the decision-making process, they do have the important job of ensuring that the Government utilizes proper procedures in the implementation of public policy. Parliament can, if it chooses, forbid the courts to undertake any judicial action with reference to specific legislation, but this ban on judicial review of administrative action is looked upon with great disfavor and is seldom utilized. Normally the courts have the power to see that administrative officials do not step beyond the jurisdiction allotted them by Parliament and to require them to follow certain procedural rules, known as the "principles of natural justice," in the course of their activities. Thus if an administrative officer takes action unauthorized by Parliament, the courts may hold him *ultra vires, i.e.,* beyond his powers, and if he takes action in a specific instance without allowing the individual concerned to state his case, the courts may rule that the official here has violated the principles of natural justice.

THE STRUCTURE OF BRITISH COURTS

Unlike the American system, in which the same Federal courts handle both civil and criminal cases, the British have one set of courts concerned with civil litigation and another for criminal matters. In minor criminal cases, the issue may well be settled by a justice of the peace, an amateur whose services are unremunerated, or by two or more justices of the peace acting as a court of petty sessions. In the cities such matters are handled by magistrates. In the event that a serious offense occurs, the case will in all probability be remanded or referred to a court of assize, or, if it is a noncapital offense, perhaps to a court of quarter sessions composed of all the J.P.'s of a county.

The court of assize has original jurisdiction over most serious offenses and all crimes punishable by death. It is presided over by a judge of the High Court, who two or three times a year visits the county seats for the purpose of hearing serious cases. While there are no juries in trials by justices of the peace, the accused may have jury trial at the assizes. The American observer is perpetually surprised at the rarity of jury trials in Britain; actually few accused criminals request a jury, for most accept the decision of the judge acting alone. This is a high tribute to the integrity and impartiality of the judges, although it also may reflect the thoroughness of the pretrial investigation which screens out doubtful cases. Incidentally, the grand jury is no longer employed in England to prepare indictments; this process is handled by the justices of the peace or magistrates who prepare "informations," the latter taking the place of the "true bill" traditionally drawn up by the grand jury.

Above the local level, the British court system gets more complex. The central organization of the judiciary is the High Court, which is primarily concerned with civil actions. However, certain of the judges have criminal-court assignments either as judges of assize or as members of the Court of Criminal Appeal, composed of three High Court justices. The Court of Criminal Appeal is normally the last stopping place of appeals in criminal cases. Occasionally a criminal case may be appealed from the Court of Criminal Appeal to the House of Lords, but only on a question of law, not on one of fact. This is to say that the House of Lords—actually only the Law Lords—will unravel a complicated legal question but will not evaluate the guilt or innocence of the accused.

The civil-court system is likewise divided into local and central categories. For minor civil issues there are county courts, staffed by judges who travel around fairly small circuits. Cases of a more complex nature are taken to the central civil court, the High Court of Justice, which sits in London. The High Court is functionally subdivided into three divisions: Queen's Bench; Chancery; and Probate, Divorce, and Admiralty, each of which takes jurisdiction over litigation within its specialized field of competence. Appeals can be taken from any division of the High Court, as well as directly from the county courts, to the Court of Appeal, which is composed of the Master of the Rolls and eight Lord Justices of Appeal. Final appeals on a very limited legal basis may be taken from the decisions of the Court of Appeal to the House of Lords.

THE QUALIFICATIONS OF JUDGES

Unlike the American Federal courts, British tribunals are staffed by men with top legal qualifications. This is not to suggest that there are not American Federal judges of legal excellence; there are, but legal excellence is not the basic criterion for appointment. Nor is it to suggest that political considerations play no part in appointments to the British bench; they do. A Conservative Lord Chancellor, the top judicial officer of the Crown and a member of the Government, when choosing between two men of roughly equal legal capability, one Conservative and the other Labor, would probably appoint the Conservative. But the emphasis in the two systems is clearly placed at different points. This is illustrated by the path to the bench in Britain.

The British legal profession is divided into two ironclad categories: the solicitors who prepare wills, arrange estates, and generally do what might be described as the legal leg-work; and the barristers, who have a monopoly on court pleading, rely on solicitors for their material, and may fairly be described as the legal elite. It is from the latter category that British judges are chosen, on the basis of their legal eminence, to serve for life. Since there are so few judges, a barrister may anticipate—assuming first-rate ability—a fifteen- or twenty-year wait before he can be appointed to the bench. These years are spent in close association with other leading barristers at one of the Inns of Court, which serve as the guild associations, and enforce rigorous standards of behavior upon their members. Thus by the time a barrister receives the cherished recognition of a place on the High Court, he is steeped in professional standards which he then expects to find in those pleading before him.

When one compares this tortuous path of legal proficiency with the basis upon which many American lawyers are elevated to the bench, the major distinction between the judicial systems of the two countries becomes apparent. For example, Judge Thomas Murphy, the former Police Commissioner of New York City, was made a Federal district judge solely on the basis of his successful prosecution of Alger Hiss. One can applaud the imprisonment of perjurers without necessarily believing that the successful prosecution of a perjury case is a sound basis for elevating a United States Attorney to a judgeship. Unfortunately in the United States considerations of this sort—in the case of Murphy, the apparent desire of the President to demonstrate that he too was glad Mr. Hiss was in jail—play far too important a role in the allocation of judicial office. As was suggested earlier, political proficiency is a necessary prerequisite for appointment to the United States Supreme Court in view of that tribunal's unique function in American politics, but this unique situation should not be generalized to make politics the primary qualification for all Federal judicial offices. And, as the case of the late Chief Justice Harlan F. Stone indicates, it is possible to combine a high degree of political sagacity with exemplary legal training.

THE FRENCH JUDICIARY

If political proficiency is the primary prerequisite for appointment to the American Federal judiciary, and if guild status is the basis for British judicial selection, the French have devised a system which in some ways combines both these criteria. French judges are civil servants, legal technicians, and the judicial career is clearly separated from the legal one—a young man must decide at the outset whether he wants to become a lawyer or a judge, and there is no switching from one category to the other. Yet the historic route to top judicial office in France has been political favoritism. Although the Fourth Republic has taken steps to prevent such political promotion, it is to be doubted whether a system so firmly ingrained and organized can be destroyed by a weak government. Even a strong government such as the British, based on party control, often has difficulty preventing the administrative class from becoming autonomous, while bureaucratic autonomy has long been the tradition in France. So long as the French judges, like other French civil servants, can operate free from strong central direction, there is little to prevent friends from taking care of each other. Paradoxically, only a vigorous political class, *i.e.*, strong political leaders, can keep the administrative class nonpolitical.

As might be inferred from the above, the French judiciary does not have the tradition of independence that the British and American have. French judges are officials of the Ministry of Justice, and have traditionally been considered as the legal arm of the state, rather than as impartial referees in disputes. Thus one official of the Ministry of Justice prosecutes a case before another, and although the old myth that in France a man is considered guilty unless he can prove himself innocent is legally incorrect, there is certainly a strong presumption in the mind of the judge that his colleague, the prosecutor, or parquet, would not bring an innocent man into court. Furthermore, on a more subtle level, there is an institutional vested interest at stake. An American Federal judge or a British judge has no institutional ties with the prosecution, *i.e.*, he does not belong to the same bureaucratic empire. Consequently, the American or British judge can demand high standards from the prosecutor, and indeed throw his case out of court, without betraying his own organization, without committing what might be called institutional treason.

FRENCH JUDICIAL STRUCTURE

The French have two distinct sets of courts: one set, the regular courts, handles criminal cases and private litigation; the other, the administrative courts, is charged with adjudicating claims against the state. Since administrative law is reserved for treatment later in this chapter, our immediate concern here is with the regular courts. The French system of codified law is also discussed, and compared with the British and American systems, in a later section on comparative legal systems.

The French have both an enormous number of judges and a highly complex court system. Since a full description of the courts, of the distinction between the Industrial Disputes Councils, the Commercial Tribunals, the Tribunals of First Instance, etc., is unnecessary for our purposes here, a few generalizations about the judicial structure will suffice. First, the judicial system, though administratively centralized, is geographically highly decentralized. There are, for instance, 360 criminal and civil courts of original jurisdiction—as contrasted with 85 United States district courts operating in the continental United States. Similarly, the French have 27 civil appeal courts, while there are only 11 United States courts of appeal. The consequence of this is that no Frenchman has to travel far for his justice. The fact that state courts in the United States have jurisdiction over many issues that are handled on a national basis in France weakens the value of the comparison between the United States Federal courts and the French system, but if one looks at the small number of British courts, operating on a highly centralized geographical basis, the decentralization of the French court system becomes apparent. When it is further considered that the separate administrative courts have extensive jurisdiction over matters subject to the jurisdiction of the normal courts in the United States and Britain, the comparison becomes striking.

Second, the Anglo-American tradition of the judge as a "universalist," as a declarer of the law, is largely absent in France. There appear to be two major reasons for this: the civil-service status of the magistry, and the system of codified law. Under the civil-service system, a young man who has decided to become a judge and passes the necessary examinations may be immediately elevated to the bench and begin hearing cases. Probably because so many judges are inexperienced, the French have adopted the collegial principle, that is, there are usually three or more judges sitting together and deciding cases as a unit. Thus the position and status of the individual judge is deemphasized and replaced by a sort of judicial anonymity. The Anglo-American "great judge," e.g., Learned Hand, Oliver Wendell Holmes, John Marshall, Edward Coke, seldom appears on the French judicial scene. Also, under conditions established by the Superior Council of the Magistry—a body which is attempting under the Fourth Republic to cut down the role of political influence in judicial promotion—a member of the magistry may be shifted from one job to another. He may serve for ten years as a magistrate, then serve as a parquet, move into the administrative aspects of the Ministry of Justice, and perhaps finally return to the bench.

The system of codified law reduces the "universalist" function of the judge tremendously. Although judicial discretion can never be entirely removed from any system employing judges, the primary task of the judge in any nation with extensive codification is essentially comparable to a phonographic reproduction of the code. Once it has been established which section of the code is applicable to the case at bar, a task which may be somewhat complex in itself, the judge puts the needle on the record of the code at the appropriate point and serves as an animated loud-speaker. The only French court with an essentially common-law function is the Court of Cassation, which has the power to rule finally on codal ambiguities, and the decisions of which are binding on all magistrates. But these ambiguities do not arise as frequently as one might imagine, for the professors of jurisprudence and other legal experts who write the codes are notorious for their precision. Indeed, many French writers have considered the codes to be the very protoypes of precise prose, and many a French college student, troubled by imprecision in his writing, has been told by his professors to study the codes. It is questionable whether a perusal of the United States Code would serve a similar function.

COMPARATIVE LEGAL SYSTEMS

A brief description of the legal systems in force in the United States, Great Britain, and France is in order at this point. As the reader will have deduced, the functions of the judge as lawmaker are most noticeable in the United States, exist under limited circumstances in Great Britain, and are virtually absent in France. This extraordinary judicial power in the United States can be explained largely in terms of the power of judicial review at the Federal level, although in those states which have retained extensive common-law jurisprudence, the power of the judges is based on a different foundation.

The tradition of the judge as "universalist" is an outgrowth of the common law. Theoretically, in the common-law system, the judge does not make law, he merely applies the principles of natural law to the case before him. Common law would appear to be a frontier phenomenon; one variety or another of common law seems to be characteristic of most primitive societies. The wise man of the tribe sits in judgment over disputes, and his decisions serve as precedents in future instances of the same sort. Often the judgments of the wise man or shaman are given a religious foundation—he speaks for the gods.

The British common law grew up on this foundation, and though the judges presumably voiced "natural law," they were frequently open to the criticism voiced by George Bernard Shaw (through the mouth of his Caesar) that they confused natural law with the primitive customs of Britain. The apogee of this tradition in Britain was reached in the era of Lord Edward Coke, who asserted that the judges were the decisive oracles of natural law. When Coke informed King James I that the sovereign was under no man, but under God and the law, he really meant that the King was subject only to God and the judges. Both the King and Parliament rejected this concept, and by the beginning of the seventeenth century, the British judges had retreated from this high promontory, never to return.

The rise of Parliament to a position of preeminence militated against the lawmaking functions of the judges, but it was not until Britain entered the industrial age that the judges found their activities really circumscribed. As

Parliament came face to face with the problems of an increasingly complex industrial civilization, more and more statutes, dealing in increasing detail with social and economic issues, took their place on the statute books. In addition, a larger and larger administration, often armed with judicial authority, moved into the field, charged with handling the specifics of legislation—a task theretofore left to the judges. Thus today the British legal system is based on written law, set forth by Parliament and by administrators acting under Parliamentary authority, rather than on judge-made or common law.

Although the American legal system developed from the same sources as the British, it did so with certain outstanding differences. In the United States, the principle of legislative supremacy has never triumphed *de jure,* although at times it has achieved *de facto* victories, and, in addition, it was determined quite early in American history that, with one exception in the field of commercial law, there was no Federal common law. The Federalists, and the great Federalist legal lights such as Kent and Story, wanted to establish a Federal common law and, indeed, succeeded for a brief period in doing so. The Jeffersonians, however, both for the theoretical reason that they believed in states' rights and legislative preeminence and for the practical reason that the Federal courts were filled with Federalists, opposed and virtually destroyed this embryonic development. Consequently, the Federal judges could not take action, except in certain commercial cases, without statutory warrant. Oddly enough, a sort of Federal common law existed in commercial matters until the Supreme Court, in 1938, ruled that it had been unconstitutional for 149 years!

However, while there was no substantial Federal common law, there was extensive use of judge-made law in most of the states. But here again the lawmaking functions of the judges declined first in those areas of industrial advance, leaving the judges operating on a common-law basis largely in those states of a predominantly rural character. In addition, some states such as Florida, California, and New Mexico had considerable infusions of Spanish law, and Louisiana had a codified system growing out of its French background.

Today, as a consequence, all Federal law, except that made by the courts in the process of judicial review, is written law devised and enacted by the Congress or by the President, acting in most cases under statutory warrant, but occasionally under his inherent constitutional powers. The states, on the other hand, present no uniform picture. Most of the heavily industrialized, urban states have extensive codification of their statutes, while the common law, although not wholly nonexistent in urban, industrial areas, lingers on largely in the rural states.

Why is judge-made law largely characteristic of rural, agrarian eras, of what we might call the frontier period? The answer does not seem too hard to find. The problems of such societies are essentially quite simple and capable of solution by "universalist" judges because the universe is so small. But as the judicial universe enlarges, the judges are faced by problems of a more and more complex nature which, in addition, require quick solution. Furthermore, the amount of litigation increases enormously. To take a concrete example, if the village blacksmith drops an anvil on his apprentice, a judge can investigate the problem, evaluate the evidence, and reach a decision of the amount of compensation to be awarded to the injured apprentice on the basis of common-law precedents. But suppose five hundred workers a day, employed in the impersonal atmosphere of factories, are injured in one way or another, can the leisurely—and expensive—process of common-law litigation cope with the problem of employers' liability? Perhaps if five thousand judges, experienced in the common law, could be appointed to the single task, a beginning could be made. But a much simpler solution, which was simultaneously expeditious and inexpensive, has been adopted in most industrial states, and in Great Britain as a whole—administrative adjudication on the basis of statutes. Here administrative bodies, workmen's compensation boards, have been established by statute, the old common-law rules of liability have largely been abandoned, and an insurance system operates in lieu of a judicial determination of rights and wrongs.

If the development of the British and American legal systems over the last century and a half has been characterized by the decline of the universalist judge, the French system of codified law, in force since Napoleon's day, was designed to prevent judges from ever becoming universalists. The structural keynote of the French Revolution was legislative supremacy, and one of the ways to keep the legislature supreme was thoroughly to domesticate the judiciary. Some of the techniques of this deemphasis on the judicial functions have already been discussed, so it is only necessary to examine briefly the codified legal system which has been one of the outstanding characteristics of French government and which has been widely imitated elsewhere. Needless to say, the idea of codifying law was not original with the French; codification was one of the major contributions of the Roman Empire to the science of government.

Implemented by a highly centralized judicial bureaucracy, the codal system, like the educational system introduced after the Revolution, was initially designed to destroy the parochialism of the *ancien régime,* which was a hodgepodge of legal institutions. It should be emphasized that the centralization here is of an administrative, not a geographical, nature; while the judicial system is decentralized geographically, it is run from the center with the purpose of enforcing a uniform set of legal principles on the whole of France.

The codes, prepared by legal scholars and perpetually under revision, are designed to set forth in clear, concise terms the exact legal consequences of any action. In other words, they are promulgated under legislative authority for the express purpose of circumscribing the judges and telling them precisely what to do under almost any foreseeable set of circumstances. Thus in France legal administration is in the hands of technicians: technicians who prepare the codes, and technicians who administer them. In contrast with the theory of the common law, which has the judge "declaring" natural law, the theory behind the codes is basically directed toward leashing the judiciary. French judges are not oracles of natural law, and the judiciary is not permitted to compete with the legislature or to search out for itself the principles of "natural justice."

Much has been written about the distinction between the Anglo-American common law and the French codal system, but it must be recognized that recent practice in the United States and Britain has tended in the direction of the French technique. More and more the Americans and British have been replacing judicial discretion with elaborate statutory provisions which, while not wholly analogous to codes, tend to resemble them more than they resemble the common-law tradition. Thus today it might be suggested that the main distinction between French and British law is not so much the form of the legal system as it is the institutions of judicial administration. To date, both the British and Americans have doggedly hung on to the myth of the judge as universalist, while the French have explicitly bureaucratized justice.

THE RISE OF ADMINISTRATIVE LAW

One of the major techniques that has been employed in Britain and the United States to sustain the myth of the universalist judge is that of depriving the courts of jurisdiction over matters for the handling of which they are manifestly unfit. This has certainly not been done consciously, but rather under the imperatives of events and changing social and economic conditions. Thus when the courts in Britain and in certain of the American states demonstrated that they could not handle the extensive problems raised by workmen's compensation, these matters were taken from their jurisdiction by the legislature and turned over to administrative bodies.

It was long contended in both Britain and the United States that the process of administrative adjudication was thoroughly undemocratic and, in the latter nation, that it was unconstitutional as well. The theory behind this assertion was that under the "principles of natural justice" one could not adjust the law to the specific circumstances of the individual by administrative action, but rather had to treat all alike under general principles of legal action. The custodians of these general principles of natural justice were felt to be the regular courts, which would apply these general rules to specific instances through the normal process of litigation. It was believed that if these restraints on the bureaucracy were lifted, the result would be administrative despotism with officials arbitrarily depriving citizens of their rights on the basis of administrative edicts.

American constitutional lawyers raised these generic objections to administrative adjudication, but they added a unique American road block—the doctrine of the separation of powers. For the administrative agencies to exercise judicial powers, they submitted, would be a usurpation by the executive department of judicial prerogatives. Only the judiciary could exercise judicial authority. That this was an unrealistic view of the separation of powers hardly needs reiterating, but it was one which nonetheless received considerable support and was even implicitly endorsed by the United States Supreme Court.

There is no room here for extensive treatment of the rise of administrative law in Britain and the United States. Suffice it to say that, first in Britain and later in the United States, administrative bodies were clothed increasingly with judicial powers. The reasons for this have already been alluded to: the expense of the normal process of litigation, the delays involved in getting a final judicial determination, and the quantitative increase in certain types of litigation growing out of industrialization. However, particularly in the United States, administrative tribunals developed in a clandestine fashion without formal recognition as such. Americans devised the term "quasi-judicial" to characterize such bodies as the independent regulatory commissions as if reluctant to admit that these organizations did indeed possess full judicial prerogatives.

To take a concrete example of administrative adjudication, the Immigration and Naturalization Service of the U.S. Department of Justice has at every legal entry point into the United States inspectors and examiners who are charged with preventing illegal entry into the United States. In the event that someone entering the country claims American citizenship, an examiner will evaluate the evidence and reach a decision as to whether or not the claimant is an American national. If the examining officer holds against the individual, an appeal may be made to the Commissioner of Immigration and Naturalization in the Department of Justice, and if the Commissioner sustains the decision of the hearing officer, a further appeal may be taken to the Board of Immigration Appeals. Finally, the Attorney General may, at his discretion, overrule the Board of Immigration Appeals. Thus on this one issue there are four possible levels of administrative adjudication. Above and beyond these administrative judicial bodies, appeals may be carried, as will be discussed later, to the regular courts.

This is but one example taken at random; there are hundreds of others that could be employed equally well. The National Labor Relations Board, the Secretary of Agriculture, the Securities and Exchange Commission, the Interstate Commerce Commission, the Attorney General, the Civil Aeronautics Board, and dozens of other government agencies are vested by law with judicial powers. Indeed, a close examination of the powers vested in such agencies constitutes a startling refutation of the doctrine of the separation of powers. Not only do these bodies exercise executive power, but they also issue rules of a legislative character, and adjudicate violations of the rules. Thus they make the rules, prosecute violations of them, and finally punish violators.

This consolidation of power profoundly disturbed many students of American law. In 1937, the President's Committee on Administrative Management recommended that the judicial powers vested in administrative bodies should be turned over to a small body, an administrative court of sorts, within the agency. The judicial division would be under the agency for housekeeping purposes only, and its members would hold their positions for a long, stated period, say, seven, nine, or eleven years. Thus the rule-making and prosecuting functions of the agency would be segregated from those of a judicial character. However, after a bitter struggle in Congress, this proposal was rejected.

The Administrative Procedures Act of 1946, although it reflected the anti-administrative-law views of the American Bar Association, did undertake to segregate to some extent the judicial from the administrative activities. While widening the grounds on which administrative decisions could be appealed to the regular courts, the act provided that those officers within the departments who exercised judicial functions must conduct their proceedings in a judicial fashion, that is, they must not, for example, hear evidence from one party without affording the other party equal access, and that to ensure them against reprisals from their departments, these officials must be granted extraordinary job security. Another similar step was taken by the Eightieth Congress when, in 1947, it separated the prosecuting functions of the National Labor Relations Board from the rule-making and adjudicating activities, turning the former over to a General Counsel who was administratively free from Board supervision. Neither of these moves has been notably successful. The segregation provisions of the Administrative Procedures Act failed to face up realistically to the facts of bureaucratic integration. The fact that the prosecutors and the examiners are basically members of the same team has far more impact than the essentially metaphysical separation engendered by giving examiners greater tenure rights than the prosecutors. In analyzing bureaucratic loyalties it is as important to know who drinks coffee with whom as it is to know formal status in tables of organization.

In the instance of the National Labor Relations Board, the major problem arose from the fact that the separation of functions was based more on political hostility to the New Deal philosophy, which purportedly dominated the Board, than on any considerations of jurisprudence. Thus a General Counsel who was hostile to the outlook of the Board was given the task of prosecuting unfair labor practices under rules laid down by the Board. A bitter internal struggle resulted, in which the Board claimed the right to establish the framework of operation for the General Counsel, while the latter maintained that he had the right to make such decisions for himself. No one seems to have profited from this civil warfare, but if any lesson can be drawn from it, it would be that the members of such an independent regulatory commission should either be responsible to the President and removable in the event that their views differ from his, or be reconstituted as an administrative court with only adjudicative functions. As in this instance, the decision making as to what cases should be prosecuted cannot be divided between two bodies without creating chaos—as Thomas Hobbes once observed, if two men ride a horse, one rides behind.

Unfortunately, Americans have not yet recognized the scope of the problem constituted by the growth of administrative adjudication. There has been much talk about the vicious character of "bureaucratic injustice," but this particular tack ignores the fact that administrative adjudication is imperative to the efficient operation of the modern industrial state. The answer to any bureaucratic injustice is not to return the tasks handled by administrative tribunals to the regular courts, which are patently unable to cope with them in quantitative terms alone, but to create institutions of bureaucratic justice. The most feasible manner in which to accomplish this would be by the segregation of the various judicial functions handled by the administrative agencies in the hands of administrative courts similar to the already existing Court of Patent Appeals. The rule-making and prosecuting activities of these agencies should be directly under the control of the President. One of the principles of democratic justice, clearly enunciated over two centuries ago by John Locke, is that no man should be the judge in his own case, and while many examining officers in the various departments have bent over backward to see that justice is done to the citizen, it would be wise to put the wielders of judicial power beyond the reach of an enraged administrative superior. The best way to do this is to give them institutional autonomy.

As was noted above, administrative decisions can be appealed to the regular judiciary and, because of congressional distrust of the process of administrative adjudication, on very broad grounds. In effect, if a court of appeals dislikes the decision of, say, the National Labor Relations Board or the Administrator of the Fair Labor Standards Act, it may retry the whole case, thus making the previous work of the administrative tribunal superfluous. However, in the great bulk of appeals, the courts of appeal accept the administrative body's findings of fact and merely review the law in the case to ensure that it has been properly applied. The decisions of the courts of appeal in such cases may, of course, be appealed to the United States Supreme Court if the latter body is prepared to grant certiorari. In no other nation are administrative decisions subject to such comprehensive review as is the case in the United States.

ADMINISTRATIVE LAW IN BRITAIN

Like their American confreres, the British lawyers and judges bitterly resisted the growth of administrative adjudication. Although one cannot help thinking that their objections were in large part based on the "closed shop" proposition that only those trained in the mysteries of the law were qualified to administer justice, the philosophical issue of bureaucrats being judges in their own cases also played a part. In Britain this was complicated by the principle of parliamentary supremacy which made it possible for Parliament to forbid judicial review of administrative decisions taken under a specific statute. Parliament could, and did, include in certain pieces of legislation a provision that "the decision of the Minister shall be final" which automatically foreclosed substantive judicial review. However, as Professor Robson has conclusively demonstrated, administrative bodies had for centuries exercised judicial powers in Britain, and conversely, judicial courts had acted in administrative capacities. The great objection to administrative law mainly developed in the late nineteenth and early twentieth centuries when administrative tribunals began to be employed extensively in regulating and restricting property rights.

The pattern of development in Britain was likewise similar to that in the United States. The legislature, acting without any preconceived plan, delegated judicial powers to administrators in a piecemeal, pragmatic fashion, and suddenly, after this process had continued over many years, British lawyers awoke to the realization that administrative law had come into existence. The occasion for this great awakening and bemoaning was the publication, in 1929, by Lord Chief Justice Hewart of *The New Despotism*. Parliament, Lord Hewart declared, was being undermined by the bureaucracy and the "rule of law" was being replaced by bureaucratic whim. Administrative law, Hewart asserted, was not law at all, but institutionalized, arbitrary antilaw, rooted in the prejudice and self-seeking nature of the administrators. In short, administrative law was thoroughly un-British.

Lord Hewart's unqualified denunciations created a furore, and the Government appointed a committee composed of eminent Conservatives, Laborites, civil servants, lawyers, and legal scholars to examine the possible inequities growing out of the extensive use of delegated rule making and of administrative adjudication. The Committee on Ministers' Powers heard evidence from spokesmen of all points of view and emerged with a report which, while rejecting Lord Hewart's thesis that the bureaucracy was conspiring against British freedom, reflected in general the traditional bias of the legal profession against administrative tribunals. The committee attempted to maintain the fictitious distinction between judicial and "quasi-judicial" authority, recommending that "true judicial functions" should not normally be entrusted to administrative bodies. The proposals of Professors Robson and Jennings that an administrative court should be established either independently or as a branch of the High Court were ignored by the Committee. While the report of the Committee on Ministers' Powers did little to clarify the technical problems created by the rise of administrative adjudication, its sane and sober tone did much to abate the distrust of the bureaucracy initially engendered by Lord Hewart's unrestrained assault.

Consequently, like the Americans, the British have refused to rationalize their system of administrative adjudication, that is, simplify the structure and create distinct administrative courts. Each Ministry continues to adjudicate within the terms of reference and by the techniques set forth in relevant Parliamentary enactments, and the outcome is a patchwork of tribunals, boards, referees, without any rhyme or reason organizationally speaking. Pragmatism is rightly considered one of the virtues of Anglo-American political procedures, but there is such a thing as carrying pragmatism too far. Students of British administrative law have long recommended that the judicial powers exercised by administrative authorities should be segregated and rationalized so as to free the adjudicating officer or tribunal from the claims of bureaucratic loyalty and to make the process more accessible to the citizen.

The right of the citizen to appeal the decision of an administrative tribunal to the regular courts, in this instance the High Court, exists in Britain, but the grounds for review are far narrower than in the United States.

FRENCH ADMINISTRATIVE LAW

French administrative law differs radically from that existing in Britain and the United States, for the term as employed in France includes most of what would be called public law in the other two nations. Shortly after the French Revolution there was established in France a separate hierarchy of administrative courts which in its current form consists of the Council of State at the top and interdepartmental Administrative Tribunals as the normal courts of first instance. Nevertheless, the hierarchical relationship is not rigid; some cases may be heard initially by the Council of State.

However, it would be a mistake to confuse French administrative courts with British and American administrative tribunals, for the former do not engage in administrative adjudication as we described it. Indeed, the function of administrative courts in France with regard to the actions of the bureaucracy is one that is exercised by the regular courts in both the United States and Britain. They do not engage in administrative adjudication, but rather act as watchdogs over the administrative process. For example, if a Frenchman believes that an administrative decision violates the French constitution, he will take action against the official concerned in the administrative courts. Similarly if a citizen believes that a bureaucrat has abused his authority, an administrative court has jurisdiction in the matter.

Thus the French have established courts for administrators rather than administrative courts. These courts exercise essentially a negative function of holding administrators in line; they do not, like the Interstate Commerce Commission or the British Transport Tribunal, adjudicate on the substance of administrative action by, say, establishing freight rates. This distinction is an important one to keep in mind.

Any Frenchman can bring action against an administrator for what he maintains is an abuse of power or an usurpation of jurisdiction. The great bulk of cases before the interdepartmental Administrative Tribunals consists of appeals against government economic regulations of one sort or another. The Tribunals, composed of a president and four councilors, receive evidence and decide the matter on the basis of a majority vote. The procedure is expeditious and inexpensive, and the decision is almost invariably final; it is possible to appeal the holding to the Council of State, but this is rarely undertaken.

The Council of State exercises jurisdiction over matters of a more serious nature as prescribed by law. Much of its work consists of hearing suits against public officials, though it also serves as a sort of civil-service commission, regulating the internal affairs of the bureaucracy, hearing appeals from dismissals, and establishing personnel procedures. A Frenchman may bring suit in the Council against an administrator either on the ground that the official was *ultra vires* in taking some action, or that he abused his power in taking it, *i.e.*, he did a legitimate thing for illegitimate purposes. Space does not permit an elaborate examination of the legal distinctions employed by the Council in assigning liability to the state for the actions of officials; suffice it to say in oversimplification that if it can be demonstrated that an official action taken in good faith is *ultra vires*, or that the official committed a *faute de service, i.e.,* a mistake based on honest incompetence or misfeasance rather than subjective dishonesty or malfeasance, the citizen may collect damages from the state. In the event that the official misconduct was based on subjective dishonesty, a *faute personnelle* has been committed and the citizen must bring action against the official as private citizen in the regular courts. Needless to add, the distinction between *faute de service* and *faute personnelle* is a very difficult one to establish in many instances, and a special body, the *Tribunal des Conflits,* is charged with the task of distinguishing one from the other.

In sum, the French administrative courts are charged with public-law functions which often verge upon what would be called constitutional law in the United States. A tribunal roughly comparable to a French administrative court which has long existed in the United States is the Court of Claims which has jurisdiction over suits for damages brought by citizens against the United States government. But in the United States similar jurisdiction, depending upon the amount at issue, is also vested in the district courts and in administrative departments. Conversely, the judicial powers exercised by administrative bodies in Britain and the United States are not vested in the French administrative courts. These powers are exercised by the bureaucracy subject to the limitations imposed by the Council of State and the Administrative Tribunals, so that the latter bodies are charged with judicial review of administrative actions, not with administrative adjudication.

THE PROTECTION OF INDIVIDUAL RIGHTS

As was suggested in Chapter 1, the success of democracy as a form of government depends upon the continual flow of individual insight into the community pool. Thus freedom of speech, of the press, of religion, and generally of the person are essential preconditions for the continuation of democracy. If the individual is told that he must not differ, or is arrested if he does, the dynamic of democracy withers away and is replaced by the stasis of conformity. The most distinguishing characteristic of the totalitarian state is that individual opinion is forced to follow a channel created by the governing elite; in the Soviet Union, for example, freedom of speech means freedom to follow the authorized "line."

Thus one of the major tasks confronting the democrat is the maintenance of the climate of freedom, the atmosphere which encourages individuals to bring forth their new ideas for consideration by the community. The pragmatic value of this climate is demonstrable: consider where industrial development might be in the United States and Britain if the views of Adam Smith had been suppressed by the mercantilists who earlier dominated the economic scene. Generally speaking, the judicial organs are charged in democracies with the specific task of delineating individual rights and distinguishing them from abuses of freedom. However, it must be kept in mind that no institution can be much stronger than the consensus that supports it, so that individual freedom can seldom be protected from an irate community by judicial authority alone.

The basic personal freedoms were incorporated by our suspicious ancestors, who were profoundly distrustful of state power, in the Bill of Rights, the first ten amendments to the Constitution. Thus they were incorporated as part of the "supreme law of the land." However, the Bill of Rights was designed only as a limitation on the power of the national government, and it was not until 1925 that the Supreme Court held that freedom of speech, of the press, of assembly, and of religion were also, through the medium of the due-process clause of the Fourteenth Amendment, limitations on state activity. In recent years, following the leadership of the late Chief Justice Stone, the Court has moved in the direction of placing these rights in an especially favored position, insisting that the burden of proof in a civil-rights case is on the state to demonstrate that it has not violated the rights of the individual concerned. In non–civil-rights cases, the burden of proof is on the individual to demonstrate that his rights have been abused, and as any lawyer can verify, the locus of the burden of proof in a case is often decisive in determining the outcome.

Although devotees of logic such as Justice Frankfurter have objected to having two sets of rules, one set for civil-rights cases and the other for non–civil-rights litigation, it is submitted that this distinction is a valid one. These specially shielded freedoms differ qualitatively from, say, the freedom to run a business free from state regulation; they are, indeed, the preconditions for government by discussion. One may disagree with a state's decision to regulate milk prices, but so long as he has freedom of speech and of the press and the right to hold meetings and petition for a change in the law, he is in a position where he can perhaps convince a majority to agree with him and change the law. Similarly, a trade-unionist may believe the Taft-Hartley law to be wrong, but his right to convince a majority to agree with him is not affected by the statute. Democracy is not any one set of economic and social policies, it is neither capitalism nor welfarism, it is rather a method of reaching community decisions on the basis of consensus. Since the personal freedoms guaranteed by the First and Fifth Amendments are basic to and antecedent to the achievement of consensus, they deserve special protection. Democrats may differ about the road they should take, the policies they should adopt, but they should not allow anyone to tinker with the motor that is providing transportation. Those who would forbid freedom of speech and the press are in effect tearing out the spark plugs of the democratic engine.

This is all very well in theory, but the fact must be faced that the judiciary cannot protect American civil rights against a hostile community. True, the United States Supreme Court can declare an Oklahoma loyalty law unconstitutional, as it did in 1952, but the great bulk of civil-rights violations are not reviewed in the Supreme Court. In the first place, many of them are not committed by state or Federal officers, but by private citizens or groups. The unofficial pressure of private governments, American Legion posts, trade-union locals, religious bodies, can be tremendous, and it is not amenable to judicial review. In the second place, one must not suffer from what Judge Jerome Frank has called "appellatitis," that is, a concentration on the decisions of the appellate courts to the exclusion of the courts of original jurisdiction at the bottom. For example, state judges, generally elected by the citizenry, often tend to restrict civil rights unduly, particularly with unpopular minorities, and relatively few decisions are appealed. An appeal costs money, and unless, say, a Negro who has been deprived of his constitutional rights can get legal subsidization from an organization like the National Association for the Advancement of Colored People or the Urban League, he is likely to go off to the road gang. The lawyers for the NAACP have publicly stated that, for every case they appeal, fifty of equal merit go unappealed.

Consequently, the protection of American civil rights cannot be left in the hands of the judiciary. It is a community concern, and one of the major functions of education in a democracy must be the development in the individual citizen of the awareness that his rights are not just facts like the air he breathes and the food he eats, but are values which his ancestors developed through centuries of travail, and which must be regenerated in each generation if a free society is to be maintained. Continued freedom requires dedication to the preconditions of existing freedom. He must also face up to the unfortunate reality that basic civil-rights issues often arise in connection with the activities of thoroughly obnoxious, not to say noxious, characters. The right of Gerald L. K. Smith or of William Z. Foster to hold a peaceable meeting must be defended equally with the right of the Paducah Stamp Club or the Save the Redwoods League, for it is the right of freedom of assembly, not the views of those assembled, that is at issue.

The British and French have not been plagued by the problem of the community on the rampage to the extent that the United States has, at least not in recent years. In the case of Britain, this can probably be explained by two factors: first, the British have a strong tradition of individual freedom; and, second, the British have a highly homogeneous community, largely free from significant minorities of either a national or a social character. Furthermore, living in crisis is old stuff to the British, who have for centuries had enemies virtually within swimming distance of their coast, and their continued survival has endowed them with a sense of national security that Americans, who suddenly awoke to find themselves living in a possible combat area only in the last generation, have not achieved. The British reaction to the menace of Mosleyite fascism in the 1930's was a yawn, and the British people have similarly refused to give the Communists the free publicity of martyrdom. Contrary to the views of some American alarmists, this is not due to the British weakness or lack of attachment to the principles of democracy, but to British confidence in British democracy. Unquestionably the Communists have as their objective the overthrow, by force if necessary, of democratic government, but the British feel that they might as well conspire to steal Buckingham Palace. To put it another way, the British distinguish between the considerable external threat presented by Soviet imperialism and the negligible internal threat offered by the British Communist party's conspiratorial activities.

This brings up a significant comparison with the United States that is worthy of brief notation. The United States has historically been culturally pluralistic, that is, it has been a nation composed of many minority groups which have on occasion fought each other bitterly. In New England there is still considerable anti–French Canadian sentiment; in Minnesota, the Swedes looked down on the Finns; in the South, whites discriminated against Negroes; on the West Coast, the Asian minorities were subject to discrimination. Thus there are considerable elements in the population which distrust each other and are often prepared to employ official or unofficial coercion against their opponents. The recent instance of the relocation of 70,000 American citizens of Japanese ancestry during World War II is a classic instance of racial prejudice being incorporated in public policy. It would seem that there is a great deal more insecurity and even distrust of democracy in the United States than is the case in Britain, and this insecurity is reflected in the passion with which the community turns on those suspected of treason or of conspiracy against the state. On the other hand, the last significant migration to Britain occurred in 1066, and British society is not only ethnically but also socially quite stable and static. The cultural, social, and economic mobility that characterizes the United States has great advantages indeed, but it simultaneously engenders instability and competitiveness, both on the individual and the group level, which are often reflected by a lashing out against the people who criticize or undermine the system. It might be suggested that it is the average American's lack of internal security that leads him to press so vigorously for internal security laws.

Because the British people have internal security, there are few demands for the scalps of subversives so long as the latter behave themselves in an orderly manner. Espionage and sabotage are, of course, criminal offenses in Britain as they are here, but the British are aware that Soviet spies seldom carry membership cards in the British Communist party or subscribe to the *Daily Worker*. Indeed, the record of communist espionage seems to indicate that the Russians profoundly distrust the foreign Communists, who have a habit of suddenly losing their faith and writing detailed and profitable autobiographies. Consequently, the British maintain that suppression of the Communist party would play no noticeable function in improving security, but would merely consume the taxpayers' money supporting jailed Communists. In any case, there have been few demands for suppression, and these have been ignored by the Public Prosecutor with the full support of both Labor and Conservative Governments.

The situation in France is more difficult to describe. Immediately after the Liberation, the French engaged in a lynching bee, shooting and hanging people who had collaborated with the Nazis. But General de Gaulle put an end to this extralegal process as rapidly as possible, and there has been no recurrence of this type of hysteria since. Paradoxical as it may sound, a major reason why there has been no organized state action against subversives may be that there are so many of them. The fragmented nature of the French community has been discussed earlier, and one of the consequences of this fragmentation appears to be a truce of sorts between the fragments. An attempt to suppress the powerful French Communist party, which received more votes in the 1951 election than any other single party, could result in civil war. At the other end of the political spectrum, right-wing subversives are not suppressed, possibly because an effort to suppress them would play into the hands of the Communists, who have been demanding a thorough purge of "fascists" for years.

Two further reasons may be suggested for the general French indifference to the problems created by disloyal minorities. First there is a certain widely held cynicism about the whole political process, well expressed by one Frenchman who observed, "All the parties are made up of talkers, and the Communists are the biggest windbags of them all." Judged from this apolitical viewpoint, the Communists do not constitute a real threat because when the chips are down their conspiracy will turn out to be all conversation and no action. Second, the French judiciary, being under the control of a bureaucracy well insulated from the passions of the community, has rigorously applied the provisions of the code. Thus Jacques Duclos, the Communist leader, was freed by a court, after being apprehended by the police for leading a welcome riot for General Matthew B. Ridgway, on the ground that his actions, narrowly and legalistically interpreted, did not abrogate his parliamentary immunity. In the United States, Duclos would probably have been given six months for disorderly conduct on the principle that he would be a good man to take out of circulation.

Consequently, it appears that the freedoms of speech, press, person, and assembly have not been seriously invaded in France. It should be noted that partly this grows out of a passionate French belief in individualism, but it also seems, at least in considerable part, to be true for unfortunate reasons. Because of the profound schisms that exist in the French community, it would seem that each group has supported the protection of civil rights for themselves and has been unwilling to risk defeat by attempting to deprive its enemies of their rights. Thus, in this pragmatic sense, freedom appears to rest more on impotence than on strength, and the peace which exists is based on a tacit non-aggression pact rather than upon consensus.

CONCLUSIONS

In all the democracies examined, judicial institutions play a significant part in the day-to-day business of government. In the United States, the courts, with their right of judicial review of legislation, have a much more powerful position than is the case in either Britain or France, where they are excluded from the legislative arena. It has been suggested that this American judicial power is in large part an outgrowth of the lack of cohesive majorities in the United States, so that if a strong two-party system did arise here, we might expect to see the right of the courts to block the decisions of the national legislature wither away. Certainly no strongly organized political party which had won an election on a precise program would permit the judiciary to frustrate the implementation of its promises. The actions of the Supreme Court at the time that the radical Congress was running roughshod over both President Johnson and the Constitution may serve as an indication of how the Court would act when faced by a determined majority: in a whole series of cases, *Mississippi v. Johnson, Georgia v. Stanton, Ex parte McCardle,* the Justices retreated to a position of rarified impotence. Indeed, in the McCardle case, they even permitted Congress to deprive them of their right to review actions taken under the Reconstruction Acts.

The British judiciary has been living with monolithic majorities for some time, while the French principle of legislative supremacy implemented during the French Revolution led to the creation of a judiciary composed of technicians which has never launched any major assault on the lawmaking process. But it must be noted in connection with the activities of the Council of State that this body has a legislative division, separate from the judicial group, which drafts legislation for the Government, so there may be an element of bureaucratic review of legislation present. An American civil servant was once known to observe that he did not care who passed the laws so long as he wrote them, and the law-drafting activities of the Council of State may fall into this pattern.

In any case, in all three democracies, the judiciary stands as the arbiter of differences between individuals and between individuals and the state. Its task is to apply social norms, whether derived by common-law techniques or from specific statutes or codes, to the conflicts that arise in society and to see that these conflicts are settled in accordance with regularized procedures. This is not only true of the so-called regular courts, but also of administrative tribunals which, while different in organization and utilizing more expeditious procedures, are fully judicial in function.

Chapter 11

THE DEMOCRATIC EXECUTIVE

AMONG THE most complex problems that rise to plague democratic government are those which relate to the extent and basis of executive power. There are those who maintain that strong, vigorous leadership is a dangerous proposition, while others, like the great political sociologists Mosca and Michels, have virtually asserted that leadership is by its very nature undemocratic. The first group opposes strong democratic executives on the ground that they are likely to run away with the government—much opposition to the late President Franklin D. Roosevelt was predicated on this assumption. The latter group looks upon democracy as a façade, a "political formula," to use Mosca's phrase, which clever leaders use to convince the mass that they are working in the best interests of the society as a whole. In this view, democracy is merely a particularly ingenious camouflage that an oligarchy has devised to conceal its activities.

Before examining the institutions of democratic leadership, these two assaults on the legitimacy of leadership must be examined. First, let us attempt briefly to answer the charge that strong democratic leadership is dangerous and tends toward dictatorship. Obviously, strong leadership can be dangerous; history is replete with examples of leaders who have become tyrants. Indeed, it was a consciousness of this that led the formulators of American constitutionalism—notably John Adams, who in his *Defense of the Constitutions* drew heavily on the experience of the Italian Renaissance city-republics to demonstrate the potentially dangerous nature of unchecked elected leadership—to hedge the Presidency about with barriers against autonomous action. But the point that must be made here is that these leaders became tyrants not because they were strong but because they were irresponsible.

The British experience would seem to support this thesis. Relatively speaking, the British Prime Minister is far stronger as an executive than is the American President. He has areas of autonomy that are unknown to the American Chief Executive, *e.g.*, in the areas of foreign affairs, appointments, reorganization of the administration. But his autonomy is responsible autonomy; he operates within an area of consensus carved out by his party, his electors, his majority in Parliament. If we may employ a somewhat unflattering analogy, the American President is comparable to a horse who can only maneuver with a rider—Congress—on his back, while the British Prime Minister is like a horse who has been given complete freedom of movement within a fairly large paddock, the boundaries of which are established by the British people through their party system. If this description of the powers of the President appears unduly restricted, it might be noted that the American executive needs senatorial assent for all his important appointments—and many minor ones as well—and for the treaties he wishes promulgated, and he can reorganize an executive department only with congressional consent. In addition, as has been described in an earlier chapter, congressional committees actively intervene in administration, in many areas challenging the President for policy control of executive agencies.

Consequently, it is submitted that strong leadership is not incompatible with democratic government so long as the leader is subject to restraint. The major restraint is, of course, the possibility of defeat in an election at the hands of outraged public opinion. Here again the importance of freedom of speech, of press, of opinion, discussed in the last chapter, emerges as the precondition of fully responsible government, for unless the opposition has the right, and the facilities, to inform the public of the deficiencies of the regime, the electoral process loses its key position as the instrument for enforcing consensus on the leaders. The reader should never forget that although this book is divided into chapters, the democratic political process is unified, and the forces described under various headings are operating simultaneously. Public opinion, parties, the legislature, the judiciary, and the administration, all play parts in the drama of responsibility.

Conversely, current experience in France as well as the history of the fall of the Weimar Republic in Germany seem to indicate that effective leadership is a vital necessity for successful democratic government. If the political class is to control the activities of the administrative class, an effective instrument is required, and neither legislatures nor legislative committees are equipped to do the job. Ironically, a strong executive, often considered as the bureaucrat's dream, is the best instrument yet devised for controlling the bureaucracy. Thus it might be suggested that strength is an integral component of a responsible executive, for unless the latter has extensive powers, he is likely to find himself at the mercy of administrative experts who take over the decision-making process. Republicans who want to see an end to what they have described as "bureaucratic tyranny" should implement this hope by giving President Eisenhower more power than he has—not by cutting down the President's prerogatives. If the Chief Executive is going to control the bureaucracy successfully, he needs the strength of ten.

The second argument against strong leadership, that it is inherently undemocratic, oligarchic, and irresponsible, also contains a grain of truth. Undoubtedly leaders, usually possessed of superior sources of information and an understanding of the whole picture that cannot be attained by either the people or the legislature, often get exasperated with the process of discussion. Sometimes they may try to break the moorings that hold them to the mass. But the advocates of the "iron law of oligarchy"—the view, notably expressed by Mosca and Michels, that leaders are inherently irresponsible—seem to have confused the part with the whole. For example, President Truman in his seizure of the United States steel industry in 1952 clearly attempted to short-cut consensus, and the Supreme Court, here acting on behalf of an irate Congress and an unconvinced populace, declared the President's action unconstitutional. Similarly British Foreign Secretary Sir Samuel Hoare had to pay the penalty in 1935 for undertaking a foreign policy without the support of the British people; the public reaction against the Hoare-Laval Pact was such that Sir Samuel lost his post and was retired to the House of Lords, with Anthony Eden, who had not supported the previous policy, becoming Foreign Secretary. In short, there are in democracies penalties which can be invoked against leaders who attempt to cut their moorings.

At this point, the defender of the "iron law of oligarchy" generally retorts by noting that the strong leaders educate the mass to follow them, thus, in effect, imposing their views. But there is a catch in this: the "in effect." In the first place, it is the job of leaders to present information to the people, and this is not, "in effect," imposing their views upon the people. One of the keystones of the democratic faith is the belief that if you present people with the facts, they will reach a correct, or at least an intelligent, decision. Thus President Eisenhower's explanation to the American people that reductions in income taxes could not precede decreases in expenditures was not an imposition of his views on the people; it was rather an attempt to bring to their attention long-run considerations which were somehow overlooked in the presidential campaign of 1952. That the Congress, which is extremely conscious of public opinion, agreed with the President, or at least acceded to his view, may be taken as some evidence that his views made sense to the people.

Following from this denial of the identity of education and imposition, it is patent that the people often refuse to be educated and proceed to vote against the leader. It should be noted that if ever a democratic leader had the field to himself, it was Prime Minister Winston Churchill in the period from 1941 to 1945—no other individual could challenge his position as the leader of Britain. But in the election of 1945, Churchill and the Conservative Government were resoundingly defeated by the Laborites. Similarly, President Franklin D. Roosevelt had just won the most decisive electoral triumph in American political history when he attempted to reorganize the Supreme Court, but the public that had voted for him in 1936 repudiated his 1937 action. Obviously the public is not mere clay that can be molded at the will of and to the shape determined by the leader, and it is their inability to appreciate this fact that has led the advocates of the "iron law of oligarchy" to overstate their case.

In summary then, the democrat is not concerned so much with the quantita-

tive fact of strength of leadership as he is with the qualitative problem of responsibility. Strong leadership, providing always that it is responsible, can be
a decided asset to the democratic cause, while weak leadership, such as that
supplied by the French Premier, can be a distinct liability which itself engenders irresponsibility. Keeping these two criteria—strength and responsibility—in mind, let us analyze the executive institutions of the leading democratic states.

THE AMERICAN PRESIDENCY

The physical separation of the Chief Executive from the legislature is the
most distinguishing characteristic of the American system. If one chooses to
define the separation of powers as the distance between the Capitol and the
White House, he is on fairly safe territory, but any attempt to distinguish executive power from legislative power, except in terms so general as to be meaningless, is doomed to frustration. The President, for example, has the pardoning power, but Congress also is authorized by the Constitution to issue amnes-
ties, which are, in effect, group pardons. Conversely, the Constitution includes
the power to suspend the writ of habeas corpus in Article I, which deals with
legislative power, and President Jefferson, when he wanted the writ suspended
at the time of the Burr conspiracy, requested Congress to do so. But usage
since President Lincoln's time has conferred this suspensory power upon the
President, so that today it is included in the Chief Executive's arsenal.

It is precisely this vagueness, this failure to delimit and define executive
power, coupled with the fact that the President and the Congress are elected
by different constituencies, that has led to the perpetual conflict between the
President and Congress. Each new President and new Congress must join battle to define their respective prerogatives. Territory won by a strong President
may be ceded by his weak successor. It may be recalled that upon President
Eisenhower's victory at the polls, many Congressmen immediately declared
that now, at last, the powers usurped from Congress by Presidents Roosevelt
and Truman would be returned to their rightful custodians. Such declarations
assume a lack of definition of executive and legislative powers, for if legislative
power is clearly legislative in nature, it could hardly, under the purported doctrine of the separation of powers, be exercised by the executive. Yet, before
the new administration had been in office six months, the new President and
the new Congress were back in the lists fighting the battle of definition, and
Congressmen were once again growling about "usurpation." Although the
President instructed his department heads to go along with Congress, he soon
found conflicts arising which necessitated that he battle with individual committee chairmen, e.g., Daniel Reed of the House Ways and Means Committee,
or resign any effective leadership.

In short, if one is going to understand the nature and effectiveness of the
American Presidency, he must abandon the almost universal misconception of

the separation of powers. In fact, governmental power in the United States is not separated but merged, and the executive, the legislature, and occasionally the judiciary, are engaged in internecine conflict, each trying to establish its jurisdiction over certain areas. There is a balance of power among the three divisions, but little separation of powers. Consequently, the powers of the President are not static and fixed, but fluid, and cannot be defined in juridical terms. The only effective way of knowing, for example, whether the President has the right to seize an industry is not to read Supreme Court decisions on the subject but to assess the power situation, the attitudes of Congress, and the state of public opinion.

Similarly, the President's control over the members of his own administration is not something that can be delineated in terms of statutory declarations or the contents of Executive orders. Legally the President has complete power over the members of his Cabinet, but in power terms some of them may be difficult to handle. For example, President Truman had little control over the activities of Secretary of State James F. Byrnes, who had a large and vociferous circle of congressional admirers, and was forced to by-pass Byrnes whenever he wanted to accomplish something the latter opposed. FBI director J. Edgar Hoover is the prize case of an untouchable administrator. Hoover runs his barony in his own efficient way with the enthusiastic cooperation of a large number of Congressmen and unquestionably has more political power than his nominal boss, the Attorney General. In fairness to Hoover, it should be noted that he has never failed to get along with his nominal chief and has not used his power to defy the administration. As Charles Hardin has demonstrated in his excellent case study *The Politics of Agriculture,* the Soil Conservation Service, although legally subordinate to the Secretary of Agriculture, was for years an autonomous duchy operating in close and fruitful contact with influential Congressmen. Once again, the powers of the President cannot be evaluated by looking at organizational charts or formal declarations, but only by carefully assessing the power factors involved in each case. No matter what figure the Bureau of the Budget may have determined as the budgetary requirement of the FBI, or how economy-minded the Congress may be, a statement by J. Edgar Hoover to a congressional committee that his funds are inadequate will bring an increased appropriation. What can the President and the Attorney General do? If they oppose the increase, they could be accused of aligning themselves with the forces of communism, gangsterism, and white slavery against the FBI's heroic struggle for law and order!

THE PRESIDENT'S CONSTITUENCY

While each Congressman is responsible to the voters of a small district, and Senators have state-sized constituencies, the President of the United States has the whole nation as his district. The direct consequence of this is that the Presidency is far more responsible to the urban electorate than is the Congress, which, as was noted earlier, is rigged in favor of rural areas. Since most minorities are politically effective in urban areas, the President is ex officio far more minority-conscious than Congress. A good example of this is the conflict between President Eisenhower and his congressional leaders over the McCarran-Walter Nationality Act. The President, following the advice of his urban-minded advisers, suggested extensive revision of some of the discriminatory provisions of that statute, but his congressional chiefs, almost without exception from homogeneous constituencies, like the enactment as it stands.

This brings up the generic problem of the President's relations with his party leaders in Congress, particularly the committee chairmen. As committee chairmen, whether Democratic or Republican, are designated on the basis of seniority, they tend to come from one-party areas, that is, from sections of the country where there is little competition. Under a Democratic regime, they come mainly from the South, while in the current Republican Congress, they are mainly representatives of rural Northern and Western constituencies. But precisely these districts have the least to say in the designation of presidential candidates. Consequently a President, whether Democrat or Republican, is nominated largely on the basis of his appeal to the marginal urban voter, who holds the balance of power in American elections, and when elected, he is invariably confronted by congressional committee chairmen from the wing of his party that he defeated at the party convention. The list of committee chairmen in the present Congress—Jenner, Capehart, McCarthy, Taber, Reed, Short, Velde, to mention only a few of the more significant—reads like a roster of the anti-Eisenhower forces at the Republican 1952 convention! Indeed, the only significant preconvention supporter of President Eisenhower to chair an important committee is Senator Saltonstall of Massachusetts. And it must be emphasized once more that the President has no institutional power over these chairmen.

Thus the President is trapped between his need to cooperate with Congress, which means in the real sense with congressional committee chairmen, and the demands of his wider constituency. If he takes a strong stand for internationalism, thus gaining high praise from the *New York Times, The New York Herald-Tribune, The Washington Post,* and other Eastern newspapers, he alienates many of his neo-isolationist committee chairmen. On the other hand, if he attempts to placate these pivotal Congressmen, representatives of the urban, industrial areas begin to grumble, and simultaneously the significant opinion-forming newspapers go into opposition. The job of President of the United States requires a hardy constitution; it could easily drive a sensitive soul to the madhouse.

The root of the problem is that the Presidency is the only American institution charged with seeing things as a whole. Congress does not operate as a whole. As Professor Schattschneider has pointed out, our legislative system institutionalizes parochialism by giving real legislative power into the hands of specialized congressional committees whose decisions are almost automatically ratified by the whole body. The President, for example, can appreciate the fact that European recovery depends in large part on an opening up of the American market, but a congressional committee reviewing tariff restrictions is far more concerned with the immediate problems raised for local constituencies by lowering import duties. The Danes whose cheese was excluded by Congress have no votes in Congressman August H. Andresen's Minnesota district, and the latter had no interest in becoming a martyr to the cause of free trade and Danish recovery. Similarly, the President can realize that repeal of the "Buy American" law, which provides that the United States government can purchase goods abroad only if they can be obtained for 25 per cent less than an American firm will bid, would save the government millions of dollars a year on clothing for our troops, industrial equipment, and other items, but Congress is not interested in saving money at the expense of votes in the areas which might be affected by this competition.

THE STRUCTURE OF THE PRESIDENCY

Unlike Britain, France, and many other nations in which the office of Chief Executive is separate from that of chief of state, the United States combines these two functions in the President. Thus in addition to being Chief Executive, chief administrator, chief of the armed forces, and formal head of his party, the President must also meet visiting Girl Scouts, launch battleships, confer medals, speak to all significant foreign potentates who visit the United States, initiate the March of Dimes campaign, and give a short speech whenever an important pressure group puts up a new building in Washington. In Britain, most of these latter functions would be handled by the royal family, which is usually appropriately large, while the Prime Minister confines himself to running the government.

Politically, the Presidency is one of the loneliest jobs in the world, for the President has no political institution, such as the British Cabinet, to share his responsibilities with him. The Vice-President is usually chosen to appease the opposite wing of the party from the President and therefore cannot be relied on in policy matters. The Cabinet offices are parceled out among the representatives of various interests in the party, or even, as is the case with President Eisenhower's first Secretary of Labor, from the opposition party. Cabinet officers are generally trying to go into business for themselves, politically speaking, and may thus constitute liabilities rather than assets to the President, who may have to spend a great deal of time keeping his official family in line. President Truman's difficulties with Secretaries Henry A. Wallace and James F. Byrnes come to mind at this point. And, until fairly recently, the President did not even have an administrative staff of any consequence to aid him in his tremendous tasks.

The absence of any trustworthy institutional aids has traditionally led American Presidents to organize so-called "kitchen cabinets," composed of personal friends and political supporters. In recent years, attempts have been made to supply the President with institutional advisers through the creation of such organizations as the Council of Economic Advisers, the Executive Office of the President, and the Joint Chiefs of Staff, all of whom are charged with giving the Chief Executive advice on matters subject to their jurisdiction. But even with these attempts to put institutional flesh and blood on the presidential office, the fact remains that the President alone is responsible to the American people, and he cannot allow any vital decision-making authority to escape from his hands. Assistants to the President can be assigned substantial chunks of authority, but the President, if he is to be politically successful, must keep them on a tight leash. President F. D. Roosevelt is said to have observed that when things got quiet in the White House, he got unsettled, suspecting that some member of his entourage was developing autonomy and attempting to take over the job. Substantial delegations of power may make for administrative efficiency, but it may also be the political equivalent of suicide.

Keeping these points in mind, it becomes apparent that the nice neat charts of the organization of the executive department have much less validity than is generally supposed. The even, formal hierarchy of bureau chiefs reporting to secretaries who in turn are responsible to the President is, in informal terms, broken by any number of unofficial channels of power and responsibility. In practice, congressional committees and pressure groups may have more authority over the decisions of some executive bureaus than do any of the formally responsible officials. Similarly, the President may circumvent or ignore his Cabinet officers by working directly with their subordinates, or with officials with no formal hierarchical position. For instance, President Roosevelt employed Undersecretary of State Sumner Welles extensively in this fashion, short-cutting Secretary of State Hull, and Harry Hopkins, who did not even appear on the chart, was far more powerful than most Cabinet members. Obviously, an understanding of the structure of the American Presidency can never be gained from the study of diagrams. Indeed, the structure is dynamic, changing from day to day, from crisis to crisis. A temporary expedient devised to solve one problem may become a permanent fixture; a permanent body may have all its vitality and power drained from it. A good case of this sort of withering on the vine is the Department of State, which has in recent years been losing control of certain aspects of foreign-policy formulation to various *ad hoc* agencies. The fiction has been maintained that, although the State Department has turned over the operation of various programs to other bodies, such as the Economic Cooperation Administration, the Foreign Operations Administration, the United States Information Agency, or the Department of Defense, it still retains policy control. But operations and policy cannot be separated, and the moment that the State Department loses control over the operation of, say, the Voice of America, it simultaneously loses its right to make policy for the Voice. Responsibility follows power, not pious assertions of fidelity.

THE OPERATION OF THE PRESIDENCY

It is apparent that the President of the United States is something less than a dictator. Indeed, a good case can be made for the point that he is not powerful enough for the job at hand. However, the case should not be overstated, for the President has at his disposal, if he is capable of employing it, a strong weapon to employ against dissident legislators or bureaucrats—public opinion. A President such as Roosevelt or Eisenhower becomes a sort of national symbol, with considerable ability to convince public opinion of the merits of his case. A President endowed with inherent leadership qualities—in Max Weber's phrase, a charismatic leader—can do a magnificent job of educating the public to his point of view, and can supply the Presidency with some much-needed leverage in the struggle with parochialism.

Furthermore, the President is the titular head of his party and can bring some pressure to bear through party channels. Presumably his party has a stake in him, for his success or failure in office may well determine the outcome of congressional elections in a presidential year. However, there is a problem here which has already been discussed above: the most powerful Congressmen have the least to fear, as they usually come from safe, one-party districts. But even they stand to lose their committee chairmanships if the opposition carries the election, so they are not immune to party pressure. The power of patronage has been much overrated as a coercive device by the "realistic" interpreters of the American scene, but from this source too the President gains some leverage.

But it is from informal rather than institutional sources that the President gains most of his power both nationally and within his own party. The fact that he is the only nationally elected official makes the President the natural focus of public opinion, and the dignity of his office always gives him headline priority in the newspapers and a clear channel over the radio and television networks. If he can mobilize public opinion behind his policies, the President holds a whip hand over Congress and over his own party, but if he is incapable of serving as a centralizing symbol, as a centripetal force in national opinion, the centrifugal forces in Congress and the bureaucracy take over. A President left high and dry by public opinion, such as Herbert Hoover in the period from 1930 to 1932, or Harry Truman in 1950 to 1952, is a sad sight to behold, for, with the failure of presidential charisma, all the divisive tendencies in American politics are exacerbated and parochialism runs rampant. On the other hand, a President with strong community support can exercise real power.

Contrary to many suppositions, the main task of the President is not issuing orders. As Herman Somers has suggested, the conflicts that require presidential settlement are of such a basic nature that most of them cannot be ordered out of existence. In a pluralistic society such as ours, group conflicts are frequently reflected in struggles between Federal agencies or even within Federal agencies, and the job facing the President is one of reconciliation. Legally he can dismiss, say, the Secretary of Agriculture, but before he acts in this hasty fashion, he had better reflect on the fact that the views advanced by the Secretary are probably those of the Secretary's constituents, the farmers. Obviously, the President cannot eliminate the farmers as a power bloc no matter how many Secretaries of Agriculture he dismisses, so another solution must be sought.

Viewed in this light, the President's role is that of the synthesist. He must take the varying and frequently conflicting demands of private interest and shape from them a working definition of the public interest. This calls for a genius at compromise as well as an ability to give compromise meaning in the forum of public opinion; it requires a willingness to lead as well as to be led. In short, in James Reston's phrase, the President must be "part executive, part actor, and part graven image." As well as Chief Executive, he is chief conciliator.

THE LIMITS OF PRESIDENTIAL POWER

Books have been written, usually in a judicial vein, analyzing the powers of the President and their limits. But to reiterate a point made earlier, the scope of presidential power is not subject to juridical analysis—at least, not in realistic terms. Presidential power is a variable which alters from day to day, from situation to situation. What may be today an unconstitutional exercise of power by the Chief Executive may be constitutional tomorrow, or ten years hence; and what was unconstitutional ten years ago may be constitutional today. In sum, the powers of the President were not wrapped up in a bundle in 1789, but have been subject to constant modification throughout the history of the Republic.

Actually it would appear that the President is free to act to the limits of consensus. To put it another way, the limits on the exercise of executive power are not set by the Constitution, but by public opinion as reflected in Congress. As Professor Clinton Rossiter has demonstrated, in an emergency which is recognized as such by the Congress and the American people, the powers of the Presidency are virtually unlimited. When Congress and the people do not believe that a "real" emergency exists, the actions of the executive may be severely circumscribed. In each instance, the rationale for expansion or limitation of executive power is not the Constitution, but community sentiment—consensus.

In the field of foreign affairs, for instance, a President may in an emergency situation take extraordinary action, e.g., Roosevelt's decision to send lend-lease to the Soviet Union after the latter was invaded by the Germans in 1941, or his "destroyers for bases" deal with the British. But unless the Congress agrees with the President, such decisions are empty of real meaning. The continuation of the lend-lease program, for instance, required extensive appropriations by Congress; and, more significantly, if the President violates the contract of consensus, Congress may take away his appropriations in other areas, or refuse to pass legislation necessary for the implementation of other programs. At Versailles in 1919, President Wilson offered France a long-term treaty of alliance which was a dead letter before the offer was made because of congressional opposition, and all attempts by President Truman to implement his "Point 4 program" of development for backward areas met with similar congressional erosion. Foreign diplomats are acutely aware of the circumscribed nature of presidential authority in foreign affairs, a fact which accounts for the skepticism with which the proposals of the American Secretary of State are frequently greeted. The truth of the matter seems to be that without congressional support, no presidential decision can achieve substantial implementation. The shade of Woodrow Wilson stands at the President's shoulder whispering warnings into his ear.

While in foreign affairs the power of the President is buttressed somewhat by nationalism, patriotism, and feelings of national honor—all sentiments to which he can appeal in support of his measures—in domestic affairs he is largely bereft of these symbolic supports. A Congressman may feel impelled by patriotism to support the Korean enterprise, but such a motivation will hardly enter into his consideration of agricultural price supports or rent control. Thus congressional support is imperative if presidential power is to be implemented.

President Truman's fate in the steel-seizure controversy is a case study of what can happen to a President who attempts to short-cut community sentiment, to issue an order instead of conciliating the conflicting interests. In an emergency, Presidents since Lincoln have exercised the power of seizing industrial facilities, both with and without statutory warrant, but in these instances there was consensus on the existence of the emergency and the Presidents had popular and congressional support for their actions. In 1952, President Truman claimed that a pressing emergency existed and took over the steel industry, listing as precedents for his decision the actions of Presidents Roosevelt, Wilson, and Lincoln. But it was immediately apparent that the American people and Congress did not consider the President's purported emergency to be a real emergency which would justify such strong action. The nation's newspapers, virtually without exception and irrespective of party affiliation, condemned the seizure. Congress began to seethe with indignation, and demands were heard that the President be impeached. The Supreme Court settled the issue by declaring the seizure to be unconstitutional. Here we have a perfect instance of limitation by public opinion, operating through the Congress indirectly and the Supreme Court directly, for the rationale of the Court's decision was not that such a seizure was invariably unconstitutional, but rather that this seizure was unconstitutional because there was not an adequate emergency. Of course, the Court did not put it in this way, but this was, nevertheless, what it said, while the three minority justices stoutly maintained that the emergency was real and did justify the action.

CONCLUSIONS

There are some who may object to the above description of the operation and prerogatives of the American President on the ground that it sounds more like the theme of a Kafka novel than like an analysis of a governmental institution. However, it is believed to be accurate, and it is in no sense aimed at denying the patent truth that the President is a powerful official. Indeed, the President is extremely powerful, but the point is that his power is not founded on his juridical position, on a technical, legal definition of his status and prerogatives. Rather, it is rooted in his relationships with Congress, pressure groups, and public opinion generally. The Presidency can be strengthened by institutional props such as the creation of an adequate staff, but the fundamental source of a President's authority is his ability to serve as a catalyst of consensus, as a mobilizer and integrator of public opinion.

In addition, because his authority rests on so tenuous a foundation, much of a President's time is taken up by attempts to avoid issuing direct orders. He is Chief Executive, chief administrator, party chief, chief of state, and commander in chief, but above all, he is chief conciliator. Thus, as President Truman once observed, he must spend hours convincing people to do what they should have done without question. In a heterogeneous, democratic society, group differences cannot be settled by recourse to the concentration camp, and it is the task of the President, who is in a sense the last level of appeal, to mediate between conflicting groups and their institutional spokesmen while simultaneously attempting to preserve the over-all imperatives of the whole society from parochial raids.

To return to our original criteria of evaluation—strength and responsibility—we find the American President to be a thoroughly responsible official. His actions are supervised not only by the official legislative and judicial institutions, but also by the unofficial institutions of party, pressure group, and, generally, public opinion. There has been much talk of the possibilities of presidential dictatorship, but in the light of the facts this appears to be nonsense. Congress could make the President into a dictator if it were so moved, but it is inconceivable that the President could go it alone. In terms of its strength, the Presidency varies from President to President and from situation to situation. Since the President does not have the support of a tightly organized political party, he is forced to build his power on a coalition of interest groups and pressure politicians. When he succeeds in developing a wide coalition, as Franklin D. Roosevelt did in the 1930's, he has considerable power, but when he must depend on a narrow segment, such as the essentially urban grouping that backed Truman in 1950 to 1952, he finds his power slipping from his hands. Thus a President, to be effective, must be broad-minded, for if he tries to build his power on a narrow and exclusive interest complex, he soon finds himself boxed in by hostile groups whose political power is sufficient to frustrate any ambitions he may have.

THE CABINET SYSTEM

Compared with the American executive, the most distinguishing feature of the cabinet system is the membership of the ministers in the legislature. Norway is the only outstanding exception to this rule; as in the United States, members of the Norwegian government are forbidden to hold legislative office. However, the chief executives of Britain, France, Italy, Austria, the Bonn Republic, and the nations of the British Commonwealth are all members of their respective legislatures. Other ministers are also initially elected as legislators. The British Cabinet is, in effect, the executive committee of the parliamentary majority, while the French Council of Ministers is composed of representatives of the parties participating in the current coalition. Consequently, the executive is not, like the President of the United States, responsible to an independent, nationwide constituency of his own, but is responsible to the legislature. The Government's continuance in office thus depends upon its ability to retain the confidence of a legislative majority for its policies.

A cabinet-type executive is not automatically either strong or responsible; an examination and comparison of the French and British experience will demonstrate that it may be both or neither. Given certain conditions the cabinet system may work exceptionally well; given other conditions, it is a mechanism that may work very badly indeed. While some Americans are vigorously urging the creation of a British type of cabinet government, some Frenchmen are equally strongly urging their fellows to establish an American-style independent president! Once again it must be emphasized that no set of governmental gadgets can guarantee the establishment of a stable, responsible government.

THE BRITISH EXECUTIVE

The British Cabinet has been developed over many centuries by a gradual process of accretion. Originally composed of the King's private councilors who gave him advice on various problems, the Privy Council gradually developed its independence and became the modern Cabinet. The great strides in this movement took place from 1689 on, after Parliamentary supremacy had definitely been established by the dismissal of King James II and the accession, by Parliamentary invitation, of William and Mary. Initially, the Cabinet was responsible more to the sovereign than to Parliament, but during the long reign of Sir Robert Walpole (1721 to 1742)—usually considered the first Prime Minister—the ties with Parliament were strengthened. Indeed, when Walpole failed to get the support of the House of Commons for his policies in 1742, he resigned, and thus set another precedent—that the Prime Minister must have the confidence of Parliament. It might be mentioned that the title "Prime Minister" did not receive official recognition until 1905; the official position of the chief minister was First Lord of the Treasury until that time.

Space does not permit an elaborate historical analysis of the rise of the modern cabinet, and those interested in more detail are referred to Sir Ivor Jennings's definitive study *Cabinet Government*. Suffice it to say that throughout the nineteenth century, as the British party system gradually evolved into its modern form, the Cabinet became a more and more homogeneous body and took an increasingly powerful position vis-à-vis Parliament. Simultaneously the discretion of the Crown in naming Prime Ministers decreased. In 1880, when the Liberal party won the general election, Queen Victoria, who detested Mr. Gladstone, the leader of the party, invited Lord Hartington to become Prime Minister, but the latter refused and advised the Queen to appoint Gladstone. Today, the only situation in which the Crown has any choice is in the event that no one party has a majority in Commons, as occurred in 1922 and 1929. In both these instances, the King sent for the previous leader of the Opposition, James Ramsay MacDonald of the Labor party. Except in these unusual situations, party organization is so strong that the designation of a Prime Minister is semiautomatic, *i.e.*, the leader of the majority takes over. No sovereign since Victoria has attempted seriously to intervene in political matters, and although Victoria tried to exercise her purported prerogative of dismissing a minister, Lord Palmerston, for whom she had a cordial dislike, she was unsuccessful. No sovereign since Queen Anne (1702 to 1714) has exercised the power of disallowing an act of Parliament, so this aspect of the royal prerogative has withered away.

THE ROLE OF THE CROWN

Americans, particularly those who watched the coronation of Elizabeth II in June, 1953, often wonder what all the fuss is about. Maintaining a Queen and a large number of royal relatives in a state of relative splendor is an expensive proposition, the thrifty American observes, particularly when you consider that they do not give any return investment. After all, if the British are such practical people, why do they insist on keeping up the elaborate masquerade of monarchy?

Some of these objections have already been met. It was noted earlier that the existence of the Queen and the royal family takes a great load of ceremonial work off the back of the Prime Minister. In one day, for example, the Queen can review a parade in honor of the Nizam of Kuwait, the Duke of Edinburgh can address a Congress of the World Health Organization, Princess Margaret and the Queen Mother can be visiting Kenya, and other uncles, aunts, and cousins can be occupied similarly elsewhere. Thus the functions of chief of state are separated from those of chief executive, with a resulting increase in the time the latter can devote to problems of state.

Also on the practical level, the sovereign can be of great assistance to the Prime Minister. In his memoirs, Winston Churchill has commented on the fine job that King George VI did during the war. The sovereign traditionally reads all important state papers and is consulted on all vital policy issues, and King George, an exceptionally conscientious and capable man, acted in the capacity of universalist, helping his overworked Prime Minister to maintain the over-all picture. Much of the effectiveness of this role depends upon the personality of the sovereign. A Queen like Victoria, with strong political and personal prejudices, was more of a nuisance than a help to her Prime Ministers, while a King like George VI, who was self-effacing and nonpolitical, could be of great help to his first Minister.

However, the real place of the Crown in the hearts of the British people cannot be explained wholly in rational terms. Democracy, as was remarked earlier, does not supply the citizen with many symbols—it is a cold, rationalistic faith that burns brightly but with little warmth. Instead of a cosmic crutch, the democrat offers the citizen a credo based on uncertainty and human fallibility; in a sense, the symbol of democracy might be a broken crutch. But in the Crown, British democracy has a symbol of unity and continuity which is above politics, and therefore not dangerous and divisive. Governments come and go, public policy is altered and realtered, individual sovereigns die or abdicate, but the Crown stands changeless as the mythological incarnation of permanence.

This association of symbolic unity with the chief of state also has pragmatic value. It makes it possible, for instance, to attack the chief executive without seeming to threaten the foundations of social unity. During the war, American Republicans were seriously hindered in their assault on President Roosevelt by the fact that he was not only a politician but also the symbolic chief of state. While they wanted only to attack the first, they found it difficult to do without seeming to endanger national unity, or at least being accused of it by the Democrats. On the other hand, in Britain, it was possible for left-wing Laborites and others bitterly to attack Prime Minister Churchill without being put in the position of undermining national unity: "God save the King, and down with Churchill."

BRITISH EXECUTIVE STRUCTURE

The over-all British executive includes, of course, both political and administrative officials, but our concern here is with the ninety-odd Members of Parliament who are appointed to executive office rather than with the permanent civil-service structure which has been discussed elsewhere. Of the ninety M.P.'s who obtain positions in the ministry, only fifteen to twenty are actually members of the Cabinet, and five or six of the latter group generally exercise the decisive voice in policy formulation.

The size and composition of the Cabinet varies from Government to Government: the 1945 Labor Cabinet included twenty officers; the Conservative Cabinet formed after the election of October, 1951, had only sixteen members. Certain Ministers, *e.g.*, the Chancellor of the Exchequer, the Minister of Defense, the Home Secretary, and the Secretaries of State for Foreign Affairs and Commonwealth Relations, are invariably included in the Cabinet, unless, as in Mr. Churchill's case, the Prime Minister also takes another portfolio—in this instance, that of Minister of Defense. The Lord Chancellor, who is the Government's chief legal official and also presides over the House of Lords, is another essential member. Other Ministers may or may not be included in the Cabinet, depending on the outlook of the Government and the exigencies of the situation. For example, in a period when the nation is faced with an acute fuel shortage, the Minister of Fuel and Power will probably be a member of the Cabinet, but if the shortage is eased, he may be dropped to lesser status.

The selections of Ministers is theoretically in the hands of the Prime Minister, but political realities may severely limit his discretion. In 1945, for example, Clement Attlee could not have refused Cabinet positions to Ernest Bevin and Herbert Morrison without creating acute political problems. Both because of his commanding personality and because the Conservative party has never attained the internal discipline of the Labor party, Mr. Churchill has far more discretion. But although the Conservative party tends to be a one-man show, even Churchill had to accommodate himself to the political realities of leading a nonmonolithic party by appointing men of differing viewpoints within the party to high office.

It must be kept in mind that British political parties are far less monolithic than is generally supposed. The Conservatives tend to appear less unified than the Laborites, but even the Labor party has great differences of opinion and potential sources of schism within its apparently united ranks. On the issue of conscription, for instance, the Labor Government received Conservative support, while many back-bench Laborites dissented and refused to vote for the draft. Conversely, in 1953, Conservative Foreign Secretary Eden's Sudanese policy caused great dissension among the more imperialist-minded Conservative M.P.'s, but gained enthusiastic Labor backing. Consequently, a Prime Minister cannot simply appoint whomever he pleases to Cabinet rank and count on party discipline to hold the line; he must adjust himself to living in a pluralistic party and must serve as a mediator between the different segments.

Once appointed, the Cabinet acts as a collectivity, that is, all members are responsible for everything that is done. If the Foreign Secretary, for example, does not like a specific policy decision, he is free to argue against it in Cabinet, but once a decision has been made, he cannot disassociate himself with it and remain in the Cabinet. All Cabinet discussions are secret, and it is a violation of the Privy Councilor's oath for a Cabinet Minister, or ex–Cabinet Minister, to reveal the substance of any Cabinet meeting. In the instance mentioned above, the Foreign Secretary may resign his position and denounce a policy proposal, but he may not go along with the proposal and then six months later state that he had opposed the decision in Cabinet. The same principle applies at all levels of the executive structure: one cannot hold office and simultaneously oppose publicly the decisions of the Government.

THE FUNCTION OF THE PRIME MINISTER

Obviously, the Prime Minister is the chief executive of Britain, but it is not sufficiently appreciated that he is also, like the American President, chief conciliator. The framework within which he must conciliate is, because of the form of the British party system and the basic social conditions that underlie it, much more limited than is that of the President. While the American President must conciliate among all significant groups in society and the French Premier, as we shall examine shortly, is a conciliator among parties that are also to some degree pressure groups, the British Prime Minister must conciliate within his party.

The consequences of this function are vital to an adequate understanding of the British Cabinet and the operation of the Prime Minister. In a very important sense, the task of the Prime Minister is to avoid taking decisions by majority vote in the Cabinet. A Labor Member of Parliament recently observed that when Cabinet decisions are made by voting, the Cabinet is in trouble. A Cabinet minority may be outvoted, but losing votes does not lessen the power of the party faction that it represents. Indeed, in a free society, the outvoted, if they are outvoted often enough on issues they consider vital, may take their political business elsewhere. Thus the task of the Prime Minister is to see that no significant group in the party is consistently overridden. Viscount Samuel, a Cabinet veteran, observed in his *Memoirs* that when a conflict arises in Cabinet, "when a knot or a tangle begins to appear, the important thing is for the Prime Minister not to let it be drawn tight; so long as it is kept loose it may still be unravelled." The real political genius of a Prime Minister lies in his keeping knots from being tightened, which is another way of saying that he must avoid rigid majority rule.

Let us examine a good case study of this sort. The Labor party is made up of an alliance of trade-unionists, socialist intellectuals, pacifists, liberals (in the American sense), cooperators, and other sundry groups. The trade-union wing of the party, while it has never supplied a high proportion of the political leadership, is the source of party finances and a huge block of votes. In the Labor Government of 1945, Mr. Ernest Bevin, the Foreign Secretary, was the only distinguished unionist to hold Cabinet office. Thus, while Mr. Bevin had only one vote in Cabinet meetings, his party strength was such that his vote had, in realistic terms, the strength of ten. Judged in these terms, what practical value would there be in outvoting Bevin?

Effective Cabinet government is thus founded on discussion and compromise rather than on nose counting. In a sense, it is comparable to the operation of a Quaker meeting, with the Prime Minister filling the shoes of the clerk of the meeting. The job of the clerk of a Quaker meeting is to formulate a decision which reflects the views of all significant elements within the meeting. This is more than a mechanical process of compromise, it is an attempt to reach a genuine meeting of minds in which those who disagree with the substance of a decision are nonetheless willing to accept it. It might even be suggested that part of this willingness to accept a decision which one dislikes grows out of the fact that it is not being stuffed down one's throat by majority tabulation. In any case, a great Prime Minister is one who prevents numerical schisms by formulating policy in such a fashion that all members of the Cabinet feel that their views have received adequate consideration, if not adoption.

If this sort of leadership depends to a great extent upon intangible factors of personality, upon charisma, there are other aspects of the Prime Minister's job which are of a more objective character. He must be a first-rate administrator who can simultaneously oversee the activities of all his important ministries and the important decisions of all ministries. It is his task to keep his team working as a team, to coordinate overlapping functions, and to supply leadership in new areas that arise. Here he is aided immensely by Cabinet committees which deal with such over-all problems as defense, economic affairs, and foreign relations. But it must be emphasized that the administrative talents of a Prime Minister are less significant in his success or failure than his charismatic qualifications. A Prime Minister such as Neville Chamberlain may be a first-class administrator but a disastrous leader.

Beyond his institutional tasks, the Prime Minister and his inner Cabinet have very important party functions. They must encourage young and talented Members of Parliament, appoint them to minor executive posts such as Parliamentary private secretaryships, and promote those who do well to higher positions. Conversely, they must eliminate the dead wood at the top, with the House of Lords frequently serving as the woodpile where aged party leaders, past their prime, can be stacked. In short, the Prime Minister must maintain the "circulation of the elite," must ensure against hardening of the political arteries, must work to keep the anabolic process of leadership development ahead of the catabolic process of death and senility. If a party's leadership fails to bring up able young men as future replacements, the handwriting is on the wall.

Furthermore, the Prime Minister is becoming more and more significant in the electoral process. Besides being party struggles, general elections have overtones of personality: it is Attlee versus Churchill as well as Labor versus Tories. Thus the Prime Minister stumps the country, speaking for his candidates in the various constituencies. As in the course of the twentieth century British political parties have tended to resemble each other more than either resembles its ancestors, the role of personality in elections has increased, particularly among the marginal, undecided voters.

CONCLUSIONS

Because of the essential stability of the British two-party system, as well as other less tangible factors, the British executive is extremely powerful. The role of the Cabinet in legislation and administration has been discussed earlier, and has therefore been passed over here, but it is important to recall the tight rein that the executive in Britain can keep on both the activities of the Parliamentary majority and those of the bureaucrats. This authority rests on the discipline of the political party, on the fact that when the chips are down, the Government's supporters will march with military precision through the lobby voting for Government policies.

However, some critics have attempted to demonstrate that this system is at base one of Cabinet dictatorship; that, in effect, the British executive is strong but irresponsible. The Prime Minister's power of dissolution, they suggest, and his internal authority in his party are of such a strong character that the lowly Member of Parliament is completely at the mercy of the leadership. Undoubtedly there is a certain amount of truth in these accusations: the formal power of the Prime Minister is tremendous, and the leadership often fails to take the backbenchers sufficiently into its confidence. But this view of the Prime Minister's authority fails to penetrate beneath the surface, fails to take into consideration the real sources of a Prime Minister's power.

First of all, it must be remembered that as in the United States there is a rigid screening process at work in the British parties, separating the men from the boys, the potential leaders from the eccentrics, the potential dictators, the demagogues. The Prime Minister is an old House of Commons man—in the twentieth century the average Prime Minister has been twenty-five years in the House before appointment! These years of apprenticeship are served under other veterans who promote young Members slowly, and largely on the basis of their performance in the House. The impatient tend to hang themselves on their own impetuosity. For example, three potential Labor Prime Ministers excluded themselves from consideration during the 1930's by reason of their unwillingness to compromise with the realities of life in a democratic nation and a democratic political party: Sir Oswald Mosley deserted the party to start a fascist movement; Sir Stafford Cripps refused to compromise his popular-front principles and was expelled from the Labor party; and George Lansbury, a much-beloved Labor pioneer, resigned as Chairman of the Parliamentary Labor Party because of his firm pacifist beliefs. Only the patent genius of Winston Churchill, and his record of unimpeachable anti-Nazism in the era of appeasement, saved him from the consequences of his erratic and undisciplined Parliamentary behavior—which included an abortive attempt to form a "King's party" at the time of Edward VIII's abdication. In short, by the time a man becomes Prime Minister, he is a veteran of government by discussion and compromise.

Second, these critics fail to appreciate the degree to which the Prime Minister is chief conciliator rather than boss: they accept a narrow juridical definition of his powers without realizing that all formal power rests, at least in a democratic society, upon a foundation of persuasion rather than coercion. Thus the Prime Minister's legislative majority is not an automatic, mechanical affair which he can count on for any policy he formulates; it is, on the contrary, a majority composed of minorities that can be welded into an effective instrument only by constant conciliation. Prime Minister Churchill, for instance, has within his legislative ranks both extremely right-wing Conservatives such as Sir Waldron Smithers, and liberal Conservatives of the R. A. Butler stripe who could easily, under different circumstances, fit into the Labor party. Consequently, the Cabinet can never, composed as it is of representatives of these various points of view, violate the basic framework of party consensus without disastrous results. The executive is strong, but it is also responsible, since the real source of executive power is a democratic, pluralistic political party.

THE FRENCH EXECUTIVE

While Britain supplies us with the typical instance of strong cabinet government, France is a fine example of a nation in which a cabinet system supplies weak leadership. This weakness is not caused by some structural defect—although the Premier's inability to dissolve the National Assembly and call for elections undoubtedly weakens his position vis-à-vis the legislature—but by the basic weakness of the French party system. Since this latter subject has been examined extensively in an earlier chapter, there is no need here to repeat the material covered there. Suffice it to say that basic schisms in the French community, perhaps exacerbated by the system of proportional representation, are reflected in the party composition of the National Assembly. Since no one viewpoint can obtain majority support, all governments must be coalitions composed of more or less closely related parliamentary factions. In the period immediately after World War II, these coalitions had a leftward orientation, with the Communist party actually participating in the government until May of 1947, but throughout the period from 1947 to 1954, the axis of coalition moved rightward until in 1953 several Gaullists actually took executive positions.

The French Cabinet, or Council of Ministers, is consequently a collective body only in the juridical sense; that is, legally it is supposed to be collective. In practice, it is a council of ambassadors, each of whom is charged by his party with protecting its special interests. These party emissaries are not responsible to the Cabinet collectivity; they are responsible to their constituents. The lack of homogeneity in the nation and in the National Assembly is thus reflected in the absence of a homogeneous executive.

THE FUNCTIONS OF THE PREMIER

This absence of homogeneity creates the framework within which the Premier must operate. Upon being asked by the President of France—the chief of state, whose activities will be noted shortly—to form a government, a party leader must scurry about among the other parties in search of majority support. He must promise important ministerial positions to various other party leaders, and make policy commitments. By the time he has obtained his majority, if indeed he is successful, he has yielded virtually all freedom of movement to the quest for support. If the large MRP bloc, for instance, is to be included in the coalition, a Premier must make certain guarantees on policy: the MRP wants state subsidies for Catholic schools, and it also believes in a considerable measure of socialism. The Radicals and their right-center allies, on the other hand, oppose subsidies to religious schools and are strong advocates of *laissez faire*. Obviously, the common denominator of any coalition must be low—it generally turns out to be anticommunism. The Communists and the Gaullist extremists will vote against anything proposed by anybody else on general principles. Furthermore, a coalition cabinet has little incentive to succeed, as its members do not have a common political future.

Once a lowest common denominator is found and a government established upon it, the Premier finds himself virtually handcuffed. Any new suggestions he may have on policy must run the gauntlet, and normally at least one member of the coalition will turn out to have strenuous objections to it. Furthermore, the legislature is so organized that functional committees, with their own empires to build and defend, play havoc with government legislative proposals. Meanwhile, the bureaucracy, operating without efficient supervision by the political class, runs the state in a semiautonomous fashion.

A successful Premier must therefore be a master conciliator even to hold his government intact against the raids of its member parties. For him to achieve positive policy leadership is virtually impossible. The simple fact of the matter is that he has position without power. If he dismisses a Minister for insubordination, that Minister's party will have its revenge and probably topple the government to the ground. If he attempts strong legislative leadership, the National Assembly, jealous of its prerogatives and populated by potential Premiers, will strike him down. Given the basic lack of consensus in the French community, the Council of Ministers can do little more than institutionalize executive impotence.

THE PRESIDENT OF FRANCE

Like the British, the French have separated the positions of chief of state and chief of government. The President of France, elected for a seven-year term by the National Assembly and the Council of the Republic meeting jointly, is the symbolic head of the French nation. Most of the President's activities are of a ritualistic character: he presides at meetings of various significant government bodies such as the Council of Ministers or the Superior Council of the Judiciary, he appoints the rectors of universities, the Grand Chancellor of the Legion of Honor, and other officials, and he exercises the pardoning power. However, Article 38 of the French constitution provides that "every act of the President of the Republic must be countersigned by the President of the Council of Ministers and by a Minister," so the President's powers are distinctly circumscribed.

But the President does have one area of freedom which is of considerable significance: he has the right to name the Premier, and although Article 38 is hardly ambiguous, he does this without the need for countersignature by the Premier and a Minister. Legally, there is no reason why this action by the President should be exempted from the countersignature requirement; in fact, it would appear to be violative of the constitution. But in practice, it is up to the President to try to designate a Premier who will receive legislative support. Of course, even here the President's discretion is limited by the political realities, for the Premier-designate must receive a vote of confidence from the National Assembly before he assumes office.

However, an able President with an inside knowledge of French party politics—and most French Presidents, both under the Third and Fourth Republics, have been old legislative hands—may himself be able to conciliate party leaders and thus aid the formation of a coalition. Similarly, the President may assume a position of moral leadership. President Vincent Auriol, the first occupant of the position under the Fourth Republic, has stated that it is the duty of the President to attain this *magistrature morale* and to aid the party leaders in understanding and acting upon the "deep and permanent will of the nation."

CONCLUSIONS

On the face of it, the French executive is weak because it is overresponsible. Because party considerations have engulfed governmental considerations, the Premier and his Ministers are at the mercy of party groups in the National Assembly. But in the fundamental sense, the French executive is both weak and irresponsible, for it does not fulfill the function of governing. Overresponsibility is, in a real sense, equivalent to irresponsibility, for the fact emerges that the French people do not have a responsible political class, a political leadership which can bridge and mediate the conflicting claims of private interest into some viable working definition of the public interest.

It must be emphasized again that this failure of leadership is not an outgrowth of dishonesty or frivolity—the French leaders are no less honest or more frivolous than British. Rather, it is a concomitant of the lack of unity in French society, of the absence of a basic framework of agreement and disagreement. Similarly, French institutions of government are not basically at fault— although they probably could be improved by, say, giving the Premier the right of dissolution—for institutions are, in the long run, no stronger than the basic social, political, and economic foundations upon which they rest. Thus the strengthening of French cabinet government, and of French political institutions generally, must emerge from a strengthening of the French community, not from political gadgetry.

THE COLLEGIAL EXECUTIVE

A discussion of democratic executives would not be complete without a brief discussion and analysis of the collegial type traditionally employed by the Swiss and recently introduced into Uruguay. Since too little time has elapsed to make possible an evaluation of Uruguay's experience, discussion will be confined to Switzerland.

The collegial executive is independent of the legislature, like the American President, but is composed of a committee which jointly exercises the executive functions. The seven members of the Swiss Federal Council are elected by a joint session of the legislature for a four-year term. No more than one member can be chosen from a single canton, or state, of the Confederation, and traditionally membership is distributed among the lingual groups of the nation with no more than five coming from German-speaking cantons. Each year, the legislature elects one of the Councilors chairman of the Council, and he is designated President of the Confederation. Normally Federal Councilors are reelected to office for fairly lengthy periods, so there is a considerable degree of stability of membership in the Council.

EXECUTIVE-LEGISLATIVE RELATIONS

In theory, the Federal Council is distinctly subordinate to the Swiss legislature. Not only are the members chosen by the Federal Assembly, but the powers delegated to the executive are ringed about with safeguards against autonomy. The Assembly can by resolution direct the Council to take certain action, and it can refuse to agree to action taken by the Council. Theoretically the Council's job is to coordinate and implement policy which has been approved by the legislature.

However, if one penetrates behind the theoretical screen, he finds that in practice the Federal Council has a good deal of power. The legislature has assigned to the Council the task of drafting needed legislation and defending it on the floor of either chamber. Furthermore, the members of the Council are usually distinguished party leaders whose views carry weight with their legislative groups. Consequently, a decision of the Federal Council will probably receive considerable legislative support. Above and beyond these considerations, each member of the Council is charged with running an administrative department, which means that within broad limits he can establish the framework of decision, "the tenor and direction of public policy," to use Zurcher's phrase. Incidentally, the long tenure of the Federal Councilors gives them time to become thoroughly acquainted with administrative problems, so there is no opportunity for bureaucratic autonomy to develop—the Swiss civil servant is thoroughly domesticated.

In recent years, because of the crisis in the world without, the Swiss have delegated more and more power to the Council. Thus the latter has been authorized to issue decrees with the force of law in the event of national emergencies, and to take plenary action to protect the nation's economy. In the judgment of Professor Arnold J. Zurcher, a careful student of Swiss affairs, this has resulted in the Federal Council's obtaining increasing ascendancy over the legislature and becoming in practice "the dominant branch of the Government."

THE PLURAL EXECUTIVE—AN EVALUATION

The very thought of a plural executive is enough to give nightmares to a specialist in public administration. Like the collegial bodies that run British local government, the Federal Council should not work. Yet the clear fact is that the Federal Council does work and seems to work well. If we are to discover why it works, we must examine the substructure of Swiss society, for only unusual conditioning factors could prevent a plural executive from developing into a slugfest between the various members.

The basic national sentiments which appear at once when one examines Swiss society are a passionate nationalism and a militant devotion to democracy. Although of ethnically different backgrounds, the Swiss have developed a pluralistic nationalism which, paradoxically, makes of them one of the most nationally homogeneous peoples in the world. The Swiss have been accused of selfishness, of greed, of a willingness to profit from any situation in the world, but whether one approves or disapproves of their policies, it is apparent that they are united in support of them. Similarly, there is a high degree of social homogeneity, of mutual trust, best exemplified by the fact that every Swiss reservist keeps his uniform, arms, and ammunition in a closet in preparation for any emergency—and every adult Swiss, with a few minor exceptions, is in the reserve until age sixty. In France, or even in the United States, a system of this sort would probably result in a lot of miscellaneous homicide, but the Swiss seem to have little difficulty with it.

The Swiss political party system reflects this national and social homogeneity. It would be too strong to say that the Swiss party system is organized nonpartisanship, but at times it seems to approach that idyllic condition. Not that there are no differences between the parties; there are, and occasionally bitter struggles occur. But all the significant Swiss parties share a tremendous area of common agreement: nationalism, democracy, prosperity, and neutrality.

This basic agreement to take certain fundamental propositions out of politics seems to set the stage for the effective operation of the plural executive. On issues of a crucial sort, arguments do not arise among the Federal Councilors for the simple reason that there is nothing to argue about. Indeed, the operation of the Council rests on so secure a foundation of consensus that if a Councilor does feel strongly and differently about some issue, he is free publicly to differ with his colleagues and need not resign his post. A tradition of this sort could not exist, at least not concomitantly with an effective government, unless differences were of a sort that did not endanger basic unity. Consequently, the Swiss have obtained from their Federal Council executive leadership that is both increasingly strong and genuinely responsible; this in spite of the fact that in the handbook of the political gadgeteers the plural executive is listed as unworkable.

THE DEMOCRATIC EXECUTIVE: SUMMARY AND EVALUATION

The institutional form of democratic leadership may vary from nation to nation, but in each the basic objective is the same: to supply strong, responsible direction to the community. Responsibility is vital, for without it the political class, to employ Mosca's phrase, may become autonomous and dictatorial. Strength is equally necessary, for without it the political class will not have the power to enforce the decisions of the community upon recalcitrant elements in the society and in the bureaucracy.

Because democratic societies are, virtually by definition, pluralistic, the primary function of the executive is to develop a tentative definition of the public interest for which he can amass support. Significant pressure groups within the community cannot be extirpated in totalitarian fashion; their views must be given consideration, their private interest must be accounted for in the establishment of a working model of the public interest. Thus, while there are undeniably extensive legal functions of an executive caliber, the basic level of effective executive operation is not juridical, but political. Interestingly enough, according to one well-informed American commentator, this is also increasingly true of the operations of the top executives in the giant corporations, which are becoming "more like federations than monolithic structures." Here, as in government, the executive finds himself mediating the demands of pressure groups within the corporation, and coordinating rather than commanding, conciliating rather than ordering. In short, reconciliation and mediation are the two major attributes of viable leadership in a pluralistic society, organization, or corporation. In a realistic analysis, the democratic leader is led as much as he leads.

PART IV. THE CRISIS IN DEMOCRATIC METHODS

Chapter 12

THE REGULATION OF ECONOMIC ACTIVITY—
A CASE STUDY OF THE PLANNING PROCESS

IN THE eleven previous chapters, the various components of the democratic process have been pulled out of context, enlarged to make more detailed examination possible, and analyzed. While this type of static analysis has great value, a book of this sort would be incomplete if it did not include material on the dynamics of the government process, the interaction of these various cogs that goes into the formulation and implementation of public policy. In order to give the reader some idea of how parties, executives, bureaucrats, legislators, and the "public" fit into the broader picture, two case studies are included here. The first, dealing with governmental regulation of economic life, is concerned with a problem primarily "domestic" in nature. The second, discussing democracy and foreign policy, which comprises the next chapter, relates to an issue in the international field. The line between "domestic" and "international" issues is fuzzy at best, but because it offers certain methodological advantages, this convenient distinction has been utilized. It should be made clear at the outset that in neither of these case studies is the emphasis on policy content, on *what* governmental regulations operate or *what* foreign policies the democracies employ. We are limiting the analysis to the political problems encountered and the political techniques employed by the United States, Britain, and France in the course of formulating and implementing *any* policy of economic regulation or *any* foreign policy. In short, these are generic studies of policy formulation and execution in democracies, and it is hoped that the insights gained from the analysis of these two examples will be applied by the student to the examination of other areas of public policy.

GOVERNMENT AND THE ECONOMY

Most current governmental problems are not merely political in essence, but have, in addition, far-reaching economic implications. This is to suggest that it is neither possible nor desirable to consider governments as being somehow apart from and unconcerned with economic activity. All governments, whether democratic or autocratic, play an active part in shaping their economies. In some nations, the form of the economy has been molded by the refusal of the government to take an active hand, while in others, government actively regulates and in some instances owns and operates economic activities. But in both cases the actions of government have contributed to the form of economic life, so that *laissez faire* is as much a product of government policy as is its converse, socialism. In the former instance, the government refuses to regulate the economy and consequently, by an act of will, turns economic power over to private hands. In the latter case, the government itself undertakes to regulate economic action.

Unfortunately, any treatment of the relationship between government and the economic process is bound to stir emotions. Almost everyone who discusses these matters seems to have a strong basic set in one direction or another, so that disputes on the subject tend to depart immediately from the realm of fact and to surge into the theological arena. Our concern here, however, is not with economic theology; we are not attempting to build a case for one viewpoint or another, but rather to analyze how democratic governments deal with their economies and to discover what factors in public opinion, party operation, and the governmental structure itself play a part in decision making in the economic sphere. In fairness to the reader it should be noted that this attitude itself conceals an ideological assumption on the part of the authors that should be brought into the light, namely, that we do not subscribe to natural-law economics of either the left- or right-wing varieties—neither to the laissez-faire assumption that if the government will only keep its hands off the economy, all will work out for the best, nor to its socialist counterpart that all we have to do is plan everything, and mankind will automatically enter utopia.

Similarly, the dedication of an entire chapter to the subject indicates that the authors do not accept the thesis that the proper way to handle economic problems is to turn them over to the economists for expert handling. While no one would for a minute deny the value of the economist's insights and of the descriptive material that he can unearth about the actual operation of the economy, still the economist, like the political scientist, has more in common with the astrologer than with the astronomer. The prediction of human behavior, whether in economic, political, or social activity, can only be undertaken on a highly tentative basis. As a consequence, political economists find themselves in basic disagreement over the implications of government programs. From this it is apparent that the relationship between democratic government and the economic sphere cannot be analyzed with the precision characteristic of a natural science. A depression cannot be predicted on the same basis as an eclipse of the sun, as was demonstrated in the United States immediately after World War II when, with the lone exception of W. S. Woytinsky, leading economists joined in predicting a severe slump which never materialized. Likewise British economists violently differed on the consequences of socialist planning, and by a strange coincidence, most economists of a socialist persuasion predicted happy consequences, while economists of a conservative complexion anticipated dire things. This would suggest that the major road block to making economics into a precise science is economists.

Thus, as in other areas of policy formulation, the citizen must make his own decisions. He can, of course, draw upon the training of the economist; indeed, in a complex industrial society, this is an imperative. But there are no buttons that can be pushed which will automatically supply correct answers to economic problems. The real issues are beyond solution by comptometer, for they lie in the realm of premises, of assumptions about what is "good." Given a certain decision, e.g., that the state is responsible for preventing unemployment, one set of techniques can be applied to give it meaning. However, if one begins at a different point, say, by denying the state's responsibility in the employment area, a different set of techniques becomes applicable. The economist can point out the possible consequences of a decision and can draw up alternate methods of implementing it, but the individual must make the basic decision.

PLANNING

Much discussion of the relationship between government and economic life wanders off on such semantic wild-goose chases as "Can freedom survive under planning?" Brief reflection will demonstrate the absurdity of following this deductive path. In ordinary usage, a plan is simply a program for the future, and certainly no individual, and assuredly no businessman, refuses to plan his future activities. Indeed, success in business is predicated upon accurate planning of future demand. Some would deny to governments this common-sense prerogative, but in reality the issue is not "plan or no plan," but to what extent, and by whom, the planning should be undertaken. Historically in the democracies, planning has largely been left in the hands of private individuals who have built industrial plants, imported raw materials, and manufactured goods in anticipation of national needs. In recent years, there has been more direct planning by governments, mostly as an outgrowth of war needs. But any way you look at it, there has always been planning by someone. Similarly, governmental planning is not all of one variety. In a narrow sense, there is governmental planning when the state fosters the development of an industry or industries—a technique which entered American public policy in 1795 with Alexander Hamilton's famous *Report on Manufactures,* and has been fostered in recent years through such methods as air-mail subsidies, industrial tax exemption, or the manifold activities of the Reconstruction Finance Corporation. In the broader sense, planning has been employed in such democratic nations as Britain, Sweden, Norway, or New Zealand in the attempt to regulate the over-all development of the economy. Consequently, the real problems that arise from planning must be analyzed in specific terms, not in socialist or antisocialist clichés. A militant socialist would probably not accept governmental planning of the press or rigid regulation of family relationships, while an equally vociferous advocate of free enterprise would generally accept a public monopoly of mail service and of atom bombs.

Nor is there any necessary consistency in the planning views of a single individual. Many a strong supporter of the American "free-enterprise" system is an equally vigorous advocate of the protective tariff, an indirect type of sub· sidization of the industries protected. Some who support public ownership of public utilities would strongly oppose governmental intervention in the affairs of, say, the clothing industry. Thus one is not necessarily either for state planning or against it; he may, and probably will, be in favor of certain governmental actions and not in favor of others.

Semantic considerations often play an interesting part in this public opinion on planning. The farmer who is opposed to planning by the state is simultaneously a militant supporter of agricultural subsidies—which are not in his eyes subsidies at all but only state recognition of the risks, perils, and dangers that the farmer faces in his struggle with nature. Magazines which editorially excoriate "planners" and encourage their readers to stand firm behind the free-enterprise system distribute their views to the public with the aid of a mailing subsidy—which is, in their view, not a subsidy but rather recognition by the public of the immeasurable value of freedom of the press and of an informed populace. And so it goes, with each group rationalizing its acceptance of state aid with some such semantic maneuver.

GOVERNMENT AND THE AMERICAN ECONOMY

The word planning has long been anathema in American politics, but the reality of state intervention in the economy has been present since the founding of the republic. Alexander Hamilton's famous project for aiding infant industries was a symbolic affirmation of the responsibility of the national government for economic development. Although the national government did undertake some activities of an economic character, such as the creation of a central banking structure, the bulk of economic interventions by government took place on the state level. As Professors Oscar Handlin and Louis Hartz have shown in their respective studies of state economic policy in Massachusetts and Pennsylvania, the state governments in the early period undertook extensive economic projects, building canals, subsidizing railroads, and forming development corporations.

Later in the nineteenth century, the national government attempted—although, as Paul W. Gates has shown, with a poorly conceived approach—to shape the agricultural economy of the West around the family farm, and the resulting Homestead Act of 1862 must be considered as a major planning measure. During the same period, huge land grants were made to railroad corporations—20 million acres were donated by Congress in 1870–1871 alone —and these corporations were able to subsidize their activities from the sale of the land. Meanwhile the tariff was becoming more and more of a weapon to be employed to eliminate competition from foreign goods, a technique of subsidization for American business that reached its apogee in 1930 with the passage of the Smoot-Hawley Tariff, which gave protection to agriculture as well as to virtually every significant business in the nation.

Space does not permit a detailed examination of American economic history, but a generalization, which can be verified by reference to any standard textbook in economic history, does emerge: the American people have traditionally felt that their governments, both state and national, have definite responsibilities in the economic area. In the nineteenth century and in the first thirty years of the twentieth, these responsibilities were largely of a negative character, that is, the states set up rules governing business conduct and licensing regulations, and both the states and the Federal government subsidized business activity. But little attempt was made to provide positive economic direction. The Interstate Commerce Commission, for instance, was established in 1887 by the Congress to prevent certain gross railroad abuses, but not to run the railroads. The tariff acted in a similar fashion, subsidizing the businesses protected but offering no direction to them. Certainly there was no over-all economic plan; agencies were created and measures were enacted in the piecemeal effort to meet specific economic problems. It should be noted that the attitude of the Supreme Court in the period from 1890 to 1936 was quite consonant with this reality: the Court developed the tradition that state regulation of economic activity, except in limited areas such as the dangerous trades, child labor, or business affected with a public interest, was violative of the due-process clause of the Fourteenth Amendment, but the justices rarely suggested that state aid to economic activity violated anything.

With the advent of the Great Depression of 1929, however, a new note was sounded. Many Americans began to demand that the national government take a positive direction of the economy, and the New Deal measures reflect this movement of public opinion away from negative economic measures toward positive, over-all government planning. But a clear distinction must be made here between the ambitions of some of the intellectual New Dealers, such as Rexford Tugwell, and the realities of New Deal planning as it emerged from Congress and was administered by the highly pragmatic President. Indeed, Roosevelt was never prepared to sacrifice votes for an abstract concept of planning, and many of the intellectuals were bitterly disappointed by the actual implementation of their planning dreams. Nonetheless, and however motivated, the creation of such government operations as the Tennessee Valley Authority, the Agricultural Adjustment Administration, the National Recovery Administration, and the National Labor Relations Board marked the beginning of a new era in national governmental intervention in economic life, and the pattern thus established has survived a change from Democratic to Republican rule without significant modification. It should be noted that the noun "plan" and the verb "to plan" are employed throughout this analysis in the sense approved by Webster, *i.e.*, a plan as a "proposed method of action" and to plan as "to devise or project a method or course of action." Thus government regulation of all sorts would fall under the heading of "planning."

Assuming then that such measures as those listed above are now firmly embedded in the American political tradition, let us attempt an analysis of the part played in the regulatory process by the various institutional components of the democratic process. What influences do pressure groups, bureaucrats, and political parties exercise over the formulation and exercise of government interventions in the economy?

PRESSURES AND PLANNING

Although some maintain that regulatory projects emerge from the fertile minds of creeping socialists, the source of these programs is generally found in the demands of pressure groups. It was the American Farm Bureau Federation, not the Socialist party, that conceived of the AAA and brought pressure to bear on Congress to get the plan adopted. Similarly, the railroad lobby has long been agitating on behalf of governmental regulation of motor carriers, and interest groups from the Western states, short of coal but long on rushing rivers, have been militant advocates of cheap public power and multipurpose dams. Each pressure group, whether it admits it or not, considers its interest to be the national interest, and looks upon Congress as a potential instrument for helping its constituents and crippling its opponents.

Thus pressure groups play an active part in the initial stage of a state economic program. Often a lobbyist actually drafts a proposal for his congressional supporters, but given the interplay that exists between the executive and Congress, the lobbyist may bring influence upon an important government agency to prepare a bill. Too often analysts of the pressure process emphasize the relationship between the pressure agent and Congress and overlook the close relationship that often exists between the pressure groups and administrative agencies. As was discussed in an earlier chapter, all the important pressure groups have allies in the administration who represent their interests within the executive department and before Congress, and to whom, in return, they provide protection and support before Congress.

Consequently, the passage by Congress of some interest group's pet measure does not end the group's activity. On the contrary, legislative enactments are meaningless unless they are implemented in a desirable fashion, so the pressure groups continue to bring pressure on the administration. If it is possible, and it often is, they get their men appointed to positions of importance in the implementation of the act. A "friendly" administrator will surround himself with advisers representing the pressure group, and if an administrator begins to act in an "unfriendly" fashion, immediately the pressure group's congressional supporters will be alerted and will begin to bring pressure on the independent bureaucrat and, if necessary, upon his superiors. For example, in the mid-1930's, when some of the administrators of the AAA began to take an undue interest in the plight of the tenant farmers, the Farm Bureau brought immediate pressure upon Secretary Henry A. Wallace, resulting in the dismissal of the men involved.

The dismissal and subsequent reinstatement in 1953 of Dr. Allen V. Astin, head of the Bureau of Standards, grew out of the Bureau's alleged "unfriendliness" to small business—in this specific instance, to the manufacturers of a chemical purporting to lengthen the life of electrical batteries. Dr. Astin, in spite of pressure on behalf of the product by twenty-four Senators, held the chemical to be useless—a judgment which was later to be vindicated by an independent committee of nationally known scientists. Although Dr. Astin was a registered Republican, he was initially dismissed from his post by Secretary of Commerce Sinclair Weeks. However, as a result of pressure brought both by scientific groups and by influential Senators, Weeks later reversed his decision and reinstated Astin.

A classic case of pressure-group vengeance on an unfriendly administrator took place in 1950, when the natural-gas producers succeeded in blocking the reappointment of Leland Olds as Chairman of the Federal Power Commission. As Professor Joseph P. Harris has shown in a fine case study of the Olds dismissal, the ostensible issues raised against Olds were his speeches and writings as a youthful radical, but the real objection to his remaining on the FPC was his forthright conviction that the Commission should take its regulatory mission seriously.

CONGRESS AND PLANNING

Because of the nature of American political parties, there is little point to an examination of the role of party in the planning process. Each party is against "planning" in theory, but in favor of rewarding certain elements in the community and of utilizing the governmental process to do it. The Democrats are of a more antibusiness complexion than the Republicans—even the Southern Democrats are prepared on occasion to denounce the evils of big business and the wickedness of Wall Street. Conversely, the Republicans have generally less respect for the labor interest and more regard for business than their opponents. But none of the current economic problems are party issues as such. Republicans and Southern Democrats united behind the Taft-Hartley Act, a measure designed to decrease the institutional power of the labor movement. Both Republicans and Democrats joined forces behind the Kerr bill, devised to free the natural-gas industry from the clutches of the Federal Power Commission. Consequently, it is to the multiparty system in Congress rather than to the purported national two-party system that we must look for realistic information about attitudes toward governmental planning.

Each major bloc in Congress is always busy, in cooperation with its pressure constellation and its bureaucratic allies, planning for its constituents. To take a case in point, in the spring of 1953, the dairy interests in the United States were in a precarious position. Oleomargarine was rapidly driving butter from the market, and to make things worse, Section 104 of the Defense Production Act, which authorized the Secretary of Agriculture to forbid the import into the United States of dairy products, was due to expire on June 30, so that foreign competition in dairy products might be anticipated after that date. The dairy lobby immediately organized its congressional stalwarts in the effort to continue the embargo on foreign dairy produce, and on April 10, Senator George Aiken, Chairman of the Senate Agriculture Committee, announced, "It's a safe bet that Congress is not going to leave the dairy industry in a helpless condition after July 1."

Secretary of Agriculture Benson was also concerned lest the American dairy industry get caught in a competitive situation, but rather than asking Congress to renew the provisions of Section 104, he wrote the President, requesting that the Federal Tariff Commission take action to exclude foreign dairy products. The Assistant Secretary of State for Economic Affairs, Harold Linder, objected mildly to this move toward a more restrictive import policy but added quickly that he was "not suggesting that the dairy farmer is not entitled to a certain amount of protection." President Eisenhower followed the suggestion of his Secretary of Agriculture, and the Tariff Commission went to work to raise the protective barrier. Needless to add, Senator Aiken and his colleagues took an acute interest in the outcome, and in particular undertook to fight off those Congressmen who objected to the new restriction and to intimidate those bureaucrats who held a similar view.

The operations of congressional committees have already been discussed, but it is important to keep in mind that they are the keystones of congressional —and pressure-group—oversight of administrative action. Most of this supervision takes place on the informal level; the committees make their views clear to the administration and then, in the event that bureaucrats become "unfriendly," threaten to cut appropriations or hold investigations. Former Senator Kenneth McKellar of Tennessee was famous for his investigatory raids against the Farm Security Administration and the Tennessee Valley Authority which were designed primarily to force "unfriendly" administrators into line. Unless an administrator has a considerable body of supporters of his own who rally behind him—or a strong President who rallies public support in his behalf—he is likely to be realistic and concede the point to the pressure politicians.

But not only does this process of congressional supervision operate on the informal level; it has also been institutionalized in certain devices of a formal nature. In the case of the Tennessee Valley Authority, for example, Congress provided that members of the board of directors could be removed from office by a concurrent resolution, that is, a resolution passed by a majority of both houses of Congress which does not need presidential signature to become effective. This provision is *sui generis* so far as an executive officer is concerned, although a similar provision applies to the Comptroller General, who is generally considered to be a congressional subordinate. No director of the TVA has ever been moved against under this proviso, and there are serious doubts as to its constitutionality. The concurrent resolution has also been employed by Congress in the drafting of other types of statutes. One type of usage was included in the Immigration and Nationality Act of 1952, which provided in Section 244 that certain suspensions of deportation by the Attorney General required congressional approval by concurrent resolution, while others went into effect unless disapproved by a resolution of either house of Congress. Similarly, under recent Reorganization Acts, presidential proposals for administrative reorganization become effective unless rejected by concurrent resolution. Another use of this technique was found in the Lend-Lease Act of 1941, which provided that the powers conferred upon the President could be terminated by concurrent resolution, and the Mutual Defense Assistance Act of 1949 stated even more specifically that aid to any nation could be cut off by Congress in this fashion.

Congressional committees have also been given statutory powers of oversight. A 1944 statute, for instance, authorized the Secretary of the Navy to acquire and dispose of real estate only after coming "into agreement with the Naval Affairs Committee of the Senate and of the House of Representatives with respect to the terms of such prospective acquisitions or disposals." A 1952 statute carried this process even further by requiring the Director of the Budget to get the approval of the Chairman of the House Appropriations Committee before changing rent policy in government-owned housing. The influence of the real-estate lobby appears to be far-reaching and effective.

These rather intricate provisions have been spelled out in some detail because they demonstrate the fact, often unrealized by students of American government, that Congress plays an active part in every stage of policy implementation. Any executive plan, for instance, to supply low-rent housing to Federal employees was subjected to prior approval by a senior Congressman who would, of course, consult with the appropriate interests before making any decisions. And this formal right of intervention is only the part of the iceberg above water, for the informal powers of congressional committees, and significant Congressmen, are nowhere given statutory foundation but are comprehensive and detailed.

THE PRESIDENT AND PLANNING

One of the main objections to governmental planning of economic activity in the United States is the centralizing effect that is purported to accompany it. While, as has been suggested earlier, planning may be centralized or decentralized, efficient or inefficient, democratic or totalitarian, American usage has generally associated the term with centralized executive authority, and, indeed, the word "planner" is often used as a synonym of totalitarian or Communist—particularly in the congressional lexicon. It is unquestionably the case that efficient planning does call for a considerable delegation of authority to the planner, but it does not follow that the plan must be nationwide, or even region-wide, in scope. Decentralized planning, as the Tennessee Valley Authority's experience demonstrates, is possible—all the strings are not necessarily pulled by administrators in Washington. Interestingly enough, there appears to be a tendency toward decentralization in the management of large business enterprises which are simultaneously strong advocates of planning. Du Pont, whose industrial empire has been built by shrewd planning, experimentation, and market analysis, has maintained its planning structure but has delegated decision-making authority in the great bulk of problems that arise to plant managers and to directors of its component industries.

However, in American politics, planning and centralization are considered the siamese twins of potential presidential dictatorship—at least, this is assuredly the view of the majority in Congress. Consequently, all suggestions for planning projects initiated by the President must run the initial gauntlet of congressional suspicion, and they are frequently condemned, irrespective of their merits, on the ground that they may increase the President's power vis-à-vis Congress. A good case of this sort was the development and subsequent decapitation of the National Resources Planning Board. Originally established by President Roosevelt in 1934 as the National Resources Board, the NRPB was charged with advising the President on the development of national resources, preparing plans for the efficient utilization of resources, and supplying Federal and state agencies with data on resource development. As the depression and the New Deal enthusiasm which accompanied its birth moved into the past, the Board came under increasing attack in Congress. The Board brought things to a head during World War II by preparing reports and recommendations on postwar problems, notably the problems that might arise in the areas of health and employment, and Congress retorted in 1943 by refusing to appropriate any funds for the agency. To make sure that the President did not simply slip the Board into another administrative department, Congress further provided that the functions of the NRPB could not be transferred to any other agency.

Another instance of the President's difficulties in getting his planning views adopted was the fate of the Brannan Plan under the Truman administration. Secretary Charles F. Brannan, with the firm support of the President, attempted to rationalize the system of agricultural price supports. The details of the plan are not important here; what is important is the fact that Brannan found himself opposed by the American Farm Bureau Federation, by the congressional forces of the farm bloc, and by significant groups in the Department of Agriculture itself. This combination was unbeatable. The difference between the fate of the AAA and that of the Brannan Plan is notable: in the case of the AAA, the plan was itself prepared by Farm Bureau experts and was adopted by the Secretary of Agriculture and the President; in the case of the Brannan Plan, the President and his Secretary tried to impose a plan without agreement from the pressure groups and pressure politicians. From the viewpoint of congressional semantics, the distinction between the two was simple: the AAA was sound, American-style support for free enterprise; the Brannan Plan was socialism.

Thus, if the President is going to be successful in getting his planning views adopted, they must also be the views of a significant body of pressure opinion. Successful presidential action is therefore based on a tremendous amount of previous preparation, on discovering and making use of the views of important pressure groups and their political spokesmen. Much of President Roosevelt's success in his relationships with Congress was due to his superb ability to lead and follow simultaneously. If he thought a measure might be useful, he would frequently begin by having one of his subordinates float a trial balloon, that is, Secretary Harold L. Ickes, say, would make a speech advocating some embryonic policy. Then the President would await the reaction. If a significant body of public opinion supported the idea, the legislative wheels would begin to move. If the reaction was strongly negative, the President would simply explain that Mr. Ickes was expressing his own views in the speech, not those of the administration.

True, the President can serve as a catalyst of national public opinion and through this leadership process bring public pressure to bear on Congress. But the effectiveness of this process can easily be overemphasized, for public opinion has both quantitative and qualitative connotations, and it is the latter which are most important in dealing with Congress. Medieval political theorists developed a concept of concurrent majority, best expounded in the writings of Marsiglio of Padua, in which it was maintained that for a measure to be adopted both a quantitative and a qualitative majority was necessary. To put it oversimply, a law affecting merchants would require for adoption both a numerical majority of the populace and a majority of the merchants. A similar process operates with respect to public opinion and Congress, for an agricultural proposal supported by a numerical majority of the American people will never receive congressional sanction unless it is also approved by the significant agricultural groups. The chairman of the Senate Agriculture Committee is far more interested in the views of the Farm Bureau than in those of 7 million New Yorkers or of 50 million industrial workers. The President's task therefore is one of influencing selected public opinions in the area specifically under discussion, and interest is more important than rhetoric in achieving this objective.

THE BUREAUCRACY AND PLANNING

Although most administrators theoretically work for the President, it has already been pointed out that in practice the President's power over his subordinates varies tremendously depending upon circumstances. Thus the bureaucracy and planning deserve consideration separate from the discussion of the President and planning, for frequently the bureaucracy is going in one direction and the President in the other. Once again it must be emphasized that the bureaucracy in the American national government is not an irresponsible clique which operates autonomously; indeed, the bureaucracy is thoroughly responsible, but not necessarily to the President. It is the fact that the bureaucracy is often responsible to pressure groups and pressure politicians in Congress which gives the legislature its unique role in the planning process.

There has been a tendency in American politics for the regulated interests to capture the agencies charged with regulating them, and this tendency appears in large part to be an outcome of the fact that the President cannot protect his administrators. The Interstate Commerce Commission, for example, which began life as the agency to curb the railroads, has for years been an institutional buffer for the railroad interests. So long as public interest, and pressure group interest, in regulating the railroads was high, the ICC could maintain its autonomy. However, once this initial enthusiasm disappeared, the ICC was faced with two alternatives: beat the railroads, or join them. Without the power to beat the railroads, the ICC found that the rail pressure groups would give it a considerable amount of support and protection if it would in return accept the railroad interest as public interest. This is not to accuse the members of the ICC of dishonesty, for it is doubtful whether any part of this process was conscious. The point is that when the President looked about for men to put on the Commission, he knew that an avowed enemy of the railroad interests could hardly win approval by the Senate—at least not after the reform furor had died down—and the Commissioners and staff of the ICC knew in return that the railroad Congressmen would look with great disfavor, budgetary as well as personal, on actions designed to curb the railroad interest. President Roosevelt learned this the hard way when, in February of 1939, he nominated Thomas P. Amlie to a vacancy on the ICC. Amlie, a Wisconsin Progressive, was publicly on record in favor of government ownership of the railroads, and his nomination raised a tremendous stir in the Senate. After two months of controversy in which Amlie was accused of being a Communist, the President, at Amlie's request, retreated from an impossible situation by withdrawing the nomination.

But there are, as Samuel P. Huntington has pointed out in a cogent analysis of the operations of the ICC, risks involved in this process. When a governmental agency becomes closely tied to a specific pressure interest, its power increases or decreases directly with the power of its pressure twin. Thus today, precisely because it has become so closely tied to the railroads, the ICC finds its authority withering away, for the railroads are a declining interest in the face of stiff competition from trucks and air transportation. Because the ICC has administratively supported the rail interests against the truckers and airmen, the two latter groups are out to get the Commission's scalp.

Each significant pressure constellation thus has both congressional and bureaucratic agents, and the struggle between pressure groups, which is the main feature of American politics, goes on at all three levels. Not only do the groups oppose each other in the newspapers or in magazine advertisements, but their respective pressure politicians argue on the floor of Congress and their bureaucratic forces join battle within the administration. For instance, a fight between the airlines and the railroads will be featured by both disputes between Congressmen and a squabble between the administrative spearheads of the two interests, the Civil Aeronautics Authority and the Interstate Commerce Commission. To take another instance which can be historically documented, when after World War II the War Shipping Administration and the United States Maritime Commission attempted to revitalize American coastwise shipping, suspended during the war, they found that the water carriers needed authorization for higher freight rates if they were to operate. These two maritime agencies, backed by shipping interests, tried to get the ICC to authorize rate increases, but the railroads, to whom the freight formerly shipped by boat had fallen during the war, objected strongly, and made their objections stick. In spite of congressional pressure brought by the maritime interests, and the apparent justice of the water carriers' position, the ICC refused to grant the shippers permission to raise their rates to the necessary level. As a consequence, American coastwise shipping is today virtually nonexistent.

Other cases could be cited at length to the same point. During the late thirties, the National Labor Relations Board became, to a large extent, the bureaucratic spearhead of the labor movement, a fact which led to many bitter congressional attacks on that agency. The line taken by the attackers was that the NLRB was "not impartial," but what the congressional assailants probably meant was that it was partial to the wrong interest. The passage of the Taft-Hartley Act was a congressional reprisal against the pro-labor decisions of the NLRB; indeed, several sections of the statute were specifically designed to overrule administrative decisions of the Board. It is needless to add that politically speaking "impartiality" is a chimera; every group in society identifies the general interest with its own specific ends and considers any opponents of this general interest to be biased and partial. While Mr. Charles Wilson of General Motors may have made a political blunder if he told Congress that the interests of GM and the United States were identical, his honesty was commendable. Certainly if Walter Reuther of the CIO did not believe that the interests of labor and the United States were identical, he would never have risen to the top of the labor movement. Like business, the trade-union movement wants no partial commitments from its leaders; it wants wholehearted loyalty.

PUBLIC AND PRIVATE INTEREST: THE NEW FEUDALISM

This leads to a point which many commentators on the American scene have noted with astonishment: the extent to which private organizations and interests are vested with public power. Indeed, the regulatory process both Federally and in the states has often consisted of turning over to private interest associations the power to regulate themselves. The National Industrial Recovery Act of 1933 was a classic instance of this sort. The Roosevelt administration, in the effort to restore the operation of the law of supply and demand, authorized each industry to draw up a code of fair competition which, after approval by the President, would have the force of law. These codes were designed to prevent needless competition and generally to eliminate overproduction, and the impact of the NRA on American industry was one of rationalization by autoregulation. In other words, the codes turned public power over to the industries themselves—in effect, to the leading firms in each area. The leaders in an industry frequently employed the codes to strengthen their position vis-à-vis small competitors. The Sun Oil Company, for example, waged a bitter fight against the Petroleum Code which it maintained was drawn up by the big oil producers in such a fashion as to squeeze the small oil companies to the wall. Public control over this syndicalistic process of self-regulation was supposed to be maintained by the requirement of presidential approval of the codes, but in practice, this task was turned over to the agency and, largely because of the tremendous number of codes that were prepared and the fact that Director Hugh Johnson staffed the NRA with ex-businessmen, approval became routine.

The extensive cloaking of private interest in public power has led to a development which might be called the new feudalism. As the map of Europe in the Middle Ages was dotted with small autonomous geographic entities, the economic map of the United States today is characterized by self-governing economic enclaves. Each of these enclaves is composed partly of pressure groups, partly of Congressmen, and partly of bureaucrats, all of whom are devoted to forwarding the functional interest which serves as the matrix of the organization. The Farm Bureau, the farm bloc in Congress, and the Department of Agriculture are the components of one of the most powerful duchies; another would be made up of the trade-union movement, the National Labor Relations Board, and the labor bloc in Congress. But there is no necessary split between labor and management: the railroad unions and the railroad operators are united in their efforts to frustrate the St. Lawrence seaway project. If, for example, Walter Reuther of the United Automobile Workers were elected Senator from Michigan, he would have far more in common with the interest of Ford and General Motors than with the farming interests, and he would probably soon be referred to as an "automobile Senator" in pressure parlance.

The reasons for this fragmentation of economic power are many, but a careful student soon realizes that the major factor conducive to the continuance of this process is the absence of any organization charged with defining the public interest and enforcing its definition. This is another way of saying that the roots of this diffusion of planning power are nourished by the lack of a strong party system in the United States. If a disciplined national political party were able to elect a President and maintain an effective majority in Congress, an enforceable definition of the public interest could emerge and be enforced on the feudal enclaves. In a sense, the same development which ended political feudalism is called for: the development of enforceable public law. There is in the United States today very little public law in economic affairs; each functional barony makes its own private law and enforces it upon its members. Recall the ICC's frustration of coastwise shipping interests as a case in point, and examine the actions of the Federal Power Commission toward the natural-gas interests for another classic instance of private government.

Indeed, the limitations on the power of these functional duchies are seldom supplied by public economic law, which we can define as a broad definition of the public interest set forth by the political class, the President and Congress. They are rather supplied by the counterforce of other duchies. The power of the railroad-ICC combination has, for instance, been limited increasingly by the growth of the trucking interests and air transportation interests. The strength of the trade-unions and their bureaucratic allies has been weakened by the resurgence of business interests. The Taft-Hartley Act, as its supporters frankly stated, was a legislative attempt to "even the balance" between labor and management in labor relations, it was not a positive attempt to establish a coherent public policy in the area of labor-management relations. This may sound like quibbling, but the distinction is significant, particularly when one is considering the nature of planning. Planning in the United States, rather than being an a priori, broadly conceived approach to public needs, tends to be the institutionalization of the demands of various pressure groups, or one group taking its revenge on others.

To say this is not to condemn the process; indeed, there is a good deal to be said for it. Given the diffusion of political power in the United States, it would be difficult to conceive of any alternate form of planning that would work at all. At the same time, it is important to realize the defects that exist. It is possible, for example, for the farmers or railroad workers or natural-gas producers to hold the public for ransom. Unless the groups being held for ransom organize effectively in their own interest, they are not likely to get much consideration. The plight of the unorganized consumers is a vivid testimony of the results of failure to organize; when agricultural or industrial subsidies are voted, few pause to worry about the impact these will have on the consumer's pocketbook. For reasons too complex to investigate here, the cooperative movement, a vigilant defender of consumer interest in nations like Britain and Sweden, has never become powerful in the United States.

But the central problem remains: how can an operational definition of the public interest be enforced against autonomous, state-endorsed, economic enclaves? Antidemocratic thinkers have solved this problem by suppressing private interest in the name of a transcendent public purpose, but the solution of Machiavelli and Rousseau can hardly be accepted by democrats. Democrats are committed to the belief that from the clash of private interest a working definition of the group interest will emerge. But this faith is in turn posited on the assumption that there will be a compromise, an amalgam, and not simply institutionalized, state-supported anarchy. It may be overly harsh to describe the American situation in the latter terms, but it is difficult to find adequate words to describe a system in which each significant interest, with state authorization, takes over the management of its own affairs subject only to the checks that opposing interests can build up. This is not a synthesis of interests; it is rather a fragmentation of public power.

The answer to the problems posed by this new feudalism has yet to be found, though there are clichés aplenty posing as answers. The utopian plea for centralized planning certainly puts the cart before the horse, since short of totalitarianism, centralized political power, necessary to implement such planning, is still far in the future. However, a long-run solution could emerge from the increasing homogeneity of American society which may, as has been suggested earlier, lead to the development of increasingly cohesive political parties. As American society becomes more uniform, more stable, the number of significant interests may decrease, and—as has occurred in Britain in the last century—two major constellations of interest may arise. At this time, a "nationalization" of private interest may develop, with clash and compromise occurring on the interparty and intraparty levels, so that the public will be confronted at election time with a choice between two national definitions of public interest instead of the present multiplicity of parochial interests.

CONCLUSIONS

In this discussion we have concentrated our attention on the procedural aspects of government regulation in the United States rather than on the substance of regulation. The student who is interested in the actual content of regulatory and planning programs can obtain full information on this subject from specialized investigations such as those of Fainsod and Gordon or Mund; what we are concerned with here is the planning process itself, the way planning is implemented and formulated rather than the nature of the plans or regulations.

Government intervention in economic affairs has, it is submitted, been an outgrowth of the pressure process which forms the substructure of American political life. Although the dominant elements in American politics are virtually unanimous in their dislike for government "planning" in the abstract, they have always been prepared to employ the apparatus of state intervention for their own purposes, to fulfill their own objectives. A priori planning, the advance preparation of a careful blueprint for future action, has been almost nonexistent in the United States, but piecemeal, pragmatic plans have been a constant feature of American politics. The consequence of this piecemeal planning has been the development in the United States of a patchwork of economic regulations with no theoretical common denominator except their common source in the demands of interest groups. To a socialist, or anyone else committed to a priori planning, this is something of a nightmare: the Middle Western farmer receives a state guarantee of high prices for his product; the Eastern dairy farmer, who must pay artificially high prices for his grain, must have his butter and eggs subsidized; the industrial worker, whose food costs are high as a consequence of price supports, demands higher wages; and, to pay higher wages, the industrialist must raise his prices to the farmer. Finally, to keep the whole show on the road, foreign competition must be barred by tariff restrictions. The socialist criticisms have considerable logical force!

But logic is not the first law of politics, and—while such criticisms as that detailed above are useful in forcing Americans to realize what they are doing— the logical attack on American-style economic intervention has had little political effectiveness. In a heterogeneous, pluralistic society like that in the United States, each group tends to go its own way subject only to the limitations that can be devised by other groups. In economic regulation the main tendency has been for functional groups to obtain the power to regulate themselves, and because of the diffusion of power and the absence of any stable interest constellations which might "nationalize" private interest, *i.e.*, develop a nationwide interest pattern, and establish thus an enforceable definition of the public interest, economic power in the United States has been fragmented. The logicians of planning can bewail this new feudalism, but it would appear that they must await increasing national and social homogeneity to supply them with a rank and file. Public economic law, as defined earlier in this chapter, will be an outgrowth of political and economic consolidation, not of the theoretical machinations of planners.

THE PLANNING PROCESS IN BRITAIN

The British welfare state is today being bitterly criticized from two directions. One school of thought, tutored by John Jewkes and F. A. Hayek, asserts that British planning is the anteroom of totalitarianism, that the British are, in Hayek's expressive phrase, on the "road to serfdom." The other critics, led by Robert A. Brady, maintain that British planning and, indeed, British socialism, are simply clever disguises that have been assumed by British capitalism in the effort to continue private capitalist government. To employ the dichotomy developed above, Jewkes, Hayek and company believe that Britain has developed public economic law of a sinister character—in fact, they seem to believe that any public economic law automatically assumes a sinister form

—while Brady and his group submit that Britain still suffers under private economic law, that is, the cloaking of private planning with public power, of a singularly ingenious character.

Since theoreticians of this sort seldom allow factual considerations to interfere with their theoretical assumptions, a specific examination of the planning process in Great Britain may give the student a far better insight into the actual state of British economic intervention, the formulation and implementation of plans, than can be found in their abstract and ex parte presentations.

Some historical background is relevant at this point. Britain, first to receive the full impact of the Industrial Revolution, was likewise first to undertake large-scale intervention in economic affairs. But as Professor John B. Brebner has observed in an acute analysis, economic activity in the nineteenth century tended to be of a piecemeal character. Pressure groups such as industrialists, farmers, artisans, and workers, in frequently shifting alliances, attempted to employ state power for their own ends and to punish their opponents. The "Tory Socialists," for example, who once included Disraeli among their number, tried to form a coalition of the landowners and the urban workers against the rising industrialists. Similarly, the industrialists attempted to build a political entente with the urban workers against the agrarian interests. The economic history of England in the nineteenth century is largely understandable in terms of the private economic law that emerged from these various coalitions.

The development of British political parties has been discussed earlier, so for our purposes here it should be sufficient to recall that over the course of the last century two major constellations of interest groups have emerged to preeminent positions. One of these, the Conservative party, is based largely on industrial and agricultural foundations; the other, the Labor party, is founded on working-class and lower-middle-class support. Each of these constellations developed, from an amalgam of its own internal interests, a definition of the national interest which it presents to the electorate at general elections and which it attempts to implement when in office. Private interest has thus been "nationalized" in Britain, *i.e.*, it has been consolidated into national patterns. Unless a pressure group casts its fortunes with one of the two major parties, it will find little support for its objectives in legislation or administrative action. Each party program is therefore not merely a collection of pious platitudes; it is a concrete statement of policy objectives which will be enforceable in the event the party becomes the Government.

THE PARTIES AND PLANNING

While in the United States the political parties as such have little role to play in the planning process, in Great Britain they hold a position of great power. The Conservative party, for example, told the electorate in 1951 that, if victorious, it would denationalize the steel industry which had been put under public ownership by the Laborites. The Conservative victory put the Churchill Government in a position where it could go through with this planning, or perhaps deplanning, measure. Similarly, the Laborites told the people in 1945 that, if elected, they would nationalize coal, electricity, transport, and the Bank of England, and once victorious, they proceeded with dispatch to implement these programs. However, the parties do not get their plans out of the blue; obviously, as in the United States, such measures of government intervention come from a specific source, and in common with American experience, the source is often a pressure group in the area concerned.

To take a case in point, the National Union of Mineworkers, affiliated with the Labor party, had long demanded the nationalization of the coal industry. While this was motivated by the self-interest of the miners, it was endorsed by socialist theoreticians as a step on the road to industrial democracy and socialism. However, some objections were immediately heard from the cooperative movement, which is also affiliated with the Labor party, on the ground that cooperatives were handling a significant portion of the retail distribution and sale of coal. Indeed, at the time of coal nationalization, the cooperatives were responsible for 15 per cent of the coal distributed. In this instance, the co-ops endorsed the nationalization measure, but as was described earlier, they took strong action later against the proposal for nationalization of insurance and succeeded in getting it modified in accordance with their views to a mutualization plan.

A similar process of compromise goes on within the Conservative party. One group in the party, for instance, has been vigorously opposed to the National Health Plan, while another group—and, as it turned out, the dominant one— supported the nationalization of medicine. A battle also raged on the subject of agricultural subsidies which ended in a draw: the subsidies were continued but decreased. The denationalization of steel was a measure near and dear to the heart of the Federation of British Industries, but the spokesmen for the Federation's point of view in the Conservative party did not succeed in winning their full position.

In short, the planning process in Britain has its roots in the same soil as is the case in the United States. The demands of pressure groups, which in Britain concentrate on the party level, emerge, if the group is significantly powerful, as proposals for public policy. If the electorate endorses these proposals, it simultaneously puts into office men committed to them and, more importantly, supplied with power to implement them.

THE GOVERNMENT AND PLANNING

At the governmental level, a significant difference exists between the planning power of the British Cabinet and that of the American President. Because the President has no stable party foundation on which to operate, his actions tend to be of a piecemeal character. He deals with one problem on its political merits, and then with the next one on its merits, but there may be no connecting thread between his two resulting policies. He must handle each situation in terms of its own political dynamics, of the congressional support he can get for his views, and not on the basis of a thought-out theoretical approach. Thus President Truman could veto the Kerr Act, freeing natural gas from regulation by the Federal Power Commission, but subsequently appoint to the FPC a member who supported the Kerr policy. The President must find support for his policies where he can, and in the event that no support is forthcoming, he finds it politically advisable to run with the wind. The mansion of presidential power is built on sand.

On the other hand, the British Cabinet draws its power from a stable, disciplined parliamentary majority. This majority is not monolithic, but it is homogeneous. While it may have severe internal struggles, it presents a united front in Commons. It is responsible and must behave; the penalty for irresponsibility may well be defeat at the next election. The furor caused by Aneurin Bevan's resignation from the Cabinet in 1951 noticeably decreased the public's confidence in the Labor Government, and contributed to the Labor defeat in the election later that year. Thus, while the party leaders cannot become too autonomous, they have a wide area of discretion and consequently can plan policy with a much greater degree of consistency than is possible in the United States. A priori planning, that is, planning which is broad and comprehensive in scope, and which attempts to deal with individual situations in terms of an over-all scheme, is thus to some extent possible in Great Britain.

The chief instrument for this planning is the annual budget. Here another brief comparison with American practice is in order. Each year, in the United States, the Bureau of the Budget, subject to presidential direction, consolidates the budgetary requests of the various Federal agencies for submission to Congress. The Bureau exercises wide discretion in paring down these departmental and agency estimates to a figure consonant with the operating requirements of the various organizations. But although final appropriations generally follow the President's request fairly closely, an individual program which is disliked by Congress, or, to be more precise, by congressional appropriations committees or subcommittees, may suffer a heavy cut. Similarly, programs favored by key Congressmen, such as those of the Army Corps of Engineers, the Department of Agriculture, or the Federal Bureau of Investigation, may receive budgetary increases above the budget level.

In Britain, the battle rages within the Government before the budget is submitted, and a change on the floor of the House of Commons is equivalent to a motion of censure, resulting in the fall of the Government or the dissolution of the Parliament and new elections. Furthermore, Parliamentary standing orders forbid increasing an appropriation. Rarely are pressure groups able to modify a proposal once it has been incorporated in the budget. In 1937, business interests were successful in getting Chancellor of the Exchequer Neville Chamberlain to withdraw a proposed national-defense business tax, although it was not forced in Commons but was brought about by informal pressure on the Cabinet. The tax was withdrawn; it was not rejected. But such concession to pressure occurs very seldom; usually the Chancellor has analyzed the opposition in advance and taken budgetary action to forestall serious revolt.

The British budget is thus the most significant planning device that exists in that nation, and the Government invariably employs it to implement some over-all conception of national policy. This is as true of the Conservatives as of the Laborites: the former often grumble as they plan, but they plan nonetheless; the latter revel in planning, although one often suspects that there is more bark than bite in their actions. Of course, international as well as internal imperatives have forced extensive economic intervention upon any Government that rules Britain. The management of a virtually bankrupt nation cannot allow things to take their natural course. The fact, for example, that British railroads are running in the red cannot be met by closing them down. Railroads are obviously necessary; in the absence of trucks, money to buy trucks, or materials to build trucks, the Government must maintain rail transportation even if it is uneconomic.

The operation of the British Cabinet has already been described in some detail elsewhere, so there is no point in repeating the material here. Suffice it to say that all significant economic measures are first discussed in a Cabinet committee and then approved by the Prime Minister and the Cabinet as a whole. Often bitter arguments take place at this level. Aneurin Bevan has revealed that he and his Cabinet colleagues in 1951 fought a long battle over the issue of increases in the defense budget and cutbacks in the allocations for the social-security programs. Compromises between various forces in the party often result in measures which are considerably less than a planner's dream, so that Britain is far less of a planner's paradise, or guinea pig, than is sometimes supposed. Rarely does a fully consistent, integrated plan survive the process of political compromise. Between 1945 and 1951, the Laborites were simultaneously engaged in developing antitrust policies and in rationalizing industry, that is, encouraging its integration. Similarly, while talking of state planning and control, the Labor Government, through such devices as Development Councils, was encouraging businesses to regulate themselves and giving them state authority to do so.

THE BUREAUCRACY AND PLANNING

Because of the nature of the British party system and the social underpinnings upon which it rests, there does exist a considerable body of public economic law as we have used the term in this analysis. However, before planning measures are presented to Commons for approval there is a gap between party aspirations and concrete proposals that must be bridged. Similarly, passage by Parliament does not automatically implement a proposal. It is in these two areas of drafting and implementing that the British bureaucracy has a real function.

Socialist critics, notably the late Professor Harold J. Laski, often criticized the operation of the British bureaucracy, maintaining that basic political policy decisions were actually in the hands of a few "knights of the Treasury" who forced their policies upon the inexpert Ministers. Although the top civil servants undoubtedly do have considerable influence upon their political chiefs, this accusation appears to be without basic merit. A strong, conscientious Minister can keep his civil servants in line, and conversely the members of the administrative class appear to have a genuine devotion to the tradition of nonpartisanship. When Labor Ministers did encounter difficulties from civil servants, it was generally at the bottom of the career ladder rather than at the top that these clashes occurred.

On the other hand, Professor R. S. Milne has developed a persuasive case to support the thesis that it is the *esprit de corps* of the administrative class which has made Britain's planning machinery workable. On paper, the machinery of planning is a hodgepodge of ministerial committees and agencies, but each of these is administratively run by a member of the administrative elite. Milne suggests that not more than fifty civil servants play significant roles in the planning process, and that these men tend to be personal friends and belong to the same clubs, thus supplying an informal dynamic to the operation that is not apparent on the surface. A problem confronted by one section which it might take weeks and a ream of carbon paper to bring to the attention of other concerned agencies can be thrashed out in half an hour at the club by the officials involved.

The formal job of the bureaucracy is to put administrative flesh on the bones supplied by the politicians. Thus a Cabinet proposal to nationalize the chemical industry would be turned over to the Economic Section of the Cabinet Office, which would in turn consult other agencies concerned. A tentative working model would be established in this fashion and then referred to the Cabinet for approval or modification. Once passed by Parliament, the enactment would be turned over to a ministry for enforcement and implementation, and a new set of civil servants would, subject to ministerial and Treasury approval of their techniques, carry on the job.

The operating administrators do, indeed, have considerable autonomy and flexibility, but their actions are carried on within a framework established by a stable political class. There is continuous interaction between administrators and Ministers and between administrators and administrators, but the general mission to be fulfilled has been defined in terms of public economic law. Thus the possibility of developing functional baronies, such as characterize the American scene, is slight.

CONCLUSIONS

Through the activities of their political parties, the British have evolved and "nationalized" concrete, though tentative, definitions of the public interest. While planning can never be implemented on a wholly a priori basis in a democracy, that is, the planners can never ruthlessly pursue an abstract goal without regard for the wishes of the people, the British have succeeded in large degree in developing public economic law. That British planners could follow the totalitarian pattern of sacrificing one generation in the interests of the next is inconceivable, but nonetheless a Government does have the ability to formulate and implement a general program within the limits of consensus.

To reiterate, the reason for this is the network of responsibility that is characteristic of British politics and administration. The party is responsible to the electorate and wants to be returned to power at the next general election. The Cabinet is responsible, even though endowed with a high degree of autonomy, to a majority in Commons which has no desire to commit political suicide by rigidly adhering to unpopular policies. The administrative class is responsible, though not in an inflexible fashion, to the Ministers. And, finally, the whole planning process operates effectively not because of the superiority of British organization charts or the work of Hoover Commissions, but because of the deeply and often inarticulately held body of shared values which compose the British democratic tradition. The process rests on the firm foundation of British social homogeneity.

THE PLANNING PROCESS IN FRANCE

No general studies have been made of the French planning process, but, from one source and another, enough material can be gathered to give an approximate picture of how the operation works. The reason for the absence of precise knowledge would seem to be indicative of the nature of the problem: the work of planning in France is largely clothed in the anonymity which the bureaucracy employs as a protective device in the defense of its commanding position. Thus, before analyzing the planning operation, it would be well to recall the institutional highlights of French society: the centralized and virtually autonomous administrative class, the decentralized and weak political class, and the lack of social homogeneity which has made of France a geographical expression populated by several rival communities of Frenchmen.

The history of economic regulation in modern France, as Professor Shepard Clough pointed out in 1939, is the history of private economic law. What state planning was undertaken, was destined to aid the group or groups which drew up the plans. As in the United States, pressure groups employed the state in the effort to achieve their objectives and frustrate the objectives of their opponents. There was no "nationalization" of private interest which could lead to an enforceable definition of the public interest; indeed, the many French political parties and groups tended to be merely pressure groups in political attire.

The political left consistently advocated national planning, and in 1934, the *Confédération Générale du Travail,* the leading trade-union center, actually published a comprehensive program for improving agricultural and industrial production. The CGT was, however, a voice crying in the wilderness; what planning there was, such as the Blum Government's attempts to develop the French armaments industry against the German threat, was undertaken on a piecemeal basis. Given the fragmented basis of French politics, it was impossible to develop a national conception of public interest either from the right or from the left. The timid nature of the measures undertaken by the socialist Blum led a syndicalist commentator to observe that there was only one thing more conservative than a conservative out of office: a socialist in office! While this is perhaps unfair to Léon Blum, the inability of his Government to make up its mind whether it should change capitalism or administer it did, as Professor Adolf Sturmthal pointed out in his *Tragedy of European Labor,* contribute to the victory of Nazism.

The collapse of France in the face of Nazism contributed to a new rise of radicalism. The Resistance refurbished the 1934 plan of the CGT and prepared to move into the postwar world with a strong national program for restoring France to her place of eminence in the world. The elections to the two Constituent Assemblies and the first National Assembly resulted in tremendous majorities for those parties favoring socialism, whether of Communist, Socialist, or Christian Democratic persuasion. In October, 1945, the *Délégation des Gauches,* a group which included representatives of the Radical Socialist party, the Communist party, the Socialist party, and the CGT—and whose recommendations were approved by the Christian Democrats (MRP)—demanded the nationalization of banking, insurance, gas and electricity, the iron and steel industry, and several other industrial sectors. It appeared, to the great trepidation of the conservative elements in the community, that a far-reaching and stringent definition of national interest was about to be imposed on the economy.

However, the left-wing coalition, so monolithic in appearance, was in actuality crisscrossed with internal schisms. Since the party history of this period has been discussed earlier, it should here suffice to note that by 1947, the MRP had moved considerably to the right, the Socialists and Communists had come to the parting of the ways, and the Radical Socialists had returned to the trenches to fight the battle of capitalism. All that remained of this economic common-law marriage were several measures of nationalization, notably those putting most banks and insurance companies, coal, electricity, and gas under public ownership, passed in late 1945 and early 1946 by the Constituent Assembly.

With the collapse of the left coalition, French politics returned to its primordial state of fragmentation, and the administrative class moved back into the positions of power from which it had momentarily been driven by the passions of the Liberation. The history of French planning since 1947 is, consequently, a history of bureaucratic operations. In effect, after a brief interlude of public economic law, France returned to private economic law administered by the administrative class.

THE BUREAUCRACY AND THE PLANNING PROCESS

Although discussed earlier under a different heading, the operation of the nationalized industries merits reanalysis, for it gives a good picture of the relationship that exists between the paper planning and the actual planning of these industrial operations. It will be recalled that when the coal industry was nationalized, a national coal board, the *Charbonnages de France,* was established to plan over-all mining procedures. Regional boards were also established in each of the major coal regions of France directly to supervise the extraction of the vital product. These boards were composed on the basis of interest representation, and because of the temporary ascendance of the left in 1946, they tended heavily to overrepresent the trade-union interest. Fourteen of the eighteen members of the *Charbonnages de France* appointed by the communist Minister of Industrial Production Marcel Paul in 1946 were actually trade-unionists, although they were assigned, for formal juridical purposes, other titles. Léon Jouhaux, at that time one of the General Secretaries of the still unified CGT, was, for example, appointed to the *Charbonnages* to represent the coal consumers!

With the change in the climate of political opinion, these left-dominated boards were soon an operating anachronism. The state had always the power to appoint the directors-general of the boards—the full-time, paid officials who were presumably to execute the policies formulated by the boards. As the political power of the left went down, the industrial power of these bureaucrats went up, until today, as Professor Sturmthal has recently demonstrated, they not only operate the mines, but they also determine, in collaboration with the officials in the central ministry, industrial policy. The boards have become impotent appendages on the bureaucratic structure of the nationalized industries.

Thus the unique aspect of the planning process in France is the dominant role played by the expert, the civil servant, the *fonctionnaire*. Here, as in other aspects of government, we can see the justice of Halévy's famous statement about the two French constitutions. Writing of the constitution of the Third Republic, the great historian noted that it juridically and formally vested power in Parliament, but that, in effect, it was subordinate to the constitution of the year VIII, the Napoleonic document which gave state power to the administrative class. Halévy's comment appears to be equally applicable to the constitution of the Fourth Republic.

THE NEW FEUDALISM: FRENCH STYLE

The main distinction between the new feudalism as it has been described operating in the United States and that existing in France is to be sought in the differing natures of the bureaucracies in the two nations. While bureaucrats in the United States have considerable authority over the planning process, there is no tradition of bureaucratic centralization or of a highly selected administrative elite such as there is in France. Furthermore, and probably in part as an outgrowth of this fact, the power of the bureaucracy vis-à-vis the legislature is considerably less in the United States than in France.

But once this has been said, the similarities between the planning forms of the two countries become apparent. In both, the government servants tend to ally themselves with the significant pressure groups in the functional area to which they have been assigned. State planning thus seems to take the form of public endorsement and support for private decisions—private economic law, as we have used the term. The formulation and implementation of the Monnet Plan, the great postwar effort to restore France's basic capital equipment, serves as a good example of this process in action.

The top officials of the *Commissariat Général du Plan de Modernisation et de l'Équipment,* the formal title of the Monnet group, were experts. They were charged by a government decree of Jan. 3, 1946, with the task of planning the revitalization of the French economy. In each significant industrial sector, a committee of experts was established to determine the goals that should be achieved in the four-year period from 1946 to 1950, and the investment levels necessary for their attainment. The over-all Plan was simply an addition of the estimates of the various expert working parties. In other words, experts in steel, picked from the industry because of their knowledge of its problems, prepared the plan for steel, and a similar procedure was followed in the other areas. The needs of each sector were calculated by men with a vested interest in it—with empires to defend, so to speak—and almost no attempt was made to reconcile the goals established in each area into an integrated whole. The Monnet Plan, in other terms, was not a plan, but a series of plans devised by interest groups for their own advancement and given state approval. This was no less than an institutionalization of private law planning. Incidentally, this is not to say that the Monnet program was bad; on the contrary, it appears to have been quite successful in restoring French basic industries. This is an analysis of the operation, not a condemnation.

THE LEGISLATURE AND THE PLANNERS

The relationship between the National Assembly and the administrative elite in France has already been examined in an earlier chapter, but some reiteration is necessary at this point. It will be recalled that the legislature is seriously disabled in its attempts to regulate the activities of the bureaucracy by its inability to forge an adequate instrument of political government, a strong cabinet. While individual Cabinet Ministers have on occasion maintained their jobs with some continuity—in the period from December, 1946 to July 1, 1951, the tenure of the Minister of the Interior, for example, averaged seventeen months, as also did the term of the Foreign Minister—the collective weapon of cabinet responsibility was not present to combat the operations of the administrative elite.

Furthermore, as the center of gravity of the French legislature has moved to the right, advocates of less government have moved into positions of power, and in France less government seems to be synonymous with government by the civil service. It was the parties of the left which traditionally opposed the *république des fonctionnaires,* for the very good reason that the *fonctionnaires* as a rule emerged from conservative backgrounds and were disposed to sabotage —or, at least, not to enforce effectively—any radical measures passed by the legislature. Thus the left, when in power, usually attempted to circumvent the civil service by establishing *ad hoc* bodies, such as the governing boards of the nationalized industries, composed of laymen, to implement its proposals. The right, on the other hand, has tended to turn the task of implementing legislation over to the administrative class with few qualms about the outcome. An interesting instance of this tendency of the right to vest power in old-line civil servants appears to emerge from the history of the *Chambre des Comptes.*

Established at the time of the nationalizations of 1946, the *Chambre* was charged with the task of overseeing the finances and administration of the coal and gas and electricity boards. The members of the *Chambre* were to be experts in accounting and industrial management and were given extensive powers over the industries concerned. However, in January, 1948, the *Chambre* was abolished, and in its place was set up the *Commission de Vérification des Comptes des Entreprises Publiques,* a body with even greater powers of administrative oversight, but composed in a significantly different fashion. While the *Chambre des Comptes* was staffed by experts of a nongovernmental character, the *Commission* was composed of members of the administrative class —magistrates of the former Court of Accounts, and high-ranking civil servants from the Ministry of Finance.

One might consequently suggest that so long as the right holds the reins of formal government power, there will be no serious attempts to break the hold of the bureaucracy on the planning process. The National Assembly does conduct an occasional foray against the nationalized industries, particularly the administration of the nationally controlled railroad corporation, but this is usually because the enterprise under discussion is losing money. The budget of such an organization as the Monnet Plan may be cut, but this does not seriously affect the control of the bureaucracy over decision making. It is simply reflected in smaller allocations to the industrial objectives of the Plan and does not alter the internal power structure of the planners. Indeed, the actions of the various French governments since 1947 have, if anything, strengthened the power of the administrative class, particularly in the nationalized sector of the economy. Partly this was due to the fact that the original nationalizing legislation was designed to create, in the words of Professor Mario Einaudi, "autonomous empires led by the Communist party," and thus any attempt to break the power of the Communists had to result in the strengthening of an opposition group in these industries. In part, it seems also to have been an outgrowth of the trust that the right has traditionally put in the administrative class as an outfit that can keep France in safe hands.

CONCLUSIONS

Private-law planning seems, on the basis of what evidence there is, to be the rule in France. As in the United States, decision making on state intervention in economic affairs appears to be in the hands of an alliance of interest groups, bureaucrats, and—although there is virtually no scholarly evidence to support this fact—probably legislators. This situation is a seeming outgrowth of the social heterogeneity that is characteristic of France generally; there are no significant "nationalizations" of private interest, or, to put it another way, there are so many "nationalizations" of interest that no two or three can dominate the stage and offer the electorate a meaningful choice among definitions of the public interest.

From the institutional point of view, the bureaucracy is therefore the locus of decision-making power, since the political class is unable to undertake this role. The planning which emerges is not necessarily bad; indeed, some of it has been excellent. But it is essentially autoregulation by the industries concerned—the Monnet Plan for electricity, for example, was drawn up by experts from the public utilities and became the operating objective of the *Électricité de France*, the public corporation running the power sector. The state planners simply endorsed the program designed by the nationalized industry itself. It appears that the emergence of a strong political class is the prerequisite for public economic law in France. Until such a development takes place—and it would seem to be far in the future—the autonomous administrative elite, working with the interests concerned, will dominate the planning process.

PLANNING IN A DEMOCRACY—CONCLUSIONS

It has been suggested in this chapter that state planning, which we have employed in its broadest sense as state intervention in economic affairs, is an outgrowth of the group process. Each group, putting forward its conception of the public interest, attempts to utilize state power to obtain its private objectives. Each group, that is, tends to identify its private interest with the public interest. So long as a democratic society is highly heterogeneous, a form of economic feudalism, of functional autonomy, seems to be characteristic of the planning process. Various groups ally themselves with legislators and bureaucrats in the attempt to build autonomous economic duchies, to cloak their private decisions with public power. Thus the economic regimes in such nations as the United States and France are characterized by what we have designated private economic law. It would not be wise to push this comparison between the United States and France too far. While the objective situations are similar, the subjective causes of these situations are vastly different. France is in the advanced stages of ideological fragmentation, which prevents the formulation of public economic law. On the other hand, fragmentation in the United States is nonideological and largely results from the diffusion of economic and political power throughout the huge, young nation.

This is not to suggest that all regulatory agencies in the United States are prisoners of the interests they are supposed to regulate. The Federal Reserve System, particularly the central Board, has not fallen into the hands of the bankers, and so far the Securities and Exchange Commission has retained its independence of the stockbrokers. But, in the absence of a strong political class, which in turn depends for its power on disciplined political parties, there is a distinct tendency in the direction of the regulation of the regulators by the regulated. A few examples have been cited in the text, but hundreds more will suggest themselves to careful students of government. It is difficult, for example, to find a state in which the milk-control board is not the private property of the dairy interests, and state public-utilities commissions are frequently dominated by the private-utility interests.

Nor are we suggesting that this process is immoral. If an electorate had cast its vote in favor of a clear definition of the public interest, then it would be immoral for legislators and bureaucrats to pursue a contrary policy. But it is precisely because there is no national definition of the public interest, formulated and enforced by a strong political class, that this fragmentation exists. The legislator and the bureaucrat cannot be expected to pull an enforceable definition of the public interest out of a hat; indeed, such an a priori formulation of a general will is characteristic of the antidemocratic regime. The legislator or the administrator in a democracy must depend upon his constituents for his views, and if his constituents are engaged in pressing their own interest as the public interest, as they are almost invariably doing, he must cast in his lot with them or pay the political consequences. Similarly, the French administrative class is not engaged in a vicious conspiracy against the public interest; it is because there is no enforceable conception of the public interest, because there is a political vacuum, that they have the authority that they possess. Indeed, it is a tribute to the integrity and dedication of the members of this elite that, given the degree of autonomy that they have, they perform their tasks, on the whole, in an excellent fashion. The bureaucratically administered French railroads, for example, are probably the finest in Western Europe.

The emergence of economic public law, conversely, is an outgrowth of fundamental social developments. Rather than being a consequence of the conspiracy of a small group of planners, it seems to be founded upon the "nationalization" of private interest, that is, a definition, or definitions, of public interest supported by a homogeneous society. This is another way of saying that economic public law depends upon a disciplined political party which has succeeded in convincing the electorate that its interpretation of the public interest is wise and should be implemented. A strong political class, such as that which currently governs Britain, can enforce public economic law and destroy the power of the autonomous duchies which formerly ran their affairs to suit themselves.

But even in a nation where public economic law is an actuality, the planning process does not lose its ties with interest groups. The groups remain as the component units of the political parties, which are cohesive precisely because the groups that make them up have a high common denominator. And, while these groups have much in common, there are also differences between them which frequently find their way into public policy. Consequently, pure a priori planning, which supplies conservative economists with material for nightmares, seems to be impossible in a democracy. Such planning would be monolithic and comprehensive, and would depend for its fruition upon techniques of enforcement that are impossible in a democracy. It must be emphasized again that democratic political parties, even cohesive ones such as the British Labor party, are far from monolithic. Thus the planner in a democracy can never, at least not for very long, tell the people that, in Lord Lindsay's metaphor, the reason the shoe is too tight is that the foot is too big. There are always other planners waiting off stage with the cheerful message that the shoe is too small, and the right to choose planners remains with the people.

This brings up the final point to be considered in this analysis: the problem of regulating the regulators. Put another way, this is the fundamental issue of popular government, the power to determine the public interest and enforce the decision once made. In order to do this adequately, the people must be informed on the matters at issue and must be aware of what is being done and by whom it is done. Here the confused lines of responsibility, if lines is the proper word, which are characteristic of American and French government make informed appraisal very difficult. If the President of the United States has very little real power over the activities of the head of the Federal Bureau of Investigation, for example, or the director of the Soil Conservation Service, there is little point in blaming the Chief Executive for their actions. On the other hand, the techniques of responsibility developed by the British are such that, if national coal requirements are not correctly assessed, the people have every right to blame the Minister of Fuel and Power, and with him the Government. A basic function of the British party system, one which it fulfills regularly in Commons, is that of public education on the issues of the day, with the Opposition offering new policies and a new political class as the solution to Government blunders. Because the Government has the power to implement its policies, it cannot pass the blame for failure to any other shoulders.

Thus the task of regulating the regulators, of keeping the planners responsible to the public, depends in the last analysis upon the existence of a strong, responsible political class. But a strong political class in turn is founded on the institutions of party government and the social structure which underlies these institutions. Consequently, the development of economic public law, which depends for its existence upon a political class capable of enforcing a definition of national interest upon pressure groups and their bureaucratic allies, is an essential precondition for public control of the planning process. Unless there is a "nationalization" of private interest, a nationwide consolidation of interests founded upon economic homogeneity, the feudal economic system will remain based on the institutionalization of parochial interest in private economic law and a concomitant fragmentation of the planning power.

Chapter 13

FOREIGN AFFAIRS—A CASE STUDY IN POLICY FORMULATION AND EXECUTION

IN THE last chapter, we examined an area of policy formulation which was largely, though not exclusively, domestic in nature. Now we turn to an analysis of the problems involved in the formulation and execution of a democratic foreign policy. It must be noted before beginning this examination that the line between domestic and foreign policy has, over the course of the past half century, grown more and more indistinct until today there is a tremendous overlap. A nation which has, for example, committed itself to a rigorous program of economic planning must consider each aspect of foreign policy in terms of its impact on the domestic plan. No British Government could consent under present circumstances to free convertibility of the pound sterling into dollars, no matter how important this question should bulk in negotiations in foreign policy. Such an action would wreck the British financial structure.

However, once this has been noted, it should be emphasized that the formulation and implementation of foreign policy is not wholly analogous to the process in effect on the domestic scene. While in each area the sources of policy are similar—the demands of pressure groups—the groups which have great power domestically do not necessarily have equal authority internationally. Conversely, some groups, notably the military and strategic planners, have a far stronger position in the decision making on international policy than they do on the national stage. Furthermore, on another level, state power over the international decision-making process has always been greater than is the case in domestic issues. While private groups such as the United Fruit Company or the British South Africa Company have at times been clothed with state power either officially or unofficially, there has been a strong tendency toward centralized, national direction of foreign policy. As long ago as 1799, the United States Congress passed the so-called Logan Act which forbade private individuals from entering into negotiations with foreign governments on matters of public policy. This statute, which is still in effect, makes clear the point that there is to be no free enterprise in the field of foreign affairs.

DEMOCRACY AND FOREIGN POLICY: SOME GENERAL DEVELOPMENTS

The problems which a democracy must face in the field of foreign affairs are of a highly complex nature and, indeed, present a real challenge to the theory of responsible government. If the American Joint Chiefs of Staff, on the basis of confidential information, reach a decision on the strategic importance of, say, Indochina, how can the general public, with its limited information, either approve or disapprove of the policy? Or, to take a similar case, suppose that reliable intelligence sources report to the President that the Chinese Communists can be split from Moscow if the United States adopts a sufficiently conciliatory policy toward the Chinese, what would be the reaction of the "man on the street" to such a policy shift? In short, in the field of foreign affairs we are confronted with the problem of the expert in its starkest form. And public control of *expertise* is made exceptionally difficult by the confidential aura that surrounds international relations and prohibits the revelation of important factual data until well after the fact.

But this is not a new problem. In fact, the history of modern democracy is in part a history of the weakening of expert control over foreign affairs. Traditionally diplomacy was a guild matter, conducted by virtually autonomous "statesmen" who played international chess at regularly arranged conferences. One of the truisms of national politics was that "politics stopped at the water's edge," with the corollary that what was done abroad in the name of the nation was "above politics." An American Secretary of State such as John Quincy Adams or a British Foreign Secretary such as Lord Palmerston operated in what was almost a nonpolitical arena, freed from the bickerings of politics and dedicated to the principles of expert diplomacy. This is not to suggest that the policies formulated by these men did not have their origins in the group interests of their respective nations, but rather that the manner in which they conducted the nation's business abroad was largely free from the interference of political considerations. They had a considerable area of autonomy.

With the exception of moments of crisis such as the Oregon boundary dispute or the Armenian massacres, the public tended to ignore international events. One good reason for this was that in those days a foreign policy was not an expensive item; another was the lack of media of mass communications which could bring to the average citizen information, or misinformation, about the state of international relations. By the time the reader of the South Mudville *Gazette* got around to reading the foreign news, it was already days, if not weeks, old, and it is rather difficult to get enraged about an event which is already two weeks old when one learns of it. Similarly, diplomats abroad could not be directed rapidly by radio or cable.

But the twentieth century has seen an end to this leisurely pace. The growth of mass-circulation newspapers, which first achieved their hysterical stride in the Spanish-American War, and later the development of radio, made it possible for the citizen to keep up with the news almost on a minute-to-minute basis. Simultaneously, foreign policy began to affect the taxpayer's most sensitive organ, his pocketbook. World War I demonstrated to all that cheap wars, fought by professional soldiers, were a thing of the past, and the aftermath of the war showed that maintaining peace, or establishing the conditions for peace, was also a costly item in the budget. As the citizen became aroused about the cost of foreign policy, as he found that a failure might require him or his son to serve in the military forces, he also found that modern communications made it possible for him to keep his finger on the pulse of international relations. Instead of meeting behind closed doors to enact secret treaties, diplomats were forced to operate in a goldfish bowl. Instead of dealing with each other in a realistic fashion, they were forced to prepare their case for home consumption, so that international conferences began to resemble oratorical contests rather than poker games. Scoring a point at the expense of an opponent became more important than attaining any sort of agreement.

This is a formidable indictment of the influence of public interest on diplomacy, but it must be kept in mind that while the experts may have given the conduct of foreign affairs an efficiency which it now lacks, their blunders were of a portentous nature. The experts had it all their own way, yet World War I was blundered into by all the initial participants. One has the feeling in reading the biographies of the statesmen of that period—Sir Edward Grey, the British Foreign Secretary, for instance—that no one was more surprised than the professionals when the war actually began. Judged empirically, it does not appear that "goldfish-bowl diplomacy" has been any less successful in averting crises and dealing realistically with international problems than was "guild diplomacy."

However, today there is little point in debating the merits or demerits of guild diplomacy unless one has antiquarian proclivities, for goldfish-bowl diplomacy appears to be a permanent fixture in the democracies. Consequently any discussion of the formulation and execution of foreign policy must be conducted against a backdrop of public interest, possibly even public frenzy. Diplomacy is "in politics," and it appears to be in to stay.

UNITED STATES FOREIGN POLICY: SOURCES

The sources of American foreign policy, like domestic policy, must be sought in the demands of interest groups in the American community. From the earliest days of the republic, the Secretaries of State were charged with the job of advancing on the international scene the claims of cotton planters, New England fishermen, New York financiers, Pennsylvania ironmongers, and Western farmers. The origin of the two-thirds majority required in the Senate for the approval of treaties was the distrust of various economic-sectional groups of each other, and the fear that they had that the Secretary of State of the new government would favor one section over another in his conduct of foreign affairs. The Louisiana Purchase of 1803 was an accidental enlargement of the effort by President Jefferson to obtain control of the mouth of the Mississippi River and the harbor of New Orleans, which was one of the major demands of the President's Western agrarian supporters.

The demands of the cotton planters likewise played a major part in the diplomacy which preceded the Mexican War and in the fighting of the war itself, and the demands of Southern railroad interests for a favorable right of way to the Pacific Ocean resulted in the Gadsden Purchase of 1853. Similarly, American mercantile interests were acutely interested in the possibility of a canal through Central America connecting the Atlantic and Pacific Oceans, and urged the United States to prevent Great Britain from gaining a position of dominance in Central America. One outcome of this interest was the Clayton-Bulwer Treaty of 1850, in which the United States and Britain agreed that neither power would exclude the other from any ship canal that might be built in that area.

To say this is not to subscribe to a naïve form of economic determinism. Although the economic demands of various pressure groups have probably played an impressive part in the weaving together of an American foreign policy, ideological pressures have also played a significant role. The Monroe Doctrine, while unquestionably supported by economic forces, was also an American declaration of approval for the independence movements in various Latin-American countries. The American belief in national independence as a moral good, which reached its apogee with President Woodrow Wilson's policy of national self-determination, has been one of the more inspiring aspects of our foreign policy over the years. The group demands that are reflected in foreign policy are not wholly confined to the level of economics, and although Americans have tended to exaggerate their altruism, there have been policies such as the Marshall Plan which give concrete evidence of unselfishness.

Frequently, as a consequence of the bitter struggling between groups which precedes policy enactment, American foreign policy is internally inconsistent. A large sum of money can be appropriated for use by the European Cooperation Administration to rebuild Italian industrial production—as was the case in 1948 to 1950—while at the same time no action is taken to permit the resulting increased production to compete favorably on the American market. When in 1952 the Department of State was urging a policy of "trade, not aid" upon the British, a British engineering firm turned in the low bid to the United States Army Engineers on a contract for hydroelectric equipment. After considerable protest from American manufacturers to the effect that the American market belonged to Americans, the Engineers, in 1953, rejected the bid on questionable technical grounds. Group pressures frequently have American policy going vigorously in several directions simultaneously.

There would be little point in a detailed examination of American foreign policy to indicate the group origins of its various components, for this would be laboring an obvious point. However, it is important to note that strategic and military factors are much more significant in the determination of foreign policy than is the case domestically. In a real sense, the Pentagon and the National Security Council are a strategic pressure group which must enter the arena and fight for its policies with the rest. In domestic affairs, the strategic lobby runs into considerable difficulty, for its objectives run counter to the views of important and powerfully situated lobbies. Note the difficulty that is involved in getting an appropriation for civil defense that would fulfill the minimum requirements of military preparation, and recall the troubles that have beset the Pentagon in its efforts to get universal military training enacted.

But in the field of foreign policy, the views of the strategic lobby are given great weight. There are probably many factors which help account for this, the outstanding one being that the military have to protect the nation from foreign enemies. Foreign policy is consequently distinctly relevant to their function. Another, which has grown greatly in recent years, is the decline in the prestige of the State Department, which resulted in the almost automatic increase in the power of the only other major government agency with large foreign commitments, the Department of Defense. Of course, a basic reason for the increase in military prestige, which underlies both the points made above, is the continued existence of a world crisis. In normal times such as the 1920's, the strategic lobby was virtually impotent, but when emergencies occur, military authority skyrockets. But it should be noted that even in normal periods, strategic factors play a greater role in foreign policy formulation than in the development of domestic programs.

THE PRESIDENT AND POLICY FORMULATION

Constitutionally as well as practically, the position of the President in the formulation of foreign policy is far stronger than is his authority in domestic matters. The constitutional source of his authority was an outgrowth of the tradition of foreign policy as a monopoly of the Crown, the "federative" power described by John Locke, which strongly influenced the framers of the Constitution. This was reinforced by early decisions of the Supreme Court which asserted that the President was the sole organ of diplomatic authority. However, although a strong legal case can be built to demonstrate the autonomy of the President in foreign policy, the real power of the President in these matters is founded far more on his psychological than on his juridical position.

It was suggested earlier that part of the President's powers stem from his position as the symbol of national unity, the "republican king," to use a phrase borrowed from the era of George Washington. When the President is dealing with foreign nations, all the forces of nationalism operate to rally support for him against the "out-group." At least twice in our history, the President has been advised by the Secretary of State to solve domestic squabbles by uniting the nation in a foreign war: once when John Adams had Jeffersonian troubles, and later when Lincoln was faced with imminent scission of the Union. While the President's domestic leadership may be bitterly attacked, it is part of the tradition to rally to his position on international relations with the justification concisely stated by Commodore Decatur, "My country, may she ever be right, but my country, right or wrong." As in the era of President Harry Truman, the opposition may attack some aspects of national policy, but it will rarely attack across the board.

In addition, there is a practical factor which gives the President considerable power in dealing with Congress in foreign policy—his superior sources of information. When a domestic matter comes before Congress, all the pressure groups concerned rush to Congressmen detailed cases to support or oppose the proposal. But in foreign policy, such groups are largely inoperative, while the President has at his disposal the information gathered by Foreign Service officers, military officers on foreign duty, the Central Intelligence Agency, and officials of allied governments. To counteract this advantage, Congressmen have at one time or another attempted to set up their own foreign-intelligence departments—Senator Borah and Senator McCarthy are two recent examples —and have undertaken elaborate personal investigations abroad. At any given moment there are probably five or six legislators investigating conditions in Western Europe on behalf of some congressional committee. But although Congressmen may not admit it, the President's preponderance in sources of information is tremendous, for he has at his disposal the services of experts and can utilize confidential materials to which Congressmen do not have access.

But having said all this, it must be emphasized that in foreign affairs as in domestic the President needs the support of Congress if he is effectively to implement his policies. His position vis-à-vis Congress is stronger, but he is in no sense autonomous. Congressional power in foreign policy is reserved for treatment later in this chapter, but it would leave a distorted picture not to note here that while the President can propose, Congress can dispose. The President's position as symbolic sovereign tends to give him more congressional support in his activities abroad than is the case at home, but it takes both the President and Congress to formulate and implement a workable foreign policy. The President's increased effectiveness in foreign affairs is a result not of his autonomy from Congress, but of inherently stronger congressional support for his views that develops in such matters.

PROBLEMS OF POLICY IMPLEMENTATION

Once a policy is formulated, the problem arises as to how to implement it, and how to implement it in such a manner that Congress will continue to back it once the initial enthusiasm has worn off. Traditionally, the department charged with foreign-policy implementation has been State, but in recent years, Americans have been witnessing what might be described as the withering away of the State Department. There has been a notable tendency, for example, to turn over policies intimately related to foreign affairs to new agencies created for that purpose. The Economic Cooperation Administration, which administered Marshall Plan aid, was one such example; the former Mutual Security Agency, now the Foreign Operations Administration, which handles both military and economic aid, the latter disguised as "defense support," to our allies is another. Gradually the State Department has been stripped of its operating functions and left with the hopeless job of formulating policy without being in a position to enforce its decisions. There has been a corresponding increase in the power over foreign policy of the Department of Defense. The reasons for this shift in the locus of decision-making power over foreign affairs are of vital significance to the student of American government.

As Herman Somers has noted in his fine analysis of this problem, the basic cause of State's decline is its lack of a constituency. While the farmers "own" the Department of Agriculture and will leap to its defense, no significant pressure groups rally around the Secretary of State. Indeed, the latter official often appears to Congressmen and to the public to be the American representative of foreign interests. He pleads for decreases in the tariff, he urges Congress to understand the French dilemma, he calls for "giveaway programs" for voteless aliens. Furthermore, the Secretary often appears to be overly considerate of foreign sensibilities, even downright cowardly. When the Guatemalans expropriate the United Fruit Company's plantations, he refuses to urge the President to send in the Marines. When the Bulgars lock up a citizen of Iowa, or Oregon, he refuses to call for a declaration of war. When action is called for, he puts on his homburg, gets out his brief case, goes to the office, and writes a note!

Thus the Secretary of State is a sitting duck for congressional and public marksmen. Who is going to support the Guatemalans or the Bulgars? Who is going to bring pressure on Congressmen on behalf of an abstract conception of over-all national interest? In short, when the State Department is attacked, few countervailing pressures seem to mobilize behind it. The Department has in recent years become further suspect because of the charges of communist sympathy leveled against some of its officials. Secretary of State Dean Acheson's defense of Alger Hiss here played into the hands of those bringing such accusations against the Department, and by dint of repetition such charges gained wide public credence. When Senator McCarthy accused General of the Armies George Marshall of communist proclivities, there was immediate congressional and public opposition to the charge, but the Senator's largely unsubstantiated attacks on career officials in the State Department ran into no such barrier. The State Department has no pressure buffer to aid it in withstanding assault.

With the Secretary of State rendered largely impotent, President Truman had to find alternate ways of implementing his policies satisfactory to Congress. He logically turned to the Department of Defense to fill this administrative vacuum, and top military officials, notably General Omar Bradley, then Chairman of the Joint Chiefs of Staff, began to appear more and more often before congressional committees to defend what were inherently foreign, rather than military, policies. Furthermore, as Somers has pointed out, all foreign policy began to be presented to Congress in military garb. Economic aid to Western Europe became in 1952, as was noted above, "defense support." Partly this was due to congressional suspicion of economic "giveaway programs," caused by an increasing emphasis on economy, but it was also probably motivated by President Truman's recognition that Congress would authorize money to be administered by MSA missions largely dominated by the military when it would not grant funds to be handled by State. It is recalled that the Mutual Security Agency was carefully given separate status and not, as would have been the case if administrative logic prevailed, made an operating agency of State.

But such a policy has bureaucratic implications. When Congress appropriates money for defense purposes, even when nonmilitary operations are for purposes of expediency temporarily put in uniform, the logical men to implement the policies are the military. Somers quotes one high military officer saying, with respect to the civilian officials purportedly responsible for MSA policy, "They told Congress that the only business they have is our business." Thus American foreign policy at the level of crucial decision making has fallen more and more into the hands of military officials, who are not under the jurisdiction even of American ambassadors abroad but report to their own military superiors.

The point of this is not that there is a plot under way by the military to take over the United States. On the contrary, the military have moved in by request to fill a vacuum created by the withering away of civilian authority over foreign policy. The point is that politically speaking the Defense Department has a constituency and can give its officers support and protection that State cannot give. An able man in a colonel's uniform can do his work and know that his superiors will go to bat for him, while an equally able man working for the Department of State is fair game for any Congressman in search of notoriety. It is hardly to be wondered that State has a difficult time finding adequate personnel; what is remarkable, and it is something for which the American people should be grateful, is the number of able colonels that the military has been able to draw on for the tasks that confront it. However, while grateful, the American people should also consider the complexion that this military predominance gives to foreign policy. At a time when communist propaganda is telling the world that the United States is a militaristic, imperialistic power, it is hardly the better part of wisdom, to say nothing of psychological warfare, to have so many diplomatic functions handled by men in uniform.

While we feel strongly that this separation of policy responsibility from operational responsibility in the area of foreign affairs is a grave administrative error, it must be noted that some able observers believe that the Department of State should be stripped of its operational responsibilities and left to function exclusively as a general staff in the formulation of foreign policy. It was this view which apparently motivated the establishment, in President Eisenhower's Reorganization Plan No. 7 which went into effect in August, 1953, of the Foreign Operations Administration. Headed by Harold Stassen, former Director of the Mutual Security Agency, the FOA absorbed the duties of the MSA and, in addition, was assigned authority over the Technical Co-operation Administration, the Institute of Inter-American Affairs, and the administration of the Battle Act, which regulates East-West trade in strategic items. The ambivalent position of the Director of the FOA can be ascertained by his assigned policy role. On the one hand, he is a member of the National Security Council, the top presidential strategy board, and has direct access to the President; on the other hand, under the terms of the Reorganization Plan, he is to derive his policy on financial and monetary matters from the Secretary of the Treasury, his defense policy from the Secretary of Defense, and his foreign policy from the Secretary of State. It remains to be seen how effectively the policies of the FOA will be directed by the distant voices of these three Secretaries. Ironically enough, the President had earlier refused to strip the three service members of the Joint Chiefs of Staff of their operational responsibilities on the ground that unless these three officers had control over their respective services they would be unable to implement their policy views. President Eisenhower has given the State Department strong support in its efforts to plan a consistent foreign policy, but it is still too early to judge how effective this general-staff approach will be.

While the relative authority of the Departments of State and Defense over policy implementation probably constitutes the major contemporary problem in the administration of American foreign policy, there is an additional problem that deserves brief mention, that of internal policy coordination within the administering agencies and cooperation with presidential policies. No agency is monolithic, and frequently bitter struggles take place behind closed doors between various subdivisions and between the bureaucracy and the political official at the top. For example, when President Truman decided to recognize the new state of Israel, a bitter argument was purported to have occurred within the Department of State between the Near Eastern specialists, who were reportedly pro-Arab, and the Secretary. A similar battle was reported within the military establishment at the time that President Truman recalled General Douglas MacArthur.

Interdepartmental squabbles are generally turned over for solution to inter-departmental committees. At the time that the Hoover Commission's Foreign Affairs Task Force examined this phenomenon, *i.e.,* in 1948, there were thirty-three interdepartmental committees on which the State Department was represented. The Secretary of State sat on thirteen of them, while the remaining representatives were from lower levels in the Department. Many of the issues turned over to committees for compromise are technical in nature and solutions emerge without too much difficulty, but committees have not proved valuable in solving top-level policy matters. If the Secretary of State and the Director of the Foreign Operations Administration, for example, get into a battle over the amount to be designated for the operation of the Technical Cooperation Administration, and a basic policy issue is involved, it is doubtful whether a committee would be able to reach any satisfactory solution.

Deadlocks of this sort must be handled by the President himself, and the bargaining power of the two contestants is likely to be more significant in the outcome than the inherent justice or logic of their positions. For example, in April, 1953, Secretary of State John Foster Dulles and MSA Director Harold Stassen came to different positions over the policy to be followed with respect to Senator McCarthy's private international negotiations with Greek shippers. Stassen forcefully opposed the Senator's usurpation of the prerogatives of the executive, while Dulles conceded that the Senator was acting in "the national interest." President Eisenhower decided the issue in favor of the Dulles approach, probably not because he accepted McCarthy's activities as a legitimate exercise of congressional power, but rather because of an unwillingness to take on the Senator and his followers at that time.

In short, the bureaucratic implementation of foreign policy often presents as many problems to the President as he initially faced in its formulation. At a time when a wide range of government agencies have responsibilities that can be included under the general heading of foreign policy—the Hoover Commission Task Force listed twenty-seven agencies besides State and Defense that have international interests and functions—the job of coordination obviously assumes major proportions. When decision-making authority is widely diffused, as it is in the executive branch, the problem of maintaining control at the center also bulks large. If too many cooks spoil the broth, they also make it exceptionally difficult to blame any one cook for the spoilage. One of the more familiar situations in Washington in recent years has been the passing of blame for a policy error, *e.g.*, the decision to evacuate American troops from Korea in 1948, from the Secretary of State to the Joint Chiefs of Staff to the President and then back to the Secretary of State, or perhaps on to another circuit of culprits. Simultaneously, Congress blames the President for not following a sound, coherent policy, while the President accuses Congress of making it impossible for him to put such a policy in action. At this point, therefore, it is advisable to shift the analysis from the executive to Congress in the effort to discover what role the legislature plays in policy formulation and execution.

CONGRESS AND FOREIGN POLICY

Congressional leverage on foreign policy is largely applied through the two key committees in each house: Foreign Affairs, and Appropriations. Since most significant foreign policies involve considerable expenditure, each house of Congress gets two chances to influence policy formulation: once when the principle, e.g., European recovery, is presented to it for approval, and later when the appropriation for the implementing agency is requested. The complications that can occur when four committees of two houses have the opportunity to conduct detailed evaluations of the same program almost defy description. For reasons discussed in an earlier chapter, the possibilities of sabotage in such a many-staged progression are tremendous. A key committee chairman can, if he so chooses, put great barriers in the way of a policy approved by three other committees, as John Taber of the House Appropriations Committee did with the Marshall Plan appropriation in 1948.

The consequence of this situation is that key Congressmen have extensive control over the conduct of foreign relations, and the psychological position of the Secretary of State is weakened in his negotiations with foreign diplomats. The latter have never forgotten the hash that Senator Henry Cabot Lodge, Chairman of the Senate Foreign Relations Committee in 1919, made of President Wilson's policies. The long-term treaty of alliance which Wilson offered the French at Versailles, for example, never emerged from the committee. Thus, while the French or British Foreign Minister will listen courteously to the American Secretary of State with one ear, they keep the other ear attuned to Congress, particularly to the views of key committee chairmen. Once again it must be recalled that Congress, in the words of a perceptive analyst, Don K. Price, "is little more than a collective noun," and in the field of foreign relations crucial authority resides in committee chairmen chosen not for their *expertise* but for their seniority.

Presidents since Wilson have taken congressional views into far greater consideration than was formerly the case, and generally today the Chief Executive attempts to associate leading congressional figures from both parties with his policies. This is often referred to as "bipartisanship," but a little reflection reveals that this term is predicated on the assumption that there are in Congress two parties—an assumption which, as James M. Burns has documented in *Congress on Trial*, is unwarranted. The significant Congressmen to associate with a foreign policy, from the viewpoint of the President, are important not because of their party position but because of their committee position. As party representatives, they have little power over their colleagues, but as committee members, they make decisions which will be given great weight by other Senators or Representatives. The simple reason, explained in some detail earlier, is that if the Senate or the House ever began to overrule the decisions of their committees, no business could ever be accomplished. The committee is the basic legislative unit.

Associating congressional committee leaders of both party labels with an executive policy may be useful in gaining passage of the measure through Congress, but it also has a considerable impact on the content of the policy. Such association can be obtained only by, in effect, allowing the Congressmen involved to write the ticket, for there is no coercive power that can be exercised to force them to go along with a policy they dislike. Furthermore, Congressmen, irrespective of party affiliation, tend to suspect the executive and feel that they are being "used." The President, with his superior sources of information, can present them with a pig in a poke, and because they have no direct control over administration, over actual operations, they often feel that they cannot adequately evaluate policy proposals. Here party considerations of a sort enter the picture, for those members of the party out of executive office must face up to the political fact that if a policy with which they have associated works out well, the President will claim credit for it, while if it fails, he will undoubtedly inform the electorate that "both parties" supported it. But still the basic schism is between Congress and the executive; a Republican committee chairman usually has more in common with the senior Democrat on his committee than he has with the Republican President.

All in all, intimate association with the executive in the formulation of policy —whether domestic or foreign—is not regarded with great enthusiasm by members of Congress. From the viewpoint of democratic theory, given American institutions with the institutional separation and differing constituencies of Congress and the President, this is probably just as well. The job of assigning responsibility for policy formulation, the vital task of rewarding success and punishing incompetence, is sufficiently difficult in the United States without merging Congress with the executive in the institutionalized preparation of policy. If the American electorate wants to repudiate a presidential policy, e.g., the Truman-Acheson China policy or the Eisenhower-Dulles Soviet policy, it is important that responsibility can be clearly assigned to the Chief Executive.

Those in search of detailed information about congressional influence on foreign policy should examine the excellent analyses presented by Daniel S. Cheever and H. Field Haviland, Jr., in their *American Foreign Policy and the Separation of Powers,* and Robert A. Dahl in his *Congress and Foreign Policy.* Here we have only the space to mention briefly some recent developments and their implications. One in particular is an outgrowth of the withering away of the State Department discussed under a different rubric: a relative decline in the power of Congress over policy. A second is the influence of ideological pressure groups such as the so-called "China lobby," and the final development to be examined is the attempt by Congressmen to develop their private state departments in an effort to achieve information equality with the executive.

The congressional assault on the purportedly irresponsible Department of State has had as an unanticipated consequence the transfer of many of State's functions to an organization which, particularly in time of crisis, Congress has great difficulty in dealing with—the Department of Defense. When the Secretary of State appears before a congressional committee, members feel free to interrogate him in a searching fashion and even, on occasion, accuse him of deception. But when the chairman of the Joint Chiefs of Staff—a four-stripe admiral with an outstanding record of service to his nation—comes before the same committee, a different atmosphere prevails. He is the key figure in the military protection of the national interest and, more significantly, he is supported by a powerful and vocal constituency, both military and civilian. When the chairman of the JCS informs the committee that he cannot reveal to it information required to justify his views because it would endanger national security to do so, the committee often gets annoyed, but seldom pursues the point. The lesson of the B-36's is still fresh in the memory of the strategic planners: in June, 1951, a military official revealed to the Senate Armed Services Committee, under injunctions of greatest secrecy, the exact number of intercontinental bombers the United States had in operation, and the figure appeared in the next morning's newspapers!

As Elias Huzar pointed out in his careful study of congressional control over military appropriations, *The Purse and the Sword,* Congress has not developed adequate techniques of investigating and regulating military policies, and now that large areas of nonmilitary foreign policy have been consigned to military operation, the same problem exists on a larger scale. Thus, when Congress weakened the Department of State, it simultaneously weakened its own position in foreign-policy matters. Incidentally, this has also resulted in a relative decrease in the prestige of the top military officials whom Congress, often justifiably, suspects of disguising political considerations in security garb. But this suspicion has not as yet resulted in improved techniques of control. The hearings on the dismissal from command of General Douglas MacArthur have been the only major attempt by Congress to revenge itself on the alleged political activities of the strategic planners, and these hearings were more of a bonus to Soviet intelligence than a practical mechanism for maintaining responsibility.

As was noted earlier, pressure groups in the United States do not operate solely on the economic level. Although it is impossible to disengage economic considerations completely, there are many groups whose objectives are primarily ideological. The peace lobby, composed of representatives of various religious groups, is one such, and others that probably fall under this heading, at least with respect to their international programs, are the veterans' lobby, the pro-Israel groups, and groups urging the liberation of various Soviet-dominated nations such as Poland and Rumania. The operation of such groups as these often seems to the foreign observer to be cloaked in mystery. Why, they may ask, do the few Poles in the United States have such a vigorous presentation of their case in the Senate? How can the relatively tiny proportion of Jews in the American population obtain such support for a pro-Israel policy?

Actually, there is little that is mysterious about the operation of these pressure organizations, but to realize this one needs an understanding of the American election and representation systems. The key role of the supposed "Jewish vote" in New York State, with its forty-five electoral votes, has given the pro-Israel lobby its political power. Similarly, the purported "Polish vote" in Detroit may have influenced Senator Homer Ferguson of Michigan to take an unusually enthusiastic interest in the fate of Poland. That such bloc votes do in fact exist has never been conclusively demonstrated, but few politicians want to experiment empirically in the matter. Furthermore, to reiterate a point made earlier, there are few counterpressures in foreign policy such as operate domestically to muffle a certain amount of congressional extravagance. A raucous denunciation of the British on the floor of the Senate may warm the hearts of one's Irish constituents, and it loses votes only in England. Needless to say, these congressional blasts complicate the life of the American diplomat abroad, who is held responsible by foreign opinion not only for official acts of statecraft, but also for the views expressed by Congressmen and by American newspapers and magazines.

The final point worthy of notation here is closely related to the action of ideological pressure groups. Congress, in an era when crises erupt almost daily in Burma, Iran, Indochina, Madagascar, Tunis, Kenya, and other geographical loci too numerous to mention, is engaged in a desperate quest for adequate information. The official sources of information, the government departments, are suspect—they have a vested interest to defend—but information Congress must have if it is to fulfill its policy functions. One of the major sources of pressure-group power grows from the fact that these organizations are prepared to supply Congressmen with a detailed brief, facts and figures, in support of their objectives.

This search for information has also led to congressional committees attempting to establish their own intelligence services. For example, in the course of its 1953 investigations of the Voice of America, Senator McCarthy's Senate Committee on Executive Expenditures sent two emissaries, Mr. Roy M. Cohn and Mr. Gerard D. Schine, to look into the European facilities of the Voice. The staffs of the Senate Foreign Relations Committee and of the House Foreign Affairs Committee likewise attempt to serve as private state departments and intelligence services.

These investigations often disturb constitutional purists, who maintain that Congress has no business interfering with the President's conduct of foreign relations. This, however, is a thoroughly unrealistic and untenable position, for Congress has every right to investigate the actions of the executive in foreign as in domestic affairs. Actually the job of the two committees specifically charged with overseeing foreign relations is one with enormous problems contained in it, particularly where the task of obtaining accurate and adequate information is concerned. One may have strenuous objections to the manner in which some committees—though neither of the two foreign-affairs committees falls in this category—have conducted investigations, but it must always be emphasized that the investigatory function is basic to free government.

CONCLUSIONS

In foreign-policy formulation, as in the domestic field, one of the major problems facing the analyst is the location, at any given moment, of decision-making power. In May, 1953, Clement Attlee, leader of the Opposition in the British Parliament, gave a speech on American foreign policy which set off forensic fireworks on both sides of the Atlantic. In the course of his remarks, Mr. Attlee noted that one of the most puzzling aspects of the American system of government was the difficulty in discovering "where effective power lies." This is a problem for American specialists too, for the locus of power is highly elusive, shifting sometimes almost from minute to minute. At one point in policy formulation, the State Department may have the upper hand, suddenly to be replaced by the Department of Defense, or by the chairman of a congressional committee.

This fact has been appreciated by recent Chief Executives, who have made attempts to create the machinery for cohesive and consistent policy formulation within the executive branch of government. The functions of the Bureau of the Budget have already been discussed, but another instrument, which President Eisenhower has put much emphasis upon, also deserves mentioning: the National Security Council. Composed of the Secretaries of State and Defense, the President and the Vice-President, the Director of the Foreign Operations Administration and the Director of the Office of Defense Mobilization, advised by the Joint Chiefs of Staff, and with frequent unofficial attendance by the Secretary of the Treasury and the Director of the Bureau of the Budget, the National Security Council is designed to give the United States one voice in international policies rather than many, often discordant, voices.

Although it is still too early to tell whether, under President Eisenhower, the NSC will succeed in this worthy ambition, one can on general grounds be skeptical about the possibility of a committee such as this achieving enforceable decisions. With the exception of the President and the Vice-President, each member is the ambassador of a significant power complex within the administration, so he can hardly act as a free agent at NSC meetings. The NSC can offer opportunities for high-level compromise and threshing out of intra-administration differences, but if its decisions are to be effective, it would seem that they would have to reflect real bargaining power rather than theoretical considerations about national security. In a sense, the NSC supplies a table on which the various agencies can put their cards, but it does not alter the strength or weakness of the cards held by the participants. Given the present pressure basis of American politics, it is doubtful whether any magical institution can be devised that will, for example, transform the Secretary of State's low cards to aces. But apparently President Eisenhower has developed the NSC into a quite useful *advisory* body by putting questions before it in such a way that internecine clashes are averted.

This brings us back to the essential point about the formulation of American foreign policy and the basic reason why the United States speaks with many voices. The absence of a strong, stable political class such as is supplied by the British party system almost forces administrative officials to find and work with their own constituencies. Because these constituencies are not in agreement on basic policy, their various spokesmen differ with each other, and the President, lacking the support of a disciplined party majority, does not himself have the power to enforce a uniform policy. While his symbolic position is great, in the concrete quest for political power he is only first among equals. Thus he can enforce his decisions by aligning himself with one interest coalition against a less powerful alliance, and conversely, if he joins the less powerful alliance, he may find himself with very circumscribed authority. Compare in this light the power of President Franklin D. Roosevelt, which rested on a wide coalition of farmers, workers, and lower middle class, with the authority of President Truman in the period from 1950 to 1952, which was supported by few pressure allies. Essentially the power of a President can be measured in terms of the power of his allies, who may or may not be closely affiliated with his political party.

But the fact that the President must build a coalition of interest to enforce his views only reinforces the point that he does not himself have the power to make decisions on many crucial matters. To put it another way, the President does not have the power, that is, the constituency, to protect officials who do what he tells them to do. Consequently, these officials must seek their own protection, their own constituency, and defend it even against the President. The political power which should sustain the President and give him the weapons with which to deal with recalcitrant administrators is fragmented among congressional committees, executive departments, and not infrequently pressure groups. It is this diffusion of power in the United States which leads to the pluralistic foreign policy which so astounds and dismays foreign observers, and it would appear that any real solution to the difficulties thus created must await the development within the United States of a homogeneous electorate and a disciplined party system. This may be a pessimistic prognosis, but it appears, on the basis of the facts, to be a realistic one.

BRITISH FOREIGN POLICY: SOURCES

It will come as no shock to the reader to learn that the British political parties and their parliamentary representatives supply the basic positions on foreign affairs and that the bureaucracy gives these positions meaning in practice. But once again it must be emphasized that the parties themselves get their ideas from constituent groups, so that if one looks deeply enough, he will discover that many of the planks in Britain's foreign program have originated in the demand of some group in the British community. For example, the demands for protection of the Anglo-Iranian Oil Company undoubtedly were a significant factor in determining Britain's policy toward the Iranian government in 1951–1952.

But, because of the existence of a stable, disciplined party system and the stable political class which has arisen from it, the British Government is in a far better position to coordinate foreign policy than is the American Government. At times, it has appeared that certain elements in British foreign policy were actually of a private character, that is, that some group with a special interest had succeeded in capturing decision-making power over certain aspects of foreign affairs. For example, in the thirties, the British oil interests seemed to have effective control over British Middle Eastern policy. However, the significant point here is that these interests took control by default. If the Governments of the day had chosen to alter the Middle Eastern policy, they could have done so, but they chose, probably on the basis of honest convictions, to identify the British interest in the Arab nations with that of the oil cartel.

This, in fact, would seem to be the answer to the generic charges that the top civil servants in the Foreign Office are autonomous, a charge that has often been leveled from the Labor benches. At times, particularly under the Conservative Governments in the interwar period, these bureaucrats did seem to exercise power with little effective check by the Prime Minister or the Foreign Secretary. But the Labor critics often, perhaps deliberately, failed to take into consideration the fact that the foregin policy that emerged from the bureaucracy was thoroughly acceptable to the Conservative Government, so that the Foreign Secretary had little cause to intervene. Although history in the conditional is a dangerous field in which to dabble, it seems safe to say that if the bureaucrats had suddenly begun to implement a socialist foreign policy, the Prime Minister and Foreign Secretary would speedily have thrust their authority into the picture. In short, the fact that control is not rigorously exercised on a day-to-day basis is no proof that control does not exist. When Ernest Bevin became Foreign Secretary in 1945, he had little difficulty with administrative sabotage, probably in part because the bureaucrats realized that he had adequate power to cope with any recalcitrance on their part.

A more striking instance of the control powers of the political class lies in the area of the military and national security. If any bureaucratic group has the opportunity to become autonomous, it is the military in time of national crisis. However, although the military planners undoubtedly have a considerable advisory role, they have certainly not attained decision-making power. Partly this is due to the strategic capabilities of Prime Minister Sir Winston Churchill, who must be ranked as one of the great architects of military strategy, and who is thoroughly cognizant of the real military situation, and therefore in a position to dominate military policy. But, Churchill's special talents aside, there is an institutional explanation for this subordination of the military: the inability of the military to develop their own constituency, either in Parliament or among pressure groups. Because the political class has a virtual monopoly of British constituencies, both geographic and functional, the administrative class cannot grow roots of its own.

BRITISH FOREIGN POLICY: FORMULATION

The formulation of British foreign policy can be divided into roughly two stages. In the first, the Conservative or Labor party adopts a position on some international problem. For example, the Labor party, for many years before it assumed office in 1945, was urging an anti-imperialist policy and advocating freedom for India. Similarly, the Conservative party in 1950–1951 let it be known that a Conservative Government would solve the crises created, particularly in the Middle East, by the blundering shortsightedness of the Laborites. Within each party there are special groups which put great emphasis on international problems, and which tend to supply leadership to the party in these matters. The British Empire League and the Empire Economic Union, though officially nonpartisan organizations, tend to rally Conservative sentiment; the Fabian Society and various of its offshoots fulfill roughly the same function for the Laborites.

But party planks, particularly in the dynamic area of foreign relations, cannot simply be put into practice; frequently very complex problems arise which necessitate adjustments and compromises. This does not, of course, constitute a problem for the Opposition, which can criticize full blast without having to face responsibility for policy implementation. But even here, the Opposition cannot afford to be overly irresponsible. When, for example, an occasional Laborite Member of Parliament announces that Prime Minister Churchill "wants war," it is doubtful whether any votes are gained for the Labor party. Indeed, the public does not seem to respect such exaggerations and may penalize the irresponsible. Furthermore, as Sir Winston discovered in 1951, the Opposition may suddenly find itself the Government, and may discover that the policies it was so bitterly criticizing earlier are the only policies that can be followed. This, of course, will rapidly be called to the attention of the electorate by the Opposition, which can claim vindication for its policies and accuse the Government of opportunism and of doing anything to win votes.

Within the Government, the actual formulation of foreign policy seems to be shared by several Cabinet committees. The defense committee, for example, takes action on policies affecting national security, and the economic-affairs committee would logically initiate programs in the field of international economic relations. The Prime Minister is the keystone of the Cabinet committee structure, and coordination and compromise between the various interested ministries lies in his jurisdiction. Once a policy has been hammered out, it is assigned to one of the ministries for execution. The designation of the ministry depends upon the subject matter of the policy, that is, the Colonial Office would handle the execution of policies affecting the colonies; the Commonwealth Relations Office, those concerned with members of the British Commonwealth of Nations; the Ministry of Defense, those relating to military relations with allies; the Foreign Office, the bulk of political and diplomatic matters on the international scene.

In any large-scale enterprise, conflicts and jurisdictional disputes inevitably arise, and there is frequent bickering between the various agencies that handle British foreign policy. At what point does an economic matter, turned over to the President of the Board of Trade for solution, impinge on the province of the Foreign Secretary? Clear boundaries can be drawn on organizational charts, but life does not conform to organizational charts, so that what may appear clearly economic to one official may seem just as patently political to another. In the United States, many a battle royal has been fought over such an issue as this, with congressional committees, executive departments, and pressure groups lining up on one side or another. But, in Britain, while tempers may flare and fierce arguments rage, and occasionally a Minister may resign, these jurisdictional squabbles are generally settled within the administration. The Prime Minister has the power to make and enforce a final decision, within broad limits discussed earlier, and because the ministries concerned do not have their own private constituencies to back them up, they must conform. It is important to remember that the functional standing committees which in the United States give the Congress a perpetual fulcrum from which to influence executive policy do not exist in Parliament. Even as powerful a personality as Aneurin Bevan, who tried in 1951 to build his own constituency in Parliament against the rearmament and related domestic policies, found himself in a position where rhetoric was virtually his only weapon. And rhetoric is no substitute for political power, although the two are sometimes confused.

CONCLUSIONS

There is little point to an elaborate reexamination of points made earlier. British foreign policy is formulated and executed in similar fashion to British domestic policy, that is, decision making is a monopoly of the stable, responsible political class, the Cabinet. Consequently, there is little room for the sort of private foreign policies that often characterize the various departments of the

American government. It is impossible, for instance, for Parliament, or a segment of Parliament, to be following one policy while the executive follows another, and it is extremely difficult, though in fact there have been cases of it happening, for different departments of the executive to follow different policies.

There have been attempts at bipartisanship in Britain—indeed, World War II was managed by a coalition Government of Conservatives and Laborites—but except in times of extreme crisis, both parties look upon this with disfavor. On the one hand, the Government feels that consulting with the Opposition unduly limits its actions; on the other hand, the Opposition tends to shy away from identification with the policies of the Government on the grounds that such joint action curbs its ability to oppose. But the strong, often bitter, differences of opinion between the two parties should not be permitted to obscure the basic framework of agreement that they share. In a fundamental sense, it is this basic consensus which makes it possible for the parties bitterly to differ on concrete proposals and yet to yield the seals of office to their opponents when defeated at the polls. If the Laborites really believed what some of their extremists say about the Tories, the only principled consequence would be civil war; similarly, if the Conservatives accepted the views of some of their spokesmen, there could be no logical justification for ever permitting the Labor party to take office again.

It is this national and social homogeneity, this corpus of shared values, which is fundamental to the formulation and execution of both British foreign and domestic policy. Its immediate consequence has been the subdivision of the British community into two great, stable political parties which, in turn, can supply to British government a stable political class endowed with sufficient power to curb the bureaucracy and to enforce broad public policy. By the same token that the British have in internal economic matters attained public economic law, they have on the international scene achieved public international policy. Individual pressure groups or pressure complexes find it nigh impossible to capture the locus of decision-making power on international issues, as they so often do in the United States, for they are faced at every turn by the well-armed political class which is charged with enforcing its operational definition of the public interest, approved by the electorate at the last election. This is not to say for a moment that the British Government is not concerned with the protection of specific interests of Britons, but rather to suggest that the groups concerned must integrate themselves and advance their interests at the party level, for they can never go it alone at the level of policy formulation and execution.

FRENCH FOREIGN POLICY: SOURCES

Prior to 1914, French foreign policy was the almost exclusive property of the professional diplomats. Under the Third Republic, although the legislature had sufficient authority to intervene in the activities of the executive, and in most areas made life pretty miserable for the Ministers, the Deputies and Senators in the pre-1914 era tended to keep their hands off foreign policy. In the view of John E. Howard, a close student of the relationships between the legislature and the process of foreign-policy formulation in the Third Republic, it was the disquieting revelations about secret treaties and the breakdown of traditional diplomacy in 1914 which brought the French legislators into the foreign policy field with a vengeance.

However, the sources of French programs in the international arena were, both in the pre-1914 period of professional diplomacy and in the post-1914 period of professional diplomacy, tempered by occasional legislative revolt, the demands of various groups in the French community. The basic locus of power in the French state, that is, in the administration as well as in the less conservative legislature, lay well to the right of center. As a consequence, the interests of those groups whose interests lay in the conservative sector of politics tended to gain a virtual monopoly of representation in the formulation and execution of foreign policy. Those groups, for example, which supported for economic and/or patriotic reasons a policy of imperialistic exploitation of colonial areas never, even under the Popular Front Government of Léon Blum, lost a significant policy battle. As one cynical French colonial observed, "Not only politics, but liberty, equality and fraternity as well, stop at the water's edge."

But it must be noted that the ministerial instability which has been characteristic of French politics for the last three-quarters of a century did not affect the Foreign Ministry to anywhere near the extent that it affected other administrative departments. Foreign Minister Briand, for example, held office, with the exception of one day, from Apr. 16, 1925, until Jan. 12, 1932; Paul-Boncour and Deblos held the post for long periods of the time in the thirties: and under the Fourth Republic, Georges Bidault and Robert Schuman have each maintained their position under many varying governments. As a consequence, the professional bureaucrats in this department have never had quite the autonomy that their colleagues in other agencies have had. However, it must also be emphasized that this tenure of Foreign Ministers has not been so much a policy tenure as a personal tenure, and in a sense, they themselves have become a species of professional experts on foreign affairs. To put it another way, because these Foreign Ministers were not agents of a strong, stable political class, they tended to become assimilated into the bureaucracy so that the whole ministry, Minister and professionals, has tended to become semiautonomous. Once again we find the phenomenon so often seen on the American scene: the political administrator who, for lack of a political constituency, must ally himself with his subordinates and join his fate with theirs.

In any case, the foreign policy of the Third and Fourth Republics has generally reflected the interests of the more conservative elements in the French community. But once again it must be recalled that this is not the outgrowth of a conspiracy of the conservatives. One could with more justice suggest that it is an outgrowth of a conspiracy on the part of the radicals and socialists to make the implementation of their policy views impossible. When the "left" has taken office, it has never supplied its Ministers with the authority necessary to alter existing policies, and there is no such thing in politics as a policy vacuum. If no new policies are enforced, the bureaucracy will simply continue to implement the old ones. The reasons for this failure of the "left" have been analyzed in some detail earlier in this book, but two points might be reiterated here which have been major contributors to this policy impotence. First, there is the generic distrust of the French "left" for strong leaders. The Communists are obviously a special case here, since they believe in strong Communist leaders, but in the objective situation, they too have opposed strong leadership by other groups.

Second, there is the conflict within left-wing majorities—always, be it noted, coalitions—between those who accept what Max Weber called the "ethic of responsibility" and those who accept the "ethic of ultimate ends." In other phraseology, this is the struggle between the "possibilists" and the "impossibilists." In the field of foreign policy, this may be reflected in a struggle between those who believe that imperialism should immediately be abolished, and those who believe that the colonies should be gradually aided in attaining self-government. The net result of these perpetual quarrels is that a left-wing government can rarely achieve inner unity on policy and is hardly in a position to enforce its halfhearted views on well-entrenched bureaucrats. Those interested in a case study of this policy schizophrenia should examine the internal battles that have raged in French left-wing parties on the problems of the North Atlantic Alliance and the European Defense Community.

The parties of the "right" are in a far happier position policywise, for, with certain limited modifications, all they generally want to do is leave well enough alone. Obviously there will be few problems involved in enforcing the *status quo* on the bureaucracy, for the bureaucracy is the personnel office of the *status quo*. Men in search of radical change seldom try to achieve high positions in the civil service, and if they do, the chances are that they will be sidetracked by cautious screening devices long before they reach positions of significance. Thus a left-wing government must be exceptionally well armed if it is going to be able to bring the bureaucracy to heel, and it is precisely this sort of armament, which the British Laborites have given to their Ministers, that the French "left" has refused to grant to its leaders.

THE LEGISLATURE AND FOREIGN POLICY

We have earlier commented on the French parliamentary committee system, its resemblance to that in the United States, and the seeming parallels that exist between committee interference in administrative affairs in the two nations.

Little concrete evidence has been presented on this vital matter for the simple reason that students of French institutions have paid little attention to it. However, a distinguished French political scientist, François Goguel, has noted that before any bill can come up for discussion on the floor of the National Assembly, it must be reported on by the appropriate functional committee, and that these committees seek assistance from the bureaucracy in their investigations. But, M. Goguel points out, the *fonctionnaires* to whom the committees generally turn are different from those who prepared the legislative proposals under examination—a fact which, in his phrase, "provokes the development of hostile cliques within the administration; . . . weakens the discipline and the authority of the ministers who have practically no control over the members of their staffs 'on detached service' with the parliamentary committees [and results in] a serious dilution of responsibilities which enables interest groups to intervene effectively, but discreetly, in the preparation of legislation."

Needless to say, the Foreign Affairs Committee is one of the most important ·of the legislative subdivisions of the National Assembly. Before any significant policy in the field of international affairs can go into effect, it must run the institutional gauntlet provided by this committee, which, it will be recalled, is composed of members of all parties in the National Assembly in number proportional to their membership in the whole legislature. Thus the Foreign Minister is in roughly the same position vis-à-vis the committee as is the American Secretary of State to the Senate Foreign Relations Committee, that is, he has no institutional control over the activities of the committee, and few weapons other than rhetoric at his disposal. A further problem may arise from the fact that the Chairman of the French Foreign Affairs Committee is not a member of a government party—a Socialist currently holds this key position.

Under both the Third and Fourth Republics, it has often appeared as though the Committees on Foreign Affairs were, as far as the Foreign Minister was concerned, the total legislature. On Jan. 11, 1922, for instance, the Committee of Foreign Affairs of the Senate, the now defunct powerful upper house, telegraphed the Foreign Minister, M. Briand, precise instructions on what policies would be acceptable to the chamber, and John E. Howard, in his study of *Parliament and Foreign Policy in France,* has examined other similar instances at length. The Committee on Foreign Affairs of the National Assembly appears to operate in a parallel, though somewhat less formal, fashion under the Fourth Republic. As in the United States, the basic reason for the power of this and other committees is the inability of the legislature to operate as a whole. Over the years, reforms have been suggested which would lessen the power of the committees and make them agents of the whole rather than substitutes for it. However, these mechanical suggestions appear to be analogous to those constitutional amendments suggested by some American commentators as the solution to the same problem in the United States, and are equally unrealistic.

The truth of the matter seems to be that these committees are powerful not as an outgrowth of poor political mechanics, but rather because of the fragmented nature of political power in France, and it is to be doubted whether the power locus in society can be significantly changed by tinkering with institutions. These institutions reflect power situations; they do not create them. It will be recalled that the attempts to give France a strong two-party system by tinkering with the electoral system have uniformly proved abortive: a multiparty legislature resulted equally from single-member districts and from proportional representation.

CONCLUSIONS

Functional committees need not necessarily usurp the prerogatives of the legislature as a whole, and Ministers could conceivably have the power to cope with recalcitrant bureaucrats. But the prerequisite for centralization of political power would be the development of a centralized, powerful political class. If, for instance, the Committee on Foreign Affairs were composed of disciplined members of two parties, the actions of members would be determined by decisions of the parties as a whole, and the committees would thus become agents rather than principals. If, similarly, the Minister spoke as an executive agent of a strong, majority party, possessed of coercive power, the bureaucrats would listen and obey. The lessons that political scientists can learn from British experience are not lessons in political engineering, in institutional gadgetry; they are lessons on the power of a responsible political class to utilize effectively whatever institutions lie at hand and make of them a responsible system of government.

Therefore, French and American difficulties in the area of foreign policy formulation and execution, as well as in domestic matters, are not an outgrowth of inferior French and American institutions. These difficulties are, in a much more fundamental sense, the offshoots of the inability of the French and American people, to date, to provide strong, stable party government—in the phrase we are employing, a strong political class. This failure is, in turn, not a consequence of inherent irresponsibility on the part of the French and American peoples, but rather of the lack of national and social homogeneity that is characteristic of the two national communities. To say this is not to indulge in an enervating fatalism, to suggest that our fate is out of our hands, for men's attitudes and actions play a great part in developing homogeneity and in working toward political responsibility. But the first step that must be taken before intelligent action can be instituted to modify and ameliorate existing situations is knowledge of the basic problem. Too often action has been directed solely at the symptoms, the institutional failures, instead of at the basic sets and community prejudices that have given rise to these symptoms.

Chapter 14

THE FUTURE OF DEMOCRATIC GOVERNMENT

IN THE course of our analysis of the various components of democratic government, we have noted a good many areas in which democratic techniques have not kept pace with democratic imperatives. During the nineteenth century this lag, while disturbing, would not have appeared to observers to be ominous, for there seemed to be plenty of time in which to redress the balance. Life was leisurely, and what was not ameliorated today could be taken care of tomorrow, or next year, or ten years hence. However, in the modern world the gap between ideal and technique has tremendous implications for the future of democratic government, for there may be no time to bridge it by slow, piecemeal reforms such as were characteristic of change in the nineteenth century. We have suggested that democracy is a system of government that repudiates historical short cuts, which rests upon the necessarily slow process of government by discussion, of developing and enlarging the area of consensus. But while we accept this as fundamental, there is no denying the fact that in many parts of the world today the demand is for historical short cuts. Colonial peoples, for example, are demanding self-government even if they do not have the institutional and social foundations to make it responsible, as distinguished from dictatorial, self-government.

Democracy, in short, is faced by a series of formidable challenges, and we should like to conclude this book by discussing some of the key issues that these challenges raise. Unfortunately, unlike the authors of texts in mathematics, we cannot supply definitive answers in the back of the book. Frankly, while we have a deep faith in the ability of democracy to surmount these obstacles, and occasionally think we have found tentative answers to these problems, we do not feel qualified to present the reader with ex cathedra solutions. It is hoped that by calling these issues to the attention of students of democratic government along with our tentative views on possible lines of solution, we may stimulate thought and discussion on them, and from this intellectual process there may emerge new and significant thinking which will aid in the discovery of solutions. For purposes of convenience, we have divided the problems into two categories: the external challenges and the internal challenges.

As is inevitably the case in subdivisions of this sort, the dichotomy is arbitrary, since the external and the internal challenges merge at many points.

THE EXTERNAL CHALLENGES TO DEMOCRACY

International relations in the twentieth century have been characterized by explosions. Two world wars, the rise of Nazism and fascism, colonial revolts, the surge of nationalism in underdeveloped areas, and the tremendous threat offered to democratic societies by Soviet imperialism are the high points of the story. World politics today is conducted in an atmosphere of rumbling—both the human rumbling of nations shaking off old traditions or reacting to the new efficient tyranny of communist dictatorships, and the inhuman rumbling of fission and fusion, the A-bomb and the H-bomb, as new techniques of mass extermination are prepared. Keeping this background in mind, let us examine in some detail four major criticisms of democracy that have been advanced on the external plane.

"DEMOCRACY IS A BOURGEOIS LUXURY"

Traditionally, democracy has been the form of government of "have" nations, rather than of "have nots." In the former, democracy was the capstone on centuries of slow development from autocracy, generally emerging with the *bourgeoisie*, the new middle class, from the obscurity of feudalism. To the Marxist, democracy, as we have employed the term, is a system of government designed to protect the *bourgeoisie* in the exercise of its property rights, but the minute that the bourgeois sees his property rights being threatened by the consequences of democracy, *e.g.*, high taxes, wage-and-hour legislation, he will abandon freedom and revert to autocracy. Thus, the Marxist looks upon political democracy as a pure luxury that can exist only in the heyday of capitalism, to be replaced by dictatorship and fascism when the capitalist economy begins to rock and decline.

But the Marxists are not the only bellwethers of this viewpoint. In the rising national states of Asia, Africa, and Latin America there can be found many intellectuals and politicians who also, though with somewhat different motivation, consider democracy to be the icing on the cake. Many of them genuinely believe in democracy as an ideal, but they assert that democratic techniques would be far too slow in attaining the national goals that they espouse. "You Americans," they may say, "took two centuries to move from 1750 to 1950; we must do it in one generation." Once they have established an industrial state, then it may be feasible to institute democratic government. But, they maintain, in a realistic analysis, democracy is a type of government for those who have already arrived—not one for those on the rise.

Let us examine a concrete, though hypothetical, instance of this sort. The new Asian state of Burmesia has a profitable agricultural economy built around rice and jute. As a colony of an industrial Western power, its capital and industrial resources were long limited, but now that it has achieved independence, its leaders and people are agreed that it must become an economically self-sufficient nation. It must escape from economic bondage to the former colonial power. In specific terms, this means that Burmesia must create an industrial sector in its economy, build a steel mill—one of the key symbols of national maturity—and make extensive population shifts from the countryside to the cities. Because the new regime began life by expropriating foreign capital, little economic assistance can be obtained from foreign investors.

What are the Burmesian leaders going to do? While the Burmesian people were militantly for independence, will they voluntarily accept a 20 per cent decrease in their standard of living to finance the building of an industrial economy—a 20 per cent decrease possibly of twenty years' duration? Furthermore, will a large population bloc willingly accept transfer to the cities and work in the factories, thus abandoning their traditional agricultural way of life? In the face of problems like this, the Burmesian elite may well decide that democracy can come, figuratively speaking, after steel mills—as, indeed, it did in Britain—rather than take the chance that the people, if given democratic institutions, will repudiate industrialization and austerity in favor of the agricultural *status quo*.

In short, can the Western democracies demonstrate to these embryonic national states that democracy and steel mills are not mutually exclusive items on the national agenda? It would be presumptuous to assert that this can be done, for the evidence to date is fragmentary. But one can hopefully look to such actions as Technical Assistance, devised by the United States, and the Colombo Plan, set up by the British Commonwealth, which may point the way toward a copartnership, in the interests of democracy, between the "haves" and the "have nots."

"DEMOCRACY IS WEDDED TO NATIONALISM"

The critics who raise this point are skeptical about the international application of democracy. These critics ask whether Americans really believe that democracy is a good system to the extent that they will be willing to make concrete sacrifices to aid democratic development in other nations. A good instance of this problem is the plight of Japanese democracy. If democracy is to gain a firm foundation in Japan, Japanese democrats must be able to demonstrate to the Japanese people that they can solve the tremendous problems that confront that nation. However, if Japanese democrats are going to have even a modicum of success, they must have international democratic support—concrete, not rhetorical, support.

First, the Japanese economy needs markets for its goods. For ideological reasons, Japan's natural market, Communist China, has been closed to her, and no new markets of equal size have opened up. Yet, a major prerequisite for the success of democracy in Japan is economic stability and full employment. Will the United States and Britain open their markets to Japanese manufactures? Or will these nations stand pat on the traditional dogmas of economic nationalism and bar Japanese competition?

Second, Japan is fearfully overpopulated. Over 83 million people live in an area slightly smaller than the state of Montana. The obvious solution to this problem is emigration to areas of sparse population. The nearby democracy Australia is virtually uninhabited but, in an effort to remain ethnically homogeneous, has immigration barriers against Asians. Will Australian democrats lift these bars and help take the pressure off the Japanese democrats? The seriousness of these two problems for the Japanese cannot be underestimated. To put the issue in its starkest terms, refusal by Americans, British, Australians, New Zealanders, and other democrats to help their Japanese allies can only lead to the collapse of Japanese democracy and encourage the desperate Japanese once again to take the path of aggression.

In other words, the success of democracy in nations like Japan, India, Pakistan, Indonesia, and the Gold Coast depends on the willingness of Americans, Britons, and French to apply their democratic beliefs in a concrete fashion to the international scene. The success of these new democratic experiments may require a voluntary decrease in the American standard of living, and one may raise the question whether the Americans, confronted by this necessity, would show a willingness to be their brother's keeper, or whether they would take refuge from responsibility behind their national boundaries. But while optimism on this point is hardly in order, neither is extreme pessimism. We have seen the British people, through their Government, encouraging self-government in Asia and Africa although this has resulted in increased British austerity, and the American people are certainly capable, if the matter is put before them in a sufficiently cogent fashion, of meeting a similar moral challenge.

"DEMOCRACY WORKS TOO SLOWLY"

The critics who make this point maintain that democratic techniques are too slow and clumsy to handle the international problems of the twentieth century. At a time when scientific developments have literally made it possible to destroy civilization, if not the Earth itself, democracies have developed no effective methods of preserving the peace, of building a world community, and controlling through international action the forces of destruction. Traditional attitudes of political nationalism have prevented a yielding of sovereignty to an international body, and the only "practical" method of obtaining permanent peace seems to be permanent war.

While few of these critics would maintain that world government can be obtained overnight—indeed, in an optimistic view, it would probably require decades of evolution—what they do assert is that democratic governments have done little to encourage the movement toward world government, little to develop the basic change in attitudes that would be the basic prerequisite for consensus on the desirability of international government. They point to the Netherlands as the lonely instance of a nation which has amended its constitution to permit the legislature to surrender sovereignty to international bodies, and ask why other democracies have not taken similar steps.

One can dismiss these critics as exaggerating pessimists, as Cassandras, but it is too often forgotten that Cassandra's prophesies were correct. Although we do not fully agree with these prophets of woe, it is important that their views be given wide consideration. We are all prospective guinea pigs in the experiments of atomic warfare, no matter how successfully we avoid admitting it or even recognizing the fact. Let us examine the possible ways out of this foreboding situation.

Perhaps because so much was claimed for the United Nations at its inception, a good deal of cynicism has developed in the United States about this potential instrument for international government. The critics of the UN are verbose and extreme, and few can be found, particularly in high places, who will go stoutly to its defense. Yet the United Nations, if properly considered and intelligently utilized, could serve as a nucleus for developing a really effective world government. We would be the last to suggest that international government could be created by gadgetry, by devising foolproof world constitutions. An international government, to be effective, must gain a constituency of its own, a public of its own, and it does appear that in a slow fashion the UN is acquiring a constituency. The fact that the Indonesians would look favorably upon UN economic assistance while remaining highly suspicious of American aid may be suggested as evidence for this point.

Social psychologists have suggested that one of the main preconditions for changing approaches to problems is to break the pattern in which these problems are presented and considered. If, for example, it is generally accepted that the solution to political rivalry is war, then people accept war as a logical outcome of political rivalry. If, on the other hand, people can visualize a different pattern of solution, *e.g.*, that political rivalry may be resolved by an international body, they are less likely to accept war as inevitable and their whole approach to the problem of political rivalry will change. Can the democracies take the lead in altering the traditional pattern of international relations by building the UN into an organization that can regulate international conflict? This is a task that will require a basic alteration in public attitudes, but the goal is worthy of strenuous effort.

Indeed, this is not just a job for the diplomats, for today public opinion has tremendous force in the conduct of a democracy's foreign policy. Thus it is public attitudes that must change, if new patterns for solving international problems are to be effectuated. It was interesting to note, in the summer of 1953, the way public opinion in the United States reacted to the negotiations for a Korean and Far Eastern settlement. The American pattern for considering negotiations of this sort was established in the 1930's, when appeasement became a synonym for compromise. Consequently, in the 1950's, a number of people seemed to think that any compromise with an opponent must be "appeasement," so that what was contemplated in the Asian negotiations was a "new Munich." Before any tradition of international negotiation can be established to replace war as the solution to conflicts, this invalid identification must be rejected. Compromise is not necessarily "appeasement."

Are the democracies prepared to assume the leadership in this movement toward establishing new patterns of solving. international problems? Do the democracies appreciate that the alternative to developing new patterns is a grim one of scientific devastation? It hardly seems as though they are thinking in these realistic terms. The bitter campaign against the United Nations launched by right-wing organizations in the United States justifies its activities on the ground that we must retain our sovereignty, and there has been no effective counterattack. Yet, sovereignty, in the sense that the Daughters of the American Revolution use the word, is surely as extinct as the passenger pigeon. Unless democracies are willing to move rapidly in the direction of building a world community strong enough to prevent national aggression, they may learn at first hand what scientists already know: that fission, fusion, and bacteria are no respecters of sovereignty.

"DEMOCRATIC IDEALS CANNOT SURVIVE POWER POLITICS"

Some democrats with strong moral or ethical views are convinced that democratic ideals cannot survive the realities of international relations, that in the course of conducting power relationships on the international scene, democratic values are compromised to the point where they become meaningless. To such a democrat, the thought of an alliance with Franco's Spain or Tito's Yugoslavia is completely repellent. "How," he will ask, "can we claim to be the supporters of a system of government based on the sacredness of the individual when we ally ourselves with brutal dictatorships that deny to their people the very essence of freedom?"

Other democrats, no less concerned with the future and success of democratic government, will maintain that this is a stupid question, that democratic policy makers must live in a world which does not conform to their ideals. They will suggest that if we require all our allies to pass an ideological blood test, we shall find ourselves with few allies—the Pan-American Union, for instance, could not last five minutes on this basis. They will conclude that survival in a world we never made requires adjustment of ideals to reality, probably reluctant adjustments, but adjustments nonetheless.

The issue between these two viewpoints is the age-old one of ends and means. There have already been far too many clichés uttered on this subject, and we shall try not to increase the total. But it does seem permissible to note that the standard division between ends and means seems unrealistic. While the hard-boiled advocate of democratic *Realpolitik* often, with conspicuous Machiavellianism, ignores the relationship that means bear to ends, the Militant Idealist, a sort of liberal yogi, frequently becomes so enmeshed in his analysis of means that he overlooks the fact that ends exist. However, to say this is to beat down straw men, and not to come to grips with the very real problem of where to draw the line between power politics and idealism. Should a democratic power, for example, be prepared to trade Japan to the Soviet Union in exchange for East Germany and Austria? Should a democratic power be willing to reach a settlement with the Soviet Union that would not alter the status of millions of slave laborers in the Soviet orbit?

To put the question in a less categorical fashion, what we are asking is to what extent is a democracy a free agent in international relations, bound only by the limits of its bargaining power and what its public will accept, and to what extent is it limited by ideological imperatives, *e.g.*, freedom, justice, equality? Obviously a problem of this complexity will not yield to simple solution, but it might be suggested that part of a solution may be found in approaching specific instances on their specific merits instead of beginning with grandiose abstractions. If issues are examined on the level of principles—whether those of the Power Politician or those of the Militant Idealist—very little can be accomplished, for no one is willing to retreat from his principles—or, in the case of the Power Politician, from his principle of having no principles. On the other hand, a careful analysis of a specific situation, the Yugoslav alliance, for instance, will bring out some facts that would support one course of action and some facts that would support another. And after the facts are in, the difficult decision can be made between various courses of action in the light of principles. A famous debater once observed that he loved arguments on principles because he never had to know any facts.

INTERNAL CHALLENGES TO DEMOCRACY

In addition to these massive problems on the international front, democracy is faced by several severe internal challenges, precipitated in large part, it should be noted, by the international situation. In a sense, the three major criticisms that we have chosen as most cogent are a direct outgrowth of life in a garrison state, a state which is perpetually hovering on the brink of hostilities. Democracy achieved maturity in the period from 1815 to 1914, a period characterized in the West by peace, at least so far as the population at large was concerned. There were wars, but with the exception of the American Civil War, they were skirmishes fought on the littoral by professional soldiers, and had little impact on the domestic scene. However, since 1914, war and the threat of war have become a problem of consequence to whole populations, and democratic government has been brought face to face with its most insidious opponent: the need for fast decision and irrevocable commitment. Let us examine the three vital criticisms of democracy that life in an international state of siege has forcefully brought to the attention of democrats.

"DEMOCRACY LACKS UNITY"

This criticism, cogently expressed by Plato two thousand years ago and echoed by other thinkers many times since, has been given new force by recent developments. Throughout the 1930's, while Hitler planned and advertised his aggressive intentions, the democratic states were divided on what course of action to take. It is trite to point out that strong British or French or American action at any one of half a dozen points between 1933 and 1938 could have ended Nazism without the type of full-scale, total war that was later necessary. But it is important to note that the reason no such action was taken was that the people of the democracies were internally divided as to what should be done.

Conversely, critics of this persuasion point out, democracy is a system of government, particularly as it operates in the United States and France, which makes it singularly difficult for the people to get prompt action once they do make up their minds. The diffusion of power, the delays that are built into the system, make it possible for a powerful interest group to fight off change. To use the specific instance of the United States, a powerful special interest group can often, through its ties with key Congressmen, particularly committee chairmen, block legislative action. If that fails, and the President cannot be prevailed upon to veto the enactment, this group, again in concert with its congressional allies, can bring pressure on the administration to frustrate the implementation of the policy. It can also institute judicial action to nullify the statute, and appeal judicial decisions almost indefinitely. In short, a tremendous effort is required to overcome the bastions of special interest. Because power is fragmented, disunity is institutionalized, the public interest is negated.

These critics can build a strong case for their viewpoint, and their case against democracy contains many criticisms that democrats should take to heart. We have the right to ask these critics to show us a system that works any better, but this is not a sufficient rejoinder. To say that democracy is founded on a vital pluralism is no justification for the power of a minority group of Southern Senators to prevent indefinitely the enactment of civil-rights legislation. While no democrat would value the type of unity which results from the dominant elite eliminating all those who differ with its interpretation of the "national interest," democracy at its best is founded on unity of a sort. This unity, perhaps comparable with the theological doctrine of the Trinity, is of many who are yet one—groups, all fulfilling their own functions freely, yet united in the spirit of freedom. Admittedly this is an ideal which actual democratic societies have only approximated, but it is one worth striving for.

"DEMOCRACY CANNOT SURVIVE CRISIS GOVERNMENT"

This criticism is, in a sense, an offshoot of the last. The critics here emphasize the fact that, while quick decisions, usually expert decisions, are necessary for national survival, democratic government is devised to make quick decisions difficult and to keep experts from making decisions. Napoleon reputedly observed that any fool could govern in a state of seige. But the existence of an emergency, to add a corollary to Napoleon's maxim, makes it extraordinarily difficult to unmask fools and replace them by able leaders. This is particularly true of military affairs, which always have a vital role in time of crisis, for the military leader has protection from exposure and attack not usually accorded to civilians. When in November, 1950, General Douglas MacArthur sent his divided army rushing to the Yalu River, he probably committed the most serious military blunder that an American army has been the victim of since General Pope's debacle at the Second Battle of Bull Run in the Civil War. Without adequate intelligence about the enemy, winter clothing, or sufficient logistical support, the Eighth Army and Tenth Corps were flung into the jaws of a Chinese Communist trap. As Colonel S. L. A. Marshall has shown in his superb analysis of the defeat of the Eighth Army, *The River and the Gauntlet*, this precipitous advance was ordered over the objections of General Walton Walker, field commander of the Eighth Army.

Yet, when the Chinese slammed the trap shut, American opinion was generally reluctant to suggest that MacArthur's strategy and tactics were at fault. On the contrary, following the General's own excuse, it was conceded that the Chinese had played a dirty trick on MacArthur—an honest, upstanding American had been taken in by Oriental guile. In sharp contrast with the sympathy extended by the public and by Congress to MacArthur was the perpetual violent criticism of Secretary of State Dean Acheson. Acheson, who was far from being omniscient and whose Far Eastern policy, or lack of one, left much to be desired, was scarified by the press and in Congress. The point here is not to condemn General MacArthur or to defend Secretary Acheson, but rather to point out the radically different treatment that was accorded to a military expert in contrast to a civilian administrator.

To put the point another way, crises reinforce the power within society of the military experts, that division of the administrative class which is charged with giving expert direction in the area of national security. When these experts prepare estimates of their needs, and inform the citizens that "adequate national security requires" the outlay of 73 cents of each tax dollar on security costs, what is the Congressman or citizen to say? Congress is in a particularly difficult spot, for while Congressmen may suspect that there is unnecessary extravagance in the military establishment, they have, as the late Senator Taft once pointed out to Secretary of Defense Forrestal, no "criterion by which efficiency could be proved or disproved."

If the Department of Health, Education, and Welfare tells the citizen that more of his tax money should go into social security or into educational subsidies to the states, the citizen and his Congressman feel free to object and denounce the Department for its wild spending policy. But when five-star generals and five-stripe admirals solemnly tell the voter that his security depends on intercontinental bombers, giant aircraft carriers, or rocket weapons, can the voter and his Congressman reach an intelligent decision on the matter? If the citizen wants to find out how well his money is being spent, he encounters the paper curtain of security classification, and though this secrecy may enrage him, he is hardly willing to endanger his nation's security by disregarding such restrictions, or by attacking them.

Furthermore, the nature of scientific experimentation, which plays so great a role in the preparations for modern warfare, often necessitates "wasting" enormous sums of money on theories that do not work before discovering one that does. One reason why the United States outstripped the Germans in the development of the atomic bomb was the American willingness to pour huge sums of money into successive attempts to build an atomic pile, even when several proved abortive, while the thrifty Germans refused to go ahead with practical experimentation until the scientific basis for a nuclear weapon was completely established. The Germans saved money, but the United States built the bomb. The interesting question arises: If the American people and Congress had realized the extent to which the Manhattan Project was "wasting" money in unsuccessful experiments with atomic energy, would they have consented to continuing the program?

In short, the problem of military survival in the atomic age, in which by the very nature of science enormous sums must be expended on unsuccessful experimentation, is not one that can be solved by homilies on the democratic method. Some readers may recall the novel and film *Command Decision*, which posed this dilemma in its starkest terms. In this story, the Air Force general, possessing top-secret information that the Germans had developed a jet fighter which could rule the skies unless immediate action was taken to stop it, ordered raids on the factories deep in Germany. He could not justify these raids to the press and to politicians because of security restrictions, though they were terribly costly in men and planes. His decision to go through with the raids cost him his job—he was considered a butcher by the press—but should he have held back his planes until the American public and Congress were educated as to the necessity of the action?

How then can the experts be kept responsible to the people without allowing short-run public prejudice to cripple the needed exercise of *expertise?* Or, to ask the same question in a different fashion, is democratic government possessed of the techniques for survival in an age of *expertise,* or is it an anachronism, lingering on the scene as a holdover from the leisurely days of the nineteenth century, when rapid and crucial decision making was seldom required? In sum, can government by discussion operate successfully in an epoch in which international relations have been characterized by shooting first and discussing afterward?

The critics of democracy who raise this cogent problem, while unhappy about their prognosis, seem to feel that in the interests of sheer physical survival, government by discussion must be replaced by government of experts. How-ever, this does not seem to be the only possibility. Both the British and the Americans have experimented with other alternatives with some success. In Britain, the political class has retained its control over the military experts by developing its own strategy elite. The classic instance of this was the strate-gic dominance of Winston Churchill over his generals and admirals during World War II. As Chester Wilmot has shown in *The Struggle for Europe,* Churchill kept his finger on the pulse of military developments to a far greater extent than did President Roosevelt, who relied heavily for his views on Gen-eral George Marshall and delegated enormous authority to the Chiefs of Staff. While Roosevelt made such crucial policy decisions as that to concentrate on defeating Germany before Japan, he left the run of important decisions to the professionals. Churchill, often to the great distaste of his experts, insisted on intervening even in tactical matters. The Labor Government, with its doctrinal tradition of antimilitarism, also kept close watch over military policy, although it employed a professional soldier, Earl Alexander of Tunis, as Minister of Defense.

In the United States, a new technique for handling this problem has recently been tried: the election of a military expert to the Presidency. While some, notably Democrats, objected to putting a general in the White House, it must be kept in mind that President Eisenhower is in no sense the typical profes-sional soldier. Indeed, in his position as Supreme Commander of the Allied armies in Europe, he was as much the diplomat as the soldier. In this instance, the political class has recruited a broad-gauged professional whose political views are anything but militaristic. In many ways, his training in World War II was for politics rather than military life, for he was dealing then—as he was later to deal in his position as President—with a coalition that he could not force to obey his orders. General Eisenhower, from all accounts, was a master of persuasion and compromise—two talents that President Eisenhower would have to depend on tremendously. Well-substantiated reports have it that, far from being delighted by the accession of their erstwhile colleague to the Presi-dency, the military experts in the Pentagon anticipated far more rigorous con-trol from the Commander in Chief than they had become accustomed to under the administration of President Truman. One symptom of this was the suc-cessful cut of 5 billion dollars from the 1953 Air Force budget as originally pre-pared by President Truman. Although the Air Force wailed and the Democrats denounced, the Republican majority in Congress united behind the President's assurance that the lower figure would be adequate.

To sum up, it can hardly be suggested that the democracies have successfully solved the problems of scientific and military *expertise* which have led some critics to suggest that democratic government is antiquated. But, in different ways, American and British democracy have taken steps toward a solution. A beginning has been made, but much remains to be done.

"CIVIL LIBERTY CANNOT SURVIVE INTERNAL SECURITY"

This criticism has been voiced in two quarters. On one hand, civil libertarians maintain that the current anticommunist hysteria is leading to the end of freedom of discussion. On the other hand, some "realists" submit that civil rights, in the old Jeffersonian sense, belong in the museum of nineteenth-century antiquities.

The civil libertarians emphasize the point, made earlier in this analysis, that freedom of speech, of the press, of religion, and of assembly are the vital foundations of the democratic way of life, the preconditions of government by discussion. They point out that unless one believes in freedom for opinions that one detests, freedom becomes a meaningless concept. It becomes "freedom of speech for those who agree with me." They maintain that freedom for communist speech is in no sense freedom for communist conspiracy, but that a clear line must be drawn between the two with the former permitted and the latter punished.

The nub of the argument against bestowing civil liberty on "subversives" is that in this day and age, the fifth column has become one of the standard characteristics of international conflict. Therefore, the democratic state should not permit its enemies to organize under its very nose. In reply to those who distinguish between communist speech and communist conspiracy, these critics assert that the line between these two activities is nonexistent. In either case, they maintain, a communist organization is built and its internal structure developed, and if it is well knit and tightly disciplined, it can shift from peaceful to violent objectives without missing a step. The organization itself is a knife pointed at the heart of the democratic society, and the matter of what objectives it espouses at any particular moment is purely academic. They point to the history of Nazi and communist fifth columns as evidence of this point: organizations originally founded as sports clubs, musical groups, or trade-unions which suddenly blossomed into paramilitary bodies in time of crisis were employed by Hitler in his conquest of Europe and by Stalin in Czechoslovakia.

While they admit the partial validity of this viewpoint, the civil libertarians retort by raising the fundamental question of the purpose and ethical values of democratic society. They note that if the democratic state eliminates communist organizations on the grounds of self-defense, it would be equally justified, by the same logic, in eliminating any organizations that, however motivated, objectively forwarded communist ends. By the terms of this escalator logic, a pacifist group which opposes the United States government's defense policy on religious grounds would be aiding the Communists and should be suppressed. If sheer physical survival is accepted as the basic objective of the democratic state, then the motivation of opponents and dissenters becomes wholly irrelevant. This would be analogous to saying that a motorist who accidentally kills a pedestrian is as felonious as the murderer who carefully planned a strangulation; after all, it is immaterial to a corpse whether he was killed intentionally or unintentionally—he is equally dead in either case.

At this point, one suddenly becomes aware that he has encountered this "hard-boiled" logic before—at the Moscow trials and the annual purges which enliven life in communist dictatorships. Indeed, the similarity between this escalator of self-defense and the escalator of the dialectic so brilliantly described by Arthur Koestler in *Darkness at Noon* is striking. In this novel, Rubashov, the old Bolshevik who disliked the dictator, was gradually led from a statement of antipathy to admitting that, since he detested Stalin, he should, by the logic of his position, have engaged in anti-Stalin activities. Then Gletkin, the secret-police interrogator, delivered the logical coup: since Rubashov *should* have engaged in anti-Stalin, anti-Soviet activities, he was objectively an ally of the enemy, the capitalist powers. The execution of Rubashov was a triumph of logic over life. One may wonder if the commissars of democratic survival have not, in the course of fighting the communist opponent, deserted life for logic and thus grown to resemble their enemy.

However, to suggest the bitter irony involved in using totalitarian techniques to prevent democracy from becoming totalitarian is not an adequate answer to the concrete and difficult questions raised by the "hard-boiled" school of thought. Obviously a democratic state has the right to defend itself against domestic and foreign enemies, but the real dilemma occurs, as it so often does in life as distinguished from logic, not in choosing between polar opposites—freedom or totalitarianism—but in making day-to-day decisions in the gray area of doubt. Quantitative changes in the content of democracy can lead to a qualitative change. That is, if, in the thousands of daily decisions that are made on internal security at all levels of government, the emphasis is always on security at the expense of liberty, democracy will eventually wither away. This could occur without the American people ever being asked to choose between liberty and totalitarianism; daily administrative and legislative erosion could eat away the content of freedom, leaving only an empty husk where a solid tradition once stood.

It is important, in this context, to remember the close connection between freedom and dynamism. A society, to remain vital and living, needs a constant inflow of ideas which, in turn, requires an atmosphere of freedom for business, science, education, and intellectual life in general. Empirically speaking, free societies have been the most dynamic and, as a consequence, have been able to support a civilization of unequaled diversity and opportunity. They have simultaneously developed what Gaetano Mosca called a high level of "juridical defense," that is, of civil and personal liberty. Mosca suggested, moreover, that civilizations could be evaluated by the level of juridical defense that they provide to their citizens. Thus, whether judged in Mosca's terms or in terms of the democratic imperative of dynamism, civil rights are a central pillar of Western civilization. Unquestionably there are risks involved in permitting totalitarians to operate within the framework of liberty, and the democratic state must exercise constant vigilance against violent conspiracies. But there are risks in overvigorous enforcement of internal-security measures. Indeed, an overemphasis on internal security may be more subversive to the long-run development of our civilization and the ideals which buttress it than are the activities of a small band of American Communists. Stagnation and decay are, in the basic sense, no less subversive of democracy than are communist actions frankly aimed at ending free government.

CONCLUSION: THE GREAT QUESTION

In examining these criticisms of democracy, the perceptive reader may have realized that they are all facets of a more basic criticism. This fundamental criticism, one which has confronted democrats since the days when Plato and Aristotle argued the nature of the good society, may best be stated in the form of a question. Are the people capable of ruling themselves? Are they capable of making a long-run decision which may work against immediate self-interest?

Antidemocratic thinkers have generally held that man is incapable of transcending immediate self-interest, that it is folly to believe that people are more than pigs. Thus antidemocrats have felt that if man was to achieve any level of civilization, to get out of "the state of nature," as some of them put it, it would be through the necessarily dictatorial efforts of a philosopher-king, a legislator, a prophet, or an elite. Because of man's inherent selfishness, he is incapable of genuinely cooperative action. The normal condition of man, in Hobbes's phrase, was the *bellum omnium in omnes,* the war of all against all. The function of the leader, or the elite, in this view is to discover the public interest, the general will, which we might define in the spirit of Rousseau, as the right answer to the question: What is *really* best for the people? Once this truth, this definition of the public interest, has been established, it is the duty of the leader, or the elite, to liberate the people from their mistaken illusions of self-interest, to free them from the bonds of individual judgment—in Rousseau's picturesque phrase, to "force them to be free."

Democrats, on the other hand, have asserted a faith in the moral quality of man, in his rationality, in his ability to strive cooperatively for higher goals. And though we freely admit its imperfections, democracy has, in our view, demonstrated that these assumptions are not without validity. Perhaps a better system of government could be devised, but judged by comparison with existing alternatives, which have institutionalized in the concentration camp and the slave-labor barracks the view that men are wholly subservient to the dictates of dictators or small elites, the democratic way of life seems to have gone a long way toward supplying man with the conditions of the good life. We may be making an unduly subjective judgment, for we assume that men do want freedom, do want room to develop their capacities, do want to live in peace with one another. But we submit that the history of the past half century, the struggles for freedom of colonial peoples, the underground battles with Nazi and Soviet oppressors, give some empirical evidence that our assumptions are sound.

While the antidemocrat builds his political structure on the analogy of the swineherd and the swine, the democrat has a vision of men cooperatively building a society in which, profiting from the free pooling of individual insight, they can together find the good life. Thus democracy is both a search and a way of searching; it is a faith that man does not live by bread, by self-interest, alone, but that in the quest for the goal, he is capable of pulling in his belt and voluntarily sacrificing personal advantage that the group may profit.

While we have suggested that there is some evidence to validate this faith, only the future, and the future actions of democrats, can supply a final answer.

NOTES AND SELECTED BIBLIOGRAPHY

IF WE were to attempt here an exhaustive statement of our intellectual indebtedness, the length of the notes and bibliography could probably equal that of the text. To avoid such extravagance and conspicuous erudition, we have listed below only two categories of material: (1) the books and articles which we drew upon as primary sources, and (2) the books and articles which we feel would be most fruitful as additional reading for the nonspecialist. Those in search of additional material should consult *The Reader's Guide to Periodical Literature* and the excellent bibliographies which appear regularly in the *American Political Science Review*.

CHAPTER 1. *The Democratic Political Process*

Two books which have been most influential in shaping our views are Sir Ernest K. Barker, *Reflections on Government*, Oxford, New York, 1942; and Gaetano Mosca, *The Ruling Class*, McGraw-Hill, New York, 1939. Other works which have been of great value are E. F. M. Durbin, *The Politics of Democratic Socialism*, Routledge, London, 1940; H. H. Gerth and C. W. Mills (eds.), *From Max Weber: Essays in Sociology*, Oxford, New York, 1946; Harold J. Laski, *A Grammar of Politics*, G. Allen, London, 1925; A. D. Lindsay, *The Modern Democratic State*, Oxford, New York, 1947; Robert M. MacIver, *The Modern State*, Oxford, New York, 1926; and Robert Michels, *Political Parties*, The Free Press, Glencoe, Ill., 1949.

For Jacques Maritain's view that democracy in politics can be reconciled with absolutism in metaphysics, see his books *Man and the State*, University of Chicago Press, Chicago, 1951; and *Freedom in the Modern World*, Scribner, New York, 1936.

David Spitz, *Patterns of Anti-democratic Thought*, Macmillan, New York, 1949, contains an excellent analysis and critique of the views of some non-Marxist American theorists. Two readable presentations of the Marxist indictment of "bourgeois democracy" are Harold J. Laski, *The State in Theory and Practice*, Viking, New York, 1935; and John Strachey, *The Coming Struggle for Power*, Covici, New York, 1934. Barker, Mosca, and Durbin (above) all present cogent cases for the primacy of political power.

The best single analysis of the stresses and strains that characterize American life is Robin M. Williams, Jr., *American Society, A Sociological Analysis*, Knopf, New York, 1951. An important contemporary study of the political implications of American social and national heterogeneity is David Truman's *The Governmental Process*, Knopf, New York, 1951. See also Reinhold Niebuhr's unique interpretation of the American "way of life" in his *The Irony of American History*, Harper, New York, 1952.

The literature on sovereignty has achieved epic proportions. A good summary of the different viewpoints can be found in Hyman E. Cohen, *Recent Theories of Sovereignty*, University of Chicago Press, Chicago, 1937. See also Harold J. Laski's two historical treatises, *Studies in the Problem of Sovereignty*, Yale University Press, New Haven, 1917; and *Foundations of Sovereignty*, Harcourt, Brace, New York, 1921; and William Y. Elliott's rejoinder, *The Pragmatic Revolt in Politics*, Macmillan, New York, 1928. Maritain's views, contained in Chap. II, "The Concept of Sovereignty," in *Man and the State* (above) strike us as being singularly cogent.

The influence of the purported "Jewish vote" in New York on the Truman administration's Israel policy can be ascertained from Walter Millis (ed.), *The Forrestal Diaries*, Viking, New York, 1951, especially pp. 309–310, 346–349, 362–364, and 440–441. President Truman's statement to Forrestal about the civil-rights issue at the 1948 Democratic convention can be found at p. 458.

The pluralistic nature of British political parties can be grasped by reading what their members say about them as well as by detached analysis. For the former, see *The Political Quarterly*, Vol. 24, Nos. 1, 2, and 3, 1953. Each of these issues is devoted to the analysis of one of the three top parties, with the articles, in the main, written by leading figures of the respective organizations. For analysis from without, see John P. Roche, "The Crisis in British Socialism," *Antioch Review*, Winter, 1952–1953, pp. 387–397; and Samuel Beer, "The Conservative Party in Great Britain," *Journal of Politics*, Vol. 14, pp. 41–71, 1952. For the parties of Western Europe, see Mario Einaudi and François Goguel, *Christian Democracy in France and Italy*, Notre Dame University Press, 1952; François Goguel, *France under the Fourth Republic*, Cornell University Press, Ithaca, N.Y., 1952; and, for those who can read French, Maurice Duverger, *Les Partis politiques*, Librairie Armand Colin, Paris, 1951.

CHAPTER 2. *Political Parties*

In addition to Erich Fromm's *Escape from Freedom*, Rinehart, New York, 1941, two other interpretations of the effects of impersonal, industrial society on human nature which are well worth reading are David Reisman, *The Lonely Crowd*, Yale University Press, New Haven, 1950; and José Ortega y Gasset, *The Revolt of the Masses*, Norton, New York, 1932.

The distinction between the policy-formulation and the policy-implementation functions and the limitations on the role of the party are drawn from Barker, though without his knowledge or permission, and, quite possibly he would not agree with our adaptation. See his *Reflections on Government* (above), Chap. II.

The material on American parties is enormous. The outstanding historical treatment, which has the additional virtue of being extremely readable, is W. E. Binkley, *American Political Parties*, Knopf, New York, 1945. Three comprehensive textbooks which will put flesh on the skeleton presented here are V. O. Key, Jr., *Politics, Parties, and Pressure Groups*, Crowell, New York, 1952; Dayton D. McKean, *Party and Pressure Politics*, Houghton Mifflin, Boston, 1949; and Hugh Bone, *American Politics and the Party System*, McGraw-Hill, New York, 1949. A brief, stimulating analysis can be found in E. E. Schattschneider, *Party Government*, Rinehart, 1942. A regional study which examines in detail the local political organisms of the South is V. O. Key, Jr., *Southern Politics*, Knopf, New York, 1949. For an analysis of American farmer and labor parties, see Murray S. Stedman, Jr., and Susan W. Stedman, *Discontent at the Polls*, Columbia University Press, New York, 1950.

For the 1952 campaign and election, see *The New York Times, Time Magazine, U.S. News & World Report, The Reporter,* and *The Economist* of London for that period. The student in search of a dispassionate analysis of the American scene will find *The Economist* indispensable. The McCarthy attack on Governor Stevenson was examined in the light of logic in *America,* Dec. 13, 1952, pp. 301–303. Social psychologists of the Survey Research Center, University of Michigan, conducted an extensive inquiry into the campaign and election in the attempt to discover why people voted as they did. The preliminary results of this analysis can be found in A. Campbell, G. Gurin, and W. E. Miller, "Political Issues and the Vote: November, 1952," *American Political Science Review,* Vol. 47, pp. 359–385, 1953.

Each of the following textbooks in comparative government contains a good discussion of the British party system: Morstein Marx (ed.), *Foreign Governments,* Prentice-Hall, New York, 1952; Robert Neumann, *European and Comparative Government,* McGraw-Hill, New York, 1951; John Ranney, Gwendolen Carter, and John Herz, *The Major Foreign Powers,* Harcourt, Brace, New York, 1952; and Taylor Cole (ed.), *European Political Systems,* Knopf, New York, 1953. The electoral system is analyzed by David E. Butler in *The Electoral System in Britain 1918–1951,* Oxford, New York, 1953. An excellent short analysis of the roots of the two-party system in Britain is Leslie Lipson, "The Two-party System in British Politics," *American Political Science Review,* Vol. 47, pp. 337–358, 1953. Hiram Stout, *British Government,* Oxford, New York, 1953, gives the role of parties in the broader governmental process a good treatment.

Herbert Morrison's statement on the "unconstitutionality" of political strikes against the Conservative Government, as well as the views of the leading figures of the Trade Union Congress, may be found in *The New York Herald Tribune,* Feb. 25, 1952, p. 1. The operation of the Parliamentary Labor party has been discussed in a fine article by James M. Burns, "The Parliamentary Labor Party in Great Britain," *American Political Science Review,* Vol. 44, pp. 855–871, 1950.

For Prime Minister Attlee's blunt statement to Harold J. Laski, the 1945 chairman of the Labor party, that Laski's presumption to make policy statements on behalf of the Government was highly improper and that "a period of silence on your part would be welcome," see Kingsley Martin, *Harold Laski,* Gollancz, London, 1953, pp. 181–182. An interesting analysis of the Conservative party's activities in the period from 1945 to 1949 is Eric Willenz, "The Conservative Party in Great Britain since 1945," *Social Research,* Vol. 16, pp. 12–30, 1949.

The textbooks by Cole, by Neumann, and by Ranney, Carter, and Herz (above) all have good analyses of French political life. In addition, see James T. Shotwell (ed.), *Governments of Continental Europe,* Macmillan, New York, 1952.

A cogent analysis of the position of French communism is contained in Mario Einaudi, Jean-Marie Domenach, and Aldo Garosci, *Communism in Western Europe,* Cornell University Press, Ithaca, N.Y., 1951. A masterly case study of the Communist party is A. Rossi, *A Communist Party in Action,* Yale University Press, New Haven, 1949. The Gaullist movement is discussed and dissected in expert fashion in Robert G. Neumann, "Formation and Transformation of Gaullism in France," *Western Political Quarterly,* Vol. 6, pp. 250–274, 1953. Goguel's *France under the Fourth Republic* (above) is the best over-all analysis of recent French political developments.

CHAPTER 3. *Interest Groups in Modern Society*

For a general analysis of the role of interest groups in democratic society, see Robert M. MacIver, *The Web of Government,* Macmillan, New York, 1947. The best specific analysis of the place these organizations have in American political life is Key, *Politics, Parties, and Pressure Groups* (above). David Truman has, relying on insights first elaborated in 1908 by Arthur F. Bentley in *The Process of Government,* attempted to develop a general theory of the group process. See *The Governmental Process* (above). An analysis of this approach may be found in Murray S. Stedman, Jr., "A Group Interpretation of Politics," *Public Opinion Quarterly,* Vol. 17, No. 2, pp. 218–229, Summer, 1953. Truman's definition of an interest group appears on p. 37 of *The Governmental Process;* Key's at p. 24 of *Politics, Parties, and Pressure Groups.*

Two studies of agricultural pressure groups from which we have drawn information for the material in the text are O. M. Kile, *The Farm Bureau through Three Decades,* Waverly Press, Baltimore, 1948; and Wesley McCune, *The Farm Bloc,* Doubleday, New York, 1943. See also Charles Hardin, *The Politics of Agriculture,* The Free Press, Glencoe, Ill., 1952.

On labor lobbies, see Lewis L. Lorwin, *The American Federation of Labor,* Brookings Institution, Washington, D.C., 1933; Harwood Childs, *Labor and Capital in National Politics,* The Ohio State University Press, Columbus, Ohio, 1930; and Joseph Gaer, *The First Round: The Story of the CIO Political Action Committee,* Duell, Sloan & Pearce, New York, 1944. There is no adequate general treatment of this subject.

For business, see Childs (above) and Kenneth Crawford, *The Pressure Boys,* Messner, New York, 1939. Two excellent studies which, while not precisely to the point, discuss the activities of businessmen in politics in their specific contexts are Dayton D. McKean, *Pressures on the Legislature of New Jersey,* Columbia University Press, New York, 1938; and Elmer E. Schattschneider, *Politics, Pressures, and the Tariff,* Prentice-Hall, New York, 1935.

The activities of professional groups have received only sporadic analysis. In general, see J. A. C. Grant, "The Guild Returns to America," *Journal of Politics,* Vol. 4, pp. 303–336, 458–477, 1942. The best specific study of a professional group is Oliver Garceau, *The Political Life of the American Medical Association,* Harvard University Press, Cambridge, Mass., 1941.

There is no good contemporary examination of the veterans' lobby. Both Marcus Duffield, *King Legion,* Cape & Smith, New York, 1931; and Justin Gray, *The Inside Story of the Legion,* Boni & Gaer, New York, 1948, are hortatory rather than analytical.

Religious pressure groups have also been neglected. Peter M. Odegard, *Pressure Politics: The Story of the Anti-saloon League,* Columbia University Press, New York, 1928, is in a sense an examination of a religious movement, and Luke E. Ebersole, *Church Lobbying in the Nation's Capital,* Macmillan, New York, 1951, is useful though brief.

A fine case study of how pressure groups actually operate, and the various levels on which they apply leverage, is Stephen K. Bailey, *Congress Makes a Law,* Columbia

University Press, New York, 1950. A similarly good job which attacks the problem from a somewhat different angle is James M. Burns, *Congress on Trial*, Harper, New York, 1949.

The material on the *Reichswirtschaftsrat* is drawn from Lindsay Rogers and W. R. Dittmar, "The Reichswirtschaftsrat: *De Mortuis*," *Political Science Quarterly*, Vol. 50, pp. 481–501, 1935. See also Ernest Barker, "British Ideas of a Social Parliament," *American Political Science Review*, Vol. 44, pp. 14–22, 1950.

Interest "representation" in administration is discussed by Avery Leiserson, *Administrative Regulation, A Study in Representation of Interests*, University of Chicago Press, Chicago, 1942; and by E. Pendleton Herring, *Public Administration and the Public Interest*, McGraw-Hill, New York, 1936.

The activities of interest groups in Britain are discussed in W. Ivor Jennings, *Parliament*, Cambridge, New York, 1939, pp. 31–50, 171–232. Because of the nature of French political parties, discussion of interest groups in that nation is largely superfluous. See, however, Gordon Wright, "Agrarian Syndicalism in Postwar France," *American Political Science Review*, Vol. 47, pp. 402–416, 1953.

On the regulation of lobbies in the United States, see George B. Galloway, *Congress at the Crossroads*, Crowell, New York, 1947; Belle Zeller, "The Federal Regulation of Lobbying Act," *American Political Science Review*, Vol. 42, pp. 239–271, 1948; and the various reports of the House of Representatives Select Committee on Lobbying Activities, 81st Cong., especially House Reports 3138 and 3239.

CHAPTER 4. *Public Opinion*

Of historical interest in understanding various approaches to the analysis of public opinion are Gustave LeBon, *The Crowd—A Study of the Popular Mind*, T. Fisher Unwin, London, 1896; Graham Wallas, *Human Nature in Politics*, 4th ed., Constable, London, 1948; Walter Lippmann, *Public Opinion*, Harcourt, Brace, New York, 1922; and A. Lawrence Lowell, *Public Opinion in War and Peace*, Harvard University Press, Cambridge, Mass., 1923.

Contemporary studies which attempt to isolate and analyze the basic determinants of public opinion are T. W. Adorno and associates, *The Authoritarian Personality*, Harper, New York, 1950; Eric Hoffer, *The True Believer*, Harper, New York, 1951; Ruth Benedict, *Patterns of Culture*, Houghton Mifflin, Boston, 1934; Erich Fromm, *Escape from Freedom* (above): Clyde Kluckhohn, *Mirror for Man*, McGraw-Hill, New York, 1949.

The concentration of ownership of the press in the United States is discussed in Morris Ernst, *The First Freedom*, Macmillan, New York, 1946. The situation in Britain is analyzed coldly in Royal Commission on the Press, *Report*, Cmd. 7700, H. M. Stationery Office, London, 1949. The statistics on concentration are cited from Norman J. Powell, *The Anatomy of Public Opinion*, Prentice-Hall, New York, 1951, p. 221; and from Frederick C. Irion, *Public Opinion and Propaganda*, Crowell, New York, 1950, p. 79. Both these textbooks give extended treatment to the various problems discussed briefly here.

The most ambitious American attempt to analyze over-all issues of mass communication in the United States was undertaken by the privately sponsored Commission on Freedom of the Press. This Commission subsidized a series of monographs on special aspects of the problem and a general report. See Commission on Freedom of the Press, *A Free and Responsible Press,* University of Chicago Press, Chicago, 1947. The monographs will be cited where appropriate.

The percentages of newspaper support for Franklin D. Roosevelt in his various campaigns for the Presidency are taken from Dayton McKean, *Party and Pressure Politics,* Houghton Mifflin, Boston, 1949, p. 144.

On the impact of radio, see Paul F. Lazarsfeld and Patricia L. Kendall, *Radio Listening in America,* Prentice-Hall, New York, 1948. Generally on radio and television, see Charles Siepmann, *Radio, Television, and Society,* Oxford, New York, 1950. Two studies of the specific impact of television are E. C. McDonagh *et al.,* "Television and the Family," *Sociology and Social Research,* Vol. 35, pp. 113–122, 1950; and J. W. Riley *et al.,* "Some Observations on the Social Effects of Television," *Public Opinion Quarterly,* Vol. 13, pp. 223–234, 1949.

On the legal problems presented by mass communications, see Zechariah Chaffee, Jr., *Government and Mass Communications,* 2 vols., University of Chicago Press, Chicago, 1947. On the motion picture and the censorship techniques that have been developed to deal with it, see Ruth Inglis, *Freedom of the Movies,* University of Chicago Press, Chicago, 1947.

The Supreme Court's decision in the *Miracle* case was *Joseph Burstyn et al. v. Wilson et al.,* 343 U.S. 495 (1952).

On the techniques of measuring public opinion, see Hadley Cantril *et al., Gauging Public Opinion,* Princeton University Press, Princeton, N.J., 1944; George Gallup and Saul F. Rae, *The Pulse of Democracy,* Knopf, New York, 1948; Leonard W. Doob, *Public Opinion and Propaganda,* Holt, New York, 1948; Mildred Parten, *Surveys, Polls, and Samples: Practical Procedures,* Harper, New York, 1950; Louis H. Bean, *How to Predict Elections,* Knopf, New York, 1948; and Paul F. Lazarsfeld *et al., The People's Choice—How the Voter Makes Up His Mind in a Presidential Campaign,* Columbia University Press, New York, 2d ed., 1948. A succinct examination of the variables that pollsters must deal with is Edward Suchman, "Socio-psychological Factors Affecting Predictions of Elections," *Public Opinion Quarterly,* Vol. 16, pp. 436–438, 1952. The extensive use of public-opinion polls by various United States government agencies is discussed in Harry Alpert, "Opinion and Attitude Surveys in the United States Government," *Public Opinion Quarterly,* Vol. 16, pp. 33–41, 1952. Further examples of the use of polls by various governments, along with data on specific research institutes, may be found in the *International Social Science Bulletin,* Vol. 5, No. 3, 1953. This issue is devoted entirely to public-opinion research.

For critiques of polling techniques, see Lindsay Rogers, *The Pollsters,* Knopf, New York, 1949; Social Science Research Council, *The Pre-election Polls of 1948,* Bulletin 60, New York, 1949; and Norman C. Meier and Harold W. Saunders (eds.), *The Polls and Public Opinion,* Holt, New York, 1949.

CHAPTER 5. *Electoral Systems*

Generally, see the comparative-government textbooks listed earlier for details on Britain and France, and the textbooks on political parties by Key and Bone (above) for the United States.

On nominations, see Joseph P. Harris, "A New Primary System," *State Government,* Vol. 21, pp. 140–143, 1948. The quotation is taken from p. 141. Cross-voting is discussed briefly by Daniel M. Ogden, Jr., "Parties Survive Cross-voting," *National Municipal Review,* Vol. 39, pp. 237–241, 1950.

The viewpoint of the Committee on Political Parties of the American Political Science Association can be found in its report, *Toward a More Responsible Two-party System,* published as a supplement to the *American Political Science Review,* Vol. 44, 1950. This report stirred up a great deal of controversy. For examples, see Murray S. Stedman, Jr., and Herbert Sonthoff, "Party Responsibility—A Critical Inquiry," *Western Political Quarterly,* Vol. 4, pp. 454–468, 1951; T. W. Goodman, "How Much Political Party Centralization Do We Want?" *Journal of Politics,* Vol. 13, pp. 536–560, 1951; Norton E. Long, "Party Government and the United States," *Journal of Politics,* Vol. 13, pp. 187–214, 1951; and Austin Ranney, "Toward a More Responsible Two-party System: A Commentary," *American Political Science Review,* Vol. 45, pp. 488–499, 1951.

Since 1945, British political scientists have prepared detailed analyses of the general elections which are invaluable for understanding the electoral process in that nation. See R. B. McCallum and Alison Readman, *The British General Election of 1945,* Oxford, New York, 1947; H. G. Nicholas, *The British General Election of 1950,* Oxford, New York, 1951; David E. Butler, *The British General Election of 1951,* Oxford, New York, London, 1953.

For those who can read French, an excellent study of the influence of electoral systems on politics is Maurice Duverger *et al., L'Influence des systèmes électoraux sur la vie politique,* Librairie Armand Colin, Paris, 1950. The material in the text on France is largely drawn from the fine chapter on the French experience which François Goguel prepared for this book. The electoral law of May 7, 1951, is discussed by Goguel in his *France under the Fourth Republic* (above), Chap. II. On the 1951 election, see Mario Einaudi, "The Crisis of Government and Politics in France," *World Politics,* Vol. 4, pp. 64–84, 1951.

On the Hare system of proportional representation, see George Hallett, *Proportional Representation—The Key to Democracy,* National Municipal League, New York, 1940. On the operation of PR in New York City, see Belle Zeller and Hugh Bone, "The Repeal of P.R. in New York City—Ten Years in Retrospect," *American Political Science Review,* Vol. 42, pp. 1127–1148, 1948. On the list system, see Ferdinand A. Hermans, *Democracy or Anarchy? A Study of Proportional Representation,* University of Notre Dame Press, 1943. Professor Hermans, a bitter opponent of PR who tends to overstate the case against the system, returned to the lists again with *Europe between Democracy and Anarchy,* University of Notre Dame Press, 1951.

The material on the Italian election of 1948 has been drawn from Mario Einaudi, "The Italian Elections of 1948," *Review of Politics,* Vol. 10, pp. 346–361, especially pp. 348–349, 1948.

On the new German electoral law, see Otto Kirchheimer and A. Price, "Analysis and Effects of the Election in Western Germany," *Department of State Bulletin,* Vol. 21, pp. 563–573, 1949.

For an analysis of spending in American presidential elections, see Louise Overacker, *Presidential Campaign Funds,* Boston University Press, 1946, and Professor Overacker's periodic analyses in the *American Political Science Review.* British campaign procedures are detailed in the three studies of recent general elections cited above.

Two standard studies, now out of date but still valuable, on registration and election administration in the United States are Joseph P. Harris, *Registration in the United States*, Brookings Institution, Washington, D.C., 1929; and Harris's *Election Administration in the United States*, Brookings Institution, Washington, D.C., 1934. For an analysis of actual voting procedures, see Spencer D. Albright, *The American Ballot*, American Council on Public Affairs, Washington, D.C., 1942.

The Lodge-Gossett proposal for changing the system of presidential election is discussed in Ruth Silva, "The Lodge-Gossett Resolution: A Critical Analysis," *American Political Science Review*, Vol. 44, pp. 86–99, 1950.

CHAPTER 6. *Legislative Structure and Organization*

The history of the British Parliament is discussed in Sir Courtney Ilbert, *Parliament, Its History, Constitution, and Practice*, Oxford, New York, 1950; and by Kenneth MacKenzie, *The English Parliament. A Study of Its Nature and Historic Development*, Pelican Books, London, 1950.

An excellent analysis of the changing relationships between the legislature and the executive in the United States since the founding of the republic is Wilfred E. Binkley, *President and Congress*, Knopf, New York, 1947.

French parliamentary practice is discussed in D. W. S. Lidderdale, *The Parliament of France*, The Hansard Society, London, 1951. The various views on legislative power at the Constituent Assembly of the Fourth Republic may be found in Gordon Wright, *The Reshaping of French Democracy*, Reynal & Hitchcock, New York, 1948.

The changing position of the House of Lords in Britain is analyzed by Jennings in *Parliament* (above), Chap. XI. See also Dell Hitchner, "The Labour Government and the House of Lords," *Western Political Quarterly*, Vol. 1, pp. 426–438, 1948.

The standard treatment of French political developments under the Third Republic is D. W. Brogan, *France under the Republic (1870–1939)*, Harper, New York, 1940. For more recent experience, see Dorothy Pickles, *French Politics: The First Years of the Fourth Republic*, Royal Institute of International Affairs, London, 1953.

On the organization of the American Congress, see Floyd M. Riddick, *The United States Congress—Organization and Procedure*, National Capital Publishers, Washington, D.C., 1949; and Ernest S. Griffith, *Congress; Its Contemporary Role*, New York University Press, 1951. Jennings's *Parliament* (above) is the definitive British study.

Legislative committee structure in the United States is discussed by Riddick in the work cited above. For France under the Third Republic, see Robert K. Gooch, *The French Parliamentary Committee System*, Appleton-Century, New York, 1935. Professor E. E. Schattschneider's incisive remarks on the unrepresentative character of congressional committees can be found in his article, "Congress in Conflict," *Yale Review*, Vol. 41, pp. 181–193, 1951. On the committee structure of the Swedish legislature, see Neil C. M. Elder, "The Parliamentary Role of Joint Standing Committees in Sweden," *American Political Science Review*, Vol. 45, pp. 464–473, 1951.

On party organization within the American Congress, see Paul D. Hasbrouck, *Party Government in the House of Representatives*, Macmillan, New York, 1927; Lawrence H. Chamberlain, *The President, Congress, and Legislation*, Columbia University Press, New York, 1946; and Harvey Walker, *The Legislative Process*, Ronald, New York, 1948. For Britain, see Jennings's *Parliament* (above); and Burns,

"The Parliamentary Labor Party in Great Britain" (above). For France, see Lidderdale's *The Parliament of France* (above).

David Thomson's analysis of the permanence of certain basic French institutions, notably the bureaucracy, is contained in his *Democracy in France,* 2d ed., Oxford, New York, 1952.

CHAPTER 7. *Legislative Operation*

Many of the sources listed in the previous chapter are also useful here, notably Jennings's *Parliament;* Lidderdale's *The Parliament of France;* Riddick's *The United States Congress—Organization and Procedure;* and Walker's *The Legislative Process.*

For a vivid examination of the intricacies of the lawmaking process in the United States, see Bertram Gross, *The Legislative Struggle,* McGraw-Hill, New York, 1953. In addition to the two excellent volumes (employing the case-study approach) cited earlier—James M. Burns, *Congress on Trial;* and Stephen K. Bailey, *Congress Makes a Law*—see the recent "cross-section" analysis by Stephen K. Bailey and Howard D. Samuel, *Congress at Work,* Holt, New York, 1952.

On the filibuster, see Franklin L. Burdette, *Filibustering in the Senate,* Princeton University Press, 1940. For a detailed description of Senate activities and prerogatives, see George H. Haynes, *The Senate of the United States; Its History and Practice,* Houghton Mifflin, Boston, 1938. See also Lindsay Rogers, *The American Senate,* Knopf, New York, 1926.

Julius Turner's analysis of party lines in Congress may be found in his *Party and Constituency: Pressures on Congress,* Johns Hopkins Press, Baltimore, 1951. Ralph Burton's study of party cohesion in the French Chamber of Deputies is cited by Turner at p. 27.

George Galloway's views on the Legislative Reorganization Act of 1946 are contained in his "The Operation of the Legislative Reorganization Act of 1946," *American Political Science Review,* Vol. 45, pp. 41–68, 1951. For Griffith's defense of Congress, see his *Congress; Its Contemporary Role* (above). The views of Professors Schattschneider and Burns may be found in their respective books *Party Government* (above) and *Congress on Trial* (above).

CHAPTER 8. *The Administrative Process*

Generally, see the public-administration textbooks: Herbert Simon, Donald W. Smithburg, and Victor A. Thompson, *Public Administration,* Knopf, New York, 1950; Leonard D. White, *Introduction to the Study of Public Administration,* 3d ed., Macmillan, New York, 1948; and Marshall E. Dimock and Gladys O. Dimock, *Public Administration,* Rinehart, New York, 1953.

Charles A. Beard's views on public administration may be found in his book *Public Policy and General Welfare,* Farrar & Rinehart, New York, 1941. The other works discussed in the text are James M. Beck, *Our Wonderland of Bureaucracy,* Macmillan, New York, 1932; Laurence Sullivan, *The Dead Hand of Bureaucracy,* Bobbs-Merrill, New York, 1940; and Paul Appleby, *Big Democracy,* Knopf, New York, 1945. The quotations are from Beck, p. 85, and Sullivan, p. 13.

On rules of public administration, see W. F. Willoughby, *Principles of Public Administration,* Johns Hopkins Press, Baltimore, 1927; James B. Mooney and Allen C. Reiley, *Onward Industry!* Harper, New York, 1931; and Luther Gulick and L. Urwick (eds.), *Papers on the Science of Administration,* Institute of Public Administration, Columbia University, New York, 1937.

On the conflict between line and staff functions, see Arthur Macmahon and John D. Millett, *Federal Administrators,* Columbia University Press, New York, 1947. On "span of control," see the paper by Graicunas in Gulick and Urwick, *Papers on the Science of Administration* (above), pp. 181–188. That "line" officers cannot operate effectively without adequate staff planning is underlined by Herman M. Somers, *Presidential Agency, OWMR,* Harvard University Press, Cambridge, Mass. 1950; and John D. Millett, *The Process and Organization of Government Planning,* Columbia University Press, New York, 1947.

The extent to which the Federalists contributed to the permanent structure of national administration can be seen in Leonard D. White, *The Federalists,* Macmillan, New York, 1948. See also Professor White's *The Jeffersonians,* Macmillan, New York, 1951, which continues the history through the administration of John Quincy Adams.

The constant shifting of political power from the President to Congress, and conversely from the legislature to the executive, which makes it virtually impossible to isolate a clear body of executive or of legislative powers in the United States government, was first emphasized by Professor Arthur F. Bentley in his classic and long-neglected *The Process of Government,* University of Chicago Press, Chicago, 1908. Two good case studies of the ties that bind administrative agencies to congressional committees are Charles M. Hardin, *The Politics of Agriculture,* The Free Press, Glencoe, Ill., 1952; and Arthur Maass, *Muddy Waters,* Harvard University Press, Cambridge, Mass., 1951.

Leonard D. White's breakdown of the administrative responsibilities of the President can be found in his *Introduction to the Study of Public Administration* (above), pp. 46*ff.*

Myers v. United States may be read in its massive entirety in 272 U.S. 52 (1926). *Rathbun v. United States* can be found in 295 U.S. 602 (1935). An excellent commentary on these decisions is Edward S. Corwin, *The President: Office and Powers,* New York University Press, 1948, pp. 102–114.

Clinton Rossiter's recommendations on putting the Vice-President to work were contained in his article, "The Reform of the Vice-Presidency," *Political Science Quarterly,* Vol. 63, pp. 383–403, 1948.

The standard work on the techniques of British government is W. Ivor Jennings, *Cabinet Government,* 2d ed., Cambridge, New York, 1951. There is a good discussion of this matter in Stout, *British Government* (above).

The degree to which the French bureaucracy operates free of political control is well brought out in Brian Chapman, *Introduction to French Local Government,* G. Allen, London, 1953.

The definitive study by Robert E. Cushman, *The Independent Regulatory Commissions,* Oxford, New York, 1941, not only analyzes American experience with these bodies, but also investigates British agencies of an analogous character. For techniques of nationalization in Britain, see William A. Robson, "The Public Corporation in Britain Today," *Harvard Law Review,* Vol. 63, pp. 1321–1348, 1950. For nationalization in France, see Mario Einaudi, "Nationalization in France and Italy," *Social Research,* Vol. 15, pp. 22–43, 1948. On bureaucratic control of the French nationalized industries, see Adolf Sturmthal, "The Structure of Nationalized Enterprises in France," *Political Science Quarterly,* Vol. 67, pp. 357–377, 1952.

CHAPTER 9. *Techniques of Administrative Management*

Generally, see the texts cited in the bibliography for Chap. 8 above. See also Chester I. Barnard, *Organization and Management,* Harvard University Press, Cambridge, Mass., 1948.

On personnel administration in the United States, see William E. Mosher, J. Donald Kingsley, and O. Glenn Stahl, *Public Personnel Administration,* 3d ed., Harper, New York, 1950. For Britain, see Herman Finer, *The British Civil Service,* G. Allen, London, 1947; Harold R. G. Greaves, *The Civil Service in the Changing State,* Harrap, London, 1947; and J. Donald Kingsley, *Representative Bureaucracy,* The Antioch Press, Yellow Springs, Ohio, 1944. The best brief treatment of the French civil service is Herman Finer, *The Theory and Practice of Modern Government,* rev. ed., Holt, New York, 1949, Chaps. 29 and 32.

The information on average length of service for British assistant secretaries is taken from Kingsley, *Representative Bureaucracy* (above), p. 247. The high degree of interchange between private and public office in the United States was pointed out by Herman M. Somers, "The Dilemma of the American Executive Branch," *Confluence,* Vol. I, pp. 63–75, 1952. The data on unionization of public employees are drawn from Sterling D. Spero, *Government as Employer,* Remsen Press, New York, 1948.

On the United States government's actions against security and loyalty risks in government employment, see the excellent analysis by Eleanor Bontecou, *The Federal Loyalty-Security Program,* Cornell University Press, Ithaca, N.Y., 1953.

An interesting analysis of how one government agency faced up to various problems of administration is John M. Gaus and Leon Wolcott, *Public Administration in the United States Department of Agriculture,* Public Administration Service, Chicago, 1940.

For a discussion of recent social psychological and social anthropological experiments of value to the student of politics, see James G. Miller (ed.), *Experiments in Social Process,* McGraw-Hill, New York, 1950; and on the specific experiments mentioned in the text, see George C. Homans, "Group Factors in Worker Productivity," and L. Kahn, "Some Recent Findings in Human Relations Research in Industry," in Guy E. Swanson *et al., Readings in Social Psychology,* 2d ed., Holt, New York, 1952, pp. 637–649, 650–665.

On administrative powers, see Ernst Freund, *Administrative Powers over Persons and Property,* University of Chicago Press, Chicago, 1928; Bernard Schwartz, *Law and the Executive in Britain,* New York University Press, 1949, which compares American and British developments at many points; and William A. Robson, *Justice and Administrative Law,* 2d ed., Stevens, London, 1947. An excellent basic analysis of the position of administrators vis à vis the law and the United States Constitution is J. Roland Pennock, *Administration and the Rule of Law,* Rinehart, New York, 1941.

CHAPTER 10. *The Functions of the Judiciary*

Generally, on the American Constitution, see Alfred H. Kelly and Winfred A. Harbison, *The American Constitution—Its Origins and Development,* Norton, New York, 1948. A classic study, now out of date but still invaluable for the period prior to 1932, is Andrew C. McLaughlin, *A Constitutional History of the United States,* Appleton-Century-Crofts, Inc., New York, 1935. Probably the best single volume for acquainting the student with the sources of American law is James Willard Hurst, *The Growth of American Law: The Lawmakers,* Little, Brown, Boston, 1950. On the role of the Supreme Court, see the standard work by Charles Warren, *The Supreme Court in United States History, 1789–1918,* 2 vols., Little, Brown, Boston, 1947.

The suggestion that American law is essentially collectivistic is made by Alexander Pekelis, *Law and Social Action,* Cornell University Press, Ithaca, N.Y., 1950, pp. 42–74. A good discussion of the various recent attempts to define, or define away, natural law is Fred V. Cahill, *Judicial Legislation,* Ronald, New York, 1952. See also Edmond Cahn, "Scepticism in American Jurisprudence," *New York University Law Review,* Vol. 28, pp. 852–865, 1953. The statement of the Milford town meeting is quoted from George F. Willison, *Saints and Strangers,* Reynal & Hitchcock, New York, 1945, p. 392.

On the lack of constitutional definition of United States citizenship, see John P. Roche, *The Early Development of United States Citizenship,* Cornell University Press, Ithaca, N.Y., 1949.

The relationships among social attitudes, political majorities, and Supreme Court decisions is discussed in John P. Roche, "Executive Power and Domestic Emergency: The Quest for Prerogative," *Western Political Quarterly,* Vol. 4, pp. 592–618, 1952; John P. Roche, "Education, Segregation and the Supreme Court—A Political Analysis," *University of Pennsylvania Law Review,* Vol. 99, pp. 949–959, 1951; and John P. Roche, "The Future of 'Separate but Equal,' " *Phylon,* Vol. 12, pp. 219–226, 1951.

The British judicial system is well discussed in Stout, *British Government* (above). See also Robson, *Justice and Administrative Law* (above). There is an excellent treatment of the French judicial system in Ranney, Carter, and Herz, *The Major Foreign Powers* (above).

A stimulating examination of the background of the Anglo-American legal tradition is Edward S. Corwin, *Liberty against Government,* Louisiana State University Press, 1948. See also Charles H. McIlwain, *Constitutionalism—Ancient and Modern,* Cornell University Press, Ithaca, N.Y., 1947. On the growing resemblance between codified law in Britain, and analogously in the United States, and the codified system in France, see W. Friedmann, "Public Law Problems in Recent English Decisions," *Current Legal Problems,* Vol. 4, pp. 370–394, 1951.

On administrative law in the United States, see Pennock, *Administration and the Rule of Law* (above). For Britain, see Robson, *Justice and Administrative Law* (above); and W. Friedmann, *Law and Social Change in Contemporary Britain,* Stevens, London, 1952. The best brief summary of French administrative law is Finer, *The Theory and Practice of Modern Government* (above), pp. 924–927. See also the discussion of this in Shotwell (ed.), *Governments of Continental Europe* (above).

The classic study of freedom of speech and the constitutional protection given to it in recent American history is Zechariah Chaffee, Jr., *Free Speech in the United States,* Harvard University Press, Cambridge, Mass., 1946. The general state of civil liberties in the United States has been examined by a series of authors under the general direction of Professor Robert E. Cushman of Cornell University. Some of the volumes that have appeared in the series, all published by the Cornell University Press, Ithaca, N.Y., are Walter Gellhorn, *Security, Loyalty and Science,* 1950; Vern Countryman, *Un-American Activities in the State of Washington,* 1951; Milton Konvitz, *The Alien and the Asiatic in American Law,* 1946; Robert K. Carr, *Federal Protection of Civil Rights,* 1947; Lawrence H. Chamberlain, *Loyalty and Legislative Action,* 1951; Bontecou, *The Federal Loyalty-Security Program* (above); Walter Gellhorn (ed.), *The States and Subversion,* 1953; Robert K. Carr, *The House Committee on Un-American Activities;* and Edward L. Barrett, Jr., *The Tenney Committee,* 1951.

CHAPTER 11. *The Democratic Executive*

The standard legal study of the powers of the President is Corwin, *The President: Office and Powers* (above). A well-written history of the relations between the White House and Capitol Hill is Binkley, *President and Congress* (above).

E. E. Schattschneider's observations on the unrepresentative quality and great power of congressional committees are in his article, "Congress in Conflict" (above).

An incisive description of the various tasks of the American President can be found in Clinton L. Rossiter, "The American President," *Yale Review,* Vol. 37, pp. 619–637, 1948. See also Eric F. Goldman, "The Presidency as Moral Leadership," *The Annals,* March, 1952, pp. 37–45, 1952.

Herman Somers' view that the President's job is essentially one of reconciling interests, see his "The President as Administrator," *The Annals,* September, 1952, pp. 104–114, 1952.

On the Supreme Court's decision in the steel case and its implications, see Roche, "Executive Power and Domestic Emergency: The Quest for Prerogative" (above). A fundamental treatment of the Court's attitude toward the President in periods of emergency is Clinton L. Rossiter, *The Supreme Court and the Commander in Chief,* Cornell University Press, Ithaca, N.Y., 1951.

On the functions of the British executive, see Jennings, *Cabinet Government* (above). A good description of the operation of the British Cabinet is contained in Stout, *British Government* (above). The quotation from Viscount Samuel's *Memoirs* is taken from Stout, p. 75.

There is a thorough treatment of the French executive in Shotwell (ed.), *The Governments of Continental Europe,* (above), President Auriol's view that he is more than a figurehead was contained in a statement to the foreign press, written up in *Le Figaro,* Paris, Nov. 16, 1951.

The material on the Swiss plural executive is largely drawn from Arnold J. Zurcher's treatment of the subject in Shotwell (ed.) *The Governments of Continental Europe* (above).

CHAPTER 12. *The Regulation of Economic Activity*

For a painstaking analysis of American attitudes toward the economy in the different historical stages of American development, see Joseph Dorfman, *The Economic*

Mind in American Civilization, 3 vols., Viking, New York, 1946, 1949. For a discussion of the positive governmental measures necessary in England to create *laissez faire,* see Karl Polanyi, *The Great Transformation,* Farrar & Rinehart, New York, 1944. The extent to which state governments intervened in economic life in the early years of the republic is discussed with reference to Pennsylvania by Louis Hartz, *Economic Policy and Democratic Thought,* Harvard University Press, Cambridge, Mass., 1948; to Massachusetts by Oscar and Mary Handlin, *Commonwealth,* New York University Press, 1947; and to Virginia by Carter Goodrich, "The Virginia System of Mixed Enterprise," *Political Science Quarterly,* Vol. 64, pp. 355–387, 1949.

Paul W. Gates's cogent analysis of the Homestead Act and its policy implications may be found in his article, "The Homestead Law in an Incongruous Land System," *American Historical Review,* Vol. 41, pp. 652–681, 1936.

On the "planning" role of pressure groups, see Bailey, *Congress Makes a Law,* (above), and Hardin, *The Politics of Agriculture* (above). Senatorial pressure on the Bureau of Standards in behalf of AD-X2, the battery additive, was reported in *The New York Times,* Apr. 15, 1953, p. 1. On the Olds dismissal, see Joseph P. Harris, "The Senatorial Rejection of Leland Olds," *American Political Science Review,* Vol. 45, pp. 674–692, 1951.

The information on the dairy industry's restrictionist demands and the quotations from Senator Aiken and Assistant Secretary of State Linder are taken from *The New York Times,* Apr. 11, 1953, p. 9.

The material on congressional oversight of administrative officers is largely drawn from Robert W. Ginnane, "The Control of Federal Administration by Congressional Resolutions and Committees," *Harvard Law Review,* Vol. 66, pp. 569–611, 1953. See also the excellent articles, which have become something of a classic, by Arthur W. Macmahon, "Congressional Oversight of Administration: The Power of the Purse," *Political Science Quarterly,* Vol. 58, pp. 161–190, 380–414, June and September, 1943.

On the Amlie case, see *Newsweek,* Feb. 6, 1939. Samuel P. Huntington's analysis of the ICC is contained in his article, "The Marasmus of the ICC: The Commission, the Railroads, and the Public Interest," *Yale Law Journal,* Vol. 61, pp. 467–509, 1952.

On the autoregulatory aspects of the NRA, see Alfred M. Bingham and Selden Rodman (eds.), *Challenge to the New Deal,* Falcon Press, New York, 1934, Chap. III.

A recent book which examines national planning in the United States from the viewpoint of procedures rather than substance and supplies a wealth of scholarly detail on the subject is Emmette S. Redford, *The Administration of National Economic Control,* Macmillan, New York, 1952.

The conservative critiques of the British welfare state referred to in the text are John Jewkes, *Ordeal by Planning,* Macmillan, London, 1948; and F. A. Hayek, *The Road to Serfdom,* University of Chicago Press, Chicago, 1944. The purist, socialist view may be found in Robert A. Brady, *Crisis in Britain,* University of California Press, 1950.

Professor John B. Brebner's analysis of nineteenth-century British economic legislation is contained in his *"Laissez-faire* and State Intervention in Nineteenth Century Britain," *Journal of Economic History, Supplement,* Vol. 8, pp. 59–73, 1948.

Some of the problems of the British cooperative movement with regard to the anticapitalist propensities of its socialist allies are discussed in N. Barou (ed.), *The*

Cooperative Movement in Labour Britain, Gollancz, London, 1948. The statistic on co-op coal distribution is taken from this book, p. 33.

Chancellor Chamberlain's withdrawal of the national-defense business tax in 1937 is discussed by Beer in "The Conservative Party in Great Britain" (above). A fine case study of the Labor Government's planning activities in a new town is Harold Orlans, *Stevenage,* Routledge, London, 1952. For a dispassionate, over-all appraisal, see Ben Lewis, *British Planning and Nationalization,* Twentieth Century Fund, New York, 1952. A little book which raises some big questions about the basic direction of socialist planning is Hugh Clegg, *Industrial Democracy and Nationalization,* Blackwell, Oxford, 1951.

Professor R. S. Milne's observations on the informal nature of liaison between the key planning officers in Britain are contained in his article, "Britain's Economic Planning Machinery," *American Political Science Review,* Vol. 46, pp. 406–421, 1952. A French observer reached similar conclusions; see A. Bertrand, "Les Techniques du travail gouvernmental en Grande-Bretagne," *Revue internationale d'histoire politique et constitutionnelle,* Vol. 1, pp. 62–76, 1951.

The best single volume on French economic history from the Revolution to the outbreak of World War II is Shepard B. Clough, *France: A History of National Economics, 1789–1939,* Harper, 1939. For the post–World War II period, see Edgar Beigel, "France Moves toward National Planning," *Political Science Quarterly,* Vol. 62, pp. 381–397, 1947; Howard Ellis (ed.), *The Economics of Freedom,* Harper, New York, 1950, Chap. VII; and the many reports of the *Commissariat Général du Plan de Modernisation et d'Equipement.* Information on the Monnet Plan has been drawn from Harold Lubell, *The French Investment Program,* private publication, Paris, 1951.

On the changes that have taken place in the operation of the nationalized industries since the left-wing coalition fell apart in 1947, see Adolf Sturmthal, "The Structure of Nationalized Enterprises in France," *Political Science Quarterly,* Vol. 67, pp. 357–377, 1952.

Halévy's remark on the two constitutions is cited by Finer in *The Theory and Practice of Modern Government* (above), p. 821.

The information on the tenure of specific Ministers in the period from 1946 to 1951 is taken from Roy Macridis, "Cabinet Instability in the Fourth Republic," *Journal of Politics,* Vol. 14, pp. 643–658, 1952.

The abolition of the *Chambre des Comptes* is discussed briefly by Mario Einaudi in "Nationalization of Industry in Western Europe: Recent Literature and Debates," *American Political Science Review,* Vol. 44, pp. 177–191, at pp. 185–186, 1950. The quotation by Einaudi may be found in this article, p. 185.

CHAPTER 13. *Foreign Affairs*

Generally, on the changes in diplomatic practice that have taken place in the last half century, see Gordon A. Craig and Felix Gilbert (ed.), *The Diplomats, 1919–1939,* Princeton University Press, Princeton, N.J., 1953. For a stimulating interpretation of the evils that grow out of public meddling with the activities of the professional diplomats, see George F. Kennan, *American Diplomacy, 1900–1950,* University of Chicago Press, Chicago, 1951. In a similar vein, see Hans J. Morgenthau, *In Defense of the National Interest; A Critical Study of American Foreign Policy,* Knopf,

New York, 1951. An incisive critique of the Morgenthau position can be found in Robert W. Tucker, "Professor Morgenthau's Theory of Political 'Realism,'" *American Political Science Review*, Vol. 46, pp. 214–224, 1952. A good general discussion of American policy formation is Dexter Perkins, *The American Approach to Foreign Policy*, Harvard University Press, Cambridge, Mass., 1952.

Herman Somer's analysis is contained in his article, "Civil-Military Relations in Mutual Security," *The Annals*, July, 1953, pp. 27–35, 1953. A similar viewpoint was recently expressed by John J. McCloy, *The Challenge to American Foreign Policy*, Harvard University Press, Cambridge, Mass., 1953.

According to Secretary of Defense James Forrestal, American policy toward Israel was made by President Truman without consultation with the State Department. See Millis (ed.), *The Forrestal Diaries* (above), pp. 440–441. The statistics on interdepartmental committees are drawn from Hoover Commission Foreign Affairs Task Force: *Staff Study of the Interdepartmental Aspects of Foreign Affairs*, Appendix V, Washington, D.C., 1948.

Don K. Price's examination of the role of Congress in foreign policy formulation and execution is contained in his monograph, *The New Dimension of Diplomacy*, Woodrow Wilson Foundation, New York, 1951. Generally on this subject, see Robert Dahl, *Congress and Foreign Policy*, Harcourt, Brace, New York, 1950; and Daniel S. Cheever and H. Field Haviland, Jr., *American Foreign Policy and the Separation of Powers*, Harvard University Press, Cambridge, Mass., 1951. Valuable, though somewhat diffuse, is William Y. Elliott *et al.*, *United States Foreign Policy—Its Organization and Control*, Columbia University Press, New York, 1952.

On the administration of American foreign policy, see the report prepared by a study group at the Brookings Institution, *The Administration of Foreign Affairs and Overseas Operations*, Brookings Institution, Washington, D.C., 1951.

On the formulation of British foreign policy, see Craig and Gilbert (eds.), *The Diplomats, 1919–1939* (above), Chaps. 1, 10, 14, and 17. An over-all discussion of some of the problems encountered by the British in the period from 1931 to 1939, and how they were handled, can be found in Nicholas Mansergh, *Survey of British Commonwealth Affairs: Problems of External Policy, 1931–39*, Oxford, New York, 1952. See also the outdated but valuable article by Eugene P. Chase, "Parliamentary Control of Foreign Policy in Great Britain," *American Political Science Review*, Vol. 25, pp. 861–880, 1931.

For France, see John E. Howard, *Parliament and Foreign Policy in France*, The Cresset Press, London, 1948; and Craig and Gilbert (eds.), *The Diplomats, 1919–1939* (above), Chaps. 2, 12, 14, and 18. The statement by François Goguel is from his *France under the Fourth Republic* (above), p. 167.

CHAPTER 14. *The Future of Democratic Government*

For the point that if we are to change our approach to certain crucial problems, we must break the pattern in which we consider these matters, we are indebted to David Krech and Richard S. Crutchfield, *Theory and Problems of Social Psychology*, McGraw-Hill, New York, 1948, Chap. XV.

A coldly dispassionate analysis of the defeat of the Eighth Army in Korea in November–December, 1950, is contained in Colonel S. L. A. Marshall, *The River and the Gauntlet*, Morrow, New York, 1953. Senator Taft's observation to Secretary

Forrestal on the difficulties faced by Congress in evaluating military efficiency may be found in Millis (ed.), *The Forrestal Diaries* (above), p. 446. Churchill's personal intervention in the operations of the British military are described by Chester Wilmot in *The Struggle for Europe,* Harper, New York, 1952. Wilmot presents a persuasive case for the point that the American refusal to give political direction to military undertakings was in large part responsible for postwar European difficulties.

The view that the process of free discussion is the basic dynamic of democratic government is eloquently expressed by Barker in *Reflections on Government* (above), Chaps. 1 and 2. Gaetano Mosca's discussion of "juridical defense" is found in *The Ruling Class* (above), Chap. 5.

The possibilities of using social science techniques to achieve democratically oriented goals are presented, with numerous examples, in the challenging work edited by Daniel Lerner and Harold D. Lasswell, *The Policy Sciences,* Stanford University Press, Stanford, California, 1951.

INDEX